CIT: CISCO®
INTERNETWORK
TROUBLESHOOTING

CIT:
Cisco®
Internetwork
Troubleshooting

Thomas M. Thomas II
Mark J. Newcomb
Andrew G. Mason

McGraw-Hill
New York   San Francisco   Washington, D.C.
Auckland   Bogotá   Caracas   Lisbon   London
Madrid   Mexico City   Milan   Montreal   New Delhi
San Juan   Singapore   Sydney   Tokyo   Toronto

McGraw-Hill

A Division of The McGraw·Hill Companies

Copyright © 2000 by The McGraw-Hill Companies, Inc. All rights reserved.
Printed in the United States of America. Except as permitted under the United
States Copyright Act of 1976, no part of this publication may be reproduced or
distributed in any form or by any means, or stored in a data base or retrieval
system, without the prior written permission of the publisher.

1 2 3 4 5 6 7 8 9 0   DOC/DOC   0 5 4 3 2 1 0

P/N 0-07-212481-4
Part of ISBN 0-07-212483-0

The executive editor for this book was Steven Elliot, the development editor
was Jennifer Perillo, the associate development editor was Francis Kelly, and the
production manager was Clare Stanley. It was set in Century Schoolbook by D&G
Limited, LLC.

Printed and bound by R.R. Donnelley & Sons Company.

This book is printed on recycled, acid-free paper containing a minimum of 50
percent recycled de-inked fiber.

I would like to take a moment to dedicate this book to my mother. I could say many things about my life with her and how she shaped me into the man I have become today. Who would have ever thought life would take me down the paths I have tread? It was through the lessons and life experiences shared with me by my mother that have given me wisdom and courage. However, mere words cannot capture these thoughts and feelings adequately. So let me simply say that my mother taught me the skills to find my way through life, fight for what's right, and respect myself no matter what. For these things and everything else that goes unspoken between a mother and her son, I dedicate this book to her.

"Mom, you are a special person . . . thank you for my life, my future, and shaping me like no one else ever could. I shall always have you in my heart. God Bless, thank you, and I love you."

THOMAS M. THOMAS II

This book is dedicated to my Uncle Dick, who fought in the war, raised a family, and had a positive influence on more people than we will ever know.

MARK J. NEWCOMB

I would like to dedicate this book to my wonderful daughter, Rosie Elizabeth Mason, who was born just after I started work on this book. Her arrival has brought new meaning to life.

ANDREW G. MASON

CONTENTS

	Preface	xxi
	Acknowledgments	xxiii
	About the Authors	xxv
	About the Reviewers	xxvii

Part 1	INTRODUCTION	1
Chapter 1	Introduction to Cisco Internet Troubleshooting	3
	Who Should Read This Book	4
	Network Engineers	4
	CCNP Candidates	4
	Topics Covered	5
	Cisco CCNP Requirements	8
	Test Objectives	10
	Study Schedule	12
	The Actual Test	12
	Dealing with Test Failures	15
	Chapter Summary	16

Part 2	METHODOLOGY, TOOLS, AND COMMANDS	17
Chapter 2	Troubleshooting Methodology	19
	Objectives Covered in the Chapter	20
	Review of Network Complexity Issues	20
	The Cisco Problem-Solving Method	22
	Defining the Problem	22
	Gather Facts and Analyze the Problem	27
	Evaluate Causes of the Problem	28
	Design an Action Plan	29
	Implement the Plan	29
	Evaluate the Results	30
	Repeat Until the Problem Is Solved	30
	Document the Solution	31
	The OSI Model and Troubleshooting	32
	Physical Layer	32
	Data Link Layer	34
	Network Layer	37

Transport Layer	38
Session Layer	40
Presentation Layer	40
Application Layer	41
Climbing the Ladder	41
Chapter Summary	47
Frequently Asked Questions (FAQ)	48
Scenarios	49
Questions	51
Answers	55

Chapter 3 Troubleshooting Tools — 57

Objectives Covered in the Chapter	58
Testing with Physical Devices	58
Multi Meters	59
Cable Testers	60
Time Domain Reflectometers (TDR) and Optical Time Domain Reflectometers (OTDR)	61
Bit/Block Error Rate Testers (BERTs)	62
Testing with Software Applications	64
Network Monitor	64
Network Analyzers	65
Cisco Works	66
Cisco NetSys Network Management Suites	69
NetSys Baseliner for Windows NT	69
NetSys SLM Suite	70
Chapter Summary	70
Frequently Asked Questions (FAQ)	71
Case Study	72
Scenario	72
Approach	72
Results	72
Questions	73
Answers	77

Chapter 4 Basic Diagnostic Commands — 79

Objectives Covered in the Chapter	80
Routing Processes	80
Process Switching	81
Fast Switching	82
Autonomous Switching	82

Contents

Netflow Switching	82
Silicon Switching	83
Optimum Switching	83
Distributed Switching	83
Cisco Express Forwarding	83
Differences Between Show and Debug Commands	84
Debug	85
Debug and Performance	85
Debug Commands	89
Serial Interface Commands	91
Show Commands	94
Global Commands	103
Interface Commands	106
Core Dumps	110
Ping Commands	112
ICMP	113
Ping	116
User Ping	120
Extended Ping	122
Windows Ping	125
Traceroute Commands	127
Chapter Summary	130
Frequently Asked Questions (FAQ)	131
Lab Exercise	132
Questions	133
Answers	137
Part 3 LOCAL AREA NETWORKS (LANS)	141
Chapter 5 Troubleshooting Local Area Networks (LANs)	143
Objectives Covered in the Chapter	144
Physical and Logical Topologies	144
Cabling Issues	146
Ethernet Topologies	151
Carrier Sense Multiple Access/ Collision Detect (CSMA/CD)	152
Collision Domains	153
Broadcast Domains	154
Jabbers	156
Runts	156
Token Ring Topologies	156

Fiber Distributed Data Interface (FDDI)   158
Chapter Summary   163
Frequently Asked Questions (FAQ)   164
Lab Exercise   166
Questions   167
Answers   171

Chapter 6   Troubleshooting Switched LANs   173

Objectives Covered in This Chapter   174
OSI Model in Switched LANs   174
  Data Link Layer   175
  Network Layer   175
ATM   175
  ATM Layers   177
  ELAN   178
Ethernet Hubs   179
Ethernet Bridges   180
Ethernet Switches   183
  VLAN   186
  Spanning Tree Protocol   188
  EtherChannel and FastEtherChannel   190
  ISL and 802.1q   192
Troubleshooting Switched Ethernet LANs   192
  Connection Speed   193
  Full- Versus Half-Duplex   194
  SPAN   195
Chapter Summary   196
Frequently Asked Questions (FAQ)   197
Questions   199
Answers   203

Chapter 7   Cisco Switches   205

Catalyst Switches   206
  1900 Series   206
  2900 Series   206
  4000 Series   207
  5000 series   207
  The 6000 Series   208
Command-Line Interface   209

Contents

RMON   223
  Statistics   224
  History   224
  Alarms   724
  Events   225
Power up Sequences and Lights   225
Internal Components   225
  The Encoded Address Recognition Logic (EARL)   226
  The Synergy Advanced Gate-Array Engine (SAGE)   226
  The Synergy Advanced Interface and Network Termination (SAINT) 226
  The Synergy Advanced Multipurpose Bus Arbiter (SAMBA)   227
  The Phoenix   227
Chapter Summary   228
Frequently Asked Questions (FAQ)   229
Questions   230
Answers   234

Part 4   WIDE AREA NETWORKS   237

Chapter 8   Serial, Frame Relay, and X.25 Connectivity   239

Objectives Covered in the Chapter   240
Overview of Serial Lines   240
  Show Commands   242
  show interface   242
  show controllers   245
  show buffers   247
  Debug Commands   248
  debug serial interface   248
  Serial Line Summary   250
Overview of Frame Relay   251
  Frame Relay Structure   252
  Frame Relay Devices   253
  Virtual Circuits   253
  Congestion Management   255
  Local Management Interface (LMI)   255
  Show Commands   256
  show frame-relay lmi   256

show frame-relay map 257

show frame-relay pvc 258

show interface 259

Debug Commands 261

debug frame-relay events 261

debug frame-relay lmi 262

debug frame-relay packet 263

debug serial interface 263

Frame Relay Summary 264

Overview of X.25 265

X.25 Protocols 265

X.25 Devices 267

Show Commands 268

show interface 269

show x25 route 270

show x25 vc 270

Debug Commands 271

debug x25 events 272

debug x25 all 273

X.25 Summary 274

Chapter Summary 274

Frequently Asked Questions (FAQ) 275

Case Study 276

Approach 276

Results 277

Questions 278

Answers 282

Chapter 9 Transmission Control Protocol/Internet Protocol (TCP/IP) 285

Objectives Covered in the Chapter 286

Overview of TCP/IP 287

TCP and IP in the OSI Model 287

Internet Protocol (IP) 288

Transmission Control Protocol (TCP) 293

User Datagram Protocol (UDP) 293

Internet Control Message Protocol (ICMP) 294

Address Resolution Protocols (ARP) 296

Broadcasts 298

Unicasts/Multicasts 299

Domain Name Server (DNS) 299

Helper Addresses 300

Common TCP/UDP Ports	301
Microsoft Windows 95/NT TCP/IP	301
Host to-Host Communication	303
Ping	304
Tracert	305
ARP Cache	306
Windows NT Routing Table	307
Name Resolution	309
Show Commands	312
show interface	312
show ip interface	314
show ip interface brief	316
show ip protocols	317
show ip arp	318
show ip route	318
show ip access-lists	319
show ip traffic	321
Debug Commands	322
debug arp	323
debug ip icmp	324
debug ip packet	325
debug ip routing	326
Other IP Commands	327
clear arp-cache	328
clear ip access-list counters	329
clear ip route	331
Packet Internet Groper (Ping)	331
Trace	333
Chapter Summary	336
Frequently Asked Questions (FAQ)	337
Case Study	338
Scenario	338
Approach	338
Results	342
Questions	343
Answers	347
Chapter 10 AppleTalk	349
Objectives Covered in the Chapter	350
Zones and Cable Ranges	350
Zones	350

Cable Ranges	352
LocalTalk and AppleTalk	354
LocalTalk	354
AppleTalk	355
Initial AppleTalk Address Assignment	355
AppleTalk Protocols	356
EtherTalk, TokenTalk, and FFDITalk	357
AppleTalk Address Resolution Protocol (AARP)	357
AppleTalk Data Stream Protocol (ADSP)	358
Datagram Delivery Protocol (DDP)	359
Name Binding Protocol (NBP)	360
Routing Table Maintenance Protocol (RTMP)	361
Apple Update-based Routing Protocol (AURP)	361
AppleTalk File Protocol (AFP)	362
AppleTalk Session Protocol (ASP)	362
Printer Access Protocol (PAP)	362
Zone Information Protocol (ZIP)	362
Show Commands	364
Show AppleTalk Globals	364
Show AppleTalk Interface	364
Show AppleTalk Traffic	365
Show AppleTalk Neighbors	366
Other Show Commands	367
Debug Commands	369
Debug Apple Events	369
Debug Apple Packet	369
Debug Apple ZIP	371
Other AppleTalk Commands	371
Chapter Summary	372
Frequently Asked Questions (FAQ)	373
Questions	374
Answers	378
Chapter 11 Novell Internet Packet Exchange/Sequenced Packet Exchange (IPX/SPX)	381
Objectives Covered in the Chapter	382
Novell Protocols	382
Internet Packet Exchange (IPX)	383
Sequenced Packet Exchange (SPX)	386
Service Advertisement Protocol (SAP)	387

Contents

Netware Core Protocol (NCP)   388
Get Nearest Server (GNS)   388
Service Advertisement Protocol (SAP)   388
SAP Management   389
IPX Routing Protocols   390
Novell Routing Information Protocol (IPX RIP)   391
NetWare Link Services Protocol (NLSP)   392
Enhanced Interior Gateway Routing Protocol (EIGRP)   394
Encapsulation Types   395
Show Commands   396
show interface   397
show ipx interface   398
show ipx interface brief   400
show ipx servers   401
show ipx traffic   402
show ipx route   403
show ipx access-lists   404
show ipx eigrp interface   405
show ipx eigrp neighbors   405
Debug Commands   406
debug ipx sap events   407
debug ipx packet   407
debug ipx routing events   408
Other IPX/Novell Commands   411
Ping   412
Trace   413
Chapter Summary   414
Frequently Asked Questions (FAQ)   415
Case Study   416
Questions   418
Answers   422

Chapter 12   Routing Protocols   425

Objectives Covered in the Chapter   427
Routing Protocols in the OSI Model   427
Classless Versus Classfull Protocols   428
Distance Vector Protocols   429
Network Discovery and Topology Changes   431
The Problems and Limitations of Distance Vector Routing   431
Routing Information Protocol (RIP)   433

Troubleshooting RIP   434
show ip protocols   435
show ip route   437
show ip rip database   438
debug ip routing   438
debug ip rip   440
Interior Gateway Routing Protocol (IGRP)   442
Troubleshooting IGRP   443
show ip protocols   444
show ip route   445
debug ip routing   446
debug ip igrp events   448
Link State Protocols   454
Network Discovery and Topology Changes   455
Problems and Limitations of Link State Routing   455
Open Shortest Path First (OSPF)   456
Troubleshooting OSPF   457
show ip protocols   458
show ip route   459
show ip ospf interface   460
show ip ospf neighbor   462
debug ip routing   463
debug ip ospf events   466
Border Gateway Protocol (BGP)   470
Troubleshooting BGP   471
Enhanced Interior Gateway Routing Protocol (EIGRP), the Hybrid Protocol   473
Neighbor Discovery/Recovery   474
Reliable Transport Protocol (RTP)   474
Diffusing Update Algorithm (DUAL) Finite State Machine   474
Protocol Dependant Modules   475
Troubleshooting EIGRP   475
show ip protocols   476
show ip route   478
show ip eigrp interface   479
debug ip routing   480
debug ip eigrp   484
Chapter Summary   488
Frequently Asked Questions (FAQ)   489
Case Study   490
Scenario   490

Contents

	Approach	490
	Results	491
	Questions	492
	Answers	495
Chapter 13	Troubleshooting ISDN Basic Rate Interface (BRI)	497
	ISDN Device and Reference Configuration Devices	499
	Termination	499
	ISDN Protocols	500
	Reference Points	500
	Service Profile Identifiers (SPIDs)	501
	Objectives Covered in This Chapter	501
	ISDN in the OSI Model	502
	Physical Layer	502
	Data-Link Layer	503
	LAPD	503
	Network Layer	505
	ISDN Q.931	505
	Dial-On-Demand Routing	505
	Snapshot Routing	507
	PPP	508
	PPP Authentication	508
	Multilink PPP (MPP)	510
	ISDN SHOW Commands	511
	show interface bri n	511
	show interface bri n:x	513
	show controllers bri	514
	show isdn status	515
	show dialer	516
	show ppp multilink	518
	ISDN DEBUG Commands	518
	debug bri	519
	debug isdn q921	520
	debug isdn q931	522
	debug ppp negotiation	523
	debug ppp authentication	525
	debug ppp packet	526
	debug dialer	527
	debug isdn	528
	Other ISDN Troubleshooting Commands	529

Chapter Summary   530
Common BRI Problems   530
Frequently Asked Questions (FAQ)   532
Case Study   533
Questions   537
Answers   540

Part 5   ADVANCED TROUBLESHOOTING   **541**

Chapter 14 Cisco Support   543

Objectives Covered in This Chapter   544
On Line Support—Cisco Connection Online (CCO)   544
   Cisco Marketplace   549
   Technical Documents   550
   Software Center   555
Technical Assistance Center (TAC)   556
Documentation CD   563
   Searching the CD   564
Support Commands   566
   Show Tech-Support   566
   Core Dumps   575
Chapter Summary   576
Frequently Asked Questions (FAQ)   577
Questions   578
Answers   581

Chapter 15 Advanced Troubleshooting Techniques   583

Objectives Covered in the Chapter   584
Reading Protocol Analyzer Outputs   584
Common Symptoms and Causes   590
Common False Assumptions   591
   The "I can see you, therefore, you can see me" Assumption   591
   The "I know how this is configured" Assumption   592
   The "I can ping, so there are no TCP/IP issues" Assumption   592
   The "I have a link light, therefore, there is a good physical
      connection" Assumption   593
   The "I took a quick look and that is not the issue" Assumption 593
Debug   593
   Debugging Access Lists   595

Routing Issues 596
Static Routes 596
Ping and Traceroute 598
Working with Your Service Provider 601
Line Monitoring 602
Escalation 602
Chapter Summary 603
Layer 1: The Physical Layer 621
Cables and Wires 621
Physical Terminations and Connectors 624
Physical Encoding Methods 628
Conclusion 631
Layer 2: The Data Link Layer 631
Data Link Layer Example 633
Conclusion 636
Layer 3: Network Layer 636
The Internet Protocol (IP) 639
IP Node Operation 639
Internetwork Packet Exchange (IPX) Operation 642
Layer 4: Transport Layer 642
Transport Layer Protocol Examples 644
Conclusion 646
Layer 5: Session Layer 646
Layer 6: Presentation Layer 648
Layer 7: Application Layer 649
Conclusion 650

Appendix A Glossary 605

Appendix B Bibliography 615

Appendix C Webliography 617

Appendix D OSI Model 621

Layer 1: The Physical Layer 621
Cables and Wires 621
Physical Terminations and Connectors 624
Physical Encoding Methods 628
Conclusion 631
Layer 2: The Data Link Layer 631
Data Link Layer Example 633

Conclusion	636
Layer 3: Network Layer	636
The Internet Protocol (IP)	639
IP Node Operation	639
Internetwork Packet Exchange (IPX) Operation	642
Layer 4: Transport Layer	642
Transport Layer Protocol Examples	644
Conclusion	646
Layer 5: Session Layer	646
Layer 6: Presentation Layer	648
Layer 7: Application Layer	649
Conclusion	650
Index	651

PREFACE

When *CIT: Cisco Internetwork Troubleshooting* was still in the design stage, the authors decided that we needed to provide the readers with three benefits to purchasing this book: introduce all the material presented in the official Cisco approved class, give enough information and examples to allow the readers to successfully pass the associated exam, and supply the tools necessary for readers to solve problems in their daily work. We feel this book has accomplished all three of these goals.

Toward realizing these goals, we have taken the Cisco network troubleshooting exam a number of times, taken the networking class again, and done extensive research about networking on numerous Web sites. Collectively, the authors have a library consisting of most, if not all, of the major publications dealing with Cisco network troubleshooting. We have researched articles dating back over 10 years to find the most common as well as the uncommon problems found in networking. We have also searched our memories for the toughest problems we have encountered during our combined years in networking.

While no single publication can possibly provide the reader with an answer to every networking problem, this book provides something even better—a means for teaching the reader how to approach a network problem, break it down into the salient points, and then correct the underlying cause. Once the reader learns how to troubleshoot, the process of learning the specifics of networking can be addressed.

Although readers are assumed to have an understanding of networking and particularly Cisco equipment, they will first be presented in each section with a discussion of the underlying technology. This is done to ensure that readers do not have a false assumption that will later cause them problems. For example, when even knowledgeable Cisco engineers are asked for the speed of the backplane on a Cisco 5500, they would usually answer: "3.6 Gbps." This answer is not totally correct. A more correct answer would be "The architecture of a Cisco 5500 chassis has three backplanes, each with a capacity of 1.2 Gbps, allowing a total theoretical combined speed of 3.6 Gbps. However, only the Supervisor III engine will utilize this technology." The difference is subtle, but extremely important for the test as well as for daily use of the switch. If the switch were originally shipped with a Supervisor II module, the theoretical capacity would be limited to 1.2 Gbps. Unless you know this fact, you may spend hours trying to figure out why your switch is unable to transfer as much data as you think it should.

If you have years of troubleshooting experience or are new to the process, *CIT: Cisco Internetwork Troubleshooting* will show you sound techniques combined with enough facts and examples to successfully troubleshoot Cisco equipment.

ACKNOWLEDGMENTS

A book is certainly a team effort and this book in particular epitomizes the value of a good team. Allow me to explain. Mark Newcomb and Andrew Mason live on literally opposite sides of our planet and they have never met in person, I have never met either of them, they have only talked on the phone once and only then because I hosted that call to congratulate them on finishing this book. They truly used the "E" everything (e-mail, e-fax, e-commerce, etc.) to communicate effectively and efficiently to write this wonderful book. This places them #1 on the list of people to acknowledge. My hat's off to these talented network engineers and communicators. They are an inspiration and a talented team. I also hope that one day we can all meet and bring our wives together so I can thank them as well, but until that time, I want to acknowledge the support of our families and the staff at McGraw-Hill for their assistance.

THOMAS M. THOMAS II

I would like to thank my lovely wife, Jacqueline, for her infinite understanding and support throughout this project. I know I never could have accomplished this without all of her love, praise, and patience. Equally important is the cooperation I received from both Tom Thomas and Andrew Mason. It is still amazing to me how much we have accomplished through the power of e-mail. I wanted to mention Robert Lusian, Derek Simmelink, and Steve Trabun, who gave me insight, a "technical ear" for ideas, technical assistance, and most of all moral support through the long nights spent on this project. Finally, I will acknowledge all of the hard work done by our technical reviewers, Cuong Vu and Mahmoud Harb, who provided a different point of view, found technical inaccuracies, and provided many great suggestions.

MARK J. NEWCOMB

Helen, my beautiful wife, deserves an award for her patience and love through this very difficult time. The arrival of our first born, Rosie, and the tight deadlines of this book took the toll on both of us.

The comradeship that I developed with the other author, Mark Newcomb, and the editor, Tom Thomas, really helped along the way. We live at opposite sides of the world but still managed to communicate very frequently along the way.

The technical reviewers Cuong Vu and Mahmoud Harb also deserve a mention, as their input was appreciated.

ANDREW G. MASON

ABOUT THE AUTHORS

Thomas M. Thomas II is the series editor and founder of NetCerts (www.netcerts.com), a leading training and education site for Cisco certification. He was previously a course developer for Cisco Systems and has worked on the Advanced Systems Solutions Engineering Team for MCI's Managed Network Services. He is currently an instructor/consultant for Chesapeake Network Solutions (www.ccci.com)

Mark J. Newcomb, CCNP, CCDP, MCSE, is a consulting network engineer working for Aurora Consulting Group (www.auroracg.com), where he provides network design, security, and implementation services for clients throughout the Pacific Northwest. He has more than 20 years' experience in the Microcomputer industry.

Andrew G. Mason, A+, Network+, CNA, Cisco Sales Expert, MCSE+ Internet, CCDP, CCNP, is the CEO of Mason Technologies Limited (www.masontech.com), a United Kingdom (UK)-based Cisco Premier He is a partner involved in Cisco consulting for numerous UK-based companies and has more than 8 years' experience in the computer industry.

ABOUT THE REVIEWERS

As the leading publisher of technical books for more than 100 years, McGraw-Hill prides itself on bringing you the most authoritative and up-to-date information available. To ensure that our books meet the highest standards of accuracy, we have asked a number of top professionals and technical experts to review the accuracy of the material you are about to read.

We take great pleasure in thanking the following technical reviewers for their insights:

Mahmoud Harb, CCNA, CCDA, is a senior network engineer at SEEK Consulting in Wakefield, Massachusetts, where he is a WAN Network specialist. He is responsible for monitoring, testing, and evaluating the USPS MNS network topology. Previously, he was a senior system network administrator in St. Paul's Hospital, Vancouver, Canada. He holds a Diploma in Computer Information Technology from Vancouver Community College (Langara Campus, Vancouver, Canada) and a Diploma in Computer Science Technology from the Business Automation Training Center (Beirut, Lebanon).

Cuong Vu, CCIE, has over nine years of networking experience with REALTECH Systems Corporation, a New York-based Integrator. He provides consultative design and support services for enterprise and carrier-based customers, involving various LAN/WAN technologies and operating systems. His current responsibilities also include supporting the sales efforts for the organization as well as leading engineering teams in implementation projects and troubleshooting efforts. Mr. Vu holds a bachelor of science in electrical engineering from Rutgers University.

Introduction

Introduction to Cisco Internet Troubleshooting

Who Should Read This Book

There are two major audiences for this book. The first includes those seeking to gain recognition of their skills by obtaining the *Cisco Certified Network Professional* (CCNP) certification. This is an intermediate-level certification sponsored by Cisco Systems. This book covers the final topics to be mastered for that certification. Every CCNP candidate pursuing this certification is required to take either the CIT or the Support exam.

Network Engineers

The second major audience for this book includes those who work in the Wide Area Network environment every day. The major challenge faced by these individuals is how to keep the network running with the minimal amount of "down-time." All networks will fail at some point. The challenge is to get the network running again quickly. This book will teach network engineers a structured approach that results in finding the problem promptly and preventing the problem from recurring. People at all levels, from the beginner to the seasoned expert, will benefit from using this book as a reference. Virtually all of the employed network engineers have at least a basic knowledge of how the systems work on a theoretical basis. However, many of them have never been taught a logical and methodic approach to problem solving.

This is the book that will bind all of the reader's previous learning and experience into a single guide used to maintain, diagnose, and troubleshoot both one-time occurrences and recurring issues on a daily basis. This book will allow the reader to combine theoretical and hands-on knowledge with these sound techniques to allow him to quickly and easily solve virtually any problem that can be encountered.

CCNP Candidates

CCNP candidates utilizing this book will also need to study for three other exams that test their knowledge in three main areas: *Advanced Cisco Router Configuration* (ACRC), *Cisco LAN Switch Configuration* (CLSC), and *Configuring Maintaining Troubleshooting Dial-up* (CMTD). The *Cisco Internet Troubleshooting* (CIT) exam is considered the most difficult of all exams because it presupposes thorough knowledge of all the areas listed here. If you are studying for the CCNP certifications, we strongly urge you to gain a solid knowledge of all of these areas before attempting the CIT or Support exam.

For those studying for the exams, this book is designed to accomplish three goals:

- Help the professional in everyday, ordinary troubleshooting situations
- Provide the reader with all the information they would receive in the official Cisco-approved course
- Provide all the resources needed for the reader to successfully pass the exam

This is generally considered a tough test. The reason it is considered tough is because it requires a strong working knowledge of all three of the study areas (router configuration, dial-up, and switches), combined with the knowledge of how to troubleshoot within each area when something is not working properly. This book will provide the reader with the knowledge required to approach the exam with confidence and an ability to succeed.

Topics Covered

Looking at the layout of this book, you may notice that the approach taken differs from other books on the market in significant ways. The most obvious way in which this book differs is that the book starts with the troubleshooting methodology, discusses available tools, covers basic commands, and then moves on to the "meat" of the book. You will not find 16 pages of output when only 20 lines will clearly show the desired items. The authors have purposefully removed most of the "fluff" in order to give you what you really need.

Most books you find on the market today jump from routing protocols, move back to how Ethernet works, and then jump forward again to AppleTalk before discussing Serial connections. This book approaches troubleshooting the way most of us have learned about networking. We start with the basics before moving to complex topics. We will discuss LANs before discussing switched LANs. Next, we will explore how WAN connections are made through the common methods of Serial connections, Frame

Relay, and X.25. We next look at how TCP/IP is used because this forms the basis of most WAN networks.

After we have looked at TCP/IP, we will look at the alternatives to TCP/IP, such as AppleTalk and IPX/SPX. After we understand how the networks talk through the WAN, we look at the routing protocols used to keep the routes current. After we understand routing protocols, we are ready to discuss Dial-on-Demand routing, which requires a thorough understanding of routing protocols and is one of the greatest benefits of ISDN.

Finally, we discuss how to get the most out of Cisco Support before giving an overview of all that was previously presented, as well as a few new tricks and tips.

Following is a list of each chapter and a short description of what is covered in the chapter.

- Chapter 1, "Introduction to Cisco Internet Troubleshooting." This chapter is the introduction to the book. It gives an overview of the book, describes the conventions used in the book, discusses why the reader should buy the book, and lists the requirements for Cisco certifications.

- Chapter 2, "Troubleshooting Methodology." This chapter may be the most critical in the book. The most important point of the chapter is to show you how to approach a problem. The main point this chapter (in fact, the whole book) stresses is that every problem is easily solved if you work from the bottom layers of the OSI model toward the top layers.

- Chapter 3, "Troubleshooting Tools." This chapter shows the basic hardware and software tools that are available for the network engineer to purchase. Although it doesn't tell you exactly how to use a cable tester, it does show you when to use one and what a cable tester will do for you.

- Chapter 4, "Basic Diagnostic Commands." This chapter discusses the "nuts-and-bolts" commands that allow the network engineer to troubleshoot a network. This is an essential chapter because the remainder of the book relies on the tools presented.

- Chapter 5, "Troubleshooting LANs." Chapter 5 introduces the reader to troubleshooting techniques used in simple LANs. This is the first practical application of Chapters 2, 3, and 4. This chapter also lays the foundation necessary for Chapters 6 and 7.

- Chapter 6, "Troubleshooting Switched LANs." Chapter 6 adds complexity to the network by introducing switches and VLANs. Building on Chapter 5, you learn how complexity does not change troubleshooting methodology.

- Chapter 7, "Cisco Switches." In Chapter 7, the specifics of dealing with Cisco switches are discussed. This is a large chapter that reflects the emphasis the exam places on these switches.

- Chapter 8, "Serial, Frame Relay, and X.25 Connectivity." Chapter 8 moves the reader from the LAN environment to the WAN environment. Although the techniques remain the same as those in the LAN environment, new commands and tools are introduced that are specific to the Serial, Frame Relay, and X.25 environments.

- Chapter 9, "Transmission Control Protocol/Internet Protocol (TCP/IP)." In Chapter 9, troubleshooting TCP/IP is discussed. Some of the issues raised include access lists, routing, and subnet masking.

- Chapter 10, "AppleTalk." Although AppleTalk is not a predominant protocol, there are still a large number of installed AppleTalk networks. This chapter looks at the issues unique to troubleshooting AppleTalk networks in both the LAN and WAN environments.

- Chapter 11, "Novell Internet Packet Exchange/Sequenced Packet Exchange (IPX/SPX)." This chapter looks at the issues of troubleshooting IPX in both the LAN and WAN environments. We also discuss how SAP filters work, how to filter them, and the unique problems associated with IPX and Novell networks.

- Chapter 12, "Routing Protocols." Chapter 12 helps you understand the issues involved in troubleshooting routing protocols. We cover IGRP, EIGRP, OSPF, and RIP. We also examine how access lists affect routing protocols.

- Chapter 13, "Troubleshooting ISDN *Basic Rate Interface* (BRI)." The emphasis in this chapter is how to troubleshoot ISDN BRI connections. It covers dial maps, access lists, dialing pools, rotary groups, and low-level debugging of ISDN connections. Although this chapter is a "must-read" for those who use ISDN, there will not be a great audience because most companies do not use ISDN. However, the tests stress ISDN debugging, which is thoroughly covered.

- Chapter 14, "Cisco Support." This chapter deals with both the support tools available from Cisco Systems and the way in which the Cisco *Technical Assistance Center* (TAC) handles problems. This is rated as the least popular chapter, mainly because most of the everyday problems will not need to be directed to Cisco after studying this book.

- Chapter 15, "Advanced Troubleshooting Techniques." This chapter "brings it all together" for the reader. The purpose of this chapter is to bring all the elements discussed in the book together in the form of complex, yet easily approachable real-world examples.

Cisco CCNP Requirements

As of this writing, Cisco has two different tracks, each of which gives you an option regarding the tests taken. According to Cisco, the original exam track will "continue to support the original curriculum through June 2000, and/or as the market demands." Interestingly, the Cisco Web sites specifically say that the ACRC, CMTD, and CLSC exams do not cover the same objectives as the new BSCN, BCMSN, and BCRAN exams. However, there is no mention at this time that the objectives for the Support test are in any way different from the current CIT test.

The original method of obtaining CCNP is shown in Figure 1-1. Notice that although the Foundation R/S exam is an alternative to taking the

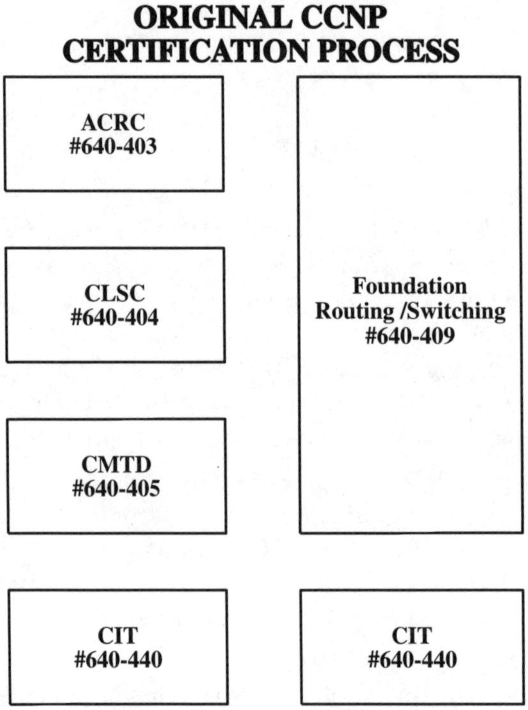

Figure 1-1
Original CCNP
requirements

**ORIGINAL CCNP
CERTIFICATION PROCESS**

ACRC #640-403	
CLSC #640-404	Foundation Routing /Switching #640-409
CMTD #640-405	
CIT #640-440	CIT #640-440

three separate ACRC, CMTD, and CLSC exams, the CIT exam must still be taken separately. This chart presupposes that the candidate already has a valid CCNA certification.

If you are moving on the new CCNP track, Figure 1-2 outlines the required exams.

Notice that on either of the tracks chosen, you have the option of taking a foundation exam instead of three separate exams. Two advantages of taking a foundation exam are that you only need to pass two tests to gain your certification instead of four, and you can save $100.00 in test costs. A disadvantage of taking the foundation exam is that this exam will cover the whole of all three exams that are replaced. It is up to the individual candidate to decide which track better suits their personal study habits and comfort level.

One of the things to consider while deciding whether you should take the foundation test is how well you know the areas covered by the exams. If, for instance, you are weak in one area, you may be able to leverage your strong areas against your weaker area and successfully pass the foundation test. On the other hand, if you are weak in more than one area, it is unlikely that you will be able to pass the foundation exam.

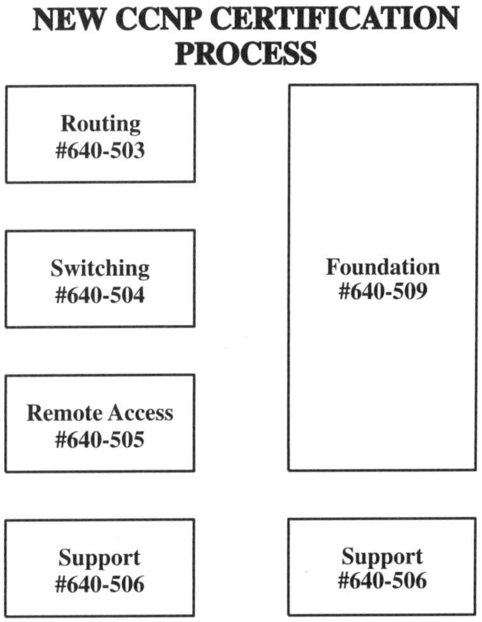

Figure 1-2
New CCNP requirements

NEW CCNP CERTIFICATION PROCESS

Routing #640-503	
Switching #640-504	Foundation #640-509
Remote Access #640-505	
Support #640-506	Support #640-506

Even if you are not planning on taking the CIT or Support test, this book will still prove valuable to you in your everyday troubleshooting efforts.

Test Objectives

Those taking the CIT (640-440) or Support (640-506) exams will benefit from looking over the following objectives. As of this writing, the exam objectives for the Support exam have not been published. However, the beta version of the Support exam has been released and the authors have taken this exam and incorporated the breadth and scope of the exam into this text. Following is a list of the published objectives for the 640-440 exam, along with the chapters associated with that objective:

Number	Objective	Chapter(s)
1.	Describe information gathering and communications to get the best use of Cisco's service and support services.	14, 15
2.	Describe an efficient problem-solving method when troubleshooting and documenting internetwork problems.	2
3.	Identify and apply generic and Cisco-specific troubleshooting tools on Cisco routers and switches.	4 through 13
4.	Analyze problem symptoms and resolve resolution strategies in TCP/IP (including the Microsoft 95/NT IP stack), Novell IPX, AppleTalk, Ethernet VLANs, Frame Relay, and ISDN BRI.	9
5.	Perform labs that troubleshoot problems (hardware, software, or configuration bugs) and then correct these bugs to restore full network operations.	2 through 15
6.	Describe the types and purposes of tools commonly used for network troubleshooting processes.	3
7.	Describe and use the Cisco information resources (especially those in the CCO CD or World Wide Web site) that can assist with troubleshooting processes.	14
8.	List the preferred methods of escalation of troubleshooting issues to Cisco's service and support programs.	14
9.	Use a problem-solving model to systematically troubleshoot a given problem and list the value of using a systematic process.	2
10.	Apply a process for documenting the steps taken to isolate potential causes and determine potential solutions.	2

Number	Objective	Chapter(s)
11.	Demonstrate knowledge of troubleshooting targets for connection-oriented and connectionless protocols.	5, 9 through 12
12.	Demonstrate knowledge of common data link layer characteristics and key troubleshooting targets likely to be found in campus LANs.	6, 7
13.	Demonstrate knowledge of connection sequences and key troubleshooting targets within TCP/IP, Novell IPX, and AppleTalk.	9, 10
14.	Handle troubleshooting tools and minimize their impact on a Cisco router's switching type and data flow.	4, 5, 15
15.	Identify and use the innate Cisco IOS software commands and debug utilities to filter, capture, and display protocol traffic flows.	4 through 13
16.	Obtain protocol troubleshooting information by capturing and interpreting data with a third-party protocol analyzer.	2, 15
17.	Use proven isolation techniques to list the symptoms of common TCP/IP problems.	9
18.	Apply diagnostic tools to trouble tickets and solve classroom network TCP/IP problems that simulate real-life internetworking malfunctions.	9
19.	Apply diagnostic tools to solve network problems that include systems running TCP/IP with Windows NT/95 clients and servers.	9
20.	Use proven problem-isolation techniques to list the symptoms of common Novell IPX problems on router networks.	11
21.	Apply diagnostic tools to trouble tickets and solve classroom network Novell IPX problems that simulate real-life internetworking malfunctions.	11
22.	Use proven isolation techniques to list the symptoms of common AppleTalk problems on routed networks.	10
23.	Apply diagnostic tools to trouble tickets and solve network AppleTalk problems that simulate real-life internetworking malfunctions.	10
24.	Use proven problem-isolation techniques to list the symptoms of Catalyst 5000 and VLAN problems on switched Ethernet networks.	6, 7
25.	Apply diagnostic tools to trouble tickets and solve classroom network Catalyst 5000 problems that simulate real-life networking malfunctions.	7

Number	Objective	Chapter(s)
26.	Apply diagnostic tools to classroom trouble tickets on switched and routed VLAN configuration problems.	6, 7
27.	Use Cisco IOS router troubleshooting commands with Catalyst 5000 switched troubleshooting commands.	7
28.	Use Cisco IOS commands and problem isolation techniques to identify the symptoms of common WAN and Frame Relay problems.	8
29.	Apply diagnostic tools to trouble tickets and solve classroom network Frame Relay problems that simulate real-life WAN malfunctions.	8
30.	Use Cisco IOS commands and problem isolation techniques to identify the symptoms of common ISDN BRI problems.	13
31.	Apply diagnostic tools to trouble tickets and solve classroom network ISDN BRI problems that simulate real-life WAN malfunctions.	8
32.	Describe the interface and functions of the FTP Software LANWatch protocol analyzer product.	3
33.	Describe the necessary steps to execute a (manual) core dump.	4

Study Schedule

If you are planning to take the certification test, consult the table on the following page for recommendations on how much time to devote to each section. Notice that there are recommendations for both a two-week (14-day) and six-week (56-day) study schedule. Be aware that the 14-day schedule is very, very aggressive and designed for those who have a good deal of experience with both Cisco equipment and troubleshooting in general. We believe that both of these schedules, if proper effort is given, will result in a successful testing experience.

The Actual Test

You can register for the CIT or Support exams by calling Sylvan Prometric at (800)829-6387 within the United States. Outside of the United States, contact the local testing center directly. If you are unsure of how to find a

Chapter	14 Day Plan	6 Week Plan
1—Introduction to Cisco Internet Troubleshooting	Day 1	Week 1
2—Troubleshooting Methodology	Day 1	Week 1
3—Troubleshooting Tools	Day 2	Week 1
4—Basic Diagnostic Commands	Days 3 and 4	Week 2
5—Troubleshooting LANs	Days 4 and 5	Week 2
6—Switched LANs	Day 6	Week 3
7—Cisco Switches	Day 7	Week 3
8—Serial, Frame Relay, and X.25 Connectivity	Day 8	Week 4
9—Transmission Control Protocol / Internet Protocol (TCP/IP)	Day 9	Week 4
10—AppleTalk	Day 10	Week 4
11—IPX/SPX and Novell	Day 11	Week 5
12—Routing Protocols	Day 12	Week 5
13—Troubleshooting ISDN Basic Rate Interface (BRI)	Day 13	Week 6
14—Cisco Support	Day 14	Week 6
15—Advanced Troubleshooting Techniques	Day 14	Week 6

testing center, your local Cisco sales representative can assist you. Sylvan will assist you by locating the nearest testing center and scheduling the exam. There are presently over 800 testing centers worldwide. Cisco exams must be scheduled at least 24 hours in advance.

The original CIT test consists of approximately 70 questions, which must be answered within 90 minutes. A score of 720 is required. Cisco has chosen to use an unusual system, in which the minimum score received is 300 and the maximum of 1000 points is available. The minimum passing score is 720.

Although subject to change, the current test allows marking a question and returning to that question at a later time. This feature can be very helpful. Most people will mark the questions they are unsure about and return to that question after all others are completed. We know of one test taker who looks through every question and makes notes regarding the category each question falls into. He will then go back and answer all of the questions within a single category before moving to the next category. This allows him to concentrate on a single area for a longer period of time. Each user must decide individually what works best. Following are a few generally accepted hints for taking the test.

Tips for taking the actual test include:

■ We have never seen a Cisco question that was purposefully designed to fool you into choosing the wrong answer. Cisco does, however, force you to know thoroughly all aspects covered in the tests. For example, you may see a question regarding access lists. Unless you know exactly the correct syntax for an access list, you will probably not be able to choose the correct answer from the available ones. Be sure that you know the subject areas you are being tested on in advance.

■ Sometimes, knowing what is incorrect is as important as knowing what is correct. Being able to eliminate two wrong answers will improve your chances on a four-answer question to 50%, even if you are only guessing.

■ If you are unsure about an answer, mark the most probable answer and note the question number. If you have time when all of the questions are answered, go back and re-work the questions you were unsure about. Be sure that the test will allow you to return to a question before using this technique.

■ Sometimes, one question will answer a previous or future question. While answering a question, try to remember if you have seen the answer to that question before on this test. Look at the following two questions below and notice how question # 2 answers question # 1.

Question # 1

Which of the following is valid for assigning an IP address to an interface?

Answers:

   A: Router(config-if)#ip address 172.30.1.1

   B: Router(config-if)#ip address 172.30.1.1 255.255.255.0

   C: Router(config-if)#ip address 172.30.1 255.255.255.0

   D: Router(config)#ip address 172.30.1.1 255.255.255.0

Question # 2

You have configured "RouterA" with the following commands:

```
RouterA(config)# int E1
RouterA(config-if)#Ip address 172.30.1.1 255.255.255.0
RouterA(config-if)#int s1.1
RouterA(config-if)#Ip address 172.28.1.3 255.255.255.252
```

What command do you use on "RouterB" to send all traffic destined for the `172.30.1.1./24` subnet to the appropriate router?

Answers:

A: . . .

Notice how question # 2 shows the proper syntax for assigning an IP address to an interface within the question itself. This is a simplified example, but you may notice a similar situation on a test. Take advantage where you can.

- Never, ever, leave a question blank. If you must guess, choose what sounds best, even if you do not have a concept regarding the correct answer. A blank answer will always be marked wrong. Choosing any answer even if you plan on revisiting a question will ensure that the question is not left blank even if you run out of time.

- Take time enough to carefully read each question. Even if you think you instantly know the answer, make sure you read and understand the question and every possible answer. A single word can change the whole meaning of a question or answer.

- Do not spend all of your time on any one question. If you do not answer all of the questions you reduce your chances of passing.

- Test taking is a troubleshooting process. As in network troubleshooting, the first rule is that you should never panic.

Dealing with Test Failures

Somewhere along the path to CCIE, you are likely to fail at least one test. You may even realize while in the middle of the test that you are likely to fail. There are some advantages to be gained from taking a test, even if you do not pass. The most important thing to remember if you do not pass a test is that this has absolutely no reflection on how smart you are, on how nice a person you are, or even on how well you know the material. It merely means that you did not answer enough questions correctly.

If you are in the middle of a test and believe that you cannot possibly pass the test, do not simply give up. Giving up will ensure that you do not pass. We have been in tests where we were convinced that we would fail. It was an amazingly pleasant feeling to learn that we had passed. Make notes on the areas that you need to study. Although you are not allowed to take the notes out of the testing room, writing them down will help you remember the areas where you need to concentrate your study efforts. Immediately upon exiting the testing room, write down on a new piece of paper the areas that you need to concentrate on. If you can remember exact questions where you had trouble, writing them down will help while studying for the next test.

There are also those who feel that taking tests is a valid form of study. They feel that the only way to really know what to expect on a test is to take that test. Because Cisco is very strict about its non-disclosure agreement, we find this philosophy hard to argue against. Although it is possible to purchase practice tests from a number of vendors, there is usually no guarantee that the questions on the practice exam are the same on the current Cisco test.

Chapter Summary

This book is designed for the engineer to work through all of the chapters consecutively. Even if you believe that you already know a subject thoroughly, it is still worth the effort to read the chapters in order. Each chapter builds on the lessons learned in the previous chapters. To successfully pass the exam, you must know all of the areas being tested. This book will cover all of these areas.

Now, move on to Chapter 2, in which we introduce the basic concepts necessary for successful troubleshooting.

Methodology, Tools, and Commands

2

Troubleshooting Methodology

When a network failure occurs, the only issue management is concerned about is how quickly the network will be running again. In the television industry, any time you have dead air the station has lost revenue because it cannot show advertisements during that time and this revenue can never be recovered. The same is true of networking. Any time the network is not functioning properly your company is losing money in the form of lost productivity, additional manpower needed to accomplish the same tasks, and data.

The question raised here is not how to prevent networks from having problems. All networks of a significant size and complexity will experience periods of instability. This is not a reflection on the quality of the personnel maintaining the network. This is a fact of life. The issue is not if the network will go down, rather, the issue is how quickly the network will come back up and how long the network will stay up.

Objectives Covered in the Chapter

We will examine the following five test objectives in this chapter:

■ Describe the information gathering and communications to get the best use of Cisco's service and support services.

■ Use an efficient problem-solving method when troubleshooting and documenting internetwork problems.

■ Use a problem-solving model to systematically troubleshoot a given problem and list the values of using a systematic process.

■ Apply a process for documenting the steps taken to isolate potential causes and determine potential solutions.

■ Demonstrate knowledge of common data link layer characteristics and key troubleshooting targets likely to be found in campus *local area networks* (LANs).

Review of Network Complexity Issues

How can any one person be expected to know all of the possible causes of a given problem? Suppose you work for a medium-sized company that has 300 routers, several switches, and several thousand users. The network uses access lists, three different routing protocols, and three different LAN protocols. Is it reasonable to expect that any one engineer can solve any issue? In short, the answer is yes if two precautions are taken and a sound troubleshooting methodology is followed.

First, a network diagram should be drawn. This does not need to be a complex diagram. Actually, it does not even need to be drawn. A spreadsheet will suffice. The purpose of this document is to give the troubleshooter a single source of all the information available regarding the network layout and configuration. The main documentation features to be included on the network map are as follows:

■ Router connections

■ Equipment serial numbers

■ Routing protocols

- IOS version
- Installed modules
- Access lists
- Addresses (both network and serial)
- Switches
- Hubs
- A copy of all configurations

If you are in the process of designing or redesigning a network, the documentation process is usually accomplished during the design stage. A thorough network design will automatically lead to efficient and logical network topology documentation. If you are designing a network, use the design documents as the basis for your network diagrams, remembering to document changes between the planned and actual implementations.

Failure to update your network map when changes are made will result in the map becoming less than useless; it will become dangerous. You must make a brand new network map in case a crisis arises rather than rely on a map that does not reflect reality.

Second, a baseline of your network performance must be accomplished while the network is performing in its usual manner. A baseline is used to record the amount of traffic on a network during periods of low, medium, and high usage. It establishes a written record of how the network performs. This record is then used for comparison to determine if a problem actually does exist. For example, a user may say that the network is running slowly. Without a baseline, the engineer cannot distinguish if the slowness is real or only perceived. Baselines should be run periodically and whenever a significant change has been made to the network. Two good tools used for baselining a network are Cisco Works and Cisco Works for Switched Internetworks. These will be discussed in Chapter 3, "Troubleshooting Tools." The main items to include in your baseline are as follows:

- The protocols running on the network
- The percentage of bandwidth used by each protocol
- The peak and average utilization by each protocol
- The packet size with percentages of each size of packet
- The peak and average number of cyclical redundancy check (CRC) errors
- The peak and average frame transmissions per second by segment
- The existence of any jabbers

- The peak and average collisions per second by the collision domain
- The peak and average runs by segment

We will next look at the Cisco troubleshooting methodology. This method will show how the correct approach to a problem is the first step in actually solving it.

The Cisco Problem-Solving Method

Cisco uses an eight-step problem-solving method. Each of these steps will be examined in turn. It should be noted that these steps tend to overlap each other and that the method is recursive in nature. For example, documenting the solution can, and probably should, be done while the plan is being implemented. The steps within the Cisco problem-solving method are as follows:

1. Define the problem.
2. Gather facts and analyze the problem.
3. Evaluate the causes of the problem.
4. Design a plan of action.
5. Implement the plan.
6. Evaluate the results.
7. Repeat until the problem is solved.
8. Document the solution.

Spend a few minutes looking at Figure 2-1, which lays out the process advocated by Cisco for solving network problems. Each of these steps will be discussed.

Defining the Problem

Defining the problem really consists of asking the correct questions. These questions should generally use the format of *Who, What, When,* and *Where.* These questions should be viewed as recursive. When you answer one question, you need to continue asking questions until you become satisfied that

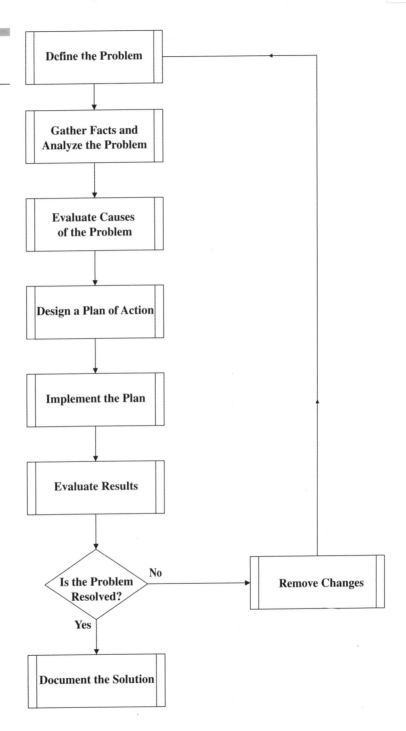

Figure 2-1
Cisco problem-
solving method

the total picture is accurately known. Users, administrators, help desk personnel, and anyone else experiencing or having knowledge of the issues should be questioned.

Following is a guideline of some of the common questions and possible causes. These guidelines are useful throughout the first four steps of the Cisco model. Many more questions may be asked and there could be many other causes possibly associated with these questions. This should not be considered an exhaustive list.

Who is affected by the problem? Is this an individual user, a group of users with something apparent in common, or is this problem experienced by all users throughout the network?

A single user experiencing problems may point to one of several issues. These include

- A physical layer problem including a bad network cable
- A hardware failure on the specific host
- Software incorrectly loaded or corrupted, especially networking protocols
- An incorrectly configured host address or subnet mask
- An incorrectly configured default gateway

A group of users sharing common properties and experiencing problems may point to several issues such as

- A network device failure, such as a hub or switch
- A router interface failure
- A server failure
- An access list configuration error
- A VLAN configuration error

Figure 2-2 shows a hypothetical university utilizing a FDDI ring for their metropolitan area network (MAN). Assume that the symptoms reported are that the business, science, and mathematics schools can all access the school of psychology's information. However, psychology cannot see any other users. This would indicate that the area we should focus on first for our solution is the school of psychology. Answering the who question allows us to concentrate our remaining questions on our area of interest.

Figure 2-2
MAN example

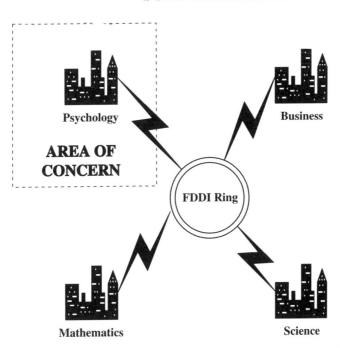

SCHOOL EXAMPLE

What is the symptom of the problem? Is this an issue of no connectivity, an issue of partial connectivity, or an issue of no connectivity? Issues concerning no connectivity can be attributed to

- A hardware failure
- A Frame Relay or other long-distance communications service failure
- A routing protocol failure

Issues concerning partial connectivity can be attributed to

- Access lists
- Incorrect subnet masks
- Routing protocol incompatibilities

When does the problem occur? Is this an intermittent problem, a problem that occurs on a regular basis, or a new problem that just started?

An intermittent problem could be caused by

- A Frame Relay or other long distance communications service failure
- Congestion
- Routing loops

A regularly occurring problem is usually caused by congestion. A new problem is liable to be caused by

- A change in an access list
- A new hardware failure
- A routing protocol change
- A newly added route

Where do the symptoms occur? The symptoms can occur in the core, distribution, or access areas, or throughout the network. Problems in the core area are generally attributed to

- Routing protocol changes, especially IGP routing protocols
- The redistribution of routes

Problems in the distribution area are usually associated with access lists or any other issue listed above. Problems in the access area can be contributed to any issue listed above.

NOTE: *We should spend a little time at this point to review the three parts of the hierarchical network design model and each of their functions. Remember that these layers may overlap each other and are not always configured in a clearly defined manner.*

The core layer usually consists of a high-speed switched backbone. Its sole purpose is to transfer packets in the fastest manner possible. No access lists or filtering should be done on this layer.

The distribution layer is used to differentiate the core from the access layers and to provide packet manipulation. This is the layer where security, VLAN routing, and translations between differing media such as Token Ring and Ethernet take place.

The access layer is where users are connected to the network. This is the layer responsible for microsegmentation (Ethernet switching) and MAC layer filtering. It may also have access lists applied.

Figure 2-3 provides an overview of how the three layers relate to each other.

Figure 2-3
Hierarchical
network model

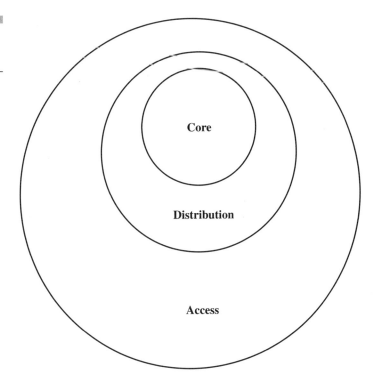

Although many more questions can and should be asked during the problem definition phase, these should give you an idea of the types of questions to ask.

Gather Facts and Analyze the Problem

Gathering the facts and analyzing the problem consists of looking at the equipment and attempting to see where exactly the problem is showing itself. This will consist of looking at interfaces and process commands similar to "show serial interfaces" and "show controllers," as well as looking at memory, buffers, and CPU utilization. This is the step where you document what you have found in order to be able to evaluate the causes. If you are experiencing an intermittent loss of connection, you would look at how many times an interface had been reset. If the issue is related to an access list problem, you would want to see exactly how the access list was set up. Compare these notes to the existing documentation to see if they agree. If an existing configuration does not agree with the documentation, you will need to review your policies on updating the documentation. After you have gathered as many facts as possible, it is time to move on to evaluating the causes of the problem.

Evaluate Causes of the Problem

Now that we know the facts and have analyzed the problem, our next task is to determine what is causing the problem. At this point, we should know exactly how the problem manifests itself and exactly who is being affected by it. If we do not know this, we will need to go back one or two steps and rethink the problem.

This is actually one of the easiest steps in the Cisco problem-solving model if we have gathered the correct information. We know who the problem is affecting, what the symptoms are, when the problem occurs, and where the problem is occurring. The only question left is why is the problem occurring. This is the point when a thorough understanding of the OSI model can become invaluable to the troubleshooter. Understanding the functions and knowing the protocols of each of the OSI model layers will provide the clues necessary to find out why the problem occurs.

For example, if the issue is that the *file transfer protocol* (FTP) services do not work for some users while all other services do, it is fairly safe to assume that the problem is an access list issue. How do we come to that conclusion? First, if all other services work, we know there are no issues with the physical or data link layers. This is due in large part to the fact that layers 1 and 2 do not know or care whether we are running FTP or the *trivial file transfer protocol* (TFTP). Second, we know that FTP is a layer 4 (transport layer) protocol. We know that FTP should not be affected by anything at layers 5, 6, or 7. FTP, like all other applications, will not work if lower-layer protocols are not working. Upper-layer protocols will not and cannot stop a lower-layer protocol from working. This only leaves layers 3 and 4. Then ask yourself what configuration issue that resides at layers 3 or 4 can cause some but not all communication to work? The access list answer should be high on your list of possible causes because the purpose of an access list is to enable some but not all communications to work.

After you believe the cause has been found, spend some extra time to determine what other causes could be responsible. Try to avoid having only a single possible cause. The more probable causes you are able to determine, the more likely you will succeed. In the example above, there could be other causes of the problem. For example, assume that the workers are using a *dynamic host configuration protocol* (DHCP) server for their IP addresses and are also using IPX/SPX on their LAN. If the only remote application they ever use is FTP and the DHCP server has failed, it is entirely possible that these symptoms would be exactly the same. The DHCP failure would cause the *Internet protocol* (IP) not to assign an address. Since tIP is a layer 3 protocol and FTP is a layer 4 protocol, having the IP stack not initialized correctly would cause FTP to fail. This is why it is critical to have your network documentation readily available. Without the documentation, it would be much easier to assume that an access list is the only possible cause of this problem. Listing the possible causes in descending order of probability will allow your action plan to be designed to find the most probable cause first.

Design an Action Plan

Only after you have determined the most probable causes of the problem can you create a plan of action. This plan should include the steps you are planning to use in your efforts to fix the problem. Be as detailed as possible while documenting the steps to be taken. The more detailed your plan, the more likely you will follow it.

In the previous step, you laid out the probable causes in descending order. Use this list to document the steps to be taken in order by the likelihood of problem resolution. Using the example from the previous step, our action plan could look like this:

1. Change the access list on 172.16.1.1 (s0.16) to allow 172.16.1.0/24 through to 172.18.2.0/24.
2. Change the access list on 172.18.2.1 (s0.1) to allow 172.16.1.0/24 into 172.18.2.0/24.
3. Verify 172.16.1.0/24 can see the DHCP server at 10.12.3.7.
4. Change the access list on 10.12.3.1 (s0.24) to allow UDP packets from 172.16.1.0/24 to 10.12.3.7.
5. Change the IP helper address on 172.16.1.1 so that it points to 10.12.3.7.

Once your plan is designed, you can start implementing it.

Implement the Plan

When implementing the plan, it is important that only one change be made at a time. The results of this change should be evaluated and documented if successful. If the change is not successful, immediately undo the change.

Equally important is that you should do what was planned. It is sometimes easy to try new things in the middle of implementing the plan because the plan is not working. The danger in this approach is that you will soon lose track of the original plan and can easily make the situation worse. Instead of diverting from the plan, step back, redesign the action plan, and then implement it.

A caution about security procedures during the implementation phase is warranted. Security is a real concern for many network administrators. Although the ideal would be to never loosen security even while troubleshooting a problem, this may not always be feasible. When you must loosen security on the network, open the network as little as possible. Also strive to loosen security for as little time as possible. The former will still thwart attempts of the less astute hacker, while the latter will lessen the chances that a hacker will be attempting to breach your network while security is lax. After the plan has been implemented, we will need to see how successful our attempts to fix the problem have been.

Evaluate the Results

The simplest method of observing the results is to test using the data gained in step one. Are the symptoms still present? Are some of the symptoms still present? If you have concisely stated the problem in step one, it is relatively easy to test if these symptoms still exist. Try to reproduce the problems as stated in step one. Talk to the users, administrators, and anyone else who experienced the problem. Try to avoid being too eager to assume that the problem has been resolved. Double-checking the results can save having to deal with the same problem later in the day. If some symptoms are solved but others still remain, document the solution and move to the next step, which directs you all the way back to the first step.

Intermittent problems may not always be tested easily. Sometimes the test merely waits until another failure occurs. In this case, it is critical to document the changes to the system before you have finalized this issue.

Repeat Until the Problem Is Solved

In a perfect world we would never need to repeat the process because our analysis of the issue would definitively point to the one and only issue. Unfortunately, we do not live in a perfect world and our analysis is seldom perfect despite how hard we strive for perfection. Let's look at what happens when we do not initially succeed with our action plan.

When an action plan does not produce the results as expected, our first objective should be to undo all the changes made during the attempt to fix the problem. Leaving the changes that have not fixed the issue in place can cause residual problems. For example, suppose an access list is changed without any apparent result. This will lead to unexpected results in the future if the list is not returned to the original state. Also, changing any one item will demand a new analysis of the problem because this is now a different configuration than the one used for the original analysis. Most problems that are not immediately obvious will require multiple passes through the problem-solving steps.

Our next objective should be to find out where the analysis failed. It is critical to restart the process by defining the problem. Often it is tempting to assume that the reason the resolution was not achieved is due to improper implementation of the plan. Use caution and don't assume any one part is at fault. Let's say you've gone from step one through step seven without resolving the issue. If you only go as far back as step three, and the real failure is at step one, you may never solve the problem. Most issues on networks occur at lower layers of the OSI model. Most issues in problem solving also occur at the lower levels. Pay extra attention to the first steps in the process.

Question all of the suppositions you made while doing your problem analysis. Redefine the problem, taking more time to examine details and dig deeper into all of the issues when you are making a second attempt at resolution. If there is something missing during the first attempt, make sure that the second attempt does not suffer from the same oversight as the first.

Assume that you have gone through the above steps several times but have been unable to resolve the problem. What do you do? The first thing *not* to do is to make the issue a matter of pride. Do not hesitate to call for assistance, which could come from coworkers, an outside consultant, or Cisco's *Technical Assistance Center* (TAC). Show whoever is helping you the documentation you have gathered to this point and what you have tried in order to resolve the issue. Having the documentation handy will not only impress them with your professionalism, but it will also save a lot of time.

Document the Solution

Earlier in this chapter we discussed the need for good network documentation. We also examined the problems associated with out-of-date network documentation. Once the issue is resolved, everyone suddenly becomes calm. Now is the time to document the changes that have been made. If you choose to wait until the next day before starting the documentation, it may never get done. Tomorrow there will other emergencies and more pressing issues.

There is also another reason for immediate documentation. Can you guarantee that the fix will still work tonight after you leave? If you do not document the changes, you run the risk of someone else changing the system without knowledge of the changes that have occurred. This can lead to other unexpected issues. Documentation is an integral part of solving the problem and should not be viewed as an optional component.

Now that we have looked at the Cisco method of problem solving, we will see how the OSI model is used within the Cisco system to quickly resolve the issues.

The OSI Model and Troubleshooting

The OSI model is the primary tool used in troubleshooting any computer-related problem, whether that problem deals with a network, a desktop PC, or an application. This is true even for systems that do not follow the OSI model because all models follow the same basic premise: no upper layer will work correctly until all of the lower layers work correctly. This is critical to remember when approaching any problem. Until you are sure that all of the lower layers are working properly, you are wasting your time in attempting to solve an upper-layer issue.

The OSI model has provided tremendous benefits for the computer industry. Among these benefits are allowing specialization, standardizing interfaces, breaking the complexity into manageable pieces, and adding to the ease of troubleshooting. Study Figure 2-4 and review the purposes of each of the seven layers of the OSI model before we do a review of each of them. Because each layer must rely upon the layer below, we will start at the bottom of the OSI model with the physical layer.

Physical Layer

The physical layer really has only three responsibilities. The first two responsibilities are to send and receive bits of data. If the physical layer does not provide the proper physical connection to another device, no data can be transferred. Let's take a moment and expand upon that last statement since it is critical in understanding exactly why we need the physical layer.

The physical layer is the layer responsible for physically connecting to another device over some sort of medium. This medium may be wires in an

Figure 2-4
OSI reference model

OSI MODEL	PURPOSE
Application **Layer 7**	Translates user to computer Compression Encryption ID communications partners
Presentation **Layer 6**	Translates Connects layer 7 to layer 5
Session **Layer 5**	Controls the dialog between nodes Flow control
Transport **Layer 4**	End-to-end communication Reliable transmission Logical connection
Network **Layer 3**	Sends packets from source to destination Routing protocols Best path
Data Link **Layer 2**	Two sub-levels - LLC & MAC Translates from layer 3 to layer 1 Framing
Physical **Layer 1**	Physical connection Sends bits across the wire Topology

Ethernet connection, radio waves in a wireless system, or light signals as in FDDI. This must be done in a way agreed upon by both devices. Included in the "connection agreement" are many items that need to be considered, such as the timing, voltage, speed of data transfer, and "keep alive" routines. All the items mentioned, as well as hardware failures, can affect the stability of the physical layer.

If the physical layer is not stable, all the layers above will suffer from this instability. For example, suppose you have Frame Relay connections that experience a repeated loss of connections. This may be manifested by an intermittent loss of routes to remote sites. The initial reaction of the network engineer could be to assume the problem resides in the routing protocol. No amount of troubleshooting or changes to the routing protocol configurations will solve the problem because it resides at a lower layer. Working from the bottom of the OSI model towards the top will prevent the engineer from making this false assumption.

The final responsibility of the physical layer is to interface with the data link layer. All layers are responsible for communication with the layers that reside above and below them. We will continue moving up the OSI model to the data link layer.

Data Link Layer

The data link layer transfers messages between the network and physical layers. The data link layer is also responsible for the formatting of binary messages into an object called a frame. Generally speaking, a frame is data that has been encapsulated with header and/or trailer information. The actual format of the frame is determined by the frame specifications. In order to understand the differing frame types, we will need to break down the data link layer into two sublayers, the *media access control* (MAC) and the *logical link control* (LLC).

Figure 2-5 shows how the data link layer is composed of the MAC and the LLC sublayers. This is done to enable manufacturers to program to the MAC layer while allowing software vendors to program to the LLC layer. Using this method, a network card manufacturer can make a single card that will work on a number of different frame types with the proper software.

The MAC layer is responsible for access to the media including issues of token passing, polling, and contention. This is where frames are built out of the binary data received from the physical layer and where the *cyclic redundancy check* (CRC) is done. The MAC layer also enables the adapter to accept broadcast and multicast packets.

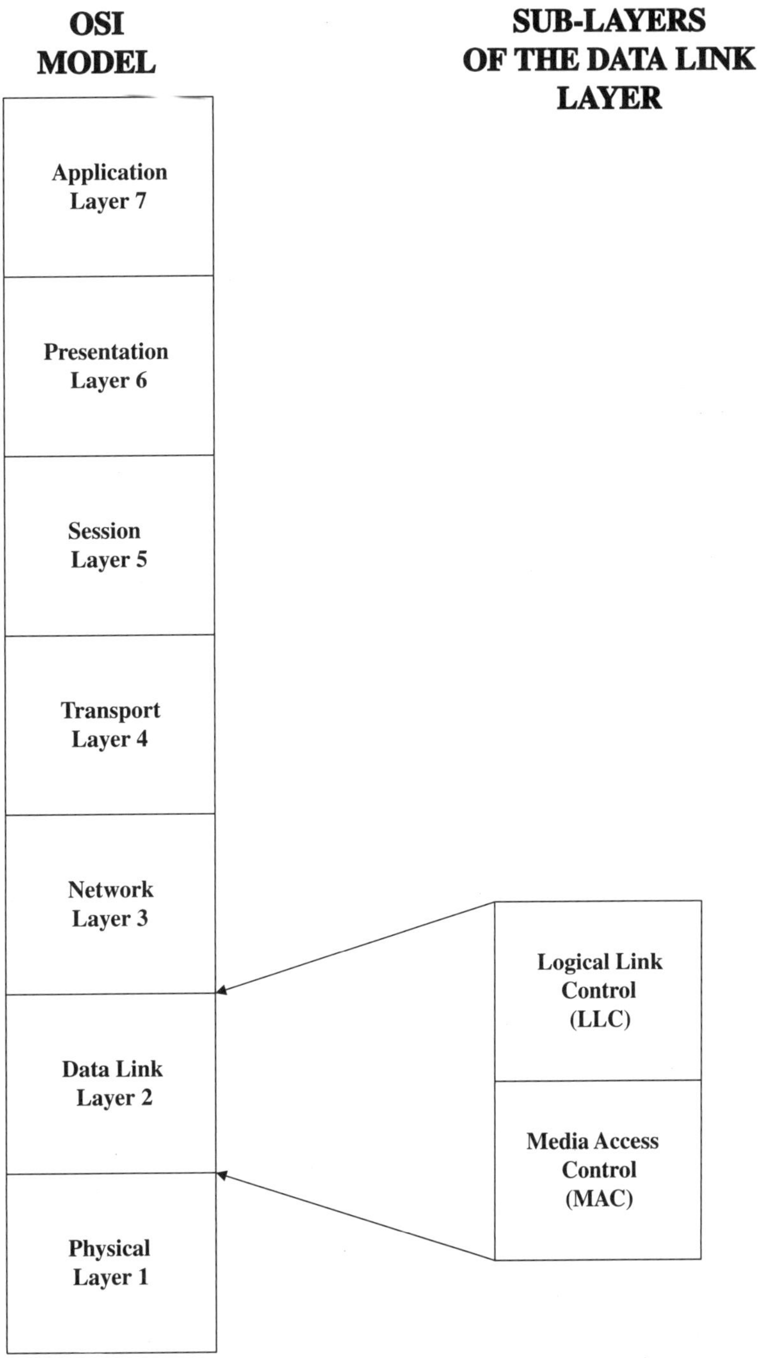

Figure 2-5
MAC. and LLC
sublayers

**OSI
MODEL**

**SUB-LAYERS
OF THE DATA LINK
LAYER**

| **Application**
Layer 7 |
| **Presentation**
Layer 6 |
| **Session**
Layer 5 |
| **Transport**
Layer 4 |
| **Network**
Layer 3 |
| **Data Link**
Layer 2 |
| **Physical**
Layer 1 |

**Logical Link
Control
(LLC)**

**Media Access
Control
(MAC)**

The LLC allows protocols at the network layer to operate independently from the hardware installed at the physical layer. This is accomplished through the use of *source service access points* (SSAPs) and *destination service access points* (DSAPs) within the Ethernet frame. SSAPs and DSAPs are used in 802.3 frame types, which operate slightly differently from Ethernet_II frame types. Figure 2-6 shows how Ethernet_II, 802.3, 802.5, and SNAP frames are related to the MAC and LLC sublayers.

Ethernet_II does not use a length field. Instead, when the frame ends, the receiver reads backwards for the four-byte frame check sequence (FCS) and extracts the data from the frame. Ethernet_II uses a two-byte type field that specifies which upper-layer protocol will receive the data. The largest length in an Ethernet frame is 1,518 bytes, including the header. Because the type field always has a value greater than 05DC hex (1,500 decimal), the adapter knows that this is a type field as opposed to a length field and therefore it is an Ethernet_II frame. This is very different from the method used in 802.3.

The Institute of Electrical and Electronics Engineers (IEEE) 802.2 frames are 802.3 frames with an LLC header. 802.3 frames use a two-byte length field. Following this field is what defines the difference between 802.3 and SNAP formats. If the first two bytes of the LLC are set to AAAA, then the

Figure 2-6
MAC and LLC compared to 802.2, 802.3, and 802.5

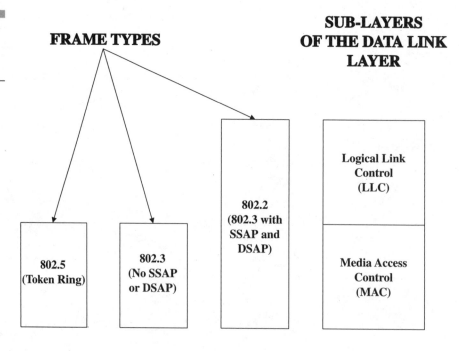

frame is considered a SNAP frame. Any other value designates the frame as an 802.3 frame. An 802.3 frame uses DSAP and SSAP fields. The DSAP field points to the memory buffer of the receiving station's application, while the SSAP specifies the source of the sending application. Figure 2-7 shows how Ethernet_II, 802.3, and SNAP frames all have similarities and differences.

Network Layer

The network layer is responsible for several tasks. First among them is determining the best path through a network. Network topology maps are built by routing protocols residing at the network layer. Protocols such as RIP, OSPF, IGRP, the *enhanced interior gateway routing protocol* (EIGRP), and BGP all utilize the network layer to determine the data pathways.

IP and IPX also reside in the network layer. IP and IPX are connection-less protocols. The connection-oriented protocols used with IP and IPX (TCP and SPX) reside at the transport layer of the OSI model. Other connection-oriented protocols may reside at the network layer. Two examples of this are X.25 and LLC-Type 2.

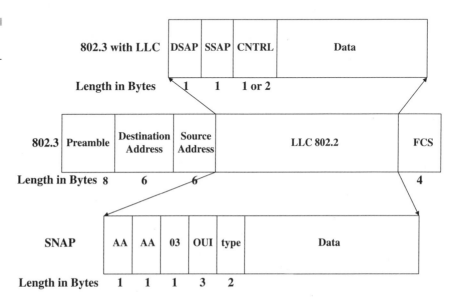

Figure 2-7
Ethernet frame types

NOTE: *A few words regarding connection-oriented and connectionless protocols is in order at this point. Many people confuse the acknowledgement of messages with a connection-oriented protocol. A connection-oriented protocol establishes a connection and receives the acknowledgement of messages while the session is still established. A connectionless protocol may receive acknowledgements, but these are received without a session being established. The difference can be compared to the ways a telephone call and an e-mail message work. Let's say your friend calls you to give directions to a party. While he is giving you directions, you acknowledge you have received the instructions to a certain point. If your friend starts telling you directions too quickly, you ask him to slow down. This is the way flow control works in a connection-oriented session. When the call is over, you say goodbye and then hang up.*

In an e-mail from your friend regarding directions to a party, if you are polite, you will thank your friend for sending the directions and tell him you will meet him at the party. If you do not understand the directions, you can send him an e-mail asking him to explain further. You could send a response to his e-mail immediately or in a week. It does not matter because there is no ongoing e-mail session. This is how a connectionless protocol operates.

The transport layer will make use of connection-oriented and connectionless protocols. We will look at this layer of the OSI model next.

Transport Layer

The transport layer is the first layer where a connection-oriented session can normally be established. TCP, SPX, and AppleTalk's ADSP are three examples of connection-oriented protocols. The transport layer will also support connectionless protocols such as a *user datagram protocol* (UDP).

One reason that connection-oriented protocols are used within this layer is that one of the responsibilities of the transport layer is to establish a reliable transmission of data between hosts. A reliable transmission becomes much easier using a connection-oriented protocol compared to a connectionless protocol.

Figure 2-8 shows a typical complete connection-oriented session. The session starts with the initiator sending a synchronize request. The receiver sends back a synchronize request. The initiator then sends an acknowledgement and the data transfer starts. During the session, the receiver may send an indication that the buffer is full. The initiator will

Figure 2-8

Flow control

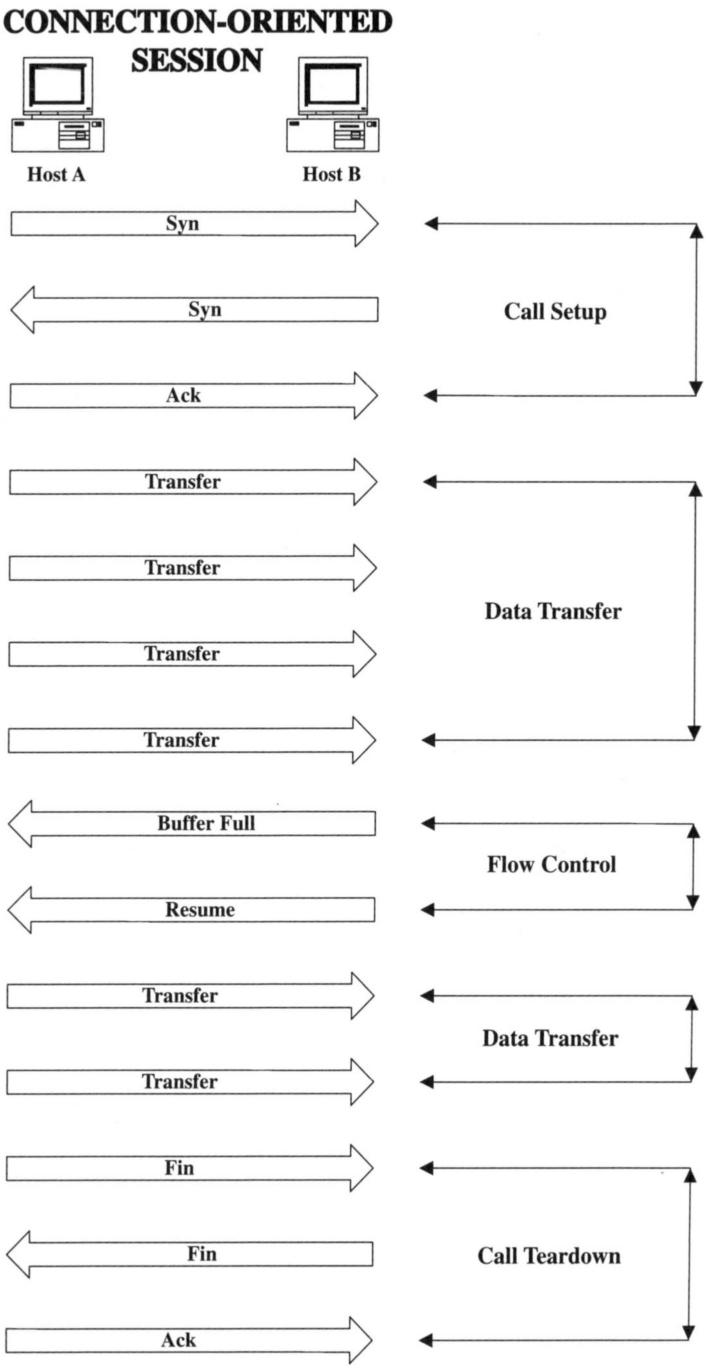

CONNECTION-ORIENTED SESSION

Host A   Host B

Syn →

← Syn

Ack →

Call Setup

Transfer →

Transfer →

Transfer →

Transfer →

Data Transfer

← Buffer Full

← Resume

Flow Control

Transfer →

Transfer →

Data Transfer

Fin →

← Fin

Ack →

Call Teardown

wait until it receives a notification that the data transfer can resume. Finally, one of the hosts will choose to end the session. This is done by one machine sending a finished command and the other sending back a finish command, followed by an acknowledgement command. This is only an example of a connection session. Further details will be given when we discuss TCP/IP and ISDN.

Session Layer

The session layer is concerned with the coordination of dialog between hosts. Session layers operate in three modes: simplex, half-duplex, and full-duplex.

Simplex is a one-way communication similar to the way a television works. The receiver has no input into what data is being received or exactly how much data is transferred. When the television show is over, the communication is finished.

Half-duplex is similar to using e-mail. One person sends information; another receives the information and then responds. Unlike full-duplex, simplex and half-duplex do not require flow control.

Full-duplex is a two-way conversation between hosts. The main requirement of full-duplex mode is that flow control is implemented. Full-duplex enables the fastest possible exchange of information between two hosts.

The session layer also breaks communications into three distinct connection-oriented phases. The stages of a connection-oriented communications session are establishment, communication, and release. Establishment is the process of agreeing upon the parameters of communication, such as setting up the initial call, choosing the protocol used, and establishing the initial data transfer size. Communication is the stage where data transfer is actually taking place. During this stage, flow control is used by the receiving system to temporarily stop transfers until the receiving buffers can be emptied. The final stage of a connection-oriented session is the release stage. This is when the connection is dropped and memory used during the communication process is freed.

Presentation Layer

The presentation layer is generally used as a translator service. The presentation layer translates data moving between the application and session layers. The presentation layer also converts data for other purposes. For example, translating from EBCDIC to ASCII is done at the presentation layer, as is translating from TN3270 to Telnet.

The presentation layer has agreed-upon standards for data storage and retrieval. These standards enable the exchange of information across differing platforms. Some of these standards include JPEG, PICT, MPEG, and MIDI. Without these standards, a Macintosh would not necessarily be able to read the same JPEG file as is read by an IBM-compatible machine.

Application Layer

The application layer sits on the top of the OSI model. In this position, the application layer translates between the presentation layer and the person running the application. The application layer is also responsible for determining the availability of local resources and combining the functionality of different programs. This layer is also used to identify communications partners and their resources.

Now that we have looked at each of the seven layers of the OSI model, we will look at how the OSI model fits into the troubleshooting process. The next section will describe two methods of approaching an issue using the OSI model. These approaches, if used properly, will enable you to solve any problem encountered on your network. The first method is to work from the bottom of the OSI model towards the top. The second method is to divide the problem to eliminate several layers of the OSI model at one time. Both of these approaches have their strengths as well as their weaknesses. We will look at each of these approaches before examining two scenarios and how each approach can be used to solve the same problem under the Cisco problem-solving method.

Climbing the Ladder

When troubleshooting a problem, this method demands that one always look at the lower layers first. Once layer-1 connectivity has been verified, layer 2 is looked at to determine if it is the problem. Only after layer-2 performance is verified is layer 3 verified. This holds for layers 4, 5, 6, and 7. The beauty of this approach is that virtually any problem can be found and solved in a logical, consistent, and easy-to-implement manner. Since most problems are associated with the lower layers, this approach can also be used to solve most problems quickly. This is especially true when groups of users are affected in the same manner. The weakness of this approach is that you cannot jump directly to the problem. This means that even if a layer-4 issue is suspected, you still need to check three other layers before getting to the heart of the problem.

In Figure 2-9, we see how this approach is used to attack a problem. Contrast this approach to the divide-and-conquer approach discussed next.

Divide and Conquer   This approach attempts to cut out large areas that could not be part of the problem. For example, if the problem is that some users cannot access certain parts of the network, then it is usually not related to a physical layer problem because physical layer problems are usually manifested by either a lack of connectivity or sporadic connectivity. The strength of this method is the same as the strength of a binary sort. If done correctly, this is the fastest method available. The weakness of this system is that it is possible to overlook a critical issue. The result of overlooking a critical issue is mainly psychological. If the engineer becomes convinced he has already considered a possible cause, he is naturally reluctant to look at that cause again. The Cisco problem-solving methodology takes this into account by requiring you to repeat the process if the proposed solution does not work.

In Figure 2-10, we see an example of how one can use the divide-and-conquer method to approach a problem. In this example, the problem is that a certain application does not run from one of the workstations. In this example, assume that we know there are no filters involved that will prevent certain applications from working properly. The first step is to ensure that connectivity is available from the workstation all the way through to the server. This is accomplished by using the traceroute command. If the traceroute is successful, we know that the problem must reside at a higher level. This allows us to check all four lower layers at one time. If the traceroute is not successful, it would be necessary to start at layer 1 in order to determine exactly where the problem resides. This is a prime example of how to correctly use the divide-and-conquer method. Look at the diagram below to see an example of the approach we have taken.

We used a single traceroute command to ensure that the four layers were all working. The question raised is exactly what did we check? If traceroute receives a response from a single device along the path, we know the following:

- The physical layer is working or we would not see any devices.
- The data link layer is working or we would not see any devices.
- TCP/IP (layers 3 and 4) are working or we would not see any devices.
- The default gateway is shown as the first hop in the trace.

As long as all of the lower layers are checked, there is no reason we cannot take the shortest route to the heart of the problem. However, be absolutely sure that any method chosen will actually check exactly what you

Figure 2-9
Climbing the ladder

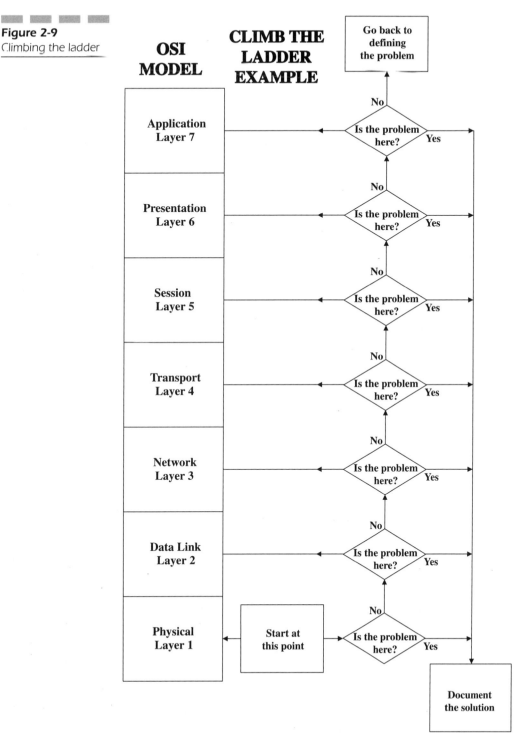

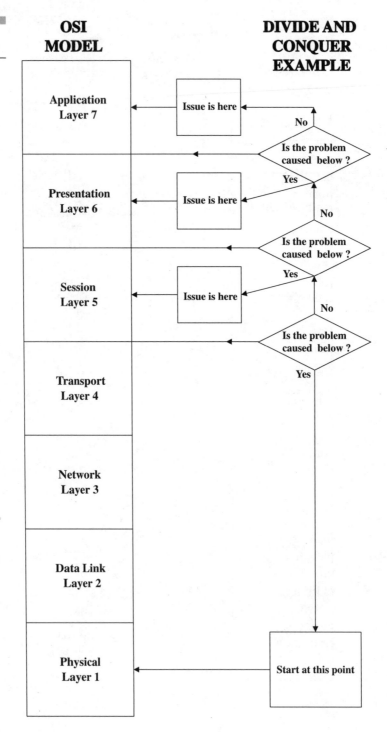

Figure 2-10
Divide and conquer

think is being checked. Again, the weakness of this approach is that it is easy to assume something has been checked when it actually has not been.

As a quick reference, we have provided Figure 2-11. You can use this chart to find the major protocols and ascertain which layer of the OSI model is associated to which protocol. Although this chart will not provide all the protocols, it is useful to quickly find the associations between protocols and OSI layers.

Look at the scenarios presented at the end of this chapter. They will show how each of these methods can be used to come to the same conclusion.

After looking at these scenarios, it is reasonable to ask which method is better. Both approaches work equally well. The decision will be largely based upon personal preference and the type of problem encountered. There is also value to be gained by combining both approaches. For example, the divide-and-conquer approach can be used to determine that the issue lies somewhere in the layer-3 or layer-4 area. Then the climbing-the-ladder approach can be used starting at layer 3. This is a quick way of resolving issues.

There is one more area to discuss regarding methodologies. This area is concerned with the psychological aspects of troubleshooting a network.

Panic   Panic is a killer, both in a test situation and in real life. Panic causes one to react instead of plan and think. Panic is what the mind will experience when it has run out of options. The more serious the situation, the more important it becomes not to panic. The professional is that person who does not panic when everyone around him does. This chapter has given you the approaches and methodology necessary to solve any networking problem. There is no need for panic if one can approach the problem, describe the symptoms, and therefore solve the problem. If you have a disaster and start to panic, read this paragraph again.

You will eventually run across a supervisor, manager, or corporate officer whose first response to a network down situation is to panic. This person will tend to demand that the problem be solved immediately, even to the point of insisting that the problem be solved before a good analysis is completed. This trait will show itself by statements similar to "It doesn't matter who is affected, just fix it!" or "I don't want to hear that you are trying to figure it out. I want to hear that it has been fixed."

How does one deal with this unreasonable demand? Keep in mind that no one can fix a problem before the nature of the problem has been discovered. One of the best ways we have found to deal with someone who makes statements similar to those stated earlier is with infinite calmness and assurance. Tell them that in order to make the system work, you need to be very methodical in your approach, and that being methodical is the quickest way to solve the issue. Become the calm spot in the middle of the storm.

Figure 2-11

Protocols in the
OSI model

OSI MODEL	MAJOR PROTOCOLS
Application	FTP, Telnet, SMTP, POP3, XWindows, HTTP, IMAP4, CDP CMOT, SNMP, TFTP, RLOGIN, RSHELL, REXEC, SSH RADIUS, RTSP, NFS, SMB, DCA, NWSERIAL XNS Filing, XNS Printing, AFP, NLP, NDS, SAP, NCP
Presentation	SCS, IPDS, 3270 Data Stream, LU6.2, ISOPP XNS Courtier, Psotscript, TOPS
Session	NetBIOS(SSN), DNS, LDAP, TUP, TCAP, RPC, Data Flow Control PAD, ISO-SP, XNS Courier, ASP, PAP, Soft Talk
Transport	TCP, SPX, XOT, ISODE, DVMRP, TPKT-OSI, NetBIOS-DGM RTCP, RAS, RTP, Mobile-IP, UDP, XTP, H.405.x, H.235, H.245 T.125(GCC), T.125/T.122(MCS), B-ISUP, B-IDSN, DUP, PEP ISUP-ISDN, TUP, GSM/CDMA, SPX2, SPP, ATP, NBP, ADSP, ASP
Network	IP, IPX, ICMP, IGMP, RTMP, AURP, DDP, DHCP, BOOTP AFP, IDP, NetB IOS, NetBEUI, RPL, APR, APPN IS-IS, EIGRP, IGRP, BGP, GGP, HSRP, OSPF NHRP, NARP, PIM, SNDCP, AEP, ZIP
Data Link	RSRB, PPTP, L2F, L2TP, ATMP. ARP, RARP, IARP SLARP, STUN-SDLC, CLIP, SLIP, FDDI-MAC, DXI DXI-ATM, AAL1, AAL2, AAL3/4, AAL5, SDLC AARP, LAP, LAPB, HDLC, LMI, Q.933
Physical	10BaseT, 10Base5, 10Base2,10BaseF, 802.3, 802.5 FDDI, CDDI, SDDI, HSSI, V.35, PPP, CDPD xDSL, MTP1, ISDN-D, ISDN-B, Frame-Relay, LAN, ATM, SMDS

Do not fall into the trap of trying whatever first comes to mind in an effort to satisfy this person's need for instant solutions. Following a solid approach will almost always ensure that the problem is solved quicker than using a best guess method.

Chapter Summary

In this chapter, we looked at the Cisco problem-solving method and two different ways to approach problem solving. Both of these approaches are valid if used properly. Both of these approaches will also fail if used improperly. Constant, methodical, documented approaches are the key to solving any network problem you will encounter. If you follow Cisco's recommended methods and use either of the approaches as shown in this chapter, you will be able to solve any network issue you encounter.

Before moving on to the next chapter, take a few minutes and review both the Cisco problem-solving methodology and the two approaches used to find where the actual problem lies.

Frequently Asked Questions (FAQ)

Question: Why do I need to check if the link light is on when I know the issue is an access list issue?

Answer: You don't. You can choose to use the divide-and-conquer method instead. However, ask yourself how you know it's an access list issue. If the user can get to some resources but not others, then it should not be a physical layer issue. Knowing that some resources are available has allowed you to instantly, and perhaps unknowingly, determine that the issue does not reside in layer 1.

Question: Why is it important to always follow the same methods when troubleshooting?

Answer: Murphy's Law. The moment you decide to skip a step in the process, you will find that this was the one step that would have saved a lot of effort. Wouldn't you feel silly if you spend three or four hours on a problem just to discover that the issue was an obvious one?

Question: Do both methodologies work when supporting users over the phone?

Answer: Yes, with a few warnings. Because you cannot see what the user is actually doing, you will need to use some tricks to get your users to follow a systematic approach. For example, instead of asking the user if the network patch cable is plugged into the network inter-face card (NIC), ask them to remove the cable and look at the end. Ask them if the end looks clean. Then ask them to replace the cable making sure that they hear a click. This ensures that the cable is well seated. If you merely ask them if the cable is securely connected, the answer will almost always be yes, regardless of whether the cable has actually been checked. The users are not lying to you; they truly believe that the cable is securely connected. They simply tend to not have the experience to know when a cable is securely connected. Therefore, extra caution is required when relying on someone else's expertise.

Question: Which approach does the author prefer, the climbing-the-ladder approach or the divide-and-conquer approach?

Answer: We usually start with the divide-and-conquer method. This enables you to quickly eliminate several layers at one time. Then, if the problem is not easily found, we can still rely on the data gathered by the first method for use with the climbing-the-ladder approach. If an author prefers to always start off connectivity issues by using the ping and traceroute commands, this will tell us if the issue is above the transport layer or below. One test can eliminate approximately one-half of the OSI model layers.

Scenarios

Scenario #1   You are told that some users in the accounting department cannot log onto the Windows NT network using the existing 10BaseT network. You go to the accounting department and discover that users get a "cannot locate domain controller" error.

Ladder approach to Scenario #1: Looking at one of the non-working computers, you notice that the link light on the NIC is out. Checking several other computers, you notice that their link lights are also out. This is almost certainly caused by a physical layer problem. There is only one probable cause. The issue is that either a hub or a group of switch ports has quit working. We know this because a number of users in a single geographic area all experience a lack of a physical connection as indicated by the link lights. Another but less likely scenario is that the all of the cables leading from the accounting department have been cut. Unless you have a construction project within the building, it is highly unlikely that all of the cables would fail at the same time.

Divide approach to Scenario #1: You assume that all the computers in the accounting department are experiencing the same type of problem. Therefore, on the way to the accounting department, you stop in the wiring closet. You notice that the hub does not have a power light showing. Since this is the hub used by the accounting department, it is reasonable to assume that the problem is with the hub.

Scenario #2   You receive a call from the help desk saying that no users can get to a remote Frame Relay site. You get onto the main router and see that the route is showing through EIGRP. You can ping the remote site and call the help desk back. At this point they can see the remote site. You assume there was a problem, but that it has disappeared. Ten minutes later you get another call from the help desk saying they cannot get to the remote site again. On your router you see that the route is still showing through EIGRP, but this time you cannot ping the remote site. Now you know this is a recurring problem. Where do you start?

Ladder approach to scenario #2: Because the connectivity appears to come and go intermittently, you start by looking at the DCU/DSU through an SNMP utility. This shows you that the line has been dropped 20 times in the last hour. If the CSU/DSU (a physical layer device) is experiencing errors, you know the issue is on the Frame Relay line. If you do not have an SNMP-compatible CSU/DSU, you can still gather the equivalent information through "show frame lmi" and "show frame pvc" commands. These commands will be discussed further in Chapter 4, "Basic Diagnostic Commands."

Divide approach to Scenario #2: Checking the routing protocols, your first command is a "show ip eigrp neighbors." This shows that the remote router is no longer connected. You ask "what can cause an EIGRP neighbor to be seen intermittently?" The first answer you come up with is a physical layer issue. If the router is seen, then not seen, then seen again, this would indicate a serial line bouncing. Checking the CSU/DSU through an SNMP utility, you see that the line has been dropped 20 times in the last hour. You call your frame provider and ask them to monitor the line.

Both of these scenarios are simplistic in their problems and the resolutions. However, their value is to show how both approaches can be used to come to the same conclusion. Caution is urged, especially when using the divide-and-conquer method, to not assume any part works unless you have a test that will ensure the lower layers of the OSI model have been tested.

Questions

1. What advantage(s) are gained by changing only one variable at a time when troubleshooting? (Choose all that apply)

   a. Having made a single change makes it easier to undo that change.
   b. It helps to isolate the problem.
   c. It lengthens the time required to solve the problem.
   d. It allows you to eliminate a single cause of the problem.

2. How do you know when you have solved a network problem?

   a. Ask the users if the symptoms are still present.
   b. Run the tests that originally determined what was the problem.
   c. Ping the remote site.
   d. Show Run.

3. Which step in the troubleshooting process occurs after a change has been implemented but did not work?

   a. Design a plan of action.
   b. Evaluate the results.
   c. Repeat until the problem is solved.
   d. Evaluate the results

4. Which step in the troubleshooting process involves talking to users in order to gain the information necessary to fix the problem?

   a. Define the problem.
   b. Gather facts and analyze the problem.
   c. Evaluate the causes of the problem.
   d. Design a plan of action.

5. Which step in the troubleshooting process involves testing to see if the changes worked?

   a. Implement the plan.
   b. Evaluate the results.
   c. Repeat until the problem is solved.
   d. Document the solution.

6. Which step in the troubleshooting process occurs after the facts have been gathered?

   a. Design a plan of action.
   b. Evaluate the results.
   c. Evaluate causes of the problem.
   d. Define the problem.

7. What is the main purpose of the "defining the problem" step of the Cisco problem-solving model?

    a. It allows us to go directly to step 4.

    b. It allows us to form a clear and concise definition of the symptoms of the problem.

    c. It allows us to find the real cause of the problem.

    d. It allows the user to find the problem without having to go through the intermediate steps.

8. Which layer of the OSI model determines whether to use Ethernet_II or SNAP?

    a. Physical

    b. Data link

    c. Network

    d. Transport

    e. Session

    f. Presentation

    g. Application

9. Which layer of the OSI model handles the conversion of ASCII to EBCDIC?

    a. Physical

    b. Data link

    c. Network

    d. Transport

    e. Session

    f. Presentation

    g. Application

10. At which layer of the OSI model do most errors occur?

    a. Physical

    b. Data link

    c. Network

    d. Transport

    e. Session

    f. Presentation

    g. Application

11. Which layer puts binary information into frames?

    a. Physical

    b. Data link

    c. Network

    d. Transport

    e. Session

    f. Presentation

    g. Application

12. TCP resides at which layer of the OSI model?

    a. Physical

    b. Data link

    c. Network

    d. Transport

    e. Session

    f. Presentation

    g. Application

13. IP resides at which layer of the OSI model?

    a. Physical

    b. Data link

    c. Network

    d. Transport

    e. Session

    f. Presentation

    g. Application

14. Which layer of the OSI model is responsible for determining the availability of a communication partner?

    a. Physical

    b. Data lLink

    c. Network

    d. Transport

    e. Session

    f. Presentation

    g. Application

15. When should a baseline for your network be run?

    a. When a serious problem occurs
    b. When new equipment has been added
    c. When all users are off the network
    d. During periods of low activity

16. Why should a baseline be run?

    a. To show how the network runs while access lists are removed
    b. To document all router configurations
    c. To convince management to add personnel
    d. To document how the network runs under normal conditions

17. What are the recommended steps for documenting your network? (Choose all that apply)

    a. Make a copy of all the router configurations.
    b. Record all the serial numbers of your routers.
    c. Record all the users on the network.
    d. Record all the versions of the router IOS.

18. Which label is used to designate the last four bytes of an 802.3 frame?

    a. Trailer
    b. Preamble
    c. Header
    d. CRC

19. Which label is used to describe an eight-byte field that appears at the beginning of an Ethernet frame?

    a. Trailer
    b. Preamble
    c. Header
    d. CRC

20. What is the difference between an Ethernet_II and an 802.3 frame?

    a. An Ethernet_II frame has a type field, while an 802.3 frame has a length field.
    b. An Ethernet_II frame has a length field, while an 802.3 frame has a type field.
    c. An Ethernet_II frame has DSAP and SSAP fields instead of a length field.
    d. There is no difference between the two frame types.

Answers

1. Answer: a, b, d.

   Having made a single change makes it easier to undo that change. If a single variable is changed and that variable solves the problem, then that was the issue. It helps isolate the problem. Eliminating a single cause of the problem will help determine where the problem lies.

2. Answer: b

   Running the tests that were originally used in the problem analysis is the best way to ensure that the issue is solved.

3. Answer: c

   Repeat until the problem is resolved. Remember to undo any changes before continuing.

4. Answer: a

   Talking to users is part of the first step called "define the problem."

5. Answer: b

   Evaluating the results involves testing to see if the changes worked.

6. Answer: c

   After you have gathered the facts, the next step is to evaluate the causes of the problem.

7. Answer: b

   The main purpose of defining the problem is to narrow down the problem until we have a clear and concise picture of exactly what symptoms the problem exhibits.

8. Answer: b

   The data link layer is concerned with whether we use Ethernet_II, SNAP, or 802.3 Ethernet frames.

9. Answer: f

   The presentation layer is basically a translator. It will translate between EBCDIC and ASCII.

10. Answer: a

    Most errors occur at the physical layer. Generally speaking, the lower in the OSI model you go, the more likely an error will occur.

11. Answer: b

    The data link layer is responsible for forming frames from binary data.

12. Answer: d

    TCP resides at the transport layer of the OSI model.

13. Answer: c

    IP resides in the network layer of the OSI model.

14. Answer: g

    The application layer is responsible for determining the availability of a communication partner.

15. Answer: b

    A baseline for your network should be run when the network is running normally, during peak usage times, and when new equipment has been added to the network.

16. Answer: d

    A baseline is run to document how the network is behaving under normal circumstances. This can be compared to how a network is running while a problem is being experienced.

17. Answer: a, b, d

    The documentation of the network should include all IOS versions, a copy of your current configurations, and the serial numbers of your equipment. All of these may be required if you are calling into the Cisco Technical Assistance Center.

18. Answer: d

    The CRC field is the last four bytes of an 802.3 frame.

19. Answer: b

    The preamble is a series of alternating zeros and ones that start an Ethernet frame.

20. Answer: a

    An Ethernet_II frame has a type field that is set to a value greater than 05DC (hex), while an 802.3 frame has a length field set to something less than 05DC (hex).

3

Troubleshooting Tools

This chapter provides an overview of the tools that are available for troubleshooting networks. Some of the tools are generic in their use and others are unique to networks that include Cisco internetworking devices. The tools are broken down into two sections, physical devices and software applications.

Network troubleshooting should follow the OSI layer in the determination of the problem. The OSI layer consists of seven layers: the application layer, presentation layer, session layer, transport layer, network layer, data link layer, and physical layer.

The best place to start when troubleshooting network problems is at the physical layer, layer 1. This consists of the actual network hardware, its media, and connectors. Failure at this layer obviously disrupts communication to all layers above. The physical layer is the logical starting point as you can visually check the status of the hardware and then progress to using physical testing devices such as multi meters and cable testers. These tools ensure that there are no problems with the media, such as attenuation, noise, faulty connectors, and illegal cable lengths.

Once the physical layer has been checked, if the problem still persists, you then move up to the next layer, the data link layer. Network monitors and analyzers work at this layer and provide a detailed view into the traffic that is crossing your network. Collisions, protocol errors, and other link-layer issues are usually identified here.

The next layer is the network layer. Here you can use network analyzers to check the packets on your network for layer-3 errors or misconfigurations. Also, simple Cisco IOS commands such as ping and trace can be used to identify routing problems at layer 3. After exhausting all of these options, you then look at the upper layers to check for software errors and misconfigurations, including errors that could have been caused by user intervention.

Objectives Covered in the Chapter

This chapter introduces you to troubleshooting tools that are used in today's internetworks. These start at simple physical layer devices such as cable testers and progress to upper layer applications such as Cisco Works. This chapter's objective is to describe the types and purposes of these tools used for network troubleshooting processes.

Testing with Physical Devices

Physical devices operate at the physical layer of the OSI model. These devices can be grouped into low-end devices, such as multi meters and cable testers, and high-end devices, such as *time domain reflectometers* (TDRs) and *bit / block error rate testers* (BERTs). These devices can be used to check the physical network connection, which should be the first starting point when troubleshooting a network problem. Always check that the network cable and connector are properly connected and use one or a combination of the following tools to check that the cable and/or connector is functioning.

Multi Meters

Multi meters and volt-ohm meters simply measure a set of electrical parameters such as cable continuity, current, resistance, and capacitance (see Figure 3-1). They work at the physical layer of the OSI model and provide a fast and easy way to check the interface and connectors. They are available from most electrical suppliers and are relatively inexpensive. They provide a base level of fault finding in checking the integrity of physical connections.

Figure 3-1
A multi meter

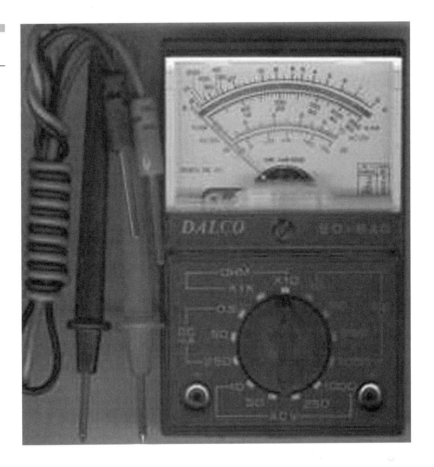

The most basic function of a multi meter is to check the continuity of a cable or connector. This provides a simple, fast check to ascertain the connection state. One use of a multi meter could be to check the corresponding pins on an X21 cable. This would prove that continuity exists between the corresponding pins and eliminates basic cable problems. However, more advanced cable problems may exist and you would need a cable tester or a TDR.

Cable Testers

Cable testers are more advanced than multi meters but generally use the same electrical principles to check continuity (see Figure 3-2). The most basic cable testers provide a variety of connectors including RJ-45, RJ-11, and BNC. These are normally doubled up on the cable tester to check the integrity of the cable and also the wiring of the UTP and STP cables. Cable testers come with multiple interfaces built in that can check a wide range of cabling including common *local area network* (LAN), *wide area network* (WAN), voice, audio, and video connectors. These range from fairly cheap specific models to expensive models that have a multitude of functions and connectors.

Most cable testers come complete with a remote node. The remote node is provided so that the cable can be checked end to end. For example, in a large office environment, you can plug the cable tester in at the LAN connector at the user's desk. The remote node can then be connected in the

Figure 3-2
Cable tester

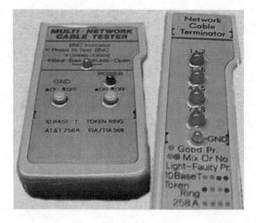

patching cabinet on the cable that corresponds to the user's network connection. This can be useful in testing for problems with the structured cabling as well as the interference or break that can occur while traversing over the patching panels.

Basic network cable testers usually have RJ-45 and RJ-11 connectors. These cable testers can be used to check the integrity of each of the twisted pairs with a visual indication from an automatically rotating source.

More advanced cable testers can also report on cable faults such as crosstalk, attenuation, and noise. Some cable testers even provide simple network statistics such as the percentage of utilization and the number of frames per second on the segment. You can also purchase cable testers that have limited layer-3 protocol functions such as ping. With these devices, you can ping remote hosts on the network to check the cable and also the performance of the network.

Cable testers generally work at the physical layer of the OSI model. However, some cable testers on the market also provide data-link-layer functionality to display information about network traffic including simple statistics such as network utilization and collision/error rates.

Time Domain Reflectometers (TDR) and Optical Time Domain Reflectometers (OTDR)

TDRs are used to locate and identify faults in all types of cable. They can locate major or minor cabling problems, including opens, shorts, splices, splits, bridged taps, ground faults, water damage, crimps, cuts, shortened conductors, and a variety of other fault conditions.

TDRs work by bouncing a signal down a cable and then listening for reflections of the signal. Common cable faults such as opens or shorts will generate a reflection or echo. The TDR can then approximate the distance to the error condition in the cable. When the signal reaches the end of the cable, it is reflected at a low amplitude. This is expected by the TDR and can be used to check the length of the cable.

TDRs are at the high end of physical troubleshooting tools and can be expensive (see Figure 3-3). However, they are excellent diagnostic tools and it is a good idea to check any new structured cabling with a TDR before the network is commissioned, as it will identify any problems at the physical layer. This can save you a lot of troubleshooting time in the future if a cabling inconsistency is the cause of a hard-to-trace network problem.

Figure 3-3
The Bicotest T810
LEXXI TDR

Optical time domain reflectometers (OTDRs) are TDRs for fiber-optic cable. They function in a similar way to standard TDRs except they transmit optical pulses instead of electrical pulses. OTDRs can measure the length of a fiber run as well as locate breaks and other problems with the cable. Both TDRs and OTDRs function at the physical layer of the OSI model.

NOTE: *TDRs are used on copper cables and OTDRs are used on fiber-optic cables.*

Bit/Block Error Rate Testers (BERTs)

BERTs are cable testers that check and visually report on digital signals received from PCs or peripheral interfaces (see Figure 3-4). They can be

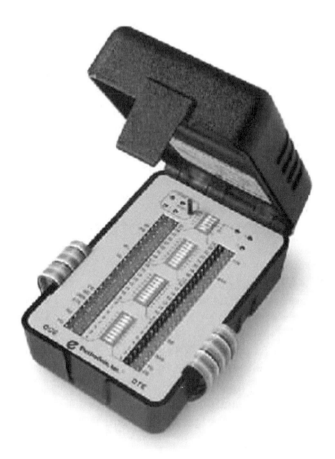

Figure 3-4
The BERT from Bert
Technologies

used on synchronous or asynchronous equipment regardless of the baud rate or data format.

BERTs are typically used on serial lines. A BERT used on a 25-pin serial connection will usually have an LED indicator linked to each pin. The LEDs will flash as data travels through the wire. This allows the user to get a visual indication that the individual line is working. This makes BERT useful as a quick troubleshooting tool.

Breakout pins and jumpers allow any of the 25 circuits to be made or broken for testing purposes. This also allows the user to cross wires for troubleshooting a problem, such as an incorrectly wired connector. The user can wire the connector in one manner and use the BERT to change the wiring while seeing the results. Once the proper configuration has been determined, the connectors can be wired in this manner.

━ ━━ ━━ ━━ ━━ ━━ ━━ ━━ ━━ ━━ ━━ ━━ ━━ ━━ ━━ ━━ ━━ ━━ ━━ ━

NOTE: Be sure to record the proper configuration of the connector for future reference. If you fail to document how the connection was made, you will need to get the BERT out again and go through the same analysis.

BERTs operate at the physical layer of the OSI model and support multiple standards such as RS-232, CCITT, EIA, or V.24.

Testing with Software Applications

Software applications generally work at the data link layer of the OSI model and upwards. Network monitors and network analyzers generally work at the data link and network layers, whereas Cisco Works, Cisco Works for Switched Internetworks, and Cisco NetSys are all upper-layer products that offer a plethora of management and configuration information across multiple OSI layers.

A lot of information can be obtained from software network troubleshooting applications. This information can be overwhelming and it is important to master the application you are using so that you can tailor it to just report on the protocols or data that you require. In this way, you will use the application to its full potential.

Network Monitor

Network monitors are software-based applications that monitor the connected network (see Fig. 3-5). They generally work at the upper layers of the OSI model. They intercept and report on frames that are present on the network segment. These monitors gather information about network performance and utilization and produce statistics with information on frame sizes, the number of frames, error frames, and the number of hosts and their *media access control* (MAC) addresses. These statistics can be correlated in order to formulate a baseline for network activity. This baseline is then the unit of measure that can be used to indicate normal or troublesome network activity.

The *simple network monitoring protocol* (SNMP) is the most popular method of gathering information. A server is usually set up as an SNMP console and SNMP agents are run on various network devices. These send traps to the SNMP server that can be reported upon at a later date.

Figure 3-5
The Microsoft
network monitor

Many other network monitors exist. Some of these are built around SNMP as a standard and others use their own propriety monitors. Cisco networking devices can be set up for SNMP. A set of commands is entered into the device, indicating the address of the SNMP server with various other information such as the community and password.

NOTE: *Network monitors differ from network analyzers in that network monitors work at the highest layers of the OSI model. They monitor the performance of the network through SNMP and keep-alives. Network analyzers break down and display individual data packets on the network.*

Network Analyzers

Network or protocol analyzers are software-based applications that monitor and analyze the connected network. A network analyzer receives all packets on the network segment and copies them all into memory for inspection.

This process is called a *capture* and these captures can be scheduled for specific durations at specific times of the day. During a capture, the analyzer will display real-time packet information that identifies the current state of the network. You will be provided with information such as the number of packets received and the average number of packets per second.

You can also apply filters to the capture to analyze the data at the protocol or host level. The analyzer can only capture data on the network segment where it is placed. It is therefore imperative to place the network analyzer on the network segment that you want to analyze.

Using the capture, you can identify packets and their source/destination addresses. This gives you an excellent view of the traffic on your network and enables you to troubleshoot protocol or communication problems on the network.

Network analyzers are a useful tool to have and a must for every network troubleshooter. In recent times, these tools are becoming more available with the abundance of excellent 32-bit, software-based network analyzers at an affordable price. These have progressed a long way from the early expensive hardware-based network analyzers.

Network analyzers can also be used to pinpoint specific network problems such as broadcast storms or flooding. The analyzer will report on every packet on the network. Filters can then be set to identify the source data link layer address and maybe even the source network layer address of the host that is causing the problem. Routing protocol updates and other broadcast-based traffic can also be tracked in the event of a problem.

Microsoft provides a network analyzer with NT server called Network Monitor. A more powerful version is included as part of the *Systems Management Server* (SMS). Network Associates Sniffer Pro is an excellent network analyzer.

Cisco Works

Cisco Works is the family of products that can be used to manage Cisco enterprise networks. It is a combination of monitoring, analyzing, configuration, and management tools that interact at the device level with Cisco networking devices. Currently, two variations of Cisco Works are available, Cisco Works 2000 and Cisco Works Blue. Cisco Works 2000 is the latest version of Cisco Works. It is a comprehensive management family of products aimed at total Cisco device management. This latest version utilizes Web-based technologies, Internet information, and extensive third-party partnering to deliver an intranet-based management tool.

Cisco Works 2000 includes the following:

■ Resource Manager Essentials

■ *Access Control List* (ACL) Manager

■ *Cisco Works for Switched Internetworks* Campus (CSWSI)

■ Cisco View

■ *Internetwork Performance Monitor* (IPM)

■ Cisco Management Connection

■ *User Registration Tool* (URT)

Resource Manager Essentials   Resource Manager Essentials is a set of Web-based applications that are designed to provide an interface for managing and configuring Cisco devices. You can automatically upgrade IOS feature sets and also fully configure remote devices via the Web-based interface. This product is built on Internet standards and facilitates the creation of a management intranet.

Access Control List (ACL) Manager   The ACL Manager is a Web-based, graphical front-end to ease the creation and management of device-based ACLs. This includes a full set of filter tools to graphically build and test the access list before deployment. This provides an alternative to error-prone command-line editing.

Cisco Works For Switched Internetworks Campus (CSWSI)   CWSI Campus is a collection of applications that are designed for the management of Cisco Catalyst and Lightstream switches. CWSI extends and works with Resource Manager Essentials to provide a complete network discovery and management/configuration utility.

CWSI provides a graphical front-end to the following:

■ Network topology discovery and display services

■ *Virtual LAN* (VLAN) management

■ Traffic monitoring and performance assessment

■ User tracking

■ *Asynchronous transfer mode* (ATM) and LANE service configuration and performance monitoring

Cisco View   Cisco View provides a complete graphical view of remote Cisco devices. This includes a front-panel and rear-panel view complete with chassis and port status indicator lights. Cisco View provides an interface to interrogate devices down to the port level to receive real-time statistics that would normally be received via the IOS CLI.

Internetwork Performance Monitor (IPM)   The IPM is a network-monitoring tool that can be used to troubleshoot network response times by utilizing real-time and historical reporting between Cisco devices. The IPM is built on Web standards and provides the network manager with a tool to diagnose and isolate a range of performance-related issues that come with large internetworks.

Cisco Management Connection   Cisco Management Connection is provided to allow third-party developers to create Web-based Cisco management applications and link these to Resource Manager Essentials. This provides a centralized administrative interface for both Cisco-provided and third-party-provided applications.

User Registration Tool (URT)   The URT is provided to simplify the administration of your VLAN. This is aimed towards users on Microsoft or Novell operating systems running TCP/IP. The URT identifies users on the network and intelligently monitors the switch port VLAN membership and protocol information pertaining to the user. URT intercepts the user logon request and automatically configures the switch port to the correct subnet, and VLAN URT integrates with *dynamic host configuration protocols* (DHCPs), NT domain controllers, and NDS servers.

Cisco Works Blue is designed to simplify the management of an integrated *Internet protocol* (IP) and *systems network architecture* (SNA) network. It has specific tools related to SNA traffic and the management interfaces can communicate and send alerts to most mainframe management applications. This enables router monitoring, reporting, and configuration from a mainframe console.

Cisco Works Blue includes the following:

- Internetwork Status Monitor
- Cisco Works Blue Maps
- SNA View
- *Internetwork Performance Monitor* (IPM)

Internetwork Status Monitor   Cisco Works Blue's Internetwork Status Monitor is designed to allow mainframe operators full visibility of a Cisco device network from a single mainframe console. Mainframe operators can use common function keys, help panels, event displays, and network logs to monitor, configure, and manage the Cisco environment from their mainframe console. Internetwork Status Monitor integrates with NetView and SOLVE:Netmaster.

Cisco Works Blue Maps   Cisco Works Blue Maps provide a dynamic view of the combined SNA and IP network. Blue Maps utilize *Management Information Base* (MIB) information to provide the user with powerful management information. Blue Maps also simplify the management of *data link switching* (DLSw), *advanced peer-to-peer networking* (APPN), and *remote source-route bridging* (RSRB) networks by monitoring the physical and logical relationships between the Cisco routers that are supporting these SNA protocols.

SNA View   SNA View is a Web-based application designed to gather information about traditional SNA sessions as well as SNA sessions using DLSw, APPN, and RSRB. The Web interface provides a graphical, color-coded representation of these connections. Session outages are identified by a red arrow that points to the resource, which is usually the cause of the problem.

Internetwork Performance Monitor (IPM)   The version of IPM that ships with Cisco Works Blue monitors the network response time for SNA traffic as well as IP traffic on a hop-by-hop basis.

Cisco NetSys Network Management Suites

The Cisco NetSys Network Management Suites are a series of tools that provide simulation-based planning and problem-solving products. These tools are provided for network managers, network analysts, and network designers. They aim to assist in the planning and design activities by providing a simulation of the proposed network. Two versions of Cisco NetSys are available: Cisco NetSys Baseliner for Windows NT and the Cisco NetSys SLM Suite.

NetSys Baseliner for Windows NT

NetSys Baseliner is provided for use on Windows NT 4.0. Its main function is to provide an accurate offline model of your network. This model is initially automatically analyzed by NetSys. The application then navigates your existing Cisco network and accesses Cisco devices to capture their configuration files. The configuration files are used to create the offline model of the network.

Network designers can then test any proposed changes to the live network on the offline model. NetSys then analyzes the offline model and reports on any errors or topology changes. This method can be used to test planned changes to the network, such as access list additions or alterations. Due to the instant configuration nature of command-line editing on a Cisco device, it is necessary to test planned changes to ascertain their impact on the live network.

If any problems are found in the proposed changes, they can be rectified on the offline model until all involved are happy with the outcome of the change. The change can then be implemented in the live network with the knowledge that it has been fully tested on the offline model. This process provides a proactive method to monitor change as part of a change management procedure.

NetSys Baseliner also checks your network for over 100 common configuration problems. These will be reported on the off-line model as well as recommendations on how to rectify the problems.

NetSys SLM Suite

The NetSys SLM suite of products is designed to run on SunOS, Solaris, HP-UX, and AIX. This suite of applications provides a policy-based service-level management solution that enables network managers to define performance policies as well as monitor and assess their effectiveness. The applications enable you to monitor your existing network and they use built-in intelligence to report on the availability of key network resources. This is provided for LAN switch monitoring as well as WAN router and switch monitoring.

Chapter Summary

In this chapter, you have been introduced to the tools that can be used to troubleshoot today's internetworks. We started with the physical tools that work at the lower layers of the OSI model such as cable testers and TDRs. We then moved on to software tools that function at the higher layers of the OSI model. Lastly, we looked at the Cisco-provided software applications that monitor and configure Cisco network devices.

Frequently Asked Questions (FAQ)

Question: What is the difference between a network monitor and a network analyzer ?

Answer: Network monitors generally work at higher layers of the OSI model and they monitor the performance of the network through SNMP and other propriety methods. Network analyzers capture and display information about data packets that are on the network.

Question: What is the difference between a cable tester and a multi meter?

Answer: Multi meters simply provide continuity and resistance information, whereas cable testers test the integrity of the cable and have specific connectors such as RJ-45 or BNC.

Question: What is the difference between a TDR and an OTDR?

Answer: An OTDR is an optical version of a TDR. OTDRs are used on fiber-optic cable and TDRs are used on copper cable.

Case Study

You, as network manager, have been been given the task of formulating a procedure to incorporate Cisco device configuration changes into the corporate change management procedure.

Scenario

You work as the network manager for a mid-sized manufacturing company that has offices and factories in 11 major U.S. cities. Every remote site is connected and the network has been designed using Cisco routers and switches. Network management teams reside in three of the 11 locations. Recently, there have been network changes implemented that have had a detrimental effect on the performance of the network. These changes have not been recorded or adequately planned and tested. The company is implementing a change management procedure and they want any Cisco configuration changes to go through the process in order to provide a written record of all the changes and to ensure certain steps have been taken. The problem is that you do not have enough spare Cisco equipment to build a test lab, and due to the instantaneous nature of the command-line changes, you are left with a problem where you cannot readily test forthcoming changes.

Approach

You are aware that you cannot physically create a test environment for testing purposes. You also know that you cannot rely on your staff to always predict the outcome of a change and let them implement it without testing. So, you decide to see if there is a software solution for this problem. You decide to use Cisco NetSys Baseliner for Windows NT.

Results

Cisco NetSys Baseliner for Windows NT automatically scans your network for Cisco devices. It interrogates the config files to provide a complete offline model of your network. Changes are then applied to the offline model before being implemented into the live network. This provides a solution to the problem. You can then test all network configuration changes before committing them to the live network.

Questions

1. Which type of tool displays packet data?

   a. Cable tester
   b. Multi meter
   c. TDR
   d. Network analyzer

2. Which tool would you use to check the wiring on a UTP cable?

   a. Cable tester
   b. Multi meter
   c. TDR
   d. Network analyzer

3. A TDR can be used for testing fiber-optic cable.

   a. True
   b. False

4. A multi meter works at which of the OSI layers?

   a. Session
   b. Transport
   c. Physical
   d. Application

5. When network troubleshooting, it is recommended to start at the _____ layer of the OSI model.

   a. Network
   b. Application
   c. Data link
   d. Physical

6. Which tool is the most useful for stress testing changes to a router configuration file?

   a. Microsoft NetMon
   b. TDR
   c. CWSI
   d. NetSys Baseliner

7. Which tool is ideal for testing signals across an RS-232 cable?

   a. Cable tester
   b. Multi meter
   c. Bit/block error rate tester
   d. Network analyzer

8. What is another name for a bit/block error rate tester?

   a. Breakout box

   b. Breakdown box

   c. Break tester

   d. Breakout tester

9. Which tool provides Web-based configurations of Cisco devices?

   a. Cisco Works

   b. Cisco Works 2000

   c. Network monitor

   d. Network analyzer

10. Which tool works by bouncing a signal down the cable and listening for reflections?

   a. Cable tester

   b. TDR/OTDR

   c. Protocol analyzer

   d. Network analyzer

11. _____ is a method of gathering information for network monitors using MIBs.

   a. SNMP

   b. SMTP

   c. NNT

   d. NFS

12. The two main versions of Cisco Works are:

   a. Cisco Works SNA

   b. Cisco Works 2000

   c. Cisco Works Blue

   d. Cisco Works Now

13. The *User Registration Tool* (URT) can dynamically map a user to a VLAN port.

   a. True

   b. False

14. Which tool can accurately measure a length of copper cable?

    a. Cable tester

    b. Multi meter

    c. Network monitor

    d. TDR

15. A broadcast storm is best identified by using a

    a. Network monitor

    b. Network analyzer

    c. Cable tester

    d. TDR

16. You are designing a new network for a client. Which tool is best for testing and proving the network before installation?

    a. Network monitor

    b. Cisco Works 2000

    c. Cisco NetSys SLM

    d. Cisco NetSys Baseline

17. You have a complicated mixed SNA and IP network. You are looking for a complete management interface that enables current mainframe operators to monitor and configure the Cisco network from their current mainframe terminals. Which is the best choice?

    a. Cisco Works 2000

    b. Cisco Works Blue

    c. Cisco NetSys Baseliner

    d. Cisco NetSys SLM

18. Your network has a complicated switched infrastructure. Which Cisco Works 2000 application is designed primarily for switched internetworks?

    a. Cisco Resource Manager

    b. CSWI

    c. Cisco View

    d. Cisco Blue Maps

19. Which Cisco Works 2000 application provides a front and rear panel view of Cisco network devices?

    a. Cisco Resource Manager

    b. CSWI

    c. Cisco View

    d. Cisco Blue Maps

20. Traffic filters and captures are associated with which tool?

    a. Network monitor

    b. Network analyzer

    c. Cable tester

    d. OTDR

Answers

1. Answer: d

   Network analyzers display packet data. The other tools work at the physical layer of the OSI model.

2. Answer: a

   Cable testers can be used to check for specific faults on cables. Multi meters can also check the continuity of the cable, but A was the best answer.

3. Answer: b

   TDRs can only be used for copper cable, as it sends an electrical pulse down the cable. An OTDR has to be used for fiber-optic cable.

4. Answer: c

   Multi meters work at the physical layer of the OSI model.

5. Answer: d

   When network troubleshooting, it is always recommended to start troubleshooting at the physical layer of the OSI model.

6. Answer: d

   Cisco NetSys Baseliner creates an offline model of the network. Any stress testing of changes can be performed in an offline manner.

7. Answer: c

   A bit/block error rate tester is specifically designed for testing signals of RS-232 and other serial/parallel cables.

8. Answer: a

   Another name for a bit/block error rate tester is a breakout box.

9. Answer: b

   Cisco Works 2000 provides Web-based configurations of Cisco devices.

10. Answer: b

    TDRs/OTDRs work by bouncing a signal down the cable and listening for reflections.

11. Answer: a

    The *simple network management protocol* (SNMP) uses MIBs to gather network information.

12. Answer: b and c

    The main two Cisco Works versions are Cisco Works 2000 and Cisco Works Blue.

13. Answer: a

    True. The *User Registration Tool* (URT) that comes with Cisco Works 2000 can dynamically map a user to a VLAN port.

14. Answer: d

    TDRs can be used to measure the length of a cable. This works by measuring how long it takes for the signal to bounce back.

15. Answer: b

    Network analyzers can identify packet information containing protocol specifics. This can lead to the identity of the broadcasting node.

16. Answer: d

    Cisco NetSys Baseline creates an offline model of your network. This can also be used to build up a new network to prove the network before installation.

17. Answer: b

    Cisco Works Blue integrates IP and SNA management and enables mainframe terminals to fully configure and monitor the Cisco device network.

18. Answer: b

    Cisco Works for Switched Internetworks is designed for managing switched internetworks.

19. Answer: c

    Cisco View provides a front and rear panel view of Cisco network devices.

20. Answer: b

    Traffic filters and captures are a part of the network analyzer. A filter can be placed either before (Capture Filter) or after (View Filter) to reduce the information onscreen.

CHAPTER

4

Basic Diagnostic Commands

This chapter will demonstrate how to use the basic diagnostic commands available with Cisco equipment. Throughout this book you will find many examples of the commands that are initially presented here. Many new commands and concepts will be presented within this chapter that will form the knowledge base required for subsequent topics covered in this book. Understanding how the debug, show, ping, and traceroute commands operate as well as the meaning of the output from these commands provides the necessary basis for troubleshooting all routing issues. We will explore Cisco-specific troubleshooting tools, hardware, software, and configuration bugs, as well as how to minimize the impact on routers during the troubleshooting process. We will also explore how and why a core dump is made.

Objectives Covered in the Chapter

The objectives covered in this chapter include the following:

- Identify and apply generic and Cisco-specific troubleshooting tools on Cisco routers and switches.

- Analyze problem symptoms and resolve resolution strategies in TCP/IP (including the Microsoft 95/NT IP stack), Novell, AppleTalk, Ethernet *virtual local area networks* (VLANs), Frame Relay, and ISDN BRI.

- Perform labs that troubleshoot problems (hardware, software, or configuration bugs) and then correct these bugs to restore full network operations.

- Handle troubleshooting tools and minimize their impact on a Cisco router's switching type and data flow.

- Identify and use the innate Cisco IOS software commands and debug utilities to filter, capture, and display protocol traffic flows.

- Apply diagnostic tools to solve network problems that include systems running TCP/IP with Windows NT/95 clients and servers.

- Use Cisco IOS commands and problem-isolation techniques to identify the symptoms of common *wide area network* (WAN) and Frame Relay problems.

- Apply diagnostic tools to trouble tickets and solve classroom network Frame Relay problems that simulate real-life WAN malfunctions.

- Describe the necessary steps to execute a (manual) core dump.

In order to understand how to properly use the diagnostic commands available, it is first necessary to understand what is happening within the router. This chapter will explore how the router works regarding both routing and switching before going into specifics as far as which command to use in a given circumstance. Finally, two of the most powerful commands at our disposal will be examined, ping and traceroute.

Routing Processes

This section will explore how a router operates. Routers rely on two basic processes in order to forward data towards the end destination. The first process is path determination. This process relies upon metrics and routing protocols to determine where the data should go. When data comes in one interface, the path determination process decides which interface, if any, the data should be forwarded through. This process will be covered in Chapter 12, "Routing Protocols."

The second process is called the switching process. This process works at layer 3 of the OSI model. Switching in the Ethernet environment is done at layer 2 of the OSI model. This is a totally different process that does not relate to router switching. For the remainder of this chapter when switching is mentioned, we will be referring to router switching at layer 3, not Ethernet switching. Router switching still needs to reference layer 2 protocols, such as ARP, to determine which *media access control* (MAC) address a packet will be sent to, while switching occurs in layer 3.

As a router receives a packet, it looks at the logical (layer 3) destination. If the route is known to the destination, the MAC address (layer 2) will be changed to reflect the current router before the packet is forwarded to the next router. The process of moving the data from the incoming interface to the outgoing interface is switching. During this process, the router will place its own interface MAC address on the packet to specify where the packet originated.

The switching process can use several different methods. The model and accessories on a router will determine which methods are available, as will the type of routing protocol currently in use. We will examine each of these methods next, starting with the most processor-intensive and moving toward the least processor-intensive.

Process Switching

Router switching is the slowest switching on Cisco equipment. The processor is used to look up the layer 3 destination. The packet is copied to the router process buffer, the routing table is consulted for the destination interface, and then the packet is encapsulated and forwarded to the destination interface. Every packet that uses router switching follows the same path. This becomes very *central processing unit*-intensive (CPU) because every packet must be copied to the buffer, the route is looked up for every packet, and then the packet is forwarded.

In order to reduce the number of processor cycles required, fast switching is normally used instead of router switching. Router switching is usually only activated during troubleshooting because of the extreme amounts of processor power required.

Fast Switching

Fast switching is basically an enhancement of process switching. In this method, the first packet is copied to the interface processor and then to the CxBus, eventually making its way to the switch processor. At this point, a check is made against caches within the router. If an entry for this destination is not found in the cache, the router processor is used to look up the destination in the routing table. The destination is placed into one of the caches.

Packets that have the same destination are handled differently. Because the fast-switching process checks the cache before going to the route processor, this method is much faster for all packets to a given destination, except for the first packet. The interface processor, instead of the route processor, calculates the *cyclical redundancy check* (CRC) on the packet and passes the packet to the interface cache. The packet is sent to the appropriate interface over the backplane of the router.

Fast switching is turned on by default. It will prevent being able to see packets that do not go through the route processor while using packet-level debugging. To overcome this, fast switching can be turned off and you can therefore resort to router switching with the following command:

```
Router(config)#no ip route-cache
```

Turning fast switching back on can be done with the following:

```
Router(config)#ip route-cache
```

Autonomous Switching

This switching method requires that the system have a high-speed controller interface card. This optional equipment is only available on the AGS and Cisco 7000 series routers. The method used is even more advanced than the fast switching method. The on-board processor and cache on the interface board do not require the packets to travel over the backplane, except to go to the exit interface.

Netflow Switching

Netflow switching is actually an accounting system built into the switching process. Netflow switching, compatible on Cisco 7200 and 7500 routers, enables the administrator to gather statistics on the protocol, port, user, source, and destination. This accounting data can be used to bill departments or individual users for their share of the network cost. This method can utilize the *versatile interface processor* (VIP) cards and is considered one of the most efficient when dealing with large access lists. Netflow switching can also utilize either fast or optimum switching.

Silicon Switching

Silicon switching utilizes the *silicon switch processor* (SSP) on Cisco 7000 routers. In this method, a *silicon switching engine* (SSE) is also required. The SSP offloads the switching process from the router processor. The switched packets pass over the backplane of the router to the SSP, and then over the backplane again to go out the interface. By traveling over the backplane twice, this method uses more system resources than optimum switching.

Optimum Switching

In optimum switching, all processing is carried out on the interface processor, including the CRC check. A packet enters the interface, is compared to the optimum switching cache, and is sent out the exit interface. This method is faster than fast switching and netflow switching. Optimum switching must be enabled on individual interfaces.

Distributed Switching

Distributed switching happens on the VIP card installed in the router. This card has switching processors on-board that in turn relieve the router processor of the responsibilities of switching. The VIP card maintains a copy of the router's routing cache. The efficiency of the system increases as multiple cards are added.

Cisco Express Forwarding

Cisco Express forwarding (CEF) is the most efficient method of switching in terms of speed. The CEF system uses two tables instead of a cache. The first table, the *forwarding information base* (FIB), is a duplicate of the router's IP routing table. Changes made to the routing table are propagated to the FIB. The second table, the adjacency table, stores the MAC addresses of the next hop routers. When a packet is received, the router will look for the next hop address and interface associated with that address in the FIB. Next, the MAC address from the adjacency table is found. The packet is then forwarded through the appropriate interface.

CEF was designed specifically for large backbone routers. CEF has many advantages, including the ability to balance loads across different interfaces. The drawbacks of CEF include the large amount of RAM required (a minimum of 128 MB) and the number of interface types that are not supported, such as ATM, Token Ring, and multipoint PPP.

Now that we have looked at some of the switching methods, we are ready to move on to the commands that will help us troubleshoot our networks. We will start with the debug and show commands.

Differences Between Show and Debug Commands

There is a major difference between the output from a show command and the output from a debug command. Although a show command gives you a picture of how the equipment looks at a given time, the debug command shows you how a piece of equipment is changing over a period of time. Sometimes you will need to use both commands if you want to understand the total picture of how the system is operating. An example of this would be the task of troubleshooting the *enhanced interior gateway routing protocol* (EIGRP). Performing a "show ip route eigrp" will only show which entries are currently in the routing tables due to the EIGRP protocol. Then, by using the "debug ip eigrp events" command, you will be able to see how the routing tables are being updated. If you do not already know what is in the routing tables, simply seeing the updates may not be sufficient. This is an extremely important point to remember. A debug command does not tell you directly what the equipment already knows, and a single show command cannot tell how the tables are changing. Only by using both together can you get a good picture of exactly what is happening.

Another difference between the show and debug commands is the affect on performance when using these commands. Although a show command will not usually affect performance, a debug command can affect performance until the debugging is stopped. This and other cautions associated with the debug commands will be explored further before the show commands are discussed.

Debug

Debug commands are entered in the privileged (#) EXEC mode. Most debug commands also do not require or enable arguments. Starting debugging is done by entering a debug command, such as:

```
Router#debug apple zip
```

The debugging of a specific protocol or interface is turned off with either the "no" form of the command or the undebug command, such as the following:

```
Router#no debug apple zip
Router#undebug apple zip
```

Alternatively, you can turn off all debugging with the following command:

```
Router#no debug all
```

Be aware that the above examples will produce no output if we have not already enabled AppleTalk on our router. The router may accept debugging commands even if that protocol is not currently in use. Adding a protocol with the debugging already enabled for that protocol will result in the debugging output to be visible. Additionally, there may be no output seen after a debugging command is entered simply because no activity related to the debugging command has occurred.

Before we explore some specific debug commands, we will discuss how debugging affects performance and how to minimize the performance issues that will occur when using debug.

Debug and Performance

The output from debugging commands will take precedence over all other network traffic, connections to be maintained, router protocols, and everything else the equipment is designed to do. Caution should be used in debugging to ensure that the debugging process is not causing additional problems. For example, if you are running a protocol such as RIP that requires updates at short intervals, it is entirely possible that running debug commands can prevent the router from receiving or sending updates within the established time limits. If this happens, you will now have two apparent problems to deal with, the original problem and the loss of router updates. We can minimize the risks of problems by using the most restrictive debugging commands as possible and by redirecting debugging output in a way that minimizes impact on the equipment.

The debug commands, especially "debug all" will affect performance no matter where the debug messages are sent. The performance hit may be serious enough to cause a loss of connections over both serial and Ethernet connections. It is not unusual that by adding debug commands an administrator will bring a system to its knees. Consideration should be given to where the messages are to be sent and the speed of these connections. For example, assume you are trying to debug a router at a remote site. You telnet into the router and turn on debugging for a given interface. At this point, you receive no responses through your telnet session other than debugging messages. What happened? Because debugging messages take priority over all other types of traffic, the serial line and the remote router are too busy sending messages to respond to the telnet session. How do you recover from this situation? You really have only two choices, either have someone at the remote site connect to the router and stop debugging, or have someone at the remote site reboot the router. Debug commands may also generate enough traffic to effectively halt all connections over Ethernet. Although these are extreme examples that should not happen on most networks, it is still possible. The point being made is that the debug command can quickly get an administrator into trouble if not used carefully.

When a debug command is entered, the default is to send the output to the console. Although this may be convenient for an administrator, this is also the most intrusive in terms of performance. Using the logging command while in configuration mode can change the impact debugging has on your equipment. The possible output points for debugging are the console, the virtual terminals, a syslog server, or the internal buffers. Outputting to the console causes the most overhead with virtual terminals producing slightly less overhead. A syslog server produces less overhead than virtual terminals, and outputting to the internal buffers causes the least overhead of all methods.

Before debug output can be redirected, you will need to enable the logging of messages from the configuration mode with the following:

```
Router(config)#enable message logging
```

Next, we must enable the messages to travel to the appropriate destination with

```
Router(config)#logging on
```

If you are logging messages to the console, monitor, or a syslog server, you can also set the level of logging from 0 through 7. The higher the number, the more information will be output. Setting the error level to 0 will result in receiving messages only when the system experiences an emergency, while level 7 is used for debugging. As the message level chosen increases, more CPU processor power is required. Table 4-1 shows the eight levels, the associated keywords, a description of each level, and the syslog definition for use with a Unix syslog server.

Limiting which messages are logged to the console is controlled by the "logging console" command. For example, to set the level to 4, enter the following within the configuration mode:

```
Router(config)#logging console 4
```

Table 4-1

Logging Levels

Message Level	Keyword	Description	Syslog
0	Emergencies	System has reached an unstable state.	LOG_EMERG
1	Alerts	Immediate action should be taken.	LOG_ALERT
2	Critical	Critical conditions exist.	LOG_CRIT
3	Errors	Error conditions that are non-critical exist.	LOG_ERR
4	Warnings	Warning conditions exist.	LOG_WARNING
5	Notification	Significant conditions (below warning level) exist.	LOG_NOTICE
6	Informational	These are informational messages only.	LOG_INFO
7	Debugging	These are debugging messages.	LOG_DEBUG

This will enable logging on all messages at levels 0 through 4. Alternatively, the keyword could be used instead of the level number, as shown here:

```
Router(config)#logging console warnings
```

By default, logging is sent to the console. To send logging to the internal buffer instead, use the following command within configuration mode:

```
Router(config)#logging buffered
```

Use the "no" form of the "logging buffered" command to revert to using the console for messages. Using the logging buffered command sends messages to the circular internal buffer. When the buffer is full, the oldest entry is written over. Using the "show logging" command will show the contents of the buffer, with the oldest message displaying first.

You can limit which messages are sent to the virtual terminals with the "logging monitor" command. This works similarly to the logging console commands. An example of the command limiting the messages displayed to levels 0 through 4 is

```
Router(config)#logging monitor warnings
```

The final place to which messages can be sent is a syslog server. The messages are sent to the server in a *Berkeley Standard Distribution* (BSD) Unix 4.3 format. The server must be able to accept this message format in order to store these messages. Sending messages to a syslog server is enabled by the following configuration command:

```
Router(config)#logging ip-address
```

The variable *ip-address* is a valid IP address of the syslog server. Using the command more than once with differing IP addresses will build a list of syslog servers. Each of the servers within the list will receive a copy of all messages. Use the "no" form of the command to remove a server from the list. The level of messages sent to a syslog server is limited by the "logging trap" command such as the following:

```
Router(config)#logging trap log_warning
```

In this example, messages ranging from level 0 through 4 will be sent to the syslog server(s) previously defined with the logging command(s). Notice that we are using the rightmost column from the table above while configuring the syslog messages.

Now that we have looked at where the debug messages can be sent, the implications of where we send the messages, and how to limit which messages are sent, we are ready to look at some of the most common debugging commands. We will start with the general commands before moving to the interface-specific commands.

Debug Commands

Debug commands can be applied to a specific serial interface. These commands will be dealt with in the next section. Those commands that do not deal with serial interfaces will be dealt with in this section. All debug commands can only be used within the enhanced mode.

Entering "debug ?" while in enhanced mode will provide a list of the areas available for debugging as shown below:

```
Router#debug ?
  aaa                 AAA Authentication, Authorization, and
                      Accounting
  access-expression   Boolean access expression
  all                 Enable all debugging
  arp                 IP ARP and HP Probe transactions
  async               Async interface information
  bsc                 BSC information
  bstun               BSTUN information
  callback            Callback activity
  cdp                 CDP information
  chat                Chat scripts activity
  cls                 CLS information
  compress            COMPRESS traffic
  confmodem           Modem configuration database
  cpp                 Cpp information
  custom-queue        Custom output queueing
  dhcp                DHCP client activity
  dialer              Dial on demand
  dlsw                Data link switching (DLSw) events
  dnsix               Dnsix information
  domain              Domain name system
  dspu                DSPU information
  dxi                 atm-dxi information
  eigrp               EIGRP protocol information
  entry               Incoming queue entries
  ethernet-interface  Ethernet network interface events
  fastethernet        Fast Ethernet interface information
  frame-relay         Frame Relay
  fras                FRAS debug
```

```
ip                    IP information
lapb                  LAPB protocol transactions
lex                   LAN Extender protocol
list                  Set interface or/and access list for the next
                      debug command
llc2                  LLC2 type II information
lnm                   LAN network manager information
lnx                   Generic qllc/llc2 conversion activity
local-ack             Local acknowledgement information
modem                 Modem control/process activation
ncia                  Native Client Interface Architecture (NCIA)
                      events
netbios-name-cache    NetBIOS name cache tracing
nhrp                  NHRP protocol
ntp                   NTP information
nvram                 Debug NVRAM behavior
packet                Log unknown packets
pad                   X25 PAD protocol
ppp                   PPP (Point-to-point protocol) information
printer               LPD printer protocol
priority              Priority output queueing
probe                 HP probe proxy requests
qllc                  qllc debug information
radius                RADIUS protocol
rif                   RIF cache transactions
rtr                   RTR monitor information
sdlc                  SDLC information
sdllc                 SDLLC media translation
serial                Serial interface information
sgbp                  SGBP debugging
smf                   Software MAC filter
sna                   SNA information
snapshot              Snapshot activity
snmp                  SNMP information
source                Source-bridging information
spanning              Spanning-tree information
standby               Hot standby protocol
stun                  STUN information
tacacs                TACACS authentication and authorization
tbridge               Transparent bridging
telnet                Incoming telnet connections
tftp                  TFTP packets
token                 Token Ring information
tunnel                Generic tunnel interface
v120                  V120 information
vlan                  VLAN information
vpdn                  VPDN information
vtemplate             Virtual template information
x25                   X.25 information
```

The available debug commands shown in the previous table are dependent upon the physical configuration of the equipment and the IOS version you are using. By choosing one option, such as "AAA" along with a "?," you can see which debug commands are available for AAA, as shown below:

```
Router#debug aaa ?
```

```
accounting      Accounting
authentication  Authentication
authorization   Authorization
```

All debug options work in the same manner. There is one powerful option that is shown in the previous outputs. This is the "debug all" command. The debug all command turns on all debugging possible for the piece of equipment to which you are attached. This is also a dangerous command that should not be used on production equipment due to the high CPU utilization that is required. Additionally, this command tends to overwhelm the administrator with the amount of data that is shown. It becomes a major task to sort through the data presented to gain the information required. For these reasons, we do not recommend the use of this command on any production router.

Debug commands can be used to watch any number of items. Finding which command you should use in a given circumstance is a combination of experience and research. Many specific examples will be dealt with throughout this book. Earlier we showed a list of the possible debug commands. Becoming familiar with this list and which areas are available for debugging is the first step toward understanding the debugging process. The commands listed earlier have a short description of the purpose of the command. This will help you decide which command is useful for your specific troubleshooting needs. Note that some of these commands may have further definitions within them. For example, "debug apple" has several options including ZIP, NBP, RTMP, and so on.

Each of these debug commands can be investigated further through the Cisco Web site, the documentation CD-ROM, or through the use of the help command. Now that we have explored some of the available debugging commands, we will spend time with the commands related to the serial interface.

Serial Interface Commands

Debugging the serial interface is one of the most useful approaches available to the engineer trying to find out exactly what is happening on a remote connection. The output from a "debug serial interface" command depends upon which form of a WAN connection is configured: Frame Relay, HDLC, HSSI, SMDS, or X.25. The output will also vary depending on the type of encapsulation used. The hardware platform also can affect debug serial interface output. In all cases, using the "no" form of the command will stop debugging on the interface.

▬ ▬

NOTE: When you are searching through the available debug commands, you may see that you can debug the Synchronous Data Link Control *(SDLC). When you read the documentation of the command, it says that this will display information on the SDLC frames received and sent by a router through the serial interface. If you did not read the documentation carefully, you may be tempted to use this command on a production interface. If you do, carefully read the documentation available on the CCO regarding this command. You will learn that this command will alter the timing within the network node. As a result, you will almost certainly lose connectivity over this serial line.*

This is another example of how debugging may cause more problems than anticipated. Many such debug commands are designed for use only within a test environment. When using any debug command on a remote router, make sure that there is a way to undo the command without having to travel to the remote site. However, this command does allow you to see what packets related to SDLC are traveling across the interface, including timing events, connects and disconnects, and polling data. It therefore may be useful in troubleshooting.

We will look at a sample debug serial interface command for an interface using Frame Relay and HDLC. Although the output varies with differing encapsulations, the following output will give an indication of what to expect with a debug serial interface command:

```
Router#debug serial interface
Serial network interface debugging is on
Router#
Serial0: HDLC myseq 268182, mineseen 268182, yourseen 268681, line up
Serial0: HDLC myseq 268183, mineseen 268183, yourseen 268682, line up
Serial0: HDLC myseq 268184, mineseen 268184, yourseen 268683, line up
Serial0: HDLC myseq 268185, mineseen 268185, yourseen 268684, line up
Serial0: HDLC myseq 268186, mineseen 268186, yourseen 268685, line up
Serial0: HDLC myseq 268187, mineseen 268187, yourseen 268686, line up
Serial0: HDLC myseq 268188, mineseen 268188, yourseen 268687, line up
Serial0: HDLC myseq 268189, mineseen 268189, yourseen 268688, line up
Serial0: HDLC myseq 268190, mineseen 268190, yourseen 268689, line up
Serial0: HDLC myseq 268191, mineseen 268191, yourseen 268690, line up
Serial0: HDLC myseq 268192, mineseen 268192, yourseen 268691, line up
```

In order to fully understand the output shown above, it is necessary to understand the meanings of both the field descriptions and the error codes associated with these fields. Table 4-2 outlines the field descriptions associated with HDLC.

Table 4-3 shows some possible error messages and their meanings.

Debugging the serial interface will show what is happening on an interface. Although not a very complex command, it does provide us with information essential to the troubleshooting process. The major advan-

Table 4-2

The HDLC Fields

Field	Description
Serial0	This is the serial interface to which the debug output is associated.
HDLC	Specifies that this is an HDLC connection.
myseq 268182	The myseq counter is used for the keep-alive packets. This should be incrementing by one each time a new packet is sent.
mineseen 268182	This is used in conjunction with the myseq and yourseen fields. When a router receives a myseq, it sends a response. This response is recorded as a minseen. If the counters in the myseq and mineseen vary by more than 3, the interface will be reset. The value of the mineseen is stored in the yourseen field.
yourseen 268681	This is the last value received with a myseen from another router.
line up	This indicates that the line is remaining in an up state. The values may be line up, line down, or looped.

Table 4-3

Error Messages

Message	Description
Illegal HDLC serial type code xxx, PC=0xnnnn	This message is only displayed if an unknown message type is received. This should not normally occur. One possible cause is an encapsulation mismatch.
Illegal serial link type code xxx, PC=0xnnnn	If the router attempts to send a packet that has an unknown packet type, this message will be shown. One possible cause is an encapsulation mismatch.
Serial x: attempting to restart	This message will be sent every time interface x tries to restart from a down state. x is the interface number.
Serial x: Received bridge packet sent to nnnnnn	When an interface that is not configured for bridging receives a bridge packet, this message will be displayed. xxx is the interface number. nnnnn is the destination of the packet.

tage of this command is that we can easily see whether the problem lies within our router or somewhere towards the remote router. For example, if we are experiencing a recurring loss of connection, we can look at the myseq and mineseen fields. If we see that we are sending myseqs but not receiving mineseens, we know the issue will tend to lay beyond our router.

NOTE: *Although the debug serial interface command typically does not generate a lot of output, it will interfere with connectivity under certain circumstances.*

Some routers, such as the Cisco 1602, 2524, or 2525, have a built-in *channel service unit / data service unit* (CSU/DSU). If you are troubleshooting serial interface issues on one of these routers, using the "debug service-module" will provide additional information about the CSU/DSU. The information presented will include the detection and clearing of network alarms.

Another debug command related to the interfaces is the "debug serial packet" command. This command provides more detailed information than the debug serial interface command. Unfortunately, this command is usable only on equipment running switched multimegabit data services (SMDS) and you must understand the inner functions of SMDS for the output to be useful. The inner functions of SMDS are beyond the scope of this book.

Show Commands

Show commands can be entered in privileged mode, depending upon the individual command. The purpose of the show command is to give the user a picture of the current state of the equipment. It is possible to see how the equipment is changing by repeatedly entering the same command and analyzing the differences between the outputs. Entering "show ?" will provide the following list of the areas available for the show command:

```
Router#show ?
  WORD                Flash device information - format
                      <dev:>[partition]
  access-expression   Lists access expression
  access-lists        Lists access lists
  accounting          Accounting data for active sessions
  aliases             Display alias commands
  arp                 ARP table
  async               Information on terminal lines used as router
                      interfaces
  bridge              Bridge forwarding/filtering database [verbose]
  buffers             Buffer pool statistics
  cdp                 CDP information
  clock               Display the system clock
  cmns                Connection mode networking services (CMNS)
                      information
```

```
compress            Show compression statistics
configuration       Contents of non-volatile memory
controllers         Interface controller status
debugging           State of each debugging option
dhcp                Dynamic host configuration protocol status
diag                WAN daughter card diagnostic information
dialer              Dialer parameters and statistics
dnsix               Shows DNSIX/DMDP information
dxi                 Atm-dxi information
entry               Queued terminal entries
flash               System flash information
flh-log             Flash load helper log buffer
frame-relay         Frame Relay information
history             Displays the session's command history
hosts               IP domain name, lookup style, nameservers, and
                    host table
interfaces          Interface status and configuration
ip                  IP information
key                 Key information
line                TTY line information
llc2                IBM LLC2 circuit information
location            Displays the system location
logging             Shows the contents of logging buffers
memory              Memory statistics
modemcap            Shows modem capabilities database
ppp                 PPP parameters and statistics
privilege           Shows current privilege level
processes           Active process statistics
protocols           Active network routing protocols
queue               Shows queue contents
queueing            Shows queueing configuration
registry            Function registry information
reload              Scheduled reload information
rhosts              Remote-host and user equivalences
rmon                rmon statistics
route-map           Route map information
running-config      Current operating configuration
service-module      Service module
sessions            Information about Telnet connections
smds                SMDS information
smf                 Software MAC filter
snapshot            Snapshot parameters and statistics
snmp                SNMP statistics
sntp                Simple network time protocol
spanning-tree       Spanning tree topology
stacks              Process stack utilization
standby             Hot standby protocol information
startup-config      Contents of startup configuration
subsys              Shows subsystem information
tacacs              Shows tacacs+ server statistics
tcp                 Status of TCP connections
tech-support        Shows system information for tech support
terminal            Displays terminal configuration parameters
traffic-shape       Traffic-rate-shaping configuration
users               Displays information about terminal lines
version             System hardware and software status
whoami              Info on current TTY line
x25                 X.25 information
x29              X.29 information
```

The available show commands in this example are dependent upon the physical configuration of the equipment and the IOS version you are using. By choosing one option, such as "async," you can see which show commands are available for async in the following listing:

```
Router#show async ?
  bootp   Extended BOOTP Information
  status  Terminal line status and summary counters
```

At this point, you may be thinking that you have heard all of this before in the area dealing with debug commands. The show commands do work similarly to the debug commands, but we need to know how a show command differs from a debug command. The main differences between a show command and a debug command are as follows:

■ Show commands do not necessarily require privileged mode.

■ Show commands often require variables.

■ Show commands do not show changes to the system.

■ Show commands are only valid at the time the show command was issued.

■ The concept of "turning off" the command does not apply.

■ Show commands usually have little impact on performance.

Similar to the debug all command, there is a show command that is often used to provide a large amount of information at one time. This is the show tech command. Often, it is easier for the *technical assistance center* (TAC) engineer to ask that the output of a show tech command be sent than go through all of the show commands to produce the same output. The show tech command is the functional equivalent of all of the following commands:

■ show version

■ show running-config

■ show controllers

■ show stacks

■ show interfaces

■ show diagbus

■ show buffers

■ show process memory

■ show process cpu

■ show context

■ show boot

- show flash
- show ip traffic
- show controllers cbus

One limitation of the show tech command is actually a limitation of some telnet packages. This limitation is that the buffers of the telnet package may not be sufficient to hold all of the output because so much information is presented. If the buffers cannot hold all of the output, some data may be lost. The beauty of this command is that it will give an engineer virtually all of the data needed to determine where a problem within a router exists.

Because these are virtually all of the major show commands concerned with the troubleshooting process, we will examine the most popular ones. The commands dealing with interfaces will be addressed in the "Interface Commands" section. The output of the individual commands will vary depending upon the equipment on which the command is run.

Show version is used to display the current versions of both the hardware and software. This command will enable us to ascertain the following information:

- The IOS version
- The firmware version
- The bootstrap IOS version
- The router uptime (the time the router has been running)
- The reason for the last restart
- Processor information
- The amount of RAM
- The configuration register settings

Looking at the following output, find all of the items mentioned earlier:

```
Router#show version
Cisco Internetwork Operating System Software
IOS (tm) 1600 Software (C1600-Y-L), Version 11.2(10a)P, RELEASE
SOFTWARE (fc1)
Copyright (c) 1986-1997 by Cisco Systems, Inc.
Compiled Wed 03-Dec-97 00:21 by ccai
Image text-base: 0x0801BFA8, data-base: 0x02005000
ROM: System Bootstrap, Version 11.1(10)AA, EARLY DEPLOYMENT RELEASE
SOFTWARE (f)
ROM: 1600 Software (C1600-BOOT-R), Version 11.1(10)AA, EARLY
DEPLOYMENT RELEASE
Router uptime is 8 hours, 35 minutes
System restarted by power-on
System image file is "flash:c1600-y-1.112-10a.P", booted via flash
```

```
Cisco 1602 (68360) processor (revision C) with 1536K/512K bytes of
memory.
Processor board ID 07082664, with hardware revision 00000000
Bridging software.
X.25 software-, Version 2.0-, NET2-, BFE-, and GOSIP-compliant.
1 Ethernet/IEEE 802.3 interface(s)
1 serial network interface(s)
Onboard switched 56K line interface.
System/IO memory with parity disabled
2048K bytes of DRAM onboard
System running from flash
8K bytes of non-volatile configuration memory.
4096K bytes of processor board PCMCIA flash (Read ONLY)

Configuration register is 0x2102
```

Show running-config is the command used to show how the equipment is currently configured. This may be copied to the startup configuration by using the copy command. This does not necessarily have any relationship to the startup configuration. There may be a difference due to changes made without writing to the startup file. If you are troubleshooting a problem and see noticeable differences between the running configuration and the startup configuration, you should be wary of writing over the startup configuration. The reason for the problems may be due to the differences of the two configurations.

Show stacks shows the processor stacks on the router. This is used almost exclusively at the request of Cisco personnel. One reason for this is that the output from a show stacks command requires a stack decoder to interpret the information.

Show buffers is used to produce a list of the memory buffers, the amount of memory used in each buffer, the number of hits and misses for the buffer, and the number of failures on a buffer. Below is a sample output from a show buffers command. Notice how this shows not only the public buffers, but also the buffers related to the individual interfaces. One indication that your router needs more memory is an increasing amount of buffer failures due to no memory.

```
Router#show buffers
Buffer elements:
     499 in free list (500 max allowed)
     18198059 hits, 0 misses, 0 created

Public buffer pools:
Small buffers, 104 bytes (total 50, permanent 50):
     49 in free list (20 min, 150 max allowed)
     30408793 hits, 5618 misses, 675 trims, 675 created
     60 failures (0 no memory)
Middle buffers, 600 bytes (total 25, permanent 25):
     22 in free list (10 min, 150 max allowed)
     7250884 hits, 20 misses, 22 trims, 22 created
     2 failures (0 no memory)
```

```
Big buffers, 1524 bytes (total 50, permanent 50):
    50 in free list (5 min, 150 max allowed)
    592795 hits, 0 misses, 0 trims, 0 created
    0 failures (0 no memory)
Very big buffers, 4520 bytes (total 10, permanent 10):
    10 in free list (0 min, 150 max allowed)
    94072 hits, 0 misses, 0 trims, 0 created
    0 failures (0 no memory)
Large buffers, 5024 bytes (total 0, permanent 0):
    0 in free list (0 min, 10 max allowed)
    19 hits, 1 misses, 2 trims, 2 created
    0 failures (0 no memory)
Huge buffers, 18024 bytes (total 0, permanent 0):
    0 in free list (0 min, 4 max allowed)
    262 hits, 2 misses, 4 trims, 4 created
    0 failures (0 no memory)

Interface buffer pools:
CD2430 I/O buffers, 1524 bytes (total 0, permanent 0):
    0 in free list (0 min, 0 max allowed)
    0 hits, 0 fallbacks

Header pools:
Header buffers, 0 bytes (total 265, permanent 256):
    9 in free list (10 min, 512 max allowed)
    253 hits, 3 misses, 0 trims, 9 created
    0 failures (0 no memory)
    256 max cache size, 256 in cache

Particle Clones:
    1024 clones, 0 hits, 0 misses

Public particle pools:
F/S buffers, 256 bytes (total 384, permanent 384):
    128 in free list (128 min, 1024 max allowed)
    256 hits, 0 misses, 0 trims, 0 created
    0 failures (0 no memory)
    256 max cache size, 256 in cache
Normal buffers, 1548 bytes (total 512, permanent 512):
    338 in free list (128 min, 1024 max allowed)
    348 hits, 0 misses, 0 trims, 0 created
    0 failures (0 no memory)
    128 max cache size, 128 in cache

Private particle pools:
Ethernet0/0 buffers, 1536 bytes (total 96, permanent 96):
    0 in free list (0 min, 96 max allowed)
    96 hits, 0 fallbacks
    96 max cache size, 96 in cache
Ethernet0/1 buffers, 1536 bytes (total 96, permanent 96):
    0 in free list (0 min, 96 max allowed)
    96 hits, 0 fallbacks
    96 max cache size, 64 in cache
Serial0/0 buffers, 1548 bytes (total 28, permanent 28):
    0 in free list (0 min, 28 max allowed)
    28 hits, 0 fallbacks
    28 max cache size, 28 in cache
Serial0/1 buffers, 1548 bytes (total 28, permanent 28):
    0 in free list (0 min, 28 max allowed)
    28 hits, 0 fallbacks
```

```
        28 max cache size, 14 in cache
FastEthernet1/0 buffers, 1548 bytes (total 192, permanent 192):
        0 in free list (0 min, 192 max allowed)
        192 hits, 0 fallbacks
        192 max cache size, 128 in cache
FastEthernet3/0 buffers, 1548 bytes (total 192, permanent 192):
        0 in free list (0 min, 192 max allowed)
        192 hits, 0 fallbacks
        192 max cache size, 128 in cache
```

Show process memory provides a list of all the processes running on the system. As shown below, the first line shows the bytes of total, used, and free memory. Following this is a list of all the processes, along with the amounts of memory allocated, freed, and holding. The name of the process is also shown. The following is an output from this command:

```
Router#show process memory
Total: 1857616, Used: 1071840, Free: 785776
PID  TTY   Allocated   Freed     Holding   Getbufs   Retbufs   Process
0    0     167844      1252      787028    0         0         *Init*
0    0     328         28292     328       0         0         *Sched*
0    0     887452      135348    1448      196540    27584     *Dead*
1    0     264         264       1732      0         0         Load Meter
2    1     19480       18600     5612      0         0         Virtual Exec
3    0     0           0         2732      0         0         Check Heaps
4    0     96          0         2828      0         0         Pool Manager
5    0     264         264       2732      0         0         Timers
6    0     348         588       2996      0         0         ARP Input
7    0     96          0         2828      0         0         SERIAL A detect
8    0     96          0         2828      0         0         CSU/DSU Trap
9    0     19492       752       6704      0         0         IP Input
10   0     38788       37944     3576      0         0         CDP Protocol
11   0     420         0         4152      0         0         IP Background
12   0     0           2256      2732      0         0         TCP Timer
13   0     30876       0         6172      0         0         TCP Protocols
14   0     96          0         2828      0         0         RARP Input
15   0     62136       61104     3764      0         0         BOOTP Server
16   0     0           14092     2732      0         0         IP Cache Ager
17   0     136         0         2868      0         0         Critical Bkgnd.
18   0     7556        0         3092      0         0         Net Background
PID  TTY   Allocated   Freed     Holding   Getbufs   Retbufs   Process
19   0     96          0         4828      0         0         Logger
20   0     264         264       2732      0         0         TTY Background
21   0     0           0         2732      0         0         Per-Second Jobs
22   0     0           0         2732      0         0         Net Periodic
23   0     192         0         2924      0         0         Net Input
24   0     264         264       1732      0         0         Compute Load as
25   0     0           280       2732      0         0         Per-minute Jobs
26   0     240         0         2972      0         0         FR LMI
27   0     240         0         2972      0         0         FR ARP
28   0     0           0         2732      0         0         FR Broadcast OT
29   0     1141816     1141848   2828      0         0         IP-EIGRP Hello
31   0     744         0         5476      0         0         IP SNMP
32   0     96          0         2828      0         0         SNMP Traps
```

33	0	192	0	2924	0	0	IP-RT Background
34	0	440740	278136	176664	0	0	IP-EIGRP Router
				1071520	Total		

Show process CPU shows where the CPU is spending its time, along with the total utilization of the CPU. You should examine two major items in the output from this command. The first item is shown in the first line, which, as will be shown later, indicates the total percentage of available *central processing unit* (CPU) power for the last five seconds, the last minute, and the last hour. The utilization for the last five seconds is easily skewed simply by running the command and therefore should not be considered heavily unless it is approaching 100 percent. The utilization for the last five minutes and the last hour, however, are good indications of how well the router is handling the amounts of traffic being generated. Consistent utilization approaching 80 percent is indicative of the need to upgrade to a more powerful router.

The second item to consider is how much utilization any given process is using. Some processes, such as *network address translation* (NAT) and access lists, can use a large amount of CPU cycles. Using the show process CPU command will enable you to check the percentage of the total CPU cycles that a specific process is using. If a given process is using too many cycles, you have two choices: offload this process to another router or upgrade this router. A truncated sample output is shown below:

```
Router#Show process cpu
CPU utilization for five seconds: 12%/9%; one minute: 13%; five
minutes: 16%
PID   Runtime(ms)  Invoked  uSecs   5Sec    1Min    5Min   TTY  Process
1     300          6227     48      0.00%   0.00%   0.00%  0    Load Meter
2     2476         248      9983    1.39%   0.18%   0.27%  1    Virtual Exec
3     799844       7625     104897  0.00%   2.68%   2.62%  0    Check Heaps
4     0            1        0       0.00%   0.00%   0.00%  0    Pool Manager
5     0            2        0       0.00%   0.00%   0.00%  0    Timers
6     1880         2122     885     0.00%   0.00%   0.00%  0    ARP Input
7     4            1        4000    0.00%   0.00%   0.00%  0    SERIAL A
                                                                Detect
8     0            1        0       0.00%   0.00%   0.00%  0    CSU/DSU Trap
9     19140        13934    1373    0.57%   0.09%   0.05%  0    IP Input
10    2968         3676     807     0.08%   0.01%   0.00%  0    CDP Protocol
11    121384       31627    3837    0.40%   0.40%   0.40%  0    IP Background
12    300          6496     46      0.08%   0.00%   0.00%  0    TCP Timer
13    32           7        4571    0.00%   0.00%   0.00%  0    TCP Protocols
14    4            1        4000    0.00%   0.00%   0.00%  0    RARP Input
15    800          147      5442    0.00%   0.00%   0.00%  0    BOOTP Server
16    172          519      331     0.00%   0.00%   0.00%  0    IP Cache Ager
17    0            1        0       0.00%   0.00%   0.00%  0    Critical
                                                                Bkgnd.
18    12           5        2400    0.00%   0.00%   0.00%  0    Net
                                                                Background
19    4            4        1000    0.00%   0.00%   0.00%  0    Logger
```

PID	Runtime(ms)	Invoked	uSecs	5Sec	1Min	5Min	TTY	Process
20	1852	31103	59	0.00%	0.00%	0.00%	0	TTY Background
21	2356	31109	75	0.00%	0.00%	0.00%	0	Per-Second Jobs
PID	Runtime(ms)	Invoked	uSecs	5Sec	1Min	5Min	TTY	Process
22	1900	31108	61	0.00%	0.00%	0.00%	0	Net Periodic
23	8116	22040	368	0.00%	0.00%	0.00%	0	Net Input
24	168	6228	26	0.00%	0.00%	0.00%	0	Compute Load Avg.
25	22808	519	43946	0.00%	0.06%	0.05%	0	Per-Minute Jobs
26	7428	6227	1192	0.00%	0.00%	0.00%	0	FR LMI
27	12	519	23	0.00%	0.00%	0.00%	0	FR ARP
28	2992	309874	9	0.00%	0.00%	0.00%	0	FR Broadcast Output
29	8932	20334	439	0.00%	0.00%	0.00%	0	IP-EIGRP Hello
31	4	1	4000	0.00%	0.00%	0.00%	0	IP SNMP
32	0	1	0	0.00%	0.00%	0.00%	0	SNMP Traps
33	1816	521	3485	0.00%	0.00%	0.00%	0	IP-RT Background
34	13732	7951	1727	0.00%	0.02%	0.00%	0	IP-EIGRP Router

Show flash is used to list the files residing on the flash memory. This is useful to make sure your IOS is current. We recommend using the full file name when copying to the flash. This removes any doubts from the Cisco TAC personnel as to which version you are using. The following output is from a show flash command:

```
PAML-3640(3)#show flash
System flash directory:
File  Length    Name/status
   1  3309816   c3640-is-mz_112-18_P.bin
[3309880 bytes used, 5078728 available, 8388608 total]
8192K bytes of processor board System flash (Read/Write)
```

Show IP traffic returns information regarding the IP traffic statistics. Some of the information presented includes the number of format errors received. Format errors can usually be attributed to a host with a different encapsulation than the router. This also shows the checksum errors received and a summary of traffic based on the protocol used. It can also show if the router is using EIGRP. EIGRP traffic is labeled as "IP-IGRP2." A sample is shown here:

```
Router#show ip traffic
IP statistics:
  Rcvd:  37664 total, 9835 local destination
         0 format errors, 0 checksum errors, 3 bad hop count
         0 unknown protocol, 0 not a gateway
         0 security failures, 0 bad options, 0 with options
  Opts:  0 end, 0 nop, 0 basic security, 0 loose source route
         0 timestamp, 0 extended security, 0 record route
         0 stream ID, 0 strict source route, 0 alert, 0 cipso
```

```
                    0 other
          Frags: 0 reassembled, 0 timeouts, 0 couldn't reassemble
                 0 fragmented, 0 couldn't fragment
          Bcast: 1975 received, 0 sent
          Mcast: 6694 received, 13519 sent
           Sent: 14666 generated, 23424 forwarded
                 23 encapsulation failed, 30 no route
      ICMP statistics:
        Rcvd: 0 format errors, 0 checksum errors, 0 redirects, 0
      unreachable
                519 echo, 0 echo reply, 0 mask requests, 0 mask replies, 0
      quench
                0 parameter, 0 timestamp, 0 info request, 0 other
                0 irdp solicitations, 0 irdp advertisements
        Sent: 0 redirects, 31 unreachable, 0 echo, 519 echo reply
                0 mask requests, 0 mask replies, 0 quench, 0 timestamp
                0 info reply, 3 time exceeded, 0 parameter problem
                0 irdp solicitations, 0 irdp advertisements

      IGRP statistics:
        Rcvd: 0 total, 0 checksum errors
        Sent: 0 total

      IP-IGRP2 statistics:
        Rcvd: 6942 total
        Sent: 13768 total

      UDP statistics:
        Rcvd: 1981 total, 0 checksum errors, 6 no port
        Sent: 0 total, 3938 forwarded broadcasts

      TCP statistics:
        Rcvd: 397 total, 0 checksum errors, 0 no port
        Sent: 349 total

      ARP statistics:
        Rcvd: 173 requests, 4 replies, 0 reverse, 0 other
        Sent: 22 requests, 93 replies (1 proxy), 0 reverse
```

There are also commands that are not included in the show tech command. These commands enable the engineer to see how the system is operating. We will explore some of these commands next.

Global Commands

The first command we will look at is the show ARP command. This command shows the contents of the ARP cache including the IP address, the age of the entry, the hardware MAC address, and the interface where this entry learned of all known connections. A truncated example is shown here:

```
Router#show arp
Protocol  Address        Age (min)  Hardware Addr.  Type  Interface
Internet  172.30.2.176   3          0010.4b69.5e5d  ARPA  FastEthernet1/0
Internet  172.30.2.177   4          0010.4b6a.3d4f  ARPA  FastEthernet1/0
```

```
Internet   172.30.2.178   0      0010.4b76.b98d   ARPA   FastEthernet1/0
Internet   172.30.1.177   158    0010.5a19.8db8   ARPA   FastEthernet1/0
Internet   172.30.2.179   1      0010.4b69.5a50   ARPA   FastEthernet1/0
Internet   172.30.1.183   5      0060.b096.2b28   ARPA   FastEthernet1/0
Internet   172.30.2.181   161    0010.4b6a.ea8f   ARPA   FastEthernet1/0
Internet   172.30.2.182   157    0010.4b6a.3cd4   ARPA   FastEthernet1/0
Internet   172.30.2.183   54     0010.4b69.5cc1   ARPA   FastEthernet1/0
Internet   172.30.1.180   92     0010.5aaa.7482   ARPA   FastEthernet1/0
Internet   172.30.2.184   130    0010.4b6b.4ad5   ARPA   FastEthernet1/0
Internet   172.30.2.185   105    0010.4b6b.4aac   ARPA   FastEthernet1/0
Internet   172.30.1.184   27     0010.4b76.b519   ARPA   FastEthernet1/0
Internet   172.30.2.187   2      0060.97c6.87fc   ARPA   FastEthernet1/0
Internet   172.30.2.160   10     0060.97c6.91a4   ARPA   FastEthernet1/0
Internet   172.30.3.160   9      0060.b086.f19d   ARPA   FastEthernet1/0
Internet   172.30.2.162   5      0060.0829.4641   ARPA   FastEthernet1/0
Internet   172.30.3.163   4      00e0.18c1.c6d7   ARPA   FastEthernet1/0
Internet   172.30.4.165   1      0010.4b2b.b6fd   ARPA   FastEthernet1/0
Internet   172.30.1.160   228    00a0.24ba.11e9   ARPA   FastEthernet1/0
```

Show debugging is used to show which debug commands are currently in effect. While troubleshooting, it can be easy to lose track of what is currently being debugged if you are not careful. When you are in doubt of which debug commands are running, this command will list them for you. Here is a sample:

```
Router#show debugging
Generic serial:
  Serial network interface debugging is on
```

Show frame-relay has a few subcommands, all of which are useful when troubleshooting Frame Relay issues. The first we will explore is the LMI command.

Show frame-relay Lmi is used to show the LMI statistics on Frame Relay connections. This will show the LMI type, the number and types of errors, and the number of LMI status messages sent and received. A sample output is as follows:

```
Router#show frame-relay lmi
LMI Statistics for Interface Serial0/0 (Frame Relay DTE) LMI TYPE
= CISCO
   Invalid Unnumbered Info 0     Invalid Prot Disc 0
   Invalid Dummy Call Ref 0      Invalid Msg Type 0
   Invalid Status Message 0      Invalid Lock Shift 0
   Invalid Information ID 0      Invalid Report IE Len 0
   Invalid Report Request 0      Invalid Keep IE Len 0
   Num Status Enq. Sent 0        Num Status Msgs Rcvd 0
   Num Update Status Rcvd 0      Num Status Timeouts 0

LMI Statistics for Interface Serial0/1 (Frame Relay DTE) LMI TYPE =
ANSI
   Invalid Unnumbered Info 0     Invalid Prot Disc 0
   Invalid Dummy Call Ref 0      Invalid Msg Type 0
   Invalid Status Message 0      Invalid Lock Shift 0
```

```
Invalid Information ID 0      Invalid Report IE Len 0
Invalid Report Request 0     Invalid Keep IE Len 0
Num Status Enq. Sent 291744  Num Status Msgs Rcvd 291725
Num Update Status Rcvd 0     Num Status Timeouts 19
```

Show frame-relay map provides a quick status of each of your Frame Relay connections (up), along with the *data link control identifier* (DLCI) numbers for each of the *permanent virtual circuits* (PVCs) and whether or not this connection is active. A sample is shown here:

```
Router#show frame-relay map
Serial0/1.2 (up): point-to-point dlci, dlci 17(0x11,0x410), broadcast
   status defined, active
Serial0/1.4 (up): point-to-point dlci, dlci 19(0x13,0x430), broadcast
   status defined, active
Serial0/1.1 (up): point-to-point dlci, dlci 16(0x10,0x400), broadcast
   status defined, active
Serial0/1.3 (up): point-to-point dlci, dlci 28(0x1C,0x4C0), broadcast
   status defined, active
```

Show frame-relay pvc lists all the PVCs on this router, the DLCI, the interface, and if the PVC is active. Additional information includes the number of packets traveling both directions across the interface and the number of dropped packets. It is worth watching the number of FECNs and BECNs on a given interface to determine line congestion. A truncated example is shown here:

```
Router#show frame-relay pvc

PVC Statistics for interface Serial0/0 (Frame Relay DTE)

PVC Statistics for interface Serial0/1 (Frame Relay DTE)

DLCI = 16, DLCI USAGE = LOCAL, PVC STATUS = ACTIVE, INTERFACE =
Serial0/1.1

   input pkts 10361044  output pkts 8478505    in bytes 1028945500
   out bytes 1955911781 dropped pkts 170       in FECN pkts 0
   in BECN pkts 0          out FECN pkts 0out BECN pkts 0
   in DE pkts 2185         out DE pkts 0
   out bcast pkts 663581       out bcast bytes 53351035
   pvc create time 6w2d, last time pvc status changed 4w0d

DLCI = 17, DLCI USAGE = LOCAL, PVC STATUS = ACTIVE, INTERFACE =
Serial0/1.2

   input pkts 8969878   output pkts 7150973    in bytes 920852461
   out bytes 1645558481 dropped pkts 344       in FECN pkts 0
   in BECN pkts 0          out FECN pkts 0out BECN pkts 0
   in DE pkts 2865         out DE pkts 0
   out bcast pkts 665647       out bcast bytes 53525166
   pvc create time 5w3d, last time pvc status changed 5d18h
```

Interface Commands

The current state of all interfaces can be shown with the "show interfaces" command. This will list all of the interfaces on the router. Sometimes you will only want to look at specific interfaces. Choosing to show a specific interface will enable you to limit the output to only the interface in which you are interested.

Show controllers is used to identify the capabilities of interfaces as well as their failures. Failures can include hardware, memory, buffer, and overflow errors. In the following sample output, we have limited the show controllers command to a single interface. One important piece of information shown with this command is the number of underruns. An *underrun* is a condition in which the router is unable to process packets fast enough for the media. The router will eventually drop these packets. This is usually indicative of a problem within the router.

This also shows us that the TX and RX clocks are being detected, the number of times the CTS has been lost, and the number of overruns. *Overruns* are when the router must wait for the media before being able to send the data. If the router must wait for too long a period, the data will be dropped. This is usually indicative of line congestion.

```
Router#sh controllers Serial 0/1
Interface Serial0/1
Hardware is Quicc 68360
DTE V.35 TX and RX clocks detected.
idb at 0x6096B644, driver data structure at 0x609704BC
WIC interrupt reg = F
SCC Registers:
General [GSMR]=0x2:0x00000030, Protocol-specific [PSMR]=0x8
Events [SCCE]=0x0000, Mask [SCCM]=0x001F, Status [SCCS]=0x0006
Transmit on Demand [TODR]=0x0, Data Sync [DSR]=0x7E7E
Interrupt Registers:
Config [CICR]=0x00C9CF00, Pending [CIPR]=0x00000000
Mask    [CIMR]=0xA0000400, In-srv  [CISR]=0x00000000
SDMA Registers:
[SDSR]=0x00, [SDAR]=0x0199CFA0, [SDCR]=0x0772
Command register [CR]=0x640
Port A [PADIR]=0x0000, [PAPAR]=0xFFFF
       [PAODR]=0x0000, [PADAT]=0xF6FF
Port B [PBDIR]=0x0013FE, [PBPAR]=0x00000E
       [PBODR]=0x000000, [PBDAT]=0x03DD5C
Port C [PCDIR]=0x0002, [PCPAR]=0x000C
       [PCSO]=0x00A0,   [PCDAT]=0x0F0D, [PCINT]=0x0001
Receive Ring
       rmd(3C0102E0): status 9000 length 34 address 1905C10
       rmd(3C0102E8): status 9000 length 34 address 1905C10
       rmd(3C0102F0): status 9000 length 34 address 190C93C
       rmd(3C0102F8): status 9000 length 34 address 190B5F8
       rmd(3C010300): status 9000 length 34 address 190CFA8
       rmd(3C010308): status 9000 length 34 address 19055A4
       rmd(3C010310): status 9000 length 42 address 1908904
```

```
        rmd(3C010318): status 9000 length 34 address 190AF8C
        rmd(3C010320): status 9000 length 34 address 190C2D0
        rmd(3C010328): status 9000 length 34 address 19075C0
        rmd(3C010330): status 9000 length 34 address 1904260
        rmd(3C010338): status 9000 length 34 address 1909C48
        rmd(3C010340): status 9000 length 34 address 1906F54
        rmd(3C010348): status B000 length 34 address 190627C
Transmit Ring
        tmd(3C010350): status 5C00 length 5E0 address 198C276
        tmd(3C010358): status 5C00 length 5E0 address 198FC42
        tmd(3C010360): status 5C00 length 32 address 1991C5E
        tmd(3C010368): status 5C00 length 35 address 1998FF6
        tmd(3C010370): status 5C00 length 42C address 1977486
        tmd(3C010378): status 5C00 length 32 address 1989582
        tmd(3C010380): status 5C00 length 5E0 address 199F04A
        tmd(3C010388): status 5C00 length 77 address 1983B9A
        tmd(3C010390): status 5C00 length 9F address 1986EFA
        tmd(3C010398): status 5C00 length 1ED address 198554A
        tmd(3C0103A0): status 5C00 length 32 address 199C356
        tmd(3C0103A8): status 5C00 length 32 address 1986222
        tmd(3C0103B0): status 5C00 length 5C address 1991C5E
        tmd(3C0103B8): status 7C00 length 5E0 address 19922CA
SCC GENERAL PARAMETER RAM (at 0x3C010D00)
Rx BD Base [RBASE]=0x2E0, Fn Code [RFCR]=0x19
Tx BD Base [TBASE]=0x350, Fn Code [TFCR]=0x19
Max Rx Buff Len [MRBLR]=1548
Rx State [RSTATE]=0x19008240, BD Ptr [RBPTR]=0x300
Tx State [TSTATE]=0x19000348, BD Ptr [TBPTR]=0x3B8
SCC  PARAMETER RAM (at 0x3C010D38)
CRC Preset [C_PRES]=0xFFFF, Mask [C_MASK]=0xF0B8
Errors: CRC [CRCEC]=453, Aborts [ABTSC]=5, Discards [DISFC]=0
Nonmatch Addr Cntr [NMARC]=0
Retry Count [RETRC]=0
Max Frame Length [MFLR]=1608
Rx Int Threshold [RFTHR]=1, Frame Cnt [RFCNT]=1
User-Defined Address 0000/0000/0000/0000
User-Defined Address Mask 0x0000

Buffer Size 1524
QUICC SCC specific errors:
43 input aborts on receiving flag sequence
0 throttles, 0 enables
0 overruns
0 transmitter underruns
0 transmitter CTS losts
```

Show interface is used to show different types of interfaces. When this is used with the optional word "ethernet" and the Ethernet interface number, this limits the interface to this one particular Ethernet interface. On an Ethernet interface, you will receive an output similar to this:

```
Router#show interfaces ethernet 0/1
Ethernet0/1 is up, line protocol is up
  Hardware is AmdP2, address is 00e0.1ee9.9042 (bia 00e0.1ee9.9042)
  Internet address is 192.168.10.1/30
  MTU 1500 bytes, BW 10000 Kbit, DLY 1000 usec, rely 255/255, load
  1/255
  Encapsulation ARPA, loopback not set, keep-alive set (10 sec)
```

```
ARP type: ARPA, ARP Timeout 04:00:00
Last input 00:06:37, output 00:00:09, output hang never
Last clearing of "show interface" counters 4w0d
Queueing strategy: FIFO
Output queue 0/40, 0 drops; input queue 0/75, 0 drops
5 minute input rate 0 bits/sec, 0 packets/sec
5 minute output rate 0 bits/sec, 0 packets/sec
   217603 packets input, 132142368 bytes, 0 no buffer
   Received 4339 broadcasts, 0 runts, 0 giants, 0 throttles
   0 input errors, 0 CRC, 0 frame, 0 overrun, 0 ignored, 0 abort
   0 input packets with dribble condition detected
   563149 packets output, 70733182 bytes, 0 underruns
   0 output errors, 34 collisions, 0 interface resets
   0 babbles, 0 late collision, 128 deferred
   0 lost carrier, 0 no carrier
   0 output buffer failures, 0 output buffers swapped out
```

The first two lines are useful in our troubleshooting efforts. The first line tells us the present status of the interface. We can also see that the interface and the line are both up. Thus, the line status has only four possibilities:

- Ethernet0/1 is up; line protocol is up.
- Ethernet0/1 is up; line protocol is down.
- Ethernet0/1 is down; line protocol is down.
- Ethernet0/1 is administratively down; line protocol is down.

Assuming you are not experiencing a hardware problem, you will never see the following:

- Ethernet0/1 is down; line protocol is up.
- Ethernet0/1 is administratively down; line protocol is up.

The reason for this is fairly simple. The first up (or down) refers to the layer 1 status of the line. The second up (or down) refers to the layer 2 status. Because layer 2 relies upon layer 1 being up, you will never see a condition where layer 1 is down but layer 2 is up. The values that are shown hold true for all types of interfaces.

The second line shows us two MAC addresses, the assigned address and the *burned-in address* (BIA). It is possible to change the assigned address to become different from the BIA. If you have done so, all packets traveling out of this interface will have the assigned address as the source address. Only the assigned address will respond to packets.

It is important to note the number of collisions experienced on Ethernet and FastEthernet interfaces. According to Cisco, and as generally accepted within the industry, the number of collisions should be less than 0.1 of the total number of output packets. In the previous example, we could calculate the percentage of collisions by dividing the 34 collision packets by the

563,149 total packets. This is well below the Cisco recommended maximum of 0.1. Therefore, this interface would not be considered to be experiencing excessive collisions. Because Token Ring and serial interfaces do not experience collisions, you should never see any on these types of interfaces.

Show interface serial is used for isolating problems on the serial interface. This command is similar to the command for an Ethernet interface. Specific serial information is provided, including the encapsulation type, LMI status, and keep-alive time. An example is shown here:

```
Router#sh interface serial 0/1
Serial0/1 is up, line protocol is up
  Hardware is QUICC Serial
  Description: Frame Relay
  MTU 1500 bytes, BW 1536 Kbit, DLY 20000 usec, rely 255/255, load
  2/255
  Encapsulation FRAME-RELAY IETF, loopback not set, keep-alive set
  (10 sec)
  LMI Enq sent  248783, LMI stat recvd 248767, LMI upd recvd 0, DTE
  LMI up
  LMI Enq recvd 0, LMI stat sent  0, LMI upd sent  0
  LMI DLCI 0  LMI type is ANSI Annex D  frame relay DTE
  Broadcast queue 0/64, broadcasts sent/dropped 1290043/0,
  interface broadcasts3
  Last input 00:00:00, output 00:00:00, output hang never
  Last clearing of "show interface" counters 4w0d
  Queueing strategy: FIFO
  Output queue 0/40, 0 drops; input queue 0/75, 0 drops
  5 minute input rate 9000 bits/sec, 13 packets/sec
  5 minute output rate 17000 bits/sec, 10 packets/sec
     18283529 packets input, 1939065895 bytes, 0 no buffer
     Received 0 broadcasts, 0 runts, 0 giants, 0 throttles
     2619 input errors, 1581 CRC, 999 frame, 0 overrun, 0 ignored,
     39 abort
     14524737 packets output, 3309479810 bytes, 0 underruns
     0 output errors, 0 collisions, 3 interface resets
     0 output buffer failures, 0 output buffers swapped out
     0 carrier transitions
  DCD=up  DSR=up  DTR=up  RTS=up  CTS=up
```

Two items in the previous output bear further explanation. The first is the three CRC errors shown. A CRC is a mathematical computation used on the data within a frame. When a frame is received, the CRC is recalculated. If the newly calculated CRC does not match the CRC sent with the frame, there is a CRC error, which is recorded and can be shown with the show interface command.

The second item is a carrier transition, the total number of which is also revealed with the show interface command. A carrier transition occurs whenever the state of the circuit changes. In other words, if the frame connection goes down, there will be a carrier transition. If an interface experiences three carrier transitions in rapid succession, the interface will be shut down and it will take a "no shut" command from the administrator to reenable the interface. All of the counters shown can be reset to zero with a "clear counters" command.

Core Dumps

Occasionally, a router will act in ways that are incomprehensible. After talking to the TAC engineers several times, asking your coworkers, and researching through various sources, you and the TAC engineer may still be clueless as to the cause of the problem. This is where the core dump commands come into play. Four commands are related to dumping the core. Before we examine each of them, we will examine exactly what a core is and why we would want to dump the core.

The *core* is the total memory used on the router. It contains all the buffers, routing tables, and dynamic variables on a running router. In other words, the core contains all the information a router knows at any given time. Dumping is merely the act of writing the contents of the core to a file. Reading and diagnosing the contents of a core dump are beyond the scope of this book. Usually, this file will be sent to Cisco for an analysis in which a specialist will analyze the contents to find out exactly what is going on within the router.

NOTE: Our experience is that the need to dump the core on a router is usually rare. The issue does appear to show up more often when a router is recently upgraded to the newest version of the IOS. Our advice is stay close to the middle of the road when upgrading the IOS version of your routers. Being on the "cutting edge" is risky with any software. Do not update your router IOS merely because a new version becomes available.

Unless there is a specific reason you need to upgrade your IOS, there is no advantage to using the latest version available. Using a version that has been tested by other users for the last six months or year allows you to avoid becoming a "beta site" for the newest versions available.

Caution should also be used to avoid lagging too far behind in upgrading your IOS. Most, if not all, new versions of the IOS do improve performance and stability. It is also easier to debug a problem on a current version of the IOS. The TAC personnel are usually adept in both the latest version and the previous one. If you call the TAC with an old version of the IOS installed, one of the first things they may request is that you upgrade to a newer version. For these reasons, we suggest sticking to a newer yet tested version of the IOS on your routers.

The reason for dumping a core is to provide a snapshot of all variables and the memory usage in a router. Because it is a snapshot of the router, every variable and table is available within the dump. Before dumping the core, we need to specify the name of the dump file. The dump file name is specified by the following global command:

```
Router#exception core-file dumpfilename
```

"dumpfilename" is the name of the file that is written when a dump is done. Using the "no" form of the command is used to remove the dumpfile-name. This file is saved on a remote device, as specified with one of the three commands that cause a core dump to occur. The first command is the "exception dump" command. This command tells the router to write the core when the router crashes. This is a global command used as follows:

```
Router#exception dump server-ip-address
```

The "server-ip-address" is the IP address of a server that will hold the dump file. This server must be able to receive a file over the network through FTP, RCP, or TFTP. The "exception dump" part of the command actually tells the router that when a crash is occurring, a dump should be made. Use the "no" form of the command to specify not to dump the core when a crash occurs. To choose which protocol is used to write the dump file, use the following global command:

```
Router#exception protocol {ftp | rcp | tftp}
```

As implied, FTP uses the FTP protocol to write the file, while RCP uses the RCP protocol, and TFTP uses the TFTP protocol. Notice that all of these protocols require the use of IP. It is advised that you must be sure the server can be reached by the protocol chosen. Double-check that access lists do not prevent the use of this protocol over the path to the server. Additionally, the path used preferably will be available using a high-speed link such as Ethernet or FastEthernet.

The previous method is used to dump the core when a router crashes. There is also a method available to dump the core when certain memory size parameters are exceeded. Therefore, you can get the data needed before a serious error occurs and at a more predictable time. To cause a router to dump the core and then reboot when a memory parameter is violated, use the "exception core-file" and "exception protocol" commands along with the "exception memory" command. To remove the exception memory command, use the no form. The format of the command is as follows:

```
Router#exception memory {fragment size | minimum size}
```

The keyword *fragment* followed by the variable *size* specifies that when the minimum contiguous block of memory in the free pool exceeds the value of *size*, a dump and reboot should occur. Alternatively, you can specify that the router should dump the core and reboot when the minimum of free memory, without regard to whether this memory is contiguous, falls below a given point. In this case, you would use the keyword *minimum* with the variable *size*. In both cases, the variable *size* is the amount of memory in bytes.

The final method available for getting a core dump is to force the core to be written immediately. This method does not require the router to reboot after the core is written. This allows you to troubleshoot a production router without bringing the whole system down. In order to use this method, a TFTP server must be available to receive the core dump and an IP must be enabled on the router. The following is a sample of how to use the "write core" command to obtain a core dump on a functioning router. The output has been truncated for brevity:

```
Router#write core
Remote host? 172.30.1.1
Name of core file to write [Router-core]?
Write file Router-core on host 172.30.1.1? [confirm]
Writing Router-core!!!!!!!! ...
```

Now that we have seen how and why a core dump is accomplished, we will move on to commands that test connectivity to hosts. The first of these is the ping command.

Ping Commands

Packet Internet groper (ping) is a command that can be used with various protocols to check the connectivity to remote hosts. Ping is not only useful for IP, but it can also be used with Apollo, AppleTalk, CLNS, DECnet, IPX, Vines, and XNS. To fully realize the potential uses of ping, we must remember not only the different protocols useable with ping, but also the two differing forms of ping. The first form, called the user form, is a single line command. The second form, called privileged or extended, is a series of commands. For the remainder of this book, we will refer to the former as merely ping and the later as extended ping. We will look at how ping operates before we explore the uses, tricks, and traps associated with ping.

Because ping relies upon the *Internet control message protocol* (ICMP) functions of *echo-request* and *echo-reply* messages, it is necessary for us to look at how ICMP works before we delve into Cisco's implementation of ping.

ICMP

We know that we can have an unreliable, connectionless delivery of data within our network. We need a method to see if the receiving host is available before flooding the network with information sent to a host that is not available. We also must have some way in which a connecting device, such as a router, tells the sending device that the receiving host is not available. Generally speaking, routers use the ICMP services to report that a destination is unreachable, while hosts use the ICMP services to check if the destination is reachable. In other words, routers tell and hosts ask about the availability of destinations.

ICMP was originally designed as an error-reporting protocol, not as an error-correcting protocol. The purpose of ICMP is to report a delivery error back to the original source of the ICMP request. In Figure 4-1, we show a hypothetical network with three routers, A, B, and C. Assume that we are sending an ICMP packet from router A to router C. If router B is not able to connect to router C, an ICMP message is sent back to router A.

ICMP does not know or care what route has been taken, except when the record route option is used. Reporting the error back only to the originator makes sense in an internetworking environment. Routers are autonomous devices. Router A usually has no control over router B. The most that ICMP can and should do is to tell router A that router B does not know how to for-

Figure 4-1
ICMP flow

ICMP Routes

Router A   Router B   Router C

ward the packet. Now that we know what ICMP is trying to accomplish, we will look at how it goes about reaching its goal.

ICMP messages are encapsulated within IP packets. Usually, only higher-level protocols are encapsulated within another protocol. However, ICMP is an integral part of the IP protocol suite but still is encapsulated within an IP packet. With one exception, ICMP packets are treated like all other IP packets. This exception occurs when an error is detected in sending or receiving an ICMP packet. Because an ICMP message is used to report errors, we should not report errors on the ICMP messages. Let's assume, for example, that we have a serious issue with connectivity where every other packet has an error. If we needed to send out messages that the ICMP messages were not flowing, we would quickly flood the network with notifications that ICMP was not working properly. Therefore, the IP specifications for ICMP state that ICMP error messages are not generated for errors caused by ICMP messages.

Even though each ICMP message format varies depending upon which service is requested, all ICMP messages have the first three fields in common. These fields are type, code, and checksum. Code is a single-byte field whose purpose is to further explain the type field. The ICMP checksum is a two-byte field that uses the same algorithm as the IP checksum field. However, the ICMP checksum only pertains to the ICMP portion of the IP message. All ICMP messages that report errors also carry the header and the first eight bytes of the datagram that caused the error. Because the most critical information of a higher-level protocol using IP is carried within these first eight bytes, this helps with detecting what caused the error.

The type field is a single-byte integer with one of the values shown in Table 4-4:

Because we are at this moment only concerned with how ping works, we will only look at a few of these types of messages. The first two types we will look at are the echo-request and echo-reply. These form the basis of the ping utility as implemented by Cisco.

A host or router sends the ICMP echo-request to a remote host or router to see if the remote is reachable. The last router that is unable to forward the packet or the destination host sends back an echo-reply. The formats of echo-request, echo-reply, and destination unreachable messages are shown in Figure 4-2. Remember that this ICMP message is imbedded within the data portion of an IP packet, which is in turn encapsulated within another protocol, such as Ethernet.

If the echo-request is successfully delivered, the sender will receive an echo-reply. On a Cisco router, this will be shown as a "!". If the ICMP reply is in the form of a destination unreachable message, it could be due to a

Table 4-4	**Type Field**	**Message Type**
Type Field Values	0	Echo-reply
	3	Destination unreachable
	4	Source quench
	5	Redirect
	8	Echo-request
	11	Time exceeded
	12	Parameter problem
	13	Timestamp request
	14	Timestamp reply
	15	Obsolete (information request)
	16	Obsolete (information reply)
	17	Address mask request
	18	Address mask reply

number of reasons. Notice within Figure 4-2 that the response can be one of 13 different values, depending upon the type of failure. The code field is a single-byte integer. Table 4-5 displays the code types that can be sent by the replying router as well as what a Cisco router will show when this code is received. This list applies to both ping and traceroute commands.

Two other common types of ICMP messages can be seen on a Cisco router: the source quench and time-exceeded messages. Both are shown below in Figure 4.3. A source quench has a type value of 4. This is also the mechanism used in FECNs and BECNs. A source quench message used within a ping will show as a C on the console. The final common ICMP message on a Cisco router is the time-exceeded message. This occurs because the *time-to-live* (TTL) component has been exceeded. This could be due to either congestion on the line or because of a circular route. In either case, when the hop count is reduced to zero, the router will send back an ICMP time-exceeded message in the format shown in Figure 4-3. A time-exceeded message received through the ping command will show as a "." on a Cisco router.

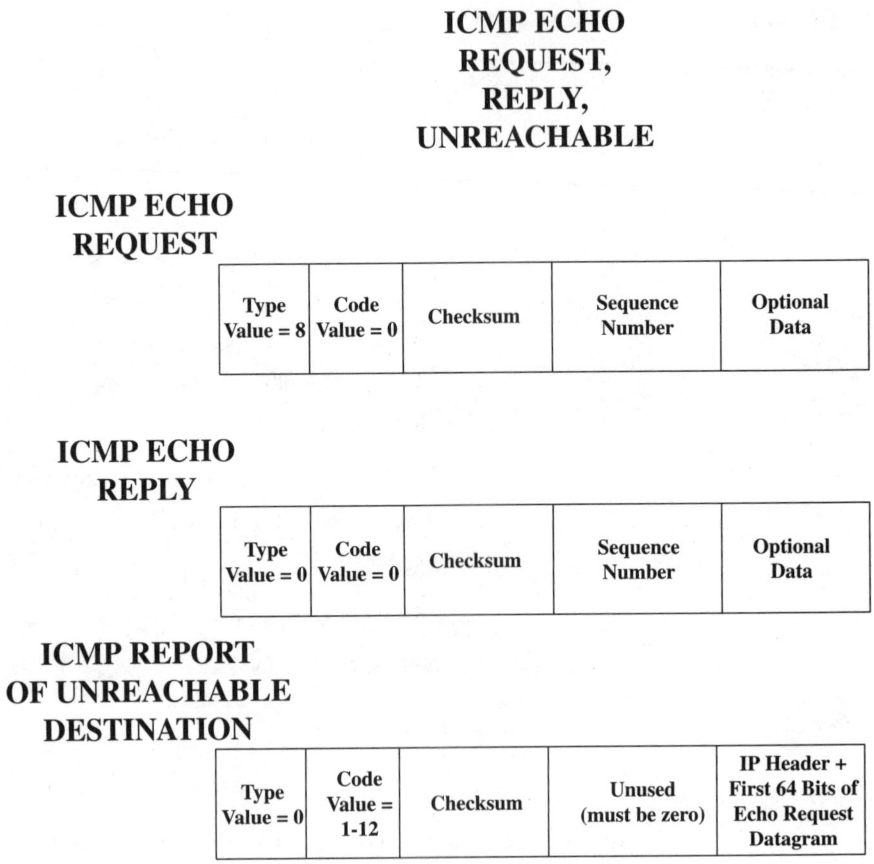

Figure 4-2
ICMP echo-request

ICMP ECHO REQUEST, REPLY, UNREACHABLE

ICMP ECHO REQUEST

Type Value = 8	Code Value = 0	Checksum	Sequence Number	Optional Data

ICMP ECHO REPLY

Type Value = 0	Code Value = 0	Checksum	Sequence Number	Optional Data

ICMP REPORT OF UNREACHABLE DESTINATION

Type Value = 0	Code Value = 1-12	Checksum	Unused (must be zero)	IP Header + First 64 Bits of Echo Request Datagram

Now that we have reviewed how the ICMP messages work, we are ready to continue with the uses, tricks, and traps associated with ping.

Ping

Ping is an extremely useful tool for testing connectivity. However, several cautions should be considered before relying on the ping command to decisively tell us if a remote host is available. We will look at several items that can affect the capability of ping to accurately judge host availability before looking at the syntax of both ping and extended ping. The first issue we will discuss is the timing-out process.

Imagine that you are home taking care of your child. The child begins to play with the electrical outlet at the same time the dog is chewing on the leg

Table 4-5

Replying Router
Code Types and
Cisco Router
Responses

Type Field	Message Type	Cisco
0	Network unreachable	U
1	Host unreachable	.
2	Protocol unreachable	P
3	Port unreachable	.
4	Fragment needed	U
5	Source route failed	?
6	Destination network unknown	U
7	Destination host unknown	.
8	Source host isolated	.
9	Communication with destination, network administratively, prohibited	!H
10	Communication with destination, host administratively prohibited	!H
11	Network unreachable for type of service	.
12	Host unreachable for type of service	.

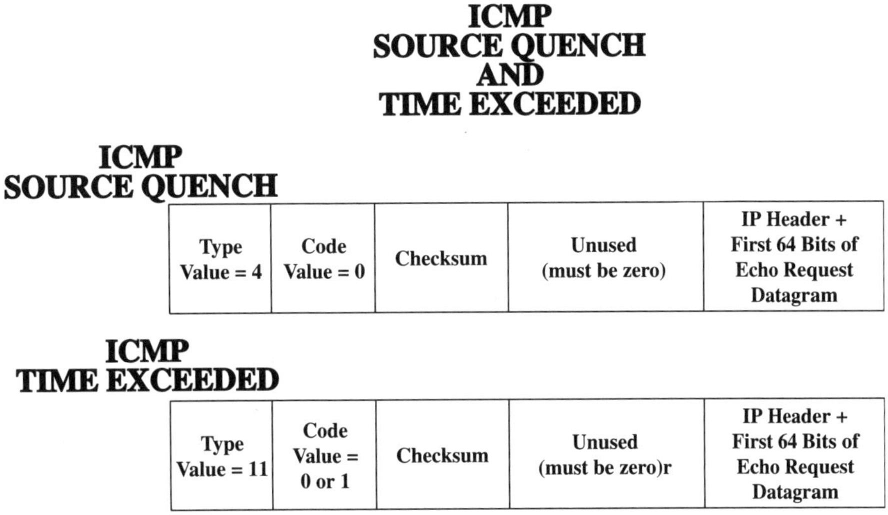

Figure 4-3
The source quench
and time-exceeded
messages

**ICMP
SOURCE QUENCH
AND
TIME EXCEEDED**

**ICMP
SOURCE QUENCH**

Type Value = 4	Code Value = 0	Checksum	Unused (must be zero)	IP Header + First 64 Bits of Echo Request Datagram

**ICMP
TIME EXCEEDED**

Type Value = 11	Code Value = 0 or 1	Checksum	Unused (must be zero)r	IP Header + First 64 Bits of Echo Request Datagram

of your antique furniture. This is also the precise moment that the pot on the stove chooses to boil over and the phone rings. You can only do one thing at a time. What do you choose to do? Chances are that you will not choose to answer the phone. Ping can be compared to this phone call. If there are sufficient resources and time to reply to the ping, the host will reply. If there are not sufficient resources or time, the ping request gets put into the queue and will be answered when there is time. When the host finally gets a chance to reply to the ping, it may be too late. In the same way that a phone will eventually stop ringing if it is not answered, a ping may have "timed out" by the time a response is sent. If ping does not receive a response within the time specified (two seconds by default), ping will act as if it had received an ICMP time-exceeded message. Timing out does not necessarily mean that the host is not available. It may merely mean that the host is too busy to answer within the time allowed. Because the default time in which a reply is expected from a ping is only two seconds, it is likely that during periods of high congestion hosts may appear to lose connectivity if ping is the only test used for connectivity.

There may be a number of reasons that a ping will not work when IP connectivity is available. One of the most common reasons is access lists. Assume that you have the following lines in an access list that is activated on the inbound serial port of your router:

```
Deny icmp any any echo-reply
Permit icmp any any echo-request
```

In this example, the echo-request will be sent out, but no replies will be let in. The pings will eventually time out. Hosts on other networks will be able to ping your hosts, but your hosts will never be able to successfully ping a host across this interface. Knowing exactly what your access lists do and do not permit is critical to knowing whether a ping should or should not succeed for a given host.

Another reason for ping to fail when connectivity is available is due to routing issues. Assume you have a series of routers set up like Figure 4-4.

Also assume, for the sake of argument, that the best path from A to C is through B. But, due to lack of consistency, the best path from C to A goes through router D. Which path do the ICMP echo-request and echo-reply packets travel? The answer is that they travel over both links. This is commonly known as *asymmetrical routing*. The route chosen in an echo-reply has no relationship to the route chosen for the echo-request. In our example, the echo-request will travel from A through B and then to C, while the echo-reply will travel from C through D and then to A. If you do not receive

Figure 4-4
Echo-reply example

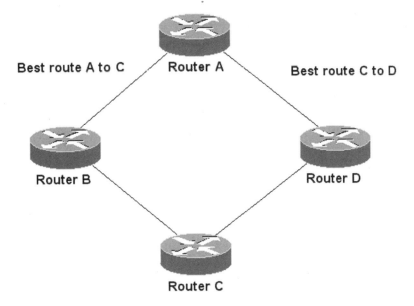

a reply, where is the issue, A-B-C or C-D-A? The problem could be in either route because we do not know if the echo-request timed out or if the echo-reply timed out.

Although this may seem like a silly example, it is actually quite common, especially when static routes have been used. Understanding which paths are chosen from both ends of a connection will significantly improve your chances of using ping to your advantage instead of merely baffling you.

NOTE: *When using static routes, it is usually advisable to be sure that the data flows through the same route regardless of which direction the data originates from, unless you have a specific reason for not doing so. Also, if you are using a metric with the static route on one side, be sure that the metric on the other side works in the same way. It is easy to unintentionally have data that flows over differing pathways depending on where the data originated if you are not careful. The same care should be applied when redistributing routes or adding metrics to routing protocols, such as EIGRP.*

Sometimes using asymmetrical routing is desired. In this case, understanding exactly how the data flow affects your troubleshooting methodologies becomes a greater issue. Keeping your troubleshooting plans in mind while designing a network in which data flows over differing paths can be a great benefit when problems arise.

One other caution should be given about ping. By default, the user form of ping sets the TTL component to 32. Each router the ping encounters decrements this by one. If the TTL becomes zero, the last router will send back an ICMP time-exceeded message. If you have extremely long paths, this may be insufficient. On a large network, it may be necessary to use the extended ping to check connectivity.

Now that we have discussed some of the most common assumptions made while using ping, we are ready to look at how to use the ping command in the user form.

User Ping

The user form of ping is actually quite a simple global command. The form is

```
Router#ping [protocol] {host | address}
```

Using this form, we can ping by typing

```
Router#ping 172.30.1.1
```

Our Cisco router assumes we mean to use the IP protocol and sends five ICMP echo-request packets to the remote host at IP address 172.30.1.1. Alternatively, we could use the name of the remote host as follows:

```
Router#ping mainrouter
```

Using the host name will require that hostname resolution be enabled. If the router does not know how to resolve "mainrouter" to an IP address, we will not be able to complete our ping. Instead we will receive the following message:

```
Routing#ping mainrouter
Translating "mainrouter"
% Unrecognized host or address, or protocol not running.
```

If we feel this is too wordy, we can specify that IP be used to ping the host at IP address 172.30.1.1 by entering

```
Router#ping ip 172.30.11.1
```

Or if we want to check an AppleTalk host, we would use "apple" instead of "ip" and use a valid AppleTalk address, such as

```
Router#ping apple 12.164
```

Similarly, we can use any other protocol that ping supports, including Apollo, AppleTalk, CLNS, DECnet, IPX, Vines, and XNS. In each case, the host address must be in the proper format as specified by the protocol. We can also use a host name instead of an address as long as name resolution for the chosen protocol has been enabled.

Let's spend a few minutes looking at the outputs we get from a ping. Here is a typical ping to an IP host:

```
Router#ping 172.31.118.1

Type escape sequence to abort.
Sending 5, 100-byte ICMP Echos to 172.31.118.1, timeout is 2 seconds:
.!!!!
Success rate is 80 percent (4/5), round-trip min/avg/max = 48/49/52 ms
```

Notice that five packets have been sent out. We receive a time-out on the first packet, however, while all the other packets only take 49 milliseconds on average to get a response. This is not necessarily a problem. As a matter of fact, this is very common. The reason the first packet timed out is easy to explain. Ethernet works on layer 2 of the OSI model. IP and ICMP are working at layer 3. We have to convert the layer 3 address to a layer 2 address before we can talk to the remote host. This will take time. The default timeout for ping is only two seconds. We did not resolve the IP address to a MAC address fast enough to prevent the first packet from timing out and subsequent packets did not need to resolve the MAC address because it was already held in the ARP table. If we try the very same ping immediately after the first ping, we should not see the first packet time out because the ARP cache still holds the MAC address of the remote host. Here is an example of the very same command executed immediately after the first ping:

```
Router#ping 172.31.118.1

Type escape sequence to abort.
Sending 5, 100-byte ICMP Echos to 172.31.118.1, timeout is 2 seconds:
!!!!!
Success rate is 100 percent (5/5), round-trip min/avg/max =
48/50/55 ms
```

Notice that this time all of the packets were received. There are circumstances where several packets might not be received. One that immediately comes to mind is an ISDN connection. If the ISDN link happens to be down when the ping is sent, all five packets may time out before the connection becomes established. The connection may also be made by a modem, which may take 30 seconds or longer to connect. This means that it may take numerous attempts before any are successful. Additionally, if a dial connection is not up at the time the ping is initiated and a ping has not been specified as interesting traffic, the line will not become activated by using the ping command. In this case, you can either change the definition of interesting traffic or you can bring the line up by another means before trying a ping.

Assuming that we have received responses from all of our pings, we still need to interpret the information we have received. Let's look closely at another ping on our Ethernet network:

```
Router#ping 172.30.2.218

Type escape sequence to abort.
Sending 5, 100-byte ICMP Echos to 172.30.2.218, timeout is 2 seconds:
!!!!!
Success rate is 100 percent (5/5), round-trip min/avg/max = 1/2/4 ms
```

In our Ethernet example, we received 100 percent responses to our ping. These responses had a minimum response time of one millisecond, an average of two milliseconds, and a maximum of four milliseconds. Is this good, bad, or indifferent? This was done over a 100-MB link. The speed at which a network responds depends upon a number of factors. We have to look at the baseline of our network for the answer. Back in Chapter 2, "Troubleshooting Methodology," we discussed how we should perform a baseline on our network. This baseline tells us how our network performs on a normal day. If there is a significant difference between the times we are seeing now and what we were seeing during the baseline, there may be a problem. Without the baseline, a set of successful pings can only tell us that we have connectivity. With a baseline, a series of pings tells us how the network is running now compared to how it was running at the time the baseline was established.

Now that we have looked at the user form of ping, we are ready to move toward a more sophisticated form of ping, the extended ping.

Extended Ping

Extended ping differs from user ping in three ways. The first difference is that we need to be in enabled mode to use extended ping. The second difference is that extended ping is only supported by IP, AppleTalk, and IPX. There is no support for extended ping while using Apollo, CLNS, DECnet, Vines, or XNS. The third and most important difference is that extended ping enables us to change the defaults that ping uses. Changing these defaults gives us the ability to run a number of different tests with the same utility.

Before we go into how extended ping can be more useful than user ping, we will walk through an extended ping. An extended ping is started by typing "ping" while in enabled mode and hitting return. You will then be prompted for variables by the ping utility:

```
Router#ping
Protocol [ip]:
Target IP address: 172.30.1.1
Repeat count [5]:
Datagram size [100]:
Timeout in seconds [2]:
Extended commands [n]: y
Source address or interface: 172.30.1.3
Type of service [0]:
Set DF bit in IP header? [no]:
Validate reply data? [no]:
Data pattern [0xABCD]:
Loose, Strict, Record, Timestamp, Verbose[none]:
Sweep range of sizes [n]:
Type escape sequence to abort.
Sending 5, 100-byte ICMP Echos to 172.30.1.1, timeout is 2 seconds:
!!!!!
Success rate is 100 percent (5/5), round-trip min/avg/max = 1/2/4 ms
```

Notice in the output above which parameters are available to us. First, we are asked which protocol to use. Pressing the return key chooses the default, which is IP. The next item is the target IP address. If we had chosen AppleTalk as our protocol, we would have been prompted for the target AppleTalk address. The same holds true for IPX.

The next parameter is the repeat count. We can set this to any reasonable integer. If we are experiencing an intermittent loss of connection, setting this value high will allow ping to keep running long enough for you to see when the connectivity is lost. This may also allow you to continuously run a ping, while on another host you run an application that appears to be losing connectivity. If both the application and ping lose connectivity at the same time, it is usually safe to assume that there is a problem with connectivity. However, if the application loses connectivity while ping does not, this would indicate a problem within the application.

The datagram size can also be changed from the default of 100 bytes. This is useful for checking the state of a connection under larger loads. Often a ping with the default size of 100 bytes will not reveal any anomalies in your network, but when you raise the packet size to 500 bytes, you may see a significant loss of connectivity or a significant change in the response time. During your baseline analysis of your network, you should document the throughput speeds of large-, medium-, and small-sized pings. This will help paint an accurate picture of how your network performs under differing loads.

Caution should be taken when setting this parameter to ensure it is not set so that other factors come into play. For example, setting the datagram size to 10,000 bytes will almost certainly give you results you did not expect. One reason for this is that your Ethernet hosts must fragment the datagram into a size that Ethernet can handle before sending the datagram over the wire. The datagram will also need to be reassembled by the remote host. This could take more time than you expect and cause your interpretation of the speed of the connection to be based on factors other than the actual time it takes to ping. Use a reasonable approach when changing the datagram size. Notice in the following output how some of the pings have timed out because the size of the datagram has been increased to the maximum of 18,024 bytes. Also, the time to respond has increased significantly again, almost certainly due to the datagram size:

```
Router#ping
Protocol [ip]:
Target IP address: 172.30.1.1
Repeat count [5]:
Datagram size [100]: 18024
Timeout in seconds [2]:
Extended commands [n]: y
Source address or interface: 172.30.1.3
Type of service [0]:
Set DF bit in IP header? [no]:
Validate reply data? [no]:
Data pattern [0xABCD]:
Loose, Strict, Record, Timestamp, Verbose[none]:
Sweep range of sizes [n]:
Type escape sequence to abort.
Sending 5, 18024-byte ICMP Echos to 172.30.1.1, timeout is 2
seconds:
!!!..
Success rate is 60 percent (3/5), round-trip min/avg/max = 40/40/40 ms
```

The next parameter we are able to adjust is the timeout parameter. If we have made the datagram size larger than the default, we should also change the timeout parameter because larger packets take longer to send and receive. Setting the timeout too low will result in what looks like either an intermittent loss of connectivity or a total loss of the connection. In reality, it may merely be that the packets are arriving after the ping has timed out. If you are experiencing what looks like intermittent loss or a total loss of connectivity, double the timeout and see how the results change:

```
Router#ping
Protocol [ip]:
Target IP address: 172.30.1.1
```

```
Repeat count [5]:
Datagram size [100]: 18024
Timeout in seconds [2]: 4
Extended commands [n]: y
Source address or interface: 172.30.1.3
Type of service [0]:
Set DF bit in IP header? [no]:
Validate reply data? [no]:
Data pattern [0xABCD]:
Loose, Strict, Record, Timestamp, Verbose[none]:
Sweep range of sizes [n]:
Type escape sequence to abort.
Sending 5, 18024-byte ICMP Echos to 172.30.1.1, timeout is 4
seconds:
!!!!!
Success rate is 100 percent (5/5), round-trip min/avg/max =
40/40/40 ms
```

Extended ping also allows for the entering of variables that are not available with the user form of ping, hence the term extended ping. These can be used for a number of differing reasons. The most interesting of these variables for our purpose is the source address variable.

It is possible to set the source address of a ping to be a different interface than the interface over which you telnet into the router. By default, if you telnet into a router on the Ethernet interface, your pings will have a source address of that Ethernet interface. Sometimes it is useful to use a different interface than the one you have chosen for telnet. For example, you may have access lists set so that only one of your Ethernet interfaces has access to a given network and that you cannot telnet to that interface. You can still test connectivity by answering "Y" to the extended commands prompt. This will cause the router to ask for the source interface address. Putting in the address of the previously unavailable interface will cause the ping to travel out of that interface. This way, you can test connectivity without changing the very access list that may be the cause of your problems.

Windows Ping

Within Microsoft Windows 95/98 and Windows NT, ping and traceroute work similarly to a router. A few differences and similarities are worth mentioning, however. The first difference is in checking the current IP configuration. On a Windows 95 system, running the winipcfg.exe program may check the IP configuration. On a Windows NT system, the equivalent command is ipconfig.exe. The second difference is that traceroute and ping enable options to be entered on the command line instead of interactively. Although the output from a ping in the Windows environment is different than a router, the basic information received is the same. Following is a sample ping from a Windows 95 host:

```
Pinging 172.30.100.1 with 32 bytes of data:

Reply from 172.30.100.1: bytes=32 time=242ms TTL=252
Reply from 172.30.100.1: bytes=32 time=239ms TTL=252
Reply from 172.30.100.1: bytes=32 time=239ms TTL=252
Reply from 172.30.100.1: bytes=32 time=239ms TTL=252
```

In both Windows systems and routers, there is a definite methodology for using ping when you cannot reach the end destination. Following this order will allow you to quickly find where the problem resides. The recommended order of troubleshooting steps when using the ping command is as follows:

1. Look at the current IP configuration using winipcfg, ipconfig, or show run. Ensure that the IP address, subnet mask, and default gateway are all correct.

2. Ping 127.0.0.1. This tests the network interface on the equipment. If this does not produce a reply, the issue is almost certainly that your IP protocols are not correctly installed. In a Windows system, this is indicative of an issue within the IP stack.

3. Ping your own IP address. This causes the ping to travel outside of your network interface, through the network, and back to your own machine. If this does not work, the issue is probably either with the physical connection to the network or, on a Windows system, the hosts file.

4. Ping the default gateway. If there is a reply, the issue is probably related to the default gateway, either in the routing tables or in the connections through the WAN.

5. Ping another host on the local subnet. If a response is received, this confirms the issue is with the default gateway. If no response is received, continue to the next step.

6. Move to another workstation and try to ping through the default gateway. If this station works, the issue is on the original station. If it does not work, the issue is with the default gateway.

Following this methodology, when a ping to a remote host is not successful, it will help you locate the origination point of the problems at least 95 percent of the time.

Now that we have seen what ping can do as well as some common traps within ping, we will look at the traceroute command that not only gives the same information as ping, but also shows the route a packet follows.

Traceroute Commands

Traceroute, like ping, is used to test connectivity. You can use traceroute instead of user ping in almost every circumstance. The disadvantage of doing this is that a traceroute takes significantly longer to process than a ping. The reason for the longer response time is that traceroute works differently and gives you additional information. Traceroute, like ping, also has an extended mode.

Ping and traceroute are both based on ICMP messages. Although they use the same underlying principles, the data received and the actual mechanisms used differ. Ping sends an ICMP echo-request with the TTL set to 32. Traceroute starts by sending three ICMP echo-request messages with the TTL set to 1. This causes the first router that processes these packets to send back ICMP time-exceeded messages. Traceroute looks into the ICMP time-exceed message and displays the router that sent the messages on the console. Then traceroute sends another set of echo-request messages, this time with the TTL increased by one more than the last TTL. The request passes through the first router to the second router. Since both routers decrement the TTL, the second router sends back a set of time-exceeded messages. The second router's information is shown on the console. This process continues until the remote host responds, or it is determined that the path cannot be found. By the time the remote host responds, traceroute will have displayed the complete path with the time between each router. If the remote host does not respond, we are still told the path that the messages took to reach the host. This is the real value of traceroute.

A typical traceroute will look similar to the traceroute shown here:

```
Router#traceroute 172.28.237.1

Type escape sequence to abort.
Tracing the route to 172.28.237.1

  1 172.30.100.2 0 msec 0 msec 4 msec
  2 172.31.252.13 92 msec 92 msec 92 msec
  3 172.31.252.6 100 msec 100 msec 100 msec
  4 172.28.233.53 140 msec *  140 msec
```

This traceroute raises two questions. The first is, why did we not get to the destination host? We actually did reach the destination host. We need to be aware of which interfaces a traceroute will show. A traceroute shows when we hit the first interface of a new device. There is no response given to indicate which interface the trace is leaving for a device. In the above traceroute, the Ethernet interface has the IP address we are looking for, while the serial interface has the last IP address shown. The second question raised is, why do we have an asterisk instead of a time in the last line? What happened here is that the originating router did not receive a response quickly enough to register the time. Therefore, an asterisk was substituted. This should be of no more concern to us than not receiving a response from an individual ping.

Figure 4-5 shows the interfaces that will respond to a traceroute.

Because we have no indication through traceroute of which interface sends out the packet, we need to know where we expect to send packets. This can easily be obtained through a network map. If a traceroute goes part of the way towards the destination and then stops, there is only one real possibility and the next hop router cannot be seen. If the route to the destination cannot be found, you will see an output similar to the one shown here:

```
Router#ping 172.28.12.1

Type escape sequence to abort.
Sending 5, 100-byte ICMP Echos to 172.28.12.1, timeout is 2 seconds:
UUUUU
```

A remote router going down can cause this, which will in turn cause the routing tables to show the destination as unreachable. A static route that points to an invalid address can also produce similar results.

Traceroute, like ping, also has an extended mode. Many of the extended mode options of ping are available with the extended traceroute. In the following extended traceroute, a few items require a little explanation. First, there are settings for both the minimum and maximum TTL. Traceroute

Figure 4-5

Traceroute flow

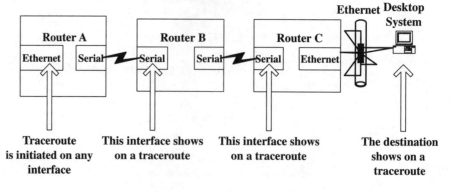

INTERFACES
RESPONDING
TO A TRACEROUTE

Traceroute
is initiated on any
interface

This interface shows
on a traceroute

This interface shows
on a traceroute

The destination
shows on a
traceroute

will not accept an echo-reply that occurs before the minimum TTL. In the following example, we have increased the maximum TTL to 60 seconds. Second, we can also adjust the number of echo-requests sent from the default of three. In the example, we increase this value to five. Third, the port number is definable. By default, traceroute sends the echo-request to an arbitrary port number. This number is actually equal to the number of the *process identifier* (PID) that sends out the traceroute. We are allowed to change this number in case only certain ports are allowed to receive traffic, such as in an access list.

```
Router#traceroute
Protocol [ip]:
Target IP address: 172.28.237.1
Source address: 172.30.100.1
Numeric display [n]: y
Timeout in seconds [3]: 3
Probe count [3]: 5
Minimum Time to Live [1]:
Maximum Time to Live [30]: 60
Port Number [33434]:
Loose, Strict, Record, Timestamp, Verbose[none]:
Type escape sequence to abort.
Tracing the route to 172.28.237.1

  1 172.30.100.2 4 msec 4 msec 4 msec 0 msec 4 msec
  2 172.31.252.13 88 msec 92 msec 92 msec 88 msec 92 msec
  3 172.31.252.6 104 msec 100 msec 100 msec 100 msec 104 msec
  4 172.28.233.53 136 msec 180 msec 140 msec 150 msec 136 msec
```

Another potential issue that is easily solved with a traceroute is a circular route. A *circular route* occurs when router A thinks that router B knows the path to a destination at the same time that router B thinks router A knows the destination. Using a ping command will merely result in receiving time-exceeded errors, while with traceroute the issue is almost instantly detectable. Looking at the following traceroute, notice where the packets travel:

```
Router#traceroute 172.28.12.1

Type escape sequence to abort.
Tracing the route to 172.28.12.1

  1 172.30.1.1 4 msec 0 msec 4 msec
  2 172.30.1.3 4 msec 0 msec 4 msec
  3 172.30.1.1 4 msec 0 msec 4 msec
  4 172.30.1.3 4 msec 0 msec 4 msec
```

The packets in this example travel from one router to the second and then back to the first. Any time a traceroute shows the same interface two or more times, you have a routing loop. Sometimes the loop will not become apparent until the packets have traveled through several different routers. Static routes improperly used or redistributed generally cause this and therefore should be one of the first things that are checked when encountering this problem. A Windows system produces a similar output on a tracert command. The following is a sample from a Windows 95 machine:

```
Tracing route to 172.30.100.1 over a maximum of 30 hops

    1    164 ms    164 ms    166 ms    172.30.2.200
    2    159 ms    156 ms    152 ms    172.30.1.3
    3    239 ms    250 ms    247 ms    172.31.252.14
    4    245 ms    247 ms    254 ms    172.30.100.1

Trace complete.
```

Chapter Summary

In this chapter, we have looked at numerous subjects. We started with the way routers switch packets between interfaces. Understanding the switching process allows us to understand the output we are receiving from debug and show commands. We explored the show and debug commands while describing the uses and cautions associated with the commands. We next explored the ping and traceroute commands. Finally, we looked at how and when to do a core dump.

Frequently Asked Questions (FAQ)

Question: Which is better for testing connectivity, ping or traceroute?

Answer: Both are equally useful in their own way. To simply test if a connection exists, ping is the quickest. To test where a connection fails, traceroute is more useful.

Question: How long should it take to receive a response from a ping?

Answer: That depends on many factors. The links are that the ping must travel over are probably the greatest factor. Any slow individual link between the source and destination will cause the response times to drop.

Question: When I try to run a core dump, I am unable to write the file. What is wrong?

Answer: If you can successfully ping where you want to write the file, the problem is usually that the machine you are trying to write to has not given you permission to write the file.

Question: While troubleshooting my 1602 router I cannot see all of the packets traveling through the router. I have debugging on. What is the problem?

Answer: The problem is that fast switching prevents you from seeing the packets. Turn off fast switching while you are debugging packets.

Lab Exercise

On an existing network, use the commands given in this chapter to find the following:

- Which Ethernet or FastEthernet interfaces are experiencing excessive collisions?
- Which serial connections, if any, show congestion through FECNs and BECNs?
- Which version of IOS are you using and what is the full file name?
- How are the buffers set up on your routers?
- When was the last time your routers were rebooted and how were they rebooted?
- Which DLCIs are you using on your connections?
- What are the average times of your routers to remote hosts?

Questions

1. What is one way to check for timing problems with mysec and mineseen events?

   a. debug interface serial
   b. debug serial interfaces
   c. show frame relay lmi
   d. debug frame-relay pvc

2. Which of the following commands can be used to show statistics regarding both buffer and hardware errors?

   a. show interface
   b. show controllers
   c. show ethernet
   d. show interface ethernet

3. Which command is used to display statistics for small memory buffers in the free pool?

   a. show memory
   b. show pools
   c. show flash
   d. show buffers

4. Which command is used to show the name of the image stored in the flash?

   a. show files
   b. show nvram
   c. show flash
   d. show files:nvram

5. Which command displays the percentage of available CPU power a given process is utilizing?

   a. show memory
   b. show process cpu
   c. show memory process cpu
   d. show cpu

6. Which port does a traceroute send an ICMP echo-request to by default?

   a. 6384
   b. any port about 1024
   c. the number of the current PID
   d. any port below 1024

7. How many ICMP echo-replies does the host that initiates a user ping send?

   a. 5

   b. 10

   c. 7

   d. none

8. Name two advantages of extended ping over user ping.

   a. The number of packets may not be increased.

   b. The time-out period may be increased.

   c. The sending interface may be changed.

   d. There are no echo-requests sent.

9. What will cause the following output to show from a show interface serial command?

   ```
   Router#sh interface serial 0/1
   Serial0/1 is down, line protocol is up
   ```

   a. Layer 1 is not properly configured.

   b. Layer 2 is not properly configured.

   c. Layer 3 is not properly configured.

   d. You will never see this.

10. The following is a truncated output from a show interface command. What MAC address will this router respond to?

    ```
    Router#show interfaces ethernet 0/1
    Ethernet0/1 is up, line protocol is up
      Hardware is AmdP2, address is 00e0.2aa8.0084 (bia 00e0.1ee9.9042)
    ```

    a. either 00e0.2aa8.0084 or 00e0.1ee9.9042

    b. 00e0.2aa8.0084

    c. 00e0.1ee9.9042

    d. neither of these will respond

11. Looking at the output below, what problem is this router encountering?

    ```
    Router#Show process cpu
    CPU utilization for five seconds: 100%/95%; one minute: 93%; five
    minutes: 90%
    PID   Runtime(ms)  Invoked  uSecs   5Sec   1Min   5Min   TTY  Process
    1     300          6227     48      0.00%  0.00%  0.00%  0    Load Meter
    2     2476         248      9983    1.39%  0.18%  0.27%  1    Virtual Exec
    3     799844       7625     104897  0.00%  2.68%  2.62%  0    Check heaps
    4     0            1        0       0.00%  0.00%  0.00%  0    Pool Manager
    5     0            2        0       0.00%  0.00%  0.00%  0    Timers
    6     1880         2122     885     0.00%  0.00%  0.00%  0    ARP Input
    7     4            1        4000    0.00%  0.00%  0.00%  0    SERIAL
                                                                 A'detect
    8     0            1        0       0.00%  0.00%  0.00%  0    CSU/DSU trap
    ```

9	19140	13934	1373	0.57%	0.09%	0.05%	0	IP Input
10	2968	3676	807	0.08%	0.01%	0.00%	0	CDP Protocol
11	121384	31627	3837	0.40%	0.40%	0.40%	0	IP Background
12	300	6496	46	0.08%	0.00%	0.00%	0	TCP Timer

   a. The pool manager process has ceased to function.

   b. The TCP timer is running too slowly.

   c. The router is experiencing high CPU utilization.

   d. The load meter is not running properly.

12. Which command can be used to obtain the current configuration on a router?

   a. show nvram

   b. show running-config

   c. show controllers

   d. show modules

13. The output from a show interface serial command is shown below. What is the meaning of this output?

```
Router#show interfaces ethernet 0/1
Ethernet0/1 is administratively down, line protocol is down
```

   a. The interface has been shut down.

   b. The connection to the remote site is down.

   c. The routing protocol has failed.

   d. This is a dial-on-demand connection.

14. A ping command shows three exclamation points (!) and two periods (.) in the output. What does this mean?

   a. The connection is experiencing intermittent problems.

   b. The remote host is not available.

   c. There is a connection to the remote host.

   d. The remote host has been shut off.

15. Where are the outputs for a debug message sent by default?

   a. To the virtual terminal connections

   b. To the the syslog server

   c. To the internal buffers

   d. To the console

16. Why should a write core command be used?

   a. To obtain a core dump from a crashed router

   b. To obtain a core dump from a running router

   c. To copy the IOS to a TFTP server

   d. To obtain a core dump and cause a reboot on a running router

17. Looking at the following snip from a show interface ethernet command, what is the problem with this router?

```
217603 packets input, 132142368 bytes, 0 no buffer
Received 4339 broadcasts, 0 runts, 0 giants, 0 throttles
3 input errors, 2 CRC, 0 frame, 0 overrun, 0 ignored, 0 abort
0 input packets with dribble condition detected
563149 packets output, 70733182 bytes, 0 underruns
0 output errors, 70000 collisions, 0 interface resets
0 babbles, 0 late collision, 128 deferred
1 lost carrier, 0 no carrier
0 output buffer failures, 0 output buffers swapped out
```

  a. The interface has experienced numerous transitions.
  b. The Ethernet buffers are too small.
  c. There is a bad NIC somewhere on the network.
  d. There are excessive collisions.

18. Which method of error logging produces the least load on a router?

  a. virtual terminal
  b. console
  c. syslog server
  d. internal buffers

19. What is the most likely cause of a single host being unable to access any other network?

  a. An incompatible link type between the router and the host
  b. No default gateway on the host
  c. The routing table is incorrect
  d. An access list is preventing connections

20. Which is never a problem on serial interfaces?

  a. Overruns
  b. Underruns
  c. Collisions
  d. Physical connections

Answers

1. **Answer:** b

   Debug serial interfaces will show the mysec, mineseen, and yourseen counters incrementing. If one of these counters is not incrementing, you have a timing problem.

2. **Answer:** b

   The show interface command will not show hardware errors, while the show controllers command will show errors that exist in the hardware.

3. **Answer:** d

   The show buffers command will display statistics for all of the memory buffers.

4. **Answer:** c

   The show flash command is used to display the contents of the flash memory. This is where the router images are stored.

5. **Answer:** b

   Show process cpu will display the percentage of available CPU power a given process is utilizing.

6. **Answer:** c

   A traceroute uses the current PID as the default port when sending an ICMP echo-request.

7. **Answer:** d

   A ping sends out five ICMP echo-request packets. ICMP echo-reply packets are sent back to the initiator.

8. **Answer:** b, c

   Extended ping enables the time-out period to be increased. This helps when pinging busy hosts and pinging hosts over busy lines. The sending interface can be changed, which may help overcome issues such as access lists.

9. **Answer:** d

   The "down" refers to layer 1, while the "up" refers to layer 2. You will never have a situation where layer 1 is down while layer 2 is up.

10. **Answer:** b

    A router will only respond to the "current" MAC address. The *burned-in address* (BIA) will not be responded to unless it is also the current address. In the example shown, the BIA was overwritten with another address. The purpose of doing this is so that the new address will become the only address that will respond.

11. Answer: c

Although the five-second utilization is not critical by itself, the one-minute and five-minute utilizations are both too high. This router is experiencing severe CPU utilization conditions.

12. Answer: b

Show running-config shows the current configuration of the router.

13. Answer: a

When an interface has been issued a shutdown command, the interface will be shown as administratively down.

14. Answer: c

A ping that shows three exclamation points (!) and two periods (.) in the output confirms that there is a connection to the remote host. A single set of pings where two echo-replies are not received in time does not necessarily show a connection problem.

15. Answer: d

By default, debug and system error messages are sent to the console.

16. Answer: b

The write core command is used to obtain a core dump from a running router. Unlike other core dumps, a write core will not cause a router to reboot.

17. Answer: d

According to Cisco, the total number of collisions compared to the total number of output packets should be less than 0.1 percent. The percentage shown here is beyond that amount. Therefore, this router's Ethernet interface is experiencing excessive collisions.

18. Answer: c

The least load amount on a router producing debug messages is done through a syslog server.

19. Answer: b

The question states that a *single* host cannot gain access outside the network. This indicates that the problem is with that host. The host is unable to gain access to *any other* network, again indicating the host is the problem, pointing to the gateway setting on the host and away from an access list issue. The question does not mention the host being unable to connect to other hosts on the same network, thereby eliminating incompatible link types.

20. Answer: c

Serial interfaces do not have collisions.

3

Local Area Networks (LANs)

5

Troubleshooting Local Area Networks (LANs)

After reading the first four chapters, you have been familiarized with the ways to approach a problem. You have been exposed to the methods used to analyze and solve almost any problem on a local or wide area network. You are also familiar with the common tools that can be used in an analysis and the basic commands that are available for use in your troubleshooting efforts.

This chapter will look at the major topologies of *local area networks* (LANs) and how they differ from each other. We will look at the bus, star, and ring topologies before exploring Ethernet, Token Ring, and the *fiber distributed data interface* (FDDI) protocol. This chapter will also build the foundation for the next chapter where switched networks will be used to build the foundation for Cisco switches.

Objectives Covered in the Chapter

The objectives covered in this chapter include the following:

- Identify and apply generic and Cisco-specific troubleshooting tools on Cisco routers and switches.
- Perform labs that troubleshoot problems (hardware, software, or configuration bugs) and then correct these bugs to restore full network operations.
- Apply diagnostic tools to solve network problems that include systems running TCP/IP with Windows NT/95 clients and servers.
- Apply diagnostic tools to trouble tickets and solve classroom network Frame Relay problems that simulate real-life *wide area network* (WAN) malfunctions.

Physical and Logical Topologies

Before we can discuss the different types of networks, we need to understand how cabling can exist on both a physical and logical level. We will start off with one of the simplest forms of cabling, the logical and physical bus system.

The bus system is considered a physical bus because the cabling is laid out in a single continuous connection with each of the hosts connected to this single connection. This is the method used in Thinnet (10Base2), which is also called Cheapernet, and in Standard Ethernet (10Base5), also called Thicknet. In this method, a wire runs from the first host to the second, then the third, and so on. There is a single, long cable that all of the hosts are connected to and through which all data must travel. If the cable is ever broken, all of the hosts lose connectivity. This is also a logical bus because there is no difference between how the cabling is arranged and how the system operates. A bus connection is shown in Figure 5-1.

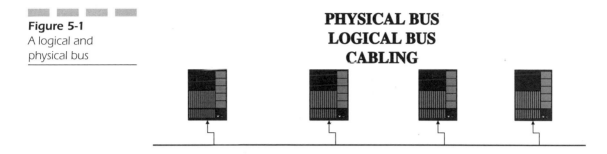

Figure 5-1
A logical and
physical bus

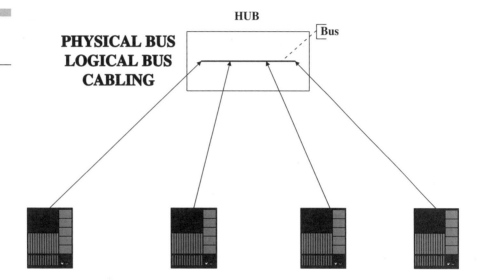

Figure 5-2
Physical star/
logical bus

A variation of the logical and physical bus appears with a 10BaseT Ethernet network. This method is more commonly used on newer installations. In this system, the physical structure is a star. The cables run from a central point out to the individual hosts. If one of these cables breaks, only the host connected to that cable loses connectivity.

A place must be made for these cables to interconnect. In the case of Ethernet, this is accomplished at a hub or switch. For simplicity's sake, we will limit this discussion to hubs. Switches will be covered in Chapter 6. What the hub actually does is provide a single connection for all of the attached hosts. Similar to a physical bus, all data must travel over this connection. This single connection is the reason a 10BaseT network is considered a logical bus system. Physical star/logical bus is shown in Figure 5-2.

The third major system is a physical star/logical ring system. In this method, the physical wires also go from a central point to each individual host. This method also requires some form of central connection equipment. In a Token Ring system, the *media access unit* (MAU) provides this connection. However, within the MAU, there is no single common bus over which the data travels. Instead, the MAU connects the wires to form a ring. The data travels around this ring, passing through each host in turn. In most systems, two rings lead to a redundancy if the primary ring breaks. If the wires leading to a single host break, the MAU is designed to bypass that station by "wrapping" the ring over to the backup ring. In this way, the ring stays active. Figure 5-3 displays a diagram of physical star/logical ring.

The fourth major system is a logical and a physical ring system. FDDI uses this schema to provide connectivity. In this system, two physical fiber-optic rings are also logical rings. Similar to Token Ring, there is one primary ring and a backup ring for redundancy. Should the primary ring break, the interfaces upstream and downstream of the break will wrap the ring to complete the circuit.

Cabling Issues

The way a building's cabling has been installed may be one of the most critical factors in the stability of a network. Because the cabling is a physical

Figure 5-3
Physical star/
logical ring

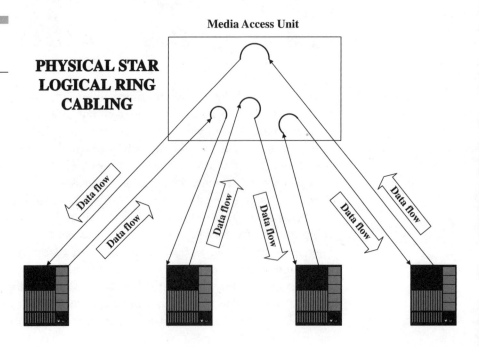

device, it deals with the physical layer of the OSI model. Although the actual numbers may be debated, most engineers agree that cabling issues account for around 80 percent of all LAN problems. This section will discuss how to analyze and fix cabling problems.

The first area of cabling to be discussed is cable length. Remember that all cabling schemes have limitations on the cable length. In 10BaseT Ethernet, the length of a segment is limited to 100 meters. When measuring cable lengths, ensure that the patch cables are at both ends and that an allowance for errors is included. This limitation is mandatory if the collision-detection mechanisms are expected to work correctly. The IEEE 802.3 Ethernet specifications state that the round-trip delay time must not exceed 576 bit periods. The number and latency of the repeaters must be added into the round-trip time calculation. Exceeding the cable length will cause this maximum time to be exceeded. This will in turn cause what are commonly called *late collisions*. A late collision occurs after the first 64 bytes of the Ethernet frame have been transmitted. Late collisions are almost always attributable to either excessive round-trip times or to a speed mismatch between a station and an Ethernet switch. Troubleshooting switches will be discussed in Chapter 6.

In a Token Ring system, an excessive cable length will also cause problems, such as a loss of signal strength. Excessive cable length can also lead to timing problems. Incorrect timing on a Token Ring can result in multiple tokens being present on the ring or in an increase in administrative tasks required to keep the ring running. Additionally, cable length specifications for copper cables are stated at specific temperatures. If a copper network cable is subject to a high heat level, the result would be the same as if the cable were longer than it actually is.

Another factor that may affect both timing and connectivity is the resistance of the cable itself. All electrical conductors have a certain resistance within themselves. Using an incorrect cable on a network can significantly affect how well the network will work. For example, the cable used for telephone systems will have a different resistance specification than an Ethernet cable. Using a telephone cable may work, but it will never work well. Using the wrong cable will usually reduce the distances allowed on a network connection. Unfortunately, no standards have been set for non-standard cable. An engineer that is installing network cabling is expected to know exactly which cable is being used and that this cable is correct for the job. A number of good books cover the specifications of network wiring.

Patch panels and patch cables also play a significant role in the number of problems experienced on an Ethernet LAN because they are where repeated connections and disconnections take place. Anytime you have a physical connection, you run the risk that the connection may fail. When connecting cable to the back of the patch panel, use the proper punch-down tool. If you must remove a cable from the back of a patch panel, double-check that the connector is thoroughly clean and that no pieces of plastic wire-coating are on the connector before reconnecting any cables.

NOTE: *We once had a connection problem with a Frame Relay circuit. We were simply not able to make the Frame Relay work. Our* channel service unit/data service unit *(CSU/DSU) did not see any connection. The phone company that extended the D-mark came back to test the circuit. All wiring tests were passed, which pointed to our equipment, yet our equipment worked fine on other circuits. The phone company eventually agreed to extend a new D-mark. The same problem occurred. We ended up in a pointing match with the phone company. We knew our equipment was good. The phone company knew their physical wiring was good.*

Eventually, after much frustration, we were able to determine exactly where the problem resided. The issue was that a very, very small piece of plastic wiring coating was stuck inside the jack for the Frame Relay connection. When the extended D-mark was replaced, the phone company reused the same jack that had previously been installed. This piece of plastic was about the size of a pin's head. Because the phone company had been testing from the wiring connectors on the back of the jack instead of through the jack itself, they were not able to find the problem quickly.

We learned two lessons from this experience. First, when you decide to replace equipment, replace all of the equipment. This should include the cables, accessories, power supplies, and jacks. If the jack had been replaced, the problem would have been solved more quickly. The second lesson we learned was that all tests ideally should be done along the exact same paths that the data will flow. If the jack had not been bypassed, the issue would have been instantly recognizable.

It is recommended that you use only factory-manufactured patch cables unless you have a lot of experience making cables. The cost difference is not enough to justify the risk that a cable might not perform up to specifications. When in doubt about the quality of a patch cable, one of the easiest troubleshooting techniques is to simply replace the cable with a new one. If you cannot easily replace the cable, ensure that the individual wires are twisted as far towards the jack as possible. This will help eliminate *near-end cross talk* (NEXT). The crimp on the jack should also be pressing into the cable sheath, not into the individual wires. Using a cable tester on every cable you are working with only takes a few minutes. You may be surprised at the number of marginal cables you find.

NOTE: *NEXT usually happens because wires have been untwisted at the connection end. Wires within cables are twisted together to minimize the affects of transporting electricity over the wire. The rates of twisting are specified similarly to the way resistance rates are specified.*

The reason wires are twisted is because this reduces a common problem experienced in electrical circuits. This problem is that when electricity is run over a wire, an electro-magnetic sphere is created. Any other wire within this sphere will experience voltage fluctuations as the sphere is created and collapse as electricity is applied and removed from the first wire. A situation in which a current in one wire affects another wire's voltage is called cross talk. *Twisting the wires can diminish the effects.*

When installing a connector on the end of a cable (called the near end), *care should be taken to untwist only as much of the cable as necessary. If too much cable is untwisted, the wires run parallel to each other for a distance that enables the effects of the electro-magnetic sphere to affect another wire.*

In addition, when laying cable, care should be taken to avoid running the cable parallel to power cables. If you must lay a network cable across an electrical cable, laying it at a 90-degree angle to the cable will minimize the affects of cross talk.

Another problem that is common on older installations is the effect of electricity on LAN cabling. Although most new installations avoid running near electrical supplies, a large number of sites were installed before the delicacies of LAN cabling were fully understood. The issue is that any electrical source or conductor produces an electro-magnetic sphere of influence around itself. This influence will affect any other electrical wires that are within this area of influence.

Usually, an electrical interference problem will manifest itself in one of two ways. The first way is through a consistent "noise" on the cable if it is a circuit with a constant load. This is usually verifiable through a cable tester or analyzer. The second manifestation is that stations lose connectivity when a certain circuit is activated, especially if this circuit draws large amounts of electricity. Most of these problems can be avoided by ensuring that the cabling does not run parallel to electrical lines and that it remains as far away from large electrical motors as possible.

NOTE: *Sometimes it is not easy to tell that an electrical device is causing a problem. We were once called to determine a recurring problem on a network. The administrator reported that once a week the backbone of their LAN experienced excessive slowness. This happened at different times during the day. The backbone of the LAN was running over a copper data distribution interface (CDDI), which is extremely similar to FDDI, except that it runs over copper wires.*

After monitoring the network for three weeks, we were only able to confirm a few things. The network did occasionally experience excessive slowness, which was not caused by any interface that we could find. The cause of the slowdown was seen as being due to excessive malformed packets, runts, and jabbers. Data examined with a packet analyzer was not in any recognizable form. This is a classic symptom of an electrical interference problem.

It took an off-hand remark by a secretary to solve the problem. She had just come out of a meeting and complained about a light dimmer switch buzzing through the whole meeting. We had just been watching the network go from extremely slow to a reasonable speed. The error count had just dropped to near zero when the meeting ended.

It turned out that a manager, during his weekly meetings, used the light dimmer switch in the meeting room. Everyone else in the company didn't like the noise produced by the switch and therefore did not use it. The CDDI cable ran directly behind the dimmer switch, which was producing enough electro-magnetic interference to cause errors on the network. Once we found the suspected cause, it was extremely easy to reproduce the symptoms. Replacing the dimmer switch and moving it to a new location solved the problem.

A quick word about cross-over cables and link lights is in order. Cross-over cables are used to connect two similar devices to each other. A cross-over cable could be used to connect one hub to another, one switch to another, or a hub to a switch. Many hubs have a provision to use either a straight or a cross-over cable. Many pre-manufactured cross-over cables have boots that are a different color than the cable sheathing. This makes them instantly recognizable. Basically, on a cross-over cable, the transmit and receive pairs are reversed or "crossed over." A good cable tester will show if a cable is straight-through or crossed. The link light on a device may still be lit even if you are using the wrong type of cable and therefore cannot be relied upon to indicate that you have the correct cable. Figure 5-4 shows how Ethernet straight-through and cross-over connectors are wired.

Figure 5-4
Straight and
crossover cables

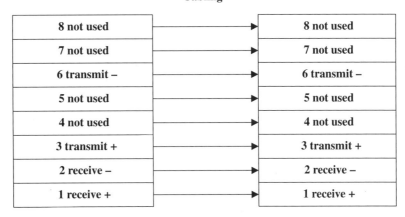

ETHERNET CABLING

Ethernet Straight Through
Cabling

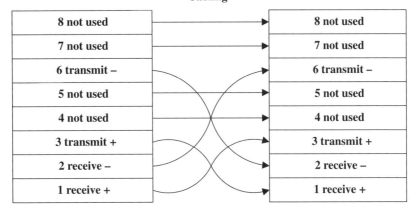

Ethernet Cross-Over
Cabling

Ethernet Topologies

Ethernet is the LAN specification that is most commonly in use today. With a base configuration of 10 Mbps and the capability to support data rates of up to a gigabit, Ethernet has become the dominant network in the industry.

Carrier Sense Multiple Access/ Collision Detect (CSMA/CD)

Originally developed in the early 1980s, Ethernet is defined as a *Carrier Sense Multiple Access / Collision Detect* (CSMA/CD) network. Carrier Sense Multiple Access means that a host will sense if the network is busy before trying to send data and that all hosts can try to access the network at any time. Collision Detect means that a host trying to transmit will detect if another host is transmitting at the same time. Each of these definitions will be examined in further detail.

CSMA is used on Ethernet because it is an effective method of enabling multiple hosts to access the same media. Carrier Sense works by having the host listen for other hosts transmitting. If no other hosts are transmitting, the host will wait a specified amount of time. This time is called the interframe gap and is set in the Ethernet specifications at 96 bit periods or 9.6 microseconds.

After waiting for the time of an interframe gap, a host starts transmitting. An Ethernet host starts by transmitting a preamble field that contains a series of bits in the form of 1010 for eight bytes. The preamble is used to allow receiving hosts to synchronize to the following data. The sending host will then continue to send the data until the rest of that frame is sent or until a collision is detected.

A collision should be detected during the time when the first 64 bytes are transmitted. The reason for this is reflected in the specifications for the allowed cable lengths. If the cable length specifications are not exceeded, all hosts are guaranteed to hear any other host within the first 64 bytes being transmitted. Assume that two hosts both choose to transmit at the same time. When this happens, the voltage on the wire exceeds a predefined threshold. When this voltage level is detected on the host that is transmitting, the hosts that are transmitting will continue to transmit for a small amount of time to ensure that all hosts see the collision.

When a collision is detected, there is a specific routine used to enable the hosts to try to transmit again. This is known as the *backoff algorithm*. A host will pause for a random amount of time (called the *backoff time*) before retransmitting. If another collision is experienced during retransmission, the host will double the backoff time, which will continue for the first 10 retransmissions. After this point, the backoff time will remain the same until a total of 15 retransmissions have been attempted. After a total of 16 attempts (the initial plus 15 retransmissions), the controller stops trying to transmit and sends an error message that transmission failed.

Many engineers worry about collisions on a network. All CSMA/CD networks will experience collisions if there is more than one host on the network. Ethernet was designed to not only have collisions, but also to be able to handle collisions without serious consequences. Collisions only warrant action if the number of collisions is causing problems on the network. Cisco has stated that the number of collisions experienced on an Ethernet port should not exceed 0.1 percent of the total number of packets transmitted.

An interesting consequence of the backoff routine is the limit that is placed upon the number of hosts allowed in an Ethernet network. The upper limit of 1,024 hosts should be enforced simply because the backoff algorithm is optimized for a system having no more than 1,024 hosts. Although an unswitched network with anywhere near 1,024 computers running programs and operating systems will generally experience unacceptable speeds, it is entirely possible to approach this number when using hosts that are not computers, such as medical instruments. The larger the number of hosts on a network, the larger the collision domain becomes.

Collision Domains

A collision domain is defined as that area of a network where an individual collision can be seen. Keeping the size of the collision domain as small as possible has several advantages. Every host on a bus network sees every data packet. If the number of data packets (including collisions) per a period of time can be reduced, there is a greater chance that a host will not experience a collision when trying to transmit.

Although the mere presence of collisions is not a problem, an excessive amount of collisions can cause extremely serious problems on a network. As the numbers of collisions increase, the likelihood of a collision occurring also raises. In other words, collisions cause collisions. The reason for this is that collisions take available time away from all of the hosts on a network. Since the amount of data intending to be transferred is not decreasing and the time available for transmission is decreasing, all of the hosts have less time in which to try to transmit and more hosts will try to transmit during the remaining available time.

In a severe enough situation, collisions can soon become a self-propagating event. It is fairly common to see a network with high collision rates move from using 30 percent of the available bandwidth up to 50 percent, 60 percent, or even higher within a matter of seconds due to excessive collisions. Approximately 30 percent of the theoretical bandwidth usage on a nonswitched Ethernet network is considered to be the maximum amount the network should be expected to carry.

One way to reduce the size of the collision domain is through the process of microsegmentation. *Microsegmentation* is the process of breaking collision domains into smaller sizes through the use of switches. Along with the added speed benefits possible from switching, collision domains are reduced because a collision domain always ends at a switch port. Adding a single 16-port switch into a network can reduce the collision domain to 1/16th of the original size. Switching will be discussed in depth in Chapter 6.

Broadcast Domains

All Ethernet, FDDI, and Token Ring adapters have a built-in 48-bit (six-byte) address. This address carries code specifying both the manufacturer and the unit number for the adapter. A combination of these is called the *media access control* (MAC) address that is guaranteed to be a unique address among all adapters.

All adapters "hear" the data traveling over a network. A protocol analyzer can be used to capture all of the data heard by putting the adapter into what is called *promiscuous mode*. In this mode, an adapter processes all heard data. Assuming that an adapter is not in promiscuous mode, an adapter will process data under the following circumstances:

- The destination address matches either the active MAC address or the adapter address.

- The destination address is a broadcast address.

- The destination is a multicast address.

Under certain circumstances it is possible to override the manufacturer's assigned MAC address with a MAC address of the user's choosing. This new address becomes the active address. In that case, any data packet sent to the new address will be processed.

If the first bit of the first byte transmitted on an Ethernet system is odd, then this is a multicast packet. A *multicast packet* is designed to go to multiple, but not all, hosts. If the destination address bits are all odd (ff-ff-ff-ff-ff-ff), then this is a broadcast packet.

Broadcasts are generally used when the transmitting host must either notify all hosts of an event or when a host does not know the MAC address of a remote host. By design, broadcasts are processed by all hosts on the network. Any time a host must process any packet, time and resources are required. Because all hosts process all broadcasts, an excessive number of broadcasts can slow hosts to unacceptable levels.

Similar to collisions, the mere presence of a broadcast is not indicative of a problem on a network. Broadcasts should only be considered a problem when they are causing adverse effects on the speed of hosts. There is no set amount of broadcasts that is considered intolerable. The only way an administrator can tell if the number of broadcasts is too high is to compare the current percentage to the percentage determined during the baseline analysis.

NOTE: *A real-life example regarding the percentage of broadcasts on a network was presented to the Cisco study group at* www.groupstudy.com. *In this example, a well-respected consultant had been called in to look at problems on a network. The consultant ran a protocol analyzer on the network and came to an instant conclusion.*

The consultant saw an unbelievable 65 percent of the packets as broadcasts. Since broadcasts generally run in the single-digit percentage rates, the consultant immediately decided that excessive broadcasts were causing the network problems. Unfortunately, the consultant was incorrect.

The network was installed in a stock brokerage firm. When any host requested the current price of a stock, the price was sent as a broadcast. This way, all hosts heard the current price and no other host would need to request the current price for this stock. For this particular software and network, using broadcasts was an extremely efficient means of updating all the hosts.

The administrator knew the consultant was wrong because he knew his network. The administrator showed the consultant the baseline analysis he had made months before. The broadcast percentages at all times on this particular network were above 60 percent of the total number of packets transmitted. When the consultant saw the baseline and learned how this network really operated, he investigated further.

The lesson learned here is twofold. First, mere percentages are not necessarily the criteria for determining that broadcasts are a problem. Second, the time spent in generating a baseline analysis is never wasted time.

Using routers can reduce broadcast domains. Since routers do not generally forward broadcasts, any time a router is inserted between two LAN segments, the broadcast domain will be reduced. This is one of the general principles that led to the evolution of *virtual local area networks* (VLANs), which will be discussed in Chapter 6. The problem with using a router is that data flowing across the router will travel at a slower rate due to the time required by the routing process.

The *80/20 rule* is generally said to be the ideal for a network. This rule states that 80 percent of the traffic should remain local, while 20 percent of the traffic is routed. As the speed of routers increases, this rule of thumb will move closer to a 50/50 spilt. Until that time, the engineer needs to be aware that broadcast domains are reduced at the cost of speed to remote devices and that a balance must be maintained. The nuances of designing the size and scope of broadcast domains are beyond the scope of this book.

Jabbers

A *jabber* is like my sister-in-law. She starts talking about absolutely nothing and will not stop talking. Jabbers can only occur when a network interface is malfunctioning. It is one of the most serious conditions that can occur on a network. A jabbering network card continuously sends data out to the network without stopping. The problem with a constantly transmitting host is that hosts listen for a quiet time on the network before trying to transmit. If there is no quiet time, no host can ever transmit. This means that a jabbering host will stop all other activity on your network. (By the way, I really like my sister-in-law and am thankful she has a sense of humor.)

A timer is started whenever an Ethernet interface starts transmitting. Because an Ethernet packet has a maximum size of 1,518 bytes, there is a definable time in which this packet should be transmitted. If the timer exceeds the maximum time allowed, the transmission should be stopped by the jabber control function. If this function fails, a jabber condition is experienced on the network and all other activity ceases. Because the network has stopped, all methods available should immediately be used to locate and remove the offending host.

Runts

A *runt* is a malformed packet that is smaller than the minimum 64-byte packet size. This is usually caused by a malfunctioning interface. This is nowhere near as serious a condition as a jabbering host. However, this situation should be taken care of whenever possible because network bandwidth is being used without any work being accomplished.

Token Ring Topologies

Token Ring is a LAN technology that is governed by the IEE 802.5 specifications. Several differences exist between Ethernet and Token Ring. The most noticeable difference is how tokens are implemented.

In Ethernet, all hosts listen on the wire before sending data. The hosts in Token Ring are attached to a logical ring laid out in a physical star topology.

In Token Ring, a data "token" is passed to each host around the ring, hence the name Token Ring. When a machine leaves the ring because it is either shut off or experiences a problem, the ring "wraps" at the MAU to bypass that machine. One host is designated as the active monitor. The *active monitor* is chosen through the *monitor contention process*. This process is started when any station on the ring fails to detect an active monitor. Every station participates in this process in an either active or passive role.

The active station with the highest ring station address is established as the active monitor. If a station detects that there is no active monitor, that station will participate in active mode. A station that has been configured to be an active participant and has not already received notification from a station with a higher ring address will also participate actively. All other stations will participate in a passive role.

When a station is an active participant, it is said to be in *contention transmit mode*. In this mode, a station will repeatedly transmit a token every 20 milliseconds without waiting for a free token. All stations read this token, which contains the ring address of the sending station. If the ring address within the token is higher than the receiving station's address, the receiving station will enter the passive mode, also called the *contention repeat mode*.

While a station is in contention repeat (passive) mode, a contention monitor timer is started. This one-second timer counts down until one of two conditions is met. The first condition is met if the timer reaches zero. In this case, the station starts the beaconing process. The second condition occurs when the station receives a ring purge token, which causes the timer to be reset. Because only an active monitor sends a ring purge token, the station becomes aware that there is now an active monitor and resumes normal operation. This includes watching for packets, indicating an active monitor, as the station remains as a standby monitor.

An active monitor is responsible for the following tasks:

- Timing the ring
- Activating the ring process
- Starting the ring poll process
- Checking for an active ring every 10 milliseconds

An active monitor is also responsible for monitoring tokens, generating new tokens as needed after errors, purging old tokens, and other ring maintenance.

An active monitor is further responsible for trying to correct errors on the ring. Two types of errors exist: hard and soft. Soft errors are temporary problems experienced on the network. These errors include such things as bad CRCs and timeouts. These are usually handled without large consequences to the network. Hard errors, however, can have more serious consequences to the network. A hard error is considered a permanent fault and causes the ring to stop functioning.

When a hard error is encountered, the ring attempts to recover by wrapping the ring. When this process does not work, a beacon is sent over the ring. A *beacon* is a broadcast packet used to tell all other stations that there is a problem. Beacons are usually sent when a station has not received a token from an upstream neighbor for a specified amount of time. The default neighbor notification is seven seconds. This beaconing process continues until the ring recovers or the station removes itself from the ring. The token is then sent around the ring. A station receiving the token has the option of passing the token back to the ring or altering the frame, adding data, and then passing the frame to the next downstream neighbor. When a station receives a frame with data and a destination address that matches its own MAC address, the data is read, the frame is marked as read, and the frame is sent back out onto the ring. The host that originally sent the data sees that the destination host has received the data and releases the frame. Some implementations enable the early release of a token.

Two different types of frames are defined by the Token Ring standards: data/command frames and tokens. A *token* is three bytes in length and contains the start delimiter, the access control byte, and the end delimiter. A *data/command frame* is shown in Figure 5-5.

Fiber Distributed Data Interface (FDDI)

FDDI is similar in concept to Token Ring in that a logical ring is utilized. In FDDI, however, the physical layout is also a ring as opposed to the physical

Figure 5-5
Token Ring frame

**TOKEN RING
DATA/CONTROL
FRAME**

Start Delimiter	Access Control	Framer Control	Destination Address	Source Address	Data	FCS	End Delimiter	Frame Status
1	1	1	6	6	Varies	1	1	1

star of Token Ring. It also differs in that fiber is used instead of copper and FDDI runs at 100 Mbps instead of the 4 Mbps or 16 Mbps of Token Ring. FDDI also uses different frame formats and interface specifications. Data in an FDDI ring can be either synchronous or asynchronous.

FDDI uses two counter-rotating rings: a primary and a secondary or backup ring. This enables the ring to wrap if there is a break in the primary ring. Figure 5-6 shows a normally operating FDDI ring. The primary ring carries the data flow in a clockwise direction. The secondary ring flows in a counterclockwise direction.

A host can be connected to an FDDI network in two different ways: as a *dual attached station* (DAS) or as a *single attached station* (SAS). One of the benefits of FDDI is that there is a redundant (backup) ring built in. When a host is critical to the operation of the LAN or to the company mission, it should be attached to both rings as a DAS device. A host that is not critical,

Figure 5-6
An FDDI ring

FDDI RING

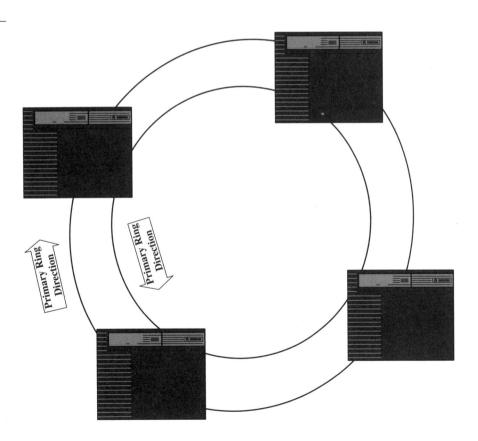

such as a PC that is turned off nightly, can be attached to only the primary ring as an SAS device.

An interface connecting to a FDDI ring connects through ports. Because of the two rings, two ports are available on DAS FDDI devices: physical port A and B. These ports can be in one of nine states:

- Off
- Active
- Trace
- Connect
- Next
- Signal
- Join
- Verify
- Break

When a break occurs, an optical bypass switch on the interfaces of the upstream and downstream neighbor connects the primary to the secondary ring. This causes the data to flow over the primary until the last host before the break. At this point, the optical bypass switch causes the data to flow over the secondary ring until reaching the second optical bypass switch where the data is again returned to the primary ring. Any DAS host should not be affected by a ring failure. However, an SAS host may lose connectivity when the primary ring fails. Figure 5-7 shows how wrapping occurs when a physical line breaks.

Four major OSI-related specifications for FDDI exist:

- *Physical layer medium dependant* (PMD)
- *Physical layer protocol* (PHY)
- *Media access control* (MAC)
- *Station management* (SMT)

The PMD specification defines the characteristics of the physical fiber connection. This includes the light levels within the fiber, the decibel loss, and the physical specifications of the equipment. The PMD specifications reside in layer 1 of the OSI model.

The PHY specifications define the data encoding and decoding schemes as well as the timing and framing requirements. The PHY specifications fit within layer 1 of the OSI model. It may seem confusing trying to decide if an issue is involved with the PMD or the PHY, but it is actually easy to separate the two. If the issue you are looking at concerns fiber optics, then this

Figure 5-7
FDDI ring wrap

FDDI RING IN A
WRAP CONDITION

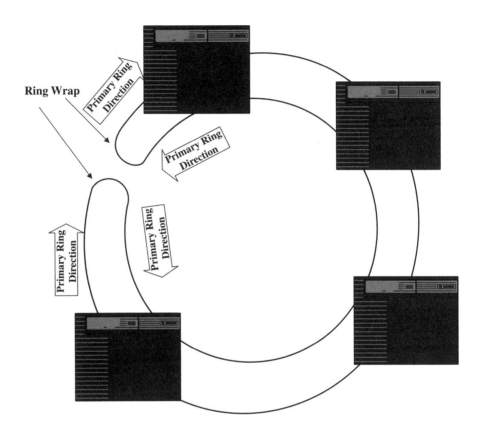

is a PMD issue. If the issue is not specifically related to fiber optics, then it is a PHY issue.

The MAC specifications deal with how the FDDI relates to OSI layer 2 functions. This includes the resolution of MAC addresses, moving data from layer 1 to layer 3, and other layer 2-related functions.

The final specification, SMT, is responsible for station management, fault recovery, and ring management, all of which are layer 1 functions. The SMT defines eight unique states a router may be in for the *entity coordination management* (ECM) process. These states are listed in Table 5-1.

A host may have one of five states on a port, depending upon who is the upstream neighbor. Table 5-2 is a list of possible host states and the meanings of each one. Notice that any status other than UNK indicates that

Table 5-1

The Router States
of the ECM Process

State	Description
Out	Isolated from the network.
In	Actively connected to the network. This is the normal state.
Trace	Trying to localize and reclaim a stuck beacon condition.
Leave	The router is allowing time for all the connections to break before leaving the network.
Path_test	The router is testing its internal paths.
Insert	The router is waiting for an optical bypass switch to be inserted.
Check	The router is waiting to ensure that the optical bypass switches are in the correct state.
De-insert	The router is waiting for an optical bypass switch to remove itself from the ring.

Table 5-2

Host States

Status	Description
A	The upstream neighbor is a physical type A DAS.
S	The upstream neighbor is a physical type A SAS.
B	The upstream neighbor is a physical type B DAS.
M	The upstream neighbor is a physical type M concentrator serving as a master to a connection station or concentrator.
UNK	The network server has not yet determined the type of the upstream neighbor. This usually indicates a physical problem with the cabling if the station has been in this state for a long time. This can also be seen from a show interface command when the upstream neighbor has an address of 0000 0000 0000.

there is a connection with the upstream neighbor and that the neighbor's type has been determined.

It is important to know both the station status and the SMT states when troubleshooting. Knowing this information enables you to determine where on the ring the problem resides. For instance, if a station does not find the upstream neighbor, the problem is almost certainly on that station or is upstream from it.

Chapter Summary

In this chapter, we have made a distinction between the logical and physical topologies of a network. We looked at the four major types of network cabling:

- Logical and physical bus
- Physical star/logical bus
- Physical star/logical ring
- Physical ring/logical ring

Knowing the differences between these types of networks enables us to focus our troubleshooting techniques on where the problems are likely to arise.

The chapter also covered cabling issues and how important it is to pay close attention to the cabling specifications for the network you are using before moving on to the common problems occurring in Ethernet networks. We had an overview of Token Ring operations and then explored FDDI networks. In the next chapter, we will use this as a basis for exploring switched Ethernet Networks.

We had an overview of Token Ring operations and then explored FDDI networks. In the next chapters, we will use this as a basis for exploring switched Ethernet Networks.

Frequently Asked Questions (FAQ)

Question: What do I do if I have a jabbering network card? How do I even find it? My network has completely stopped and everyone is panicking.

Answer: First, remain calm. Second, look at your hubs. One of your hubs should have significantly more traffic than the others. This is a good indication. If all the hubs show traffic, disconnect the hubs from each other. Some of the portions of the network will start to work. The section that does not work is where the malfunctioning network card is located. Also, adding switches to the network will provide some protection from jabbers because most switches have the capability to shut down a port when the number of bytes received exceeds a pre-set amount.

Question: My department is on a small budget and can't afford to spend $2,000 on a cable tester. Are the less expensive cable testers worth buying?

Answer: Definitely. Having a cable tester without all the features of a great cable tester is still worthwhile. Any testing equipment is better than no testing equipment. Even if all the tester can do is to tell you that there is connectivity, it will prove useful.

Question: I am experiencing a lot of collisions on my network. I think it is time to break up the collision domains. I didn't make a baseline of network performance, so I have no real data, but the network "feels" slow. How can I tell for sure?

Answer: Make a baseline for the network today. As your network grows, you will begin to see trends that will point more accurately towards network issues. Unfortunately, most managers are not willing to spend money simply because the network seems slow. You will need data to support your case for new equipment.

Question: I know that an Ethernet network can have a maximum of 1,024 hosts, but what is the maximum number of hosts I can have without suffering speed problems.

Answer: That question cannot be easily answered. A great number of variables go into the speed equation. For example, are you running only TCP/IP or are you running TCP/IP, IPX, and AppleTalk on the same network? Are you using a lot of broadcasts? Are you running applications that send small packets or large packets? How much memory does each host have? What is the physical layout of the network? All of these and many other factors go into the process of determining how many hosts should be on a LAN.

Lab Exercise

Using a protocol analyzer, create a new baseline for your network. Refer to Chapter 2, "Troubleshooting Methodology," for what should be recorded. Find out the following:

- At what time of day is the most network traffic experienced?
- What day of the week has the most traffic?
- What percentage of errors are you experiencing?
- How does this baseline compare to an earlier baseline?
- What protocols are you running on the network?
- If you are running multiple protocols, why?
- Where are the bottlenecks in your network?
- How can you remove the bottlenecks?

Questions

1. Which of the following has a physical ring and operates with a token mechanism?

   a. 100BaseT

   b. Token Ring 100

   c. 10BaseT

   d. FDDI

2. Which of the following are valid FDDI specifications?

   a. MAC, PHY, PMD, SMT

   b. MAC, UDP, LLC, SMT

   c. MAC, PMD, PHS, SMT

   d. NIC, PMD, SMT, PHY

3. Which type of FDDI station would you choose for a host such as a file server that will rarely, if ever, be turned off?

   a. RAS

   b. DAS

   c. SAS

   d. UNK

4. Which is a state that indicates that a host on an FDDI system has not yet established a connection with a neighbor?

   a. A

   b. S

   c. B

   d. M

   e. UNK

5. What state indicates that the upstream neighbor is a type B DAS connection?

   a. A

   b. S

   c. B

   d. M

   e. UNK

6. What state indicates that the upstream neighbor is a type A SAS connection?

   a. A
   b. S
   c. B
   d. M
   e. UNK

7. What are the two types of frames possible on a Token Ring network? Choose two.

   a. Controls
   b. Tokens
   c. Delimiters
   d. Data/command

8. While troubleshooting a FDDI problem, you issue a show interface command. You see all zeroes as the address of the upstream and downstream neighbors. What is the problem?

   a. There is a routing problem.
   b. The active monitor has been unplugged.
   c. There is a beaconing host.
   d. There is a physical connection problem.

9. What are you likely to see on your Ethernet network if cable lengths have been exceeded?

   a. Runts
   b. Late collisions
   c. Jabbers
   d. No connection for some hosts

10. What is the term used for the alternating ones and zeroes that start an Ethernet transmission?

    a. CRC
    b. Source address
    c. Destination address
    d. Preamble

11. Which of the following specifications is concerned with controlling the ring?

    a. PMD
    b. PHY
    c. SMT
    d. MAC

12. Which of the following specifications is concerned with the decibel loss on a fiber connection?

   a. PMD
   b. PHY
   c. SMT
   d. MAC

13. Which of the following specifications is concerned with layer-2 functionality such as addressing?

   a. PMD
   b. PHY
   c. SMT
   d. MAC

14. Which FDDI ECM state means that the router is waiting for an optical bypass switch to join the ring?

   a. Check
   b. Insert
   c. Trace
   d. Path_test

15. Which FDDI ECM state means that the router is trying to reclaim a stuck beacon?

   a. Check
   b. Insert
   c. Trace
   d. Path_test

16. Which FDDI ECM state means that the router is checking the internal paths?

   a. Check
   b. Insert
   c. Trace
   d. Path_test

17. Which two types of physical network topology can be associated with a logical bus? Pick two.

   a. Physical star
   b. Physical ring
   c. Physical bus
   d. Token Ring

18. Which type of network uses both a logical and a physical star?

    a. Token Ring
    b. Ethernet
    c. FDDI
    d. 10BaseT

19. Why does the amount of collisions affect network performance?

    a. Collisions force all hosts to process the packet.
    b. Collisions prevent the current packets on the network from being received.
    c. Collisions do not affect network performance

20. Which process is used to lessen a collision domain?

    a. Routing
    b. Adding hubs
    c. Microsegmentation
    d. VLAN

Answers

1. Answer: d

   FDDI operates with a physical and a logical dual ring. Similar to Token Ring, FDDI uses a token.

2. Answer: a

3. Answer: b

   Using a *dual-attached station* (DAS) makes the most sense for a critical server.

4. Answer: e

5. Answer: c

6. Answer: b

7. Answer: b, d

   The two types of frames on a Token Ring are tokens and data/control frames.

8. Answer: d

   Seeing all zeroes for both neighbors through a show interfaces command usually indicates a poor or non-existent physical connection.

9. Answer: b

   The reason that Ethernet cable length is limited is to ensure proper collision detection.

10. Answer: d

    The preamble is a series of ones and zeroes used to synchronize the interface.

11. Answer: b

12. Answer: a

13. Answer: d

14. Answer: b

15. Answer: c

16. Answer: d

17. Answer: a, c

    A logical bus can have either a physical bus or a physical star topology.

18. Answer: c

19. Answer: b

Collisions prevent the current packets on the network from being received. When two packets collide, neither of them is received properly by any host.

20. Answer: c

Collision domains are made smaller through the use of switches. This is also known as microsegmentation.

6

Troubleshooting Switched LANs

This chapter introduces the concept of switching in LANs. LAN switching is available in two different forms: cell switching and frame switching. Cell switching is used in *Asynchronous Transfer Mode* (ATM) networks, whereas frame switching is used in Ethernet networks. The difference between the two forms of switching is related to how each network handles data. Ethernet sends data over the LAN in a series of bytes, varying in size from 64 to 1518. These "series of bytes" are called frames. ATM uses a method in which all data is sent in the form of cells, which are always 53 bytes long. ATM relies heavily on cell switching to determine the path a cell will travel. Any ATM network must have an ATM switch. Ethernet, on the other hand, does not necessarily need switches present in order to work, as discussed in the previous chapter.

This chapter will discuss both cell and frame switching and lay the foundation for troubleshooting Cisco switches, discussed in the next chapter. After you learn the basic concepts of how switches work, you will be able to move quickly through the specifics of Cisco's implementation. This chapter also discuss VLANs, Spanning Tree Protocol, FastEtherChannel and ISL.

The purpose of this chapter is not to make you an expert on switching. The purpose here is to lay the groundwork necessary for Chapter 7, which discusses in detail how the Cisco family of switches work and how to troubleshoot them.

Objectives Covered in This Chapter

The objectives covered in this chapter include the following:

- Identify and apply generic and Cisco-specific troubleshooting tools on routers and switches.

- Demonstrate knowledge of common Data Link Layer characteristics and key troubleshooting targets likely to be found in campus LANs.

- Use proven problem-isolation techniques to list the symptoms of Catalyst 5000 and VLAN problems on switched Ethernet Networks.

- Apply diagnostic tools to trouble tickets and solve classroom network Catalyst 5000 problems that simulate real-life networking malfunctions.

- Apply diagnostic tools to classroom trouble tickets on switched and routed VLAN configuration problems.

OSI Model in Switched LANs

As in all computer systems, switching is accomplished in accordance with a networking model. Cisco has chosen to adhere to the OSI model for switching for Ethernet while adopting the ATM model for ATM. Although most of the work is done in the Data Link Layer of the OSI model, some functions are performed at the Network Layer.

Data Link Layer

The Data Link Layer is used extensively in both frame and cell switching. Ethernet relies solely upon the Data Link layer for forwarding packets.

ATM has used the Physical and Data Link Layers to break down the *ATM Adaptation Layer* (AAL) into five separate protocols. All of the ATM protocols fit within the Data Link and Physical Layers of the OSI model, as you will see in the discussion of ATM.

Network Layer

The Network Layer is used in switched LANs primarily in routing between Virtual LANs (VLANs). Although VLANs themselves only work on the Layer 2 level of the OSI model, the capability to move data between the different VLANs is a routing function. Therefore, when a network with VLANs is required to transport data between the VLANs, a router must be used.

When routing between VLANs, all of the normal routing procedures and troubleshooting procedures apply.

ATM

Asynchronous Transfer Mode (ATM) is based on the Broadband Integrated Services Data Network (B-ISDN) protocol standards. ATM relies on cell switching rather than frame switching because ATM packets are broken down into 53-byte-long structures called cells. The first 5 bytes of a cell contain the header, whereas the last 48 bytes contain data. The header information changes, depending upon which of two standards are used: either User *to Network Interface* (UNI) or *Network Node Interface* (NNI). Figure 6-1 shows both the structures. The only noticeable difference is that the UNI format reserves the first 4 bits of the VPI field for the GFC field.

The fields used in ATM cells are as follows:

- *Generic Flow Control* (GFC)   Used for controlling flow. This is only locally significant.
- *Virtual Path Identifier* (VPI)   Identifies the locally significant path for this packet.

ATM CELL FORMATS

	GFC 4 bits	VPI 8 bits	VCI 16 bits	PT 3 bits	CLP 1 bit	HEC 8 bits	Data 48 bytes
UNI	GFC 4 bits	VPI 8 bits	VCI 16 bits	PT 3 bits	CLP 1 bit	HEC 8 bits	Data 48 bytes

	VPI 12 bits	VCI 16 bits	PT 3 bits	CLP 1 bit	HEC 8 bits	Data 48 bytes
NNI	VPI 12 bits	VCI 16 bits	PT 3 bits	CLP 1 bit	HEC 8 bits	Data 48 bytes

- *Virtual Circuit Identifier* (VCI)   Identifies the locally significant virtual circuit number.

- *Payload Type* (PT)   Used optionally to identify the type of payload, such as voice or data. Also shows whether the cell has experienced delays due to congestion.

- *Cell Loss Priority* (CLP)   This determines if the cell may be dropped due to network congestion.

- *Header Error Check* (HEC)   This provides for a CRC check and provides delineation of the cell.

It is commonly known that large TCP/IP Ethernet packets are more efficient than small packets because the percentage of header compared to data is smaller in a large packet. This raises the question of why a protocol would purposefully be designed with an overhead approaching 10 percent. The answer lies in what and how ATM was designed to transport. First, ATM was designed to carry any type of data that was required. This includes voice, video, IP, or any other traffic that the administrator desires to transport. Many types of data, such as voice data, require very little latency. Thus, the equipment must not store large amounts of data before sending. Instead, it is most important that the data reach the end destination in a sequential manner as quickly as possible. Small data units such as a cell are optimal for this purpose.

NOTE: *The size of the data field was actually a compromise between two factions on the standards committee. One faction wanted a 64-byte data field; the other faction wanted a 32-byte data field.*

Second, by having a small fixed cell size, it becomes easier to optimize the equipment to process these cells extremely quickly. Most ATM devices are extremely efficient at moving 53-byte cells and can approach "wire speed" in their transfer rates.

The way in which an ATM switch processes cells is virtually identical to the way an Ethernet switch processes frames. The destination address is looked up in a table and the cell is forwarded to the interface to which that destination address belongs. One major difference between ATM and Ethernet is that all ATM cells are 53 bytes long, whereas Ethernet has varying sizes of packets.

ATM Layers

ATM protocols span both the Physical and Data Link Layers of the OSI model. As shown in Figure 6-2, the ATM protocols are broken into three main categories: the AAL, the ATM Layer, and the PHY Layer. The ATM and PHY Layers are equivalent to the Physical Layer in the OSI model. The AAL is equivalent to the Data Link Layer of the OSI model.

The encapsulation chosen within the AAL is dependant upon which type of service is required. There are five different types of service available. These types are as follows:

Service	Description
AAL0	AAL0 is a non-standard extension used for experimentation purposes.
AAL1	AAL1 is used on DS1, fractional DS1, E1, fractional E1, and any other circuit that emulates a conventional telecommunication circuit.
AAL2	AAL2 is designed for carrying voice data. The equipment to support AAL2 is still under development at the time this was written.
AAL3/ AAL4	AAL3 and AAL4 are traditionally grouped together because they are extremely similar and were designed to be used over the same types of connections. These encapsulations were designed for use over connectionless *Switched Multimegabit Data Service* (SMDS) circuits. They also support connection-oriented services, but are seldom used at present.
AAL5	AAL5 is the most commonly seen form of ATM and works similarly to most other Data Link Layer protocols. Data is encapsulated within cells. If the data is too large to fit into the 48-byte data field, the data is "sliced" to the appropriate size. If the data is too small for a single cell, the data is buffered until it reaches 48 bytes in size.

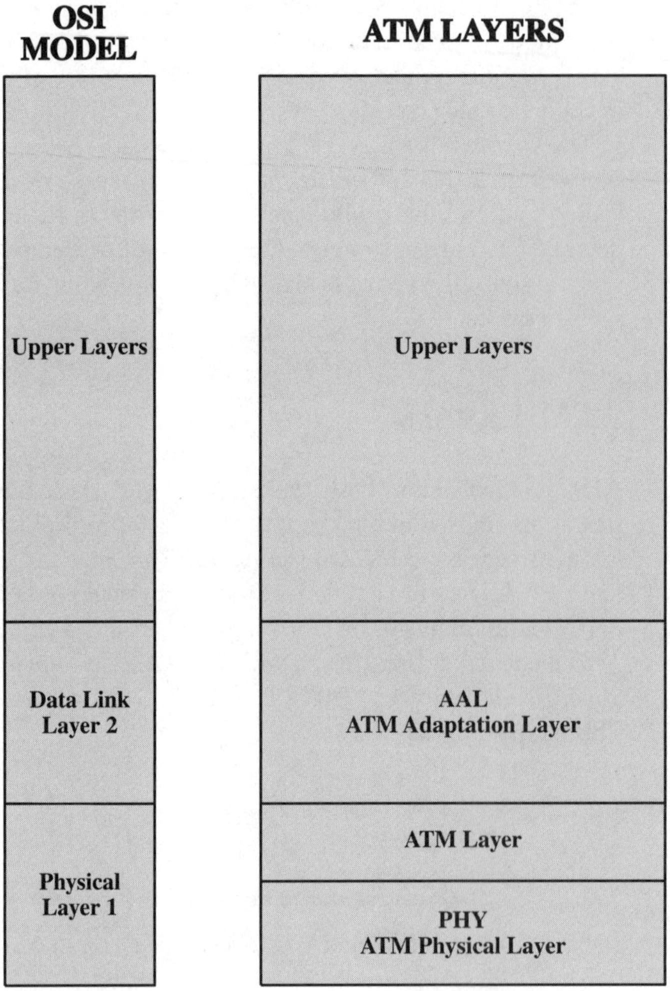

Figure 6-2
ATM layers

OSI MODEL	ATM LAYERS
Upper Layers	Upper Layers
Data Link Layer 2	AAL ATM Adaptation Layer
Physical Layer 1	ATM Layer
	PHY ATM Physical Layer

ELAN

Emulated LAN (ELAN) over ATM is a methodology wherein an ATM network is constructed to look like either an Ethernet or Token Ring system to the machines attached to this network. Essentially, ELAN was designed to extend an Ethernet segment over a WAN link. This is a very powerful tool to use over backbones in a campus environment. ELAN is commonly used in conjunction with VLANs and *LAN Emulation* (LANE), which is another form of encapsulation. Together, these tools provide virtually the same capabilities as an Ethernet system while retaining one of the greatest assets of ATM—speed.

Ethernet Hubs

As was discussed in Chapter 5, a hub is a device that provides a connection between hosts. This connection relies upon a shared common connection that all hosts must use. This is a shared (non-dedicated) medium that uses the CSMA/CD algorithms. There are two main factors limiting usability of a hub system. The first limiting factor is that a hub system has a single collision domain; the second is that a hub system has a single broadcast domain. Although this may be sufficient for smaller networks, collisions and broadcasts in large networks may become a problem because of the amount of time the network is spending on processing these collisions and broadcasts.

NOTE: *As previously stated, the mere percentage of collisions or broadcasts, when considered by themselves, is not indicative of a network problem. Collisions and broadcasts are only a problem if they adversely affect the performance and objectives of the network.*

As shown in Figure 6-3, when data enters one port of a hub, the data is sent out over all the ports of that hub. Thus, every other device connected through this hub sees collisions and broadcasts. These devices include other hubs connected to the first hub and all hosts connected to the second hub.

When a network uses only hubs for connectivity, that network is considered to have a single collision domain and a single broadcast domain (see Figure 6-4).

Many hub manufacturers allow for cascading hubs through a separate interface, such as through a 50-pin SCSI connector on the back of the hub.

Figure 6-3
Hub

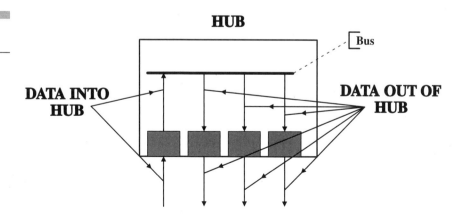

Figure 6-4

Collision1

SINGLE COLLISION DOMAIN
SINGLE BROADCAST DOMAIN

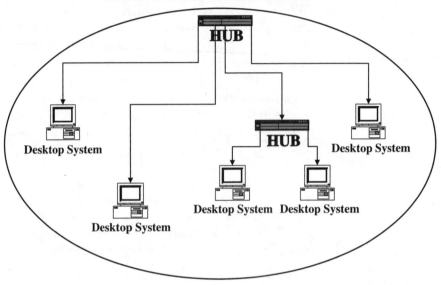

Cascading hubs usually provides a larger bandwidth between the hubs but does not solve the collision issue. Additionally, it is very easy to mistake the collision light with the power light when a system has six or seven 48-port hubs cascaded together. Bridges allow the network engineer to reduce collision domains. Routers allow the engineer to limit broadcast domains. *Virtual Local Area Networks* (VLANs) are used to limit both collision domains and broadcast domains. We will explore bridges before switches, which are actually multi-port bridges.

Ethernet Bridges

Bridges are Layer 2 devices that have the effect of reducing the collision domain on a network. They do this by using two separate ports to connect the different segments of the network. For this discussion, we will assume that the bridges are considered "intelligent," meaning that the MAC addresses do not need to be manually entered. A bridge that has more than two ports is sometimes referred to as a multi-port bridge.

Because bridges have their ports set to promiscuous mode, the port will attempt to process every frame received. When a frame is received on any port, the bridge will read the destination address of that frame. An address table residing in the bridge will be consulted. If the address is known, the frame will be forwarded to the appropriate port. If the address is not known, the bridge will replicate this frame over all interfaces other than the one on which it was received.

NOTE: *When Spanning Tree is in use, this process varies slightly. See the section on Spanning Tree later in this chapter for more details.*

When we look at how a frame is being forwarded by a bridge, there are several things to remember, as follows:

- The source address of the frame is not changed.
- The sending and receiving hosts are unaware that a bridge resides between the two.
- A bridge will not forward a frame over the same port in which the frame was received.
- There is a delay involved in the forwarding of the frame (this topic is discussed further in this chapter in the section on switches).
- The bridge must obey all the rules of Ethernet, including those regarding collisions and back-off algorithms.

The major benefit of a bridge is that the collision domain of a network is reduced (shown in Figure 6-5). Notice that the broadcast domain is not affected by adding a bridge because when a broadcast frame is received, the bridge will merely replicate the frame as if the bridge did not know the destination address. That is, the broadcast frame will be replicated over all the ports other than the port through which the frame was received.

The collision domain when using a bridge extends from the bridge port through all the devices attached to that LAN segment, including hosts, hubs, and other switch ports that are connected to this LAN segment.

The collision domain is reduced because the bridge does not merely carry the frame through a connection between the two ports. Instead, the frame received is read into memory, where it is stored until the address table has been consulted (which accounts for the delay inherent in using a bridge). It also requires memory inside the bridge. The bridge discards collisions, runts, and other non-acceptable frames. Discarding collisions is the

Figure 6-5
Collision2

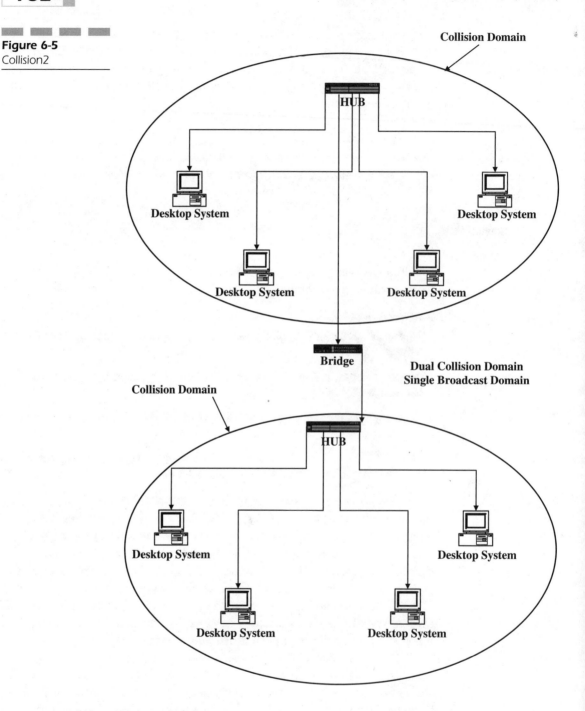

way the collision domain is reduced. The reduction of collision domains is called segmentation.

Ethernet Switches

There is one major difference between a bridge and a switch. The marketing personnel at switch manufacturers have found out that it is easier and more profitable to sell switches than bridges. Other than this distinction, there are no real differences between a bridge and a switch. A switch operates in exactly the same manner as a bridge: building address tables, forwarding frames, and reducing collision domains.

Although the actual chip-level interactions within switches are beyond the scope of this book, you will still need to know the basic concepts upon which all switches rely. The first of these concepts is that multiple paths are built and removed as needed within the switch. When there is no data attempting to flow through a switch, there are no connections between the ports. Then, when data come into a port, the destination port is determined by using the address table. A connection is created between the inbound and the outbound port, as shown in Figure 6-6.

The data travels over the "switch fabric," which is usually the factor that limits the amount of data that can be transferred through a switch in a specified amount of time. The "switch fabric" is connected to the backplane and is measured in Gigabits per second. It is called a "switch fabric" because it really is a mesh of connections, not a single connection. The fabric allows the connection from any port directly to any other port within the switch. Additionally, the switch can make several of these connections at the same

Figure 6-6
Switch1

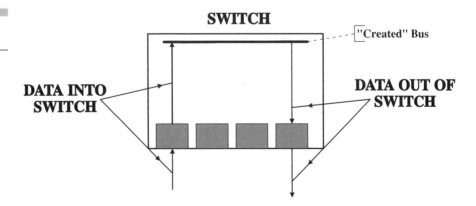

Figure 6-7
Switch2

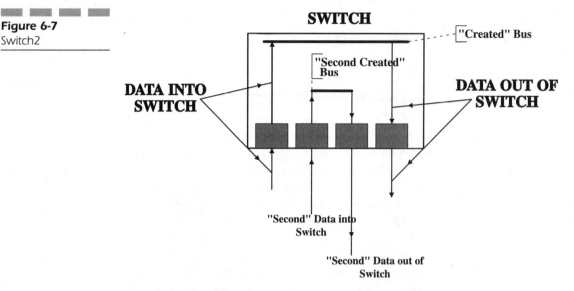

time. From a user's perspective, when two ports receive data at the same time, the switch will create two completely separate connections between the inbound and outbound ports as shown in Figure 6-7. This process differs drastically from a hub, in which data can only be accepted from one port at a given time and where data is sent to all ports at the same time. If the outbound port is not immediately available, the switch will either buffer the data or send a collision notice to the sending host, depending upon the switch manufacturer.

The method a switch uses to forward frames is also dependent upon the manufacturer. Some switches allow the administrator to choose between the switching methods. There are three major forms of switching, each of which will be investigated in turn:

■ Cut-Through

■ Fragment-Free Cut-Through

■ Store-and-Forward

Cut-Through switching is the switching method that experiences the least latency. As soon as the frame is read through the destination address (64 bytes), the switch will start looking up the destination port in the address table. While the outbound port is being determined, the frame continues to be received through the port and placed into the buffer. After the outbound port has been determined, the frame is forwarded. This method causes the least amount of delay in forwarding frames at the expense of a heightened likelihood of forwarding poorly formed frames.

When a frame is transmitted, there are three possibilities that may occur. First, there may be a collision. The collision should occur within the first 64 bytes or it is considered a "late" collision. The second possibility is that the CRC may fail. The third possibility is that the frame will be properly formed. Using Cut-Through switching will start sending data through the outbound port under any of these three possibilities. If a collision is detected on the inbound port while a frame is being sent, the switch will generate a collision signal on the outbound port. This will cause all hosts connected to the outbound port to ignore the frame.

While using Cut-Through switching, it is possible to determine the amount of time the switch adds while transferring data through the network. Fragment-Free switching also allows the administrator to determine how much additional time (latency) the switch will add.

Fragment-Free switching addresses the issue of collisions. This method buffers the first 64 bytes of a frame before starting to send the frame through the outbound port. Because a collision should occur during the first 64 bytes, the switch will notice the collision occurring before starting to output the frame. Therefore, the switch spends less time processing frames that will ultimately not be traversing the switch. It is still possible for a late collision to occur; in which case the switch will generate a late collision to overwrite the frame that is in the process of being sent out the port. The Fragment-Free method adds more latency than the Cut-Through method, but not as much as the Store-and-Forward method.

The Store-and-Forward method of switching causes the most amount of latency but also provides the fewest number of errors being propagated through the LAN. In this method, the entire frame is read into the buffer, the CRC is checked, and then the frame is forwarded. This prevents all malformed packets due to collisions, late collisions, and failed CRC checks from traversing the switch. The cost of ensuring that bad frames do not cross the switch is paid for in additional latency. Because the size of an Ethernet frame varies, so will the latency experienced using the Store-and-Forward method. This method may also demand more memory resources than the other two methods in order to store the whole frame.

An overview of the three major types of Ethernet switching is shown in Figure 6-8. Cut-Through switching causes the least amount of latency, but provides the least protection from poorly formed frames. Store-and-Forward switching provides the most protection from poorly formed frames, but also provides for the greatest latency. Fragment-Free switching is a compromise between the other two methods and provides some protection from poorly formed frames and does not demand as great a latency period as does Store-and-Forward switching.

Figure 6-8

Switching methods

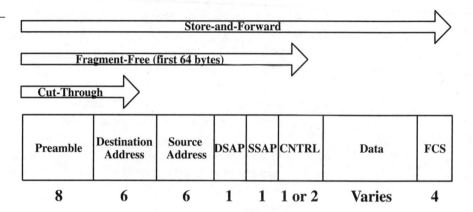

SWITCHING METHODS

Preamble	Destination Address	Source Address	DSAP	SSAP	CNTRL	Data	FCS
8	6	6	1	1	1 or 2	Varies	4

VLAN

Creating *Virtual LANs* (VLANs) allows the administrator to separate a single physical LAN into multiple logical LANs based upon virtually any criteria that the administrator chooses. Membership in a specific VLAN can be based upon MAC address, the switch port connected to, department, physical location, or even which day of the week a machine was put into place. This gives the administrator the ability to create many separate networks using the existing wiring, and thereby reducing broadcast domains.

By default, a VLAN cannot talk to a different VLAN without a router. On larger Cisco switches, this may be in the form of a *Router Switching Module* (RSM). Using a router may rely upon the ISL protocol, which can allow a single port to belong to multiple VLANs at the same time. The disadvantage of using ISL instead of two ports is that the single port is capable of handling only a certain amount of traffic. If the traffic between the VLANs exceeds the capability of a single port, using two separate ports will tend to alleviate the congestion associated with a single port.

There are several reasons to create VLANs, including reducing broadcast domains, easing administration, and distributing network services. Broadcast limitation is usually the primary reason that administrators choose to implement VLANs. Broadcasts are limited because a router does not generally transport broadcasts. This means that each VLAN will see only the broadcasts associated with its own VLAN. On a network of several hundred PCs, this can make a significant difference in the available bandwidth. Figure 6-9 shows how a VLAN limits the broadcast domain.

Figure 6-9
VLAN

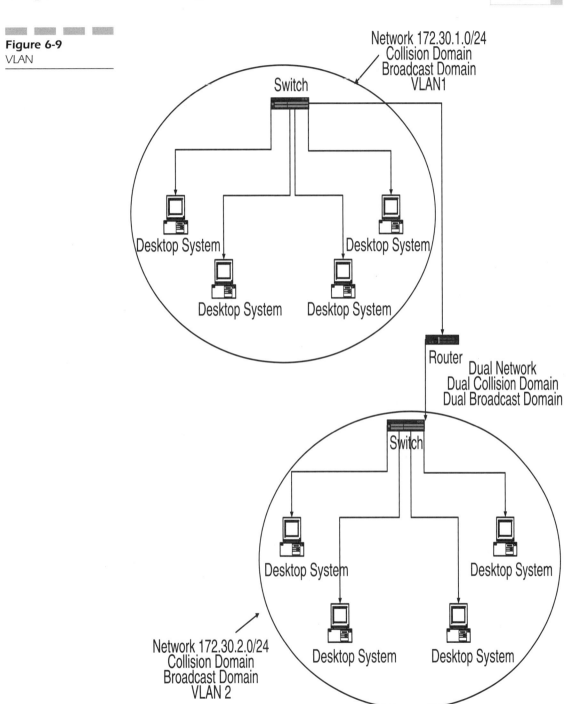

There are, however, some design issues that must be considered before implementing VLANs. The first design consideration is the number of VLANs in use. Although there may be up to 1024 VLANs on a network, Cisco equipment only allows significantly less-active VLANs on a network. Second, the *Maximum Transmission Unit* (MTU) size should be set to 1500 on all interfaces. This will cause fragmentation of Token Ring and FDDI frames because of the limitations inherent on the backplane of Cisco switches. The third consideration, the "80-20 rule," says that 80 percent of the traffic should be local to the VLAN and only 20 percent should be not local. This "rule" is becoming more relaxed as higher-speed routers are becoming more common. However, the administrator should still strive to keep most of the resources local to the VLAN.

VlanDirector is a Cisco tool that allows you to gather data regarding VLANs as well as manage the VLANs within your organization. This tool allows you to monitor the activity in a VLAN and find potential problems within a VLAN. VlanDirector relies on the *Cisco Discovery protocol* (CDP) to find the current state of the VLANs. This product provides an alternative to the command line interface method, configuring VLANs through the use of a GUI interface.

Spanning Tree Protocol

The Spanning Tree protocol allows for multiple physical paths within a network while establishing only a single logical path. Normally, in Ethernet, you can have only a single path between two devices, which prevents redundancy from being built into the network physical structure. If a cable should break, whole areas of the network will be disconnected. The Spanning Tree Algorithm that runs on Cisco switches allows for such things as cable breaks and hub failures.

The Spanning Tree protocol is defined by the IEEE 802.1 standards. This protocol utilizes Spanning Tree Frames that are called *Bridge Protocol Data Units (BPDUs)*. BPDUs are sent and received by all switches at specified intervals and are used by the switches to determine the topology of the network. There are actually two Spanning Tree Protocols available for use: IEEE and DEC. All switches dealing with Spanning Tree must use the same protocol; using different protocols will cause a network loop to occur. A network loop is shown in Figure 6-10.

In Figure 6-11, a network with three switches is shown. The connection between switches B and C is kept inactive as long as the path from C through A and then to B is active.

Figure 6-10
Network loop

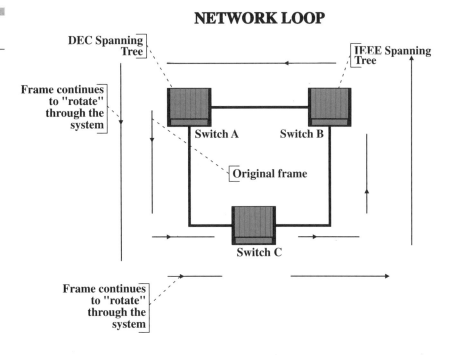

Figure 6-10
Network loop

NETWORK LOOP

Figure 6-11
Spanning Tree1

SPANNING TREE PROTOCOL IN NORMAL MODE

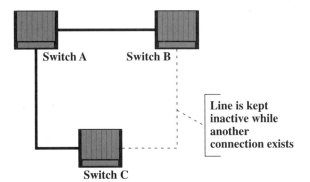

Figure 6-11
Spanning Tree1

If the cable between switches A and C becomes broken or disconnected, as shown in Figure 6-12, the Spanning Tree algorithm will activate the link between switches B and C. There will still only be a single path between any two devices on the network.

The administrator can create a fully meshed network, as shown in Figure 6-13. While creating a meshed network, you will use more switch ports

Figure 6-12
Spanning Tree2

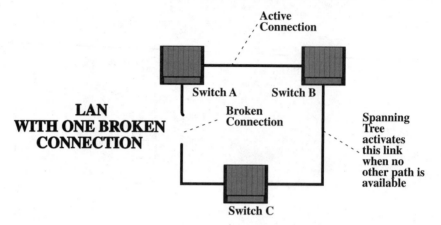

**SPANNING TREE PROTOCOL
CHOOSING NEW PATH**

but gain the advantage of being able to lose any given connection between devices and still retain connectivity.

The previous examples showed Spanning Tree between switches. However, all that is required is that each redundant connection be made to a switch port. In other words, you may have redundant connections between a switch and another switch, between multiple switches, between multiple switches and a single hub, or between a single switch and a single hub. You may not have redundant connections between a hub and another hub without a Spanning Tree-capable switch between the two hubs. Chapter 7 will discuss how Spanning Tree is configured on Cisco switches and the options that are available.

EtherChannel and FastEtherChannel

EtherChannel is a Cisco proprietary method of link aggregation that is usually used in combination with a full-duplex connection. When 100Mbps ports are used, this is referred to as FastEtherChannel. The principles and specifics of EtherChannel and FastEtherChannel differ only in the speed of the connections. EtherChannel is available on most Cisco switches and runs over 10Mbps, 100Mbps, and 1000Mbps ports. For the remainder of this section, we will refer to FastEtherChannel.

By combining a set of ports to act as if they were a single port with a larger bandwidth, FastEtherChannel allows connection between two

Figure 6-13
Spanning Tree3

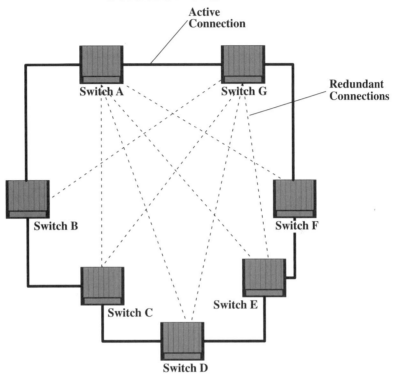

SPANNING TREE PROTOCOL UNDER NORMAL CONDITIONS WITH MANY MESHED CONNECTIONS

switches or between a switch and a high-end server. Ports may be combined in groups of two, four, or eight ports with the "Port Group" command. All of the ports within a group must be on the same slot. This allows a connection speed of up to 800Mbps between switches, not counting the additional speed made available through the use of full-duplex connections.

High-end servers benefit from FastEtherChannel by using NIC cards that have two or more ports. Most of the dual or four-port cards available at this time allow the administrator to combine multiple cards into a single FastEtherChannel group.

Because all of the ports within a FastEtherChannel group act as a single port, this is an exception to the rule that spanning tree must be enabled if there is more than one connection to a single device.

ISL and 802.1q

InterSwitch Link (ISL) is a Cisco proprietary protocol that is similar to the IEEE 802.1q standard. However, there are some noticeable differences. For example, ISL allows for automatically balancing loads between parallel paths while having a higher overhead than IEEE 802.1q. ISL allows a port to belong to multiple VLANs at the same time. To enable load balancing, the administrator must set differing VLAN priorities.

ISL encapsulates a frame with a header and additional CRC field, which are stripped off when the frame exits the receiving switch. The header and CRC add a total of 30 bytes to the frame, making the larger legal ISL frame a size of 1548 bytes when carrying Ethernet. The additional data flowing through the network should be considered when using ISL. Figure 6-14 shows the format of an ISL frame.

Notice that the original frame is encapsulated within the ISL frame and the original frame is unchanged. The list on the following page shows the fields used in ISL and a brief discussion of their usage.

802.1q does not encapsulate the original frame. Instead, four bytes are added after the source address. The CRC is then recalculated to include the new field. This saves 26 bytes overhead per frame. Some protocol analyzers are not capable of decoding 802.1q frames, so use caution when choosing a manufacturer.

Troubleshooting Switched Ethernet LANs

The major troubleshooting problems that arise with switched networks are no different from the issues found with non-switched networks. All of the rules, techniques, and tips previously discussed are valid when using switches in an Ethernet LAN. There are, however, some additional troubleshooting options as well as problems that are seen when switches are used in a network.

Figure 6-14
ISL Frame

ISL FRAME FORMAT

MCA	Type	User	Source	Length	Binary	ORG ID	VLAN ID	Index	Reserved	Original	CRC

Symbol	Name	Usage
MCA	ISL Multi-Cast Address	ISL uses the multi-cast address of 01:00:0C:00:00. This is a 40-bit field.
Type	Type Code	This 4-bit field is used to determine the encapsulated frame's type. The values can be 0000 for Ethernet, 0001 for Token Ring, 0010 for FDDI, and 0011 for ATM.
User	User-defined bits	This 4-bit field is used to determine the priority of a frame. 0000 indicates normal priority, whereas 0011 indicates a high priority.
Source	Source Address	The MAC address of the source port. Length is 48 bits.
Length	Length of ISL Frame	The length of the ISL frame minus 18 bits.
Binary	Binary Expression	The same as a SNAP header because ISL uses SNAP LLC. It is set to AA:AA:03.
ORG ID	Organizational Identifier	The first three bytes of the MAC address of the source port.
VLAN ID	Virtual LAN Identifier	Each VLAN has a unique identifier associated with itself. This field is used to identify the VLAN the frame belongs to. It is 15 bits in length.
Index	Index	The index field is used for troubleshooting. It contains the source port value of the frame.
Reserved	Reserved Bits	The value of this field depends upon which type of frame is being carried. For Ethernet, this field is 0. Token Ring copies the Access Control and Frame Information fields here. FDDI places an 0x00 into this field and then copies in the frame control field.
Original	Original Frame	Contains the original frame (Ethernet, ATM, FDDI, or Token Ring) that ISL is transporting.
CRC	ISL CRC	The ISL adds this 32-bit CRC as the final field in the ISL frame. This CRC is calculated for the entire ISL frame, including the original (encapsulated) frame.

Connection Speed

Most new Cisco switches have the capability to operate ports at either 10Mbps or 100Mbps port speeds. Most new NICs can automatically sense that the switch has the capability to operate at either speed and will negotiate with the switch to obtain the highest speed possible. The technique used is similar to the technique used by modems to obtain the highest connection speed possible.

Problems can arise when the negotiation does not work correctly or if the two devices are not set to automatically negotiate the speed and both devices are also set to differing values. Sometimes, it is desirable to manually set the connection speeds. For example, there are some Windows NT servers that did not reliably keep an automatically negotiated 100Mbps connection until a recent service pack for NT was released. Prior to the service pack, a connection would be initially made at 100Mbps, and within a few hours the connection slowed to 10Mbps. The only way to prevent this from happening was to configure the switch port for 100Mbps only and force the server to connect at 100Mbps.

When forcing a connection to occur only at a specific speed, one of two viable options are available for use on the opposing end of the connection. The first option is to set the opposing end to automatically negotiate the connection speed. In this case, the speed set on the port will be the only speed available, so it will be used. The second option is to set the opposing end to the same setting as the switch port. In this case, the speed will not be negotiated and the connection will be made at the specified speed. If the opposing ends of the connection are not set to the same speed, several results may be seen. The most common symptom is that no Layer 2 connection will be made, although the link lights will indicate a Layer 1 connection. This will usually cause the interface to repeatedly attempt to connect without success.

Full- Versus Half-Duplex

It is possible to double the theoretical bandwidth of an Ethernet connection by using a type of connection called "full-duplex." In normal (half-duplex) Ethernet, data flows in only one direction at a time. However, as you learned in Chapter 5, Ethernet cable uses wires 1, 2, 3, and 6. Wires 1 and 2 are both receive, and wires 3 and 6 are both transmit. Therefore, it is possible to use wires 1 and 3 at the same time wires 2 and 6 are being used. This allows data to flow in one direction over one pair of wires while simultaneously flowing over the other pair of wires in the opposite direction.

To utilize a full-duplex connection, there must be a dedicated connection between the two interfaces. In other words, you may have a full-duplex connection between two switches, between two hosts, or between a switch and a host. Full-duplex may not be used with a hub because a hub has a non-dedicated (shared) connection between all the attached hosts. A full-duplex connection should never experience any collisions because data is transmitted over a different pair of wires than data is received upon.

Full-duplex can be specified or automatically negotiated similar to the way speed is determined. The rules for applying full-duplex are the same as those for setting speed. Full-duplex can be automatically negotiated, set on one side and negotiated on the second side, or set the same on both sides. A good way to tell if both sides are not set properly is to look for a large amount of late collisions.

SPAN

Switched Port Analyzer (SPAN) and *Enhanced Switched Port Analyzer* (ESPAN) enable the administrator to monitor the traffic passing through the switch, regardless of the destination port. This can prove essential to an administrator because, by default, any host attached to a switch port will see only traffic destined for that particular host. As shown in Figure 6-15, when SPAN is enabled, a connection is made not only between the source and destination ports, but also to the port designated as the monitor port.

Although it is possible on most switches to enable a single port to monitor all other ports, this is seldom as useful as it sounds. Assume that you

Figure 6-15
SPAN

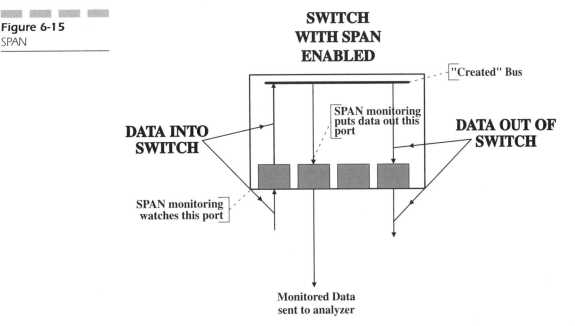

wish to monitor 144 ports through a single 100Mbps port. The amount of data flowing between all of the monitored ports will easily overwhelm a single 100Mbps connection. This will result in packets being dropped and there is no control over exactly which packets will be dropped. Therefore, the analysis that relies upon the data gathered through the monitoring process would be flawed.

With SPAN, a port being monitored must be within the same VLAN as the monitoring port. ESPAN overcomes this limitation.

Chapter Summary

In this chapter, you got an overview of ATM and looked at how switching affects Ethernet. You discovered the basic concepts of switching and some of the more obvious problems associated with switching.

In the next chapter, you will use the information presented here to help in your troubleshooting efforts on Cisco switches.

Frequently Asked Questions (FAQ)

Question:: How much will a switch speed up my network?

Answer:: Assuming that you have very few collisions and that you are not changing from 10 Mbps to 100 Mbps, the answer is "very little" if any speed increase will be noticed. This is because switches do not add bandwidth to your network. They merely exchange a reduction in the collision domain with an increase in the latency on the network.

Question:: Are you saying that a switch can slow down my network?

Answer:: Yes. Because a switch must store at least part of the frame and look up the destination address before sending the frame out the appropriate port, there will be an added latency in frames traversing the network. Although this limitation is usually overcome by a reduction in the amount of collisions, this is not always the case.

Question:: I can't afford to switch my whole network. What areas of the network will benefit most from switching?

Answer:: Switching will help those areas that have the highest numbers of hosts trying to access them. In other words, if you have several servers that communicate between themselves and also to client PCs, these may be the items you want to add to a switch. This allows the communication between the switches to be separated from the communication between the servers and the hosts.

Question:: Does FastEtherChannel really help on a heavily used server?

Answer:: Absolutely. We have experienced up to a 55% increase in throughput after hooking a server to a dual-port FastEtherChannel capable card.

Question:: I want to switch our whole network so that it will run at top speed. My boss says it is too expensive for the amount of additional speed received. Who is correct?

Answer:: Unfortunately, your boss may be more correct. There is seldom the need to switch every host on a network. Equipment purchases must be based on need balanced against cost. Assume that you are currently experiencing 5 percent collisions and that switches cost approximately $100.00 per port. Switching may reduce the amount to virtually no collisions. However, you need to ask if spending around

$100.00 per port is really worth a 5 percent speed increase minus the added latency. Our advice is to add switches where they are needed the most, unless the cost difference between a hub and a switch is negligible. If the cost is justified by the speed increase, make the purchase. If the cost is not justified, do not make the purchase.

Questions

1. Which of the following are allowed encapsulations on an ATM network?

    a. AAL5, PVC, SVC

    b. VPC, VC

    c. AAL5, LANE

    d. AAL2

2. Which product allows you to gather data about VLANs as well as manage your VLANs?

    a. System Monitor

    b. TrafficDirector

    c. VlanDirector

    d. VLAN Works

3. Which type of frame switching guarantees a consistent latency as well as the lowest latency?

    a. Store-and-Forward

    b. Cut-Through

    c. Fragment-Free

4. Which type of frame switching does not guarantee a consistent latency?

    a. Store-and-Forward

    b. Cut-Through

    c. Fragment-Free

5. Which type of frame switching guarantees that no runts will be forwarded and has a guaranteed latency?

    a. Store-and-Forward

    b. Cut-Through

    c. Fragment-Free

6. Which type of frame switching guarantees that no packets failing the CRC will be forwarded?

    a. Store-and-Forward

    b. Cut-Through

    c. Fragment-Free

7. How many ports may be connected by using a FastEtherChannel connection?

   a. 2

   b. 4

   c. 8

   d. 2, 4, or 8

   e. up to 8

8. Which protocol allows the administrator to monitor ports on a switch?

   a. FastEtherChannel

   b. Spanning Tree

   c. Span

   d. Monitor

9. Which IEEE protocol allows for physical loops in an Ethernet network?

   a. 802.5

   b. 802.1

   c. 802.3

   d. 802.1q

10. What is the result of using the IEEE Spanning Tree protocol on some switches and the DEC Spanning Tree Protocol on other switches?

   a. Spanning Tree will work, but not well.

   b. It optimizes the Spanning Tree protocol.

   c. The network will not work.

   d. Spanning Tree will be disabled on all switches.

11. Switches are designed to accomplish one of the following (choose the best answer):

   a. Speed up the network.

   b. Reduce the broadcast domain.

   c. Reduce the collision domain.

   d. Make LAN administration easier.

12. What is required to transport data between two different VLANs?

   a. Router

   b. VlanDirector

   c. Nothing

   d. Two VLANs can never exchange data.

13. Which of the following will allow a full-duplex connection? (Choose 2.)

    a. Switch to Switch
    b. Switch to Hub
    c. Hub to Hub
    d. Switch to PC

14. Which of the following is an asynchronous connection?

    a. 10BaseT
    b. 100baseT
    C. Full-duplex

15. ATM is an acronym for what?

    a. AppleTalk Media
    b. Automatic Transport Method
    c. Asynchronous Transfer Mode
    d. Automatic Teller Machines

16. ATM is similar to which technology?

    a. Ethernet
    b. B-ISDN
    c. Frame-Relay
    d. D-ISDN

17. ATM works at which layers of the OSI Model? (Choose 2.)

    a. Application
    b. Presentation
    c. Session
    d. Transport
    e. Network
    f. Data Link
    g. Presentation

18. Ethernet switching works at which layer of the OSI Model?

    a. Application
    b. Presentation
    c. Session
    d. Transport
    e. Network
    f. Data Link
    g. Presentation

19. When working with VLANs, which layers of the OSI model should you concentrate on? (Choose 2.)

   a. Application
   b. Presentation
   c. Session
   d. Transport
   e. Network
   f. Data Link
   g. Presentation

20. When using VlanDirector, which protocol must be running?

   a. IP
   b. ISL
   c. CDP
   d. BGP

Answers

1. Answer: c.

2. Answer: c.

   VlanDirector is designed to ease the maintenance of VLANs through the use of a graphical User Interface.

3. Answer: b.

   Cut-Through switching guarantees the smallest amount of latency and a consistent amount of latency.

4. Answer: a.

   Store-and-Forward switching reads the whole frame before forwarding the frame. Because Ethernet frames vary in size, the latency added cannot be guaranteed.

5. Answer: c.

   Fragment-Free switching guarantees that the frame sent out will be no fewer than 64 bytes. Therefore, there are no runts. Because the switch will start forwarding the frame after the first 64 bytes have been read, there is a definable amount of latency.

6. Answer: a.

   Store-and-Forward switching reads the whole frame before forwarding the frame. The CRC is checked before the frame is forwarded.

7. Answer: d.

   FastEtherChannel allows the administrator to group ports in sets of two, four, or eight ports.

8. Answer: c.

   SPAN (Switched Port Analyzer) allows the administrator to monitor ports on a switch.

9. Answer: b.

   The 802.1 standard defines the Spanning Tree Protocol, which allows for physical loops in an Ethernet environment. The IEEE 802.1q is similar to the ISL protocol and defines the connections between switches, not Spanning Tree.

10. Answer: c.

    The IEEE and the DEC Spanning Tree protocols do not communicate with each other. The network will experience loops and will cease to work.

11. Answer: c.

Ethernet switches are used to reduce the collision domain. An added benefit may be that the network will run faster due to the lack of collisions.

12. Answer: a.

A router or Route Switch Module (RSM) is used to move traffic between two VLANs.

13. Answer: a, d.

Full-duplex can be obtained only with a dedicated connection. Because hubs are non-dedicated, they cannot achieve a full-duplex connection.

14. Answer: c.

Full-duplex allows two conversations to occur at the same time.

15. Answer: c.

ATM stands for Asynchronous Transfer Mode.

16. Answer: b.

ATM is similar to B-ISDN because there is a single channel dedicated to maintenance of circuits.

17. Answer: f, g.

ATM works at the Physical and Data Link Layers of the OSI model.

18. Answer: f.

Ethernet switching works at the Data Link Layer of the OSI model.

19. Answer: e, f.

If you are using VLANs, you need to be concerned with the Data Link Layer for the switching part as well as the Network Layer for the routing part of VLANs.

20. Answer: c.

VlanDirector requires the use of the Cisco Discovery Protocol.

## CHAPTER 7

Cisco Switches

This chapter will start with a quick overview of some of the members of the Cisco Catalyst switch family. We will then explore the command-line interface associated with Cisco switches and how switches differ and are comparable to routers in their troubleshooting. We will then look at the major internal *Application Specific Integrated Circuits* (ASICs) within the Cisco 5500 switch.

Catalyst Switches

This section will explore some of the members of the Catalyst family of switches. We will give a quick overview of the most popular switches merely to familiarize the reader with some of the capabilities. The Catalyst switches are constantly undergoing revisions in the models available and in the features of the individual models.

1900 Series

The Catalyst 1900 series is on the lower end of the switches available. The main features of the 1900 are as follows (see Figure 7-1):

- 12 or 24 switched 10BaseT ports
- Two 100BaseT ports
- Two 100BaseFX ports (Catalyst 1924F)
- A one-Gbps bus
- Shared memory architecture with a three-Mb packet buffer
- A FastEtherChannel up to four ports
- Support for four *virtual local area networks* (VLANs)

2900 Series

The Catalyst 2900 series of switches is a larger and more powerful switch than the 1900 series (see Figure 7-2). The major features are as follows:

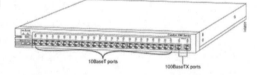

Figure 7-1
The Cisco 1900

Figure 7-2
The Cisco 2924

- 12, 22, 16 and 24 auto-sensing 10BaseT/100BaseTX ports
- Four-port 10BaseT/100BaseTX add-on switch modules
- Two-port and four-port 100BaseFX switch modules (two slots available)
- Future support for Gigabit Ethernet (1000BaseX) and OC-3 *Asynchronous Transfer Mode* (ATM)
- Up to 64 port-based VLANs per switch
- 3.2-Gbps switching fabric
- A FastEtherChannel up to eight ports
- Four-MB shared memory architecture

4000 Series

The Catalyst 4000 series is a larger and more powerful switch than the 2900 series and slightly less powerful than the 5000 series. The major features are as follows:

- Three-slot chassis
- A 10BaseT/100BaseTX with up to 96 ports
- A 1000BaseX Gigabit Ethernet with up to 36 ports
- Up to 64 port-based VLANs per switch
- A FastEtherChannel up to eight ports

5000 series

The Catalyst 5000 series is the mainstay of the Catalyst switch family (see Figure 7-3). The main features include

- Up to 264 10BaseT Ethernet interfaces
- Up to 134 100BaseFX Fast Ethernet interfaces
- Up to 134 100BaseTX Fast Ethernet Interfaces
- Up to 11 *Copper Data Distribution Interfaces* (CDDIs) or *Fiber Distributed Data Interfaces* (FDDI)
- Three 1.2-Gbps backplanes (see the following note)
- Up to 64 port-based VLANs per switch
- A FastEtherChannel up to eight ports
- Redundant Supervisor engines

Figure 7-3

The Cisco 5500

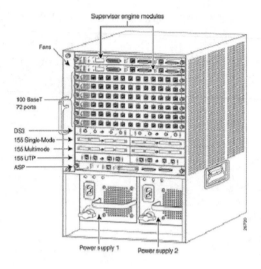

- Redundant, load-sharing power supplies
- Redundant sharing fans
- Redundant uplinks

NOTE: *The Cisco 5000 has a single 1.2-Gbps backplane. The Cisco 5500 is available with three separate 1.2-Gbps backplanes.*

The 6000 Series

The Catalyst 6000 series is one of the newest additions to the Catalyst family. This series of switches provides far more power than the 5000 series. Some of the major features include

- Six or nine slots, depending on the model
- Up to 48 ports per slot
- A Fast EtherChannel, up to eight ports
- A scalable backplane from 32 to 256 Gbps
- 130 Gigabit Ethernet ports
- 192 100FX Ethernet ports

- 384 10/100 Ethernet ports
- 192 10BaseFL ports
- Eight ATM OC-12 ports
- Redundant Supervisor engines
- Redundant, load-sharing power supplies
- Redundant sharing fans
- Redundant system clocks
- Redundant uplinks
- Redundant switch fabrics (Catalyst 6500 series only)

Command-Line Interface

Cisco switches enable configurations in two different ways: through a Web browser or through the *command-line interface* (CLI). Some people prefer to use the CLI because it can accomplish certain tasks more quickly than a Web browser.

The syntax for the CLI is extremely similar to the one used in Cisco routers. Chapter 4 dealt with how to diagnose issues with the Ethernet ports of routers. Virtually all of the same techniques, tips, and commands apply to switches. Any Ethernet interface on any Cisco equipment works in virtually the same way. The rules do not change when you move between a switch and a router.

The main differences between a router and a switch that are noticeable immediately deal with the serial interfaces and routing. Switches, generally speaking, do not have serial interfaces, so the commands associated with serial interfaces do not apply. Switches also do not route. Therefore, routing commands will not apply. For example, no command can show an IP route in a switch. The switch does not know or care about routing. If you are using an RSM within a switch, then the RSM supports the routing. However, the RSM is not really a switch. It is really a router that is mounted within the same physical box as the switch for convenience and speed. The only noticeable difference between an internal RSM and an external router is that the RSM connects in a virtual fashion to the VLANs and does not occupy a port like an external router. The RSM connects to the backplane of the switch at 400 Mbps with a half-duplex connection. Other than these two areas, treat an RSM as you would any other router.

The other differences you will notice on a switch are that added commands are available for use with technology that is switch-specific. For example, you will not be able to configure Spanning Tree on a router. Since Spanning Tree is specific to the *local area network* (LAN), a router is not concerned with the establishment or configuration of Spanning Tree.

On the CLI of a switch, the same as on a router, the most useful command is the "show" command. The output of a show command varies depending upon which options you have installed and the version of IOS running on the switch.

The following is output from a show command. Notice that this looks almost exactly like the output from a show command on a router. Some differences are apparent, such as the VLAN option, which is not available on routers:

```
switch#show ?
  access-lists         List access lists
  accounting           Accounting data for active sessions
  aliases              Display alias commands
  arp                  ARP table
  boot                 Show boot attributes
  buffers              Buffer pool statistics
  cdp                  CDP information
  cgmp                 Display CGMP information
  clock                Display the system clock
  configuration        Contents of Non-volatile memory
  controllers          Interface controller status
  debugging            State of each debugging option
  file                 Show filesystem information
  forward              Show Controller forwarding map
  history              Display the session command history
  hosts                IP domain-name, lookup style, nameservers, and
                       host table
  html                 HTML helper commands
  interfaces           Interface status and configuration
  ip                   IP information
  line                 TTY line information
  location             Display the system location
  logging              Show the contents of logging buffers
  mac-address-table    MAC forwarding table
  memory               Memory statistics
  port                 Show switch port configuration
  privilege            Show current privilege level
  processes            Active process statistics
  queue                Show queue contents
  queueing             Show queueing configuration
  registry             Function registry information
  reload               Scheduled reload information
  rhosts               Remote-host+user equivalences
  rmon                 rmon statistics
  running-config       Current operating configuration
  sessions             Information about Telnet connections
  snmp                 snmp statistics
  spanning-tree        Spanning tree topology
  stacks               Process stack utilization
  startup-config       Contents of startup configuration
  subsys               Show subsystem information
  tcp                  Status of TCP connections
```

```
tech-support      Show system information for tech support
terminal          Display terminal configuration parameters
users             Display information about terminal lines
version           System hardware and software status
vlan              VTP VLAN status
```

As with the CLI on routers, you can also "drill down" through the commands. One example is the "show cdp" command. You can use this command without a question mark to get the global information, as shown here:

```
switch#show cdp
Global CDP information:
        Sending CDP packets every 180 seconds
        Sending a holdtime value of 255 seconds
```

Alternatively, you can use a question mark to help you find the exact syntax of the command. Below, we first find all the options of the "show cdp" command, choose "neighbors" as the option we want, find the syntax for the "show neighbors detail," and get output from that command. Notice also that one of the options when working with switches is VLAN. This is not an option on a router. The output from the "show cdp neighbors detail" command has been truncated.

```
switch#show cdp ?
  entry      Information for specific neighbor entry
  holdtime   Time CDP info kept by neighbors
  interface  CDP interface status and configuration
  neighbors  CDP neighbor entries
  run        CDP Process running
  timer      Time CDP info is resent to neighbors
  traffic    CDP statistics
  <cr>

switch#show cdp neighbors ?
  FastEthernet  FastEthernet IEEE 802.3
  Null          Null interface
  VLAN          Switch VLAN Virtual Interface
  detail        Show detailed information
  <cr>

switch#show cdp neighbors detail

-------
Device ID: Switch.McGraw-Hill
Entry address(es):
  IP address: 172.30.2.11
Platform: Cisco WS-C2916M-XL,  Capabilities: Switch
Interface: FastEthernet0/2,  Port ID (outgoing port):
FastEthernet1/2
Holdtime : 133 sec

Version :
Cisco Internetwork Operating System Software
IOS (tm) C2900XL Software (C2900XL-H-M), Version 11.2(8)SA5,
RELEASE SOFTWARE ()
```

```
Copyright (c) 1986-1999 by Cisco Systems, Inc.
Compiled Tue 23-Mar-99 11:52 by rheaton


————————-
Device ID: Switch.McGraw-Hill
Entry address(es):
  IP address: 172.30.2.11
Platform: Cisco WS-C2916M-XL,  Capabilities: Switch
Interface: FastEthernet0/10,  Port ID (outgoing port):
FastEthernet1/3
Holdtime : 134 sec

Version :
Cisco Internetwork Operating System Software
IOS (tm) C2900XL Software (C2900XL-H-M), Version 11.2(8)SA5,
RELEASE SOFTWARE ()
Copyright (c) 1986-1999 by Cisco Systems, Inc.
Compiled Tue 23-Mar-99 11:52 by rheaton


————————-
Device ID: Switch.McGraw-Hill
Entry address(es):
  IP address: 172.30.2.11
Platform: Cisco WS-C2916M-XL,  Capabilities: Switch
Interface: FastEthernet0/1,  Port ID (outgoing port):
FastEthernet1/1
Holdtime : 131 sec

Version :
Cisco Internetwork Operating System Software
IOS (tm) C2900XL Software (C2900XL-H-M), Version 11.2(8)SA5,
RELEASE SOFTWARE ()
Copyright (c) 1986-1999 by Cisco Systems, Inc.
Compiled Tue 23-Mar-99 11:52 by rheaton


————————-
Device ID: Switch.McGraw-Hill
Entry address(es):
  IP address: 172.30.2.11
Platform: Cisco WS-C2916M-XL,  Capabilities: Switch
Interface: FastEthernet0/11,  Port ID (outgoing port):
FastEthernet1/4
Holdtime : 132 sec

Version :
Cisco Internetwork Operating System Software
IOS (tm) C2900XL Software (C2900XL-H-M), Version 11.2(8)SA5,
RELEASE SOFTWARE ()
Copyright (c) 1986-1999 by Cisco Systems, Inc.
Compiled Tue 23-Mar-99 11:52 by rheaton


————————-
Device ID: Cisco3640
Entry address(es):
  IP address: 172.30.1.3
Platform: Cisco 3640,  Capabilities: Router
Interface: FastEthernet2/4,  Port ID (outgoing port):
FastEthernet1/0
```

```
Holdtime : 134 sec

Version :
Cisco Internetwork Operating System Software
IOS (tm) 3600 Software (C3640-IS-M), Version 11.2(18)P,  RELEASE
SOFTWARE (fc1)
Copyright (c) 1986-1999 by Cisco Systems, Inc.
Compiled Mon 12-Apr-99 19:53 by ashah


--------
Device ID: second main room switch00902B52F380
Entry address(es):
  IP address: 172.30.2.9
Platform: Cisco 1900,  Capabilities: Trans-Bridge Switch
Interface: FastEthernet1/1,  Port ID (outgoing port): A
Holdtime : 142 sec

Version :
V8.00


--------
Device ID: McGraw-Hillddr
Entry address(es):
  IP address: 172.30.1.4
Platform: Cisco 2520,  Capabilities: Router
Interface: FastEthernet2/1,  Port ID (outgoing port): Ethernet0
Holdtime : 151 sec

Version :
Cisco Internetwork Operating System Software
IOS (tm) 3000 Software (IGS-IR-L), Version 11.0(9), RELEASE
SOFTWARE (fc1)
Copyright (c) 1986-1996 by Cisco Systems, Inc.
Compiled Tue 11-Jun-96 01:21 by loreilly
```

In the previous output, a single Cisco 2916 switch with the IP address of 172.30.2.11 is shown four times. The reason for this is that FastEther-Channel has been enabled with four ports connecting these switches. Each connection on a port group is shown separately. A Cisco 1924 switch is only shown once because there is a single connection to that switch instead of a port group. Two routers are also listed because they are Cisco equipment and partake in the CDP process.

Using the Show MAC command will reveal a number of facts about the switch. In the following example, notice that the maximum number of media access control (MAC) addresses is 2,048. This is because the command was run from a Cisco 2916 switch. Running the same command on a Cisco 5500 would reveal that the table could maintain 128,000 MAC addresses. The truncated example also shows the MAC addresses of each VLAN. In this case, there is a single VLAN. The same command on a router will not show any VLAN information.

```
switch#show mac
Dynamic Address Count:                      147
Secure Address (User-defined) Count:        0
Static Address (User-defined) Count:        0
System Self Address Count:                  50
Total MAC Addresses:                        197
Maximum MAC Addresses:                      2048
Non-static Address Table:
Destination Address   Address Type   VLAN   Destination Port
───────────────────   ────────────   ──     ────────────────
0000.0c91.83f1        Dynamic         1     FastEthernet2/1
0000.8501.13ec        Dynamic         1     FastEthernet1/3
0006.29ba.0627        Dynamic         1     FastEthernet0/6
0010.29e4.4b80        Dynamic         1     FastEthernet1/3
0010.29e4.4b9b        Dynamic         1     FastEthernet1/3
0010.4b2b.b632        Dynamic         1     FastEthernet0/14
0010.4b2b.b633        Dynamic         1     FastEthernet0/13
```

The "show config" command can be used on a switch as well as the "show run" or "show start" commands. The output received is similar to output from a router, with the exception of routing or switching specific information.

Looking at the following truncated output, several items deserve extra attention. First, notice the interface named VLAN1. It is connected to another switch that has established a VLAN1. The address of the switch that established the VLAN is shown within the VLAN1 interface. If there were more than one VLAN on this system, we would see multiple VLAN statements, each with a different number.

Second, notice that each individual port has a command that reads "spanning-tree portfast." This command sets the Spanning Tree protocols to take on a slightly different Cisco-proprietary form of Spanning Tree. We will discuss Spanning Tree and portfast further after this output has been examined.

Look through the sample configuration below carefully. We will discuss more items that bear notice after the configuration.

```
switch#show config
Using 4218 out of 32768 bytes
!
version 11.2
no service pad
no service udp-small-servers
no service tcp-small-servers
!
hostname switch
!
enable password cisco
!
!
ip domain-name McGraw-Hill
ip name-server 172.30.1.55
ip name-server 172.30.1.57
!
interface VLAN1
 ip address 172.30.1.9 255.255.0.0
```

```
 no ip route-cache
 !
interface FastEthernet0/1
 description 172.30.2.11
 speed 100
 duplex full
 port group 2
 spanning-tree portfast
 !
interface FastEthernet0/2
 description 172.30.2.11
 speed 100
 duplex full
 port group 2
 spanning-tree portfast
 !
interface FastEthernet0/3
 description 172.30.3.9
 speed 100
 duplex full
 port group 1
 spanning-tree portfast
 !
interface FastEthernet0/4
 description 172.30.3.9
 speed 100
 duplex full
 port group 1
 spanning-tree portfast
 !
interface FastEthernet0/5
 description 172.30.3.9
 speed 100
 duplex full
 port group 1
 spanning-tree portfast
 !
interface FastEthernet0/6
 description 172.30.3.9
 speed 100
 duplex full
 port group 1
 spanning-tree portfast
 !
interface FastEthernet0/7
 description 172.30.1.14
 speed 100
 duplex full
 port group 4
 !
interface FastEthernet0/8
 spanning-tree portfast
 !
interface FastEthernet0/9
 description 172.30.1.14
 speed 100
 duplex full
 port group 4
 !
interface FastEthernet0/10
```

```
 description 172.30.2.11
 speed 100
 duplex full
 port group 2
 spanning-tree portfast
!
interface FastEthernet0/11
 description 172.30.2.11
 speed 100
 duplex full
 port group 2
 spanning-tree portfast
!
interface FastEthernet0/12
 port monitor FastEthernet0/1
 port monitor FastEthernet0/2
 port monitor FastEthernet0/3
 port monitor FastEthernet0/4
 port monitor FastEthernet0/5
 port monitor FastEthernet0/6
 port monitor FastEthernet0/7
 port monitor FastEthernet0/8
 port monitor FastEthernet0/9
 port monitor FastEthernet0/10
 port monitor FastEthernet0/11
 port monitor FastEthernet0/13
 port monitor FastEthernet0/14
 port monitor FastEthernet0/15
 port monitor FastEthernet0/16
 port monitor FastEthernet1/1
 port monitor FastEthernet1/2
 port monitor FastEthernet1/3
 port monitor FastEthernet1/4
 port monitor FastEthernet2/1
 port monitor FastEthernet2/2
 port monitor FastEthernet2/4
 spanning-tree portfast
!
interface FastEthernet0/13
 description 172.30.2.14
 speed 100
 duplex full
 port group 3
 spanning-tree portfast
!
interface FastEthernet0/14
 description 172.30.2.14
 speed 100
 duplex full
 port group 3
 spanning-tree portfast
!
interface FastEthernet0/15
 description 172.30.2.14
 speed 100
 duplex full
 port group 3
 spanning-tree portfast
!
interface FastEthernet0/16
```

```
 description 172.30.2.14
 speed 100
 duplex full
 port group 3
 spanning-tree portfast
!
interface FastEthernet1/1
 description 172.30.2.9
!
interface FastEthernet1/2
 description 172.30.2.15
 speed 100
 duplex full
!
interface FastEthernet1/3
 description 172.30.2.9
 speed 100
 duplex full
!
interface FastEthernet1/4
 description 172.30.1.14
 speed 100
 duplex full
 port group 4
!
interface FastEthernet2/1
!
interface FastEthernet2/2
 description 172.30.1.14
 speed 100
 duplex full
 port group 4
!
interface FastEthernet2/3
 port monitor FastEthernet0/1
 port monitor FastEthernet0/2
 port monitor FastEthernet0/3
 port monitor FastEthernet0/4
 port monitor FastEthernet0/5
 port monitor FastEthernet0/6
 port monitor FastEthernet0/7
 port monitor FastEthernet0/8
 port monitor FastEthernet0/9
 port monitor FastEthernet0/10
 port monitor FastEthernet0/11
 port monitor FastEthernet0/12
 port monitor FastEthernet0/13
 port monitor FastEthernet0/14
 port monitor FastEthernet0/15
 port monitor FastEthernet0/16
 port monitor FastEthernet1/1
 port monitor FastEthernet1/2
 port monitor FastEthernet1/3
 port monitor FastEthernet1/4
 port monitor FastEthernet2/1
 port monitor FastEthernet2/2
 port monitor FastEthernet2/4

!
interface FastEthernet2/4
```

```
!
ip default-gateway 172.30.1.1
no logging buffered
no logging console
cdp timer 180
cdp holdtime 255
snmp-server community private RW
snmp-server community public RO
snmp-server location main server room
snmp-server contact Tom Thomas/Mark J. Newcomb/Andrew Mason
snmp-server chassis-id switch
!
line con 0
 exec-timeout 0 0
 stopbits 1
line vty 0 4
 password cisco
 login
line vty 5 9
 login
!
end
```

In the output, notice that several port groups are defined with the "port group" command. These are FastEtherChannel port groups. Every member of the group acts as if they were a single port. As long as at least one of the ports remains connected, the port group will continue to function. In other words, losing one connection in a group consisting of four ports will mean that the remaining three ports will carry the data as if they were one port. Four groups are defined, three of them with four ports belonging to each group, and one group with two members. In this case, group 4, with two members, is connected to a server (its IP address is 172.30.1.14) with a dual port Ethernet card, while the other groups are connected to switches. This server is also an example of a server that does not tend to hold a full-duplex 100-Mbps connection well. Therefore, the connection speed and duplex mode are enforced by putting in the "speed 100" and "duplex full" commands. It is not required that ports belonging to a port group be sequentially numbered.

If you want to quickly ascertain the ports belonging to a group, the "show port group" command enables you to gain the information quickly. The following example shows the four port groups on this switch and which ports are associated with each group:

```
switch#show port group
Group   Interface                 Transmit Distribution
-----   ---------                 --------------------
    1   FastEthernet0/3           source address
    1   FastEthernet0/4           source address
    1   FastEthernet0/5           source address
```

```
1    FastEthernet0/6           source address
2    FastEthernet0/1           source address
2    FastEthernet0/2           source address
2    FastEthernet0/10          source address
2    FastEthernet0/11          source address
3    FastEthernet0/13          source address
3    FastEthernet0/14          source address
3    FastEthernet0/15          source address
3    FastEthernet0/16          source address
4    FastEthernet0/7           source address
4    FastEthernet0/9           source address
4    FastEthernet1/4           source address
4    FastEthernet2/2           source address
```

Interface FastEthernet 2/4 is different than all of the other interfaces because it does not have a description, a speed, a port group, a portfast, or a duplex mode set. None of these commands are required by a switch to work. The description field is merely a way for the administrator to document what is connected to that port. In this configuration example, the descriptions are the IP addresses of the equipment connected to that port. The speed is automatically negotiated, as is the duplex mode. A port does not need to belong to a group, and portfast is enabled on a port-by-port basis. Port 2/4 is not currently in use.

Now let's look at interfaces FastEthernet 0/12 and FastEthernet 2/3. Notice that both of these have a list of ports that have SPAN enabled on them. The "port monitor" command is used to enable a port to watch the activity on any other port or ports. A port cannot monitor itself. A strange result of this SPAN configuration will become apparent after closely studying the way port monitoring is set up. When analyzers are connected to FastEthernet 0/12 and FastEthernet 2/3 simultaneously, their outputs are extremely different. The analyzer on port 2/3 shows twice the traffic as the one on 0/12. The reason for this is that port 2/3 is monitoring port 0/12, but port 0/12 is not monitoring port 2/3.

When using any analyzer, make sure you know exactly which ports you are looking at and their significance. For example, if we were to monitor ports 0/4, 0/5, and 0/6, we would not have an accurate analysis because these all belong to a single port group. However, the port group also contains port 0/3, which is not being monitored. When monitoring a member of a port group, it is advised that the whole group be monitored unless you are trying to troubleshoot something particular to that specific port. Even when this is the case, it is best to remove the port from the group and then analyze what the port is dong.

A quick way of finding out which ports are being monitored and which ports are monitoring is to use the "show port monitor" command. Here is a truncated example:

```
switch#show port monitor
Monitor Port                    Port Being Monitored

FastEthernet0/12                FastEthernet0/1
FastEthernet0/12                FastEthernet0/2
FastEthernet0/12                FastEthernet0/3
FastEthernet0/12                FastEthernet0/4
FastEthernet0/12                FastEthernet0/5
FastEthernet0/12                FastEthernet0/6
FastEthernet0/12                FastEthernet0/7
FastEthernet0/12                FastEthernet0/8
```

The original Spanning Tree may take over 30 seconds to recognize that a new loop has occurred or that a link has been broken. Part of how Spanning Tree works is by monitoring the status of ports and watching which ports are active and which are inactive. Enabling portfast makes Spanning Tree act upon changes in a port quickly, usually within five seconds. However, this is risky and some situations require portfast to be disabled. Specifically, these are usually situations where a connection is made, broken, and then reconnected, followed by an immediate request for a data transfer that does not work well with portfast. The reason for this is that Spanning Tree is being recalculated when the request for data is sent. This usually results in the program timing out because the port will not be able to communicate until Spanning Tree has completed the recalculation. Disabling portfast is one of the first things to try in the troubleshooting process if a connection cannot be established on the port. This causes the Spanning Tree protocol to revert its default state.

The "show spantree" command can be used to see the current Spanning Tree configuration, including the protocol used. If a port is in portfast mode, a line will indicate this, as in port FA0/4, but not in port FA0/1. A truncated example is shown here:

```
switch#show spantree

Spanning tree 1 is executing the IEEE compatible Spanning Tree
protocol
  Bridge Identifier has priority 32768, address 0010.0b3e.4240
  Configured hello time 2, max age 20, forward delay 15
  We are the root of the spanning tree
  Topology change flag not set, detected flag not set, changes 1598
  Times:  hold 1, topology change 35, notification 2
          hello 2, max age 20, forward delay 15
  Timers: hello 0, topology change 0, notification 0

Interface Fa0/4 (port 1) in Spanning tree 1 is FORWARDING
   Port path cost 8, Port priority 128
   Designated root has priority 32768, address 0010.0b3e.4240
   Designated bridge has priority 32768, address 0010.0b3e.4240
   Designated port is 1, path cost 0
   Timers: message age 0, forward delay 0, hold 0
```

```
    BPDU: sent 3742978, received 204
    The port is in the portfast mode

Interface Fa0/1 (port 2) in Spanning tree 1 is FORWARDING
    Port path cost 8, Port priority 128
    Designated root has priority 32768, address 0010.0b3e.4240
    Designated bridge has priority 32768, address 0010.0b3e.4240
    Designated port is 2, path cost 0
    Timers: message age 0, forward delay 0, hold 0
    BPDU: sent 3743918, received 1064
```

The "show interfaces" command works the same as on a router except that no serial interfaces exist and the additional interfaces associated with the VLANs and bridging are in effect. The "show interface ?" command lists the types of interfaces available on this particular switch. For example, a switch with Token Ring capabilities would also show "Token" as one of the options. A sample is shown here:

```
switch#show interface ?
  FastEthernet  FastEthernet IEEE 802.3
  Null          Null interface
  VLAN          Switch VLAN Virtual Interface
  accounting    Show interface accounting
  crb           Show interface routing/bridging info
  irb           Show interface routing/bridging info
  link-trap     Show interface traps on no link
  <cr>
```

The following is a truncated example of the "show interfaces" command. All of the references made in previous chapters regarding Ethernet interfaces hold true for switches. Note that the VLAN interface is shown first.

```
switch#show interface
VLAN1 is up, line protocol is up
  Hardware is CPU Interface, address is 0010.0b3e.4240 (bia
0010.0b3e.4240)
  Internet address is 172.30.1.9/16
  MTU 1500 bytes, BW 10000 Kbit, DLY 1000 usec, rely 255/255, load
1/255
  Encapsulation ARPA, loopback not set, keepalive not set
  ARP type: ARPA, ARP Timeout 04:00:00
  Last input 00:00:00, output 00:00:00, output hang never
  Last clearing of "show interface" counters never
  Queueing strategy: fifo
  Output queue 0/40, 0 drops; input queue 0/75, 0 drops
  5 minute input rate 8000 bits/sec, 8 packets/sec
  5 minute output rate 0 bits/sec, 0 packets/sec
      36770583 packets input, 3933542519 bytes, 0 no buffer
      Received 35742143 broadcasts, 0 runts, 2278 giants, 0
      throttles
      0 input errors, 0 CRC, 0 frame, 0 overrun, 671554 ignored, 0
      abort
      0 input packets with dribble condition detected
```

```
        1023243 packets output, 152063953 bytes, 0 underruns
        0 output errors, 0 collisions, 0 interface resets
        0 babbles, 0 late collision, 0 deferred
        0 lost carrier, 0 no carrier
        0 output buffer failures, 0 output buffers swapped out
FastEthernet0/1 is up, line protocol is up
   Hardware is Fast Ethernet, address is 0010.0b3e.4241 (bia
0010.0b3e.4241)
   Description: 172.30.2.11
   MTU 1500 bytes, BW 100000 Kbit, DLY 100 usec, rely 255/255, load
   1/255
   Encapsulation ARPA, loopback not set, keepalive not set
   Full-duplex, 100Mb/s, 100BaseTX/FX
   ARP type: ARPA, ARP Timeout 04:00:00
   Last input 00:01:14, output 00:00:00, output hang never
   Last clearing of "show interface" counters never
   Queueing strategy: fifo
   Output queue 0/40, 0 drops; input queue 0/75, 0 drops
   5 minute input rate 10000 bits/sec, 3 packets/sec
   5 minute output rate 5000 bits/sec, 4 packets/sec
        33964426 packets input, 412968702 bytes, 0 no buffer
        Received 1958291 broadcasts, 0 runts, 0 giants, 0 throttles
        0 input errors, 0 CRC, 0 frame, 0 overrun, 50 ignored, 0 abort
        0 watchdog, 81548 multicast
        0 input packets with dribble condition detected
        53703240 packets output, 765406926 bytes, 0 underruns
        0 output errors, 0 collisions, 3 interface resets
        0 babbles, 0 late collision, 0 deferred
        0 lost carrier, 0 no carrier
        0 output buffer failures, 0 output buffers swapped out
FastEthernet0/2 is up, line protocol is up
   Hardware is Fast Ethernet, address is 0010.0b3e.4242 (bia
0010.0b3e.4242)
   Description: 172.30.2.11
   MTU 1500 bytes, BW 100000 Kbit, DLY 100 usec, rely 255/255, load
   1/255
   Encapsulation ARPA, loopback not set, keepalive not set
   Full-duplex, 100Mb/s, 100BaseTX/FX
   ARP type: ARPA, ARP Timeout 04:00:00
   Last input 00:01:16, output 00:02:48, output hang never
   Last clearing of "show interface" counters never
   Queueing strategy: fifo
   Output queue 0/40, 0 drops; input queue 0/75, 0 drops
   5 minute input rate 0 bits/sec, 0 packets/sec
   5 minute output rate 0 bits/sec, 0 packets/sec
        40832820 packets input, 1463682290 bytes, 0 no buffer
        Received 3056442 broadcasts, 0 runts, 0 giants, 0 throttles
        6 input errors, 0 CRC, 6 frame, 0 overrun, 74 ignored, 0 abort
        0 watchdog, 659675 multicast
        0 input packets with dribble condition detected
        44746630 packets output, 2666412542 bytes, 0 underruns
        0 output errors, 0 collisions, 3 interface resets
        0 babbles, 0 late collision, 0 deferred
        0 lost carrier, 0 no carrier
        0 output buffer failures, 0 output buffers swapped out
```

To check on the IOS version currently running on the switch, use the "show ver" command. As in a router, this provides details about the switch, which version of the software you are running, the name of the flash file, how long the switch has been running, and the amount of memory on the switch. Here is a sample:

```
Switch#show ver
Cisco Internetwork Operating System Software
IOS (tm) C2900XL Software (C2900XL-H-M), Version 11.2(8)SA5,
RELEASE SOFTWARE ()
Copyright (c) 1986-1999 by cisco Systems, Inc.
Compiled Tue 23-Mar-99 11:52 by rheaton
Image text-base: 0x00003000, data-base: 0x001D0068

ROM: Bootstrap program is C2900XL boot loader

Switch uptime is 12 weeks, 2 days, 18 hours, 33 minutes
System restarted by power-on
System image file is "flash:c2900XL-h-mz-112.8-SA5.bin", booted via
interface


cisco WS-C2916M-XL (PowerPC403GA) processor (revision 0x11) with
4096K/640K byt.
Processor board ID 0x06, with hardware revision 0x00
Last reset from power-on

Processor is running Standard Edition Software
24 Ethernet/IEEE 802.3 interface(s)

32K bytes of flash-simulated non-volatile configuration memory.
Base Ethernet MAC Address: 00:90:F2:45:1D:40
Motherboard assembly number: 73-2193-09
Motherboard serial number: FAA02300214
System serial number: FAA0228V1FJ
Configuration register is 0xF
```

Probably the most important of the CLI commands on any piece of Cisco equipment is the "show tech" command. This command combines several other commands and results in single, consolidated output. As with routers, this command is usually run at the request of TAC personnel.

RMON

Remote Monitoring (RMON) can be enabled on the Catalyst 5000 family of routers through the use of an optional imbedded RMON agent residing in software on the supervisor engine. This agent, in conjunction with the corresponding *Management Information Base* (MIB), can be useful for the administrator interested in remotely monitoring his switches. Although

RFC 1757, which defines RMON, enables nine different categories of services, the Catalyst 5000 family only supports four types of services: Statistics, History, Alarms, and Events.

Statistics

The Statistics RMON service obviously delivers statistics. Specifically, statistics are available regarding frames and cells. Included in these statistics are numbers of collisions, runts, and jabbers. Also available are statistics regarding bandwidth utilization, broadcasts, and multicasts.

NOTE: *RMON statistics are also useful when creating the baseline for your network.*

History

History provides statistics for previous events. Although the Statistics RMON is concerned with the present moment, the History RMON is concerned with previously occurring data. This is useful for studying network trends and to let the administrator see how the network is performing over time. Third-party utilities are available that can greatly increase the usability of the History RMON.

Alarms

The Alarms RMON enables the administrator to set thresholds that, when exceeded, notify the administrator of certain events occurring in real time. This is typically used for items such as broadcast and collision levels or levels of excessively long Ethernet frames (jabbers). When the threshold set is exceeded, the RMON agent notifies the administrator. This enables the administrator to act quickly, usually before a person has reported the problem.

Events

The Events RMON relies on RMON traps to provide a log of issues in real time.

Power up Sequences and Lights

Most Cisco equipment has built-in indicator lights or lights built into the add-on modules that are placed in the slots. These indicator lights mean different things based upon the current state of the equipment. For example, a red light during the initialization phase means something entirely different than a red light after the initialization has completed.

It is helpful to remember some rules when using indicator lights to help in the troubleshooting process. The first rule is that lights can and will change colors during the initial booting process. The second rule is that once the process has completed, no red lights should be showing.

During normal operations, green lights indicate that all is well. Yellow lights indicate a potential problem and red indicates a real problem, usually a failure. For example, a yellow light on a switch port indicates a problem, such as the wrong speed or an incorrect duplex mode. However, when a single host directly connected to a port is turned on, the light will move between yellow, red, and green during the speed and duplex negotiation phases.

There is an exception to the above when working with the RSM module. The RSM module has a CPU halt light. This light will blink during normal operations. If the light stops blinking, this is an indication that the CPU has ceased to function.

Internal Components

It is necessary for us to know the major internal components of the Catalyst 5000 series switches if we expect to be able to troubleshoot them when they are not working. The Catalyst switch family has five major ASICs that are used in the frame switching process: the *Encoded Address Recognition Logic* (EARL), the *Synergy Advanced Gate-Array Engine* (SAGE), the *Synergy Advanced Interface and Network Termination* (SAINT), the *Synergy Advanced Multipurpose Bus Arbiter* (SAMBA), and the Phoenix.

An administrator really has no way to troubleshoot these individual components, but knowing which components control which aspects of the switch can help the overall troubleshooting process. For example, knowing that the Phoenix is responsible for transferring between backplanes may help if the problem is that Ethernet data does not appear to be showing up on the ATM *LAN emulation* (LANE). Using the appropriate show and debug commands can help the administrator isolate the problem.

The Encoded Address Recognition Logic (EARL)

The EARL chip coordinates with the bus arbitration system to control access to the data-switching bus. Additionally, the EARL is responsible for determining the destination port of a frame. Technically, the EARL is responsible for giving permission to a frame to leave a port. See the section on the SAINT for more details.

The EARL watches each frame crossing over all the ports and uses the destination and source addresses within the frames to build a table containing the MAC address, the port the MAC address sits on, and the VLAN ID associated with the MAC address. This table checks the ages of the entries and removes them after 300 seconds by default. The administrator may change this default to a value between one and 20 minutes. The EARL is considered intelligent because it "learns" the port and VLAN associated with the MAC address.

The Synergy Advanced Gate-Array Engine (SAGE)

The SAGE handles switching for FDDI, ATM LANE, and Token Ring, as well as ISL encapsulation. The SAGE consists of individual buffers for each port on both the inbound and outbound sides.

The Synergy Advanced Interface and Network Termination (SAINT)

The SAINT works similarly to the SAGE except only on Ethernet. Each Ethernet port has a 168-KB outbound buffer and a 24-KB inbound buffer for Ethernet frames. These two buffers together total 192 KB and are used to hold the frames during the store-and-forward switching on the Catalyst 5000.

NOTE: *The Catalyst 5000 and 5500 use only the store-and-forward method of frame switching. In this family of switches, each frame is actually sent to every port on the switch. The EARL enables a port or ports to transmit the frame based upon the MAC/VLAN/port table. The EARL telling the master SAMBA to release or purge data from a port does this. One of the reasons that each port has so much buffer space is to hold these frames until the EARL either releases them through the port or tells the port to discard the frame.*

The Synergy Advanced Multipurpose Bus Arbiter (SAMBA)

The SAMBA is actually a group of ASICs with a single ASIC located on each supervisor and line module. SAMBA works in either master or slave mode depending where it is located. The purpose of the SAMBA is to suppress broadcasts above the thresholds set by the administrator.

The SAMBA on the supervisor module acts as the master, while all others act as slaves. In master mode, SAMBA can address 13 line modules. In slave mode, SAMBA can serve a maximum of 48 ports. This is the reason line cards are limited to 48 ports per card and a Catalyst 5500 may only have 13 line cards. A slave must wait for permission from the master SAMBA, which has received the information from the EARL, before releasing data or purging from a port.

The Phoenix

The Phoenix ASIC is responsible for connecting the three 1.2-Gbps backplanes within the Catalyst 5500 chassis. This connection is known as the *crossbar fabric* of the switch and transfers data between the three backplanes.

The Phoenix also enables legacy-line modules such as line modules from a Catalyst 5000 to be used in the Catalyst 5500. This saves the administrator some money by enabling them to upgrade the chassis without being forced to purchase all new cards.

NOTE: *Some confusion may exist over how much data the Catalyst 5500 can carry over the backplane. The reason for this appears to be centered between single and multiple backplanes.*

Newer Catalyst 5500s, utilizing the Supervisor III module, actually have three backplanes. Each backplane can carry up to 1.2 Gbps of data. If all three backplanes are running without transferring data between themselves, then the Catalyst 500 can indeed carry a theoretical 3.2 Gbps. However, when data is transferred from one backplane to another, the limit of both backplanes must be observed. For example, if the Ethernet backplane is full and ATM data must be transferred, there must be a waiting period until the Ethernet backplane can handle the load. Older Catalyst 5500s, shipped with the Supervisor II Module, have a single 1.2 Gbps backplane.

Chapter Summary

This chapter has shown you the information necessary to troubleshoot switches. You should have noticed that topics such as how to troubleshoot Ethernet have not been addressed in this chapter. The reason for this is that such topics are covered in previous chapters. An Ethernet interface works the same on a router as on a switch.

A few items need reinforcement as this chapter ends and before moving to the next section, which deals with *wide area networks* (WANs). First, Ethernet is easy to troubleshoot if you know how it works. Chapter 4, "Basic Diagnostic Commands," provided the background necessary to effectively approach basic Ethernet issues. Second, Ethernet works the same whether you are using hubs, switches, or a combination of them. Third, any Cisco device can utilize the same debug and show commands for troubleshooting an Ethernet interface. Finally, the main new issues introduced by switches are VLANs, Spanning Tree, and SPAN.

Frequently Asked Questions (FAQ)

Question: Does SPAN affect switch performance?

Answer: Yes. Because each frame must be duplicated and carried across the backplane, SPAN may adversely affect the throughput of switches, especially the lower end switches.

Question: I still haven't made a baseline for my network. I do have a new 2900 switch at the center of my network. Can I still make a baseline?

Answer: It is never too late to create a baseline for your network. The added capabilities of RMON may make your job a lot easier than it was without the switch.

Question: Is it better to get one large switch or several smaller switches?

Answer: Although a larger switch may provide more ports, this is not always a benefit. It may be easier to convince the decision-maker to buy one small switch at a time and then connect them together using FastEtherChannel.

Question: Are there any disadvantages to using a FastEtherChannel link between two switches?

Answer: The only disadvantage is the number of ports used. If you have a medium-sized switch in the center of your network, you may use most or even all of your ports connecting to other switches via FastEtherChannel.

Questions

1. Which command can be used to show port groups?

    a. show port
    b. show group
    c. show port group
    d. show modules

2. Which command can be used to show both the Ethernet and ATM interfaces on a switch?

    a. show ethernet
    b. show interfaces
    c. show controllers
    d. show ip route

3. Which command will show the version of the software running on a switch?

    a. show run
    b. show port
    c. show config
    d. show ver

4. How many ports are on a Cisco 1924 switch?

    a. 24
    b. 16
    c. 12
    d. 8

5. Which of the following is responsible for connecting the backplanes in a Cisco 5500 switch?

    a. SAMBA
    b. SAINT
    c. EARL
    d. Phoenix

6. Which of the following is an intelligent ASIC that is responsible for determining the destination port for an Ethernet frame?

    a. SAMBA
    b. SAINT
    c. EARL
    d. Phoenix

7. Which of the following is responsible for bus arbitration on a Cisco 5500?

   a. SAMBA

   b. SAINT

   c. EARL

   d. Phoenix

8. Which command can be used to quickly determine the ports being monitored with SPAN?

   a. show port

   b. show port monitor

   c. show monitor

   d. show monitor port

9. What is shown when using the "show cdp neighbor detail" command on a switch?

   a. All directly connected Cisco equipment running the CDP protocol

   b. All directly connected Cisco switches running the CDP protocol

   c. All directly connected Cisco equipment

   d. All directly connected Cisco switches

10. Which command will add a port into FastEtherChannel group 1?

   a. fastetherchannel group 1

   b. fast group 1

   c. port group 1

   d. port fast 1

11. Which command is used to show the port that a MAC address is associated with?

   a. show span

   b. show mac

   c. show mac port

   d. show port mac

12. Which command will ensure that you are running the IEEE version of the Spanning Tree protocol?

   a. show ver

   b. show span

   c. show tree

   d. show span-tree protocol-type

13. You have just done a "show cdp neighbor detail" command. You see a single switch listed three times. What is the problem?

    a. There is no problem. This is normal.
    b. The CDP protocol is running incorrectly.
    c. One port has gone down.
    d. Two ports have gone down.

14. What command will force a port to run only at 100 Mbps?

    a. speed 100mbps
    b. speed full
    c. speed 10
    d. speed 100

15. What command will force a port to run at full duplex?

    a. duplex full
    b. duplex half
    c. full duplex
    d. full-duplex

16. What are the four types of service supported by Cisco switches?

    a. Statistics, History, Alarms, Events
    b. Statistics, Alarms, Triggers, Events
    c. Statistics, Triggers, Events, Alternatives
    d. Thresholds, Previous, Current, Baseline

17. Which answer corresponds to the type(s) of frame switching that are available on a Cisco 5500 switch?

    a. cut-through
    b. fragment-free
    c. store-and-forward
    d. All of the above

18. Which ASIC is responsible for releasing a frame through a port?

    a. SAMBA
    b. SAINT
    c. EARL
    d. Phoenix

19. Which ASIC limits the number of ports on a card to 48?

    a. SAMBA

    b. SAINT

    c. EARL

    d. Phoenix

20. What does a flashing red CPU halt light on an RSM module mean?

    a. The RSM is running.

    b. The RSM has a minor problem.

    c. The RSM has a major problem.

Answers

1. Answer: c

   Although answer A is almost correct, the full syntax is shown in answer c.

2. Answer: b

   The "show interfaces" command will show the Ethernet and ATM interfaces on a switch.

3. Answer: d

4. Answer: b

   Although not specifically addressed in this book, most lower-end Cisco routers use the last two digits of the model number to designate the number of ports.

5. Answer: d

6. Answer: c

7. Answer: a

8. Answer: b

   "show port monitor" is the correct command.

9. Answer: a

   "show cdp neighbors detail" will show all directly connected Cisco equipment that is using the CDP protocol.

10. Answer: c

    "port group 1" will add the port to port group number 1. FastEther-Channel is another way of saying port group.

11. Answer: b

    "show mac" will show all known MAC addresses and the port over which the address is known.

12. Answer: b

    "show span" will show configuration information about the Spanning Tree protocol, including the fact that IEEE Spanning Tree is running.

13. Answer: c

    Answer c is the only possible answer. A neighbor connected through a port group will be listed once for each connection in that port group. Since port groups must be made with groups of two, four, or eight ports, this indicates that one port within the original group of four has gone down. The only other alternative, which was not listed as a possible answer, is that five of the original eight ports have gone down.

14. Answer: d

"speed 100" will force the port to run at 100 Mbps. "speed 10" will force a port to run at 10 Mbps.

15. Answer: a

"duplex full" will force the port to run at full duplex. "duplex half" will force a port to run at half duplex.

16. Answer: a

The four types of RMON services available on Cisco switches are Statistics, History, Alarms, and Events.

17. Answer: c

Cisco 5500 switches can only use the store-and-forward method of frame switching.

18. Answer: c

The EARL is responsible for determining when a frame may be delivered through a port.

19. Answer: a

A SAMBA in slave mode can operate up to 48 ports.

20. Answer: a

The RSM is an exception to the rule that a red light means a failure. The CPU halt light flashing red on the RSM means that the RSM is still running.

Wide Area
Networks

## CHAPTER 8

Serial, Frame Relay, and X.25 Connectivity

This chapter provides an overview of serial, Frame Relay, and X.25 connectivity, as well as the troubleshooting methods that are available for common problems relating to the use of these protocols. We will cover the technical attributes of each protocol, explaining the way it is integrated on Cisco hardware, before looking at specific troubleshooting commands that resolve the majority of common problems. We'll cover router diagnostic tools and explain the show and debug commands that are available.

The best place to start when troubleshooting any network-related problem is at the physical layer of the OSI model. We will adopt this layered systematic troubleshooting approach in this chapter to reduce the amount of time it takes to resolve a serial, Frame Relay, or X.25-related network problem.

Objectives Covered in the Chapter

This chapter introduces you to troubleshooting serial, Frame Relay and X.25 connectivity. The following objectives will be covered:

■ Analyze problem symptoms and resolve resolution strategies in TCP/IP (including the Microsoft 95/NT IP stack), Novell IPX, AppleTalk, Ethernet virtual local area networks (VLANs), Frame Relay, and ISDN Basic Rate Interface (BRI).

■ Use Cisco IOS commands and problem-isolation techniques to identify the symptoms of common wide area network (WAN) and Frame Relay problems.

■ Apply diagnostic tools to trouble tickets and solve classroom network Frame Relay problems that simulate real-life WAN malfunctions.

Overview of Serial Lines

Cisco routers come with many interface types. These can roughly be broken down into two distinct areas: LAN interfaces and WAN interfaces.

LAN interfaces are usually Ethernet, Fast Ethernet, and Token Ring. These interfaces are high-speed and are provided over a similar physical connection. LAN-based connections normally connect the router to the local LAN segments and they provide routing between the LAN segments as well as routing to the WAN.

WAN interfaces generally operate at slower speeds and usually interconnect LANs. The WAN provides connectivity between the LANs at the numerous sites within an organization. WAN interfaces are usually serial interfaces. These are available in Asynchronous (Async) and Synchronous (Sync) flavors. The Async version is usually slower and used in legacy connectivity. Serial interfaces usually are presented in newer Cisco routers as DB-60 connectors and they support speeds of up to 4,096 Kbps. A range of services are available over these interfaces. These include *High-Level Data Link Control* (HDLC), Frame Relay, X.25, and *Switched Multimegabit Data Service* (SMDS).

The physical layer interface is common to all of these differing WAN connectivity methods with only the encapsulation and framing at the data-link layer differing. The default encapsulation type for these interfaces is HDLC and no command is required to configure this.

The *encapsulation* command is the first step in setting the type of WAN protocol that the interface uses. As previously stated, the default type is HDLC. For example, we can take this simple configuration for Serial0:

```
interface Serial0
 ip address 194.73.134.222 255.255.255.0
 no ip mroute-cache
 no ip route-cache
```

When we look at the interface with the show interface s0 command, we get the following output:

```
Router#sh int s0
Serial0 is down, line protocol is down
  Hardware is HD64570
  Internet address is 194.73.134.222/24
  MTU 1500 bytes, BW 1544 Kbit, DLY 20000 usec, rely 255/255, load
  1/255
  Encapsulation HDLC, loopback not set, keepalive set (10 sec)
  Last input never, output never, output hang never
  Last clearing of "show interface" counters never
  Input queue: 0/75/0 (size/max/drops); Total output drops: 0
  Queueing strategy: weighted fair
  Output queue: 0/64/0 (size/threshold/drops)
     Conversations  0/0 (active/max active)
     Reserved Conversations 0/0 (allocated/max allocated)
  5 minute input rate 0 bits/sec, 0 packets/sec
  5 minute output rate 0 bits/sec, 0 packets/sec
     0 packets input, 0 bytes, 0 no buffer
     Received 0 broadcasts, 0 runts, 0 giants
     0 input errors, 0 CRC, 0 frame, 0 overrun, 0 ignored, 0 abort
     0 packets output, 0 bytes, 0 underruns
     0 output errors, 0 collisions, 10 interface resets
     0 output buffer failures, 0 output buffers swapped out
     0 carrier transitions
     DCD=down  DSR=down  DTR=down  RTS=down  CTS=down
Router#
```

It is apparent that the HDLC encapsulation has been used, even though there is no mention of it in the interface configuration.

Other encapsulation types available from the interface configuration mode include the following:

```
Router(config-if)#encapsulation ?
  atm-dxi      ATM-DXI encapsulation
  frame-relay  Frame Relay networks
  hdlc         Serial HDLC synchronous
  lapb         LAPB (X.25 Level 2)
  ppp          Point-to-Point protocol
```

```
smds          Switched Megabit Data Service (SMDS)
x25           X.25

Router(config-if)#
```

The advent of new technologies is now seeing traditional, slow WAN links being replaced with faster links that utilize LAN ports. For example, a service is available in the U.K. that connects offices using Ethernet over a Fast Ethernet port. This provides 100 Mbps of full duplex between two remote offices.

This first section is going to look at the default HDLC encapsulation and explain a useful troubleshooting methodology for resolving HDLC problems. For a more technical overview of HDLC, refer to the Cisco Press *Internetworking Technologies Handbook* or visit www.cisco.com.

Show Commands

Several show commands can be used to view the current serial interface configuration of the router. These commands are useful for checking the status of the configuration as well as troubleshooting a range of serial interface problems (see Table 8-1).

show interface

The *show interface* command displays information about the configured interfaces on the router along with basic network layer settings such as IP

Table 8-1	Command	Description
Frequently Used Show Commands for Troubleshooting Serial Interfaces	show interface	Displays the current configured interfaces on the router.
	show controllers	Displays the status of the interface controllers on the router.
	show buffers	Displays detailed information about the buffer pool statistics on the router.

and IPX addressing. Only the serial interfaces are shown in the following router listing:

```
Router#sh int
Serial0 is up, line protocol is up
  Hardware is HD64570
  Description: MEGASTREAM LINK TO HEAD OFFICE
  Internet address is 197.35.38.18 255.255.255.252
  MTU 1500 bytes, BW 2000 Kbit, DLY 20000 usec, rely 255/255, load
  4/255
  Encapsulation HDLC, loopback not set, keepalive set (10 sec)
  Last input 0:00:00, output 0:00:00, output hang never
  Last clearing of "show interface" counters never
  Input queue: 0/75/0 (size/max/drops); Total output drops: 12959
  Output queue: 0/64/12959 (size/threshold/drops)
     Conversations  0/9 (active/max active)
     Reserved Conversations 0/0 (allocated/max allocated)
  30 second input rate 13000 bits/sec, 24 packets/sec
  30 second output rate 34000 bits/sec, 34 packets/sec
     10802604 packets input, 752275278 bytes, 77305 no buffer
     Received 621744 broadcasts, 0 runts, 0 giants
     0 input errors, 0 CRC, 0 frame, 0 overrun, 0 ignored, 0 abort
     19899630 packets output, 2037713881 bytes, 0 underruns
     0 output errors, 0 collisions, 2 interface resets, 0 restarts
     0 output buffer failures, 0 output buffers swapped out
     0 carrier transitions
     DCD=up  DSR=up  DTR=up  RTS=up  CTS=up
Serial1 is up, line protocol is up
  Hardware is HD64570
  Description: MEGASTREAM LINK TO NODE1
  Internet address is 197.35.37.26 255.255.255.252
  MTU 1500 bytes, BW 2000 Kbit, DLY 20000 usec, rely 255/255, load
  3/255
  Encapsulation HDLC, loopback not set, keepalive set (10 sec)
  Last input 0:00:00, output 0:00:00, output hang never
  Last clearing of "show interface" counters never
  Input queue: 0/75/0 (size/max/drops); Total output drops: 1039
  Output queue: 0/64/1039 (size/threshold/drops)
     Conversations  0/7 (active/max active)
     Reserved Conversations 0/0 (allocated/max allocated)
  30 second input rate 11000 bits/sec, 26 packets/sec
  30 second output rate 31000 bits/sec, 20 packets/sec
     13794059 packets input, 839509385 bytes, 75793 no buffer
     Received 329259 broadcasts, 0 runts, 0 giants
     3 input errors, 3 CRC, 0 frame, 0 overrun, 0 ignored, 1 abort
     12229800 packets output, 1706860106 bytes, 1 underruns
     0 output errors, 0 collisions, 1 interface resets, 0 restarts
     0 output buffer failures, 0 output buffers swapped out
     0 carrier transitions
     DCD=up  DSR=up  DTR=up  RTS=up  CTS=up
Serial2 is up, line protocol is up
  Hardware is HD64570
  Description: EPS9 LINK TO CHARLES RO
  Internet address is 164.35.48.9 255.255.255.252
  MTU 1500 bytes, BW 128 Kbit, DLY 20000 usec, rely 255/255, load
  1/255
```

```
    Encapsulation HDLC, loopback not set, keepalive set (10 sec)
    Last input 0:00:05, output 0:00:01, output hang never
    Last clearing of "show interface" counters never
    Input queue: 0/75/0 (size/max/drops); Total output drops: 0
    Output queue: 0/64/0 (size/threshold/drops)
        Conversations  0/3 (active/max active)
        Reserved Conversations 0/0 (allocated/max allocated)
    5 minute input rate 0 bits/sec, 0 packets/sec
    5 minute output rate 0 bits/sec, 0 packets/sec
        550277 packets input, 40092684 bytes, 0 no buffer
        Received 298712 broadcasts, 0 runts, 0 giants
        17551 input errors, 17492 CRC, 912 frame, 0 overrun, 1
        ignored, 3154 abort
        1156612 packets output, 344567680 bytes, 0 underruns
        0 output errors, 0 collisions, 1 interface resets, 0 restarts
        0 output buffer failures, 0 output buffers swapped out
        772 carrier transitions
        DCD=up  DSR=up  DTR=up  RTS=up  CTS=up
Serial3 is administratively down, line protocol is down
    Hardware is HD64570
    Internet address is 197.35.48.13 255.255.255.252
    MTU 1500 bytes, BW 64 Kbit, DLY 20000 usec, rely 255/255, load 1/255
    Encapsulation HDLC, loopback not set, keepalive set (10 sec)
    Last input never, output never, output hang never
    Last clearing of "show interface" counters never
    Input queue: 0/75/0 (size/max/drops); Total output drops: 0
    Output queue: 0/64/0 (size/threshold/drops)
        Conversations  0/0 (active/max active)
        Reserved Conversations 0/0 (allocated/max allocated)
    5 minute input rate 0 bits/sec, 0 packets/sec
    5 minute output rate 0 bits/sec, 0 packets/sec
        0 packets input, 0 bytes, 0 no buffer
        Received 0 broadcasts, 0 runts, 0 giants
        0 input errors, 0 CRC, 0 frame, 0 overrun, 0 ignored, 0 abort
        0 packets output, 0 bytes, 0 underruns
        0 output errors, 0 collisions, 0 interface resets, 0 restarts
        0 output buffer failures, 0 output buffers swapped out
        0 carrier transitions
        DCD=down  DSR=down  DTR=down  RTS=down  CTS=down
Router#
```

This command gives general statistics for every configured interface on the router. You can further restrict this command by entering the interface type and number after the command. Here's an example:

```
Router#show int ser 0
```

This would display the interface statistics for only Serial0. A lot of troubleshooting information can be obtained from this command. We can see that interface Serial0 is up as well as the line protocol. Take a look at Serial3 and you will notice that this interface is administratively down and so is the line protocol. When an interface is administratively down, it is usually due to the *shutdown* command that has been entered against the interface in the configuration. This is an important point to check as some interfaces are in the down state upon initial configuration.

The network layer address for the interface is also shown. In this instance for Serial0, the network addressing protocol is IP and the address is 197.35.38.18 with a mask of 255.255.255.252.

We can also see that the encapsulation method on this interface is HDLC, which is the default encapsulation method for all serial interfaces found on Cisco equipment. The earlier code also indicates that the current counters have been running since the router was powered on and have never been cleared. It is sometimes a good idea to clear the interface counters when you are troubleshooting interface problems.

The next two sections, starting with 0/75/0 and 0/64/12959, represent the input and output statistics for the interface. The input statistics are shown as size/max/drops and the output statistics are shown as size/threshold/drops. The values to be concerned with in both instances are the drops. Output drops occur when the router passes a packet to a transmit buffer, but no buffer is available. In this instance, it is important to check broadcast traffic, such as SAP announcements, and alter the size of the output hold queue. Input drops occur when the rate of information inbound to an interface is more than it can process. This can occur when switching from a fast interface to a slower one or from a fast Ethernet interface to a ISDN BRI.

show controllers

The *show controllers* command displays the status of the interface controllers on the router:

```
Router#sh contr
HD unit 0, NIM slot 1, NIM type code 12, NIM version 5
idb = 0x6082FC48, driver structure at 0x60834118, regaddr =
0x3C100000
buffer size 1524   Universal Serial: DTE V.35 cable
cpb = 0x17, eda = 0x90A0, cda = 0x90B4
RX ring with 32 entries at 0x40179000
00 bd_ptr=0x9000 pak=0x60836E20 ds=0x40184CBC status=80 pak_size=64
...
Output Omitted
...
32 bd_ptr=0x9280 pak=0x6083A670 ds=0x401931B4 status=80 pak_size=12
cpb = 0x17, eda = 0x9828, cda = 0x9828
TX ring with 2 entries at 0x40179800
00 bd_ptr=0x9800 pak=0x000000 ds=0x4022004A status=80 pak_size=534
01 bd_ptr=0x9814 pak=0x000000 ds=0x4022E550 status=80 pak_size=148
02 bd_ptr=0x9828 pak=0x000000 ds=0x401B358C status=80 pak_size=20
0 missed datagrams, 0 overruns
0 bad datagram encapsulations, 0 memory errors
```

```
0 transmitter underruns
HD unit 1, NIM slot 1, NIM type code 12, NIM version 5
idb = 0x6083E210, driver structure at 0x608426E0, regaddr =
0x3C100000
buffer size 1524   Universal Serial: DTE V.35 cable
cpb = 0x1A, eda = 0x292C, cda = 0x2940
RX ring with 32 entries at 0x401A2800
00 bd_ptr=0x2800 pak=0x608441B0 ds=0x401A9AA8 status=80 pak_size=10
...
Output Omitted
...
32 bd_ptr=0x2A80 pak=0x60843B10 ds=0x401A7FB8 status=80 pak_size=12
cpb = 0x1A, eda = 0x3014, cda = 0x3014
TX ring with 2 entries at 0x401A3000
00 bd_ptr=0x3000 pak=0x000000 ds=0x402357BE status=80 pak_size=277
01 bd_ptr=0x3014 pak=0x000000 ds=0x40001A9C status=80 pak_size=39
02 bd_ptr=0x3028 pak=0x000000 ds=0x40191D80 status=80 pak_size=143
0 missed datagrams, 0 overruns
0 bad datagram encapsulations, 0 memory errors
1 transmitter underruns
HD unit 2, NIM slot 1, NIM type code 12, NIM version 5
idb = 0x6084C7D8, driver structure at 0x60850CA8, regaddr =
0x3C110000
buffer size 1524   Universal Serial: DTE V.11 (X.21) cable
cpb = 0x1C, eda = 0xC26C, cda = 0xC280
RX ring with 32 entries at 0x401CC000
00 bd_ptr=0xC000 pak=0x608516E8 ds=0x401CEF50 status=80
pak_size=386
...
Output Omitted
...
32 bd_ptr=0xC280 pak=0x608539B0 ds=0x401D7CBC status=80
pak_size=386
cpb = 0x1C, eda = 0xC828, cda = 0xC828
TX ring with 2 entries at 0x401CC800
00 bd_ptr=0xC800 pak=0x000000 ds=0x401A2DA4 status=80 pak_size=64
01 bd_ptr=0xC814 pak=0x000000 ds=0x401A2DA4 status=80 pak_size=24
02 bd_ptr=0xC828 pak=0x000000 ds=0x402726A4 status=80 pak_size=1422
1 missed datagrams, 0 overruns
0 bad datagram encapsulations, 0 memory errors
0 transmitter underruns
HD unit 3, NIM slot 1, NIM type code 12, NIM version 5
idb = 0x6085ADA0, driver structure at 0x6085F270, regaddr =
0x3C110000
buffer size 1524   Universal Serial: No cable
cpb = 0x1F, eda = 0x5A80, cda = 0x5800
RX ring with 32 entries at 0x401F5800
00 bd_ptr=0x5800 pak=0x6085F468 ds=0x401F65A4 status=80 pak_size=0
...
Output Omitted
...
32 bd_ptr=0x5A80 pak=0x60862968 ds=0x40203D24 status=80 pak_size=0
cpb = 0x1F, eda = 0x6000, cda = 0x6000
TX ring with 2 entries at 0x401F6000
00 bd_ptr=0x6000 pak=0x000000 ds=0x000000 status=80 pak_size=0
01 bd_ptr=0x6014 pak=0x000000 ds=0x000000 status=80 pak_size=0
02 bd_ptr=0x6028 pak=0x000000 ds=0x000000 status=80 pak_size=0
0 missed datagrams, 0 overruns
0 bad datagram encapsulations, 0 memory errors
```

```
        0 transmitter underruns
    Router#
```

The output of this command indicates the state of the interface channels and whether a cable is attached to the interface. This is useful for remote troubleshooting a serial interface at the physical layer. If a cable fault occurs, no cable is shown in the output of this command. We can see at the beginning of the section that the first serial interface uses a Data Terminal Equipment (DTE) V.35 cable.

show buffers

The *show buffers* command displays detailed information about the buffer pool statistics on the router:

```
Router#sh buff
Buffer elements:
     499 in free list (500 max allowed)
     135657197 hits, 0 misses, 0 created

Public buffer pools:
Small buffers, 104 bytes (total 50, permanent 50):
     50 in free list (20 min, 150 max allowed)
     39530180 hits, 492078 misses, 15190 trims, 15190 created
     425077 failures (439 no memory)
Middle buffers, 600 bytes (total 25, permanent 25):
     23 in free list (10 min, 150 max allowed)
     4006550 hits, 924 misses, 1246 trims, 1246 created
     78 failures (0 no memory)
Big buffers, 1524 bytes (total 50, permanent 50):
     49 in free list (5 min, 150 max allowed)
     1813606 hits, 250 misses, 349 trims, 349 created
     26 failures (0 no memory)
VeryBig buffers, 4520 bytes (total 10, permanent 10):
     10 in free list (0 min, 100 max allowed)
     527679 hits, 85 misses, 85 trims, 85 created
     0 failures (0 no memory)
Large buffers, 5024 bytes (total 0, permanent 0):
     0 in free list (0 min, 10 max allowed)
     0 hits, 0 misses, 0 trims, 0 created
     0 failures (0 no memory)
Huge buffers, 18024 bytes (total 0, permanent 0):
     0 in free list (0 min, 4 max allowed)
     0 hits, 0 misses, 0 trims, 0 created
     0 failures (0 no memory)

Interface buffer pools:
Serial0 buffers, 1524 bytes (total 96, permanent 96):
     63 in free list (0 min, 96 max allowed)
     10133395 hits, 0 fallbacks
     0 max cache size, 0 in cache
Serial1 buffers, 1524 bytes (total 96, permanent 96):
```

```
      63 in free list (0 min, 96 max allowed)
      13752126 hits, 0 fallbacks
      0 max cache size, 0 in cache
Serial2 buffers, 1524 bytes (total 96, permanent 96):
      63 in free list (0 min, 96 max allowed)
      550314 hits, 0 fallbacks
      0 max cache size, 0 in cache
Serial3 buffers, 1524 bytes (total 96, permanent 96):
      63 in free list (0 min, 96 max allowed)
      33 hits, 0 fallbacks
      0 max cache size, 0 in cache
Router#
```

This command displays information relating to the internal public buffers as well as the interface-specific buffers. Only the public buffers can be administered and great care should be taken because alterations can greatly reduce system performance.

Small buffers are 104-byte-long buffers that are used during switching from one interface to another. A large number of misses in any buffer indicates that the minimum number of buffers and the number of permanent buffers should be increased.

Debug Commands

The Debug commands are an excellent way to interrogate the router and receive real-time information regarding the state of serial interface connections at various OSI layers. As always, only use debug commands when it is necessary to do so and be careful when using them on busy core production routers. Debugging puts a load on the router's central processing unit (CPU) and can have a detrimental effect on the network. After every debugging session, always use the "Router#no debug all" command to turn off all debug events.

debug serial interface

The *debug serial interface* command is the most frequently used debug command when troubleshooting serial interfaces. It displays debug information about serial interface events:

```
Router#debug serial inter
Serial network interface debugging is on
Serial0: HDLC myseq 213481, mineseen 213481, yourseen 213418, line up
Serial1: HDLC myseq 886562, mineseen 886562, yourseen 886555, line up
Serial3: HDLC myseq 886562, mineseen 886562, yourseen 248617, line up
```

```
Serial4: HDLC myseq 1930334, mineseen 1930334, yourseen 164240,
line up
Serial5: HDLC myseq 2216739, mineseen 2216739, yourseen 220355,
line up
Serial0: HDLC myseq 213482, mineseen 213482, yourseen 213419, line up
Serial1: HDLC myseq 886563, mineseen 886563, yourseen 886556, line up
Serial3: HDLC myseq 886563, mineseen 886563, yourseen 248618, line up
Serial4: HDLC myseq 1930335, mineseen 1930335, yourseen 164241,
line up
Serial5: HDLC myseq 2216740, mineseen 2216740, yourseen 220356,
line up
Serial0: HDLC myseq 213483, mineseen 213483, yourseen 213420, line up
Serial1: HDLC myseq 886564, mineseen 886564, yourseen 886557, line up
Serial3: HDLC myseq 886564, mineseen 886564, yourseen 248619, line up
Serial4: HDLC myseq 1930336, mineseen 1930336, yourseen 164242,
line up
Serial5: HDLC myseq 2216741, mineseen 2216741, yourseen 220357,
line up
Serial0: HDLC myseq 213484, mineseen 213484, yourseen 213421, line up
Serial1: HDLC myseq 886565, mineseen 886565, yourseen 886558, line up
Serial3: HDLC myseq 886565, mineseen 886565, yourseen 248620, line up
Serial4: HDLC myseq 1930337, mineseen 1930337, yourseen 164243,
line up
Serial5: HDLC myseq 2216742, mineseen 2216742, yourseen 220358,
line up
Serial0: HDLC myseq 213485, mineseen 213485, yourseen 213422, line up
Serial1: HDLC myseq 886566, mineseen 886566, yourseen 886559, line up
Serial3: HDLC myseq 886566, mineseen 886566, yourseen 248621, line up
Serial4: HDLC myseq 1930338, mineseen 1930338, yourseen 164244,
line up
Serial5: HDLC myseq 2216743, mineseen 2216743, yourseen 220359,
line up
Serial0: HDLC myseq 213486, mineseen 213486, yourseen 213423, line up
Serial1: HDLC myseq 886567, mineseen 886567, yourseen 886560, line up
Serial3: HDLC myseq 886567, mineseen 886567, yourseen 248622, line up
Serial4: HDLC myseq 1930339, mineseen 1930339, yourseen 164245,
line up
Serial5: HDLC myseq 2216744, mineseen 2216744, yourseen 220360,
line up
Router#
```

This command can be used to troubleshoot serial timing problems that cause connection failures. The most important part of this output is the sequence numbers that are displayed for each serial interface.

Three fields are used against counters in this output. These are the myseq, mineseen, and yourseen counters:

- **Myseq** This counter increases by one each time the router sends a keepalive packet to the remote router.

- **Mineseen** This counter reflects the last myseq sequence number the remote router has acknowledged receiving from the router. The remote router stores this value in its yourseen counter and sends that value in a keepalive packet to the router.

■ **Yourseen**　This counter reflects the value of the myseq sequence number the router has received in a keepalive packet from the remote router.

We can see in the earlier output that the router has five configured serial interfaces: Serial0, Serial1, Serial3, Serial4, and Serial5. These all run the HDLC encapsulation. Notice that the myseq, mineseen, and yourseen values all increment by one each time, indicating normal operations of the serial interface. A timing problem would be indicated by these values incrementing by more than one each time. If the values increment more than three, the line goes down and the interface is reset. The interface resets are shown in the following output of a show interface command for serial interfaces:

```
Serial2 is up, line protocol is up
  Hardware is HD64570
  Description: EPS9 LINK TO CHARLES RO
  Internet address is 164.35.48.9 255.255.255.252
  MTU 1500 bytes, BW 128 Kbit, DLY 20000 usec, rely 255/255, load
  1/255
  Encapsulation HDLC, loopback not set, keepalive set (10 sec)
  Last input 0:00:05, output 0:00:01, output hang never
  Last clearing of "show interface" counters never
  Input queue: 0/75/0 (size/max/drops); Total output drops: 0
  Output queue: 0/64/0 (size/threshold/drops)
     Conversations  0/3 (active/max active)
     Reserved Conversations 0/0 (allocated/max allocated)
  5 minute input rate 0 bits/sec, 0 packets/sec
  5 minute output rate 0 bits/sec, 0 packets/sec
     550277 packets input, 40092684 bytes, 0 no buffer
     Received 298712 broadcasts, 0 runts, 0 giants
     17551 input errors, 17492 CRC, 912 frame, 0 overrun, 1
     ignored, 3154 abort
     1156612 packets output, 344567680 bytes, 0 underruns
     0 output errors, 0 collisions, 1 interface resets, 0 restarts
     0 output buffer failures, 0 output buffers swapped out
     772 carrier transitions
     DCD=up  DSR=up  DTR=up  RTS=up  CTS=up
```

We can see that one interface reset has occurred on this interface. The output of this command varies depending on the encapsulation used on the interface. The example given is based on HDLC encapsulation.

Serial Line Summary

This has looked at the basics of serial interfaces and explained the Cisco IOS commands available to troubleshoot the default encapsulation, HDLC. We looked at the basic show and debug commands and explained their uses in the troubleshooting process.

In the next two sections, we are going to look at Frame Relay and X.25 and cover the basic troubleshooting commands associated with these two common WAN protocols. For more detailed instructions on how to configure serial interfaces, consult the Cisco Web site or the Advanced Cisco Router Configuration course book.

Overview of Frame Relay

Frame Relay is a high-performance WAN protocol that functions at the physical and data-link layers of the OSI model. Originally, Frame Relay was designed for use across ISDN interfaces, but today it is also used over a variety of other interfaces.

Frame Relay is a packet-switching protocol that is used between user devices such as routers, bridges, host machines, and network devices such as switching nodes. The user equipment is usually referred to as DTE and the network equipment is usually referred to as *Data Circuit-Terminating Equipment* (DCE). Frame Relay can operate over a private or a public network provided by a Telco.

Frame Relay has a lot of similarities to X.25, but Frame Relay differs in ways that make it a more streamlined protocol that facilitates higher performance and greater efficiency.

One way that Frame Relay differs from X.25 is the way it handles error corrections. X.25 has built-in error-correction algorithms because X.25 was created when unreliable WAN communication links were common. This resulted in error-correction algorithms that were implemented at the data-link layer to correct bad data and perform retransmissions. All of this had an overhead on the performance of the protocol over the WAN. Frame Relay does include a *Cyclic Redundancy Check* (CRC) algorithm for the detection of corrupt bits, but it does not include any mechanisms for correcting bad data or performing retransmissions when a data error is identified. Frame Relay leaves these time- and performance-consuming functions to the higher-layer protocols that have been designed or streamlined since the conception of X.25.

X.25 provides flow control on a per-virtual-circuit basis. Frame Relay also removed this overhead from its framing. This is due to the advances of upper layer protocols to now include effective flow control algorithms. Hence, the need for this functionality at the link layer has diminished. Frame Relay just includes simple congestion notification mechanisms to enable communication between the network device and the user device, which is informed that the network resources are close to a congested state. This congestion notification can be intercepted by higher-layer protocols if required to instigate flow control.

In the early 1990s, a collection of companies including Cisco Systems, StrataCom, Northern Telecom, and Digital Equipment Corporation joined to focus on the development of interoperable Frame Relay products. A specification was developed that conformed to the basic Frame Relay protocol as outlined by the International Telecommunication Union (ITU-T) but extended it with features that provide additional capabilities for complex internetworking environments. Collectively, these Frame Relay extensions are referred to as the *Local Management Interface* (LMI).

Frame Relay Structure

Frame Relay has associated standards devised by both the American National Standards Institute (ANSI) and the International Telegraph and Telephone Consultative Committee (CCITT). The Frame Relay structure is based upon the *Link Access Procedure-D Channel* (LAPD) protocol. The frame header in the Frame Relay frame is altered slightly to contain the *Data Link Connection Identifier* (DLCI) and congestion bits in place of the normal address and control fields (see Figure 8-1). This creates a two-byte header for Frame Relay frames.

The Frame Relay header structure can be broken down into the following components:

Figure 8-1

Frame Relay header

FRAME RELAY HEADER STRUCTURE

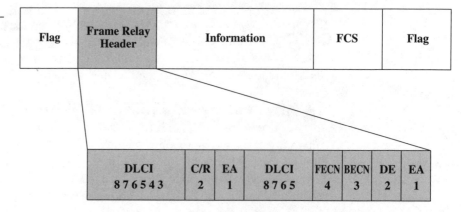

- The DLCI is a 10-bit field that represents the address of the frame. It always corresponds to a *Permanent Virtual Circuit* (PVC).

- The *Command / Response* (C/R) frame is a one-bit frame that indicates whether the frame is a command or a response.

- The *Extended Address* (EA) field is a two-bit field that extends the current address field. This provides for an increased range of addresses.

- The *Forward Explicit Congestion Notification* (FECN) field is a one-bit field that is concerned with congestion management.

- The *Backward Explicit Congestion Notification* (BECN) field is a one-bit field that is concerned with congestion management.

- The *Discard Eligibility* (DE) field is a one-bit field that is concerned with congestion management.

Frame Relay Devices

Devices that are connected to a Frame Relay WAN are categorized as either DTE or DCE. DTE devices are usually customer-owned and are located at the customer's premises. These devices can be PCs, file servers, or the routers that connect the customer network to the Frame Relay WAN (see Figure 8-2).

DCE devices are responsible for the upkeep and transit of the Frame Relay network. These are usually advanced WAN switches located in the Telco's premises. These devices provide the clocking and switching for the Frame Relay circuit and are usually packet switches. DTE and DCE devices are connected both at the physical and data-link layers of the OSI model. The physical connection is usually a cable to the X.21, V35, or RS232 standards used on most vendor's equipment, including that of Cisco Systems, Inc. The data-link layer defines the protocol responsible for communication between the DTE and DCE devices.

Virtual Circuits

Frame Relay frames are transmitted from the source DTE to the destination DTE over DCE equipment by way of a virtual circuit. A *virtual circuit* is defined as a logical connection between two DTE devices over a packet-switched (DCE) network.

These virtual circuits provide a bidirectional path between communicating DTE devices. A DLCI identifies virtual circuits. This value is locally unique to

Figure 8-2
Frame Relay devices

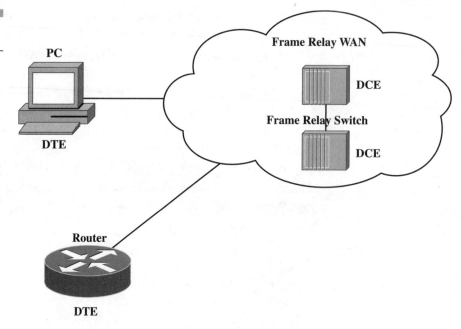

every PVC and is normally assigned by the Frame Relay service provider. The DLCI may not be unique in the Frame Relay WAN and it is important to note that the DTE at the other end of the Frame Relay WAN may refer to the same virtual circuit using a different DLCI value. These virtual circuits can be either *Permanent Virtual Circuits* (PVCs) or *Switched Virtual Circuits* (SVCs).

PVCs are connections across the Frame Relay WAN that are permanently connected. These virtual circuits are usually used for high volume and frequent data transfers that require an intrinsic communication medium. PVCs are either in the Data Transfer or Idle states, so no call setup and termination is required. Most of today's Frame Relay devices operate over PVCs.

SVCs are defined as temporary connections across the Frame Relay WAN that are created when the circuit is required. These virtual circuits are used when sporadic, bursty communication is required between DTE devices across the Frame Relay WAN.

A Frame Relay SVC session has to be initiated and disconnected in a similar way to a BRI ISDN connection utilizing similar call setup protocols. This adds overhead to the communication and a slight lag in the initial connection time. SVCs are seldom used or supported in modern Frame Relay installations.

Congestion Management

When congestion occurs in a network, the network device discards frames. These frames are usually identified as not reaching their intended destinations by upper-layer protocols and they are normally re-sent, adding to the congestion problem.

Frame Relay contains three fields in the header that are concerned with congestion management: the FECN field, the BECN field, and the DE field. The FECN field is a one-bit field that exists in the Frame Relay header. Communication from a DTE over the Frame Relay network initiates congestion management if the DCE devices are congested. The DCE device would set the FECN to 1. This indicates to the receiving DTE that congestion occurred during transit. The receiving DTE can pass this information to a higher layer protocol to instigate flow control over the network.

The BECN field is a one-bit field that exists in the Frame Relay header. When congestion occurs and is identified by the receiving DTE with the FECN field being set to 1, the receiving DTE sets the BECN field to 1 in all responses to the source DTE. This instructs the source DTE to slow down its transmission until the BECN field resets itself to the usual state.

The DE field is a one-bit field that exists in the Frame Relay header. DTE devices can use the DE field to prioritize traffic. If the DE field contains the value 1, then that frame is deemed to be of a lower importance than other traffic on the Frame Relay network.

When congestion occurs, the DCE device would drop frames with the DE field set to 1 first. This is a way to mark critical data and prevent it from being dropped during periods of congestion.

Local Management Interface (LMI)

In 1990, Cisco Systems, StrataCom, Northern Telecom, and DEC formed a consortium to improve the Frame Relay standards. This consortium developed the LMI extensions to Frame Relay. The LMI extensions added features to the standard Frame Relay standards to enhance the performance and manageability of the Frame Relay protocol. These new features include global addressing, virtual circuit status messages, and multicasting.

Cisco routers support three values for the LMI type:

- Cisco (the default value)
- ANSI
- Q944a

These LMI types are assigned by entering the following command in the interface configuration mode:

```
Router(config-if)#frame-relay lmi-type ansi
```

This would set the LMI type for this interface to ANSI.

NOTE: *Frame Relay LMI types must be set the same across directly connected interfaces. Care has to be taken when differing vendors' equipment is used. Cisco equipment automatically defaults to the Cisco LMI type. Other network vendors will not support this LMI type. This is also true of the Frame Relay encapsulation method.*

Show Commands

Several show commands can be used to view the current Frame Relay configuration of the router. These commands are useful for checking the status of the configuration as well as for troubleshooting a range of Frame Relay problems (see Table 8-2).

show frame-relay lmi

The *show frame-relay lmi* command displays information about the configured LMI on the router:

Table 8-2

Frequently Used Show Commands for Troubleshooting Frame Relay

Command	Description
Show frame-relay lmi	Displays information about the configured LMI on the router.
Show frame-relay map	Displays the mappings between the network-layer protocols and the DLCI.
Show frame-relay pvc	Displays detailed information about the configured DLCIs on the router.
Show interface	Displays information about the serial interfaces on the router.

```
Router#sh frame-relay lmi

LMI Statistics for interface Serial0 (Frame Relay DCE) LMI TYPE =
CISCO
   Invalid Unnumbered info 0           Invalid Prot Disc 0
   Invalid dummy Call Ref 0            Invalid Msg Type 0
   Invalid Status Message 0            Invalid Lock Shift 0
   Invalid Information ID 0            Invalid Report IE Len 0
   Invalid Report Request 0           Invalid Keep IE Len 0
   Num Status Enq. Rcvd 112           Num Status msgs Sent 112
   Num Update Status Sent 0           Num St Enq. Timeouts 20

LMI Statistics for interface Serial1 (Frame Relay DCE) LMI TYPE =
CISCO
   Invalid Unnumbered info 0           Invalid Prot Disc 0
   Invalid dummy Call Ref 0            Invalid Msg Type 0
   Invalid Status Message 0            Invalid Lock Shift 0
   Invalid Information ID 0            Invalid Report IE Len 0
   Invalid Report Request 0           Invalid Keep IE Len 0
   Num Status Enq. Rcvd 105           Num Status msgs Sent 105
   Num Update Status Sent 0           Num St Enq. Timeouts 17
Router#
```

The LMI provides communication between the Frame Relay DCE and DTE. This command can be run on either the DCE or DTE device to display the current LMI type as well as information about the integrity of each configured PVC on the router.

We can see from the earlier output that the above router is the DCE or Frame Relay switch and it has two interfaces configured for Frame Relay, Serial0 and Serial1. The first section shows that the interface is the DCE end and that the default Cisco type LMI is being used. Each end of a Frame Relay connection should be using a similar LMI type. One note of importance is that if the Frame Relay network utilizes non-Cisco equipment then you must use the ANSI or Q944a LMI types and not the CISCO type.

The next section is concerned with the number of status enquiries sent and received. These should always be the same. A difference here can indicate a problem with the LMI type on the Frame Relay network, the encapsulation type, physical line errors, or deactivation of the PVC.

show frame-relay map

The *show frame-relay map* command displays the mappings between the network-layer protocols and the DLCI. The following examples show the mapping below the IP address 194.73.134.1 and the DLCI 100:

```
Router#sh frame-relay map
Serial0 (up): ip 194.73.134.1 dlci 100(0x64,0x1840), static,
```

```
                    CISCO, status defined, active
Router#
```

We can see by the highlighted area that this mapping has been defined and is active. This confirms that 194.73.134.1 can be reached over Serial0 using DLCI 100. The CISCO keyword indicates that CISCO Frame Relay encapsulation is being used. We then change the DLCI value on the *frame-relay map* command to 110 from 100. This is the incorrect DLCI for the interface. We now enter the *show frame-relay map* command and the following output is displayed:

```
Router#sh frame-relay map
Serial0 (up): ip 194.73.134.1 dlci 110(0x6E,0x18E0), static,
             CISCO, status deleted
Router#
```

We now see that the status is shown as deleted by the highlighted section. This indicates that an incorrect DLCI has been entered for the interface. These Frame Relay map entries are manual and therefore prone to simple errors such as this. A quick check using the *show frame-relay map* command can be useful for checking both ends of a Frame Relay network and it simplifies the Frame Relay troubleshooting process.

show frame-relay pvc

The *show frame-relay pvc* command displays detailed information about the configured DLCIs on the router:

```
Router#sh frame-relay pvc

PVC Statistics for interface Serial0 (Frame Relay DCE)

DLCI = 110, DLCI USAGE = SWITCHED, PVC STATUS = ACTIVE, INTERFACE =
Serial0

    input pkts 18              output pkts 0          in bytes 5094
    out bytes 0               dropped pkts 1         in FECN pkts 0
    in BECN pkts 0            out FECN pkts 0        out BECN pkts 0
    in DE pkts 0              out DE pkts 0
    out bcast pkts 0          out bcast bytes 0      Num Pkts Switched 18

    pvc create time 00:23:23, last time pvc status changed 00:18:16

PVC Statistics for interface Serial1 (Frame Relay DCE)

DLCI = 100, DLCI USAGE = SWITCHED, PVC STATUS = ACTIVE, INTERFACE =
Serial1

    input pkts 1              output pkts 18         in bytes 46
    out bytes 5094            dropped pkts 0         in FECN pkts 0
```

```
in BECN pkts 0          out FECN pkts 0        out BECN pkts 0
in DE pkts 0            out DE pkts 0
out bcast pkts 0        out bcast bytes 0      Num Pkts Switched 0

pvc create time 00:22:35, last time pvc status changed 00:19:34
Router#
```

The show *frame-relay pvc* command displays details about all of the PVCs that are configured on a router. This is shown on a per-interface basis. We can see from the previous output that this router has two interfaces that are configured with PVCs: Serial0 and Serial1.

The first section shows the PVC interface and its role. We can see that this is interface Serial0 and it is operating as a Frame Relay DCE device. The second section is related to the built-in congestion management features of Frame Relay. As previously discussed, Frame Relay utilizes FECN, BECN, and DE bits to control traffic congestion. The number of instances of these bits is shown in the output of the *show frame-relay pvc* command. A high number of FECN, BECN, and DE bits represents a network bandwidth problem and this normally correlates with a high number of dropped packets. In this situation, it would be advisable to increase the bandwidth available to the network.

The third section shows the PVC create time and the last time that the status of the PVC changed. This is a useful value for determining if the interface or PVC has recently undergone a change that could have forced it into the error state.

show interface

The *show interface* command displays information about the serial interfaces on the router:

```
Router#sh int
Serial0 is up, line protocol is up
  Hardware is HD64570
  MTU 1500 bytes, BW 1544 Kbit, DLY 20000 usec, rely 255/255, load
  1/255
  Encapsulation FRAME-RELAY, loopback not set, keepalive set (10 sec)
  LMI enq sent  1, LMI stat recvd 0, LMI upd recvd 0
  LMI enq recvd 197, LMI stat sent  197, LMI upd sent  0, DCE LMI up
  LMI DLCI 1023  LMI type is CISCO  frame relay DCE
  Broadcast queue 0/64, broadcasts sent/dropped 0/0, interface
  broadcasts 0
  Last input 00:00:03, output 00:00:03, output hang never
  Last clearing of "show interface" counters never
  Input queue: 0/75/0 (size/max/drops); Total output drops: 0
  Queueing strategy: weighted fair
  Output queue: 0/1000/64/0 (size/max total/threshold/drops)
     Conversations  0/1/256 (active/max active/max total)
```

```
     Reserved Conversations 0/0 (allocated/max allocated)
  5 minute input rate 0 bits/sec, 0 packets/sec
  5 minute output rate 0 bits/sec, 0 packets/sec
     420 packets input, 24772 bytes, 0 no buffer
     Received 54 broadcasts, 0 runts, 0 giants, 0 throttles
     0 input errors, 0 CRC, 0 frame, 0 overrun, 0 ignored, 0 abort
     248 packets output, 5697 bytes, 0 underruns
     0 output errors, 0 collisions, 12 interface resets
     0 output buffer failures, 0 output buffers swapped out
     28 carrier transitions
     DCD=up  DSR=up  DTR=up  RTS=up  CTS=up

Serial1 is up, line protocol is up
  Hardwre is HD64570
  MTU 1500 bytes, BW 1544 Kbit, DLY 20000 usec, rely 255/255, load
  1/255
  Encapsulation FRAME-RELAY, loopback not set, keepalive set (10 sec)
  LMI enq sent   1, LMI stat recvd 0, LMI upd recvd 0
  LMI enq recvd 190, LMI stat sent  190, LMI upd sent  0, DCE LMI up
  LMI DLCI 1023  LMI type is CISCO  frame relay DCE
  Broadcast queue 0/64, broadcasts sent/dropped 0/0, interface
  broadcasts 0
  Last input 00:00:00, output 00:00:01, output hang never
  Last clearing of "show interface" counters never
  Input queue: 0/75/0 (size/max/drops); Total output drops: 0
  Queueing strategy: weighted fair
  Output queue: 0/1000/64/0 (size/max total/threshold/drops)
     Conversations  0/4/256 (active/max active/max total)
     Reserved Conversations 0/0 (allocated/max allocated)
  5 minute input rate 0 bits/sec, 0 packets/sec
  5 minute output rate 0 bits/sec, 0 packets/sec
     252 packets input, 5175 bytes, 0 no buffer
     Received 0 broadcasts, 0 runts, 0 giants, 0 throttles
     0 input errors, 0 CRC, 0 frame, 0 overrun, 0 ignored, 0 abort
     236 packets output, 11621 bytes, 0 underruns
     0 output errors, 0 collisions, 23 interface resets
     0 output buffer failures, 0 output buffers swapped out
     48 carrier transitions
     DCD=up  DSR=up  DTR=up  RTS=up  CTS=up
Router#
```

This command was also shown in the previous section. This time we are looking at the output of the *show interface* command for a serial interface that is using Frame Relay encapsulation. The ouput indicates that Frame Relay is the selected encapsulation method. You can then see information relating to the LMI configured on that interface and also the status of the LMI on the interface. We can see that the LMI is up on this interface. This output also shows us that we are using the CISCO LMI type and that the interface is operating as a Frame Relay DCE device.

This command is a starting point for checking the status of a Frame Relay interface. The first line in the output tells us that the interface and line protocols are both up. We can then see information relating to the status and configuration of the LMI on the interface.

Debug Commands

The debug commands are an excellent way to interrogate the router and receive real-time information regarding the state of Frame Relay connections at various OSI layers (see Table 8-3).

debug frame-relay events

The *debug frame-relay events* command displays debug information about transmission and reception events relating to Frame Relay interfaces on the router. Frame Relay ARP requests are shown using this debug command:

```
Router#deb frame-relay events
Frame Relay events debugging is on
Router#
Serial1(i): reply rcvd 194.73.134.26 122
Serial1(i): reply rcvd 194.73.134.28 126
Serial1(i): reply rcvd 194.73.134.34 128
Serial1(i): reply rcvd 194.73.134.38 134
Serial1(i): reply rcvd 194.73.134.41 194
Router#
```

This command doesn't produce much output and is only really useful in ascertaining that Frame Relay ARP packets are crossing the DLCI. The output indicates that Serial1 has received five ARP replies for the given IP addresses. The last numeric value on each line represents the DLCI to use when communicating with the responding router.

Table 8-3

Frequently Used Debug Commands for Troubleshooting Frame Relay

Command	Description
debug frame-relay events	Displays debug information about transmission and reception events relating to Frame Relay interfaces on the router.
debug frame-relay lmi	Displays debug information about the LMI packets that are sent between the local DTE and the remote DTE devices.
debug frame-relay packet	Displays debug information about all the Frame Relay packets that are processed by the router over the Frame Relay interfaces.
debug serial interface	Displays debug information about events occurring on the configured serial interfaces on the router.

debug frame-relay lmi

The *debug frame-relay lmi* command displays debug information about the LMI packets that are sent between the local DTE and the remote DTE devices:

```
Router#debug frame-relay lmi
Frame Relay LMI debugging is on
Displaying all Frame Relay LMI data
Router#
01:25:42: Serial0(in): StEnq, myseq 6
01:25:42: RT IE 1, length 1, type 1
01:25:42: KA IE 3, length 2, yourseq 4 , myseq 6
01:25:43: Serial0(out): Status, myseq 7, yourseen 4, DCE up
01:25:46: Serial1(in): StEnq, myseq 191
01:25:46: RT IE 1, length 1, type 1
01:25:46: KA IE 3, length 2, yourseq 194, myseq 191
01:25:46: Serial1(out): Status, myseq 192, yourseen 194, DCE up
01:25:52: Serial0(in): StEnq, myseq 7
01:25:52: RT IE 1, length 1, type 1
01:25:52: KA IE 3, length 2, yourseq 5 , myseq 7
01:25:53: Serial0(out): Status, myseq 8, yourseen 5, DCE up
01:25:56: Serial1(in): StEnq, myseq 192
01:25:56: RT IE 1, length 1, type 1
01:25:56: KA IE 3, length 2, yourseq 195, myseq 192
01:25:56: Serial1(out): Status, myseq 193, yourseen 195, DCE up
01:26:02: Serial0(in): StEnq, myseq 8
01:26:02: RT IE 1, length 1, type 1
01:26:02: KA IE 3, length 2, yourseq 6 , myseq 8
01:26:03: Serial0(out): Status, myseq 9, yourseen 6, DCE up
01:26:06: Serial1(in): StEnq, myseq 193
01:26:06: RT IE 1, length 1, type 0
01:26:06: KA IE 3, length 2, yourseq 196, myseq 193
01:26:06: Serial1(out): Status, myseq 194, yourseen 196, DCE up
01:26:12: Serial0(in): StEnq, myseq 9
01:26:12: RT IE 1, length 1, type 0
01:26:12: KA IE 3, length 2, yourseq 7 , myseq 9
01:26:13: Serial0(out): Status, myseq 10, yourseen 7, DCE up
01:26:16: Serial1(in): StEnq, myseq 194
01:26:16: RT IE 1, length 1, type 1
01:26:16: KA IE 3, length 2, yourseq 197, myseq 194
01:26:16: Serial1(out): Status, myseq 195, yourseen 197, DCE up
01:26:22: Serial0(in): StEnq, myseq 10
01:26:22: RT IE 1, length 1, type 1
01:26:22: KA IE 3, length 2, yourseq 8 , myseq 10
01:26:23: Serial0(out): Status, myseq 11, yourseen 8, DCE up
01:26:26: Serial1(in): StEnq, myseq 195
01:26:26: RT IE 1, length 1, type 1
01:26:26: KA IE 3, length 2, yourseq 198, myseq 195
01:26:26: Serial1(out): Status, myseq 196, yourseen 198, DCE up
Router#
```

The *debug frame-relay lmi* command provides detailed output about the communications that occur between the customer's DTE device and the

Frame Relay carrier's DCE devices. As explained in the section on the *debug serial interface* command, it is important to ensure that the sequence numbers run chronologically. This command also provides another method of establishing that the DCE is up.

This command can be used to ascertain if the problem is local or is caused by a problem in the carrier's network. Although it is not of great use, it is another tool that can be used to deduce the cause of a problem.

debug frame-relay packet

The *debug frame-relay packet* command displays debug information about all of the Frame Relay packets that are processed by the router over the Frame Relay interfaces:

```
01:25:46: Serial0: broadcast - 0, link 809B, addr 10.2
01:25:46: Serial0(o):DLCI 100 type 809B size 104:
01:25:52: Serial1: broadcast search
01:25:52: Serial1(o):DLCI 400 type 800 size 288
01:25:53: Serial0: broadcast search
01:25:54: Serial0(o):DLCI 300 type 809B size 24
```

The broadcast keyword is quite important in this output. There can be three variations to this keyword. *Broadcast - 0* indicates that this packet is destined for a specific destination, *Broadcast - 1* indicates that this is a true broadcast and that the broadcast address will follow. *Broadcast - search* searches all Frame Relay map entries for this particular protocol that include the keyword *broadcast*.

The information provided in this output can be used to troubleshoot the Frame Relay connection and data stream by ensuring that the packets are correctly addressed both at the network address and the DLCI.

Care has to be taken in the use of this debug command. A lot of output can be produced and it can severely impact the operation of the router upon which it is run. Ensure that the *no debug all* or *undebug all* command is entered after using this debug command.

debug serial interface

The *debug serial interface* command displays debug information about events occurring on the configured serial interfaces on the router. In this instance, we are concerned with interfaces that are running the Frame

Relay encapsulation and participating in a Frame Relay WAN. The router shown here is running Frame Relay over Serial0 and Serial1:

```
Router#
01:33:37: Serial1(in): StEnq, myseq 238
01:33:37: Serial1(out): Status, myseq 239, yourseen 241, DCE up
01:33:42: Serial0(in): StEnq, myseq 54
01:33:43: Serial0(out): Status, myseq 55, yourseen 52, DCE up
01:33:47: Serial1(in): StEnq, myseq 239
01:33:47: Serial1(out): Status, myseq 240, yourseen 242, DCE up
01:33:52: Serial0(in): StEnq, myseq 55
01:33:53: Serial0(out): Status, myseq 56, yourseen 53, DCE up
01:33:57: Serial1(in): StEnq, myseq 240
01:33:57: Serial1(out): Status, myseq 241, yourseen 243, DCE up
01:34:03: Serial0(in): StEnq, myseq 56
01:34:03: Serial0(out): Status, myseq 57, yourseen 54, DCE up
01:34:07: Serial1(in): StEnq, myseq 241
01:34:07: Serial1(out): Status, myseq 242, yourseen 244, DCE up
01:34:12: Serial0(in): StEnq, myseq 57
01:34:13: Serial0(out): Status, myseq 58, yourseen 55, DCE up
01:34:17: Serial1(in): StEnq, myseq 242
01:34:17: Serial1(out): Status, myseq 243, yourseen 245, DCE up
01:34:23: Serial0(in): StEnq, myseq 58
01:34:23: Serial0(out): Status, myseq 59, yourseen 56, DCE up
01:34:27: Serial1(in): StEnq, myseq 243
01:34:27: Serial1(out): Status, myseq 244, yourseen 246, DCE up
01:34:33: Serial0(in): StEnq, myseq 59
01:34:33: Serial0(out): Status, myseq 60, yourseen 57, DCE up
01:34:37: Serial1(in): StEnq, myseq 244
01:34:37: Serial1(out): Status, myseq 245, yourseen 247, DCE up
01:34:43: Serial0(in): StEnq, myseq 60
01:34:43: Serial0(out): Status, myseq 61, yourseen 58, DCE up
Router#
```

The *debug serial interface* command can be used to troubleshoot serial timing problems that cause connection failures. The most important part of this output is the sequence numbers that are displayed for each serial interface.

We can see in this output that the router has two configured serial interfaces, Serial0 and Serial1. It is important to note that the myseq and yourseen values all increment by one each time for the corresponding interface. This indicates normal operations for the Serial interface. A timing problem would be indicated by these values incrementing by more than one each time. If the values increment more than three, the line goes down and the interface is reset. This is explained in more detail in the debug serial interface in the preceding section.

Frame Relay Summary

Frame Relay is a popular WAN connectivity method. Knowledge of the essentials and the specific, intricate features is required to troubleshoot

Frame Relay problems. In this section, we have looked at the basics of Frame Relay and described the Cisco-provided commands in IOS to facilitate the troubleshooting of common Frame Relay problems. For more detailed instructions on how to configure Frame Relay interfaces, consult the Cisco Web site or the Advanced Cisco Router Configuration course book.

Overview of X.25

X.25 is a WAN protocol that was devised by the CCITT in the 1970s as a protocol that could operate over public switched networks. X.25 has a lot of similarities to Frame Relay, but Frame Relay differs in ways that make it a more streamlined protocol that facilitates higher performance and greater efficiency.

X.25 Protocols

X.25 is made up of a protocol suite that spans the bottom three layers of the OSI model (see Figure 8-3). At the network layer you have the *Packet-Layer Protocol* (PLP), at the data-link layer you have the *Link-Access Procedure Balanced* (LAPB) protocol, and at the physical layer you have various serial interface protocols, such as the X.21bis protocol.

Figure 8-3
X.25 in the OSI model

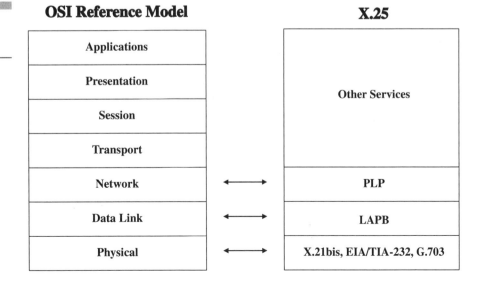

OSI Reference Model	X.25
Applications	Other Services
Presentation	
Session	
Transport	
Network ⟷	PLP
Data Link ⟷	LAPB
Physical ⟷	X.21bis, EIA/TIA-232, G.703

PLP is the X.25 network-layer protocol that is responsible for the transportation of packets between DTE devices across X.25 virtual circuits. As well as running over X.25, PLP can also be run over ISDN, utilizing the LAPD protocol. PLP looks after the call setup and termination for X.25 communications. The call setup mode utilizes the X.121 addressing scheme to set up the virtual circuit. The PLP packet is encapsulated within the LAPB frame and then the LAPB frame is converted to an X.21bis frame for transmission onto the network as a bit stream (see Figure 8-4).

A PLP packet is made up of the following elements:

- The *General Format Identifier* (GFI) identifies whether the packet is a control packet or if it contains user data. Other control options such as windowing and confirmation are established.

- The *Logical Channel Identifier* (LCI) identifies the virtual circuit between the two communicating DTE devices.

- The *Packet Type Identifier* (PTI) identifies the PLP packet type, of which there are 17.

- The *User Data field* contains encapsulated data from upper layer protocols if the GFI indicates a data packet.

LAPB operates at the data-link layer of the OSI model and is concerned with communications between the DTE and DCE devices (see Figure 8-5).

Figure 8-4
A PLP packet

Field Length

4	12	8	Variable
GFI	**LCI**	**PTI**	**USER DATA**

|← Packet Header →|← User Data →|

Figure 8-5
LAPB frame

Field Length

1	1	1	Variable	2	1
Flag	Address	Control	Data	FCS	Flag

Three LAPB frame types exist to provide this mechanism: *Information*, *Supervisory*, and *Unnumbered*. The Information or I Frame is responsible for flow control operations between the devices as well as error detection and recovery. The Supervisory or S Frame is responsible for the control information associated with the communication. I Frame receipts are carried by S Frames. The Unnumbered or U Frame only carries control information that pertains to the link setup, disconnection, or associated error reporting.

An LAPB frame is composed of the following fields:

- *Flag*   This field in the LAPB header delimits the beginning and end of every LAPB frame.

- *Address*   This field identifies to the DTE and DCE devices whether the frame is a command or a response.

- *Control*   This field indicates whether the frame is an I, S, or U frame. The frame's sequence number is also stored in the control field.

- *Data*   The PLP packet is encapsulated into this field of the LAPB frame.

- *Frame Check Sequence* (FCS)   This field is responsible for checking the integrity of the frame.

The X.21bis protocol is located at the physical layer of the OSI model and is responsible for the X.25 communication onto the physical medium. The X.21bis protocol defines the electrical and mechanical procedures for connecting the DTE device to the DCE device at speeds of up to 19.2 Kbps.

X.25 Devices

X.25 devices can be divided into three classifications: DTE, DCE, and *Packet Switching Equipment* (PSE). DTE devices are the end devices that communicate across the X.25 network. These devices can be terminals, PCs, and network hosts and they are normally located on the premises of the X.25 subscriber. DCE equipment is connected to the DTE equipment and looks after passing frames between the DTE and the PSE. X.25 DCEs are usually modems or other circuit-terminating hardware and are normally located at the X.25 provider's premises. PSE equipment is the actual switching fabric that the X.25 network traverses. Differing subscribers can utilize this network at the same time and the network may also support multiple services.

X.25 was designed when the DTE was not powerful enough to support the full X.25 protocol suite. In this instance, an X.25 *Packet Assembler/Disassembler* (PAD) was used in-between the DTE and DCE devices. The PAD

Figure 8-6

The relationship between X.25 equipment

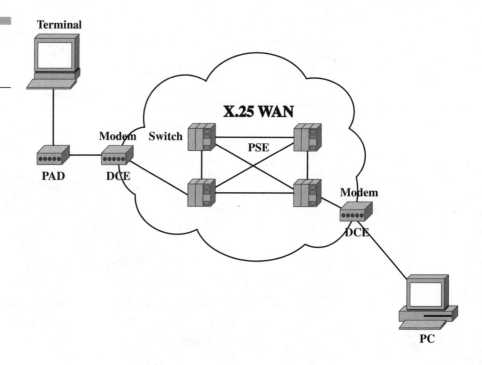

Table 8-4

Frequently Used Show Commands for Troubleshooting X.25

Command	Description
Show interface	Displays information about the configured interfaces on the router.
Show x25 route	Displays the X.25 routing table on the router.
Show x25 vc	Displays detailed parameters and statistics about the X.25 virtual circuit.

would perform the X.25 protocol functions to ensure transparent connectivity between the local and remote DTE devices (see Figure 8-6).

Show Commands

Several show commands can be used to view the current X.25 configuration of the router (see Table 8-4). These commands are useful for checking the status of the configuration as well as troubleshooting a range of X.25 problems.

show interface

The *show interface* command displays information about the configured interfaces on the router. In the following code, we examine a serial interface that is configured for X.25:

```
Router#sh int s2
Serial2 is up, line protocol is up
  Hardware is HD64570
  Description: HIGH SPEED X25 CARD
  MTU 1500 bytes, BW 64 Kbit, DLY 20000 usec, rely 255/255, load 1/255
  Encapsulation X25, loopback not set
  LAPB DTE, modulo 8, k 7, N1 12056, N2 20
      T1 3000, interface outage (partial T3) 0, T4 0
      State CONNECT, VS 3, VR 2, Remote VR 3, Retransmissions 0
      Queues: U/S frames 0, I frames 0, unack. 0, reTx 0
      IFRAMEs 5170643/5387231 RNRs 0/0 REJs 0/0 SABM/Es 0/1 FRMRs
      0/0 DISCs 0/1
  X25 DTE, address 00000000, state R1, modulo 8, timer 0
      Defaults: cisco encapsulation, idle 0, nvc 1
        input/output window sizes 7/7, packet sizes 128/128
      Timers: T20 180, T21 200, T22 180, T23 180, TH 0
      Channels: Incoming-only 512-522, Two-way none, Outgoing-only
      1536-1546
      RESTARTs 1/0 CALLs 418+3/16449+2198/16867+2198 DIAGs 0/0
  Last input never, output 0:00:01, output hang never
  Last clearing of "show interface" counters 0:00:00
  Output queue 0/40, 0 drops; input queue 0/75, 0 drops
  5 minute input rate 1000 bits/sec, 4 packets/sec
  5 minute output rate 0 bits/sec, 4 packets/sec
      10208046 packets input, 480793658 bytes, 55340 no buffer
      Received 0 broadcasts, 0 runts, 0 giants
      0 input errors, 0 CRC, 0 frame, 0 overrun, 0 ignored, 0 abort
      10441345 packets output, 112052543 bytes, 0 underruns
      0 output errors, 0 collisions, 1 interface resets, 0 restarts
      0 output buffer failures, 0 output buffers swapped out
      2 carrier transitions
      DCD=up  DSR=up  DTR=up  RTS=up  CTS=up
Router#
```

The *show interface* command was also shown in the previous section. This time we are looking at the output of the show interface command for a serial interface that is using X.25 encapsulation. This section indicates that X.25 is the selected encapsulation method. You can then see information relating to the X.25 configuration including detailed LAPB information.

This command is a starting point for checking the status of an X.25 interface. The first line in the output tells us that the interface and line protocols

are both up. We can then see information relating to the status and configuration of X.25 on the interface.

show x25 route

The *show x25 route* command displays the X.25 routing table on the router:

```
Router#sh x25 route
Number          X.121              CUD        Forward To
   1     ^100100500306                        137.37.27.1, 0 uses
   2     ^100101600806                        137.37.35.1, 18817 uses
   3     ^100101600906                        137.37.35.1, 20702 uses
   4     ^100103200002                        Serial2, 1030 uses
Router#
```

The output here shows the X.25 routing table on the router. This routing table is used to route between the X.121 address and the IP address
or interface. We can see that any X.25 traffic destined for the X.121
address 100103200002 would be sent to Serial2. The last piece of information at the end of every line is the number of times that this has been
used. Note that the first route hasn't been used. If you are experiencing
X.25 communication problems, this could be an indication of an incorrect
route or some other connectivity problem that is halting the transference
of frames.

show x25 vc

The *show x25 vc* command displays detailed parameters and statistics
about the X.25 virtual circuit:

```
Router#sh x25 vc
SVC 1544,  State: D1,  Interface: Serial2
 Started 1d02, last input 0:00:03, output 0:00:03
 Connects 100101600806 <--> 100103200002 from
 XOT between 197.37.26.1, 1998 and 194.35.36.30, 11075
 Window size input: 7, output: 7
 Packet size input: 128, output: 128
 PS: 2  PR: 3  ACK: 2  Remote PR: 1  RCNT: 1  RNR: FALSE
 Retransmits: 0  Timer (secs): 0  Reassembly (bytes): 0
 Held Fragments/Packets: 0/0
 Bytes 252691/1976854 Packets 18770/17955 Resets 0/0 RNRs 0/0 REJs
 0/0 INTs 0/0

SVC 1545,  State: D1,  Interface: Serial2
 Started 2:53:05, last input 0:10:41, output 0:10:41
```

```
Connects 100101600906 <-> 100103200002 from
XOT between 197.37.26.1, 1998 and 194.35.36.30, 11076
Window size input: 7, output: 7
Packet size input: 128, output: 128
PS: 0  PR: 3  ACK: 3  Remote PR: 0  RCNT: 0  RNR: FALSE
Retransmits: 0  Timer (secs): 0  Reassembly (bytes): 0
Held Fragments/Packets: 0/0
Bytes 12391/142021 Packets 1336/1307 Resets 0/0 RNRs 0/0 REJs 0/0
INTs 0/0

SVC 1546,  State: D1,  Interface: Serial2
Started 3:19:06, last input 0:00:09, output 0:00:09
Connects 100100500306 <-> 100103200002 from
XOT between 194.35.37.17, 1998 and 194.35.37.18, 22060
Window size input: 2, output: 2
Packet size input: 128, output: 128
PS: 0  PR: 0  ACK: 0  Remote PR: 0  RCNT: 0  RNR: FALSE
Retransmits: 0  Timer (secs): 0  Reassembly (bytes): 0
Held Fragments/Packets: 0/0
Bytes 171278/1087138 Packets 10760/10088 Resets 0/0 RNRs 0/0 REJs
0/0 INTs 0/0
Router#
```

The *show x25 vc* command can be used to check the existence and consistency of the X.25 virtual circuit. The output shows the virtual circuits that are configured on the router. We can see from this output that three virtual circuits exist: 1544, 1545, and 1546.

The first section shows that the SVC is active on the interface. The D1 state indicates that the circuit is activated on the interface. The second section confirms that the X.25 address is correctly associated to the IP address of the X.25 interface.

Debug Commands

The debug commands are an excellent way to interrogate the router and receive real-time information regarding the state of X.25 connections at various OSI layers (see Table 8-5).

Table 8-5

Frequently Used Debug Commands for Troubleshooting X.25

Command	Description
debug x25 events	Displays debug information about X.25 traffic except data and ack packets.
debug x25 all	Displays debug information about all X.25 traffic.

debug x25 events

The *debug x25 events* command debugs information about X.25 traffic except data and ack packets:

```
Router#
Serial2: X25 I P1 CALL REQUEST (24) 8 lci 522
From(12): 100103200002 To(12): 100101600906
  Facilities: (3)
    Window size: 2 2
  Call User Data (4): 0xC4000000 (unknown)
XOT: X25 O P1 CALL REQUEST (27) 8 lci 522
From(12): 100103200002 To(12): 100101600906
  Facilities: (6)
    Packet size: 128 128
    Window size: 2 2
  Call User Data (4): 0xC4000000 (unknown)
XOT: X25 I P3 CALL CONNECTED (23) 8 lci 1545
From(12): 100103200002 To(12): 100101600906
  Facilities: (6)
    Packet size: 128 128
    Window size: 2 2
Serial2: X25 O P4 CALL CONNECTED (5) 8 lci 522
From(0):  To(0):
  Facilities: (0)
Serial2: X25 I D1 CLEAR REQUEST (5) 8 lci 522 cause 0 diag 0
XOT: X25 O D1 CLEAR REQUEST (5) 8 lci 522 cause 0 diag 0
Serial2: X25 O D1 CLEAR CONFIRMATION (3) 8 lci 522
Serial2: X25 I P1 CALL REQUEST (24) 8 lci 522
From(12): 100103200002 To(12): 100101600906
  Facilities: (3)
    Window size: 2 2
  Call User Data (4): 0xC4000000 (unknown)
XOT: X25 O P1 CALL REQUEST (27) 8 lci 522
From(12): 100103200002 To(12): 100101600906
  Facilities: (6)
    Packet size: 128 128
    Window size: 2 2
  Call User Data (4): 0xC4000000 (unknown)
XOT: X25 I P3 CALL CONNECTED (23) 8 lci 1545
From(12): 100103200002 To(12): 100101600906
  Facilities: (6)
    Packet size: 128 128
    Window size: 2 2
Serial2: X25 O P4 CALL CONNECTED (5) 8 lci 522
From(0):  To(0):
  Facilities: (0)
Serial2: X25 I D1 CLEAR REQUEST (5) 8 lci 522 cause 0 diag 0
XOT: X25 O D1 CLEAR REQUEST (5) 8 lci 522 cause 0 diag 0
Serial2: X25 O D1 CLEAR CONFIRMATION (3) 8 lci 522
Router#
```

This command provides output associated with X.25 events over all X.25-configured interfaces. It is useful for debugging X.25 problems due to the fact that it shows changes that occur in the virtual circuits handled by the router. Most X.25 connectivity problems stem from errors that either clear or reset virtual circuits, and you can use debug x25 events to identify these errors. Although debug x25 all output includes both data and control messages for all the router's virtual circuits, debug x25 events output includes only control messages for all of the router's VCs.

debug x25 all

The *debug x25 all* command displays debug information about all X.25 traffic:

```
Router#debug x25 all
X25 packet debugging is on
XOT: X25 I D1 DATA (131) 8 lci 512 PS 3 PR 2
Serial2: X25 O D1 DATA (131) 8 lci 1546 PS 3 PR 2
Serial2: X25 I D1 RR (3) 8 lci 1546 PR 4
XOT: X25 O D1 RR (3) 8 lci 1546 PR 4
XOT: X25 I D1 DATA (131) 8 lci 512 PS 4 PR 2
Serial2: X25 O D1 DATA (131) 8 lci 1546 PS 4 PR 2
XOT: X25 I D1 DATA (131) 8 lci 512 PS 5 PR 2
Serial2: X25 O D1 DATA (131) 8 lci 1546 PS 5 PR 2
Serial2: X25 I D1 RR (3) 8 lci 1546 PR 6
XOT: X25 O D1 RR (3) 8 lci 1546 PR 6
Serial2: X25 I D1 DATA (8) 8 lci 1546 PS 2 PR 6
XOT: X25 O D1 DATA (8) 8 lci 1546 PS 2 PR 6
XOT: X25 I D1 DATA (32) 8 lci 512 PS 6 PR 2
Serial2: X25 O D1 DATA (32) 8 lci 1546 PS 6 PR 2
Serial2: X25 I D1 DATA (131) 8 lci 1546 PS 3 PR 7
XOT: X25 O D1 DATA (131) 8 lci 1546 PS 3 PR 7
XOT: X25 I D1 RR (3) 8 lci 512 PR 4
Serial2: X25 O D1 RR (3) 8 lci 1546 PR 4
XOT: X25 I D1 DATA (8) 8 lci 512 PS 7 PR 4
Serial2: X25 O D1 DATA (8) 8 lci 1546 PS 7 PR 4
Serial2: X25 I D1 DATA (131) 8 lci 1546 PS 4 PR 7
XOT: X25 O D1 DATA (131) 8 lci 1546 PS 4 PR 7
Serial2: X25 I D1 DATA (131) 8 lci 1546 PS 5 PR 7
XOT: X25 O D1 DATA (131) 8 lci 1546 PS 5 PR 7
XOT: X25 I D1 DATA (8) 8 lci 512 PS 0 PR 5
Serial2: X25 O D1 DATA (8) 8 lci 1546 PS 0 PR 5
Serial2: X25 I D1 RR (3) 8 lci 1546 PR 1
XOT: X25 O D1 RR (3) 8 lci 1546 PR 1
Router#
```

This command is particularly useful for diagnosing problems encountered when placing X.25 calls. The debug x25 all output includes data, control messages, and flow control packets for all of the router's virtual circuits.

X.25 Summary

In this section, we have discussed the X.25 protocol and looked at the Cisco IOS commands available to troubleshoot X.25 interfaces and connections. We looked at the basic show and debug commands and explained their uses in the troubleshooting process. For more detailed instructions on how to configure X.25 interfaces, consult the Cisco Web site or the Advanced Cisco Router Configuration course book.

Chapter Summary

In this chapter, we have looked at serial interfaces, Frame Relay, and X.25 and the available troubleshooting commands. These connectivity methods are among the most common used in today's WANs and a fundamental knowledge of each is essential.

We started with a technical overview of each method and moved on to Cisco's show and debug commands that can be used to interrogate the router to receive real-time reports that will help us in the troubleshooting process. As in any other troubleshooting situation, always start at the physical layer and work your way up. This method of troubleshooting is logical and can save you a lot of time in the field.

Frequently Asked Questions (FAQ)

Question: What is the default encapsulation type on Cisco serial interfaces?

Answer: The default encapsulation type is High-Level Data Link Control (HDLC).

Question: When connecting two Frame Relay devices that are from differing manufactures, which default settings should be changed to facilitate communication?

Answer: In this case, you should make sure that the Cisco router is using the standard IETF Frame Relay encapsulation.

Question: What is the maximum transmission speed that a standard DB-60 serial interface will support?

Answer: A standard DB-60 serial interface will support up to 4096 Kbps.

Case Study

You are the network engineer for a small engineering company with two main sites and have been assigned to identify the problem that has been encountered when trying to establish a leased line connection between the sites. The sites are referred to as Leeds and Castleford, named after their geographical locations. In the past, they were connected over ISDN using DDR. Increased traffic has made the option of a 256-Kbps line more affordable due to the escalating ISDN call charges.

You currently have a Cisco 1603 router at both sites. The ISDN is connected to the local Telco's ISDN network to provide access to the other site. You decide to go for a serial WAN interface card in each 1603 to provide you with the DB-60 serial interface required to connect to the Telco's *Network Terminating Unit* (NTU).

The Telco visits both sites and installs the NTU. You plug the DB-60 into V.35 cables for both routers and get to work on the router's configuration. After you have set up the configuration, the serial interfaces on both 1603 routers will not come up. They are both showing as being down.

Approach

You instantly presume that something in your configuration must be wrong as you are not very skilled in working with serial interfaces. You call Telco for assistance and they talk you through checking the configuration of both routers. These appear fine and no configuration errors occur. You then decide to adopt a systematic troubleshooting approach based on the OSI model.

You begin by looking at the physical interfaces on the router and the NTU. Everything seems in order. The green OK light is on the NTU and Telco has checked the line for faults. Then you remember reading about a command that displayed the cable status that was physically attached to the DB-60 interface on the router. You remember this command as *show controllers*.

You go to both routers and run a show controllers command. The following is the result from the show controllers command on the Leeds router:

```
Leeds#sh contr
HD unit 0, NIM slot 1, NIM type code 12, NIM version 5
idb = 0x6082FC48, driver structure at 0x60834118, regaddr =
0x3C100000
buffer size 1524  Universal Serial: DCE V.35 cable
cpb = 0x17, eda = 0x90A0, cda = 0x90B4
RX ring with 32 entries at 0x40179000
00 bd_ptr=0x9000 pak=0x60836E20 ds=0x40184CBC status=80 pak_size=64
```

```
...
Output Omitted
...
32 bd_ptr=0x9280 pak=0x6083A670 ds=0x401931B4 status=80 pak_size=12
cpb = 0x17, eda = 0x9828, cda = 0x9828
TX ring with 2 entries at 0x40179800
00 bd_ptr=0x9800 pak=0x000000 ds=0x4022004A status=80 pak_size=534
01 bd_ptr=0x9814 pak=0x000000 ds=0x4022E550 status=80 pak_size=148
02 bd_ptr=0x9828 pak=0x000000 ds=0x401B358C status=80 pak_size=20
0 missed datagrams, 0 overruns
0 bad datagram encapsulations, 0 memory errors
0 transmitter underruns
Leeds#
```

The following is the result from the show controllers command on the
Castleford router:

```
Castleford#sh contr
HD unit 0, NIM slot 1, NIM type code 12, NIM version 5
idb = 0x6082FC48, driver structure at 0x60865438, regaddr =
0x3C105743
buffer size 1524  Universal Serial: DCE V.35 cable
cpb = 0x17, eda = 0x90A0, cda = 0x90B4
RX ring with 32 entries at 0x40179000
00 bd_ptr=0x9000 pak=0x66436E20 ds=0x401564BC status=80 pak_size=64
...
Output Omitted
...
32 bd_ptr=0x9280 pak=0x6083A670 ds=0x4654631B4 status=80
pak_size=12
cpb = 0x17, eda = 0x9828, cda = 0x9828
TX ring with 2 entries at 0x40179800
00 bd_ptr=0x9800 pak=0x000000 ds=0x4022004A status=80 pak_size=534
01 bd_ptr=0x9814 pak=0x000000 ds=0x4022E550 status=80 pak_size=148
02 bd_ptr=0x9828 pak=0x000000 ds=0x401B358C status=80 pak_size=20
0 missed datagrams, 0 overruns
0 bad datagram encapsulations, 0 memory errors
0 transmitter underruns
Castleford#
```

You instantly notice that the cables are showing as V.35 DCE cables. You
require V.35 DTE cables because the router is acting as a DTE device.

Results

After you replace the DCE cables for DTE cables, the serial interfaces
instantly return to the Interface Up, Protocol Up state. You can now communicate over the line between sites.

Questions

1. In a Frame relay network, the Frame Relay switches are considered to be what type of equipment?

   a. DTE

   b. DCE

2. In X.25, which addressing is mapped to the network address and displayed with the show x25 vc command?

   a. X.25

   b. X.121

   c. Q.931

   d. X.28

3. Which show command displays the cable type attached to the interface?

   a. show serial cable

   b. show controllers

   c. show interface

   d. show buffers

4. Which of the following would you class as a DTE device?

   a. Frame Relay switch

   b. X.25 switch

   c. PC workstation

   d. Terminal

5. Which command displays the number of FECN and BECN packets received?

   a. show frame-relay accounting

   b. show frame-relay congestions

   c. show frame-relay lmi

   d. show frame-relay pvc

6. What happens on a serial interface if the myseq counters increment by more than three?

   a. The interface is shut down.

   b. The interface is reset.

   c. The interface is put into holddown.

   d. The interface protocol goes down.

7. Within Frame Relay, the acronym DLCI stands for what?

   a. Data Level Connection Identifier

   b. Data Link Connection Identifier

   c. Data Line Control Interface

   d. Discard Loss Correction Indicator

8. What is the default encapsulation type on Cisco serial interfaces?

   a. Frame Relay

   b. HDLC

   c. SDLC

   d. X.25

9. Which Cisco command must be run in global configuration mode for the router to operate as a DCE device?

   a. frame-relay switching

   b. frame-relay dce

   c. frame-relay intf-type dce

   d. frame-relay dce

10. In X.25, which network layer protocol is responsible for the transportation of packets between DTE devices across X.25 virtual circuits?

   a. PLP

   b. LAPB

   c. LAPD

   d. X.121

11. Which command displays the correlation between network-layer addresses and the configured DLCI on an interface?

   a. show frame-relay map

   b. show frame-relay pvc

   c. show frame-relay dlci

   d. show interface serial

12. Which command displays detailed information about the X.25 virtual circuit?

   a. show x25 circuit

   b. show x25

   c. show x25 vc

   d. show x25 pvc

13. Which command displays debug information about the LMI packets that are sent between the local DTE and the remote DTE devices?

   a. debug frame-relay interface

   b. debug frame-relay packet

   c. debug frame-relay lmi

   d. debug frame-relay events

14. Which of the following is not a WAN protocol?

   a. SMDS

   b. Frame Relay

   c. Token Ring

   d. X.25

15. What is the default Frame Relay LMI type on Cisco routers?

   a. Cisco

   b. Q944a

   c. ANSI

   d. IETF

16. If the source DTE receives a packet back from the destination DTE, what occurs?

   a. The source DTE slows down the transmission.

   b. The destination DTE slows down the transmission.

   c. The DCEs slow down the transmission.

   d. Transmission commences as normal.

17. Which command would display the X.25 routing table on a router?

   a. Router(config)#show X.25 route

   b. Router(config-if)#show X.25 route

   c. Router#show X.25 routing

   d. Router#show X.25 route

18. At which layer of the OSI reference model does LAPB function at?

   a. Application

   b. Presentation

   c. Network

   d. Data Link

19. What is the default Frame Relay encapsulation on Cisco Routers?

   a. Cisco

   b. IETF

   c. Q944a

   d. ANSI

20. In a Frame Relay congested network, which field in the Frame Relay header discriminates between high- and low-priority traffic?

    a. BECN

    b. FECN

    c. Discard eligibility

    d. Flag

Answers

1. Answer: b

   The Frame Relay switch in a Frame Relay network is a DCE.

2. Answer: b

   The X.25 addressing that is mapped to the network layer addressing is X.121.

3. Answer: b

   To display the cable type that is connected to a serial interface, you would enter the command *show controllers*. This displays the cable and interface types at the physical layer of the OSI reference model.

4. Answer: c and d

   Both the PC workstation and the terminal can be classified as DTE devices. The Frame Relay switch and the X.25 switch would both be considered DCE devices.

5. Answer: d

   The command *show frame-relay pvc* shows the number of BECN, FECN, and DE packets sent and received over a Frame Relay-enabled interface.

6. Answer: b

   If the myseq counter increments by more than three, the interface is reset. The reset can be displayed with the *show interface* command.

7. Answer: b

   DLCI stands for Data Link Connection Identifier.

8. Answer: b

   The default encapsulation on all Cisco serial interfaces is HDLC. HDLC stands for High-Level Data Link Control.

9. Answer: a

   To operate a Cisco router as a DCE device, you must enter the *frame-relay switching* command in global configuration mode.

10. Answer: a

    The Packet-Layer Protocol (PLP) is the X.25 network layer protocol that is responsible for the transportation of packets between DTE devices across X.25 virtual circuits.

11. Answer: a

   The *show frame-relay map* command displays the mappings between the network-layer protocols and the DLCI.

12. Answer: c

   The command *show x25 vc* displays detailed information about the X.25 virtual circuit.

13. Answer: c

   The *debug frame-relay lmi* command displays debug information about the LMI packets that are sent between the local DTE and the remote DTE devices.

14. Answer: c

   Token Ring is not a WAN protocol. It is a specification for a Token-based LAN and it is outlined in the IEE standard 802.5.

15. Answer: a

   The default LMI type is Cisco. The other red herring in here is option D. IETF is a Frame Relay encapsulation type and not an LMI type.

16. Answer: a

   If the source DTE receives a packet back from the destination DTE, this indicates to the source DTE that the destination DTE has received a packet loss due to congestion. The source DTE will then slow down the transmission.

17. Answer: d

   The command *Router#show x25 route* would display the X.25 routing table on the router. The important aspect to grasp here is that this command must be run from global configuration mode.

18. Answer: d

   LAPB operates at the data-link layer of the OSI reference model.

19. Answer: a

   The default Frame Relay encapsulation type is Cisco. The options C and D were both red herrings as Q944a and ANSI are not Frame Relay encapsulation types but Frame Relay LMI types.

20. Answer: c

   The DE field is a one-bit field that exists in the Frame Relay header. DTE devices can use the DE field to prioritize traffic. If the DE field contains the value 1, then that frame is deemed to be of a lower importance than other traffic on the Frame Relay network. When congestion occurs, the DCE device would drop frames with the DE field set to 1 first. This is a way to mark critical data and prevent it from being dropped during periods of congestion.

## CHAPTER 9

Transmission Control Protocol/ Internet Protocol (TCP/IP)

This chapter provides an overview of the *Transmission Control Protocol/Internet Protocol* (TCP/IP) and the tools that are available for troubleshooting TCP/IP networks. We will be covering the fundamentals of TCP/IP and examining the role of the major protocols that are contained in the suite.

The chapter will also focus on TCP/IP troubleshooting in relation to Cisco networking devices. Router diagnostic tools such as the *packet Internet groper* (ping) and trace will be covered as well as the show and debug commands that are available. We will also briefly cover the basic Microsoft Windows 95/NT TCP/IP diagnostic and troubleshooting commands.

The best place to start when troubleshooting any network-related problem is at the physical layer of the OSI model. We will adopt this layered, systematic troubleshooting approach to reduce the amount of time it takes to resolve a TCP/IP-related network problem. Generally, TCP/IP operates at the network and transport layers of the OSI model; however, protocols in the TCP/IP suite operate in the application layer, such as the *file transfer protocol* (FTP) and Telnet. Also, protocols in the TCP/IP suite operate at the data link layer of the OSI model, such as the *address resolution protocol* (ARP).

Objectives Covered in the Chapter

This chapter introduces you to troubleshooting the TCP/IP protocol suite with the following objectives:

- Analyze problem symptoms and resolve resolution strategies in TCP/IP (including the Microsoft 95/NT IP stack), Novell IPX, AppleTalk, Ethernet *virtual local area networks* (VLANs), Frame Relay, and ISDN *basic-rate interface* (BRI).

- Demonstrate knowledge of connection sequences and key troubleshooting targets within TCP/IP, Novell IPX, and AppleTalk.

- Identify and use the innate Cisco IOS software commands and debug utilities to filter, capture, and display protocol traffic flows.

- Use proven problem isolation techniques to list the symptoms of common TCP/ICP problems.

- Apply diagnostic tools to trouble tickets and solve classroom network TCP/IP problems that simulate real-life internetworking malfunctions.

- Apply diagnostic tools to solve network problems that include systems running TCP/IP with Windows NT/95 clients and servers.

Overview of TCP/IP

TCP/IP was originally developed by the *Defense Advanced Research Projects Agency* (DARPA) to interconnect various defense department computer networks. DARPA was assigned by the *Department Of Defense* (DOD) to build a robust communications protocol that could automatically recover from any node or communications failure. This built-in redundancy, which was originally designed for the battlefield, was to create the network protocol of the future and spawn the existence of the Internet.

Initially, TCP/IP included a few basic service protocols that were essential to any communications network. These were file transfer, e-mail, remote login, and remote printing. These functions enabled communication and collaboration across a large number of client and server systems.

TCP/IP can be run over a LAN or *wide area network* (WAN). It also provides LAN and WAN interconnections that have given rise to educational and corporate research WANs. These networks have grown and become interconnected using the *Internet protocol* (IP) to route between them. Today these networks form what we call the Internet. TCP/IP is the backbone of today's Internet and is the protocol of choice for corporate LANs and WANs.

Major network operating system vendors such as Novell and Microsoft have standardized the TCP/IP protocol for their operating systems. This eases and simplifies migrations and co-existences with other systems, allowing common services such as FTP and SMTP to be platform- and vendor-independent. For Novell, this was a large and strategic step, as Novell had used its propriety IPX/SPX protocol for over a decade.

TCP and IP in the OSI Model

The OSI model is a seven-layered model consisting of the following in descending order:

7. Application layer

6. Presentation layer

5. Session layer

4. Transport layer

3. Network layer

2. Data link layer

1. Physical layer

These seven layers interact and communicate with both the layers directly above and layer below. Above the application layer is the user and below the physical layer is the network cable.

In contrast to the OSI model, TCP/IP was built around a four-layer model, referred to as the DOD or DARPA model. We will refer to it as the DOD model. The simple reasoning for this is that TCP/IP was developed well before the advent of the OSI reference model and the DOD standards had already been set. However, the DOD model closely maps to the OSI reference model through the following layers:

- *Application layer*   The DOD application layer defines the upper-layer functionality included in the application, presentation, and session layers of the OSI model. Support is included for application communications, code formatting, session establishment, and maintenance between applications.

- *Transport layer*   The DOD transport layer maps directly to the transport layer of the OSI model. This layer defines connectionless and connection-oriented transport functionality.

- *Internet layer*   The DOD Internet layer maps directly to the network layer of the OSI model. The network layer defines the internetworking functionality for routing protocols. This layer is responsible for the routing of packets between hosts and networks.

- *Network interface layer*   The DOD network interface layer maps to the data link and physical layers of the OSI model (see Figure 9-1). Data link properties, media access methods, and physical connections are defined at this layer.

We will refer to TCP/IP in relation to the OSI model and not the DOD model for the rest of this chapter. The industry as a whole uses the OSI model as a reference and it is necessary to learn the correlation of the TCP/IP protocol suite to the OSI model. This also helps in following the structure of this book's coverage on troubleshooting.

Internet Protocol (IP)

IP is defined by RFC 791. It is the network-layer datagram service of the TCP/IP suite. IP is used by all other protocols in the TCP/IP suite to route

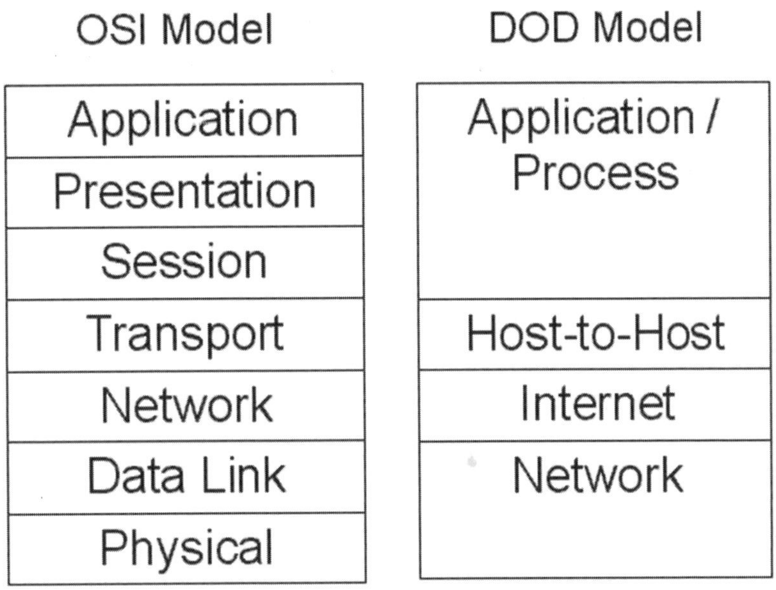

Figure 9-1
The four-layer DOD
model and the seven-
layer OSI model

OSI Model	DOD Model
Application	Application / Process
Presentation	
Session	
Transport	Host-to-Host
Network	Internet
Data Link	Network
Physical	

packets from host to host over an internetwork, except the *address resolution protocol* (ARP) and the *reverse address resolution protocol* (RARP). IP operates at the network layer of the OSI model and the Internet layer of the DOD model.

IP defines the set of rules for communicating across the network. Addressing and control information is included that enables the IP packets to be routed to their intended destinations over the internetwork. IP has two main functions:

- To provide a connectionless, best-effort packet delivery service across an internetwork.

- To provide fragmentation and the reassembly of packets to support data links with differing *maximum transmission unit* (MTU) sizes. This is also described as basic congestion control.

The main function of IP is to route packets across the internetwork. This function is unique to IP and isn't displayed by any other of the protocols contained in the TCP/IP suite. The other feature of IP, congestion control, is found on nearly every layer of the OSI model. IP performs basic congestion control because the control is primitive in comparison with the congestion control offered by TCP.

Routing is described as the delivery of packets or datagrams from the source node to the destination node, possibly across multiple heterogeneous intermediate networks. When the hosts are on the same physical network or subnet, they can be delivered using the routing services provided by their own IP modules. When the hosts are located on separate connected networks or different subnets, the delivery is made via a number of routers that interconnect the networks.

IP, as discussed earlier, provides a connectionless, best-effort packet delivery system. This facilitates the delivery of packets from the source to the destination. This service has three conceptual characteristics that are important for understanding the behavior of IP routing:

- *Connectionless*   IP is considered to be a connectionless protocol. Thus, each packet is delivered independently of all other packets. The packets can be sent along different routes and may arrive out of sequence at the destination. No acknowledgements are sent to indicate that the IP packets were received by the intended destination.

- *Unreliable*   Due to the connectionless nature of IP, we also categorize it as an unreliable protocol. IP does not guarantee that every packet that is transmitted will be received by the host intact and in the original sequence in which it was sent.

- *Best effort*   IP uses its "best effort" to deliver the packets to their intended destinations. IP only discards packets if it is forced to do so due to hardware issues such as resource allocation problems or errors caused at the physical layer.

IP packets or datagrams consist of the IP header and the data (see Figure 9-2). The data is received from the upper-layer protocols, such as

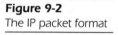

Figure 9-2
The IP packet format

0			15 16		31
version	length	type of service	total length		
identification			flags	fragment offset	
time to live		protocol	header checksum		
source IP address					
destination IP address					
data					

TCP or UDP, and encapsulated into the IP packet. The IP header is created by the IP and is used by IP on intermediary systems to route the packet to its final destination. The IP header contains complete routing information to enable IP to route the packet independent of any other process. This stems from the connectionless nature of IP.

The following sections outline the various fields within IP.

Version   The Version field has four bits and it represents the version of IP to which the packet belongs. Currently, we use IP version 4. In the future, we will use *IP version 6* (Ipv6) or *IP Next Generation* (IPng).

IP Header Length (IHL)   The IHL field defines the length of the IP header. The Options field that will be discussed is optional and can affect the length of the header. The IHL field occupies four bits of the IP header.

Type of Service (TOS)   The TOS field occupies eight bits of the IP header. This field specifies how the packet should be handled.

Total Length   The Total Length field occupies 16 bits of the IP header. This field refers to the total length of the packet measured in octets.

Identification   The Identification field occupies 16 bits of the IP header. This field is used in conjunction with the Flags and Fragment Offset fields to aid in the packet fragmentation and packet reassembly processes.

A packet is fragmented when the original packet size is larger than the MTU at the receiving node or any router along the route. IP fragments the packet into smaller packets that are within the MTU limitations. These fragmented packets are true IP packets in their own sense and contain both an IP header and IP data.

When a packet is generated at the transmitting node, a unique number is entered into the 16-bit Identification field. If the packet has to be fragmented to be received by the destination node, the original IP header is copied into the new fragmented packets. This copying process creates packets with similar Identification fields in the IP header. The receiving host then uses this to identify the original packets when it reassembles the packet into its original form.

Flags   The Flags field occupies three bits of the IP header. Its only purpose is in fragmentation. Each bit is interpreted independently as follows:

- Bit 0: This is reserved.
- Bit 1: This is the "Don't Fragment" or DF bit. When this bit is cleared, it is an indicator that the packet can be fragmented. When the bit is set, it indicates that the packet cannot be fragmented.
- Bit 2: This is the "More Fragments" or MF bit. When this bit is cleared, it indicates that this is the last fragment of the packet. When the bit is set, it indicates that more fragments are to follow.

Fragment Offset   The Fragment Offset field occupies 13 bits of the IP header. This field identifies which part of the original packet this fragment is carrying.

Time to Live (TTL)   The TTL field occupies eight bits of the IP header. This field indicates how long the packet can exist before being dropped or copied to the bit bucket by an intermediate router. When a router receives a packet, it decrements the TTL value by one. If this value is 0, then the router discards the packet by copying it to the bit bucket. Otherwise, it forwards the packet on to the next hop router or the destination network if the destination network is directly connected. The main function of the TTL field is to prevent network congestion through routing loops. The TTL ensures that even if a misconfiguration creates a loop, the packet will be dropped when its TTL expires.

Protocol   The Protocol field occupies eight bits of the IP header. This field is used to identify the protocol that should receive the data contained in the packet. Eight bits facilitates 255 different protocols and these are represented as a numeric value.

Header Checksum   The Header Checksum field occupies 16 bits of the IP header. This field is calculated as a checksum for the IP header and not for the data contained within the packet. Upper-layer protocols should have their own data integrity verification for the data contained in the IP packet.

Source and Destination Addresses   The Source and Destination Addresses both occupy 32 bits of the IP header. These are the actual 32-bit IP addresses of the source and destination nodes.

Options and Padding   The Options and Padding fields are only used for debugging and do not prove very useful.

Transmission Control Protocol (TCP)

TCP is defined in RFC 761 and operates at the transport layer of the OSI model. TCP sits on top of IP and provides IP with a reliable transport protocol that is used when communications have to be reliable. Various services utilize TCP, such as the *hypertext transfer protocol* (HTTP), *simple main transport protocol* (SMTP), *post office protocol 3* (POP3), and *file transfer protocol* (FTP). TCP is connection-oriented and provides reliability with checksums and sequencing, as well as flow control through source quench and sliding windows. The fields in the TCP header are shown in Figure 9-3.

Flow control is required to control the transmission speeds between the source and destination host. Flow control is designed to slow down the transmission of packets if the receiving host is unable to keep up with the transmission speed. Well-known TCP ports are shown later in Table 9-3.

User Datagram Protocol (UDP)

The *user datagram protocol* (UDP) is defined in RFC 768. UDP operates at the transport layer of the OSI model. UDP is a simple packet-oriented transport layer protocol that is connectionless and therefore unreliable.

UDP packets are sent with no sequencing or flow control, so there is no guarantee that they will reach their intended destination. The receiving host compares the UDP header checksum, and if a problem is detected, the packet is dropped without reporting the error back to the sending host.

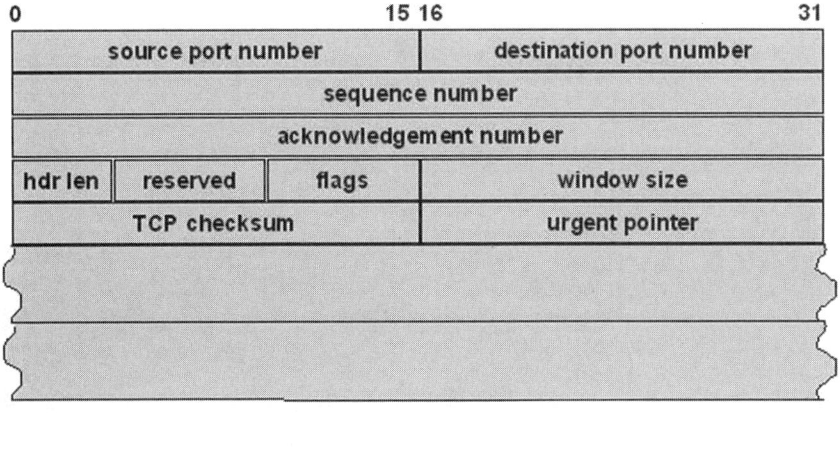

Figure 9-3
TCP header

UDP is a fast transport protocol due to the fact that no acknowledge-ments or advanced sequencing is carried out at the transport layer. Upper-layer protocols may enforce their own error-detection and recovery tasks to utilize the speed of UDP. UDP is typically used when the data is not essen-tial, such as in video or voice streaming of live content over the Internet (see Figure 9-4). The trivial file transfer protocol that is used to upgrade soft-ware images on Cisco routers and switches is also based on UDP. Well-known UDP ports are shown later in Table 9-2.

Internet Control Message Protocol (ICMP)

The *Internet control message protocol* (ICMP) is defined by RFC 792 and RFC 1700. ICMP is considered an integral part of IP. ICMP is a separate protocol, although it does use IP transmission services. It operates at the network layer of the OSI model and the Internet layer of the DOD model. Unlike IP, ICMP does not provide any services for the transport layer pro-tocols. The ICMP message is sent encapsulated in IP datagrams as data; these are sent on the network layer and are transmitted with the same best-effort, connectionless transportation used by IP.

ICMP mainly provides a reporting function that identifies error condi-tions on network devices. Routers usually generate ICMP messages as they receive and route the IP packet. These ICMP messages contain three fields at the beginning of the packet:

- *Type field*   A Type field is an eight-bit field that identifies the message. Type fields are displayed in Table 9-1.
- *Code field*   A Code field is an eight-bit field that provides further information about the ICMP message.
- *Checksum field*   A Checksum field is a 16-bit field that is used to verify the integrity of the entire ICMP message.

Figure 9-4
The UDP header

0	15	16	31
source port number		destination port number	
UDP length		UDP checksum	

Table 9-1	**Type Field**	**Type Description**
ICMP Message Types	0	Echo reply
	1	Unassigned
	2	Unassigned
	3	Destination unreachable
	4	Source quench
	5	Redirect
	6	Alternate host address
	7	Unassigned
	8	Echo
	9	Router advertisement
	10	Router selection
	11	Time exceeded
	12	Parameter problem
	13	Timestamp
	14	Timestamp reply
	15	Information request
	16	Information reply
	17	Address mask request
	18	Address mask reply
	19	Reserved
	20–29	Reserved
	30	Traceroute
	31	Datagram conversion error
	32	Mobile host redirect
	33	IPv6 where are you
	34	IPv6 I am here
	35	Mobile registration request
	36	Mobile registration reply
	37-255	Reserved

In network troubleshooting, one of the most frequently used tools is the Packet Internet Groper or ping command. The ping command utilities ICMP echo messages to provide a simple way of testing whether a remote node is up and running a TCP/IP protocol stack.

When you issue a ping command, you are sending an IP packet to the destination address. The destination will translate the IP packet and use the built-in reply functionality of IP to issue an ICMP type-eight echo message back to the source address. This command is frequently used as a first line of troubleshooting and can prove many configurations at levels 1, 2, and 3 of the OSI layer.

The command

```
Router#debug ip icmp
```

can be used to turn on ICMP debugging on the router and help you to troubleshoot end-to-end connectivity problems. This is explained further in the debugging section in this chapter.

NOTE: *ICMP can be blocked by an inbound or outbound access list as part of a firewall or similar security measure. ICMP is essential if you want to ping and trace network nodes behind the router interface.*

Address Resolution Protocols (ARP)

ARP is defined by RFC 1122. It operates at the data link layer of the OSI model and its primary function is to convert IP addresses to network layer addresses, such as a *media access control* (MAC) address.

Routers and hosts both operate ARP to convert IP addresses to MAC addresses. All network communications eventually take place over the network layer of the OSI model and a network layer address such as a MAC address is required for this to take place. The MAC address corresponding to the IP address can be either statically entered prior to any communication by adding a static ARP entry or ARP can dynamically learn the MAC address.

To dynamically learn a MAC address, ARP sends out a broadcast frame requesting the MAC address of a host with a specified IP address. All hosts on the segment will receive the broadcast, but only the host with the specified IP address will respond with its MAC address. At this point, layer-3 communication can begin.

However, if the destination address is on a remote segment or subnet, there is a slightly different process. The source host will check the destination host's IP address and subnet mask to ascertain if the host is local or remote. If the destination host is local, then a broadcast frame is sent as described above. If the destination host is remote, the source host will eventually have to pass the frame to the default gateway or router. The MAC address will have to be sent to the router, so an ARP broadcast is sent specifying the routers IP address.

Both routers and hosts have an ARP cache, which is always checked before an ARP packet is broadcast onto the network. The ARP cache contains previously learned MAC address and holds them for a predetermined duration of time before flushing them out of the cache. On Cisco routers, the ARP cache can be displayed by entering

```
Router#show arp
```

The following listing shows the results of this command:

```
Router#sh arp
Protocol   Address          Age (Min.)   Hardware Addr.   Type   Interface
Internet   192.168.10.65    14           0010.5a30.b146   ARPA   Ethernet0/0
Internet   192.168.10.35    4            00c0.f049.dea9   ARPA   Ethernet0/0
Internet   192.168.10.38    2            0080.c88e.2aed   ARPA   Ethernet0/0
Internet   192.168.10.39    2            0040.952d.02fa   ARPA   Ethernet0/0
Internet   192.168.10.43    0            00c0.f048.04f4   ARPA   Ethernet0/0
Internet   192.168.10.40    0            0090.2793.7cdd   ARPA   Ethernet0/0
Internet   192.168.10.47    2            0080.c8e5.98a4   ARPA   Ethernet0/0
Internet   192.168.10.44    1            0060.088e.b088   ARPA   Ethernet0/0
Internet   192.168.10.50    0            0000.e87e.9010   ARPA   Ethernet0/0
Internet   192.168.10.48    10           00e0.293d.5bd5   ARPA   Ethernet0/0
Internet   192.168.10.49    9            0040.952d.02f0   ARPA   Ethernet0/0
Internet   192.168.10.55    8            0090.27c2.ac63   ARPA   Ethernet0/0
Internet   192.168.10.58    0            0090.27c2.abf9   ARPA   Ethernet0/0
Internet   192.168.10.59    7            0040.952d.0b5a   ARPA   Ethernet0/0
Internet   192.168.10.56    0            0090.27c2.a498   ARPA   Ethernet0/0
Internet   192.168.10.57    3            0090.27c2.ab74   ARPA   Ethernet0/0
Internet   192.168.10.62    2            0090.27c2.57f7   ARPA   Ethernet0/0
Internet   192.168.10.60    0            0090.27c2.a49a   ARPA   Ethernet0/0
Internet   192.168.10.1     -            00d0.ba59.17a0   ARPA   Ethernet0/0
Internet   192.168.10.22    0            0040.952d.023c   ARPA   Ethernet0/0
Internet   192.168.10.23    2            00e0.2942.43de   ARPA   Ethernet0/0
Internet   192.168.10.26    0            0010.a403.ec70   ARPA   Ethernet0/0
Internet   192.168.10.27    23           0040.952d.15f2   ARPA   Ethernet0/0
Internet   192.168.10.24    4            00e0.293d.30d7   ARPA   Ethernet0/0
Internet   192.168.10.25    0            00e0.293d.7bb3   ARPA   Ethernet0/0
Internet   192.168.10.31    40           0000.e883.b99b   ARPA   Ethernet0/0
```

Due to the normally dynamic nature of ARP, you wouldn't expect it to cause many problems in a networking environment. However, static ARP entries can lead to problems if they are configured incorrectly. More ARP show and debug commands are explained at the end of the chapter.

Broadcasts

Broadcasts are data packets that are destined for all hosts on the network segment. Broadcasts are grouped into two main classifications: directed broadcasts and flooding.

Directed Broadcasts   Directed broadcasts are packets that are sent to a specific network or a series of networks that are determined by the destination IP address. All IP networks have a subnet or network broadcast address. This is always the last address in the subnet range. For example, a subnet with an IP address of 172.18.8.0 and a subnet mask of 255.255.248.0 would have a subnet broadcast address of 172.18.15.255. Further information on subnetting can be found in the course notes for the *advanced Cisco router configuration* (ACRC) class.

Flooding   A flooded broadcast uses 255.255.255.255 as its destination address. This packet will be destined for every host on every connected network.

The abundance of broadcast packets on the network can lead to a *broadcast storm*, which can literally bring down a network as it pushes the network utilization up to an unacceptable amount. Routers by nature will prevent broadcast storms from happening by limiting the storm to the local cable. Bridges, however, will pass broadcasts because a bridge is a layer-2 device and either a layer-2 or layer-3 address can define broadcasts. The layer-2 address for a broadcast is FF-FF-FF-FF-FF-FF. The best way to identify a broadcast problem is by connecting a protocol analyzer to the local segment. The analyzer can then identify and provide statistics on the types of traffic on the network.

NOTE: *Further information on protocol analyzers can be found in Chapter 3, "Troubleshooting Tools."*

Controlling broadcast messages is an essential part of IP network administration, and a thorough knowledge of the broadcast process is required for a network troubleshooter. Some UDP broadcasts such as BootP and the *dynamic host configuration protocol* (DHCP) are often required for the proper operation of a network. These can be allowed by the use of an *ip helper address*, which will be covered later in the chapter.

Unicasts/Multicasts

Unicasts are IP packets that are destined for a single location on the network. This location is indicated by the destination's host IP address being placed into the destination field in the IP header. Unicast addresses make up the largest portion of the IP address space. This address space is subdivided into three non-overlapping groups that define which part of the IP address is allocated for the host ID and the network ID. These are known as Class A, Class B, and Class C addresses. Also, host-to-host communication normally occurs over multicast addresses, that is, direct from one host to another.

Multicasts are IP packets that are destined for a group of hosts on the network. This group is indicated by the destination address in the IP header. Multicast addresses utilize Class D addresses, which fall in the 224.0.0.–239.255.255.255 range. Multicasts enable IP traffic to be sent from one source or multiple sources to multiple destinations. Unicasts require a single packet to be sent to each destination, while multicasts send a single packet to a multicast group that is identified by a single IP address.

Hosts generally listen for multicast packets on a predetermined address and port. This can be compared to the broadcasting of radio waves. Radio waves are all around us. We can simply pick up a radio transmission by tuning our radio receivers to the correct frequency. In a similar way, routers listen for specific packets by tuning in to the specific multicast address.

Multicasting is an efficient way to deliver packets to multiple destinations. It reduces traffic on the network as one packet is received and processed by a group of addresses. Routers have an internal multicast routing table as well as a standard routing table that can be classified as unicast. Further information on unicasts and multicasts can be found in the course notes for the *advanced Cisco router configuration* (ACRC) class.

Domain Name Server (DNS)

A *domain name server* (DNS) is a hierarchical way to resolve host names to IP addresses. The Internet uses DNS to resolve host names. DNS is specified in RFC 1034 and RFC 1035. Originally, the Internet used host files on all clients to facilitate name resolution. Obviously, as the Internet grew, this became impossible to administer, so DNS was created to create a hierarchical structure that enabled the namespace to be divided into subsets of names for distributing and delegating parts of the namespace to others. This eased the administrative burden of DNS and made the namespace or domain owners responsible for this administration. A full understanding of DNS is desirable but beyond the scope of this book. Many books have been written solely on DNS.

Most DNS problems result from the improper configuration of the DNS servers on the client. These servers can be manually added or dynamically added via DHCP. If the client is using a proxy server, the client does not need specific DNS services, as the proxy server will host the name resolution for the proxy client. The problems will manifest themselves into situations where you cannot reach a host by name, but you can by IP address. Issuing a ping command is a simple way to check the DNS configuration of a client.

You can configure a Cisco router to use a DNS server for hostname resolution. You can also set the command-line interface to use DNS. The command to enable DNS name resolution on a Cisco router is

```
Router(config)#ip name-server A.B.C.D
```

where A.B.C.D is the IP address of an Internet DNS server. You can specify a maximum of six DNS servers per router.

To enable IP name resolution from the command-line interface, you would enter

```
Router(config)#ip domain-lookup
```

Microsoft also use DNS on NT servers, although with NT Server 4.0, Net-Bios name resolutions are standard. NT Server 4.0 uses the *Windows Internet naming service* (WINS) along with directed broadcasts to resolve NetBios names.

Helper Addresses

Network hosts occasionally need to transmit and receive UDP broadcasts for various discovery-based services. Obviously, the standard router configuration will block these broadcasts and this will result in a service failure. One example of this is DHCP, which is used on workstations and network devices to automatically configure the TCP/IP settings to reflect the currently connected network. If a router sits between the DHCP client and the DHCP server, the server will never hear the client's DHCP discover broadcast. In this situation, you would configure an IP helper address.

Helper commands schange a broadcast address to a unicast address to enable the message to be routed to a specific destination. This directs the request to a specific network host rather than broadcasting to all network hosts.

Entering the following command in the interface configuration mode configures IP helper addresses:

```
Router(config-if)#ip helper-address A.B.C.D
```

A.B.C.D is the IP address of the remote server. By default, this configuration will send all eight default UDP ports to the same address. These ports are TFTP (69), DNS (53), Time (37), NetBios name service (137), NetBios datagram service (138), BOOTP/DHCP server (67), BOOTP/DHCP client (68), and TACACS (49).

This can be controlled by the *ip forward-protocol* command. This command specifies which ports to allocate for the helper address. Here's an example:

```
Router(config)#interface ethernet0/0
Router(config-if)#ip helper-address 192.168.10.1
Router(config-if)#ip forward-protocol udp 67
Router(config-if)#ip forward-protocol udp 68
```

This configuration would enable UDP broadcasts from DHCP clients and servers to be directed via a unicast to the host with an IP address of 192.168.10.1.

Helper addresses are a useful tool to master to help you troubleshoot your network. The introduction of routers to a predominately flat network can have serious implications to broadcast-based services. IP helper addresses are one approach to this situation.

Common TCP/UDP Ports

TCP and UDP utilize ports at the transport layer to differentiate between services (see Table 9-2). These ports are often located in the services file, which is located in the `%systemdrive%\winnt\system32\drivers\etc` folder on a Windows NT server.

Microsoft Windows 95/NT TCP/IP

Microsoft Windows platforms have evolved over the last decade. They started by utilizing broadcast-based protocols such as *NetBios extended*

Table 9-2

Common TCP/
UDP Ports

Port	Service
20/TCP	FTP data
21/TCP	FTP
23/TCP	Telnet
25/TCP	SMTP
37/UDP	Time
49/UDP	TACACS
53/TCP/UDP	Domain (DNS)
67/UDP	BootP/DHCP server
68/UDP	BootP/DHCP client
69/UDP	TFTP
80/TCP	WWW
110/TCP	POP3
137/UDP	NetBios name
138/UDP	NetBios datagram

user interfaces (NetBEUIs) and are now running TCP/IP as their core protocol. Many organizations still use NetBEUI due to its ease of use and minimal configuration. This causes problems, however, when an organization wants to implement network segmentation. The router would have to operate as a transparent bridge and therefore the full benefit of a routed network would not be realized.

Basic troubleshooting on Microsoft Windows platforms combines operating system troubleshooting and network troubleshooting. The network is the underlying medium that all operating system communication is based upon. A network configuration error can cause a perfectly configured operating system to fail or act erratically, while an operating system configuration error can cause a failure that an inexperienced troubleshooter may blame on the network. A thorough understanding of both the network and the operating system is required to become a truly proficient troubleshooter.

The majority of this book is concerned with network troubleshooting. In this section, we are going to look specifically at common troubleshooting commands and practices that can be used to troubleshoot a Windows NT TCP/IP environment.

Host-to-Host Communication

To enable host-to-host communication on a Windows NT system, you need to assign a valid IP address and subnet mask to the interface card to which TCP/IP is bound. If you have multiple networks connected by routers, you also need to have a default gateway assigned. The IP address and subnet mask are mandatory, whereas the default gateway is not. This information can be confirmed by entering the *ipconfig* command a console prompt:

```
Microsoft(R) Windows NT(TM)
(C) Copyright 1985-1996 Microsoft Corp.

C:\>ipconfig

Windows NT IP Configuration

Ethernet Adapter E100B1:

        IP Address. . . . . . . . . : 192.168.10.54
        Subnet Mask . . . . . . . . : 255.255.255.0
        Default Gateway . . . . . . : 192.168.10.1

C:\>
```

As you can see from the previous listing, the IP address bound to the Ethernet adapter E100B1 is 192.168.10.54 with a subnet mask of 255.255.255.0. The default gateway or router address is 192.168.10.1.

The ipconfig command only provides basic information about the IP configuration. The *ipconig/all* command provides more detailed information about the IP configuration:

```
C:\>ipconfig /all

Windows NT IP Configuration
        Host Name . . . . . . . . . : pc10
        DNS Servers . . . . . . . . : 212.1.128.157
                                      212.1.128.156
                                      212.1.128.165
        Node Type . . . . . . . . . : Hybrid
        NetBIOS Scope ID. . . . . . :
        IP Routing Enabled. . . . . : No
        WINS Proxy Enabled. . . . . : No
        NetBIOS Resolution Uses DNS : No

Ethernet Adapter E100B1:

        Description . . . . . . . . : Intel(R) PRO PCI Adapter
        Physical Address. . . . . . : 00-90-27-C2-A4-99
        DHCP Enabled. . . . . . . . : Yes
        IP Address. . . . . . . . . : 192.168.10.54
        Subnet Mask . . . . . . . . : 255.255.255.0
        Default Gateway . . . . . . : 192.168.10.1
        DHCP Server . . . . . . . . : 192.168.10.4
```

```
            Primary WINS Server . . . . : 192.168.10.4
            Lease Obtained. . . . . . . : Tuesday, October 26, 1999
                                          9:16:52 AM
            Lease Expires . . . . . . . : Friday, October 29, 1999
                                          9:16:52 AM
    C:\>
```

From this listing we can see a lot more information about the TCP/IP configuration, such as that the above Windows NT machine is using DHCP as its method of IP address assignment.

The ipconfig command is the initial starting point in Windows NT network troubleshooting. The first step you should take is to ensure that you have the correct IP address, subnet mask, and default gateway. The following is the command syntax for the ipconfig command:

```
C:\>ipconfig /?

Windows NT IP Configuration

usage: ipconfig [/? | /all | /release [adapter] | /renew [adapter]]

    /?       Display this help message.
    /all     Display full configuration information.
    /release Release the IP address for the specified adapter.
    /renew   Renew the IP address for the specified adapter.

The default is to display only the IP address, subnet mask, and
default gateway for each adapter bound to TCP/IP.

For Release and Renew, if no adapter name is
specified, then the IP address leases for all
adapters bound to TCP/IP will be released or renewed.

C:\>
```

Ping

The ping command that is included with Windows NT is similar in operation to the ping command supported on Cisco routers. Ping is used to check the protocol-reaching capabilities of a remote host. Here is an example of ping in action:

```
C:\>ping www.masontech.com

Pinging masontech.com [216.156.40.88] with 32 bytes of data:

Reply from 216.156.40.88: bytes=32 time=210ms TTL=110
Request timed out.
Reply from 216.156.40.88: bytes=32 time=200ms TTL=110
Reply from 216.156.40.88: bytes=32 time=201ms TTL=110

C:\>
```

The previous listing shows a ping to www.masontech.com. Note that the second reply times out, indicating that the remote host is running the TCP/IP protocol stack and there is probably a latency somewhere between the source and destination hosts. For more information on ping, check out the "Packet Internet Groper (Ping)" section. Following is the command syntax for the ping command:

```
C:\>ping

Usage: ping [-t] [-a] [-n count] [-l size] [-f] [-i TTL] [-v TOS]
            [-r count] [-s count] [[-j host-list] | [-k host-list]]
            [-w timeout] destination-list

Options:
    -t              Ping the specified host until interrupted.
    -a              Resolve addresses to hostnames.
    -n count        Number of echo requests to send.
    -l size         Send buffer size.
    -f              Set Don't Fragment flag in packet.
    -i TTL          Time to Live.
    -v TOS          Type of Service.
    -r count        Record route for count hops.
    -s count        Timestamp for count hops.
    -j host-list    Loose source route along host list.
    -k host-list    Strict source route along host list.
    -w timeout      Timeout in milliseconds to wait for each reply.

C:\>
```

Tracert

The *tracert* command that is included with Windows NT is similar in operation to the trace command supported on Cisco routers. The tracert command tracks the route that a packet traverses to reach its final destination, such as the following:

```
C:\>tracert www.masontech.com

Tracing route to masontech.com [216.156.40.88]
over a maximum of 30 hops:

  1    <10 ms    <10 ms    <10 ms   192.168.10.1
  2      *         *         *      Request timed out.
  3     30 ms     30 ms     30 ms   chel-access-4-f2-
       0.router.telinco.net [212.1.128.252]
  4     30 ms     30 ms    200 ms   chel-border-1-f1-
       0.router.telinco.net [212.1.133.194]
  5     30 ms     30 ms     40 ms   man1gw2.telinco2-gw.uk.insnet.net
       [195.89.254.125]
  6     30 ms     41 ms     40 ms   lon2gw2-ukatm.uk.insnet.net
       [195.89.1.12]
  7    421 ms    781 ms    651 ms   195.66.225.69
```

```
 8     50 ms     40 ms     40 ms    dcr01-s5-0-0.lndn01.exodus.net
             [212.62.0.145]
 9   1002 ms    731 ms      *       bbr02-p0-2.jrcy01.exodus.net
             [216.32.132.37]
10      *       191 ms     210 ms   dcr04-g3-0.jrcy01.exodus.net
             [209.67.45.98]
11   1161 ms    972 ms    1242 ms   rsm03-vlan992.jrcy02.exodus.net
             [216.32.222.115]
12    350 ms    190 ms      *       216.33.35.30
13    210 ms   1152 ms      *       216.156.0.17
14      *       200 ms      *       216.156.0.13
15    210 ms    201 ms     220 ms   masontech.com [216.156.40.88]

Trace complete.

C:\>
```

The previous listing shows a tracert that has been directed to www. masontech.com. You can see that this tracert has taken 15 hops to reach its final destination. For more information on tracert, see the trace section in this chapter. The following is the command syntax for the tracert command:

```
C:\>tracert

Usage: tracert [-d] [-h maximum_hops] [-j host-list] [-w timeout]
target_name

Options:
   -d                   Do not resolve addresses to hostnames.
   -h maximum_hops      Maximum number of hops to search for target.
   -j host-list         Loose source route along host list.
   -w timeout           Wait timeout milliseconds for each reply.

C:\>
```

ARP Cache

Windows NT has a built-in ARP cache that functions similar to the ARP cache in a Cisco router. ARP is responsible for the IP address to MAC address conversion. Static ARP entries can be added to a Windows NT client that can cause communication problems. The ARP cache is displayed with the following command:

```
C:\>arp -a

Interface: 192.168.10.54 on Interface 2
  Internet Address      Physical Address        Type
```

```
192.168.10.1          00-d0-ba-59-17-a0     Dynamic
192.168.10.201        00-90-27-93-7d-5c     Dynamic

C:\>
```

The above listing shows the ARP cache of the host. For more information on ARP, check out the ARP section in this chapter. The following is the command syntax for the arp command:

```
C:\>arp
Displays and modifies the IP-to-physical address translation tables
used by
address resolution protocol (ARP).
ARP -s inet_addr eth_addr [if_addr]
ARP -d inet_addr [if_addr]
ARP -a [inet_addr] [-N if_addr]

  -a           Displays current ARP entries by interrogating the
               current
               protocol data. If inet_addr is specified, the IP and
               physical
               addresses for only the specified computer are
               displayed. If
               more than one network interface uses ARP, entries
               for each ARP
               table are displayed.
  -g           Same as -a.
  inet_addr    Specifies an Internet address.
  -N if_addr   Displays the ARP entries for the network interface
               specified
               by if_addr.
  -d           Deletes the host specified by inet_addr.
  -s           Adds the host and associates the Internet address
               inet_addr
               with the physical address eth_addr. The physical
               address is
               given as six hexadecimal bytes separated by hyphens.
               The entry
               is permanent.
  eth_addr     Specifies a physical address.
  if_addr      If present, this specifies the Internet address of the
               interface whose address translation table should be
               modified.
               If not present, the first applicable interface will
               be used.

C:\>
```

Windows NT Routing Table

Windows NT can perform static and dynamic routing using the *routing information protocol* (RIP) or *open shortest path first* (OSPF) so a multihomed NT host can act as a simple router to connect networks. This NT router can even exchange routing information with Cisco routers over RIP and OSPF.

The following code shows the routing table for a Windows NT host. You can see that network 0.0.0.0, which is classified as the default route, is forwarded to the default gateway that is 192.168.10.1:

```
C:\>route print
===============================================================================
Interface List
0x1 ......................... MS TCP Loopback Interface
0x2 ...00 90 27 c2 a4 99 ...... Intel(R) PRO PCI Adapter
===============================================================================
===============================================================================
Active Routes:
Network Destination      Netmask           Gateway         Interface      Metric
        0.0.0.0          0.0.0.0           192.168.10.1    192.168.10.54  1
        127.0.0.0        255.0.0.0         127.0.0.1       127.0.0.1      1
        192.168.10.0     255.255.255.0     192.168.10.54   192.168.10.54  1
        192.168.10.54    255.255.255.255   127.0.0.1       127.0.0.1      1
        192.168.10.255   255.255.255.255   192.168.10.54   192.168.10.54  1
        224.0.0.0        224.0.0.0         192.168.10.54   192.168.10.54  1
        255.255.255.255  255.255.255.255   192.168.10.54   192.168.10.54  1
===============================================================================
C:\>
```

Following is the command syntax for the route command:

```
C:\>route

Manipulates network routing tables.

ROUTE [-f] [-p] [command [destination]
                [MASK netmask]   [gateway] [METRIC metric]   [IF
                interface]

    -f          Clears the routing tables of all gateway entries. If
                this is used in conjunction with one of the commands,
                the tables are cleared prior to running the command.
    -p          When used with the ADD command, this makes a route
                persistent across boots of the system. By default,
                routes are not preserved
                when the system is restarted. When used with the
                PRINT command, this displays the list of registered
                persistent routes. Ignored for all other commands,
                which always affect the appropriate persistent
                routes. This option is not supported Windows 95.
    command     One of these:
                    PRINT     Prints a route
                    ADD       Adds a route
                    DELETE    Deletes a route
                    CHANGE    Modifies an existing route
    destination Specifies the host.
    MASK        Specifies that the next parameter is the "netmask"
                value.
```

```
       netmask     Specifies a subnet mask value for this route entry.
                   If not specified, it defaults to 255.255.255.255.
       gateway     Specifies gateway.
       interface   The interface number for the specified route.
       METRIC      Specifies the metric, i.e. cost for the destination.

   All symbolic names used for the destination are looked up in the
   network database file NETWORKS. The symbolic names for gateway are
   looked up in the host name database file HOSTS.

   If the command is PRINT or DELETE, the destination or gateway can
   be a wildcard (wildcard is specified as a star '*') or the gateway
   argument may be omitted.

   If Dest contains a * or ?, it is treated as a shell pattern, and
   only matching destination routes are printed. The '*' matches any
   string, and '?' matches any one char. Examples: 157.*.1, 157.*,
   127.*, *224*.
   Diagnostic Notes:
       Invalid MASK generates an error, that is when (DEST & MASK) !=
       DEST.
       Example> route ADD 157.0.0.0 MASK 155.0.0.0 157.55.80.1 IF 1
                The route addition failed: 87

   Examples:

       > route PRINT
       > route ADD 157.0.0.0 MASK 255.0.0.0  157.55.80.1 METRIC 3 IF 2
               destination^      ^mask        ^gateway     metric^    ^
                                                                 Interface^
         If IF is not given, it tries to find the best interface for a
         given
         gateway.
       > route PRINT
       > route PRINT 157*            .... Only prints those matching 157*
       > route DELETE 157.0.0.0
       > route PRINT

   C:\>
```

Name Resolution

Windows NT uses two distinct types of name resolution. These are for
NetBios name resolution and hostname resolution. NetBios names are
also known as the computername in Windows NT environments. These
stem from the NetBios protocol and are currently required for Windows
NT to operate. Windows 2000 has the option of completely removing Net-
Bios from the Windows environment. NetBios name resolutions use
WINS and LMHOSTS files, both of which are discussed in many
Microsoft publications.

The following is the sample LMHOSTS file that ships with Windows NT. This file is called LMHOSTS.SAM and is located in the `%systemdrive%\ winnt\system32\drivers\etc` folder:

```
# Copyright (c) 1993-1995 Microsoft Corp.
#
# This is a sample LMHOSTS file used by the Microsoft TCP/IP for
# Windows NT.
#
# This file contains the mappings of IP addresses to NT computernames
# (NetBIOS) names. Each entry should be kept on an individual line.
# The IP address should be placed in the first column followed by
# the corresponding computername. The address and the comptername
# should be separated by at least one space or tab. The "#" character
# is generally used to denote the start of a comment (see the
# exceptions below).
#
# This file is compatible with Microsoft LAN Manager 2.x TCP/IP
# lmhosts files and offers the following extensions:
#
#      #PRE
#      #DOM:<domain>
#      #INCLUDE <filename>
#      #BEGIN_ALTERNATE
#      #END_ALTERNATE
#      \0xnn (non-printing character support)
#
# Following any entry in the file with the characters "#PRE" will
# cause the entry to be preloaded into the name cache. By default,
# entries are not preloaded but are parsed only after dynamic name
# resolution fails.
#
# Following an entry with the "#DOM:<domain>" tag will associate
# the entry with the domain specified by <domain>. This affects how
# the browser and logon services behave in TCP/IP environments. To
# preload the host name associated with #DOM entry, it is necessary
# to also add a #PRE to the line. The <domain> is always preloaded
# although it will not be shown when the name cache is viewed.
#
# Specifying "#INCLUDE <filename>" will force the RFC NetBIOS (NBT)
# software to seek the specified <filename> and parse it as if it
# were local. <filename> is generally a UNC-based name, allowing a
# centralized lmhosts file to be maintained on a server.
# It is ALWAYS necessary to provide a mapping for the IP address of
# the server prior to the #INCLUDE. This mapping must use the #PRE
# directive.
# In addition, the share "public" in the example below must be in
# the LanManServer list of "NullSessionShares" in order for client
# machines tobe able to read the lmhosts file successfully. This
machines tokey is under
# \machine\system\currentcontrolset\services\lanmanserver\
# parameters\nullsessionshares
# in the registry. Simply add "public" to the list found there.
#
# The #BEGIN_ and #END_ALTERNATE keywords allow multiple #INCLUDE
# statements to be grouped together. Any single successful include
# will cause the group to succeed.
```

```
#
# Finally, non-printing characters can be embedded in mappings by
# first surrounding the NetBIOS name in quotations and then using
# the \0xnn notation to specify a hex value for a non-printing
# character.
#
# The following example illustrates all of these extensions:
#
102.54.94.97    rhino      #PRE#DOM:networking   #net group's DC
102.54.94.102   "appname   \0x14"                #special app server
102.54.94.123   popular    #PRE                  #source server
102.54.94.117   localsrv   #PRE                  #needed for the
include
#
# #BEGIN_ALTERNATE
# #INCLUDE \\localsrv\public\lmhosts
# #INCLUDE \\rhino\public\lmhosts
# #END_ALTERNATE
#
# In the above example, the "appname" server contains a special
# character in its name, the "popular" and "localsrv" server names
# are preloaded, and the "rhino" server name is specified so it can
# be used to later #INCLUDE a centrally maintained lmhosts file if
# the "localsrv" system is unavailable.
#
# Note that the whole file is parsed, including comments on each
# lookup, so keeping the number of comments to a minimum will
# improve performance.
# Therefore, it is not advisable to simply add lmhosts file entries
# to the end of this file.
```

Internet names and hostnames are resolved in a different way than Net-Bios names. Hostnames are resolved using DNS and HOSTS files, both of which are discussed in many Microsoft publications.

The following is the sample HOSTS file that ships with Windows NT. It is located in the %systemdrive%\winnt\system32\drivers\etc folder:

```
# This is a sample HOSTS file used by Microsoft TCP/IP for Windows NT.
#
# This file contains the mappings of IP addresses to host names. Each
# entry should be kept on an individual line. The IP address should
# be placed in the first column followed by the corresponding host
# name.
# The IP address and the host name should be separated by at least
# one space.
#
# Additionally, comments (such as these) may be inserted on individual
# lines or following the machine name denoted by a '#' symbol.
#
# For example:
#
#     102.54.94.97   rhino.acme.com   # source server
#     38.25.63.10    x.acme.com       # x client host
```

```
127.0.0.1      localhost
212.1.157.7    server2
212.1.157.8    server3
```

Show Commands

Several show commands can be used to view the current TCP/IP configuration of the router. These commands are useful for checking the status of the configuration as well as for troubleshooting a range of TCP/IP problems (see Table 9-3).

show interface

The *show interface* command displays information about the configured interfaces on the router along with basic TCP/IP settings:

```
Router#sh int
Ethernet0 is up, line protocol is up
  Hardware is Lance, address is 0010.7b80.fdee (bia 0010.7b80.fdee)
  Internet address is 194.73.134.24/24
```

Table 9-3

Frequently Used
Show Commands
for Troubleshooting
TCP/IP

Command	Description
show interface	Displays information about the configured interfaces on the router and basic IP information.
show ip interface	Displays the current status of interfaces that have been set up to use TCP/IP. Also provides TCP/IP information on the interface over and above the show interface command.
show ip interface brief	Displays a brief summary of the information presented in the show ip interface command.
show ip protocols	Displays information pertaining to the IP routing protocols that are installed and configured on the router.
show ip arp	Displays the ARP cache on the router.
show ip route	Displays the routing table and identifies how each route was learned.
show ip access-lists	Displays the content of all configured IP access lists on the router.
show ip traffic	Displays traffic information for well-known TCP/IP protocols.

```
MTU 1500 bytes, BW 10000 Kbit, DLY 1000 usec,
   reliability 255/255, txload 1/255, rxload 1/255
Encapsulation ARPA, loopback not set
Keep-alive set (10 sec)
ARP type: ARPA, ARP Timeout 04:00:00
Last input 00:00:00, output 00:00:00, output hang never
Last clearing of "show interface" counters never
Queueing strategy: FIFO
Output queue 0/40, 0 drops; input queue 1/75, 0 drops
5 minute input rate 1000 bits/sec, 2 packets/sec
5 minute output rate 0 bits/sec, 0 packets/sec
   681613 packets input, 50510769 bytes, 0 no buffer
   Received 657619 broadcasts, 0 runts, 0 giants, 0 throttles
   1 input errors, 0 CRC, 0 frame, 0 overrun, 1 ignored
   0 input packets with dribble condition detected
   282259 packets output, 29254559 bytes, 0 underruns
   0 output errors, 1 collisions, 2 interface resets
   0 babbles, 0 late collision, 10 deferred
   0 lost carrier, 0 no carrier
   0 output buffer failures, 0 output buffers swapped out
Ethernet1 is administratively down, line protocol is down
 Hardware is Lance, address is 0010.7b80.fdef (bia 0010.7b80.fdef)
 MTU 1500 bytes, BW 10000 Kbit, DLY 1000 usec,
   reliability 252/255, txload 1/255, rxload 1/255
Encapsulation ARPA, loopback not set
Keep-alive set (10 sec)
ARP type: ARPA, ARP Timeout 04:00:00
Last input never, output 2w0d, output hang never
Last clearing of "show interface" counters never
Queueing strategy: FIFO
Output queue 0/40, 0 drops; input queue 0/75, 0 drops
5 minute input rate 0 bits/sec, 0 packets/sec
5 minute output rate 0 bits/sec, 0 packets/sec
   0 packets input, 0 bytes, 0 no buffer
   Received 0 broadcasts, 0 runts, 0 giants, 0 throttles
   0 input errors, 0 CRC, 0 frame, 0 overrun, 0 ignored
   0 input packets with dribble condition detected
   1 packets output, 60 bytes, 0 underruns
   1 output errors, 0 collisions, 1 interface resets
   0 babbles, 0 late collision, 0 deferred
   1 lost carrier, 0 no carrier
   0 output buffer failures, 0 output buffers swapped out
Serial0 is up, line protocol is up
 Hardware is HD64570
 Internet address is 172.19.1.2/16
 MTU 1500 bytes, BW 1544 Kbit, DLY 20000 usec,
   reliability 255/255, txload 1/255, rxload 1/255
Encapsulation HDLC, loopback not set
Keep-alive set (10 sec)
Last input 00:00:02, output 00:00:01, output hang never
Last clearing of "show interface" counters never
Queueing strategy: FIFO
Output queue 0/40, 0 drops; input queue 0/75, 0 drops
5 minute input rate 0 bits/sec, 0 packets/sec
5 minute output rate 0 bits/sec, 0 packets/sec
   208264 packets input, 14707734 bytes, 0 no buffer
   Received 208263 broadcasts, 0 runts, 0 giants, 0 throttles
   0 input errors, 0 CRC, 0 frame, 0 overrun, 0 ignored, 0 abort
   208260 packets output, 14708364 bytes, 0 underruns
   0 output errors, 0 collisions, 2 interface resets
```

```
     0 output buffer failures, 0 output buffers swapped out
     0 carrier transitions
     DCD=up  DSR=up  DTR=up  RTS=up  CTS=up
 Serial1 is up, line protocol is up
  Hardware is HD64570
  Internet address is 172.20.1.2/16
  MTU 1500 bytes, BW 1544 Kbit, DLY 20000 usec,
     reliability 255/255, txload 1/255, rxload 1/255
  Encapsulation HDLC, loopback not set
  Keep-alive set (10 sec)
  Last input 00:00:03, output 00:00:01, output hang never
  Last clearing of "show interface" counters never
  Input queue: 0/75/0 (size/max/drops); Total output drops: 0
  Queueing strategy: weighted fair
  Output queue: 0/1000/64/0 (size/max total/threshold/drops)
     Conversations  0/1/256 (active/max active/max total)
     Reserved Conversations 0/0 (allocated/max allocated)
  5 minute input rate 0 bits/sec, 0 packets/sec
  5 minute output rate 0 bits/sec, 0 packets/sec
     188075 packets input, 8994508 bytes, 0 no buffer
     Received 188074 broadcasts, 0 runts, 0 giants, 0 throttles
     0 input errors, 0 CRC, 0 frame, 0 overrun, 0 ignored, 0 abort
     188079 packets output, 8997141 bytes, 0 underruns
     0 output errors, 0 collisions, 0 interface resets
     0 output buffer failures, 0 output buffers swapped out
     0 carrier transitions
     DCD=up  DSR=up  DTR=up  RTS=up  CTS=up
```

The previous code indicates the IP configuration on the router interfaces. As you can see, the show interface command only displays limited information relating to the IP configurations.

show ip interface

The *show ip interface* command displays detailed TCP/IP information about the configured interfaces on the router:

```
Router#show ip interface
Ethernet0/0 is up, line protocol is up
 Internet address is 192.168.10.1/24
 Broadcast address is 255.255.255.255
 Address determined by non-volatile memory
 MTU is 1500 bytes
 Helper address is not set
 Directed broadcast forwarding is disabled
 Multicast reserved groups joined: 224.0.0.9
 Outgoing access list is not set
 Inbound access list is not set
 Proxy ARP is enabled
 Security level is default
 Split horizon is enabled
 ICMP redirects are always sent
 ICMP unreachables are always sent
 ICMP mask replies are never sent
 IP fast switching is enabled
```

```
  IP fast switching on the same interface is disabled
  IP flow switching is disabled
  IP feature fast switching turbo vector
  IP multicast fast switching is enabled
  IP multicast distributed fast switching is disabled
  Router discovery is disabled
  IP output packet accounting is disabled
  IP access violation accounting is disabled
  TCP/IP header compression is disabled
  RTP/IP header compression is disabled
  Probe proxy name replies are disabled
  Policy routing is disabled
  Network address translation is enabled, interface in domain inside
  Web cache redirect is disabled
  BGP policy mapping is disabled

BRI0/0 is up, line protocol is up
  Internet protocol processing disabled

Serial0/0 is up, line protocol is up
  Internet address is 192.168.30.1/24
  Broadcast address is 255.255.255.255
  Address determined by non-volatile memory
  MTU is 1500 bytes
  Helper address is not set
  Directed broadcast forwarding is disabled
  Outgoing access list is not set
  Inbound access list is not set
  Proxy ARP is enabled
  Security level is default
  Split horizon is enabled
  ICMP redirects are always sent
  ICMP unreachables are always sent
  ICMP mask replies are never sent
  IP fast switching is enabled
  IP fast switching on the same interface is enabled
  IP flow switching is disabled
  IP feature fast switching turbo vector
  IP multicast fast switching is disabled
  IP multicast distributed fast switching is disabled
  Router discovery is disabled
  IP output packet accounting is disabled
  IP access violation accounting is disabled
  TCP/IP header compression is disabled
  RTP/IP header compression is disabled
  Probe proxy name replies are disabled
  Policy routing is disabled
  Network address translation is disabled
  Web cache redirect is disabled
  BGP policy mapping is disabled

BRI0/0:1 is down, line protocol is down
  Internet protocol processing disabled

BRI0/0:2 is down, line protocol is down
  Internet protocol processing disabled

Dialer1 is up, line protocol is up
  Internet address will be negotiated using IPCP
  Broadcast address is 255.255.255.255
```

```
      MTU is 1500 bytes
      Helper address is not set
      Directed broadcast forwarding is disabled
      Outgoing access list is not set
      Inbound  access list is not set
      Proxy ARP is enabled
      Security level is default
      Split horizon is disabled
      ICMP redirects are always sent
      ICMP unreachables are always sent
      ICMP mask replies are never sent
      IP fast switching is enabled
      IP fast switching on the same interface is enabled
      IP flow switching is disabled
      IP feature fast switching turbo vector
      IP multicast fast switching is enabled
      IP multicast distributed fast switching is disabled
      Router discovery is disabled
      IP output packet accounting is disabled
      IP access violation accounting is disabled
      TCP/IP header compression is disabled
      RTP/IP header compression is disabled
      Probe proxy name replies are disabled
      Policy routing is disabled
      Network address translation is enabled, interface in domain
      outside
      Web cache redirect is disabled
      BGP policy mapping is disabled
      Router#
```

You can see that the previous command provides a great deal of information relating to the TCP/IP configuration for the configured interfaces on a router. IP-specific information such as helper addresses as well as inbound and outbound access lists are also shown by this command. This information makes the show ip interface command an excellent command for troubleshooting helper addresses and access lists.

show ip interface brief

The *show ip interface brief* command displays brief TCP/IP information about the configured interfaces on the router:

```
Router#sh ip interface brief
Interface     IP Address     OK?    Method    Status    Protocol
Ethernet0/0   192.168.10.1   YES    NVRAM     up        up
BRI0/0        unassigned     YES    unset     up        up
Serial0/0     192.168.30.1   YES    NVRAM     up        up
BRI0/0:1      unassigned     YES    unset     down      down
BRI0/0:2      unassigned     YES    unset     down      down
Dialer1       unassigned     YES    NVRAM     up        up
```

This command provides information about the interface, IP address, method, interface status, and protocol status. The Interface field lists the interface type and number. The IP Address field shows the IP address for all assigned interfaces. The Method field indicates where the configuration is stored. The Status field indicates the status of the interface, and the Protocol field indicates the status of the protocol running on the interface. This command displays a quick, short comparison of all interfaces on the router. This is excellent if you have many IP configured interfaces on the router you are diagnosing.

show ip protocols

The *show ip protocols* command displays information about all IP routing protocols that are currently configured on the router:

```
Router#sh ip prot
Routing protocol is "rip"
 Sending updates every 30 seconds, next due in 23 seconds
 Invalid after 180 seconds, hold down 180, flushed after 240
 Outgoing update filter list for all interfaces is
 Incoming update filter list for all interfaces is
 Redistributing: rip
 Default version control: send version 2, receive version 2
   Interface        Send   Recv   Key chain
   Ethernet0/0       2      2
 Routing for Networks:
   192.168.10.0
 Passive Interface(s):
   Dialer1
 Routing Information Sources:
   Gateway          Distance        Last Update
 Distance: (default is 120)

Routing Protocol is "ospf 1"
 Sending updates every 0 seconds
 Invalid after 0 seconds, hold down 0, flushed after 0
 Outgoing update filter list for all interfaces is
 Incoming update filter list for all interfaces is
 Redistributing: ospf 1
 Routing for Networks:
   192.168.10.0
   192.168.30.0
 Passive Interface(s):
   Dialer1
 Routing Information Sources:
   Gateway          Distance        Last Update
 Distance: (default is 110)
```

This command is used to identify the routing protocols in operation on the router along with each protocols' associated settings. You can see in the listing that this router has RIP and OSPF running. You can also see that RIP is advertising 192.168.10.0 with Dialer1 as its passive interface, and OSPF is advertising 192.168.10.0 as well as 192.168.30.0 with Dialer1 as its passive interface. *Dialer1* is a dialer profile interface for use over the BRI connection. Obviously, you do not want the BRI line to be established every time a routing update is sent out. The passive interface command does not enable routing updates to be propagated over this interface. This show ip protocols command is useful in troubleshooting problems associated with dynamic routing over any of the supported routing protocols.

show ip arp

The *show ip arp* command displays the router's ARP cache that contains all of the previously learned IP-to-MAC address resolutions:

```
      Router#show ip arp
Protocol  Address        Age (Min.)  Hardware Addr.  Type  Interface
Internet  192.168.10.65  16          0010.5a30.b146  ARPA  Ethernet0/0
Internet  192.168.10.35  6           00c0.f049.dea9  ARPA  Ethernet0/0
Internet  192.168.10.38  4           0080.c88e.2aed  ARPA  Ethernet0/0
Internet  192.168.10.39  4           0040.952d.02fa  ARPA  Ethernet0/0
Internet  192.168.10.43  2           00c0.f048.04f4  ARPA  Ethernet0/0
Internet  192.168.10.40  0           0090.2793.7cdd  ARPA  Ethernet0/0
Internet  192.168.10.47  4           0080.c8e5.98a4  ARPA  Ethernet0/0
Internet  192.168.10.44  4           0060.088e.b088  ARPA  Ethernet0/0
Internet  192.168.10.50  2           0000.e87e.9010  ARPA  Ethernet0/0
Internet  192.168.10.48  12          00e0.293d.5bd5  ARPA  Ethernet0/0
Internet  192.168.10.49  1           0040.952d.02f0  ARPA  Ethernet0/0
Internet  192.168.10.55  10          0090.27c2.ac63  ARPA  Ethernet0/0
Internet  192.168.10.58  0           0090.27c2.abf9  ARPA  Ethernet0/0
Internet  192.168.10.59  9           0040.952d.0b5a  ARPA  Ethernet0/0
Internet  192.168.10.56  0           0090.27c2.a498  ARPA  Ethernet0/0
Internet  192.168.10.57  6           0090.27c2.ab74  ARPA  Ethernet0/0
Internet  192.168.10.62  4           0090.27c2.57f7  ARPA  Ethernet0/0
Internet  192.168.10.60  2           0090.27c2.a49a  ARPA  Ethernet0/0
Internet  192.168.10.1   -           00d0.ba59.17a0  ARPA  Ethernet0/0
Internet  192.168.10.22  2           0040.952d.023c  ARPA  Ethernet0/0
Internet  192.168.10.23  0           00e0.2942.43de  ARPA  Ethernet0/0
Internet  192.168.10.26  2           0010.a403.ec70  ARPA  Ethernet0/0
Internet  192.168.10.27  25          0040.952d.15f2  ARPA  Ethernet0/0
Internet  192.168.10.24  2           00e0.293d.30d7  ARPA  Ethernet0/0
Internet  192.168.10.25  2           00e0.293d.7bb3  ARPA  Ethernet0/0
Internet  192.168.10.31  42          0000.e883.b99b  ARPA  Ethernet0/0
```

This command can be useful if you are having problems with host connectivity by checking if the IP address correlates to the host's actual MAC address. This identifies any problems with ARP or RARP configurations.

show ip route

The *show ip route* command displays the internal routing table entries of all the IP routing protocols:

```
Router#sh ip route
Codes: C - connected, S - static, I - IGRP, R - RIP, M - mobile, B
- BGP
      D - EIGRP, EX - EIGRP external, O - OSPF, IA - OSPF inter area
      N1 - OSPF NSSA external type 1, N2 - OSPF NSSA external type 2
      E1 - OSPF external type 1, E2 - OSPF external type 2, E - EGP
      i - IS-IS, L1 - IS-IS level-1, L2 - IS-IS level-2, * -
      candidate default
      U - per-user static route, o - ODR

Gateway of last resort is 192.168.20.2 to network 0.0.0.0

C    192.168.30.0/24 is directly connected, Serial0/0
C    192.168.10.0/24 is directly connected, Ethernet0/0
S    192.168.20.0/24 [1/0] via 192.168.30.2
R    10.1.0.0/24 [120/1] via Ethernet0/0
O    212.1.157.0/24 [110/151] via Serial0/0
S*   0.0.0.0/0 [1/0] via 192.168.20.2
```

From this listing you can identify each internal route in the router and ascertain which protocol this route was discovered by and which interface contains the next hop to this remote network. The codes at the top of the listing act as an index to the type of routing protocol shown in the display. We can see that we have connected RIP, OSPF, and static routes in this routing table.

The first section refers to the gateway of last resort. This is also called the default route and is set by entering the static command:

```
Router(config)#ip route 0.0.0.0 0.0.0.0 192.168.20.2
```

This static command will set 192.168.20.2 as the default route. Any traffic that is on the router that cannot be routed via the routing table will be forwarded to this address. This is a handy technique to use if the router has a single route such as a router used for Internet connectivity. You can further restrict this display by entering a protocol after the show ip route command such as

```
Router#show ip route ospf
```

This would display only the routing information for the OSPF protocol.

show ip access-lists

The *show ip access-lists* command displays information regarding the IP access lists that are set on the router:

```
Router#sh ip access-lists
Standard IP access list 2
   permit 192.168.10.0, wildcard bits 0.0.0.255
   permit 192.168.20.0, wildcard bits 0.0.0.255
```

```
Standard IP access list 5
   permit 192.168.20.0, wildcard bits 0.0.0.255
   permit 192.168.10.0, wildcard bits 0.0.0.255
Extended IP access list Firewall
   deny ip 192.168.0.0 0.0.255.255 any log (5283 matches)
   deny ip 172.16.0.0 0.15.255.255 any log (3 matches)
   deny ip 10.0.0.0 0.255.255.255 any log
   deny ip 192.0.2.0 0.0.0.255 any log
   deny ip 127.0.0.0 0.255.255.255 any log
   deny ip 255.0.0.0 0.255.255.255 any log
   deny ip host 0.0.0.0 any log
   deny ip host 222.1.157.1 any log
   deny ip host 222.1.157.2 any log
   deny ip host 222.1.157.3 any log (1479 matches)
   permit tcp any host 224.0.0.2 eq 1985
   permit icmp any 222.1.157.0 0.0.0.255 net-unreachable
   permit icmp any 222.1.157.0 0.0.0.255 echo-reply (6 matches)
   permit icmp any 222.1.157.0 0.0.0.255 echo
   permit icmp any 222.1.157.0 0.0.0.255 host-unreachable
   permit icmp any 222.1.157.0 0.0.0.255 port-unreachable
   permit icmp any 222.1.157.0 0.0.0.255 packet-too-big
   permit icmp any 222.1.157.0 0.0.0.255 administratively-prohibited
   permit icmp any 222.1.157.0 0.0.0.255 source-quench
   permit icmp any 222.1.157.0 0.0.0.255 ttl-exceeded
   permit tcp any 222.1.157.0 0.0.0.255 eq www
   permit tcp any 222.1.157.0 0.0.0.255 eq 443
   permit tcp any 222.1.157.0 0.0.0.255 eq smtp
   permit tcp any 222.1.157.0 0.0.0.255 eq pop3
   permit tcp any 222.1.157.0 0.0.0.255 eq 143
   permit tcp any 222.1.157.0 0.0.0.255 eq ftp-data
   permit tcp any 222.1.157.0 0.0.0.255 eq ftp
   permit tcp any 222.1.157.0 0.0.0.255 eq nntp
   permit tcp any 222.1.157.0 0.0.0.255 eq 8081
   permit tcp any 222.1.157.0 0.0.0.255 eq domain
   permit udp any 222.1.157.0 0.0.0.255 eq domain
   permit tcp any 222.1.157.0 0.0.0.255 established (481 matches)
   permit udp any eq domain any (76 matches)
   deny ip any any log (15713 matches)
```

This listing shows the standard and extended access lists that are in place on the router. The show ip access-lists command is useful to identify the components of each IP access list on the router. Note that this router has two standard access lists, 5 and 2, and one extended access list that is called Firewall. A similar command that would produce this is the *show running-config* command, but this would also show you the rest of the router configuration, whereas the show ip access-list command is very specific.

NOTE: *Access lists always have an implicit "deny all" at the end. If you apply an access list, make sure you let the traffic through that you require because access lists work on a deny-all basis.*

You can also use the show ip interface command to display what access list number or name is associated to inbound and outbound interfaces.

show ip traffic

The *show ip traffic* command displays traffic information regarding several IP protocols:

```
Router#sh ip traffic
IP statistics:
  Rcvd:  92341 total, 3542 local destination
         0 format errors, 0 checksum errors, 0 bad hop count
         0 unknown protocol, 1 not a gateway
         0 security failures, 0 bad options, 0 with options
  Opts:  0 end, 0 nop, 0 basic security, 0 loose source route
         0 timestamp, 0 extended security, 0 record route
         0 stream ID, 0 strict source route, 0 alert, 0 cipso
         0 other
  Frags: 0 reassembled, 0 timeouts, 0 couldn't reassemble
         0 fragmented, 0 couldn't fragment
  Bcast: 725 received, 8 sent
  Mcast: 0 received, 98 sent
  Sent:  2757 generated, 88788 forwarded
  Drop:  9 encapsulation failed, 0 unresolved, 0 no adjacency
         3 no route, 0 unicast RPF, 0 forced drop

ICMP statistics:
  Rcvd: 0 format errors, 0 checksum errors, 0 redirects, 0
  unreachable
        2160 echo, 0 echo reply, 0 mask requests, 0 mask replies, 0
        quench
        0 parameter, 0 timestamp, 0 info request, 0 other
        0 irdp solicitations, 0 irdp advertisements
  Sent: 0 redirects, 3 unreachable, 0 echo, 2157 echo reply
        0 mask requests, 0 mask replies, 0 quench, 0 timestamp
        0 info reply, 0 time exceeded, 0 parameter problem
        0 irdp solicitations, 0 irdp advertisements

UDP statistics:
  Rcvd: 745 total, 0 checksum errors, 717 no port
  Sent: 106 total, 0 forwarded broadcasts

TCP statistics:
  Rcvd: 640 total, 0 checksum errors, 2 no port
  Sent: 494 total

Probe statistics:
  Rcvd: 0 address requests, 0 address replies
        0 proxy name requests, 0 where-is requests, 0 other
  Sent: 0 address requests, 0 address replies (0 proxy)
        0 proxy name replies, 0 where-is replies

EGP statistics:
  Rcvd: 0 total, 0 format errors, 0 checksum errors, 0 no listener
  Sent: 0 total
```

```
IGRP statistics:
 Rcvd: 0 total, 0 checksum errors
 Sent: 0 total

OSPF statistics:
 Rcvd: 0 total, 0 checksum errors
        0 hello, 0 database desc, 0 link state req
        0 link state updates, 0 link state acks

  Sent: 0 total

IP-IGRP2 statistics:
 Rcvd: 0 total
 Sent: 0 total

PIMv2 statistics: Sent/Received
 Total: 0/0, 0 checksum errors, 0 format errors
 Registers: 0/0, Register Stops: 0/0,  Hellos: 0/0
 Join/Prunes: 0/0, Asserts: 0/0, grafts: 0/0
 Bootstraps: 0/0, Candidate_RP_Advertisements: 0/0

IGMP statistics: Sent/Received
 Total: 0/0, Format errors: 0/0, Checksum errors: 0/0
 Host Queries: 0/0, Host Reports: 0/0, Host Leaves: 0/0
 DVMRP: 0/0, PIM: 0/0

ARP statistics:
 Rcvd: 320 requests, 9 replies, 0 reverse, 0 other
 Sent: 9 requests, 109 replies (0 proxy), 0 reverse
```

This command provides traffic statistics for several TCP/IP protocols: IP, ICMP, UDP, TCP, Probe, EGP, IGRP, OSPF, IP-IGRP2, PIMv2, IGMP, and ARP. This command really breaks down the interface statistics that the show interface command provides. This command provides an easy-to-view set of statistics for each protocol that can be used for troubleshooting purposes.

Debug Commands

The debug commands are an excellent way to interrogate the router and receive real-time information regarding the state of TCP/IP connections at various OSI layers. As always, only use debug commands when it is necessary to do so and be careful when using them on busy, core production routers. Debugging puts a load on the router CPU and can have a detrimental effect on the network. After every debugging session, always use the Router#no debug all command to turn off all debug events. Table 9-4 displays a list of frequently used debug commands.

Table 9-4	Command	Description
Frequently Used Debug Commands for Troubleshooting TCP/IP	debug arp	Displays debug information about the ARP transactions.
	debug ip icmp	Displays debug information about ICMP.
	debug ip packet	Displays debug information about IP packets and IP security.
	debug ip routing	Displays debug information about the internal IP routing table updates.

debug arp

The *debug arp* command displays debug information about the ARP transactions:

```
Router#debug arp
ARP packet debugging is on
00:18:25: IP ARP: rcvd req src 192.168.10.4 0008.c7e1.556e, dst
192.168.10.68 Ethernet0/0
00:18:37: IP ARP: rcvd req src 192.168.10.49 0040.952d.02f0, dst
192.168.10.1 Ethernet0/0
00:18:37: IP ARP: sent rep src 192.168.10.1 00d0.ba59.17a0,
             dst 192.168.10.49 0040.952d.02f0 Ethernet0/0
00:18:40: IP ARP: rcvd req src 192.168.10.56 0090.27c2.a498, dst
192.168.10.1 Ethernet0/0
00:18:40: IP ARP: sent rep src 192.168.10.1 00d0.ba59.17a0,
             dst 192.168.10.56 0090.27c2.a498 Ethernet0/0
00:18:41: IP ARP: rcvd req src 192.168.10.59 0040.952d.0b5a, dst
192.168.10.40 Ethernet0/0
00:18:42: IP ARP: rcvd req src 192.168.10.201 0090.2793.7d5c, dst
192.168.10.4 Ethernet0/0
00:18:54: IP ARP: rcvd req src 192.168.10.57 0090.27c2.ab74, dst
192.168.10.1 Ethernet0/0
00:18:54: IP ARP: sent rep src 192.168.10.1 00d0.ba59.17a0,
             dst 192.168.10.57 0090.27c2.ab74 Ethernet0/0
00:18:58: IP ARP: rcvd req src 192.168.10.58 0090.27c2.abf9, dst
192.168.10.201Ethernet0/0
00:19:06: IP ARP: rcvd req src 192.168.10.59 0040.952d.0b5a, dst
192.168.10.201Ethernet0/0
00:19:20: IP ARP: rcvd req src 192.168.10.31 0000.e883.b99b, dst
192.168.10.1 Ethernet0/0
00:19:20: IP ARP: sent rep src 192.168.10.1 00d0.ba59.17a0,
             dst 192.168.10.31 0000.e883.b99b Ethernet0/0
00:19:23: IP ARP: rcvd req src 192.168.10.48 00e0.293d.5bd5, dst
192.168.10.1 Ethernet0/0
00:19:23: IP ARP: sent rep src 192.168.10.1 00d0.ba59.17a0,
             dst 192.168.10.48 00e0.293d.5bd5 Ethernet0/0
00:19:24: IP ARP: rcvd req src 192.168.10.4 0008.c7e1.556e, dst
192.168.10.40 Ethernet0/0
00:19:25: IP ARP: rcvd req src 192.168.10.4 0008.c7e1.556e, dst
192.168.10.38 Ethernet0/0
```

```
00:19:26: IP ARP: rcvd req src 192.168.10.35 00c0.f049.dea9, dst
192.168.10.4 Ethernet0/0
00:19:26: IP ARP: rcvd req src 192.168.10.35 00c0.f049.dea9, dst
192.168.10.201 Ethernet0/0
Router#
```

The previous listing shows various ARP requests received on the router.
Note that the debug line always starts with a *sent* or *rcvd*. The sent means
that the router has sent an ARP reply to a client's ARP request. All sent
requests are linked to the IP address 192.168.10.1 and the MAC address
00d0.ba59.17a0 of a router interface. We can see that this interface is Ether-
net0/0. All rcvd requests are entries that are added into the router's ARP cache
because these are built by hosts transmitting and receiving data through the
router. This includes the interface on which the MAC address was learned.

debug ip icmp

The *debug ip icmp* command displays debug information about ICMP
transactions:

```
Router#debug ip icmp
ICMP packet debugging is on
00:20:20: ICMP: echo reply rcvd, src 212.1.157.2, dst 212.1.159.155
00:20:22: ICMP: echo reply rcvd, src 212.1.157.2, dst
            212.1.159.155.
00:20:24: ICMP: echo reply rcvd, src 212.1.157.2, dst 212.1.159.155
00:20:51: ICMP: dst (212.1.130.20) host unreachable sent to
            212.1.159.155
00:20:54: ICMP: dst (212.1.130.20) host unreachable sent to
            212.1.159.155
00:21:00: ICMP: dst (212.1.130.20) host unreachable sent to
            212.1.159.155
00:21:04: ICMP: dst (212.1.130.20) host unreachable sent to
            212.1.159.155
00:21:08: ICMP: dst (212.1.130.20) host unreachable sent to
            212.1.159.155
00:21:12: ICMP: dst (212.1.130.20) host unreachable sent to
            212.1.159.155
00:21:14: ICMP: dst (212.1.130.20) host unreachable sent to
            212.1.159.155
00:21:27: ICMP: dst (212.1.130.20) host unreachable sent to
            212.1.159.155
00:21:54: ICMP: echo reply rcvd, src 192.168.20.2, dst 192.168.30.1
00:21:54: ICMP: echo reply rcvd, src 192.168.20.2, dst 192.168.30.1
00:21:54: ICMP: echo reply rcvd, src 192.168.20.2, dst 192.168.30.1
00:21:55: ICMP: echo reply rcvd, src 192.168.20.2, dst 192.168.30.1
00:21:55: ICMP: echo reply rcvd, src 192.168.20.2, dst 192.168.30.1
00:22:06: ICMP: echo reply rcvd, src 212.1.157.1, dst 212.1.159.155
00:22:06: ICMP: echo reply rcvd, src 212.1.157.1, dst
            212.1.159.155!
00:22:07: ICMP: echo reply rcvd, src 212.1.157.1, dst 212.1.159.155
00:22:07: ICMP: echo reply rcvd, src 212.1.157.1, dst
            212.1.159.155!
```

```
00:22:08: ICMP: echo reply rcvd, src 212.1.157.1, dst 212.1.159.155
00:22:08: ICMP: echo reply rcvd, src 212.1.157.1, dst 212.1.159.155
00:22:08: ICMP: echo reply rcvd, src 212.1.157.1, dst 212.1.159.155
00:22:08: ICMP: echo reply rcvd, src 212.1.157.1, dst
          212.1.159.155!
00:22:09: ICMP: echo reply rcvd, src 212.1.157.1, dst 212.1.159.155
00:22:09: ICMP: echo reply rcvd, src 212.1.157.1, dst
          212.1.159.155
```

The previous listing shows you ICMP echoes that were received by the router from various IP addresses. Debugging ICMP messages can help you troubleshoot end-to-end connectivity problems such as access lists prohibiting communication or an inconsistency in IP addressing on the network.

debug ip packet

The *debug ip packet* command displays debug information on IP packets and IP security:

```
Router#debug ip packet
IP packet debugging is on
00:22:24: IP: s=195.153.85.3 (Dialer1), d=192.168.10.57
              (Ethernet0/0), g=192.168.10.57, len 44,
              forward
00:22:24: IP: s=212.1.159.155 (Ethernet0/0),
              d=195.67.49.96 (Dialer1), g=195.67.49.96,
              len 40, forward
00:22:24: IP: s=212.1.159.155 (Ethernet0/0), d=62.20.91.94
              (Dialer1), g=62.20.91.94, len 48, forward
00:22:24: IP: s=212.1.128.157 (Dialer1), d=192.168.10.35
              (Ethernet0/0), g=192.168.10.35, len 224,
              forward
00:22:24: IP: s=212.1.128.156 (Dialer1), d=192.168.10.35
              (Ethernet0/0), g=192.168.10.35, len 224,
              forward
00:22:24: IP: s=38.200.221.50 (Dialer1), d=192.168.10.35
              (Ethernet0/0), g=192.168.10.35, len 44,
              forward
00:22:24: IP: s=38.200.221.50 (Dialer1), d=192.168.10.35
              (Ethernet0/0), g=192.168.10.35, len 44,
              forward
00:22:25: IP: s=62.20.91.94 (Dialer1), d=192.168.10.25
              (Ethernet0/0), g=192.168.10.25, len 44,
              forward
00:22:26: IP: s=38.200.221.50 (Dialer1), d=192.168.10.35
              (Ethernet0/0), g=192.168.10.35, len 44,
              forward
00:22:26: IP: s=192.168.10.25 (Ethernet0/0), d=192.168.10.255
              (Ethernet0/0), len 202, rcvd 3
00:22:26: IP: s=192.168.10.25 (Ethernet0/0), d=192.168.10.255
              (Ethernet0/0), len 202, rcvd 3
00:22:27: IP: s=212.1.130.20 (Dialer1), d=192.168.10.49
              (Ethernet0/0), g=192.168.10.49, len 40,
              forward
```

```
00:22:29: IP: s=216.32.243.57 (Dialer1), d=212.1.159.155 (Dialer1),
             len 40, rcvd 3
00:22:29: IP: s=212.1.159.155 (local), d=216.32.243.57 (Dialer1),
             len 40, sending
00:22:29: IP: s=192.168.10.67 (Ethernet0/0), d=192.168.10.255
             (Ethernet0/0), len 229, rcvd 3
00:22:30: IP: s=212.1.159.155 (Ethernet0/0),
             d=38.200.221.50 (Dialer1), g=38.200.221.50,
             len 40, forward
00:22:30: IP: s=212.1.159.155 (Ethernet0/0),
             d=38.200.221.90 (Dialer1), g=38.200.221.90,
             len 44, forward
00:22:30: IP: s=212.1.159.155 (Ethernet0/0),
             d=207.46.18.108 (Dialer1), g=207.46.18.108,
             len 40, forward
00:22:30: IP: s=212.1.159.155 (Ethernet0/0),
             d=38.200.221.90 (Dialer1), g=38.200.221.90,
             len 44, forward
00:22:31: IP: s=38.200.221.50 (Dialer1), d=192.168.10.35
             (Ethernet0/0), g=192.168.10.35, len 40,
             forward
00:22:31: IP: s=38.200.221.90 (Dialer1), d=192.168.10.35
             (Ethernet0/0), g=192.168.10.35, len 44,
             forward
Router#
```

The debug ip packet command can be a useful tool for troubleshooting host-to-host communication. Details are shown for every IP packet that is generated or forwarded by the router. Obviously, this generates a lot of output and is difficult to spot the exact information you require. The information captured includes source and destination addresses, the length of the packet, and whether the packet was forwarded or received by the router.

NOTE: *The debugging of all IP packets across the router is resource-intensive and shouldn't be carried out unless totally necessary because it may have a detrimental effect on the performance of the router.*

debug ip routing

The *debug ip routing* command displays debug information about the internal IP routing table updates:

```
Router# debug ip routing
RT: add 172.25.168.0 255.255.255.0 via 172.24.76.30, igrp metric
[100/3020]
```

```
RT: metric change to 172.25.168.0 via 172.24.76.30, igrp metric
    [100/3020]
        new metric [100/2930]
IP: cache invalidation from 0x115248 0x1378A, new version 5736
RT: add 172.26.219.0 255.255.255.0 via 172.24.76.30, igrp metric
    [100/16200]
RT: metric change to 172.26.219.0 via 172.24.76.30, igrp metric
    [100/16200]
        new metric [100/10816]
RT: delete route to 172.26.219.0 via 172.24.76.30, igrp metric
    [100/10816]
RT: no routes to 172.26.219.0, entering holddown
IP: cache invalidation from 0x115248 0x1378A, new version 5737
RT: 172.26.219.0 came out of holddown
RT: garbage collecting entry for 172.26.219.0
IP: cache invalidation from 0x115248 0x1378A, new version 5738
RT: add 172.26.219.0 255.255.255.0 via 172.24.76.30, igrp metric
    [100/10816]
RT: delete route to 172.26.219.0 via 172.24.76.30, igrp metric
    [100/10816]
RT: no routes to 172.26.219.0, entering holddown
IP: cache invalidation from 0x115248 0x1378A, new version 5739
RT: 172.26.219.0 came out of holddown
RT: garbage collecting entry for 172.26.219.0
IP: cache invalidation from 0x115248 0x1378A, new version 5740
RT: add 172.26.219.0 255.255.255.0 via 172.24.76.30, igrp metric
    [100/16200]
RT: metric change to 172.26.219.0 via 172.24.76.30, igrp metric
    [100/16200]
        new metric [100/10816]
RT: delete route to 172.26.219.0 via 172.24.76.30, igrp metric
    [100/10816]
RT: no routes to 172.26.219.0, entering holddown
IP: cache invalidation from 0x115248 0x1378A, new version 5741
```

In this case, the information shown by this command displays the *interior gateway routing protocol* (IGRP) exchanging messages between routers. The beginning area of the code indicates that a route to network 172.25.168.0/24 has been added via 172.34.76.30. This is the addition of a new route to the routing table. Later in the code you can see that the route to network 172.26.219.0 via 172.24.76.30 has been removed from the routing table. This is a useful tool to display for interrogating routing information between routers. Routing update timers can also be checked along with the show ip protocols command to verify the configuration.

Other IP Commands

As well as the show and debug commands, a few *clear* commands can also be used to aid the network troubleshooter.

clear arp-cache

The *clear arp-cache* command removes all dynamic items from the router's internal ARP cache and it also clears the fast-switching cache:

```
Router#sh arp
Protocol   Address          Age (Min.)  Hardware Addr.   Type   Interface
Internet   212.1.157.94     0           00e0.2b5e.5c00   ARPA   FastEthernet0/0
Internet   212.1.157.8      -           0030.804e.d440   ARPA   FastEthernet0/0
Internet   212.1.157.9      -           0030.804e.d440   ARPA   FastEthernet0/0
Internet   212.1.157.10     -           0030.804e.d440   ARPA   FastEthernet0/0
Internet   212.1.157.11     -           0030.804e.d440   ARPA   FastEthernet0/0
Internet   212.1.157.12     -           0030.804e.d440   ARPA   FastEthernet0/0
Internet   212.1.157.13     -           0030.804e.d440   ARPA   FastEthernet0/0
Internet   212.1.157.14     -           0030.804e.d440   ARPA   FastEthernet0/0
Internet   212.1.157.15     -           0030.804e.d440   ARPA   FastEthernet0/0
Internet   212.1.157.1      -           0000.0c07.ac64   ARPA   FastEthernet0/0
Internet   212.1.157.2      -           0030.804e.d440   ARPA   FastEthernet0/0
Internet   212.1.157.3      1           0030.8070.a580   ARPA   FastEthernet0/0
Internet   212.1.157.6      -           0030.804e.d440   ARPA   FastEthernet0/0
Internet   212.1.157.7      -           0030.804e.d440   ARPA   FastEthernet0/0
Internet   212.1.157.29     101         0010.a403.ec70   ARPA   FastEthernet0/0
Internet   212.1.157.30     3           00e0.2b5e.5c00   ARPA   FastEthernet0/0
Internet   212.1.157.16     -           0030.804e.d440   ARPA   FastEthernet0/0
Internet   212.1.157.17     -           0030.804e.d440   ARPA   FastEthernet0/0
Internet   212.1.157.18     -           0030.804e.d440   ARPA   FastEthernet0/0
Internet   212.1.157.19     -           0030.804e.d440   ARPA   FastEthernet0/0
Internet   192.168.20.15    0           0010.a403.ec70   ARPA   FastEthernet0/1
Internet   192.168.20.7     9           0090.2793.7cdf   ARPA   FastEthernet0/1
Internet   192.168.20.1     -           0000.0c07.ac65   ARPA   FastEthernet0/1
Internet   192.168.20.2     -           0030.804e.d441   ARPA   FastEthernet0/1
Internet   192.168.20.3     1           0030.8070.a581   ARPA   FastEthernet0/1
Internet   212.1.130.254    0           00e0.2b5e.5c00   ARPA   FastEthernet0/0
Router#clear arp

Router#sh arp

Protocol   Address          Age (min)   Hardware Addr.   Type   Interface
Internet   212.1.157.8      -           0030.804e.d440   ARPA   FastEthernet0/0
Internet   212.1.157.9      -           0030.804e.d440   ARPA   FastEthernet0/0
Internet   212.1.157.10     -           0030.804e.d440   ARPA   FastEthernet0/0
Internet   212.1.157.11     -           0030.804e.d440   ARPA   FastEthernet0/0
Internet   212.1.157.12     -           0030.804e.d440   ARPA   FastEthernet0/0
Internet   212.1.157.13     -           0030.804e.d440   ARPA   FastEthernet0/0
Internet   212.1.157.14     -           0030.804e.d440   ARPA   FastEthernet0/0
Internet   212.1.157.15     -           0030.804e.d440   ARPA   FastEthernet0/0
Internet   212.1.157.1      -           0000.0c07.ac64   ARPA   FastEthernet0/0
Internet   212.1.157.2      -           0030.804e.d440   ARPA   FastEthernet0/0
Internet   212.1.157.3      0           0030.8070.a580   ARPA   FastEthernet0/0
Internet   212.1.157.6      -           0030.804e.d440   ARPA   FastEthernet0/0
Internet   212.1.157.7      -           0030.804e.d440   ARPA   FastEthernet0/0
Internet   212.1.157.16     -           0030.804e.d440   ARPA   FastEthernet0/0
Internet   212.1.157.17     -           0030.804e.d440   ARPA   FastEthernet0/0
Internet   212.1.157.18     -           0030.804e.d440   ARPA   FastEthernet0/0
Internet   212.1.157.19     -           0030.804e.d440   ARPA   FastEthernet0/0
Internet   192.168.20.15    0           0010.a403.ec70   ARPA   FastEthernet0/1
Internet   192.16820.7      0           0090.2793.7cdf   ARPA   FastEthernet0/1
Internet   192.16820.1      -           0000.0c07.ac65   ARPA   FastEthernet0/1
```

```
Internet    192.16820.2     -           0030.804e.d441   ARPA    FastEthernet0/1
Internet    192.16820.3     0           0030.8070.a581   ARPA    FastEthernet0/1
Internet    212.1.130.254   0           00e0.2b5e.5c00   ARPA    FastEthernet0/0
```

In the previous listing, we display the ARP cache with the *show arp* command. We then clear the ARP cache with the *clear arp* command. Upon displaying the ARP cache again, we can see that the three dynamically learned entries have now been removed. The other entries are static and exist due to static *network address translation* (NAT) on the router. Clearing the ARP cache can be useful if using a *hot standby routing protocol* (HSRP) or if you have recently added or changed a host's *network interface card* (NIC).

clear ip access-list counters

When troubleshooting a problem with an access list, it may be a good idea to reset the access list counters to zero in order to facilitate an easier visual observation of the counters. In the following listing, we first display the IP access lists with the *show ip access-list* command. We then clear the IP access list counters with the *clear ip access-list counters* command. Finally, we redisplay the IP access lists. You can clearly see that the access list counters have been reset:

```
Router#sh ip access
Standard IP access list 2
    permit 192.168.10.0, wildcard bits 0.0.0.255
    permit 192.168.20.0, wildcard bits 0.0.0.255
Standard IP access list 5
    permit 192.168.20.0, wildcard bits 0.0.0.255
    permit 192.168.10.0, wildcard bits 0.0.0.255
Extended IP access list Firewall
    deny ip 192.168.0.0 0.0.255.255 any log (5810 matches)
    deny ip 172.16.0.0 0.15.255.255 any log (3 matches)
    deny ip 10.0.0.0 0.255.255.255 any log
    deny ip 192.0.2.0 0.0.0.255 any log
    deny ip 127.0.0.0 0.255.255.255 any log
    deny ip 255.0.0.0 0.255.255.255 any log
    deny ip host 0.0.0.0 any log
    deny ip host 212.1.157.1 any log
    deny ip host 212.1.157.2 any log
    deny ip host 212.1.157.3 any log (1611 matches)
    permit tcp any host 224.0.0.2 eq 1985
    permit icmp any 212.1.157.0 0.0.0.255 net-unreachable
    permit icmp any 212.1.157.0 0.0.0.255 echo-reply (6 matches)
    permit icmp any 212.1.157.0 0.0.0.255 echo
    permit icmp any 212.1.157.0 0.0.0.255 host-unreachable
    permit icmp any 212.1.157.0 0.0.0.255 port-unreachable (12
matches)
    permit icmp any 212.1.157.0 0.0.0.255 packet-too-big
    permit icmp any 212.1.157.0 0.0.0.255 administratively-prohibited
    permit icmp any 212.1.157.0 0.0.0.255 source-quench
    permit icmp any 212.1.157.0 0.0.0.255 ttl-exceeded
    permit tcp any 212.1.157.0 0.0.0.255 eq www
```

```
    permit tcp any 212.1.157.0 0.0.0.255 eq 443
    permit tcp any 212.1.157.0 0.0.0.255 eq smtp
    permit tcp any 212.1.157.0 0.0.0.255 eq pop3
    permit tcp any 212.1.157.0 0.0.0.255 eq 143
    permit tcp any 212.1.157.0 0.0.0.255 eq ftp-data
    permit tcp any 212.1.157.0 0.0.0.255 eq ftp
    permit tcp any 212.1.157.0 0.0.0.255 eq nntp
    permit tcp any 212.1.157.0 0.0.0.255 eq 8081
    permit tcp any 212.1.157.0 0.0.0.255 eq domain
    permit udp any 212.1.157.0 0.0.0.255 eq domain
    permit tcp any 212.1.157.0 0.0.0.255 established (608 matches)
    permit udp any eq domain any (78 matches)
    deny ip any any log (17124 matches)
Router#
Router#
Router#clear ip access-list counters

Router#show ip access-list
Standard IP access list 2
    permit 192.168.10.0, wildcard bits 0.0.0.255
    permit 192.168.20.0, wildcard bits 0.0.0.255
Standard IP access list 5
    permit 192.168.20.0, wildcard bits 0.0.0.255
    permit 192.168.10.0, wildcard bits 0.0.0.255
Extended IP access list Firewall
    deny ip 192.168.0.0 0.0.255.255 any log (15 matches)
    deny ip 172.16.0.0 0.15.255.255 any log
    deny ip 10.0.0.0 0.255.255.255 any log
    deny ip 192.0.2.0 0.0.0.255 any log
    deny ip 127.0.0.0 0.255.255.255 any log
    deny ip 255.0.0.0 0.255.255.255 any log
    deny ip host 0.0.0.0 any log
    deny ip host 212.1.157.1 any log
    deny ip host 212.1.157.2 any log
    deny ip host 212.1.157.3 any log (3 matches)
    permit tcp any host 224.0.0.2 eq 1985
    permit icmp any 212.1.157.0 0.0.0.255 net-unreachable
    permit icmp any 212.1.157.0 0.0.0.255 echo-reply
    permit icmp any 212.1.157.0 0.0.0.255 echo
    permit icmp any 212.1.157.0 0.0.0.255 host-unreachable
    permit icmp any 212.1.157.0 0.0.0.255 port-unreachable
    permit icmp any 212.1.157.0 0.0.0.255 packet-too-big
    permit icmp any 212.1.157.0 0.0.0.255 administratively-prohibited
    permit icmp any 212.1.157.0 0.0.0.255 source-quench
    permit icmp any 212.1.157.0 0.0.0.255 ttl-exceeded
    permit tcp any 212.1.157.0 0.0.0.255 eq www
    permit tcp any 212.1.157.0 0.0.0.255 eq 443
    permit tcp any 212.1.157.0 0.0.0.255 eq smtp
    permit tcp any 212.1.157.0 0.0.0.255 eq pop3
    permit tcp any 212.1.157.0 0.0.0.255 eq 143
    permit tcp any 212.1.157.0 0.0.0.255 eq ftp-data
    permit tcp any 212.1.157.0 0.0.0.255 eq ftp
    permit tcp any 212.1.157.0 0.0.0.255 eq nntp
    permit tcp any 212.1.157.0 0.0.0.255 eq 8081
    permit tcp any 212.1.157.0 0.0.0.255 eq domain
    permit udp any 212.1.157.0 0.0.0.255 eq domain
    permit tcp any 212.1.157.0 0.0.0.255 established
    permit udp any eq domain any
    deny ip any any log (87 matches)
Router#
```

clear ip route

The *clear ip route* command can be used to force routing table recalculations by clearing all routes out of the internal routing table on the router. This can be useful if you have just added a new interface to the router, changed the state of an interface, or changed a routing protocol setting on an interface. Here is an example:

```
Router2514#clear ip route ?
*         Delete all routes
A.B.C.D   Destination network route to delete
vrf       Clear routes for a VPN Routing/Forwarding instance
```

You have the option of clearing the entire table by entering a "*" or a specific host by entering the hostname or IP address.

Packet Internet Groper (Ping)

As already discussed, one of the most frequently used debugging tools for troubleshooting network problems is the ping command. This command invokes the ICMP echo request and the ICMP echo reply messages. A host or router sends an ICMP echo request to a specified destination by entering a ping command. The destination host or router receives the echo request and replies with an ICMP echo reply. This is returned to the sending host or router.

The echo request and its associated echo reply can be used to test whether a destination is reachable and responding. Both the echo request and echo reply are encapsulated in IP packets. Therefore, the successful receipt of an echo reply can be used to verify many factors pertaining to IP communication:

- IP must be running on the source host to route the packet.
- Routers between the source and destination must be routing the packet correctly.
- The destination host must be at least running IP and ICMP.
- All routers along the return path must be routing correctly.

Thus, a lot can be discovered from simply pinging a remote host. If you ping the remote host via the host name and not the IP address, this also verifies the host name resolution via the local HOST file or DNS.

The ping command can be entered either on a Microsoft Windows NT machine or a Cisco router. The command syntax varies between these systems and so does the output. On a Cisco router, you can use the standard ping command from the user exec mode, the privileged exec mode, or the extended ping command from the privileged exec mode only. Here is an example of a standard ping:

```
Router#ping 194.73.134.2

Type escape sequence to abort.
Sending 5, 100-byte ICMP Echos to 194.73.134.2, timeout is 2
seconds:
!!!!!
Success rate is 100 percent (5/5), round-trip min/avg/max = 1/18/84 ms
Router#
```

You can see that we issued a ping to the address 19.73.134.2. The five exclamation marks indicate a successful receipt of an echo reply.

Notice the difference with the following router output:

```
Router#ping 212.1.130.11

Type escape sequence to abort.
Sending 5, 100-byte ICMP Echos to 212.1.130.11, timeout is 2
seconds:
.....
Success rate is 0 percent (0/5)
Router#
```

The above output has five periods. This indicates that the router timed out waiting for a datagram reply. Table 9-5 shows the characters returned by ping and their definitions.

The extended ping command has other options that relate to the IP header information. The following is an example of output from a successful extended IP ping:

Table 9-5

Ping Characters and Definitions

Character	Definition
!	A successful receipt of an echo reply
.	Timed out waiting for a response
U	Destination network unreachable
C	Congestion experienced
I	Interrupted by user
?	Packet type unknown
&	Packet TTL exceeded

```
Router#ping
Protocol [ip]:
Target IP address: 194.73.134.2
Repeat count [5]:
Datagram size [100]:
Timeout in seconds [2]:
Extended commands [n]: y
Source address or interface:
Type of service [0]:
Set DF bit in IP header? [no]:
Validate reply data? [no]:
Data pattern [0xABCD]:
Loose, Strict, Record, Timestamp, Verbose[none]:
Sweep range of sizes [n]:
Type escape sequence to abort.
Sending 5, 100-byte ICMP Echos to 194.73.134.2, timeout is 2
seconds:
!!!!!
Success rate is 100 percent (5/5), round-trip min/avg/max = 1/10/40 ms
Router#
```

As you can see, more options can be used to further refine the ping command.

Trace

The trace command is also a widely used command for troubleshooting connectivity problems on internetworks. This command enables you to see the complete end-to-end path that the packets take to reach their destination.

The trace command works by sending an ICMP echo request message with the TTL set to 1. By setting the TTL to 1, all routers that process this packet decrement the TTL by 1. This causes the routers to send back an ICMP time-exceeded message along with the name and IP address of the router sending the message. This router then sends the ICMP echo request packet to the next hop with the TTL set to 1 again. The destination router decrements the TTL by 1 and sends back an ICMP time-exceeded message along with the name and IP address of the router. This loop occurs until the network is deemed unreachable or the destination host is reached. From this information we can see every hop the packet takes to reach its final destination. Be sure to permit ICMP ttl-exceeded on any access list to allow the trace traffic to be reported.

Here is an example of a trace to 212.1.157.1:

```
1 194.73.134.1 4 msec 4 msec 4 msec
2 Frame-Relay-customers-Hssi0-0-01.79.74.194.in-addr.arpa
  (194.74.79.1) 76 msec 48 msec 28 msec
3 core2-ATM1-1-02.ealing.bt.NET (194.74.16.230) 48 msec 36 msec
  32 msec
```

```
 4 core2-H-5-0-0.telehouse.bt.NET (195.99.120.190) 96 msec 32 msec
   40 msec
 5 transit1-fe-4-0.telehouse.bt.NET (194.74.16.3) 32 msec 44 msec
   32 msec
 6 linx.core.exodus.NET (195.66.224.69) 40 msec 100 msec 40 msec
 7 dcr02-s5-0-0.lndn01.exodus.NET (212.62.0.77) 44 msec 140 msec
   56 msec
 8 dcr01-g4-0-0.lndn01.exodus.NET (212.62.0.65) 36 msec 96 msec
   148 msec
 9 bbr02-p0-2.jrcy01.exodus.NET (216.32.132.37) 864 msec 836 msec
   852 msec
10 dcr04-g4-0.jrcy01.exodus.NET (209.67.45.226) 140 msec 132 msec *
11 *    rsm03-vlan992.jrcy02.exodus.NET (216.32.222.115) 192 msec *
12 *    216.33.35.30 248 msec *
13 *   *   *
14 *   *   *
15 *   *   *
16 *   *   *
17 *   *   *
18 *   *   *
19 *   *   *
20 *   *   *
21 *   *   *
22 *   *   *
23 *   *   *
24 masontech.com (216.156.40.88) 136 msec 120 msec 144 msec
```

As you can see from the listing, all of the intermediary routers that the packet has traversed are displayed. This is an excellent tool for diagnosing if a problem exists on a remote router. The previous trace was carried out over the Internet from the U.K. to the U.S. and you wouldn't imagine that a normal-sized corporate WAN would include so many intermediary routers. The "*" indicates that a timeout was received between these routers. Table 9-6 outlines the main trace characters.

Table 9-6	Character	Definition
Trace Characters and Definitions	!H	The probe was received but not forwarded. This is usually caused by an access list on the router.
	P	The protocol was unreachable.
	N	The network was unreachable.
	U	The port was unreachable.
	*	Timeout.

Table 9-7

Common TCP/IP Problems

Symptom	Action
Hosts cannot access hosts on another network or subnet.	Check the default gateway on the local and remote hosts, check the subnet mask on the local and remote hosts, or check that the router between the hosts is functioning correctly.
Hosts can access some remote networks but not others.	Check the subnet mask on the local host or check the access lists on the router.
Some services are available on remote networks and some services do not work on remote networks.	Check the extended access lists on the router for the denial of a specific service. Remember the implicit "deny all."
Hosts cannot connect when one redundant route is down.	Check the dynamic routing on the router. Convergence may have not occurred.
Hosts cannot communicate with other local hosts.	Check the subnet mask and IP addresses on all local hosts.
Protocols such as http work, but others such as ftp do not.	Check the extended access lists on the router. You may be denying certain protocols due to the implicit "deny all."
Hosts cannot resolve DNS names.	Check the hosts' DNS configuration.
Hosts cannot ping the default gateway.	Check the subnet mask and IP address on the host. Or check the inbound interface on the router against access lists that would deny icmp echo replies.
Hosts can access other hosts on remote networks, but they cannot ping these hosts.	Check all access lists between the host and destination for entries that would deny icmp echo replies.

On a Cisco router, you can enter the trace command from either the user or privileged exec mode.

NOTE: *The Web site* `www.tracert.com` *provides a set of remote locations all over the world from where you can trace a host.*

Chapter Summary

In this chapter, we looked at TCP/IP and the available troubleshooting commands. TCP/IP is the backbone of all modern communications and the protocol of choice for the Internet. A thorough conceptual understanding is crucial for succeeding in troubleshooting TCP/IP communications.

We started with a technical overview of TCP/IP and moved on to Cisco's show and debug commands, which can be used to interrogate the router to receive real-time reports that help us in the troubleshooting process. We also looked at other commands such as ping and trace. We then looked at the TCP/IP configuration from a Microsoft perspective to be thorough. As in any other troubleshooting situation, always start at the physical layer and work your way up. This method of troubleshooting is the most logical and can save you a lot of time.

Frequently Asked Questions (FAQ)

Question: What is the difference between a unicast and a multicast?

Answer: A unicast is a packet that is destined for a single host on the internetwork. It has a unicast address that is either a Class A, B, or C IP address. A multicast is a packet that is sent to a group of computers on the internetwork. This is identified by a multicast address that is a Class D IP address.

Question: What protocol does ping use?

Answer: Ping uses ICMP echoes to communicate. These ICMP echoes are encapsulated in an IP frame.

Question: How does a trace return each router name traversed?

Answer: A trace sends an ICMP echo request message with the TTL set to 1. Upon receipt of this packet, the router decrements the TTL by 1. Therefore, the router thinks the TTL has expired and it sends back an ICMP time-exceeded message along with the name and IP address of the router.

Answer: Helper addresses convert specific UDP broadcasts into a unicast packet and direct the packet to a specific host. Without helper addresses, services such as DHCP and TFTP would not be able to cross a router.

Case Study

You, as a network engineer, have been assigned to identify a problem with the connectivity to one of your remote retail stores.

Scenario

You work for a small retail company with seven remote retail outlets and a central office. You are based at the central office. All remote retail outlets are running PC till-based *Electronic Point-of-Sale* (EPOS) and these connect to the head office every hour to upload sales figures. The outlets use Cisco 801 ISDN routers. The central office is running a Cisco 2621 with an 8 port BRI network module installed.

Recently, you have lost communication with one of the outlets in Tucson, Arizona. This has led to sales data been sent through the postal service on floppy disk on a daily basis. All of the other stores are still communicating with the central office on an hourly basis. A junior technician was doing some work on the 801 router at Tucson and was trying to get an outbound access list working to restrict the type of traffic that crosses the ISDN line. When the router was reloaded, you lost communication.

Approach

It seems pretty obvious to you that the problem lies with the configuration of the 801 ISDN router at Tucson. You cannot even ping the router at Tucson, so you decide that a site visit is the only way to resolve this problem. Figure 9-5 outlines the configuration between the central site and Tucson.

Once on site, you try a ping from a local Windows 98 machine. The results you get are as follows:

```
C:\>ping 10.1.1.1

Pinging 10.1.1.1 with 32 bytes of data:

Reply from 10.1.1.1: bytes=32 time=1ms TTL=255
Reply from 10.1.1.1: bytes=32 time=1ms TTL=255
Reply from 10.1.1.1: bytes=32 time=1ms TTL=255
Reply from 10.1.1.1: bytes=32 time=1ms TTL=255

Ping statistics for 10.1.1.1:
    Packets: Sent = 4, Received = 4, Lost = 0 (0% loss),
```

Figure 9-5
Network topology

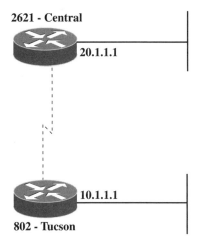

2621 - Central

20.1.1.1

10.1.1.1

802 - Tucson

```
Approximate round trip times in milliseconds:
    Minimum = 1ms, Maximum =  1ms, Average =  1ms

C:\>
```

This indicates that the Ethernet0 interface of the 801 router was working correctly with no configuration problems. You then decide to ping the central office router on IP address 20.1.1.1. This is the result you receive:

```
C:\>ping 20.1.1.1

Pinging 20.1.1.1 with 32 bytes of data:

Request timed out.
Request timed out.
Request timed out.
Request timed out.

Ping statistics for 20.1.1.1:
    Packets: Sent = 4, Received = 0, Lost = 4 (100% loss),
Approximate round trip times in milli-seconds:
    Minimum = 0ms, Maximum =  0ms, Average =  0ms

C:\>
```

You would have probably expected this result due to the fault you noticed from the central office. You now know that all communication between the Tucson outlet and the central office is down. This is true for both directions. You decide to look at the configurations from the central office router and the Tucson outlet router. The following configuration is from the central office router:

```
version 12.0
service udp-small-servers
service tcp-small-servers
!
hostname Central
!
enable secret cisco
!
username Tucson password shoedepot
isdn switch-type basic-5ess
!
interface Ethernet0
ip address 20.1.1.1 255.0.0.0
!
interface BRI0
no ip address
encapsulation ppp
dialer rotary-group 0
isdn spid1 0155533330 5553333
isdn spid2 0155533330 5554444
!
interface Dialer0
ip unnumbered Ethernet0
encapsulation ppp
dialer in-band
dialer idle-timeout 300
dialer map ip 10.1.1.1 name Tucson speed 56 14045551111
dialer map ip 10.1.1.1 name Tucson speed 56 14045552222
dialer hold-queue 10
dialer load-threshold 200 either
dialer-group 1
no fair-queue
 no cdp enable
 ppp authentication chap
ppp multilink
!
ip classless
ip route 10.0.0.0 255.0.0.0 Dialer0
ip http server
!
dialer-list 1 protocol ip permit
!
line con 0
password console
login
line aux 0
line vty 0 4
password telnet
login
!
end
```

The configuration here is from the Tucson router:

```
version 12.0
service udp-small-servers
service tcp-small-servers
!
```

```
hostname Tucson
!
enable secret cisco
!
username Central password shoedepot
ip subnet-zero
isdn switch-type basic-ni1
!
interface Ethernet0
ip address 10.1.1.1 255.0.0.0
!
interface BRI0
no ip address
 encapsulation ppp
dialer rotary-group 0
isdn spid1 014045551111000 5551111
isdn spid2 014045552222000 5552222
!
interface Dialer0
ip unnumbered Ethernet0
encapsulation ppp
dialer in-band
dialer idle-timeout 300
dialer map ip 20.1.1.1 name Central speed 56 16175553333
dialer map ip 20.1.1.1 name Central speed 56 16175554444
dialer hold-queue 10
dialer load-threshold 200 either
dialer-group 1
ip access-group 10 in
ip access-group 10 out
no fair-queue
 no cdp enable
 ppp authentication chap
ppp multilink
!
ip classless
ip route 20.0.0.0 255.0.0.0 Dialer0
ip http server
!
access-list 10 permit 10.0.0.0 255.0.0.0
dialer-list 1 protocol ip permit
!
line con 0
password console
login
line aux 0
line vty 0 4
password telnet
login
!
end
```

You can see from the Tucson router configuration that the junior technician has made an error with an access list that has caused all inbound and
outbound packets to be blocked. It would appear that the technician was
attempting to ensure that only traffic from the source network crossed the

ISDN connection. The problem lies with the syntax of the access list command. The access list command entered by the technician was

```
access-list 10 permit 10.0.0.0 255.0.0.0
```

This has the effect of only allowing hosts X.0.0.0, where X can be any valid IP first octet. The correct command should have been:

```
access-list 10 permit 10.0.0.0 0.255.255.255
```

This would enable any host on the 10.X.X.X network to be allowed over the interface.

Results

You make the required change to the access list and the connection is immediately established. This is a classic lock-out case where a real-time configuration change locks you out of making the necessary changes to restore service. Proper planning and testing or the use of Cisco NetSys baseliner can help reduce these occurrences.

Questions

1. Which protocol is responsible for IP-to-MAC address conversion?

    a. ARP

    b. FTP

    c. WINS

    d. CLNX

2. Which of the following protocols operate at TCP port 25?

    a. FTP

    b. SNMP

    c. SMTP

    d. WWW

3. On a Cisco router, which command displays the contents of the internal ARP cache?

    a. display arp

    b. show arp

    c. show arpcache

    d. show cache

4. On a Cisco router, which command displays the internal IP routing table?

    a. show routing-table

    b. show route

    c. show ip route

    d. show all routes

5. What are the two types of broadcasts?

    a. Directed

    b. Unicast

    c. Lateral

    d. Flooding

6. On a Cisco router, which command displays real-time IP-to-MAC address resolution requests?

    a. debug arp events

    b. debug arp

    c. debug all arp

    d. debug ip mac

7. What is the Windows NT trace command called?

   a. trace

   b. tracert

   c. tracer

   d. mstrace

8. What is the maximum number of DNS servers you can set on a Cisco router?

   a. 2

   b. 3

   c. 8

   d. 6

9. On a Cisco router, which commands would clear the dynamically learned ARP entries?

   a. clear arp

   b. clear arp dynamic

   c. clear arp *

   d. clear arp-cache

10. Which command will display statistics about several IP protocols?

    a. show ip traffic

    b. show ip interface

    c. show interface

    d. show ip

11. Which command displays basic information about IP-enabled interfaces on a Cisco router?

    a. show interface

    b. show interface brief

    c. show ip interface

    d. show ip interface brief

12. At which OSI layer does ARP function?

    a. Physical

    b. Data link

    c. Transport

    d. Network

13. Which debug command would display information about routing table updates?

   a. debug routing
   b. debug ip routing
   c. debug routing-updates
   d. debug route

14. What is an helper address used for?

   a. To help IP packets find their destination
   b. To direct specific UDP broadcasts to a specific host
   c. To reduce routing loops
   d. To speed up convergence

15. On a trace issued by a Cisco router, what does a P represent?

   a. That the network is unreachable
   b. That the packet was rejected
   c. That the protocol is unreachable
   d. That the operation timed out

16. On a ping issued by a Cisco router, what does a ! represent?

   a. The successful receipt on an echo reply
   b. The destination is unreachable
   c. Congestion was experienced
   d. The packet was lost

17. Which statement is true about access lists?

   a. Access lists permit all traffic by default.
   b. An implicit permit all is at the end of every access list.
   c. An implicit deny all is at the end of every access list.
   d. Access lists are only available for IP.

18. At which OSI layer does TCP function?

   a. Physical
   b. Application
   c. Transport
   d. Network

19. What is the command to set a DNS server on a Cisco router?

   a. Router#ip name-server 10.10.10.10
   b. Router(config-if)#ip dns 10.10.10.10
   c. Router(config)#ip name-server 10.10.10.10
   d. Router#ip dns-server 10.10.10.10

20. At which OSI layer does IP function?

    a. Physical
    b. Application
    c. Transport
    d. Network

Answers

1. Answer: a

   The *address resolution protocol* (ARP) is responsible for IP-to-MAC address resolution.

2. Answer: c

   The *simple mail transfer protocol* (SMTP) operates at the TCP port 25.

3. Answer: b

   The show arp command displays the internal ARP cache on the router. The other three commands are illegal.

4. Answer: c

   The command show ip route displays the internal routing table on the router.

5. Answer: a and d

   The two types of broadcasts are directed and flooding.

6. Answer: b

   The debug arp command displays real-time IP-to-MAC address resolution requests.

7. Answer: b

   The Windows NT trace command is called tracert.

8. Answer: d

   The maximum number of DNS servers you can configure on a Cisco router is six. These are configured with the ip name-server command from the global configuration mode on the router.

9. Answer: a and d

   The command to clear the ARP cache on a Cisco router is clear arp-cache. The command clear arp is also allowed as it is a shortened version.

10. Answer: a

    The show ip traffic command displays information and statistics about several IP protocols. The show interface command just gives you an overview of all traffic on the interface.

11. Answer: b

    The show interface brief command displays basic information about the configuration of IP-enabled interfaces on the router.

12. Answer: b

ARP functions at the data link layer of the OSI model.

13. Answer: b

The command debug ip routing would display real-time updates of routing table additions and changes.

14. Answer: b

An IP helper address directs specific UDP broadcasts to a specific host.

15. Answer: c

On a trace issued by a Cisco router, a P represents that the protocol is unreachable.

16. Answer: a

On a ping issued by a Cisco router, a ! represents the successful receipt of an echo reply.

17. Answer: c

An implicit "deny all" is at the end of every access list. The other statements are all untrue.

18. Answer: c

TCP functions at the transport layer of the OSI model.

19. Answer: c

The command Router(config)#ip name-server 10.10.10.10 sets a DNS server on a Cisco router. You must be in global configuration mode to enter this command.

20. Answer: d

IP functions at the network layer of the OSI model.

10

AppleTalk

Apple Computer made significant strides in establishing itself within the computer industry during the early 1980s. They were one of the first to successfully implement a *local area network* (LAN) that was easy for the end user to configure and use. Unfortunately, their success has not matched the success of the IBM-compatible systems. Significantly fewer Macintosh computers are in business today than IBM compatibles. However, a large installed base of Apple computers still exists on both LANs and *wide area networks* (WANs). Therefore, it is important for us to know the concepts behind the Apple routing protocols and how these protocols affect our network. This chapter will prepare the reader to effectively troubleshoot AppleTalk protocols.

Objectives Covered in the Chapter

We will examine the following test objectives in this chapter:

■ Use proven isolation techniques to list the symptoms of common AppleTalk problems on router networks.

■ Apply diagnostic tools to trouble tickets and solve classroom network AppleTalk problems that simulate real-life networking malfunctions.

In the previous chapter, we discussed the basic troubleshooting techniques used in TCP/IP. Here we will examine how AppleTalk differs from and is similar to TCP/IP and IPX/SPX, the latter of which will be covered in the next chapter. Like IPX, AppleTalk was originally designed for LANs but has successfully been used in WAN environments. Like IP, AppleTalk is based on the network/node addressing scheme, except that AppleTalk uses the concept of cable ranges instead of subnets. This chapter will focus on how to approach a problem while using AppleTalk. When reading this chapter, keep in mind of how the Apple protocols map to the OSI seven-layer model. A comparison of the Apple protocols to the OSI model is shown in Figure 10-1.

Zones and Cable Ranges

Zones and cable ranges work together, allowing an administrator to break the network into manageable segments. We will examine these areas and then look at how to set up the router to enable AppleTalk to flow over the network.

Zones

AppleTalk uses *zones*, which are similar to an Ethernet *virtual local area network* (VLAN). A zone is merely a logical grouping of computers. This

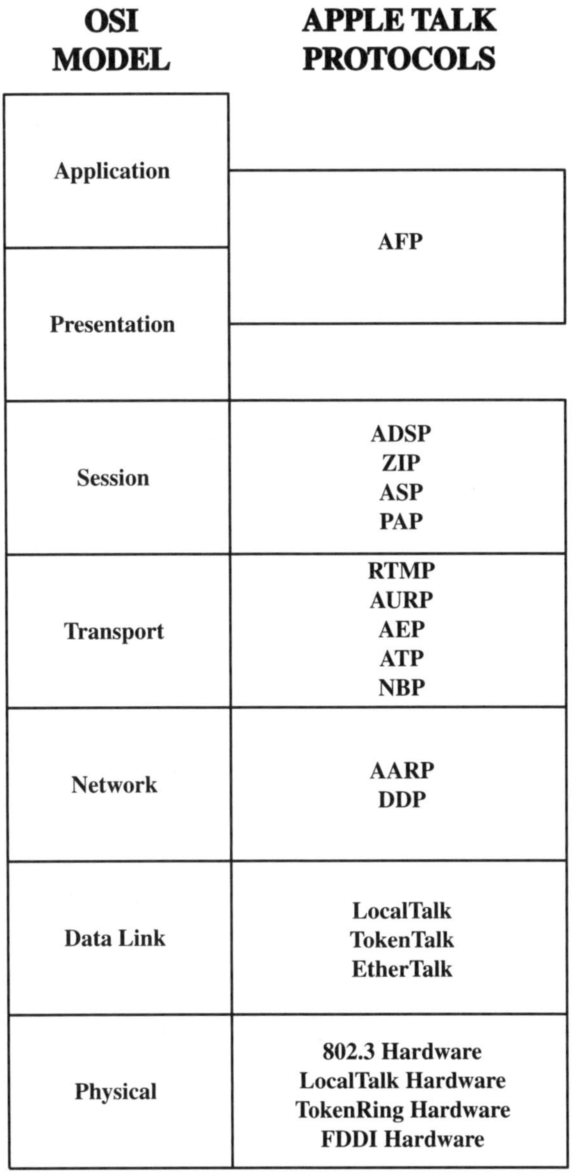

Figure 10-1
A comparison of the Apple protocols to the OSI model

OSI MODEL	APPLE TALK PROTOCOLS
Application	AFP
Presentation	
Session	ADSP ZIP ASP PAP
Transport	RTMP AURP AEP ATP NBP
Network	AARP DDP
Data Link	LocalTalk TokenTalk EtherTalk
Physical	802.3 Hardware LocalTalk Hardware TokenRing Hardware FDDI Hardware

grouping may contain multiple networks and multiple zones may be assigned to a single physical network segment. In other words, a zone is merely a multicast domain that may cross routers without regard to network numbers. The actual definition of a network, which is determined by the cable range, will be discussed in the section on cable ranges.

Users can choose the zone they belong to by using the Chooser application. The information on who belongs to which zone is propagated through the network by the *zone information protocol* (ZIP) and is stored in the *zone information table* (ZIT). A zone can be associated with single or multiple cable ranges. The cable ranges do not have to be contiguous or associated with each other in any way.

Zones are useful for both the administrator and the user for several reasons. First, using zones enables the administrator to group users in the same way that VLAN users can be grouped. Similar to VLANs, zones can be created based upon *media access control* (MAC) addresses, user duties, departments, networks, and so on. Second, users do not necessarily want or need to see all the resources on the network. The resources available to a user are based upon the zone to which they belong. Third, and arguably the greatest benefit of zones, is that the administrator is not limited by the physical topology when applying zones. This means that if a user moves from the fourth-floor accounts payable department to the third-floor accounts payable department, the only issue the administrator deals with is making sure the router interface on the third floor belongs to the correct zone.

Cable Ranges

A cable range is used to determine a network number. The combinations of a network number and a host address uniquely identify a host within an AppleTalk system. Cable ranges, only used in AppleTalk Phase II, are defined on the router interface. The cable range can be a single network number or a consecutive group of network numbers. The network numbers can range from 0 to 65,279. Combining the cable range (16 bits) with the node address (eight bit) gives us the 24-bit address of the host.

Use caution when deciding on the size of a cable range. Since a single cable range can have up to 255 nodes, choosing one that is too large can result in too many hosts on a network, which in turn could degrade performance.

Setting up AppleTalk on a router is actually a simple task. Some concepts, such as the ZIT, will be discussed later in this chapter. First, we will go into the interface and set the cable range:

```
Router(config-if)#appletalk cable-range 32-33
```

This command tells the interface to build a ZIT with entries for the networks 32 and 33. We could also tell the router to build a single network number as follows:

```
Router(config-if)#appletalk cable-range 150-150
```

This would build the ZIT for network 150. At this point, we have only numbered the networks. Assume for a moment that we would like to associate two cable ranges with a given interface. This can be accomplished as follows:

```
Router(config-if)#appletalk cable-range 187-190 200-200
```

This will associate networks 187 through 190 and network 200 with this router interface.

The next step is to assign a zone name to the interface. This is accomplished with the following:

```
Router(config-if)#appletalk zone name Chromozone
```

If we wish to associate multiple zones with a given cable range, we merely use the same command with a different name:

```
Router(config-if)#appletalk zone name orbitzone
```

At this point, we have associated the zone names "chromosone" and "orbitzone" with both the interface and the previously defined cable range. To eliminate orbitzone from our zone list, we would use the "no" form of the zone name command:

```
Router(config-if)#no appletalk zone name orbitzone
```

Or, to remove all zones at once, simply enter

```
Router(config-if)#no appletalk zone
```

We also need to define our routing protocol as a *routing table maintenance protocol* (RTMP), an *enhanced interior gateway routing protocol* (EIGRP), or an *Apple update-based routing protocol* (AURP). RTMP and AURP will be discussed in this chapter. EIGRP will be discussed in Chapter 12, "Routing Protocols."

When we want to see which zones a router knows about, we issue the command as follows:

```
Router# Show Apple Zone
Network(s)oldzone     32-33
FramePgh              150-150
```

```
Chromozone            130-130
Ozone                 999 6-10
CaliZone              20-25
Bozone                15-16
pittsburgh            54-57
orbitzone             19-19
xFrame156             156-156
dallas                50-53
Dozone                12000-12000 120-122
Endzone               50012-50012 12-12
60                    60-60
wazone                30-31 39158
Accounting            6-10
Frame151              151-151
Frame160              160-160
frame152
Frame154              154-154
Frame157              157-157
WY-ZONE               13-13
Zone A                25707
longisland            70-71
beanzone              59-59
Marketing             6-10
TwilightZone          1-5
twin-cities           45-47
Total of 27 zones
```

Notice that the output lists all known zone names and the cable ranges associated with those names. Also note that some names are associated to multiple discontiguous networks.

LocalTalk and AppleTalk

LocalTalk, originally named AppleBus, was the first attempt by Apple to allow computers to communicate. It has largely been supplanted by use of the AppleTalk protocol, but we will still need to know a few simple facts about LocalTalk.

LocalTalk

LocalTalk ran over a serial connection at 230.4 Kbps with a limitation of 32 nodes on a segment. A LocalTalk device works only on layer 2 of the Apple model, with the operating system being responsible for the remaining layers. Because there is no way to preset the network address, a means of dynamically assigning a unique network address had to be devised. The scheme Apple came up with was simple, even if it is inefficient in large networks. This method is still used in AppleTalk.

AppleTalk

AppleTalk is divided into two implementations called Phase I and Phase II. One advantage of AppleTalk over LocalTalk is the number of available network nodes. In Phase I, there is a limitation of a single network with a maximum of 127 hosts and 127 servers. Phase II was introduced in 1989, making Phase I nearly obsolete, although you may still be able to find some implementations. Phase II enables multiple networks (up to a theoretical limit of 65,535 networks), each with up to 254 nodes. Phase II uses the term "cable ranges" to designate network numbers. The AppleTalk address consists of a 16-bit network number followed by an eight-bit node address. This gives us a total of 24 bits to uniquely identify a node and network (cable range). This gives us the same number of networks and hosts as an IP address with a class C subnet mask. Nodes are numbered from 0 to 255, while networks are numbered from 0 to 65,353. Some addresses are reserved, as we will show later in this chapter.

Always be sure that both devices are using the same phase of AppleTalk because a Phase I device cannot talk to a Phase II device. If one node does not see any others, or only sees some nodes on the network, check that the phase is the same on all machines. If nodes cannot see outside of the network, check to see if the router is using the same phase as the nodes. Since Cisco equipment does not support LocalTalk, we will only discuss Phase II for the remainder of the chapter.

Initial AppleTalk Address Assignment

Because there is no way to guarantee that the previous host address is available, AppleTalk has implemented the following five-step process for address assignments:

1. An AppleTalk-capable device chooses AppleTalk as the network protocol.

2. A network address is chosen at random (see the following note).

3. An *AppleTalk address resolution protocol* (AARP) broadcast packet is sent over the network with the chosen address.

4. The device either receives a notification that this address is already being used or no notification is received and the process experiences a time-out failure.

5. If a notification is received that this address is in use, another address is chosen at random.

NOTE: *The AppleTalk network address is not a totally random scheme. AppleTalk stores the last used address in* parameter RAM *(PRAM) and tries to use this address the next time there is an attempt to connect to the network.*

Although you may be able to manually set the address on some interfaces, most devices still use this process to determine an AppleTalk address. You will encounter two issues on large networks using this scheme. First is the amount of time it can take to successfully choose an unused address. Assume that you have a network with 250 active machines. Because AppleTalk does not keep track of which addresses it has already tried, the machine may spend an inordinate amount of time randomly choosing an address before it finally stumbles upon one of the four remaining addresses. The second issue is the number of broadcasts caused by a machine trying to initialize on a large network. Imagine what happens to network performance due to the sheer number of broadcasts on a Monday morning at 9:00 A.M. when 50 users are all trying to find an available address on a network that already has 200 users active.

AppleTalk Protocols

AppleTalk consists of several different protocols. We will focus on those used within the internetworking environment. Before studying these thoroughly, we will first have a short definition of each of the major protocols used in AppleTalk.

EtherTalk, TokenTalk, and FFDITalk

EtherTalk, TokenTalk, and FDDITalk are the AppleTalk implementations at layer 2. These layer 2 protocols enable AppleTalk to communicate over differing media at the physical layer. These support Ethernet using ELAP, Token Ring using LAPB, and FDDI using FLAP. LocalTalk uses LLAP.

AppleTalk Address Resolution Protocol (AARP)

AARP is a connectionless layer 2 protocol that works in manner similar to ARP. AARP maps a known layer 2 address to a previously unknown layer 3 address. When a node needs to find the layer 3 AppleTalk address of another node, it sends out an AARP broadcast that requests the name. The process is the same on Ethernet, Token Ring, or the *fiber distributed data interface* (FDDI). At the node, the addresses are stored within the *address maintenance table* (AMT). Cisco chooses to call this the *Apple ARP table*. Old entries eventually are timed out of the table and new entries may overwrite the least used entries.

Checking the contents of the ARP cache can be accomplished by using the Show APPLE ARP command. A typical output would look as follows:

Router#	Show Apple	ARPAddress	Age (Min.)		Type	Hardware Addr.
Encap Interface1.4	24	Dynamic	0010.8328.21e1.0000		SNAP	Ethernet2
1.5	107	Dynamic	0010.832c.a6c5.0000		SNAP	Ethernet2
1.6	25	Dynamic	0060.b021.0fe4.0000		SNAP	Ethernet2
1.25	180	Dynamic	0000.c51b.4d8b.0000		SNAP	Ethernet2
1.95	209	Dynamic	00a0.c911.56ef.0000		SNAP	Ethernet2
1.128	0	Dynamic	0060.b018.9024.0000		SNAP	Ethernet2
1.131	33	Dynamic	0060.b044.d52e.0000		SNAP	Ethernet2
1.133	180	Dynamic	0800.0734.f7ea.0000		SNAP	Ethernet2
1.137	180	Dynamic	0800.0704.6f7f.0000		SNAP	Ethernet2
1.138	52	Dynamic	0060.b002.6795.0000		SNAP	Ethernet2
1.143	180	Dynamic	0800.0784.be4a.0000		SNAP	Ethernet2
1.159	100	Dynamic	0800.07c4.46d8.0000		SNAP	Ethernet2
1.163	180	Dynamic	0800.0784.643a.0000		SNAP	Ethernet2
1.190	180	Dynamic	0800.07d4.fbb7.0000		SNAP	Ethernet2
1.224	180	Dynamic	0800.0704.045f.0000		SNAP	Ethernet2
1.246	180	Dynamic	0800.07c4.6643.0000		SNAP	Ethernet2
2.158	5	Dynamic	0005.0249.ff81.0000		SNAP	Ethernet2

Several things should be noted from this output. In the first column, notice the address. It consists of a network (16 bits) and a node (eight bits) separated by a period. Next is the age of the ARP entry in minutes. As with all ARP caches, AppleTalk ARP caches will time out an entry that is not used after a definable amount of time. The entry type in the cache follows this and can be either dynamic or static. The MAC address of the host is also shown, followed by the encapsulation type. In this example, the encapsulation types are all SNAP. Finally, the interface that the ARP entry was learned from is shown.

NOTE: *Mixing encapsulation types will result in some devices not being shown on the network. A good rule of thumb to remember is that all devices on the network will need the same encapsulation type or a method of routing between the encapsulation types. For example, suppose you have three hosts called A, B, and C. Hosts A and B have the same encapsulation type, while host C has a different type. Hosts A and B will not be able to directly communicate with host C. Although it is possible to add a router with two interfaces, each running a different encapsulation type, this is only recommended if you have specific reasons for needing to run different encapsulation types.*

Table 10-1 provides a list of some of the commands related to the AppleTalk ARP and a short description of their purpose.

AppleTalk Data Stream Protocol (ADSP)

The *AppleTalk data stream protocol* (ADSP) is a layer 5 (session) protocol used to establish and maintain full-duplex data streams between two hosts in an AppleTalk network. Using a connection-oriented and reliable method-

Table 10-1

AppleTalk ARP
Commands

AppleTalk Arp [probe/request] interval	Specifies the interval used by AARP.
AppleTalk Arp [probe/request] retransmit	Specifies the number of retransmissions of an AARP.
Apple ARP-TIMEOUT	Specifies the time after which an entry is removed from the AARP table.

ology, ADSP uses a windowing system where the receiving host notifies the sender of the available buffer size.

Datagram Delivery Protocol (DDP)

The *datagram delivery protocol* (DDP) is AppleTalk's layer 3 implementation of a connectionless, unreliable protocol. DDP is extremely similar to IP in its approach to communications and the fields associated with each. This is also the protocol responsible for gaining a unique network node address. Two types of DDP packets exist: short and extended. Short DDP packets do not have a source destination network field and are an older format that is not commonly used today. An illustration of the extended DDP header is shown in Figure 10-2.

As you can see, a DDP packet contains several fields. The most important fields for our purposes are as follows:

- Hop Count: This is a six-bit field holding a counter with a maximum value of 15. This field is incremented by one every time a router forwards the packet. If the field value reaches 16 and the router receiving that packet is not directly connected to the destination, the packet is dropped.

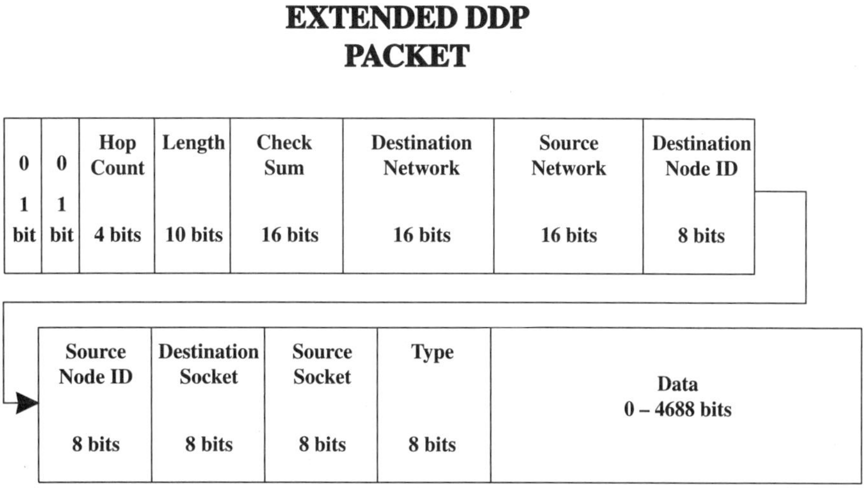

Figure 10-2
The extended
DDP header

EXTENDED DDP PACKET

0 1 bit	0 1 bit	Hop Count 4 bits	Length 10 bits	Check Sum 16 bits	Destination Network 16 bits	Source Network 16 bits	Destination Node ID 8 bits

Source Node ID 8 bits	Destination Socket 8 bits	Source Socket 8 bits	Type 8 bits	Data 0 – 4688 bits

- Destination Network: This is the network number associated with the ultimate destination of the packet.

- Source Network: This is the network number from which the packet originated.

- Source Node: This is the node that originated the packet.

- Source Socket: This is extremely similar to a source socket in IP. However, AppleTalk uses layer 3 to determine socket numbers, while IP uses layer 4 to determine socket numbers.

- Destination Socket: This is similar to the destination socket in IP. However, like the DDP source socket, this is determined at layer 3.

Name Binding Protocol (NBP)

The *name binding protocol* (NBP) is a layer-4 connectionless protocol and its main purpose is to build a list of hosts by mapping the hostnames to the network address. It actively searches the network for hosts that the user needs to access. NBP is the functional equivalent of a DNS server in a TCP/IP network. The four types of NBP packets are broadcast request, lookup request, lookup reply, and forward request.

Names in AppleTalk are not case-sensitive. Names take the form of *object: type @ zone.* Each object, type, and zone can be up to 32 characters in length. The colon (:) and ampersand (@) are required delimiters. Special characters can also be used as wildcards. Acceptable wildcards include the tilde (~) to represent single or multiple characters within the object or type fields, an asterisk (*) to represent the requester's default zone, or an equals sign (=) to represent all possible values.

One useful command is the Debug APPLE NBP command. This can be used to verify that NBP packets are crossing the network. The output from a Debug APPLE NBP follows:

```
Router# Debug Apple NBP
AppleTalk NBP packets debugging is on
Sep 20 12:32:19.241 PDT: AT: NBP, LkUp handler, ntups=1Sep 20
12:32:19.241 PDT: AT: NBP ctrl = LkUp, ntuples = 1, id = 1
Sep 20 12:32:19.241 PDT: AT: 6.118, skt 129, enum 0, name:
=:NRL@Endzone
Sep 20 12:32:21.209 PDT: AT: NBP, LkUp handler, ntups=1
Sep 20 12:32:21.209 PDT: AT: NBP ctrl = LkUp, ntuples = 1, id = 1
Sep 20 12:32:21.209 PDT: AT: 6.118, skt 129, enum 0, name:
=:NRL@Endzone
Sep 20 12:32:21.693 PDT: AT: NBP, LkUp handler, ntups=1
```

```
Sep 20 12:32:21.693 PDT: AT: NBP ctrl = LkUp, ntuples = 1, id = 155
Sep 20 12:32:21.693 PDT: AT: 1.133, skt 129, enum 1, name: Sly
One:LaserWriter@TwilightZone
Sep 20 12:32:22.685 PDT: AT: NBP, LkUp handler, ntups=1
Sep 20 12:32:22.685 PDT: AT: NBP ctrl = LkUp, ntuples = 1, id = 155
Sep 20 12:32:22.685 PDT: AT: 1.133, skt 129, enum 1, name: Sly
One:LaserWriter@TwilightZone
Sep 20 12:32:23.189 PDT: AT: NBP, LkUp handler, ntups=1
```

Routing Table Maintenance Protocol (RTMP)

RTMP is a layer-4 routing protocol using the distance-vector algorithm that utilizes Split Horizon. It has a limit of 16 hops. By default, a routing table is broadcast from every router every 10 seconds. Routes are marked as invalid after 20 seconds and removed from the routing tables after 40 seconds. RTMP may use an associated routing protocol called AURP. The RTMP routing table contains the following information regarding each of the known destination networks:

- The cable range of the destination network
- The number of hops to the destination network, which is a maximum of 16
- The port for the destination network
- The next-hop router address
- The routing entry state, which is labeled as good, suspect, or bad

RTMP routing is enabled with a global command:

```
Router#Appletalk routing RTMP
```

Apple Update-based Routing Protocol (AURP)

This layer-4 protocol is used in conjunction with RTMP. In essence, AURP creates a tunnel through TCP/IP that bypasses RTMP's hop-count limitation. AURP utilizes Split-Horizon to limit where routes are learned. Two types of AURP tunnels exist: point-to-point and multi-point. As their names imply, a point-to-point tunnel goes from a single point (router interface) to another single point, while a multi-point tunnel connects a single point to more than one other point.

While exchanging routing information using AURP, the source router encapsulates the RTMP and ZIP packets into TCP/IP *user datagram protocol* (UDP) packets. The remote router strips off the encapsulation. AURP routing is enabled with a global command:

```
Router#(config)Appletalk routing AURP
```

AppleTalk File Protocol (AFP)

The *AppleTalk file protocol* (AFP) enables the sharing of file resources across an AppleTalk network. AFP works at both layers six and seven of the OSI model.

AppleTalk Session Protocol (ASP)

The *AppleTalk session protocol* (ASP) is the AppleTalk layer-5 (session) protocol that establishes and maintains sessions between AppleTalk clients and servers. It is a connectionless protocol.

Printer Access Protocol (PAP)

The *printer access protocol* (PAP) is another layer-5 protocol used by AppleTalk clients. Its main purpose is to establish and maintain printing sessions. It is a connection-oriented protocol.

Zone Information Protocol (ZIP)

As previously discussed, ZIP is a layer-5 protocol that is used to map the network address to a specific zone. A router sends out a ZIP request that contains one or many network numbers. The remote router responds with the zones and associated networks that are known. This information is stored in a ZIT. An example of a ZIT is shown in Figure 10-3.

Figure 10-3

An example of a
zone information
table (ZIT)

APPLETALK ZONE INFORMATION TABLE

Network Number	Zones
20	Accounting
50	Marketing, Sales
84	Management
100 – 110	Research

We can watch ZIP packets cross the network by using Debug. Here is an example of a ZIP packet:

```
Router# Debug Apple ZIPAppleTalk ZIP Packets
debugging is onSep 20 12:37:54.721 PDT: AT: Recvd ZIP
cmd 5 from 15.137-6Sep 20 12:37:54.721 PDT: AT:
Answering ZIP GetNetInfo rcvd from 15.137 via
Ethernet0
Sep 20 12:37:54.721 PDT: AT: Sent GetNetInfo reply to 15.137 via
                             Ethernet0
Sep 20 12:39:11.105 PDT: AT: Recvd ZIP cmd 5 from 15.138-6
Sep 20 12:39:11.105 PDT: AT: Answering ZIP GetNetInfo rcvd from
15.138 via Ethernet0
```

Notice that first our router received a ZIP GetNetInfo, which is a request for information regarding a network, then the router answered the request. When a router repeatedly resets an AppleTalk interface, it is possible to flood the network with requests for ZIT information. This is referred to as a ZIP storm.

Show Commands

Many AppleTalk-related show commands are available. The most common ones are detailed in this section.

Show AppleTalk Globals

Show AppleTalk Globals shows the configurations that apply to all interfaces on this router. Of specific interest are the number of routes, the number of zones, and the default timers. These are critical to know for both everyday use and for the CIT test. Here is some sample output:

```
Router# Show AppleTalk GLOBALS
AppleTalk global information:
   Internet is incompatible with older, AT Phase1, routers.
   There are 28 routes in the Internet.
   There are 27 zones defined.
   Logging of significant AppleTalk events is disabled.
   ZIP resends queries every 10 seconds.
   RTMP updates are sent every 10 seconds.
   RTMP entries are considered BAD after 20 seconds.
   RTMP entries are discarded after 60 seconds.
   AARP probe retransmit count: 10, interval: 200 msec.
   AARP request retransmit count: 5, interval: 1,000 msec.
   DDP datagrams will be checksummed.
```

Show AppleTalk Interface

Show AppleTalk Interface enables us to see the AppleTalk configuration of a given interface. In the following output, notice the settings for cable range, interface address, and zone.

```
Router# Show AppleTalk Interface e0
Ethernet0 is up, line protocol is up
   AppleTalk cable range is 15-16
   AppleTalk address is 15.134, Valid
   AppleTalk zone is "Bozone"
   AppleTalk address gleaning is disabled
   AppleTalk route cache is enabled
```

NOTE: *AppleTalk address gleaning has been turned off by default for this interface. Gleaning is a process in which the router examines all the DDP packets in order to learn the source and destination addresses. The information is then sent to the AMT. Enabling Gleaning tends to reduce the number of AARP requests required in exchange for the CPU cycles required to strip the DDP packets. This is not generally used.*

Show AppleTalk Traffic

Show AppleTalk Traffic gives us a snapshot of how the Appletalk traffic is affecting our network. Several elements in this output require our attention. Take a look at the following output before we discuss what should become noticeable with practice:

```
Router#Show AppleTalk Traffic
AppleTalk statistics:  Rcvd:  365030714 total, 0 checksum
errors,
        0 bad hop count 10187382 local destination, 0 access denied
        0 for MacIP, 0 bad MacIP, 0 no client
        66 port disabled, 0 no listener
        0 ignored, 0 martians
  Bcast: 173971 received, 7785343 sent
  Sent:  9199992 generated, 1418203 forwarded, 352532880 fast
         forwarded, 872549
loopback
        0 forwarded from MacIP, 0 MacIP failures
        16459 encapsulation failed, 3670 no route, 0 no source
  DDP:   13370751 long, 0 short, 0 macip, 5 bad size
  NBP:   4381684 received, 24 invalid, 0 proxies
        4 replies sent, 3425581 forwards, 2668770 lookups, 248
        failures
  RTMP:  6983362 received, 238 requests, 7 invalid, 0 ignored
        6234016 sent, 0 replies
  ATP:   0 received
  ZIP:   365045 received, 367661 sent, 364080 netinfo
  Echo:  2963 received, 0 discarded, 0 illegal
        0 generated, 110 replies sent
  Responder:  0 received, 0 illegal, 0 unknown
        0 replies sent, 0 failures
  AARP:  181642 requests, 4103 replies, 13285 probes
        362379 martians, 20 bad encapsulation, 0 unknown
        85944 sent, 0 failures, 4100 delays, 16459 drops
  Lost: 0 no buffers
  Unknown: 0 packets
  Discarded: 8 wrong encapsulation, 0 bad SNAP discriminator
  AURP: 0 Open Requests, 0 Router Downs
        0 Routing Information sent, 0 Routing Information received
        0 Zone Information sent, 0 Zone Information received
        0 Get Zone Nets sent, 0 Get Zone Nets received
```

```
0 Get Domain Zone List sent, 0 Get Domain Zone List
  received
0 bad sequence
```

Among the first things to notice is that this router has seen eight packets with incorrect encapsulations. Although this is a small enough number not to cause concern, a large number would indicate that at least one device on the network does not agree with the rest of the network regarding encapsulation types.

Second, compare the counters in the RTMP section with those in the AURP section. This tells us that this router is running RTMP without AURP because all of the AURP counters are at zero.

Third, calculate what percentage of traffic is devoted to broadcasts. The percentage of broadcast packets compared to total packets received is under one-half of one percent. This is an excellent statistic that shows us the network is not being burdened by broadcasts.

Fourth, this router uses extended DDP packets. The number of long packets under the DDP section shows this. We should treat the five "bad" DDP packets as anomalies until they begin to rise steadily. If we have both types in significant quantities, it indicates that there is a device that is using AppleTalk Phase I, which does not include the source and destination networks in the DDP header.

Show AppleTalk Neighbors

Show AppleTalk Neighbors works just like any other show neighbor command. It shows you the neighbors that this router is directly connected to as well as how they are connected and how long the interface has been active.

Here is some sample output:

```
Router# Show AppleTalk Neighbors
AppleTalk neighbors:  15.174
Ethernet0, uptime 7w5d, 7 secs
       Neighbor has restarted 2 times in 8w1d.
       Neighbor is reachable as a RTMP peer
  6.176        Ethernet1, uptime 8w1d, 1 sec
       Neighbor is reachable as a RTMP peer
  6.197        Ethernet1, uptime 8w1d, 2 secs
       Neighbor is reachable as a RTMP peer
  6.240        Ethernet1, uptime 8w1d, 8 secs
       Neighbor is reachable as a RTMP peer
  9.62         Ethernet1, uptime 1w6d, 6 secs
       Neighbor has restarted 3 times in 8w1d.
       Neighbor is reachable as a RTMP peer
  1.95         Ethernet2, uptime 8w1d, 3 secs
       Neighbor is reachable as a RTMP peer
```

```
120.174        Ethernet3, uptime 8w0d, 3 secs
      Neighbor has restarted 3 times in 8w1d.
      Neighbor is reachable as a RTMP peer
12.164         Ethernet5, uptime 8w1d, 3 secs
      Neighbor is reachable as a RTMP peer
150.210        Serial0.1, uptime 8w1d, 8 secs
      Neighbor has restarted 1 time in 8w1d.
      Neighbor is reachable as a RTMP peer
151.2          Serial0.2, uptime 8w1d, 8 secs
      Neighbor is reachable as a RTMP peer
154.102        Serial0.4, uptime 17:23:57, 1 sec
      Neighbor has restarted 8 times in 8w1d.
      Neighbor is reachable as a RTMP peer
157.210        Serial0.7, uptime 1w0d, 5 secs
      Neighbor is reachable as a RTMP peer
156.210        Serial0.9, uptime 3w4d, 8 secs
      Neighbor has restarted 3 times in 8w1d.
      Neighbor is reachable as a RTMP peer
160.210        Serial0.10, uptime 1w2d, 7 secs
      Neighbor has restarted 5 times in 8w1d.
  Neighbor is reachable as a RTMP peer
```

This output immediately tells us three significant items. The first is that we are using RTMP as the routing protocol to see our neighbors.

The second is that there seem to be problems with keeping the interfaces running. This is indicated by the fact that most neighbor connections have been reset at least twice in the past eight weeks. Without any other historical information, it appears that there has been a continuing problem on the network. In this case, the network administrator has replaced a Catalyst 5500 switch within his network. This is the cause of the interfaces resetting. However, we would never know this if we did not ask what changes had occurred in the network within the last eight weeks. Also, when the number of interface resets is nearly consistent across neighbors, it is usually safe to assume that the issue is caused by something that affects the whole network.

Third, what is the problem with the router on network 157.210, which is connected through Serial port 0.7? The router on the far end has been down for maintenance. Therefore, the "uptime" is only a single week.

Other Show Commands

Many other AppleTalk show commands are useful in everyday administration. Table 10-2 displays a comprehensive list of all the show commands with short explanations. See the Cisco IOS documentation for a full explanation of each command.

Table 10-2

Command	Usage
show appletalk access-lists	Displays the currently defined AppleTalk access lists.
show appletalk adjacent-routes	Displays routes one hop away or directly connected.
show appletalk ARP	Displays entries in the AARP cache.
show appletalk AURP events	Shows AURP events.
show appletalk AURP topology	Displays entries in the AURP private path database.
show appletalk cache	Displays routes in the AppleTalk fast-switching table.
show appletalk domain	Displays all of the domain-related information.
show appletalk EIGRP	Displays AppleTalk interfaces configured for EIGRP. interfaces
show appletalk EIGRP neighbors	Displays neighbors running EIGRP.
show appletalk EIGRP topology	Displays the AppleTalk EIGRP topology table.
show appletalk globals	Displays information about the AppleTalk network.
show appletalk interface	Displays the status of an interface running AppleTalk.
show appletalk macip-clients	Displays the status of all known MacIP clients.
show appletalk macip-servers	Displays the status of all known MacIP servers.
show appletalk macip-traff	Displays statistics about MacIP traffic.
show appletalk name-cache	Displays a list of NBP services offered by nearby routers.
show appletalk NBP	Displays the contents of the NBP name registration table.
show appletalk neighbors	Displays information about directly connected AppleTalk routers.
show appletalk remap	Displays domain remapping information.
show appletalk route	Displays entries in the AppleTalk routing table.
show appletalk sockets	Displays information about process sockets on an AppleTalk interface.
show appletalk static	Displays information about statically defined routes.
show appletalk traffic	Displays statistics about AppleTalk traffic.
show appletalk zone	Displays entries in the ZIT.

Debug Commands

The following section outlines three debug commands of crucial importance for troubleshooting purposes: Debug Apple Events, Debug Apple Packet, and Debug Apple ZIP.

Debug Apple Events

Debug Apple Events is one of the primary commands used to look at the actions of a routing protocol within an AppleTalk network. The following output shows a typical output:

```
Router# Debug Apple Events
AppleTalk Events debugging is on
Sep 20 12:28:41.866 PDT: AT: RTMP GC complete (0 PDBs freed, 0 PDBs
                            waiting)
Sep 20 12:28:41.886 PDT: AT: Connected GC complete (0 PDBs freed, 0
                            PDBs waiting)
Sep 20 12:29:41.906 PDT: AT: RTMP GC complete (0 PDBs freed, 0 PDBs
                            waiting)
Sep 20 12:29:41.926 PDT: AT: Connected GC complete (0 PDBs freed, 0
                            PDBs waiting)
Sep 20 12:30:41.938 PDT: AT: RTMP GC complete (0 PDBs freed, 0 PDBs
                            waiting)
Sep 20 12:30:41.954 PDT: AT: Connected GC complete (0 PDBs freed, 0
                            PDBs waiting)
Sep 20 12:31:41.986 PDT: AT: RTMP GC complete (0 PDBs freed, 0 PDBs
                            waiting)
Sep 20 12:31:42.010 PDT: AT: Connected GC complete (0 PDBs freed, 0
                            PDBs waiting)
```

In a Debug Apple Event dump, two major areas indicate problems. The first is that the requests for updates are not fulfilled. This would have been discovered by not receiving the "Connected GC complete" message and would indicate a problem with the RTMP protocol. The second issue to look for is an increasing number of PDBs waiting. This could indicate that the router is not keeping up with demands.

Debug Apple Packet

Debug Apple Packet shows all AppleTalk traffic traveling over the network. This is one of the most powerful tools available. The following output is an example of this tool at work:

```
Router# Debug Apple Packet
AppleTalk packets debugging is on
Sep 20 12:35:42.197 PDT: Ethernet1: encap'ed output packet AT
                        packet: enctype SNAP, size 186
Sep 20 12:35:42.197 PDT: AT: src=Ethernet1:9.34, dst=6-10,
                        size=151, 24 rtes, RTMP pkt sent
Sep 20 12:35:42.197 PDT: Ethernet2: encap'ed output packet AT
                        packet: enctype SNAP, size 198
Sep 20 12:35:42.201 PDT: AT: src=Ethernet2:4.8, dst=1-5, size=163,
                        27 rtes, RTMP pkt sent
Sep 20 12:35:42.201 PDT: Ethernet3: encap'ed output packet AT
                        packet: enctype SNAP, size 192
Sep 20 12:35:42.201 PDT: AT: src=Ethernet3:120.189, dst=120-122,
                        size=157, 26 rtes, RTMP pkt sent
Sep 20 12:35:42.205 PDT: AT: src=Ethernet4:130.189, dst=130-130,
                        size=163, 27 rtes, RTMP pkt sent
Sep 20 12:35:42.217 PDT: Ethernet5: encap'ed output packet AT
                        packet: enctype SNAP, size 192
Sep 20 12:35:42.221 PDT: Serial0.1: encap'ed output packet AT
                        packet: enctype FRAME-RELAY-IETF, size 180
Sep 20 12:35:42.221 PDT: AT: src=Serial0.1:150.1, dst=150-150,
                        size=157, 26 rtes, RTMP pkt sent
Sep 20 12:35:42.221 PDT: Serial0.2: encap'ed output packet AT
                        packet: enctype FRAME-RELAY-IETF, size 159
Sep 20 12:35:42.221 PDT: AT: src=Serial0.2:151.1, dst=151-151,
                        size=136, 22 rtes, RTMP pkt sent
Sep 20 12:35:42.225 PDT: Serial0.4: encap'ed output packet AT
                        packet: enctype FRAME-RELAY-IETF, size 180
What did we learn from this? We know that the Ethernet 1 port is
using SNAP as the encapsulation by this lines:
Sep 20 12:35:42.197 PDT: Ethernet1: encap'ed output packet AT
                        packet: enctype SNAP, size 186
This router knows how the route to Cable-Range 6-10 and Ethernet
port 1 has an AppleTalk address of 9.34 based on:
Sep 20 12:35:42.197 PDT: AT: src=Ethernet1:9.34, dst=6-10,
                        size=151, 24 rtes, RTMP pkt sent
Ethernet 2 uses SNAP, has an AppleTalk address of 4.8, and the
router knows the destination to Cable-range 1-5. This is based on
these two lines:
Sep 20 12:35:42.197 PDT: Ethernet2: encap'ed output packet AT
                        packet: enctype SNAP, size 198Sep 20
                        12:35:42.201 PDT: AT: src=Ethernet2:4.8,
                        dst=1-5, size=163, 27 rtes, RTMP pkt sent
Serial Sub-interface 0.1 uses Frame-Relay with IETF, uses RTMP, and
Cable-range 150 based upon these two lines:
Sep 20 12:35:42.221 PDT: Serial0.1: encap'ed output packet AT
                        packet: enctype FRAME-RELAY-IETF, size
                        180Sep 20 12:35:42.221 PDT: AT:
                        src=Serial0.1:150.1, dst=150-150,
                        size=157, 26 rtes, RTMP pkt sent
```

This is quite a lot of information to gather in a short amount of time.
Extreme caution should be used with this command. Issuing this command
on a router that is running close to maximum capacity will bring your network down.

Debug Apple ZIP

Debug Apple ZIP generates output from ZIP updates. This output tells us several interesting things, including where routers are connected and how often ZIP GetNetInfo requests occur.

```
Router# Debug APPLE ZIP
AppleTalk ZIP Packets debugging is on
Sep 20 12:37:54.721 PDT: AT: Recvd ZIP cmd 5 from 15.137-6
Sep 20 12:37:54.721 PDT: AT: Answering ZIP GetNetInfo rcvd from
                             15.137 via Ethernet0
Sep 20 12:37:54.721 PDT: AT: Sent GetNetInfo reply to 15.137 via
                             Ethernet0
Sep 20 12:39:11.105 PDT: AT: Recvd ZIP cmd 5 from 15.138-6
Sep 20 12:39:11.105 PDT: AT: Answering ZIP GetNetInfo rcvd from
                             15.138 via Ethernet0
Sep 20 12:39:11.109 PDT: AT: Sent GetNetInfo reply to 15.138 via
                             Ethernet0
Sep 20 12:39:25.245 PDT: AT: Recvd ZIP cmd 5 from 1.128-6
Sep 20 12:39:25.245 PDT: AT: Answering ZIP GetNetInfo rcvd from
                             1.128 via Ethernet2
Sep 20 12:39:25.245 PDT: AT: Sent GetNetInfo reply to 1.128 via
                             Ethernet2
Sep 20 12:39:54.577 PDT: AT: Recvd ZIP cmd 5 from 15.137-6
Sep 20 12:39:54.577 PDT: AT: Answering ZIP GetNetInfo rcvd from
                             15.137 via Ethernet0
Sep 20 12:39:54.577 PDT: AT: Sent GetNetInfo reply to 15.137 via
                             Ethernet0
Sep 20 12:41:10.960 PDT: AT: Recvd ZIP cmd 5 from 15.138-6
Sep 20 12:41:10.960 PDT: AT: Answering ZIP GetNetInfo rcvd from
                             15.138 via Ethernet0
Sep 20 12:41:10.960 PDT: AT: Sent GetNetInfo reply to 15.138 via
                             Ethernet0
Sep 20 12:41:11.180 PDT: AT: GetZoneList request rcvd from 19.138
                             via Ethernet6
Sep 20 12:41:11.180 PDT: AT: GetZoneList startindex 1, src 19.138
Sep 20 12:41:24.048 PDT: AT: Recvd ZIP cmd 5 from 1.128-6
Sep 20 12:41:24.048 PDT: AT: Answering ZIP GetNetInfo rcvd from
                             1.128 via Ethernet2
Sep 20 12:41:24.048 PDT: AT: Sent GetNetInfo reply to 1.128 via
                             Ethernet2
```

Other AppleTalk Commands

Like most other protocols, AppleTalk is associated with a wide array of commands. For example, ping is available for AppleTalk in the form Ping Appletalk [network.node]. The AppleTalk protocol suite has commands to assign access lists, change update intervals, assign unique identifiers to an

Table 10-3

Access List
Commands

access-list additional-zones	Defines the default action to take for access checks that apply to zones.
access-list cable-range	Defines an AppleTalk access list for a cable range.
access-list includes	Defines an AppleTalk access list that overlaps any part of a range of network numbers or cable ranges.
access-list NBP	Defines an AppleTalk access list entry for NBP entities by class or zone.
access-list network	Defines an AppleTalk access list for a single network number.
access-list other-access	Defines a default action for access checks that apply to networks or cable ranges.
access-list other-nbps	Defines a default action for access checks that apply from entities not otherwise defined.
access-list within	Define an access list whose network number or cable range is included entirely within the specified cable range.
access-list zone	Defines an access list that applies to a zone.
Appletalk access-group	Assigns an access list to an interface.

interface, and filter packets through an interface. Table 10-3 is a list of access list commands with short descriptions. Again, reference the Cisco IOS manual for a complete explanation of the commands.

Chapter Summary

In this chapter, we have looked at the major protocols related to AppleTalk networks. We have also seen how the effective use of show and debug commands can give us insights into which packets are traveling through the network. As in any other situation, it is important to work from the bottom layers of the OSI model towards the top. Making sure that there is a physical connection before debugging the routing protocols will save large amounts of time.

Frequently Asked Questions (FAQ)

Question: How do access lists in AppleTalk differ from IP access lists?

Answer: Several differences exist between IP and AppleTalk access lists. The most obvious is the number associated with the access list (600–699). Another difference is that either a zone or cable range can be denied or permitted with an AppleTalk access list.

Question: I need to have 400 devices on my network, which limits the number of devices to 253. What can I do?

Answer: Increase the cable range to enable multiple network numbers.

Question: Which routing protocol should I use?

Answer: The answer depends upon many factors. Things to look for include the routing protocols you are currently using, whether you want a distance vector protocol or link state, and how the size of your network.

Question: I work in TCP/IP networks. Why should I even care about AppleTalk networks?

Answer: You will eventually run into a situation where you must incorporate an existing AppleTalk network into an IP network. If you do not understand how an AppleTalk network operates, you will not be successful when trying to work with them.

Question: If AppleTalk will disappear within the next few years, why should it be studied?

Answer: That is the same type of statement that was made a few years ago about IPX networks. Both are still widely entrenched in networking. It is important for us to know all of the common protocols. That is what makes an expert.

Questions

1. Which protocol is used to associate an AppleTalk address with a MAC address?

   a. ZIP

   b. ZIT

   c. DDP

   d. NBP

   e. AARP

2. Which protocol resides in layer 7 of the OSI model?

   a. RTMP

   b. AURP

   c. AARP

   d. AFP

   e. DDP

3. Which show command is used to see AURP open requests?

   a. show appletalk interface

   b. debug appletalk interface

   c. show appletalk traffic

   d. debug appletalk traffic

4. Which command displays a list of NBP services offered by nearby routers?

   a. show appletalk ARP

   b. show name cache

   c. show appletalk name-cache

   d. show appletalk name-cache

5. An AppleTalk name is composed in which format:

   a. object: type @ zone

   b. type: object @ zone

   c. object: zone @ type

   d. object @ zone: type

6. Which of the following protocols establishes a full-duplex data stream between sockets?

   a. AFP

   b. PAP

   c. ADSP

   d. FDDITalk

   e. ASP

7. Which of the following establishes and maintains sessions between clients and servers?

   a. AFP

   b. PAP

   c. ADSP

   d. FDDITalk

   e. ASP

8. Which of the following establishes and maintains connection-oriented sessions between clients and servers?

   a. AFP

   b. PAP

   c. ADSP

   d. FDDITalk

   e. ASP

9. Which of the following protocols shares files across an AppleTalk network?

   a. AFP

   b. PAP

   c. ADSP

   d. FDDITalk

   e. ASP

10. Which of the following is a valid AppleTalk address?

    a. 14.12

    b. 12

    c. 14.12.13

    d. 14.12.13.18

    e. 172.30.1.1

11. Which of the following protocols uses a tunnel to route packets?

    a. DDP
    b. AURP
    c. EIGRP
    d. RTMP

12. Select the correct order from the following list of choices for how an AppleTalk address is chosen.

    1. A network address is chosen at random.
    2. An *AppleTalk address resolution protocol* (AARP) broadcast packet is sent over the network with the chosen address.
    3. If a notification is received that this address is in use, another address is chosen at random.
    4. If the device either receives a notification that this address is already being used or no notification is received and the process experiences a time-out failure.
    5. An AppleTalk-capable device chooses AppleTalk as the network protocol.

    a. 3, 1, 2, 4, 5
    b. 5, 2, 1, 3, 4
    c. 5, 1, 2, 4, 3
    d. 1, 3, 2, 4, 5

13. Which of the following are layer-1 protocols?

    a. ADSP, AFP, PAP
    b. FDDITalk, LocalTalk, EtherTalk, TokenTalk
    c. FLAP, LLAP, ELAP, TLAP
    d. AURP, RTMP, EIGRP

14. What is the speed of a LocalTalk network?

    a. 10 Mbps
    b. 230.4 Kbps
    c. 2.5 Mbps
    d. 1 Mbps

15. Which AppleTalk protocol can be compared to DNS?

    a. ASP
    b. AFP
    c. NBP
    d. AURP

16. Where would you find the following table?

16   Managers

17   Accounting

18   Supervisors

19   Finance

a. ZIT

b. ZIP

c. Zone Map

d. Zone List

17. What is the most likely cause of some users on an AppleTalk network not being able to see some zones and services on remote networks?

a. No default gateway has been set

b. Phase I and Phase II incompatibility

c. Too many cable ranges have been set

d. Too many hosts on the local network

18. Which command is used to show that a new zone is discovered?

a. debug apple routing

b. show apple route

c. debug apple ZIP

d. show apple ZIP

19. What is the purpose of the debug apple ARP command?

a. It displays the AARP contents.

b. It shows if the ZIP is storing information to the *address mainte-nance table* (AMT).

c. It shows if a routing is sending or receiving AARP requests.

d. It shows if AARP requests are stored in the NBP.

20. Which command will show directly connected routers running AppleTalk?

a. show Appletalk routers

b. show neighbors

c. show CDP neighbors

d. show Appletalk neighbors

Answers

1. Answer: e

   The *AppleTalk address resolution protocol* (AARP) is used to associate an AppleTalk address to a layer-2 MAC address.

2. Answer: d

   The *AppleTalk file protocol* (AFP) resides in layer 7 of the OSI model. It is the protocol used for sharing files in an AppleTalk network.

3. Answer: c

   Show Appletalk traffic is the show command that will show AURP open requests. Note that the question asked which show command, a specific type of command.

4. Answer: d

   Show Appletalk name-cache is used to display a list of NBP services offered by nearby routers.

5. Answer: a

   An AppleTalk name is composed as *object: type @ zone*. Capitalization is ignored and each can be up to 32 characters.

6. Answer: c

   The *AppleTalk data stream protocol* (ADSP) establishes a full-duplex, connection-oriented stream.

7. Answer: e

   The *AppleTalk session protocol* (ASP) establishes connections between servers and hosts. Note that the question did not ask for a connection-oriented protocol.

8. Answer: b

   The *printer access protocol* (PAP) is a connection-oriented protocol that establishes connections between clients and servers.

9. Answer: a

   The *AppleTalk file protocol* (AFP) shares files across an AppleTalk network.

10. Answer: a

    AppleTalk addresses are established in the form of network.node. The network number is 16 bits, while the node is eight bits.

11. Answer: b

The *AppleTalk update routing protocol* (AURP) uses a tunnel when connecting through a foreign network.

12. Answer: c

The correct order is 5, 1, 2, 4, 3.

    5. An AppleTalk-capable device chooses AppleTalk as the network protocol.

    1. A network address is chosen at random.

    2. An *AppleTalk Address Resolution Protocol* (AARP) broadcast packet is sent over the network with the chosen address.

    4. If the device either receives a notification that this address is already being used or no notification is received and the process experiences a time-out failure.

    3. If a notification is received that this address is in use, another address is chosen at random.

13. Answer: c

FLAP is used by FDDITalk, TLAP is used by TokenTalk, ELAP is used by EtherTalk, and LLAP is used by LocalTalk. These are all layer-1 protocols.

14. Answer: b

LocalTalk runs over a serial line with the speed limited to 230.4 Kbps.

15. Answer: c

The *name binding protocol* (NBP) associates AppleTalk names with AppleTalk addresses. DNS associates fully qualified domain names with IP addresses.

16. Answer: a

The *zone information table* (ZIT) contains a list similar to the one shown.

17. Answer: b

Because an AppleTalk network's gateway is automatically detected and all routers on the network must be configured to use one or the other, the most probable cause is an incompatibility between Phase I and Phase II hosts.

18. Answer: c

    Only a debug command will tell us when something happens. The correct command is debug apple ZIP because the ZIP is used to discover new zones.

19. Answer: c

    Debug apple ARP is used to see if a device is sending and receiving AARP requests. The results of an AARP are stored in the *address maintenance table* (AMT).

20. Answer: d

    Show Appletalk neighbors shows all the directly connected routers that are running AppleTalk.

11

Novell Internet Packet Exchange/ Sequenced Packet Exchange (IPX/SPX)

This chapter provides an overview of the Internet Packet Exchange /Sequenced Packet Exchange (IPX/SPX) protocol that was developed by Novell and used with NetWare. We also examine the tools and commands that are available for troubleshooting IPX/SPX networks. We will be covering all the fundamentals of these protocols and examining the role of the major protocols that are contained in the suite. This will cover router diagnostic tools as well as explaining the show and debug commands that are available.

The best place to start when troubleshooting any network-related problem is at the physical layer of the OSI model. We will adopt this layered systematic troubleshooting approach in this chapter to reduce the amount of time it takes to resolve an IPX/SPX-related network problem. Generally, IPX/SPX operates at the network and transport layer of the OSI model.

Objectives Covered in the Chapter

This chapter introduces you to troubleshooting the IPX/SPX protocol suite. The following objectives will be covered:

- Analyze problem symptoms and resolve resolution strategies in TCP/IP (including the Microsoft 95/NT IP stack), Novell IPX, AppleTalk, Ethernet virtual local area networks (VLANs), Frame Relay, and ISDN basic rate interface (BRI).

- Demonstrate knowledge of connection sequences and key troubleshooting targets within TCP/IP, Novell IPX, and AppleTalk.

- Use proven problem-isolation techniques to list the symptoms of common Novell IPX problems on router networks.

- Apply diagnostic tools to trouble tickets and solve classroom network Novell IPX problems that simulate real-life internetworking malfunctions.

Novell Protocols

Novell introduced NetWare as a network operating system (NOS) in the early 1980s. It was derived from the *Xerox Network System* (XNS) that was created by the Xerox Corporation in the late 1970s. NetWare is based upon a client/server architecture where clients request services and resources from servers but carry out local processing power. This architecture became the de facto standard for personal computer networking and grew with the same intensity as the desktop PC market.

Novell standardized upon their own IPX/SPX protocol stack for many years. Only recently has TCP/IP been included with releases of NetWare, and the latest versions have bowed to industry pressure and utilized TCP/IP as the core protocol. The NetWare protocol suite maps to the upper five layers of the OSI reference model. This enables NetWare to run on virtually any media access protocol and/or topology as defined at OSI layer 2 and layer 1.

The IPX/SPX addressing scheme uses the hardware or media access control (MAC) address as the host address with a manually assigned network address. This facilitates a smoother transition between layer 3 and layer 2 protocols because no MAC-address-to-network-address resolution is required. With TCP/IP, you have to resolve the IP address to the MAC address using the *Address Resolution Protocol* (ARP) before communication can take place. This increases the broadcast rate on the local segment and adds another step in the communication process.

Internet Packet Exchange (IPX)

IPX is the NetWare protocol that is used to route packets through an internetwork. This is a connectionless packet-based protocol that operates at the network layer of the OSI model. IPX operates in a similar manner to the Internet Protocol (IP) from the TCP/IP suite.

Due to its connectionless nature, IPX offers no guarantee that the source packets will reach their destination or that they will be in the order in which they were sent. IPX depends upon upper-layer protocols to provide packet retransmissions and sequencing to ensure the reliability of the data delivery.

IPX supports multiple encapsulation schemes and is responsible for assigning this encapsulation type before sending the packet down to the data-link layer for framing. This is an important point to remember with IPX networks, as differing encapsulation types are incompatible.

NetWare supports the following four encapsulation types (see Figure 11-1):

- *Novell Proprietary (802.2):*   This is the default encapsulation type that NetWare uses. It includes an 802.3-length field but not an 802.2 header. The IPX header follows the 802.3 length field.

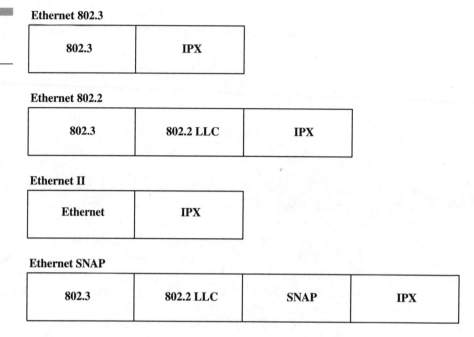

Figure 11-1

IPX encapsulation types

- *802.3:* This is the standard 802.3 frame format as outlined by the IEEE. This is usually referred to as *Novell-Ether encapsulation*.

- *Ethernet Version 2:* This is also referred to as Ethernet II. This encapsulation consists of the standard Ethernet Version 2 header and the IPX header.

- *Subnetwork Access Protocol (SNAP):* SNAP extends the 802.2 header to provide a type of code similar to the definition in the Ethernet Version 2 specification.

IPX addressing is based on a hierarchical structure that uses a four-byte number for the network address and a six-byte number for the host address. The six-byte host address is usually the hardware or MAC address of the connecting network interface card (NIC). MAC addresses have to be unique and all communication eventually takes place using MAC addresses, so the utilization of the MAC address in NetWare removes the need for any host-address-to-MAC-address resolution similar to the function of ARP in the TCP/IP suite. The four-byte network address is usually manually assigned by the network administrator and must be unique on the internetwork.

For example, to enable IPX on interface Ethernet0 and assign it to network 100, you would enter the following command:

```
Router(config-if)#ipx network 100
```

You don't need to enter the IPX address because the IPX address is automatically assigned as the Ethernet0 MAC address. A *show ipx int* command will display the following output:

```
Router#sh ipx int
Ethernet0 is up, line protocol is up
  IPX address is 100.0050.736b.c338, NOVELL-ETHER [up]
  Delay of this IPX network, in ticks is 1 throughput 0 link delay 0
  IPXWAN processing not enabled on this interface.
  IPX SAP update interval is 60 seconds
  IPX type 20 propagation packet forwarding is disabled
  Incoming access list is not set
  Outgoing access list is not set
  IPX helper access list is not set
  SAP GGS output filter list is not set
  SAP GNS processing enabled, delay 0 ms, output filter list is
  not set
  SAP Input filter list is not set
  SAP Output filter list is not set
  SAP Router filter list is not set
  Input filter list is not set
  Output filter list is not set
  Router filter list is not set
  Netbios Input host access list is not set
  Netbios Input bytes access list is not set
  Netbios Output host access list is not set
  Netbios Output bytes access list is not set
  Updates each 60 seconds aging multiples RIP: 3 SAP: 3
  SAP interpacket delay is 55 ms, maximum size is 480 bytes
  RIP interpacket delay is 55 ms, maximum size is 432 bytes
  RIP response delay is not set
  IPX accounting is disabled
  IPX fast switching is configured (enabled)
  RIP packets received 0, RIP packets sent 1, 0 Throttled
  RIP specific requests received 0, RIP specific replies sent 0
  RIP general requests received 0, 0 ignored, RIP general replies
  sent 0
  SAP packets received 0, SAP packets sent 1, 0 Throttled
  SAP GNS packets received 0, SAP GNS replies sent 0
  SAP GGS packets received 0, 0 ignored, SAP GGS replies sent 0
Router#
```

From this output, you can see that the IPX address of the Ethernet0 interface is 100.0050.736b.c338. The 100 pertains to the network address and the 0050.736b.c338 is the host address. Leading zeros are removed from the network address but not the host address (see Figure 11-2).

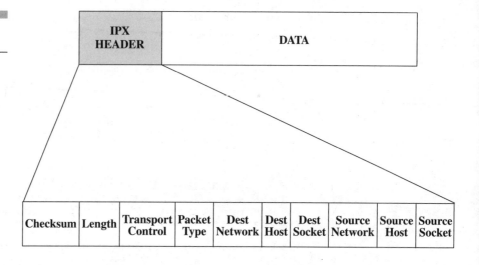

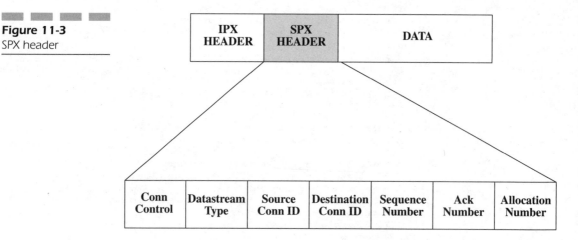

Sequenced Packet Exchange (SPX)

SPX is the NetWare transport layer protocol that provides guaranteed end-to-end connections. SPX operates in a similar way to the Transmission Control Protocol (TCP) that is part of the TCP/IP suite. SPX is Novell's version of the Xerox *Sequenced Packet Protocol* (SPP).

SPX is responsible for the acknowledgement and successful packet delivery of all packets from source to destination (see Figure 11-3). A *Cyclic Redundancy Check* (CRC) is used to also check the integrity of the data at the receiving end against the data that was transmitted.

Service Advertisement Protocol (SAP)

The *Service Advertisement Protocol* (SAP) advertises all known servers and resources available on the servers throughout the internetwork. NetWare clients require prior knowledge of the resources available on the network before they can establish communications with that server.

Servers advertise their services via a SAP broadcast every 60 seconds by default. The SAP packet contains a SAP identifier field that consists of a four-bit hexadecimal number that identifies the distinct service. Table 11-1 displays the common SAP types.

Cisco routers participate in the SAP advertisement process. An IPX-enabled router will by default listen to all SAP broadcasts received on all connected interfaces to build up a table of SAP services local to the router. The SAP service is entered into the SAP table along with the network address of the server that advertised the service. This SAP table is then broadcast by the router every 60 seconds. A NetWare client can query a particular service and the router will intercept this query and reply to the client with the network address of the requested service. The client then contacts the server directly. This is essential for internetwork operability with NetWare. If the server is local to the client, then this would not cause a problem, but the SAP packet by its broadcast nature will not traverse the internetwork. This is why the router acts as a SAP provider to ensure that service advertisements are fulfilled.

SAP is used extensively with NetWare 3.x, but NetWare 4.x utilizes NDS to facilitate service discoveries. The SAP process is similar in operation to the Microsoft Browser Service that runs on Windows 9x and NT.

Table 11-1	Decimal	Hex	Service Description
Common SAP Types	4	0004	File server
	7	0007	Print server
	32	0020	NetBIOS
	567	0237	NMS IPX discovery
	632	0278	Novell Directory Services (NDS) (NetWare 4.x)
	1659	067b	Microsoft Windows file/print sharing
	1660	067c	Microsoft Windows file/print sharing
	34238	85be	Cisco Enhanced Interior Gateway Routing Protocol (EIGRP)

Netware Core Protocol (NCP)

The NetWare Core Protocol (NCP) is similar in operation to the Microsoft *Server Message Block* (SMB) protocol that is used to share resources in a Microsoft Windows environment. NCP is responsible for managing access to the primary NetWare server resources. This is accomplished with the use of information learned through SAP broadcasts.

NCP is a high-level protocol that works at the presentation layer of the OSI model. NCP uses IPX, not SPX, as its transport. Reliability is provided by a built-in mechanism within NCP that provides a one-to-one acknowledgement for every packet sent.

Get Nearest Server (GNS)

When NetWare clients boot up, they send a *Get Nearest Server* (GNS) request to the local network to ascertain which servers are local. They also attach to this server for resources. The GNS request uses information that has been gathered in SAP updates to identify the local servers and also the resources on these servers.

If no local servers to the client exist, the Cisco router acts as a proxy GNS server and responds to the GNS request. This is similar to the proxy ARP role that a router performs in TCP/IP internetworking. The router replies to the GNS request with a list of servers and resources that is gathered from the receipt of SAP updates. Obviously, SAP filtering using access lists can restrict the services that are advertised to the NetWare client. The client is completely unaware of the router between itself and the NetWare server.

Service Advertisement Protocol (SAP)

As previously discussed, SAP advertises all known servers and resources available on these servers throughout the internetwork. NetWare clients require prior knowledge of the resources available on the network before they can establish communications with that server. SAP broadcasts are sent every 60 seconds by default. As the size of the NetWare internetwork grows, a potential problem can occur with respect to the amount of bandwidth consumed by the SAP updates.

NetWare servers periodically send clients SAP broadcasts to advertise the services that they are providing. These updates are broadcast to the local area network (LAN) to which the server belongs. Routers are required to propagate these SAP updates throughout the IPX network so that all IPX clients can see all the service messages to obtain a view of the NetWare services.

SAP Management

Cisco employs two main methods for reducing the bandwidth overhead of SAP broadcasts in a large internetwork. These methods include filtering the SAP updates and configuring incremental SAP updates.

Filtering SAP Updates   SAP updates can be filtered with the use of access lists. Access lists can control which routers receive SAP updates and which routers do not send or receive SAP updates. SAP access lists can be defined to filter SAP updates based upon the source network address of a SAP entry, the type of SAP entry, and the name of the SAP server. A SAP access list has the following format:

```
access-list x [deny/permit] network[.node] [service-type[server-
name]]
```

The x correlates to a number between 1000 and 1099. This number range is reserved for SAP access lists. The network number of -1 would indicate any network and a service type of 0 would indicate any service.

The following SAP access list example would permit any type 4 (file server) and any type 7 (print server) SAP updates to any network. An implicit "deny all" exists, as in every other access list. Therefore, only type 4 and type 7 SAP broadcasts would pass the filter:

```
access-list 1001 permit -1 4
access-list 1001 permit -1 7
```

Once this access list has been established, it then requires to be bound to an interface in the same way as an IP or IPX access list does. The command to bind the access list to the interface is either ipx input-sap-filter or ipx output-sap-filter.

To add the above access list 1001 to the outbound Ethernet0 interface, the correct configuration would be

```
Router#conf t
Router(config)#int e0
Router(config-if)#ipx output-sap-filter 1001
```

This would add the IPX SAP filter 1001 to the outbound queue on the Ethernet0 interface.

Incremental SAP Updates   Incremental SAP updates enable all SAP updates to be sent and received over the internetwork with reduced network SAP overhead. Instead of eliminating the receipt of SAP updates, as in the SAP filtering, all IPX services can be broadcast to remote sites only as changes in the SAP tables occur.

EIGRP is required to facilitate incremental SAP updates. Complete SAP updates are sent periodically on each interface until an EIGRP neighbor is found. As soon as the neighbor is established, SAP updates are sent only when there are changes to the SAP table. This conserves bandwidth and the advertisement of services is reduced without being eliminated.

Incremental SAP updates are automatically configured for EIGRP's participating serial interfaces. The command *ipx sap-incremental eigrp x* has to be entered for other interfaces where x is the autonomous system number of the EIGRP process. Here's an example:

```
interface ethernet 0
ipx network 20
ipx sap-incremental eigrp 100
!
interface serial 0
ipx network 30
!
ipx router eigrp 100
network 10
network 20
```

This would facilitate incremental SAP updates on both Serial0 and Ethernet0. Remember that serial interfaces are automatically configured for incremental SAP updates.

IPX Routing Protocols

The NetWare IPX/SPX protocol has three main routing protocols that are implemented on Cisco networking devices:

- The Novell Routing Information Protocol (IPX RIP)
- The Netware Link State Protocol (NLSP)
- EIGRP

IPX RIP and NLSP are routing protocols that are part of the IPX/SPX protocol suite. EIGRP is a Cisco propriety routing protocol that has multiprotocol capabilities. IPX RIP is also a distance vector-based routing protocol and NLSP is a link state routing protocol. EIGRP is classified as a hybrid routing protocol that has both distance vector and link state properties.

Novell Routing Information Protocol (IPX RIP)

IPX RIP is a distance vector routing protocol that is the same in operation as the IP RIP routing protocol. RIP is a distance vector-based dynamic routing protocol that uses a hop count as its metric. The hop count is defined as the number of routers or hops a packet has to traverse to reach its destination.

RIP is an *Interior Gateway Protocol* (IGP) and therefore performs routing within a single *Autonomous System* (AS). RIP has two main versions. RIP version 1 is a classfull routing protocol that strictly follows the classfull addressing scheme of IP. RIP version 2 is the latest version of RIP and is a classless routing protocol that enables more information to be included in the RIP packet header and supports *Variable Length Subnet Masks* (VLSMs). RIP is also available for both IP routing and also IPX routing.

RIP is formally defined in RFC 1058 and 1723. RFC 1058 was defined in 1988 and describes the first implementation of RIP. RFC 1723 was defined in 1994 and this revision defines RIPv2 and the extended carrier features supported in the RIP packet header.

RIP operates by sending routing updates at regular intervals out of all configured interfaces. The default time for this update is every 30 seconds. These routing updates contain the complete routing table minus any routes removed due to the split horizon rule. When a routing update is received from a direct neighbor, route information is checked against the current routing table and any better routes, that is, with a lower metric or hop count, are updates in the routing table. RIP uses the hop count as the routing metric and the maximum allowable hop count using RIP is 15. The 16th hop is deemed unreachable.

On a Cisco router, simply adding the following command in global configuration mode enables IPX RIP routing:

```
Router(config)#ipx router rip
```

Networks are advertised and participate in IPX RIP routing by entering

```
Router(config-ipx-router)network A
```

where A is the network address of the network to be advertised via IPX RIP. Other IPX RIP configuration commands include the following:

- `default` Sets a command to its defaults.
- `distribute-list` Filters networks in routing updates.
- `distribute-sap-list` Filters services in SAP updates.
- `exit` Exits from IPX routing protocol configuration mode.
- `network` Enables routing on an IPX network.
- `no` Negates a command or sets its defaults.
- `redistribute` Enables routing protocol redistribution.

NetWare Link Services Protocol (NLSP)

NLSP is a link state routing protocol designed by Novell to overcome some of the limitations associated with the IPX version of RIP. NLSP is based on the OSI Intermediate-System-to-Intermediate-System (IS-IS) protocol and it is primarily designed to replace RIP and SAP. RIP and SAP were designed for routing when the internetwork complexity was relatively simple. Today's networks pose a much more complex scenario and the RIP/SAP implementation suffers at this scale. NLSP is an IGP and therefore performs routing within a single AS.

NLSP utilizes a reliable delivery protocol that guarantees the delivery of routing updates. The protocol is also link state so that it facilitates the storage of a complete map of the network, not just next hop information such as in RIP-based routing processes. Routing information is exchanged only when the network topology changes. This differs from RIP, which sends out periodic updates that contain the full routing table. The benefits in this model are a lower bandwidth overhead and a faster convergence due to instantaneous triggered updates. NLSP also includes service updates that SAP usually manages. This removes the need for regular SAP updates in the network and reduces bandwidth overhead in doing so. NLSP sends service-based updates only when services change. This also differs from the regular SAP updates that send the full service list every 60 seconds by default.

NLSP-based routes are also backwards-compatible with IPX RIP routers. This eases the migration to NLSP as an automatic route redistribution occurs between these protocols.

On a Cisco router, simply adding the following command in global configuration mode enables the NLSP routing process:

```
Router(config)#ipx router nlsp
```

Networks are advertised and participate in NLSP routing by entering

```
Router(config-router)network A.B.C.D E.F.G.H
```

where A.B.C.D is the network address of the network to be advertised via EIGRP. E.F.G.H. is the wildcard mask and this operates as in the access list command.

Other NLSP configuration commands include the following (refer to the previous configuration list as well):

- `area-address` configures the NLSP area address.
- `log-adjacency-changes` logs changes in the adjacency state.
- `lsp-data-hashing` uses hash algorithms to populate LSPs.
- `lsp-gen-interval` sets a minimum LSP generation interval.
- `lsp-mtu` sets the maximum size of a link state packet.
- `lsp-refresh-interval` sets LSP refresh intervals.
- `max-lsp-lifetime` sets the maximum LSP lifetime.
- `multicast` selects the multicast or broadcast addressing on LANs.
- `name-display-disable` displays system IDs rather than names.
- `prc-interval` is the minimum interval between partial route calculations.
- `route-aggregation` enables NLSP route aggregation.
- `spf-interval` is the minimum interval between SPF calculations.

Enhanced Interior Gateway Routing Protocol (EIGRP)

EIGRP is the evolution of the *Interior Gateway Routing Protocol* (IGRP). EIGRP combines both of the capabilities of distance vector dynamic routing protocols and link state dynamic routing protocols to create a hybrid protocol that meets the demands of diverse large-scale internetworks.

Cisco Systems created EIGRP to improve upon IGRP and to provide an enterprise multi-protocol routing protocol. EIGRP supports AppleTalk, IP, and Novell's IPX/SPX. This integration occurs through the redistribution of routing information between common protocols. AppleTalk support is provided through redistribution with the *Routing Table Maintenance Protocol* (RTMP). IP redistributes routes from OSPF, RIP, IS-IS, or BGP. The Novell implementation provides support through redistribution with Novell RIP or SAP.

EIGRP provides seamless compatibility with routers that are currently running IGRP. This occurs via an automatic redistribution mechanism that converts IGRP routes to EIGRP routes and vice versa. This makes the implementation of EIGRP less of an administrative and technical burden as it can co-exist with nearly all major routing protocols. EIGRP is a classless routing protocol that supports route summarization and VLSMs.

EIGRP utilizes four key technologies that differentiate it from other routing protocols. These are neighbor discovery/recovery, the *Reliable Transport Protocol* (RTP), the *Diffusing Update Algorithm* (DUAL) finite state machine, and protocol-dependant modules.

On a Cisco router, simply adding the following command in global configuration mode enables EIGRP:

```
Router(config)#ipx router eigrp 101
```

The above command would enable EIGRP for the AS 101. You must specify the AS number when implementing EIGRP.

Networks are advertised and participate in EIGRP routing by entering

```
Router(config-router)network A
```

where A is the network address of the network to be advertised via EIGRP. Other EIGRP configuration commands include the following (please refer to the earlier configuration command lists for other commands that would be of use here):

- `log-neighbor-changes` enables/disables the IPX-EIGRP neighbor logging.
- `redistribute` enables routing protocol redistribution.
- `timers` adjusts routing timers.

A full explanation of EIGRP is found in Chapter 12, "Routing Protocols."

Encapsulation Types

As discussed previously, NetWare IPX supports multiple encapsulation schemes on a single router interface. The encapsulation type relates to the framing method in which the data is encapsulated for transmission onto the physical media. Each physical media such as Ethernet, Token Ring, and the *Fiber Distributed Data Interface* (FDDI) has its own framing formats. NetWare IPX supports four frame types for Ethernet networks:

- Ethernet 802.2
- Ethernet 802.3
- Ethernet SNAP
- Ethernet II

The choice of the frame type to be used on a network is an important decision that is unique to IPX networks. The choice can be based upon the version of NetWare and the other protocols that will be running on the network. Table 11-2 outlines the four different encapsulation types.

Remember that frame types are incompatible if configured differently within an internetwork. A major problem was caused when the default frame type on version 3.12 was changed from 802.3 to 802.2, which was used before 3.12.

On a Cisco router, the encapsulation type is set at the interface level. Only one encapsulation type can be set for any given Ethernet interface, but a NetWare server can have up to four encapsulation types assigned to each network interface. Each frame type would have its own IPX network address and the router can have differing encapsulation types within the

Table 11-2

IPX Encapsulation
Types

Encapsulation Type	Properties
Ethernet 802.2	Default frame type on NetWare 3.12 and above. Supports IPX/SPX.
Ethernet 802.3	Default frame type on NetWare 3.11 and below. Only supports IPX/SPX.
Ethernet SNAP	Supports IPX/SPX, TCP/IP, and AppleTalk phase II.
Ethernet II	Supports IPX/SPX, TCP/IP, and AppleTalk phase I.

router. For example, Ethernet0 can be 802.2 and Ethernet1 can be 802.3. A packet from Ethernet0 will be re-encapsulated into an 802.3 packet before it is sent out on Ethernet1 and vice versa.

The following configuration would set the interface to use Ethernet II encapsulation:

```
Router(config-if)#ipx encapsulation arpa
```

The following configuration would set the interface to use Ethernet 802.3 encapsulation:

```
Router(config-if)#ipx encapsulation novell-ether
```

The following configuration would set the interface to use Ethernet 802.2 encapsulation:

```
Router(config-if)#ipx encapsulation sap
```

The previous configuration would set the interface to use Ethernet SNAP encapsulation:

```
Router(config-if)#ipx encapsulation snap
```

Show Commands

Several show commands can be used to view the current IPX/SPX configuration of the router. These commands are useful for checking the status of the configuration as well as for troubleshooting a range of IPX/SPX problems (see Table 11-3).

	Command	Description
Table 11-3 Frequently Used Show Commands for Troubleshooting IPX/SPX	Show interface	Displays information about the configured interfaces on the router and basic IPX information.
	Show ipx interface	Displays the current status of interfaces that have been set up to use IPX/SPX. Also provides IPX/SPX information on the interface over and above the show interface command.
	Show ipx interface brief	Displays a brief summary of the information presented in the show ipx interface command.
	Show ipx servers	Displays information about the IPX servers.
	Show ipx traffic	Displays information about IPX traffic on the router. A statistical breakdown of each IPX protocol is displayed.
	Show ipx route	Displays the IPX internal routing table and identifies the means by which each route was learned.
	Show ipx access-lists	Displays the content of all configured IPX access lists on the router.
	Show ipx eigrp interface	Displays traffic information for well-known TCP/IP protocols.
	Show ipx eigrp neighbors	Displays a list of all EIGRP neighbors that were discovered by IPX EIGRP.
	Show ipx nlsp neighbors	Displays a list of all NLSP neighbors that were discovered by NLSP.

show interface

The *show interface* command displays information about the configured interfaces on the router along with basic IPX/SPX settings:

```
Router#sh int
Ethernet0 is up, line protocol is up
  Hardware is Lance, address is 0010.7b7e.f1fa (bia 0010.7b7e.f1fa)
  Internet address is 150.200.200.62/16
  MTU 1500 bytes, BW 10000 Kbit, DLY 1000 usec, rely 255/255, load
  1/255
  Encapsulation ARPA, loopback not set, keepalive set (10 sec)
  ARP type: ARPA, ARP Timeout 04:00:00
  Last input 00:00:19, output 00:00:04, output hang never
  Last clearing of "show interface" counters never
  Queueing strategy: fifo
  Output queue 0/40, 0 drops; input queue 0/75, 0 drops
  5 minute input rate 0 bits/sec, 0 packets/sec
```

```
5 minute output rate 0 bits/sec, 0 packets/sec
    4266877 packets input, 507927529 bytes, 0 no buffer
    Received 522473 broadcasts, 0 runts, 0 giants, 0 throttles
    1 input errors, 0 CRC, 0 frame, 0 overrun, 1 ignored, 0 abort
    0 input packets with dribble condition detected
    4400111 packets output, 1787611790 bytes, 0 underruns
    4 output errors, 1069 collisions, 1 interface resets
    0 babbles, 0 late collision, 2419 deferred
    0 lost carrier, 0 no carrier
    0 output buffer failures, 0 output buffers swapped out
Serial0 is up, line protocol is up
  Hardware is HD64570
  Internet address is 10.39.248.7/24
  Backup interface Dialer1, kickin load not set, kickout load not set
      failure delay 5 sec, secondary disable delay 5 sec
  MTU 1500 bytes, BW 200 Kbit, DLY 20000 usec, rely 255/255, load
  1/255
  SMDS hardware address is c449.1813.3603.81ff
  Encapsulation SMDS, loopback not set, keepalive set (10 sec)
  ARP type: SMDS, ARP Timeout 04:00:00
  Mode(s):  D15 compatibility, DXI 3.2
  DXI heartbeat sent 412542,  DXI heartbeat received 412542
  Last input 00:00:00, output 00:00:00, output hang never
  Last clearing of "show interface" counters never
  Queueing strategy: fifo
  Output queue 0/40, 0 drops; input queue 2/75, 1 drops
  5 minute input rate 5000 bits/sec, 5 packets/sec
  5 minute output rate 1000 bits/sec, 2 packets/sec
    21720714 packets input, 3906325512 bytes, 1 no buffer
    Received 195 broadcasts, 0 runts, 0 giants, 0 throttles
    0 input errors, 0 CRC, 0 frame, 0 overrun, 0 ignored, 0 abort
    4564680 packets output, 690296602 bytes, 0 underruns
    0 output errors, 0 collisions, 1 interface resets
    0 output buffer failures, 0 output buffers swapped out
    0 carrier transitions
    DCD=up  DSR=up  DTR=up  RTS=up  CTS=up
Router#
```

From this output you can verify the hardware address of the interface.
Remember that this hardware address is also used as the host address in
the IPX address.

show ipx interface

The *show ipx interface* command provides more detailed information on all
IPX-enabled interfaces:

```
Router#sh ipx int
Dialer1 is standby mode, line protocol is down
  IPX address is 44804006.0010.7b7e.f1fa [up]
  Delay of this IPX network, in ticks is 6 throughput 0 link delay 0
  IPXWAN processing not enabled on this interface.
  IPX SAP update interval is 1 minute(s)
  IPX type 20 propagation packet forwarding is disabled
  Incoming access list is not set
```

```
      Outgoing access list is not set
      IPX helper access list is not set
      SAP GNS processing enabled, delay 0 ms, output filter list is
      not set
      SAP Input filter list is not set
      SAP Output filter list is not set
      SAP Router filter list is not set
      Input filter list is not set
      Output filter list is not set
      Router filter list is not set
      Netbios Input host access list is not set
      Netbios Input bytes access list is not set
      Netbios Output host access list is not set
      Netbios Output bytes access list is not set
      Updates each 60 seconds, aging multiples RIP: 3 SAP: 3
      SAP interpacket delay is 55 ms, maximum size is 480 bytes
      RIP interpacket delay is 55 ms, maximum size is 432 bytes
      Watchdog processing is disabled, SPX spoofing is disabled, idle
      time 60
      IPX accounting is disabled
      IPX fast switching is configured (enabled)
      RIP packets received 0, RIP packets sent 0
      SAP packets received 0, SAP packets sent 0
    Ethernet0 is up, line protocol is up
      IPX address is 1.0010.7b7e.f1fa, NOVELL-ETHER [up]
      Delay of this IPX network, in ticks is 1 throughput 0 link delay 0
      IPXWAN processing not enabled on this interface.
      IPX SAP update interval is 1 minute(s)
      IPX type 20 propagation packet forwarding is disabled
      Incoming access list is 801
      Outgoing access list is not set
      IPX helper access list is not set
      SAP GNS processing enabled, delay 0 ms, output filter list is
      not set
      SAP Input filter list is not set
      SAP Output filter list is not set
      SAP Router filter list is not set
      Input filter list is not set
      Output filter list is not set
      Router filter list is not set
      Netbios Input host access list is not set
      Netbios Input bytes access list is not set
      Netbios Output host access list is not set
      Netbios Output bytes access list is not set
      Updates each 60 seconds, aging multiples RIP: 3 SAP: 3
      SAP interpacket delay is 55 ms, maximum size is 480 bytes
      RIP interpacket delay is 55 ms, maximum size is 432 bytes
      IPX accounting is enabled
      IPX fast switching is configured (enabled)
      RIP packets received 82805, RIP packets sent 69324
      SAP packets received 69885, SAP packets sent 67461
    Serial0 is up, line protocol is up
      IPX address is 44804001.0010.7b7e.f1fa [up]
      Delay of this IPX network, in ticks is 6 throughput 0 link delay 0
      IPXWAN processing not enabled on this interface.
      IPX SAP update interval is 1 minute(s)
      IPX type 20 propagation packet forwarding is disabled
      Incoming access list is not set
      Outgoing access list is not set
      IPX helper access list is not set
```

```
      SAP GNS processing enabled, delay 0 ms, output filter list is
      not set
      SAP Input filter list is not set
      SAP Output filter list is not set
      SAP Router filter list is not set
      Input filter list is not set
      Output filter list is not set
      Router filter list is not set
      Netbios Input host access list is not set
      Netbios Input bytes access list is not set
      Netbios Output host access list is not set
      Netbios Output bytes access list is not set
      Updates each 60 seconds, aging multiples RIP: 3 SAP: 3
      SAP interpacket delay is 55 ms, maximum size is 480 bytes
      RIP interpacket delay is 55 ms, maximum size is 432 bytes
      Watchdog processing is disabled, SPX spoofing is disabled, idle
      time 60
      IPX accounting is disabled
      IPX fast switching is configured (enabled)
      RIP packets received 5, RIP packets sent 1
      SAP packets received 14, SAP packets sent 1
   Router#
```

From this output we can see information about access lists, filters, and routing processes that are configured on each IPX-enabled interface. This provides a lot more IPX-specific information than the standard *sh interface* command. This command is useful in the troubleshooting of IPX/SPX problems. You attain an excellent view of each IPX-enabled interface along with all of the filtering, addressing, and routing information.

show ipx interface brief

The *show ipx interface brief* command displays a brief summary of each IPX-enabled interface on the router:

```
Router#sh ipx int brief
Interface IPX Network Encapsulation Status              IPX State
BRI0      unassigned  not config'd  up                  n/a
BRI0:1    unassigned  not config'd  down                n/a
BRI0:2    unassigned  not config'd  down                n/a
Dialer1   44804006    PPP           standby mode        [up]
Ethernet0 1           NOVELL-ETHER  up                  [up]
Serial0   44804001    SMDS          up                  [up]
Serial1   unassigned  not config'd  administratively down n/a
Router#
```

This command provides details on the IPX network, the encapsulation method, the interface status, and the IPX status for every IPX-enabled interface on the router. This is a useful command as it provides a simple breakdown of all the essential IPX information for every interface on the router.

show ipx servers

The *show ipx servers* command displays a list of all IPX servers that the router has knowledge about. These servers are all discovered from the receipt of SAP advertisements that have been generated by NetWare servers:

```
Router#sh ipx servers
Codes: S - Static, P - Periodic, E - EIGRP, N - NLSP, H -Holddown, + = detail
27 Total IPX Servers

Table ordering is based on routing and server info

Type  Name                      Net             Address         Port Route   Hops Itf
E     4 NOVELL1                 44741001.0000.0000.0001:0451   269824000/02  2    Se0
E     4 OXF                     44631003.0000.0000.0001:0451   269824000/02  2    Se0
E     4 PSEC1                   A1A1A1A1.0000.0000.0001:0451   269824000/02  2    Se0
E     4 UKFCD1                  44641001.0000.0000.0001:0451   269824000/02  2    Se0
E     4 UKFONOSI1               44001028.0000.0000.0001:0451   269824000/02  2    Se0
E     4 UKODF001                44631001.0000.0000.0001:0451   269824000/02  2    Se0
E     4 UKOXFNSGW-NWCONNEC      44631002.0000.0000.0001:0451   269824000/02  2    Se0
E     4 UKRGA1                  44191001.0000.0000.0001:0451   269824000/02  2    Se0
E     4 UKGEA2                  44191002.0000.0000.0001:0451   269824000/02  2    Se0
E     4 URSHEH1                 44711001.0000.0000.0001:0451   269824000/02  2    Se0
E     4 UKWARL1                 44731001.0000.0000.0001:0451   269824000/02  2    Se0
E     4 UKWERT1                 44671001.0000.0000.0001:0451   269824000/02  2    Se0
E     4 UKWJKT2_NOVELL          44671002.0000.0000.0001:0451   269824000/02  2    Se0
E     4 CRRGHA01                44201019.0000.0000.0001:0451   271232000/03  3    Se0
E     4 UKMILER001              44201001.0000.0000.0001:0451   271232000/03  3    Se0
E     4 UKDEREO006              44201006.0000.0000.0001:0451   271232000/03  3    Se0
E     4 URMILLANRS              44201013.0000.0000.0001:0451   271232000/03  3    Se0
E     4 UKFDLSAR04              44201015.0000.0000.0001:0451   271232000/03  3    Se0
E     107 OXR                   44631003.0000.0000.0001:8104   269824000/02  3    Se0
E     107 PGFC1                 A1A1A1A1.0000.0000.0001:8104   269824000/02  2    Se0
E     107 UKRRD1                44641001.0000.0000.0001:8104   269824000/02  3    Se0
E     107 RRLONOSI1             44001028.0000.0000.0001:8104   269824000/02  3    Se0
E     107 UKRRF001              44631001.0000.0000.0001:8104   269824000/02  3    Se0
E     107 UKORRNSNW             44631002.0000.0000.0001:8104   269824000/02  2    Se0
E     107 UKRRA1                44191001.0000.0000.0001:8104   269824000/02  3    Se0
E     107 UKRRR2                44191002.0000.0000.0001:8104   269824000/02  3    Se0
E     107 UKSHERR               44711001.0000.0000.0001:8104   269824000/02  3    Se0
Router#
```

The first section shows information regarding the NetWare server NOVELL1. We can see that NOVELL1 has been advertised as a file server by the type of 4. This relates to the SAP type of 4 that is a file server. We can then see that the network address is 44741001. This server is two hops away and is located over interface Serial0.

A problem or inconsistency with this output is probably an indication of a problem with SAP management on a router in the internetwork. This table is built from SAP updates that are received by the router. A SAP filter (access list) may be in place either on this router or on a directly connected router. This filter may have restricted a SAP broadcast from a server that a NetWare client on your local network may require.

show ipx traffic

The *show ipx traffic* command displays information regarding IPX traffic that the router has sent and received:

```
Router#sh ipx traffic
System Traffic for 0.0000.0000.0001 System-Name: Router#
Rcvd:    9044657 total, 16 format errors, 0 checksum errors, 0 bad
         hop count,
         106617 packets pitched, 8818599 local destination, 0
         multicast
Bcast:   8821061 received, 213730 sent
Sent:    317480 generated, 110469 forwarded
         0 encapsulation failed, 1 no route
SAP:     42 SAP requests, 0 SAP replies, 46 servers
         0 SAP Nearest Name requests, 0 replies
         0 SAP General Name requests, 0 replies
         69857 SAP advertisements received, 67404 sent
         56 SAP flash updates sent, 0 SAP format errors
RIP:     12955 RIP requests, 3 RIP replies, 42 routes
         69856 RIP advertisements received, 69266 sent
         54 RIP flash updates sent, 0 RIP format errors
Echo:    Rcvd 0 requests, 0 replies
         Sent 0 requests, 0 replies
         0 unknown: 0 no socket, 0 filtered, 0 no helper
         0 SAPs throttled, freed NDB len 0
Watchdog:
         0 packets received, 0 replies spoofed
Queue lengths:
         IPX input: 0, SAP 0, RIP 0, GNS 0
         SAP throttling length: 0/(no limit), 0 nets pending lost
         route reply
         Delayed process creation: 0
EIGRP:   Total received 8665885, sent 110676
         Updates received 2645, sent 7965
         Queries received 3314, sent 753
         Replies received 3137, sent 3675
         SAPs received 10943, sent 3687
NLSP:    Level-1 Hellos received 0, sent 0
         PTP Hello received 0, sent 0
         Level-1 LSPs received 0, sent 0
         LSP Retransmissions: 0
         LSP checksum errors received: 0
         LSP HT=0 checksum errors received: 0
         Level-1 CSNPs received 0, sent 0
         Level-1 PSNPs received 0, sent 0
         Level-1 DR Elections: 0
         Level-1 SPF Calculations: 0
         Level-1 Partial Route Calculations: 0
Router#
```

This provides detailed information on various IPX/SPX protocols including SAP, RIP, Echo, Watchdog, EIGRP, and NLSP. We can see from this listing that the above router is running IPX RIP and EIGRP as its routing protocols. No received or sent packets exclude NLSP.

Careful monitoring of the SAP values is handy for testing the effectiveness of SAP filters against the amount of SAP traffic received on the router. This traffic analysis is for the entire router and isn't broken down for each interface.

show ipx route

The *show ipx route* command displays the internal IPX routing table on the router:

```
CSL_Barrow>sh ipx route
Codes: C - Connected primary network,    c - Connected secondary
       network
       S - Static, F - Floating static, L - Local (internal), W -
       IPXWAN
       R - RIP, E - EIGRP, N - NLSP, X - External, A - Aggregate
       s - seconds, u - uses

15 Total IPX routes. Up to 1 parallel paths and 16 hops allowed.

No default route known.

C         1 (NOVELL-ETHER),   Et0
C         44804001 (SMDS),         Se0
E         AA [271232000/3] via 44804001.00e0.1ea9.abde, age
          1d10h,1u, Se0
E         CC0002 [13337600/1] via 44804001.00e0.1eb9.2307, age 1d13h,
          1u, Se0
E         44001028 [269824000/2] via 44804001.0050.735d.97e1, age 1w4d,
          11831u, Se0
E         44191001 [269824000/2] via 44804001.00e0.1ea0.d361, age 1d13h,
          935u, Se0
E         44191002 [269824000/2] via 44804001.00e0.1ea0.d361, age 1d13h,
          935u, Se0
E         44192004 [13337600/1] via 44804001.00e0.1ea0.d361, age 1d13h,
          1u, Se0
E         44194003 [21024000/0] via 44804001.00e0.1ea0.d361, age 1d13h,
          1u, Se0
E         44201001 [271232000/3] via 44804001.00e0.b08e.39d1, age 1d13h,
          1837u, Se0
E         44201013 [271232000/3] via 44804001.00e0.b08e.39d1, age 1d13h,
          1603u, Se0
E         44201015 [271232000/3] via 44804001.00e0.b08e.39d1, age 1d13h,
          1153u, Se0
E         44201019 [271232000/3] via 44804001.00e0.b08e.39d1, age 1d13h,
          2454u, Se0
```

```
E     44202001 [269824000/2] via 44804001.00e0.b08e.39d1, age 1d13h,
      614u, Se0
E     44202010 [271232000/3] via 44804001.00e0.b08e.39d1, age 1d13h,
      2u, Se0
Router#
```

Directly connected interfaces are shown as well as routes that are learned via EIGRP, IPX RIP, and NLSP. In the previous listing, we can see two connected interfaces and 13 routes that have been learned via EIGRP.

The first section shows an EIGRP route to network 44201001. The 271232000 relates to the delay or metric and the /3 is the number of hops to the destination. This information is used by the router to make its routing decisions. The age is shown as 1d13h; this is one day and 13 hours since the route was discovered. The 1837u relates to the number of times this route has been used. We can see that this route is over Serial0. The *Se0* at the end of the line indicates this.

This show ipx route command can be further restricted by entering *show ipx route x* where x is the network number you want to interrogate. This command is one of the first places you would start looking when users are complaining or when you experience communication problems on remote networks.

show ipx access-lists

The *show ipx access-lists* command displays the current configured IPX access lists on the router:

```
Router#sh ipx access-lists
IPX access list 800
     permit 44202001
     permit 44202003
     permit 44202010
     permit 44201001
     permit 44201010
     permit 44201012
     permit 44201019
     permit 44201013
IPX access list 801
     permit 1.0010.5aa5.d6bb FFFFFFFF
     permit 1.0010.5aa5.e2c7 FFFFFFFF
     permit 1.0010.5aa5.d590 FFFFFFFF
     permit 1.0010.7b7e.f1fa
     permit 44691001
IPX access list 802
     permit 1
     permit 44691001
IPX SAP access list 1000
```

```
        permit 44201001 4 UKMGFEO001
        permit 44201019 4 CSLSAA01
        permit 44201012 4 UKMILLANRS
        permit 44201019 130 CDFSAA01
        permit 44202001 39B MILB01
        permit 44201013 4 UKMILFDNRS
Router#
```

We can see from this listing that the router has three standard IPX access lists and one IPX SAP filter. When troubleshooting IPX/SPX problems, remember that there is always an implicit "deny all" at the end of every access list. Ensure that, if you are creating an access list to deny traffic, you also include a permit statement or else all traffic will be denied by the access list. This is a common configuration error that results in a loss of network availability.

show ipx eigrp interface

The *show ipx eigrp interface* command displays all interfaces configured within the EIGRP routing process:

```
Router#sh ipx eigrp inter

IPX EIGRP Interfaces for process 2

                    Xmit Queue    Mean   Pacing Time  Multicast   Pending
Interface   Peers   Un/Reliable   SRTT   Un/Reliable  Flow Timer  Routes
Se0         9       0/0           59     4/484        244         0
Di1         0       0/0           0      6/10         0           0
Router#
```

From this output we can see that Serial0 and Dialer1 are both participating in EIGRP. These are both in EIGRP process number 2. We can see that the Serial0 interface has nine adjacent neighbors. The *Peers* field identifies this. This *show ipx eigrp interface* command and its associated output can be useful for verifying that EIGRP has been configured correctly and that the correct routing updates are being sent or delivered.

show ipx eigrp neighbors

The show *ipx eigrp neighbors* command displays all the directly connected EIGRP neighbors that have been identified by the EIGRP routing process:

```
Router#sh ipx eigrp neigh

      IPX EIGRP Neighbors for process 2
H     Address                   Interface    Hold Uptime   SRTT   RTO    Q    Seq
                                             (sec)         (ms)          Cnt  Num
4     44804001.00e0.1ea9.abde   Se0          11  1d10h     68     2904   0    12435
7     44804001.00e0.b08e.39d1   Se0          11  1d13h     60     2904   0    9990
5     44804001.00e0.1ea0.d361   Se0          14  1d13h     58     2904   0    46588
1     44804001.00e0.1eb9.2307   Se0          13  5d22h     60     2904   0    783
0     44804001.0010.7bfe.a4e1   Se0          13  6d15h     58     2904   0    8507
8     44804001.00e0.1e3e.0239   Se0          13  1w4d      77     2904   0    60879
2     44804001.0050.735d.97e1   Se0          12  1w4d      65     2904   0    9167
6     44804001.00d0.bbee.f900   Se0          14  1w5d      63     2904   0    5253
3     44804001.00e0.1eb4.1e41   Se0          12  1w5d      30     2904   0    14796
Router#
```

This information correlates with the *show ipx eigrp interfaces* command that we have just covered. This output is from the same router and, if you recall, the Serial0 interface had nine peers. These peers or directly connected neighbors are shown here.

The *ipx eigrp neighbors* command is useful for checking the consistency of the EIGRP routing process and ensuring that all directly connected neighbors are visible. A problem here may be the cause of an incorrectly configured access list or misconfigurations of the EIGRP routing process.

Debug Commands

The Debug commands are an excellent way to interrogate the router and receive real-time information regarding the state of TCP/IP connections at various OSI layers (see Table 11-4). As always, only use debug commands when it is necessary to do so and be careful when using them on busy core production routers. Debugging puts a load on the router CPU and can have

Table 11-4 Frequently Used Debug Commands for Troubleshooting TCP/IP	**Command**	**Description**
	debug ipx sap events	Displays debug information about the SAP updates that are sent and received by the router.
	debug ipx packet	Displays debug information about all the IPX packets that are processed by the router.
	debug ipx routing events	Displays debug information about the IPX routing activity. This produces debug output for all IPX routing protocols.

a detrimental effect on the network. After every debugging session, always use the `Router#no debug all` command to turn off all debug events.

debug ipx sap events

The *debug ipx sap events* command displays debug information about SAP updates that are sent and received by the router:

```
IPXSAP: at 0023F778:
I SAP Response type 0x2 len 160 src:160.0000.0c00.070d
dest:160.ffff.ffff.ffff(452)
   type 0x4, "Hello2", 199.0002.0004.0006 (451), 2 hops
   type 0x4, "Hello1", 199.0002.0004.0008 (451), 2 hops
IPXSAP: sending update to 160
IPXSAP: at 00169080:
   O SAP Update type 0x2 len 96 ssoc:0x452
dest:160.ffff.ffff.ffff(452)
IPX: type 0x4, "Magnolia", 42.0000.0000.0001 (451), 2hops
```

SAP updates are by default sent out every 60 seconds. There can be up to seven service entries in every SAP packet. This results in numerous packets been sent from routers that advertise large numbers of services. Each SAP update contains the service type, name, network address, socket number, and number of hops to the server hosting the service.

This *debug ipx sap events* command can be used to identify problems when users complain that some IPX services are not available in some areas of the network, but they are available from others. Misconfigured SAP filters (in the access-list range of 1000 to1099) are the main problem that causes these service interruptions.

debug ipx packet

The *debug ipx packet* command displays debug information about all the IPX packets that are processed by the router:

```
Router#
8w5d: IPX: Se1:450.0050.736b.c338->450.ffff.ffff.ffff ln= 88 tc=00
      pt=01 ds=0453 ss=0453, rcvd
8w5d: IPX: Se1:450.0050.736b.c338->450.ffff.ffff.ffff ln= 88 tc=00
      pt=01 ds=0453 ss=0453
8w5d: IPX: Et0:100.0050.736b.c338->100.ffff.ffff.ffff ln= 40 tc=00
      pt=01 ds=0453 ss=0453, rcvd
8w5d: IPX: Et0:100.0050.736b.c338->100.ffff.ffff.ffff ln= 40 tc=00
      pt=01 ds=0453 ss=0453
```

```
8w5d:  IPX: Se0:400.0050.736b.c338->400.ffff.ffff.ffff ln= 40 tc=00
       pt=01 ds=0453 ss=0453, rcvd
8w5d:  IPX: Se0:400.0050.736b.c338->400.ffff.ffff.ffff ln= 40 tc=00
       pt=01 ds=0453 ss=0453, local
8w5d:  IPX: Se1:450.0050.736b.c338->450.ffff.ffff.ffff ln= 40 tc=00
       pt=01 ds=0453 ss=0453, rcvd
8w5d:  IPX: Se1:450.0050.736b.c338->450.ffff.ffff.ffff ln= 40 tc=00
       pt=01 ds=0453 ss=0453
8w5d:  IPX: Lo0:800.0010.7b80.fdee->800.ffff.ffff.ffff ln= 40 tc=00
       pt=01 ds=0453 ss=0453, rcvd
8w5d:  IPX: Lo0:800.0010.7b80.fdee->800.ffff.ffff.ffff ln= 40 tc=00
       pt=01 ds=0453 ss=0453
8w5d:  IPX: Et0:100.0050.736b.c338->100.ffff.ffff.ffff ln= 96 tc=00
       pt=01 ds=0453 ss=0453, rcvd
8w5d:  IPX: Et0:100.0050.736b.c338->100.ffff.ffff.ffff ln= 96 tc=00
       pt=01 ds=0453 ss=0453
8w5d:  IPXSAP: positing update to 700.ffff.ffff.ffff via Serial1
       (broadcast) (full)
8w5d:  IPX: Lo0:800.0010.7b80.fdee->800.ffff.ffff.ffff ln= 96 tc=00
       pt=01 ds=0453 ss=0453, rcvd
8w5d:  IPX: Lo0:800.0010.7b80.fdee->800.ffff.ffff.ffff ln= 96 tc=00
       pt=01 ds=0453 ss=0453
8w5d:  IPXSAP: positing update to 800.ffff.ffff.ffff via Loopback0
       (broadcast) (full)
Router#
```

This command can quickly overload the router with information and also place a considerable loading on the router CPU. Every IPX packet that the router processes will be displayed along with the source interface and address, the destination address, the packet length, and the next hop or gateway address.

In real-world situations, the *debug ipx packet* command is not of a great use due to the amount of information produced. However, it is an excellent source for debugging new links or verifying the route of packets that the router is processing.

debug ipx routing events

The *debug ipx routing events* command displays debug information about the IPX routing activity. This produces debug output for all the IPX routing protocols. Here we'll look at the routing events provided for a debug when we add an IPX network and remove the network using IPX RIP:

```
RouterA#debug ipx routing events
IPX routing events debugging is on
RouterA#
RouterA#sh ipx route
Codes: C - Connected primary network,    c - Connected secondary
network
```

```
          S - Static, F - Floating static, L - Local (internal), W -
IPXWAN
          R - RIP, E - EIGRP, N - NLSP, X - External, A - Aggregate
          s - seconds, u - uses, U - Per-user static

10 Total IPX routes. Up to 1 parallel paths and 16 hops allowed.

No default route known.

C        400 (HDLC),            Se0
C        500 (NOVELL-ETHER),    Et0
C        700 (HDLC),            Se1
C        800 (UNKNOWN),         Lo0
R        100 [07/01] via        400.0050.736b.c338,    29s, Se0
R        200 [07/01] via        400.0050.736b.c338,    29s, Se0
R        250 [07/01] via        400.0050.736b.c338,    29s, Se0
R        300 [07/01] via        400.0050.736b.c338,    29s, Se0
R        450 [07/01] via        400.0050.736b.c338,    29s, Se0
R        1000 [07/01] via       400.0050.736b.c338,    29s, Se0
RouterA#

8w5d: IPXRIP: positing full update to 400.ffff.ffff.ffff via
      Serial0 (broadcast)
8w5d: IPXRIP: positing full update to 500.ffff.ffff.ffff via
      Ethernet0 (broadcast)
8w5d: IPXRIP: Marking network 999 FFFFFFFF for Flash Update
8w5d: IPXRIP: positing flash update to 500.ffff.ffff.ffff via
      Ethernet0 (broadcast)
8w5d: IPXRIP: positing flash update to 400.ffff.ffff.ffff via
      Serial0 (broadcast)
8w5d: IPXRIP: positing flash update to 700.ffff.ffff.ffff via
      Serial1 (broadcast)
8w5d: IPXRIP: positing flash update to 800.ffff.ffff.ffff via
      Loopback0 (broadcast)
8w5d: IPXRIP: suppressing null update to 400.ffff.ffff.ffff
      (Serial0)

RouterA#
RouterA#sh ipx route
Codes: C - Connected primary network,     c - Connected secondary
       network
       S - Static, F - Floating static, L - Local (internal), W -
       IPXWAN
       R - RIP, E - EIGRP, N - NLSP, X - External, A - Aggregate
       s - seconds, u - uses, U - Per-user static

11 Total IPX routes. Up to 1 parallel paths and 16 hops allowed.

No default route known.

C        400 (HDLC),            Se0
C        500 (NOVELL-ETHER),    Et0
C        700 (HDLC),            Se1
C        800 (UNKNOWN),         Lo0
R        100 [07/01] via        400.0050.736b.c338,    28s, Se0
R        200 [07/01] via        400.0050.736b.c338,    28s, Se0
R        250 [07/01] via        400.0050.736b.c338,    28s, Se0
R        300 [07/01] via        400.0050.736b.c338,    28s, Se0
R        450 [07/01] via        400.0050.736b.c338,    28s, Se0
```

```
R       999  [07/01] via      400.0050.736b.c338,   24s, Se0
R      1000  [07/01] via      400.0050.736b.c338,   28s, Se0
RouterA#
RouterA#

8w5d: IPXRIP: positing full update to 800.ffff.ffff.ffff via
      Loopback0 (broadcast)
8w5d: IPXRIP: Marking network 999 FFFFFFFF for Flash Update
8w5d: IPXRIP: poison route to 999 FFFFFFFF via 0050.736b.c338,
      delay 65535, hops 255
8w5d: IPXRIP: positing flash update to 500.ffff.ffff.ffff via
      Ethernet0 (broadcast)
8w5d: IPXRIP: positing flash update to 400.ffff.ffff.ffff via
      Serial0 (broadcast)
8w5d: IPXRIP: positing flash update to 700.ffff.ffff.ffff via
      Serial1 (broadcast)
8w5d: IPXRIP: positing flash update to 800.ffff.ffff.ffff via
      Loopback0 (broadcast)
8w5d: IPXRIP: suppressing null update to 400.ffff.ffff.ffff
      (Serial0)
8w5d: IPXRIP: positing full update to 400.ffff.ffff.ffff via
      Serial0 (broadcast)
8w5d: IPXRIP: positing full update to 500.ffff.ffff.ffff via
      Ethernet0 (broadcast)
RouterA#
RouterA#sh ipx route
Codes: C - Connected primary network,    c - Connected secondary
       network
       S - Static, F - Floating static, L - Local (internal), W -
       IPXWAN
       R - RIP, E - EIGRP, N - NLSP, X - External, A - Aggregate
       s - seconds, u - uses, U - Per-user static

11 Total IPX routes. Up to 1 parallel paths and 16 hops allowed.

No default route known.

C       400 (HDLC),          Se0
C       500 (NOVELL-ETHER),  Et0
C       700 (HDLC),          Se1
C       800 (UNKNOWN),       Lo0
R       100  [07/01] via     400.0050.736b.c338,   8s, Se0
R       200  [07/01] via     400.0050.736b.c338,   8s, Se0
R       250  [07/01] via     400.0050.736b.c338,   8s, Se0
R       300  [07/01] via     400.0050.736b.c338,   8s, Se0
R       450  [07/01] via     400.0050.736b.c338,   8s, Se0
RH      999  [**/**] via     400.0050.736b.c338,  63s, Se0
R      1000  [07/01] via     400.0050.736b.c338,   8s, Se0

8w5d: IPXRIP: garbage collecting entry for 999 FFFFFFFF
8w5d: IPXRIP: Marking network 999 FFFFFFFF for Flash Update

RouterA#
RouterA#sh ipx route
Codes: C - Connected primary network,    c - Connected secondary
       network
       S - Static, F - Floating static, L - Local (internal), W -
       IPXWAN
       R - RIP, E - EIGRP, N - NLSP, X - External, A - Aggregate
       s - seconds, u - uses, U - Per-user static
```

```
10 Total IPX routes. Up to 1 parallel paths and 16 hops allowed.

No default route known.

C      400 (HDLC),           Se0
C      500 (NOVELL-ETHER),   Et0
C      700 (HDLC),           Se1
C      800 (UNKNOWN),        Lo0
R      100 [07/01] via       400.0050.736b.c338,   29s, Se0
R      200 [07/01] via       400.0050.736b.c338,   29s, Se0
R      250 [07/01] via       400.0050.736b.c338,   29s, Se0
R      300 [07/01] via       400.0050.736b.c338,   29s, Se0
R      450 [07/01] via       400.0050.736b.c338,   29s, Se0
R      1000 [07/01] via      400.0050.736b.c338,   29s, Se0
RouterA#
```

This listing shows the successful addition and removal of network 999 from the router's IPX routing table. We start by issuing a *show ipx route* command to ensure that we do not already have an entry for the 999 network. As you can see, no entry exists for this network.

The first section shows the newly received RIP update that includes the 999 network. This information is added into the routing table and another show ipx route displays the routing information to network 999. At this point, we can ascertain that the entry of the 999 network has been successful. We now want to remove the network at the remote end from the RIP routing process and see what happens.

The listing also shows that this route to network 999 has been poisoned. We then look at the IPX routing table once more and the route to 999 is shown as **/**. Also note that the routing entry type has changed from *R* to *RH*. This is for RIP and the H represents a hold down state.

Next we see the garbage collection for the route to network 999. As you can see in the last IPX routing table, the route has now been removed. This shows the successful entry and removal of a route into the IPX routing table. This command can be used either to monitor the current routing events or a sample network can be added, as in the example, to ensure that the routing process on the router is functioning correctly.

Other IPX/Novell Commands

As well as the show and debug commands, a few others can be used to aid in troubleshooting a Novell network. These include *ping* and *trace*. We usually associate ping and trace with TCP/IP networks, as these tools are core with the TCP/IP protocol suite. However, Cisco implements ping and trace functionality for IPX as well as other protocols. This gives you a simple method of testing the reliability and integrity of the internetwork.

Ping

One of the most frequently used debugging tools for troubleshooting network problems is the ping command. Cisco routers support pings over IPX, Decnet, and AppleTalk, as well as IP. The ping command provides a method of ensuring that a remote host is responding and that the IPX protocol stack is loaded correctly. This is also an easy method for checking that communication between one host and another is working through the internetwork.

Many situations arise where a ping can prove communication. The ping will travel through the internetwork passing every router to the destination and back. This is an excellent way to test routing and visibility through access lists. On a Cisco router, you can use the standard ping command from user exec or privileged exec mode, or the extended Ping command from the privileged exec mode only. Table 11-5 provides a list of ping characters. Here is an example of an extended IPX ping:

```
Router#ping
Protocol [ip]: ipx
Target IPX address: 400.0050.736b.c338
Repeat count [5]:
Datagram size [100]:
Timeout in seconds [2]:
Verbose [n]:
Type escape sequence to abort.
Sending 5, 100-byte IPXcisco Echoes to 400.0050.736b.c338, timeout
is 2 seconds:
!!!!!
```

Table 11-5

Ping Characters and Definitions

Character	Definition
!	A successful receipt of an echo reply
.	Timed-out wait for a response
U	The destination network is unreachable
C	Congestion is experienced
I	Interrupted by user
?	Packet type unknown
&	Packet TTL exceeded

```
Success rate is 100 percent (5/5), round-trip min/avg/max =
48/50/52 ms
Router#
```

Trace

The trace command is also a widely used command for troubleshooting connectivity problems on internetworks. This command enables you to see the complete end-to-end path that the packets take to reach their destination. Here is a sample IPX trace:

```
Router#trace
Protocol [ip]: ipx
Target IPX address: 100.0050.736b.c338
Numeric display [n]:
Timeout in seconds [3]:
Probe count [3]:
Minimum Time to Live [0]:
Maximum Time to Live [1]:
Verbose [n]:
Type escape sequence to abort.
Tracing the route to 100.0050.736b.c338

  1 200.0051.736b.c338 20 msec 20 msec 20 msec
  2 101.0052.736b.c338 24 msec 22 msec 22 msec
  3 100.0050.736b.c338 24 msec 24 msec 24 msec
Router#
```

As you can see from the previous listing, all the intermediary routers that the packet has traversed are displayed. This is an excellent tool to diagnose if a problem exists on a remote router. Table 11-6 displays the trace characters and their meanings.

On a Cisco router, you can enter the trace command from either user or privileged exec mode.

	Character	Definition
Table 11-6 *Trace Characters and Definitions*	!H	The probe was received but not forwarded. This is usually caused by an access list on the router.
	P	The protocol was unreachable.
	N	The network was unreachable.
	U	The port was unreachable.
	*	Time-out.

Chapter Summary

In this chapter, we have looked at the NetWare IPX/SPX protocol suite and the troubleshooting commands available with Cisco IOS. We started by looking at the basics of IPX/SPX and the associated protocols, giving us a technical overview of the way these protocols integrate to provide the Net-Ware services.

We then looked at NetWare-specific routing protocols and explained their attributes and associated problems. Next, we looked at the Cisco show and debug commands that can interrogate the router to receive real-time reports that will help us in the troubleshooting process. As in any other troubleshooting situation, always start at the physical layer and work your way up. This method of troubleshooting is logical and can save you a lot of time.

Frequently Asked Questions (FAQ)

Question: Does the IPX address have to be resolved to the hardware address as in IP (ARP)?

Answer: No, the IPX address is the hardware or MAC address of a node, so this eliminates the need for a hardware address-resolving process.

Question: Which routing protocol will automatically support IP and IPX?

Answer: The Enhanced Interior Gateway Routing Protocol (EIGRP) is multi-protocol capable and will work with IP and IPX.

Question: On which interfaces are incremental SAP updates automatically configured when using EIGRP for IPX?

Answer: Serial interfaces are automatically configured for incremental SAP updates. Other interfaces have to be enabled by entering the command *ipx sap-incremental eigrp x* where x is the AS number of the EIGRP process.

Case Study

You, as a network engineer for a small financial services company, have been assigned to identify the connectivity problem in one of your remote retail stores. You have a predominately IP network that employs two routers to connect the two main offices. The routers are Cisco 2501s running IOS 11.3 IP/IPX. A 256Kbps leased line connects the two buildings and is connected to the Serial0 interface on both 2503 routers.

You only look after the router in your building. You have recently added IPX routing to the configuration and you have a problem communicating over IPX to the remote network. IP communications are fine. You are only having a problem with IPX.

Approach It seems pretty obvious that the problem lies with the configuration of one of the serial interfaces in your building or at the remote site. You get a config file from both 2503 routers.

The following is the 2503 configuration in your office:

```
Interface Serial0
 ip address 172.19.1.2 255.255.0.0
 no ip directed-broadcast
 no ip mroute-cache
 ipx network 400
 ipx encapsulation hdlc
```

Here is the 2503 configuration in the remote office:

```
Interface Serial0
 ip address 172.19.1.1 255.255.0.0
 no ip directed-broadcast
 no ip mroute-cache
 ipx network 400
 ipx encapsulation hdlc
```

You notice that the encapsulation method is the same on both interfaces. You originally thought that this might have been the problem due to all you have heard about encapsulation types. You try to change the encapsulation type on the Serial0 interface and you find that you only have the HDLC choice. Any of the others return an error due to the interface type.

After you have exhausted this possibility, you then look at the rest of the config on both routers. You notice that the remote 2503 router has the following access list configuration:

```
access-list 1 permit any
access-list 101 deny tcp any any eq ftp
```

```
access-list 101 deny tcp any any eq web
access-list 101 deny tcp any any eq domain
access-list 801 deny -1
```

You know about the access lists numbered 1 and 101 but are unsure about the access list 801. You check it out and realize that this is blocking all IPX traffic over the serial link. This was originally put in place to block any IPX traffic before the remote site required access to the IPX servers.

Results   You collaborate with the local support staff at the remote site and you remove the access list numbered 801. After you do this, all IPX traffic passes over the serial connection.

Questions

1. Which NetWare protocol is responsible for routing a packet through the internetwork?

   a. SPX
   b. IPX
   c. NCP
   d. NLSP

2. The host address is usually the same as the _____.

   a. network address
   b. hardware or MAC address
   c. interface number
   d. IP address

3. Which NetWare routing protocol is backward-compatible with IPX RIP?

   a. SAP
   b. IS-IS
   c. EIGRP
   d. NLSP

4. How many bytes are in an IPX network number?

   a. 2
   b. 3
   c. 5
   d. 4

5. Which troubleshooting command will display the IPX servers that the router is aware of?

   a. show ipx sap
   b. show ipx servers
   c. show servers
   d. show ipx services

6. Which command displays the IPX routing table?

   a. show route
   b. show ipx route
   c. show ip route
   d. show route ipx

7. The command *show ipx servers* displays a list of servers that the router knows about. Which NetWare protocol is responsible for building this list of servers?

    a. SAP

    b. IPX

    c. SPX

    d. NCP

8. What are the two ways to reduce SAP bandwidth utilization? (Choose two.)

    a. SAP filters

    b. SAP holdowns

    c. Incremental SAP updates

    d. SAP Split Horizon

9. Which IPX routing protocol is based on distance vector principles?

    a. RIP

    b. NLSP

    c. EIGRP

    d. AURP

10. What is the access-list number range for an extended IPX access list?

    a. 800-899

    b. 900-999

    c. 1000-1099

    d. 100-199

11. Which debug command displays SAP information?

    a. debug ipx sap events

    b. debug ipx servers

    c. debug ipx routing

    d. debug ipx packets

12. Incremental SAP updates are automatically configured on _____ interfaces.

    a. Fast Ethernet

    b. Ethernet

    c. Token Ring

    d. serial

13. To perform a detailed IPX ping, which router mode must you be in?

    a. User
    b. Privileged
    c. Router
    d. Global

14. In an IPX access list, what does a -1 indicate?

    a. Any network
    b. Any host
    c. No networks
    d. No hosts

15. What is the access list number range for a SAP filter?

    a. 800-899
    b. 900-999
    c. 100-199
    d. 1000-1099

16. Which command would produce detailed IPX-routing process information?

    a. debug ipx routing
    b. debug ipx sap
    c. show ipx route
    d. show ipx servers

17. The command *show ipx servers* indicates that you have 82 service entries. How many SAP updates will be broadcast every 60 seconds on a network that is running NLSP as the IPX routing protocol?

    a. 82
    b. 164
    c. 0
    d. 255

18. Which command must be entered to enable incremental SAP updates on an Ethernet interface where the router is participating in EIGRP AS 101?

    a. Router(config) ipx sap-incremental eigrp 101
    b. Router(config-if) ipx sap-incremental eigrp
    c. Router(config-if) ipx sap-incremental eigrp 101
    d. Router(config-if) ipx sap-incremental

19. Which NetWare routing protocol is based upon the OSI IS-IS protocol and was designed to replace RIP and SAP?

   a. IPX RIP

   b. NLSP

   c. EIGRP

   d. OSPF

20. A client issues a _____ request upon bootup to discover the network services.

   a. IPX

   b. SAP

   c. NCP

   d. GNS

Answers

1. Answer: b

   IPX is responsible for routing a packet through the internetwork. It is a network-layer protocol that is similar in operation to IP from the TCP/IP protocol suite.

2. Answer: b

   The IPX host address is usually the same as the hardware or MAC address. This has the advantage of removing the need for network-address-to-hardware-address resolution. IP requires ARP to carry out this resolution.

3. Answer: d

   The NetWare Link Services Protocol (NLSP) is backward-compatible with IPX RIP. This helps ease the transition to NLSP from RIP-based networks.

4. Answer: d

   Four bytes are in the IPX network number.

5. Answer: b

   The command *show ipx servers* displays all of the IPX servers that the router is aware of. These entries are made from SAP broadcast packets that advertise servers and resources.

6. Answer: b

   The command *show ipx route* displays the routing table for the IPX protocol.

7. Answer: a

   The Service Advertisement Protocol (SAP) is responsible for building the list of servers that the *show ipx servers* command displays.

8. Answer: a and c

   The two ways to reduce SAP bandwidth utilization are SAP filters (access lists) and incremental SAP updates.

9. Answer: a

   RIP is a distance vector routing protocol.

10. Answer: b

    The extended IPX access list range is 900-999. 800-899 is the standard IPX access list range.

11. Answer: a

   The command *debug ipx sap events* displays real-time debug information about SAP packets that are sent and received by the router.

12. Answer: d

   Incremental SAP updates are by default automatically configured on serial interfaces that have IPX network numbers associated with them.

13. Answer: b

   To perform a detailed ping to an IPX device, you must be in privileged exec mode. In user exec mode, you can only ping the device by name.

14. Answer: a

   A *-1* in an IPX access list refers to any network. This is used to specify any source network or any destination network.

15. Answer: d

   The SAP filter access list range is 1000-1099.

16. Answer: a

   The command *debug ipx routing* displays detailed information about the IPX routing process.

17. Answer: c

   NLSP implements incremental SAP updates. An update is only sent when a service change occurs. Therefore, no SAP updates will be sent over the network at periodic intervals.

18. Answer: c

   To enable incremental SAP updates on an Ethernet interface, you have to enter the command *Router(config-if) ipx sap-incremental eigrp 101*. This sets the interface within EIGRP AS 101 to use incremental SAP updates. You must be in the interface configuration mode to run this command.

19. Answer: b

   NLSP is based upon the OSI IS-IS routing protocol.

20. Answer: d

   A client issues a GNS request upon bootup to discover the network services.

12

Routing Protocols

This chapter provides an overview of routing protocols and the tools that are available for troubleshooting these protocols. We will be covering the fundamentals of routing protocols and their relation to the OSI model. We will look at classless and classfull routing protocols and examine their differences. We then move onto the various link state and distance vector routing protocols. Each protocol will be examined and explained and then we will cover common configuration problems associated with the protocol.

Networks traditionally were separate entities that connected computers together to share resources and collaborate. As technology advanced, networks sparked the advent of bridges to interconnect separate networks and increase network performance. With the introduction of TCP/IP as the protocol of choice, more and more networks were getting segmented at the network layer of the OSI model and these networks were interconnected by routers. Routers, as we know, interconnect separate networks and each network has its own address space, as defined by a layer-3 protocol such as an *Internet protocol* (IP) or *Internetwork packet exchange* (IPX).

Routers operate by looking at the layer-3 protocol destination address and making a routing decision based on entries in the internal routing table. Obviously, the larger and more complex the internetwork gets, the larger and more difficult it is to administer the internal routing table.

Routes can be added in two ways. They can be added either manually or dynamically. If all of the network segments are connected to a single router, the routing process would be easy for the router because it knows every network address that is configured on every interface that exists on the router. The challenge arises when the packet has to cross multiple routers to reach its destination. By default, each router only knows about networks that are located on a physically connected interface. To enable routers to pass packets that have distant network addresses, it is necessary to configure routes on the router.

Manually entered routes are known as *static routes*. The network administrator enters static routes to every router. This approach may be ideal for small internetworks, but as the internetwork increases in size, the administration of these routes becomes complex. Another problem with manually entered routes is convergence. Convergence is defined as the time it takes for an internetwork to recalculate routing information after a link goes down. With static routes, you have to take a reactive approach and manually change routing information on all of the relevant routers when a link is broken or a new router is added to the internetwork.

Dynamic routes are automatically discovered and entered into the router's internal routing table. This provides a pro-active solution to routing maintenance that is automatic once configured. Any change in the network topology causes the routing tables to be dynamically updated when necessary. This procedure is carried out by a routing protocol. Several routing protocols are in operation. Some of these are open protocols, such as *open shortest path first* (OSPF), and others are propriety, such as the *enhanced interior gateway routing protocol* (EIGRP).

Routing protocols are grouped into two main classifications: link state and distance vector. These classifications describe how the protocol operates and how convergence takes place in the event of a network topology change. Large networks, or networks that have frequent topology changes, benefit from the dynamic nature of implementing these routing protocols rather than using static routing. Once the routing protocol is configured, it should require little or no maintenance to continue operating correctly. Each routing protocol has its own characteristics, and a protocol used in one scenario may not be suitable for use in another. It is therefore important to give the design process a lot of thought to select the routing protocol that will be best suited to the internetwork on which it will be running.

The best place to start when troubleshooting any network-related problem is at the physical layer of the OSI model. We will adopt this layered systematic troubleshooting approach in this chapter in order to reduce the amount of time it takes to resolve a routing protocol-related network problem. All routing protocols operate at the network layer of the OSI model. They must, however, have a reliable network infrastructure at layers 1 and 2 to communicate effectively.

Objectives Covered in the Chapter

This chapter introduces you to troubleshooting IP routing protocols with the following objectives:

- Analyze problem symptoms and resolve resolution strategies in TCP/IP (including the Microsoft 95/NT IP stack), Novell IPX, AppleTalk, Ethernet VLANs, Frame Relay, and ISDN BRI.
- Demonstrate knowledge of connection sequences and key troubleshooting targets within TCP/IP, Novell IPX, and AppleTalk.
- Identify and use the innate Cisco IOS software commands and debug utilities to filter, capture, and display protocol traffic flows.

Routing Protocols in the OSI Model

We know from earlier studies and from previous chapters in this book that the network layer (layer 3) of the OSI model is responsible for routing packets across an internetwork. We associate protocols such as IP and IPX with the network layer. Therefore, it is self-explanatory that routing protocols also reside at the network layer of the OSI model. The routing protocols that we are going to cover in this chapter are as follows:

- *Routing information protocol* (RIP)
- *Interior gateway routing protocol* (IGRP)
- *Open shortest path first* (OSPF)
- *Border gateway protocol* (BGP)
- *Enhanced interior gateway routing protocol* (EIGRP)

Classless Versus Classfull Protocols

IP follows a classfull addressing scheme where all unicast IP addresses are grouped into three main classifications: Class A, B, and C. Each class of addresses specifies a range of IP addresses and have a default subnet mask that identifies the network and host portion of the IP address:

- *Class A (0.0.0.0 to 126.255.255.255)*   Class A addresses have a default subnet mask of 255.0.0.0 This provides for 255 networks and 16,777,214 hosts per network.
- *Class B (128.0.0.0 to 191.255.255.255)*   Class B addresses have a default subnet mask of 255.255.0.0 This provides for 65,536 networks and 65,534 hosts per network.
- *Class C (192.0.0.0 to 223.255.255.255)*   Class C addresses have a default subnet mask of 255.255.255.0 This provides for 16,777,216 networks and 254 hosts per network.

As you can see, the original classfull addressing scheme provides far too many hosts per network for Class A and B addresses and too few hosts per network for Class C addresses. The solution around this is to partition large networks internally into subnetworks or subnets. This enables you to create subnetworks (subnets) of the original network address.

Routing protocols are either classfull or classless in their design and operation. This doesn't correlate with the distance vector and link state grouping, but most link state routing protocols are also classless. As always, there are exceptions to this rule.

Classfull dynamic routing protocols strictly adhere to the rules and restraints of the IP addressing scheme. Subnets and subnet masks are supported by classfull routing protocols, but they require that all subnet masks are the same for all IP addresses belonging to the same classfull network address. This point is key in understanding the difference between classfull and classless routing protocols. A network address of 172.18.1.0 and a subnet mask of 255.255.255.0 provide subnets for every change on the third octet. These would be 172.18.1.0, 172.18.2.0, 172.18.3.0, and so on. In this instance, a classfull dynamic routing protocol would insist that the subnet mask be the same for every subnet of 172.18.0.0. This would mean that the corporate-wide network address scheme would have to be based on the same subnet mask. To use another subnet mask, you would have to use a different network address. For example, 172.19.1.0 is a different Class B network and could have a subnet mask of 255.255.248.0

The reason why classfull protocols only support one subnet mask is due to the fact that classfull dynamic routing protocols do not have the facility to include the subnet mask in the routing update. Because classfull routing protocols assume that the subnet mask is the same for all subnets of a network, they acquire the subnet mask from interfaces over which they send and receive routing updates.

Classless dynamic routing protocols have the capability to send the subnet mask along with the subnet information as part of the routing update. This lets variable length subnet masks (VLSM) and route summarization conserve network resources.

Table 12-1 outlines various routing protocols and specifies whether they are classfull or classless.

Distance Vector Protocols

As previously discussed, dynamic routing protocols can be split into two main categories: distance vector routing protocols and link state routing

Table 12-1	**Routing Protocol**	**Classfull or Classless**
Classfull and Classless Routing Protocols	*Routing information protocol* (RIP)	Classfull
	Routing information protocol V2 (RIPv2)	Classless
	Interior gateway routing protocol (IGRP)	Classfull
	Open shortest path first (OSPF)	Classless
	Border gateway protocol (BGP)	Classless
	Enhanced interior gateway routing protocol (EIGRP)	Classless

protocols. This difference is in the way that the routing protocols learn about topology changes and the way this topology is recorded in the internal routing table of the router.

Distance vector routing is based around an algorithm called the Bellman-Ford algorithm, named after its creators. The basis of the distance vector routing is that all participating routers periodically pass copies of their routing table to other directly connected routers. These updates also communicate network topology changes as soon as they occur.

A router running a distance vector routing protocol receives route information from routers that are directly connected (see Figure 12-1). By directly connected, we mean routers that are at the other end of a *local area newtork* (LAN) or a *wide area network* (WAN) interface on the router. These can be thought of as the routers' direct neighbors. This route information includes the direct neighbor information of the routers that are direct neighbors of the router that has received the routing information. In this way, the router learns about remote networks.

As you can see from Figure 12-1, Router A would not know about network 3 by default. It would only know about networks 1 and 2. However, Router B does know about network 3. In fact, Router B knows about networks 2 and 3. So, we can see that Router A learns about network 3 from a routing update sent by Router B. This process occurs all over the network until each router knows every route to every remote network. One important point is that with distance vector routing, a single router can only see as far as its direct neighbors. It doesn't have a complete view of the network topology. It relies upon second-hand information.

Each router knows which networks are directly connected and it assigns a value of zero to these networks. This value is used as the metric for making routing decisions in distance vector routing. When a router receives a routing update from its direct neighbors, it automatically increments all of the route metric values by one. As this propagates throughout the network,

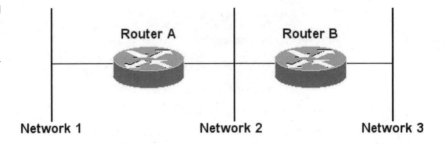

Figure 12-1
Distance vector
routing information.

Chapter 12: Routing Protocols

Chapter 12: Routing Protocols

the metric increases and this is called the hop count. The *hop count* is the number of routers that have to be passed to reach the destination network.

Distance vector routing uses the hop count as the metric of choice for routing decisions. If you have a remote network of 172.18.16.0 and two routing entries in the routing table, one over interface Ethernet0 with a distance of five and one over Serial1 with a distance of three, the distance vector routing algorithm will choose the route with the lowest hop count. In this case, the packets will be sent over the Serial1 interface. This is a limitation of the distance vector algorithm due to the fact that no decision is made on bandwidth but on distance alone. The route to 172.18.16.0 may have been available over five hops, but because all of these are 10 Mbps, the serial route could have been transmitted over 64-Kbps lines. As the packets traverse the network, they stop at every router and get forwarded by that router depending on the best available (shortest) route in that router's routing table.

Network Discovery and Topology Changes

When a distance vector routing protocol is enabled on an interface, the router automatically discovers its direct neighbors based on a network or subnet broadcast. These broadcasts stay local to the network or subnet and all other routers running the same distance vector routing protocol will respond.

Distance vector routing protocols operate by sending their complete routing table to all their direct neighbors. This identifies the state of the connected interfaces and it furnishes the direct neighbors with routing information for remote networks. The update includes the metric or hop count to the remote networks as well as the address of the first router on the path to each network. When a direct neighbor receives these updates, the neighboring router compares the update to its own routing table. If the newly received update contains any routes that are considered a better (with a lower metric or hop count), then the router updates its routing table with this information.

The Problems and Limitations of Distance Vector Routing

The main problem with distance vector routing is the convergence time in large networks. This delay can cause routing loops. All distance vector-based routing protocols contain built-in controls that protect against routing loops in the routing tables. They are as follows:

- Maximum hop count
- Split horizon
- Hold-down timers
- Triggered updates

Maximum Hop Count One way in which distance vector routing protocols prevent routing loops from going on infinitely is by imposing a maximum hop count into the routing protocol. For example, RIP has a maximum hop count of 15. This means that the router considers any destination of more than 15 hops unreachable. This can obviously have serious ramifications for large networks that have more than 15 hops and is a major reason why RIP isn't used in these installations. This control ensures that any routing loops do not propagate for longer than the maximum hop count. This control is similar to the *Time to Live* (TTL) field in the IP header that was covered in Chapter 9, "Transmission Control Protocol/Internet Protocol (TCP/IP)."

Split Horizon The implementation of Split Horizon is another control to prevent routing loops. This works by ensuring that route information is never sent back over the interface on which it was received. If a route is identified from a routing update received from the direct neighbor on Ethernet0, it is unnecessary to send this routing information back to the router on Ethernet0. This reduces routing loops and speeds up convergence.

Hold-Down Timers Routers have hold-down timers that correspond to routes in the routing table. The routes in the routing table are valid for the duration of the hold-down timer. When the hold-down timer expires, the garbage collection timer is started and the route's metric is set to infinity. Until the garbage collection timer expires, the route cannot be removed from the routing table, nor can it be modified if another routing update for the route is received.

Triggered Updates Triggered updates are routing updates that are sent or triggered by a metric or route change. By default, distance vector routing protocols advertise routing updates every 30 or 60 seconds. This can cause a latency in convergence over a sizable network. Triggered updates speed up the convergence of routing information by immediately announcing the metric or route change as soon as it occurs.

We'll now turn out attention to the two distance vector routing protocols that we will examine in detail: RIP and IGRP.

Routing Information Protocol (RIP)

RIP is a distance vector-based dynamic routing protocol that uses a hop count as its metric. The hop count is defined as the number of routers or hops a packet has to traverse to reach its destination. RIP is an *interior gateway protocol* (IGP) and therefore it performs routing within a single *autonomous system* (AS).

RIP has two main versions. RIP version 1 is a classfull routing protocol that strictly follows the classfull addressing scheme of IP. RIP version 2 is the latest version of RIP, is a classless routing protocol that enables more information to be included in the RIP packet header, and supports *variable length subnet masks* (VLSMs). RIP is also available for both IP routing and also IPX routing. RIP is formally defined in RFC 1058 and 1723. RFC 1058 was defined in 1988 and describes the first implementation of RIP. RFC 1723 was defined in 1994 and this revision defines RIPv2 and the extended carrier features supported in the RIP packet header.

RIP operates by sending routing updates at regular intervals out of all configured interfaces. The default time for this update is every 30 seconds. These routing updates contain the complete routing table minus any routes removed due to the split horizon rule. When a routing update is received from a direct neighbor, route information is checked against the current routing table and any better routes with a lower metric or hop count are updated in the routing table. RIP uses the hop count as the routing metric and the maximum allowable hop count using RIP is 15. The 16th hop is deemed unreachable.

On a Cisco router, simply adding the following command in global configuration mode enables RIP:

```
Router(config)#router rip
```

Networks are advertised and participate in RIP routing by entering the following command:

```
Router(config-router)network A.B.C.D
```

where A.B.C.D is the network address of the network to be advertised via RIP.

Other RIP configuration commands include the following:

- address-family: Activates address family command mode
- auto-summary: Enables automatic network number summarization
- default: Sets a command to its defaults
- default-information: Controls the distribution of default information
- default-metric: Sets the metric of redistributed routes
- distance: Defines an administrative distance
- distribute-list: Filters networks in routing updates
- exit: Exits from routing protocol configuration mode
- flash-update-threshold: Specifies the flash update threshold in seconds
- help: Describes the interactive help system
- input-queue: Specifies the input queue depth
- maximum-paths: Forwards packets over multiple paths
- neighbor: Specifies a neighbor router
- network: Enables routing on an IP network
- no: Negates a command or sets its defaults
- offset-list: Adds or subtracts an offset from IGRP or RIP metrics
- output-delay: An interpacket delay for RIP updates
- passive-interface: Suppresses routing updates on an interface
- redistribute: Redistributes information from another routing protocol
- timers: Adjusts routing timers
- validate-update-source: Performs sanity checks against the source address of routing updates
- version: Sets the routing protocol version

For more information on configuring RIP, refer to the ICRC or ACRC course notes.

Troubleshooting RIP

We are now going to look at troubleshooting RIP and the Cisco IOS commands that are available to assist us in RIP problem resolution. RIP can be both a classfull and classless routing protocol. Care must be taken to ensure that you are using a constant version throughout, as the packet types are incompatible. If RIPv1, the classfull version, is used, it is imperative to ensure that every interface within the routable network has the same subnet mask. This is because masking information is not propagated within the routing tables of classfull protocols. This is one of the main faults with RIP routing and the first item to check.

If routing inaccuracies occur, it is also advisable to check the router for any misconfigured distribute lists. A *distribute list* is a routing update filter that is related to an access list. The wrongful configuration of such a list can render the routing process inoperable.

The debug commands are an excellent way to interrogate the router and receive real-time information regarding the state of RIP updates and configuration. As always, only use debug commands when it is necessary to do so and be careful when using them on busy, core production routers. Debugging puts a load on the router CPU and can have a detrimental effect on the network. After every debugging session, always use the `Router#no debug all` command to turn off all debug events. Table 12-2 outlines some of the RIP troubleshooting commands.

show ip protocols

The *show ip protocols* command displays all enabled routing protocols and the associated values relating to the routing protocol. This command is useful for displaying whether inbound or outbound distribution lists have been set. Distribution lists are a common cause of routing table abnormalities. The distribution lists filter the routing traffic that flows over the interface and is related to an access list. Here is an example of a distribution list at work:

Table 12-2	**Command**	**Description**
RIP Troubleshooting Commands	show ip protocols	Displays information about the configured IP routing protocols.
	show ip route	Displays the IP routing table for all routes. This includes the static and dynamic routes learned by all configured dynamic routing protocols.
	show ip rip database	Displays the IP RIP database for all advertised routes and all learned routes.
	debug ip routing	Displays events pertaining to routing protocol updates and changes to the internal routing table.
	debug ip rip	Displays debug information about RIP updates and routing table entries.

```
Router#sh ip prot
Routing Protocol is "rip"
  Sending updates every 30 seconds, next due in 25 seconds
  Invalid after 180 seconds, hold down 180, flushed after 240
  Outgoing update filter list for all interfaces is 10
  Incoming update filter list for all interfaces is
  Redistributing: rip
  Default version control: send version 2, receive version 2
    Interface   Send   Recv   Triggered RIP   Key-chain
    Ethernet0   2      2
    Loopback0   2      2
    Serial0     2      2
    Serial1     2      2
  Routing for Networks:
    172.18.0.0
    172.19.0.0
    172.20.0.0
    194.73.134.0
    212.1.1.0
  Routing Information Sources:
  Gateway          Distance      Last Update
  194.73.134.24    120           05:10:45
  194.73.134.22    120           00:00:01
  172.18.0.12      120           05:10:45
  Gateway          Distance      Last Update
  172.20.1.2       120           05:10:46
  172.19.1.2       120           05:10:46
  Distance: (default is 120)

Routing Protocol is "ospf 1"
  Sending updates every 0 seconds
  Invalid after 0 seconds, hold down 0, flushed after 0
  Outgoing update filter list for all interfaces is
  Incoming update filter list for all interfaces is
  Redistributing: ospf 1
  Routing for Networks:
    172.18.0.0
    172.19.0.0
    172.20.0.0
  Routing Information Sources:
  Gateway          Distance      Last Update
  Distance: (default is 110)

Routing Protocol is "bgp 1"
  Sending updates every 60 seconds, next due in 0 seconds
  Outgoing update filter list for all interfaces is
  Incoming update filter list for all interfaces is
  IGP synchronization is enabled
  Automatic route summarization is enabled
  Routing for Networks:
  Routing Information Sources:
  Gateway          Distance      Last Update
  Distance: external 20 internal 200 local 200

Router#
```

You can see from the previous listing that RIP, OSPF, and BGP are all enabled on this router. RIP is advertising networks 172.18.0.0, 172.19.0.0, 172.20.0.0, 194.73.134.0, and 212.1.1.0. OSPF is advertising networks

172.18.0.0, 172.19.0.0, and 172.20.0.0. BGP is configured but currently not advertising any networks. The only distribution list is the outgoing RIP update filter that corresponds to access list number 10. It is also apparent that we are using RIP version 2 to both send and receive updates. This is important to confirm that all routers running RIP have the same version. RIP version 1 and version 2 updates are not compatible due to differing packet types. It is therefore imperative that all participating routers are all running the same version.

show ip route

The *show ip route* command displays the internal IP routing table for all enabled routing protocols. Static routes and connected routes are also displayed, as can be seen in this example:

```
Router#sh ip route
Codes: C - connected, S - static, I - IGRP, R - RIP, M - mobile, B
- BGP
       D - EIGRP, EX - EIGRP external, O - OSPF, IA - OSPF inter area
       N1 - OSPF NSSA external type 1, N2 - OSPF NSSA external type 2
       E1 - OSPF external type 1, E2 - OSPF external type 2, E - EGP
       i - IS-IS, L1 - IS-IS level-1, L2 - IS-IS level-2, ia - IS-
       IS inter area
       * - candidate default, U - per-user static route, o - ODR
       P - periodic downloaded static route

Gateway of last resort is 172.19.1.2 to network 0.0.0.0

C    194.73.134.0/24 is directly connected, Ethernet0
C    172.19.0.0/16 is directly connected, Serial0
C    172.18.0.0/16 is directly connected, Ethernet0
C    172.20.0.0/16 is directly connected, Serial1
R*   0.0.0.0/0 [120/1] via 172.19.1.2, 05:22:57, Serial0
               [120/1] via 172.20.1.2, 05:22:57, Serial1
               [120/1] via 194.73.134.22, 00:00:03, Ethernet0
R    172.22.0.0/16 [120/1] via 172.19.0.1, Serial0
S    172.24.0.0/16 is directly connected, Ethernet0
C    212.0.0.0/8 is directly connected, Loopback0
Router#
```

The first part of this listing indicates all the codes that are used to identify the routing protocols in the actual routing table. You can see from the routing table that we have five connected networks that are over multiple interfaces. The connected interface is identified by a C. We also have two networks that have been received via RIP. One of these is 172.22.0.0 and the other is 0.0.0.0 or the default route. This default route is also identified by an asterisk next to the R. There is also one static route to network 172.24.0.0. This is a small routing table and it is not uncommon for routing tables to be a hundred or more lines long depending on the size of the network. The *show ip route* command can be further divided by entering the exact route after the command or entering the routing protocol after the command. For example, Router#show ip route rip would just display routes learned by RIP. Router#show ip route 172.18.10.0 would just display protocol information about network 172.18.10.0

show ip rip database

The *show ip rip database* command displays the IP RIP database for all advertised routes and all learned routes, as shown here:

```
Router#sh ip rip database
0.0.0.0/0          auto-summary
0.0.0.0/0          redistributed
172.18.0.0/16      auto-summary
172.18.0.0/16      directly connected, Ethernet0
172.19.0.0/16      auto-summary
172.19.0.0/16      directly connected, Serial0
172.20.0.0/16      auto-summary
172.20.0.0/16      directly connected, Serial1
194.73.134.0/24    auto-summary
194.73.134.0/24    directly connected, Ethernet0
Router#
```

This command is similar in output to show ip route rip, except that this command also shows all the RIP configured networks for the local router.

NOTE: *The show ip rip database command is a new feature included with IOS 12.0.*

debug ip routing

The *debug ip routing* command displays routing information events for the IP routing protocols. To show this in operation, we are going to examine the following two router listings that show a new network has been added to RIP and then removed.

Router A Listing

```
RouterA#debug ip routing
IP routing debugging is on
RouterA#conf t
Enter configuration commands, one per line. End with CNTL/Z.
RouterA(config)#int s0
RouterA(config-if)#ip address 172.24.0.1 255.255.0.0 sec
RouterA(config-if)#
4w0d: RT: add 172.24.0.0/16 via 0.0.0.0, connected metric [0/0]
4w0d: is_up: 1 state: 4 sub state: 1 line: 0
RouterA(config-if)#exit
RouterA(config)#router rip
RouterA(config-router)#network 172.24.0.1
RouterA(config-router)#exit
RouterA(config)#exit
RouterA#
RouterA#conf t
Enter configuration commands, one per line.  End with CNTL/Z.
RouterA(config)#router rip
RouterA(config-router)#no network 172.24.0.0
RouterA(config-router)#exit
RouterA(config)#exit
RouterA#
```

Router B Listing

```
RouterB#debug ip routing
IP routing debugging is on
RouterB#
07:02:37: RT: add 172.24.0.0/16 via 194.73.134.23, rip metric
              [120/1]
07:02:37: RT: add 172.24.0.0/16 via 172.18.0.11, rip metric [120/1]
RouterB#
07:03:15: RT: del 172.24.0.0 via 194.73.134.23, rip metric [120/1]
07:03:15: RT: del 172.24.0.0 via 172.18.0.11, rip metric [120/1]
07:03:15: RT: delete network route to 172.24.0.0
RouterB#
```

These listings show the addition of the secondary ip address 172.24.0.1/16 to the Serial0 interface on Router A. Note that this adds an RT: to the internal routing table. This is included as a connected route as is it attached to a directly connected interface. Next, we add this network to the RIP configuration so that it will be advertised using RIP. As soon as this is done, the routing update is received by Router B and a RT: addition is performed, including the route as a RIP route. Thus, two routes to this network exist.

We then remove the route from the RIP configuration on Router A, and Router B deletes both of the corresponding entries from the routing table. This command is an excellent real-time tool for diagnosing routing update and topology change problems.

debug ip rip

The *debug ip rip* command displays routing information events for the RIP routing protocol. To show this in operation, we are going to examine the following two router listings that show that a new network has been added to RIP and then been removed. We are also going to change Router A to RIP version 1 to show the problems it creates.

Router A Listing

```
RouterA#conf t
Enter configuration commands, one per line. End with CNTL/Z.
RouterA(config)#int s0
RouterA(config-if)#ip address 172.24.0.1 255.255.0.0 sec
RouterA(config-if)#exit
RouterA(config)#router rip
RouterA(config-router)#network 172.24.0.1
RouterA(config-router)#exit
RouterA(config)#router rip
RouterA(config-router)#version 1
RouterA(config-router)#exit
RouterA(config)#router rip
RouterA(config-router)#ver 2
RouterA(config-router)#no network 172.24.0.0
RouterA(config-router)#exit
RouterA(config)#int s0
RouterA(config-if)#no ip add 172.24.0.1 255.255.0.0 sec
RouterA(config-if)#^Z
RouterA#
```

Router B Listing

```
RouterB#debug ip rip
RIP protocol debugging is on
RouterB#
07:23:22: RIP: sending v2 update to 224.0.0.9 via Ethernet0
              (194.73.134.22)
07:23:22: RIP: build update entries
07:23:22: 0.0.0.0/0 metric 1, tag 0
07:23:25: RIP: received v2 update from 194.73.134.23 on Ethernet0
07:23:25: 172.19.0.0/16 via 0.0.0.0 in 1 hops
07:23:25: 172.20.0.0/16 via 0.0.0.0 in 1 hops
07:23:25: RIP: received v2 update from 172.18.0.11 on Ethernet0
07:23:25: 172.19.0.0/16 via 0.0.0.0 in 1 hops
07:23:25: 172.20.0.0/16 via 0.0.0.0 in 1 hops
07:23:50: RIP: sending v2 update to 224.0.0.9 via Ethernet0
              (194.73.134.22)
07:23:50: RIP: build update entries
07:23:50: 0.0.0.0/0 metric 1, tag 0
07:23:55: RIP: received v2 update from 194.73.134.23 on Ethernet0
07:23:55:      172.19.0.0/16 via 0.0.0.0 in 1 hops
07:23:55:      172.20.0.0/16 via 0.0.0.0 in 1 hops
07:23:55: RIP: received v2 update from 172.18.0.11 on Ethernet0
```

```
07:23:55:        172.19.0.0/16 via 0.0.0.0 in 1 hops
07:23:55: 172.20.0.0/16 via 0.0.0.0 in 1 hops
07:24:19: RIP: sending v2 update to 224.0.0.9 via Ethernet0
          (194.73.134.22)
07:24:19: RIP: build update entries
07:24:19: 0.0.0.0/0 metric 1, tag 0
07:24:21: RIP: received v2 update from 194.73.134.23 on Ethernet0
07:24:21: 172.19.0.0/16 via 0.0.0.0 in 1 hops
07:24:21: 172.20.0.0/16 via 0.0.0.0 in 1 hops
07:24:21: RIP: received v2 update from 172.18.0.11 on Ethernet0
07:24:21: 172.19.0.0/16 via 0.0.0.0 in 1 hops
07:24:21: 172.20.0.0/16 via 0.0.0.0 in 1 hops
07:24:39: RIP: received v2 update from 194.73.134.23 on Ethernet0
07:24:39: 172.24.0.0/16 via 0.0.0.0 in 1 hops
07:24:39: RIP: received v2 update from 172.18.0.11 on Ethernet0
07:24:39: 172.24.0.0/16 via 0.0.0.0 in 1 hops
07:24:41: RIP: sending v2 flash update to 224.0.0.9 via Ethernet0
          (194.73.134.22)
07:24:41: RIP: build flash update entries - suppressing null update
07:24:46: RIP: sending v2 update to 224.0.0.9 via Ethernet0
          (194.73.134.22)
07:24:46: RIP: build update entries
07:24:46: 0.0.0.0/0 metric 1, tag 0
07:24:51: RIP: received v2 update from 194.73.134.23 on Ethernet0
07:24:51: 172.19.0.0/16 via 0.0.0.0 in 1 hops
07:24:51: 172.20.0.0/16 via 0.0.0.0 in 1 hops
07:24:51: 172.24.0.0/16 via 0.0.0.0 in 1 hops
07:24:51: RIP: received v2 update from 172.18.0.11 on Ethernet0
07:24:51: 172.19.0.0/16 via 0.0.0.0 in 1 hops
07:24:51: 172.20.0.0/16 via 0.0.0.0 in 1 hops
07:24:51: 172.24.0.0/16 via 0.0.0.0 in 1 hops
07:25:15: RIP: sending v2 update to 224.0.0.9 via Ethernet0
          (194.73.134.22)
07:25:15: RIP: build update entries
07:25:15: 0.0.0.0/0 metric 1, tag 0
07:25:16: RIP: ignored v1 packet from 194.73.134.23 (illegal
          version)
07:25:16: RIP: ignored v1 packet from 172.18.0.11 (illegal version)
07:25:42: RIP: sending v2 update to 224.0.0.9 via Ethernet0
          (194.73.134.22)
07:25:42: RIP: build update entries
07:25:42: 0.0.0.0/0 metric 1, tag 0
07:25:43: RIP: received v2 update from 194.73.134.23 on Ethernet0
07:25:43: 172.19.0.0/16 via 0.0.0.0 in 1 hops
07:25:43: 172.20.0.0/16 via 0.0.0.0 in 1 hops
07:25:43: 172.24.0.0/16 via 0.0.0.0 in 1 hops
07:25:43: RIP: received v2 update from 172.18.0.11 on Ethernet0
07:25:43: 172.19.0.0/16 via 0.0.0.0 in 1 hops
07:25:43: 172.20.0.0/16 via 0.0.0.0 in 1 hops
07:25:43: 172.24.0.0/16 via 0.0.0.0 in 1 hops
07:25:46: RIP: received v2 update from 194.73.134.23 on Ethernet0
07:25:46: 172.24.0.0/16 via 0.0.0.0 in 16 hops  (inaccessible)
07:25:46: RIP: received v2 update from 172.18.0.11 on Ethernet0
07:25:46: 172.24.0.0/16 via 0.0.0.0 in 16 hops  (inaccessible)
07:25:48: RIP: sending v2 flash update to 224.0.0.9 via Ethernet0
          (194.73.134.22)
07:25:48: RIP: build flash update entries
07:25:48: 172.24.0.0/16 metric 16, tag 0
RouterB#
```

These listings show the addition of the secondary IP address 172.24.0.1/16 to the Serial0 interface on Router A. Next, we add this network to the RIP configuration so that it will be advertised using RIP. As soon as this is done, the next RIP routing update received by Router B includes this network in the update.

We then change the RIP version on Router A to be version 1. As we can see from the listing, this packet is considered illegal and is ignored. We remove the route from the RIP configuration on Router A, and Router B receives the notification, and marks it in the routing table as inaccessible. At this stage, the hold-down timer would start.

The *debug ip rip* command is of paramount importance when debugging a RIP routing problem. A common RIP problem is version misconfigurations. The debug ip rip command identifies every RIP packet and provides output that can be used for diagnosing the problem.

Interior Gateway Routing Protocol (IGRP)

IGRP is a distance vector-based dynamic routing protocol that uses a combination of metrics. IGRP is an *interior gateway protocol* (IGP). Therefore, it performs routing within a single AS. IGRP is formally defined in RFC and was designed in the mid-1980s by Cisco Systems to provide a more robust, scaleable intra-autonomous system routing protocol to replace the de facto standard routing protocol, RIP. The problem with RIP was that its hop count was limited to 15 and this was the only metric used. No consideration was given to the bandwidth or reliability of a line for the computation of the best route to a given destination. The route was decided upon the lowest number of hops alone. IGRP is a propriety-routing protocol designed and utilized by Cisco internetworking devices.

IGRP operates by sending routing updates at regular intervals out of all the configured interfaces. These routing updates contain the complete routing table minus any routes removed due to the split horizon rule. When a routing update is received from a direct neighbor, route information is checked against the current routing table and any better routes with a lower metric or hop count are updated in the routing table. IGRP uses a combination of factors to create the routing metric. These include the following:

- Internetwork delay
- Bandwidth

- Reliability
- Load
- *Maximum transmission unit* (MTU)

All of the above are all factored into the routing decision. The network administrator can set weights for each of these values or you can accept the defaults. This inclusion of multiple values into the routing decision provides the router with a much more powerful means of establishing routing decisions. IGRP also has a faster convergence than RIP. This is due to the IGRP implementation of flash updates. Flash updates are the IGRP equivalent of distance vector-triggered updates. A flash update is sent whenever a network topology change is noticed.

On a Cisco router, simply adding the following command in global configuration mode enables IGRP:

```
Router(config)#router igrp 101
```

This command enables IGRP for the AS 101. You must specify the AS number when implementing IGRP. Networks are advertised and participate in IGRP routing by entering the following command:

```
Router(config-router)network A.B.C.D
```

where A.B.C.D is the network address of the network to be advertised via IGRP.

In addition to the configuarion commands listed earlier in the RIP section, the IGRP configuration commands include the following:

- metric: Modifies IGRP routing metrics and parameters.
- variance: Controls load-balancing variance.

For more information on configuring IGRP, refer to the ICRC or ACRC course notes.

Troubleshooting IGRP

We'll now examine the task of troubleshooting IGRP and the Cisco IOS commands that are available to assist us in IGRP problem resolution. IGRP is a classfull routing protocol. It is imperative to ensure that every interface within the routable network has the same subnet mask. This is because masking information is not propagated within the routing tables of classfull protocols. This is one of the main faults with IGRP routing and the first item to check.

The commands show ip protocols, show ip route, and debug ip routing are all in use here. For specific information on them, refer to Table 12-1 in the RIP section. One new command is used here, the debug ip igrp events command. It displays debug information about IGRP updates and routing table entries.

show ip protocols

As stated earlier, the *show ip protocols* command displays all the enabled routing protocols and the associated values. This command is useful for displaying inbound or outbound distribution lists. Here is an example of the show ip protocols command at work:

```
Router#sh ip prot
Routing Protocol is "rip"
  Sending updates every 30 seconds, next due in 1 seconds
  Invalid after 180 seconds, hold down 180, flushed after 240
  Outgoing update filter list for all interfaces is
  Incoming update filter list for all interfaces is
  Redistributing: rip
  Default version control: send version 2, receive version 2
    Interface    Send    Recv    Triggered RIP    Key-chain
    Ethernet0    2       2
    Ethernet1    2       2
    Serial0      2       2
    Serial1      2       2
  Routing for Networks:
    172.18.0.0
    172.19.0.0
    172.20.0.0
    172.30.0.0
    194.73.134.0
  Routing Information Sources:
    Gateway         Distance    Last Update
    194.73.134.23   120         00:00:17
    194.73.134.22   120         11:43:51
    172.18.0.11     120         00:00:17
    Gateway         Distance    Last Update
    172.20.1.1      120         00:00:18
    172.19.1.1      120         00:00:18
  Distance: (default is 120)

Routing Protocol is "ospf 1"
  Sending updates every 0 seconds
  Invalid after 0 seconds, hold down 0, flushed after 0
  Outgoing update filter list for all interfaces is
  Incoming update filter list for all interfaces is
  Redistributing: ospf 1
  Routing for Networks:
```

```
       172.18.0.0
       172.19.0.0
       172.20.0.0
    Routing Information Sources:
      Gateway        Distance  Last Update
    Distance: (default is 110)

Routing Protocol is "bgp 1"
  Sending updates every 60 seconds, next due in 0 seconds
  Outgoing update filter list for all interfaces is
  Incoming update filter list for all interfaces is
  IGP synchronization is enabled
  Automatic route summarization is enabled
  Routing for Networks:
  Routing Information Sources:
    Gateway        Distance  Last Update
  Distance: external 20 internal 200 local 200
Routing Protocol is "igrp 101"
  Sending updates every 90 seconds, next due in 60 seconds
  Invalid after 270 seconds, hold down 280, flushed after 630
  Outgoing update filter list for all interfaces is
  Incoming update filter list for all interfaces is
  Default networks flagged in outgoing updates
  Default networks accepted from incoming updates
  IGRP metric weight K1=1, K2=0, K3=1, K4=0, K5=0
  IGRP maximum hopcount 100
  IGRP maximum metric variance 1
  Redistributing: igrp 101
  Routing for Networks:
    172.18.0.0
    172.19.0.0
    172.30.0.0
    194.73.134.0
  Routing Information Sources:
    Gateway        Distance  Last Update
    Gateway        Distance  Last Update
    194.73.134.23  100       00:01:46
    172.19.1.1     100       00:00:13
  Distance: (default is 100)
Router#
```

From this listing, we can see that RIP, OSPF, BGP, and IGRP are all
enabled on this router. IGRP is advertising networks 172.18.0.0, 172.19.0.0,
172.30.0.0, and 194.73.134.0. We can see that no distribution lists have
been set for IGRP. This command is useful for getting a holistic view of a
router.

show ip route

The *show ip route* command, as discussed earlier, displays the internal IP
routing table for all enabled routing protocols. Here is an example of this
command:

```
Router#sh ip route
Codes: C - connected, S - static, I - IGRP, R - RIP, M - mobile, B
       - BGP
       D - EIGRP, EX - EIGRP external, O - OSPF, IA - OSPF inter area
       N1 - OSPF NSSA external type 1, N2 - OSPF NSSA external type 2
       E1 - OSPF external type 1, E2 - OSPF external type 2, E - EGP
       i - IS-IS, L1 - IS-IS level-1, L2 - IS-IS level-2, ia - IS-
       IS inter area
       * - candidate default, U - per-user static route, o - ODR
       P - periodic downloaded static route

Gateway of last resort is 172.19.1.2 to network 0.0.0.0

C    194.73.134.0/24 is directly connected, Ethernet0
C    172.19.0.0/16 is directly connected, Serial0
C    172.18.0.0/16 is directly connected, Ethernet0
C    172.20.0.0/16 is directly connected, Serial1
I    172.30.0.0/16 [100/1200] via 194.73.134.24, 00:00:29,
     Ethernet0
R*   0.0.0.0/0 [120/1] via 172.19.1.2, 1d05h, Serial0
               [120/1] via 172.20.1.2, 1d05h, Serial1
C    212.0.0.0/8 is directly connected, Loopback0
Router#
```

The first part of this listing indicates all the codes that are used to identify the routing protocols in the actual routing table. You can see from the
routing table that we have five connected networks, which are over multiple interfaces. The connected interface is identified by a C. We also have one
network that has been received via RIP. This is 0.0.0.0, or the default route.
This default route is also identified by an asterisk next to the R. There is
one static route to network 172.24.0.0. We can also see that 172.30.0.0 has
been received over IGRP. Notice the values in the brackets after the route.
These are [100/1200]. The first part, 100, refers to the administrative distance of IGRP, and the second part, 1200, refers to the metric of the route.
This metric has been calculated by the IGRP algorithm.

debug ip routing

To show this command in operation, we are going to examine two router
listings that show a new network has been added to IGRP and then been
removed. This is an IGRP-specific event.

Router A Listing

```
RouterA#conf t
Enter configuration commands, one per line.  End with CNTL/Z.
RouterA(config)#int s0
RouterA(config-if)#ip address 172.24.0.1 255.255.0.0 sec
RouterA(config-if)#
```

```
4w1d: RT: closer admin distance for 172.24.0.0, flushing 0 routes
4w1d: RT: add 172.24.0.0/16 via 0.0.0.0, connected metric [0/0]
4w1d: is_up: 1 state: 4 sub state: 1 line: 0
RouterA(config-if)#exit
RouterA(config)#router igrp 101
RouterA(config-router)#network 172.24.0.1
RouterA(config-router)#exit
RouterA(config)#router igrp 101
RouterA(config-router)#no network 172.24.0.0
RouterA(config-router)#exit
RouterA(config)#int s0
RouterA(config-if)#no ip add 172.24.0.1 255.255.0.0 sec
RouterA(config-if)#^Z
RouterA#
4w1d: RT: del 172.24.0.0 via 0.0.0.0, connected metric [0/0]
4w1d: RT: delete network route to 172.24.0.0
4w1d: is_up: 1 state: 4 sub state: 1 line: 0
4w1d: %SYS-5-CONFIG_I: Configured from console by vty0
                      (212.1.157.20)
RouterA#
4w1d: RT: add 172.24.0.0/16 via 172.19.1.1, igrp metric [100/10576]
4w1d: RT: delete route to 172.24.0.0 via 172.19.1.1, igrp metric
          [100/10576]
4w1d: RT: no routes to 172.24.0.0, entering holddown
RouterA#
```

Router B Listing

```
RouterB#
4w1d: RT: add 172.24.0.0/16 via 194.73.134.24, igrp metric
[100/8576]
RouterB#
4w1d: RT: delete route to 172.24.0.0 via 194.73.134.24, igrp metric
          [100/8576]
4w1d: RT: no routes to 172.24.0.0, entering holddown
RouterB#
4w1d: RT: 172.24.0.0 came out of holddown
4w1d: RT: garbage collecting entry for 172.24.0.0
RouterB#
```

In the previous listing, we add a new route to the IGRP routing process between two routers and track the events with the debug ip routing command. We start by adding a secondary IP address to Serial0 on Router A. As soon as this is added, we can see the RT: addition, which adds the route to the local internal routing table. We then configure the IGRP to advertise this new network. We can immediately see Router B pick up the route over IGRP. If you follow the listing down, you can see that the network is removed from IGRP routing with the *no network 172.24.0.0* command. This deletes the route on both routers and they enter into a state of hold-down. After a period of time, the route comes out of hold-down and is garbage-collected or deleted. This command is an excellent real-time tool for diagnosing routing update and topology change problems.

debug ip igrp events

The *debug ip igrp events* command displays routing information events for the IGRP routing protocol. To show this in operation, we are going to examine two router listings. They show that a new network has been added to IGRP and then been removed.

Router A Listing

```
RouterA#conf t
Enter configuration commands, one per line. End with CNTL/Z.
RouterA(config)#int s0
RouterA(config-if)#ip address 172.24.0.1 255.255.0.0 sec
RouterA(config-if)#

4w1d: RT: add 172.24.0.0/16 via 0.0.0.0, connected metric [0/0]
4w1d: is_up: 1 state: 4 sub state: 1 line: 0

RouterA(config-if)#exit
RouterA(config)#router igrp 101
RouterA(config-router)#network 172.24.0.0
RouterA(config-router)#exit
RouterA(config)#exit
RouterA#sh ip route
Codes: C - connected, S - static, I - IGRP, R - RIP, M - mobile, B
       - BGP
       D - EIGRP, EX - EIGRP external, O - OSPF, IA - OSPF inter area
       N1 - OSPF NSSA external type 1, N2 - OSPF NSSA external type 2
       E1 - OSPF external type 1, E2 - OSPF external type 2, E - EGP
       i - IS-IS, L1 - IS-IS level-1, L2 - IS-IS level-2, ia - IS-
       IS inter area
       * - candidate default, U - per-user static route, o - ODR
       P - periodic downloaded static route

Gateway of last resort is 194.73.134.1 to network 0.0.0.0

C    194.73.134.0/24 is directly connected, Ethernet0
C    172.19.0.0/16 is directly connected, Serial0
C    172.18.0.0/16 is directly connected, Ethernet0
C    172.20.0.0/16 is directly connected, Serial1
C    172.24.0.0/16 is directly connected, Serial0
C    172.30.0.0/16 is directly connected, Ethernet1
S*   0.0.0.0/0 [1/0] via 194.73.134.1

RouterA#conf t
Enter configuration commands, one per line.  End with CNTL/Z.
RouterA(config)#router igrp 101
RouterA(config-router)#no network 172.24.0.0
RouterA(config-router)#exit
RouterA(config)#int s0
RouterA(config-if)#no ip add 172.24.0.1 255.255.0.0 sec
RouterA(config-if)#
```

```
4w1d: RT: del 172.24.0.0 via 0.0.0.0, connected metric [0/0]
4w1d: RT: delete network route to 172.24.0.0
4w1d: is_up: 1 state: 4 sub state: 1 line: 0


RouterA(config-if)#^Z


RouterA#
4w1d: RT: add 172.24.0.0/16 via 172.19.1.1, igrp metric [100/10576]
4w1d: RT: delete route to 172.24.0.0 via 172.19.1.1, igrp metric
      [100/10576]
4w1d: RT: no routes to 172.24.0.0, entering holddown


RouterA#sh ip route
Codes: C - connected, S - static, I - IGRP, R - RIP, M - mobile, B
       - BGP
       D - EIGRP, EX - EIGRP external, O - OSPF, IA - OSPF inter area
       N1 - OSPF NSSA external type 1, N2 - OSPF NSSA external type 2
       E1 - OSPF external type 1, E2 - OSPF external type 2, E - EGP
       i - IS-IS, L1 - IS-IS level-1, L2 - IS-IS level-2, ia - IS-
       IS inter area
       * - candidate default, U - per-user static route, o - ODR
       P - periodic downloaded static route

Gateway of last resort is 194.73.134.1 to network 0.0.0.0

C    194.73.134.0/24 is directly connected, Ethernet0
C    172.19.0.0/16 is directly connected, Serial0
C    172.18.0.0/16 is directly connected, Ethernet0
C    172.20.0.0/16 is directly connected, Serial1
I    172.24.0.0/16 is possibly down, routing via 172.19.1.1,
     Serial0
C    172.30.0.0/16 is directly connected, Ethernet1
S*   0.0.0.0/0 [1/0] via 194.73.134.1


4w1d: RT: 172.24.0.0 came out of holddown
4w1d: RT: garbage collecting entry for 172.24.0.0


RouterA#sh ip route
Codes: C - connected, S - static, I - IGRP, R - RIP, M - mobile, B
       - BGP
       D - EIGRP, EX - EIGRP external, O - OSPF, IA - OSPF inter area
       N1 - OSPF NSSA external type 1, N2 - OSPF NSSA external type 2
       E1 - OSPF external type 1, E2 - OSPF external type 2, E - EGP
       i - IS-IS, L1 - IS-IS level-1, L2 - IS-IS level-2, ia - IS-
       IS inter area
       * - candidate default, U - per-user static route, o - ODR
       P - periodic downloaded static route

Gateway of last resort is 194.73.134.1 to network 0.0.0.0

C    194.73.134.0/24 is directly connected, Ethernet0
C    172.19.0.0/16 is directly connected, Serial0
C    172.18.0.0/16 is directly connected, Ethernet0
C    172.20.0.0/16 is directly connected, Serial1
C    172.30.0.0/16 is directly connected, Ethernet1
S*   0.0.0.0/0 [1/0] via 194.73.134.1


RouterA#no debug all
All possible debugging has been turned off
```

Router B Listing

```
RouterB#debug ip igrp events
IGRP event debugging is on
RouterB#

4w1d: IGRP: sending update to 255.255.255.255 via Serial0
      (172.19.1.1)
4w1d: IGRP: Update contains 0 interior, 3 system, and 0 exterior
      routes.
4w1d: IGRP: Total routes in update: 3
4w1d: IGRP: sending update to 255.255.255.255 via Serial1
      (172.20.1.1)
4w1d: IGRP: Update contains 0 interior, 3 system, and 0 exterior
      routes.
4w1d: IGRP: Total routes in update: 3
4w1d: IGRP: received update from 194.73.134.24 on Ethernet0
4w1d: IGRP: Update contains 0 interior, 2 system, and 0 exterior
      routes.
4w1d: IGRP: Total routes in update: 2
4w1d: IGRP: received update from invalid source 172.30.0.1 on
      Ethernet0
4w1d: IGRP: received update from 172.19.1.2 on Serial0
4w1d: IGRP: Update contains 0 interior, 3 system, and 0 exterior
      routes.
4w1d: IGRP: Total routes in update: 3
4w1d: IGRP: sending update to 255.255.255.255 via Serial0
      (172.19.1.1)
4w1d: IGRP: Update contains 0 interior, 3 system, and 0 exterior
      routes.
4w1d: IGRP: Total routes in update: 3
4w1d: IGRP: sending update to 255.255.255.255 via Serial1
      (172.20.1.1)
4w1d: IGRP: Update contains 0 interior, 3 system, and 0 exterior
      routes.
4w1d: IGRP: Total routes in update: 3
4w1d: IGRP: received update from 194.73.134.24 on Ethernet0

4w1d: RT: add 172.24.0.0/16 via 194.73.134.24, igrp metric
      [100/8576]

4w1d: IGRP: Update contains 0 interior, 3 system, and 0 exterior
      routes.
4w1d: IGRP: Total routes in update: 3
4w1d: IGRP: edition is now 4
4w1d: IGRP: sending update to 255.255.255.255 via Serial0
      (172.19.1.1)
4w1d: IGRP: Update contains 0 interior, 4 system, and 0 exterior
      routes.
4w1d: IGRP: Total routes in update: 4
4w1d: IGRP: sending update to 255.255.255.255 via Serial1
      (172.20.1.1)
4w1d: IGRP: Update contains 0 interior, 4 system, and 0 exterior
      routes.
4w1d: IGRP: Total routes in update: 4
4w1d: IGRP: received update from invalid source 172.30.0.1 on
      Ethernet0
4w1d: IGRP: received update from 172.19.1.2 on Serial0
```

```
4w1d: IGRP: Update contains 0 interior, 3 system, and 0 exterior
        routes.
4w1d: IGRP: Total routes in update: 3

RouterB#sh ip route
Codes: C - connected, S - static, I - IGRP, R - RIP, M - mobile, B
    - BGP
    D - EIGRP, EX - EIGRP external, O - OSPF, IA - OSPF inter area
    N1 - OSPF NSSA external type 1, N2 - OSPF NSSA external type 2
    E1 - OSPF external type 1, E2 - OSPF external type 2, E - EGP
    i - IS-IS, L1 - IS-IS level-1, L2 - IS-IS level-2, ia - IS-
    IS inter area
    * - candidate default, U - per-user static route, o - ODR
    P - periodic downloaded static route

Gateway of last resort is 172.19.1.2 to network 0.0.0.0

C    194.73.134.0/24 is directly connected, Ethernet0
C    172.19.0.0/16 is directly connected, Serial0
C    172.18.0.0/16 is directly connected, Ethernet0
C    172.20.0.0/16 is directly connected, Serial1
I    172.24.0.0/16 [100/8576] via 194.73.134.24, 00:00:52,
     Ethernet0
I    172.30.0.0/16 [100/1200] via 194.73.134.24, 00:00:52,
     Ethernet0
R*   0.0.0.0/0 [120/1] via 172.19.1.2, 1d06h, Serial0
               [120/1] via 172.20.1.2, 1d06h, Serial1
C    212.0.0.0/8 is directly connected, Loopback0
RouterB#

4w1d: IGRP: sending update to 255.255.255.255 via Serial0
        (172.19.1.1)
4w1d: IGRP: Update contains 0 interior, 4 system, and 0 exterior
        routes.
4w1d: IGRP: Total routes in update: 4
4w1d: IGRP: sending update to 255.255.255.255 via Serial1
        (172.20.1.1)
4w1d: IGRP: Update contains 0 interior, 4 system, and 0 exterior
        routes.
4w1d: IGRP: Total routes in update: 4
4w1d: IGRP: received update from 194.73.134.24 on Ethernet0

4w1d: RT: delete route to 172.24.0.0 via 194.73.134.24, igrp metric
        [100/8576]
4w1d: RT: no routes to 172.24.0.0, entering holddown

4w1d: IGRP: Update contains 0 interior, 3 system, and 0 exterior
        routes.
4w1d: IGRP: Total routes in update: 3
4w1d: IGRP: edition is now 5
4w1d: IGRP: sending update to 255.255.255.255 via Serial0
        (172.19.1.1)
4w1d: IGRP: Update contains 0 interior, 4 system, and 0 exterior
        routes.
4w1d: IGRP: Total routes in update: 4
4w1d: IGRP: sending update to 255.255.255.255 via Serial1
        (172.20.1.1)
4w1d: IGRP: Update contains 0 interior, 4 system, and 0 exterior
        routes.
```

```
4w1d: IGRP: Total routes in update: 4
4w1d: IGRP: received update from invalid source 172.30.0.1 on
            Ethernet0
4w1d: IGRP: received update from 172.19.1.2 on Serial0
4w1d: IGRP: Update contains 0 interior, 3 system, and 0 exterior
            routes.
4w1d: IGRP: Total routes in update: 3
4w1d: IGRP: received update from 194.73.134.24 on Ethernet0
4w1d: IGRP: Update contains 0 interior, 3 system, and 0 exterior
            routes.
4w1d: IGRP: Total routes in update: 3
4w1d: IGRP: received update from invalid source 172.30.0.1 on
            Ethernet0
4w1d: IGRP: received update from 172.19.1.2 on Serial0
4w1d: IGRP: Update contains 0 interior, 4 system, and 0 exterior
            routes.
4w1d: IGRP: Total routes in update: 4

RouterB#sh ip route
Codes: C - connected, S - static, I - IGRP, R - RIP, M - mobile, B
       - BGP
       D - EIGRP, EX - EIGRP external, O - OSPF, IA - OSPF inter area
       N1 - OSPF NSSA external type 1, N2 - OSPF NSSA external type 2
       E1 - OSPF external type 1, E2 - OSPF external type 2, E - EGP
       i - IS-IS, L1 - IS-IS level-1, L2 - IS-IS level-2, ia - IS-
       IS inter area
       * - candidate default, U - per-user static route, o - ODR
       P - periodic downloaded static route

Gateway of last resort is 172.19.1.2 to network 0.0.0.0

C    194.73.134.0/24 is directly connected, Ethernet0
C    172.19.0.0/16 is directly connected, Serial0
C    172.18.0.0/16 is directly connected, Ethernet0
C    172.20.0.0/16 is directly connected, Serial1
I    172.24.0.0/16 is possibly down, routing via 194.73.134.24,
     Ethernet0
I    172.30.0.0/16 [100/1200] via 194.73.134.24, 00:00:11,
     Ethernet0
R*   0.0.0.0/0 [120/1] via 172.19.1.2, 1d06h, Serial0
               [120/1] via 172.20.1.2, 1d06h, Serial1
C    212.0.0.0/8 is directly connected, Loopback0
RouterB#

4w1d: IGRP: received update from 194.73.134.24 on Ethernet0

4w1d: RT: 172.24.0.0 came out of holddown

4w1d: IGRP: Update contains 0 interior, 3 system, and 0 exterior
            routes.
4w1d: IGRP: Total routes in update: 3
4w1d: IGRP: received update from invalid source 172.30.0.1 on
            Ethernet0
4w1d: IGRP: received update from 172.19.1.2 on Serial0
4w1d: IGRP: Update contains 0 interior, 4 system, and 0 exterior
            routes.
4w1d: IGRP: Total routes in update: 4
4w1d: IGRP: sending update to 255.255.255.255 via Serial0
            (172.19.1.1)
```

```
4w1d: IGRP: Update contains 0 interior, 4 system, and 0 exterior
             routes.
4w1d: IGRP: Total routes in update: 4
4w1d: IGRP: sending update to 255.255.255.255 via Serial1
             (172.20.1.1)
4w1d: IGRP: Update contains 0 interior, 4 system, and 0 exterior
             routes.
4w1d: IGRP: Total routes in update: 4
4w1d: IGRP: received update from 194.73.134.24 on Ethernet0
4w1d: IGRP: Update contains 0 interior, 3 system, and 0 exterior
             routes.
4w1d: IGRP: Total routes in update: 3
4w1d: IGRP: received update from invalid source 172.30.0.1 on
             Ethernet0
4w1d: IGRP: received update from 172.19.1.2 on Serial0
4w1d: IGRP: Update contains 0 interior, 4 system, and 0 exterior
             routes.
4w1d: IGRP: Total routes in update: 4

4w1d: RT: garbage collecting entry for 172.24.0.0

RouterB#sh ip route
Codes: C - connected, S - static, I - IGRP, R - RIP, M - mobile, B
       - BGP
       D - EIGRP, EX - EIGRP external, O - OSPF, IA - OSPF inter area
       N1 - OSPF NSSA external type 1, N2 - OSPF NSSA external type 2
       E1 - OSPF external type 1, E2 - OSPF external type 2, E - EGP
       i - IS-IS, L1 - IS-IS level-1, L2 - IS-IS level-2, ia - IS-
       IS inter area
       * - candidate default, U - per-user static route, o - ODR
       P - periodic downloaded static route

Gateway of last resort is 172.19.1.2 to network 0.0.0.0

C    194.73.134.0/24 is directly connected, Ethernet0
C    172.19.0.0/16 is directly connected, Serial0
C    172.18.0.0/16 is directly connected, Ethernet0
C    172.20.0.0/16 is directly connected, Serial1
I    172.30.0.0/16 [100/1200] via 194.73.134.24, 00:01:20,
     Ethernet0
R*   0.0.0.0/0 [120/1] via 172.19.1.2, 1d06h, Serial0
                [120/1] via 172.20.1.2, 1d06h, Serial1
C    212.0.0.0/8 is directly connected, Loopback0
RouterB#
Router2501#no debug all
All possible debugging has been turned off
```

In the above listing, we add a new route to the IGRP routing process
between two routers and track the events with the debug ip igrp events
command. We start by adding a secondary IP address to Serial0 on Router
A. You can see this addition to the internal routing table on Router A. We
then add this new network to the IGRP routing process with the command
network 172.24.0.0. We can see the periodic IGRP updates occurring on
Router B. Unlike RIP, the debug ip igrp events command does not show the
individual route information in the debug output. So, we leave the process

running for a few seconds and then enter a *show ip route* on Router B. You can see that the network 172.24.0.0 is connected via 194.73.134.24, Ethernet0. This is also indicated as an IGRP route. This proves that Router B has received the routing update from Router A.

We then remove the route from the IGRP routing process on Router A by entering no network 172.24.0.0. This forces Router A to put the route into hold-down. This propagates to Router B and a show ip route command on both routers indicates that this route is possibly down. Eventually, the route comes out of hold-down on Router A and the garbage collection removes the route. A show ip route command on both routers displays that the route is absent from the routing table. This command provides a wealth of information for debugging IGRP problems. From the output, however, you can see that this level of debugging in a large network can be time-consuming and generate superfluous amounts of debug listings.

Link State Protocols

We have just looked at the distance vector routing process and the troubleshooting tools available. We are now going to look at the other category of routing protocols, link state routing protocols. Unlike distance vector routing protocols, link state routing protocols know the complete topology of the network they operate in or the complete topology of the area they are members of, depending upon the configuration. Link state protocols include the OSPF routing protocol and the *intermediate system-to-intermediate system* (IS-IS) routing protocol. Link state protocols were designed to improve on the limitations of distance vector routing protocols to provide more scaleable solutions as networks grow. Link state routing algorithms maintain a complex database of topology information that includes full details about all distant routers and how they interconnect. This differs from distance vector protocols that only store remote network information against a simple metric.

One major feature of link state routing protocols is that they are classless. This enables discontiguous subnets and VLSMs to be used to improve router performance by reducing the number of advertised routes that are propagated into the network as routing updates or *link state packets* (LSPs).

Network Discovery and Topology Changes

Link state dynamic routing protocols operate by sending out LSPs. These packets are sent upon the introduction of a new router and also at frequent intervals or when a change occurs. LSPs are sent as multicasts. All link state routers within the network or area receive these packets that are used to create a common topology database that is held on every router within the network or area. The LSPs identify the direct neighboring routers as well as the distant routers. The SPF algorithm uses this information to work out the best route to these distant networks and maintains this information in the internal routing table. Once this information is in the routing table, the router uses this information to route packets.

Distance vector routing protocols send out regular routing table updates normally every 30 seconds. This can also be forced as a triggered update if a network topology change occurs. Link state routing protocols work together and the first router that identifies a topology change would inform all the other routers participating in link state routing of the topology change. This is done by sending a multicast packet or a unicast packet to a designated router that is configured to inform all other participating routers of the update. All participating routers receive this information and again use the SPF algorithm to recalculate the route to the remote network.

Problems and Limitations of Link State Routing

Link state routing, although appearing to be extremely advantageous, still has inherent problems that must be considered. Link state protocols are more resource-hungry than distance vector routing protocols. Therefore, routers participating in link state routing require more memory and more processing power in order to not burden the routers' performance. A great deal of information is held about remote networks by link state protocols, and as the size of the network grows, so does the performance implications of the SPF algorithm in making routing decisions.

The initial link state operation of adding a new router can cause *link state flooding*. This is when all participating routers send LSPs to each other advertising their existence and their connected networks. This floods the network with LSPs and reduces the overall network bandwidth for other network hosts. This initial flooding also takes a toll on router performance while the CPU-intensive SPF algorithm is calculating.

Open Shortest Path First (OSPF)

OSPF is a link state dynamic routing protocol designed for medium to large internetworks. OSPF is an IGP and therefore it performs routing within a single AS. Along with IGRP, OSPF was created in the mid-1980s to provide a more robust intra-AS routing protocol to replace RIP. OSPF is based on the SPF algorithm that was developed in 1978 for the ARPANET as well as work by Dr. Radia Perlman and the early versions of OSI's IS-IS routing protocol. This algorithm is also referred to as the Dijkstra algorithm.

OSPF is formally defined in RFC 1247 and, as the name suggests, is an open specification that is in the public domain. This is unlike IGRP and EIGRP that are both the propriety of Cisco Systems. OSPF is a link state dynamic routing protocol that operates by the sending and receiving of *link state advertisements* (LSAs) to all of the other routers that are located in the same hierarchical area. The LSAs include information about the connected interfaces and metrics used, and these LSAs are used by the SPF algorithm on each router to calculate the shortest path to each network.

OSPF operates in a hierarchy within the AS. Although OSPF is classed as an intra-AS or interior gateway protocol, it can receive and send routes to other autonomous systems. An AS can be subdivided into a number of OSPF areas. These areas are hierarchical groupings of routers that are used to break down and simplify routing updates for large internetworks. Interfaces on routers can only be a member of one area, although a router with multiple interfaces can belong to multiple areas.

Each router within an area builds up a topological view of the entire area, which is a great advantage of this method. This information is gathered from LSAs that are sent to the area multicast address. All routers in the area listen for and receive these multicast packets. The LSA is taken and the SPF algorithm works out the shortest route to the remote network based upon all of the other SPF computations. This contrasts with distance vector routing protocols such as RIP where each router only can see as far as its direct neighbors and the topological view is all secondhand information.

On a Cisco router, simply adding the following command in global configuration mode enables OSPF:

```
Router(config)#router ospf 1
```

This command enables OSPF on the router. The value 1 represents the OSPF process ID. This is an internally used number to identify when you have multiple OSPF processes running on a single router. This process ID does not need to match other routers in the same area, but multiple instances of OSPF on the same router do require different process IDs.

Networks are advertised and participate in OSPF routing by entering the following command:

```
Router(config-router)network A.B.C.D E.F.G.H area 0
```

where A.B.C.D is the network address of the network to be advertised via OSPF. E.F.G.H. is the wildcard mask and this operates as in the access list command. The area 0 command instructs the router that the interface pertaining to this network address is part of the OSPF area 0.

The following commands

```
Router(config-router)network 172.18.0.0 0.0.255.255 area 0
Router(config-router)network 10.0.0.0 0.255.255.255 area 0
```

would place networks 172.18.x.x and 10.x.x.x into OSPF area 0.

Other OSPF configuration commands include the following:

- area: OSPF area parameters.
- auto-cost: Calculates OSPF interface cost according to bandwidth.
- ignore: Does not complain about a specific event.
- log-adjacency-changes: Logs changes in the adjacency state.
- summary-address: Configures IP address summaries.

For more information on configuring OSPF, refer to the ICRC or ACRC course notes. Also see the configuration commands in the RIP section.

Troubleshooting OSPF

If routing inaccuracies occur, it is advisable to check the router for any misconfigured distribute lists. The following commands are specific to OSPF:

■ show ip ospf interface: Displays OSPF routing protocol information for all OSPF-configured interfaces.

■ show ip ospf neighbor: Displays a list of adjacent OSPF neighbors.

■ debug ip ospf events: Displays debug information about OSPF updates and routing table entries.

show ip protocols

As stated earlier, the *show ip protocols* command displays all enabled routing protocols and the associated values relating to the routing protocol. Here is an example of this command in use:

```
Router#sh ip prot
Routing Protocol is "rip"
  Sending updates every 30 seconds, next due in 21 seconds
  Invalid after 180 seconds, hold down 180, flushed after 240
  Outgoing update filter list for all interfaces is
  Incoming update filter list for all interfaces is
  Redistributing: rip
  Default version control: send version 2, receive version 2
    Interface    Send   Recv  Triggered RIP  Key-chain
    Ethernet0    2      2
    Ethernet1    2      2
    Serial0      2      2
    Serial1      2      2
  Routing for Networks:
    172.18.0.0
    172.19.0.0
    172.20.0.0
    172.30.0.0
    194.73.134.0
  Routing Information Sources:
    Gateway         Distance   Last Update
    194.73.134.23   120        00:00:08
    194.73.134.22   120        23:57:45
    172.18.0.11     120        00:00:08
    Gateway         Distance   Last Update
    172.20.1.1      120        00:00:09
    172.19.1.1      120        00:00:09
  Distance: (default is 120)

Routing Protocol is "igrp 101"
  Sending updates every 90 seconds, next due in 14 seconds
  Invalid after 270 seconds, hold down 280, flushed after 630
  Outgoing update filter list for all interfaces is
  Incoming update filter list for all interfaces is
  Default networks flagged in outgoing updates
  Default networks accepted from incoming updates
  IGRP metric weight K1=1, K2=0, K3=1, K4=0, K5=0
  IGRP maximum hopcount 100
  IGRP maximum metric variance 1
  Redistributing: igrp 101
```

```
    Routing for Networks:
      172.18.0.0
      172.19.0.0
      172.30.0.0
      194.73.134.0
    Routing Information Sources:
      Gateway          Distance   Last Update
      Gateway          Distance   Last Update
      194.73.134.23    100        12:15:40
      172.19.1.1       100        00:00:58
    Distance: (default is 100)

Routing Protocol is "ospf 1"
  Sending updates every 0 seconds
  Invalid after 0 seconds, hold down 0, flushed after 0
  Outgoing update filter list for all interfaces is
  Incoming update filter list for all interfaces is
  Redistributing: ospf 1
  Routing for Networks:
    172.18.0.0
    172.19.0.0
    172.20.0.0
    172.30.0.0
    194.73.134.0
  Routing Information Sources:
    Gateway          Distance   Last Update
    194.73.134.23    110        00:01:00
  Distance: (default is 110)
Router#
```

From this listing, we can see that RIP, IGRP, and OSPF are configured on this router. The OSPF is running at process ID number 1. Note that the updates are sent every zero seconds because OSPF is a link state routing protocol that relies upon hello packets and is event-driven. We can see that network 172.18.0.0, 172.19.0.0, 172.20.0.0, 172.30.0.0, and 194.73.134.0 are advertised over OSPF.

show ip route

The following example shows the *show ip route* command in use:

```
Router#sh ip route
Codes: C - connected, S - static, I - IGRP, R - RIP, M - mobile, B
       - BGP
       D - EIGRP, EX - EIGRP external, O - OSPF, IA - OSPF inter area
       N1 - OSPF NSSA external type 1, N2 - OSPF NSSA external type 2
       E1 - OSPF external type 1, E2 - OSPF external type 2, E - EGP
       i - IS-IS, L1 - IS-IS level-1, L2 - IS-IS level-2, ia - IS-IS
       inter area
         * - candidate default, U - per-user static route, o - ODR
         P - periodic downloaded static route

Gateway of last resort is 194.73.134.1 to network 0.0.0.0
```

```
C    194.73.134.0/24 is directly connected, Ethernet0
C    172.19.0.0/16 is directly connected, Serial0
C    172.18.0.0/16 is directly connected, Ethernet0
C    172.20.0.0/16 is directly connected, Serial1
C    172.30.0.0/16 is directly connected, Ethernet1
     212.0.0.0/32 is subnetted, 1 subnets
O       212.0.0.1 [110/65] via 172.20.1.1, 00:06:09, Serial1
                   [110/65] via 172.19.1.1, 00:06:09, Serial0
S*   0.0.0.0/0 [1/0] via 194.73.134.1
Router#
```

The first part of this listing indicates all the codes that are used to identify the routing protocols in the actual routing table. You can see from the
routing table that we have five connected networks over multiple interfaces.
The connected interface is identified by a C. The static route entry is 0.0.0.0
or the default route, which is also identified by an asterisk next to the S.
There is one route to 212.0.0.1 that has been received over OSPF. Notice the
values in the brackets after the route, [110/65]. The first part, 110, refers to
the administrative distance of OSPF. The second part, 65, refers to the metric of the route that has been calculated by the OSPF Dijkstra algorithm.

show ip ospf interface

The *show ip ospf interface* command displays OSPF routing protocol information for all OSPF-configured interfaces:

```
Router#sh ip ospf interface

Ethernet0 is up, line protocol is up
  Internet Address 194.73.134.24/24, Area 1
  Process ID 1, Router ID 194.73.134.24, Network Type BROADCAST,
  Cost: 10
  Transmit Delay is 1 sec, State DR, Priority 1
  Designated Router (ID) 194.73.134.24, Interface address
  194.73.134.24
  No backup designated router on this network
  Timer intervals configured, Hello 10, Dead 40, Wait 40,
  Retransmit 5
    Hello due in 00:00:00
  Index 4/4, flood queue length 0
  Next 0x0(0)/0x0(0)
  Last flood scan length is 0, maximum is 0
  Last flood scan time is 0 msec, maximum is 0 msec
  Neighbor Count is 0, Adjacent neighbor count is 0
  Suppress hello for 0 neighbor(s)
Ethernet1 is up, line protocol is up
  Internet Address 172.30.0.1/16, Area 1
  Process ID 1, Router ID 194.73.134.24, Network Type BROADCAST,
  Cost: 10
  Transmit Delay is 1 sec, State DR, Priority 1
  Designated Router (ID) 194.73.134.24, Interface address
  172.30.0.1
```

```
       No backup designated router on this network
       Timer intervals configured, Hello 10, Dead 40, Wait 40,
       Retransmit 5
         Hello due in 00:00:03
       Index 3/3, flood queue length 0
       Next 0x0(0)/0x0(0)
       Last flood scan length is 0, maximum is 0
       Last flood scan time is 0 msec, maximum is 0 msec
       Neighbor Count is 0, Adjacent neighbor count is 0
       Suppress hello for 0 neighbor(s)

   Loopback0 is up, line protocol is up
       Internet Address 201.0.0.1/24, Area 1
       Process ID 1, Router ID 194.73.134.24, Network Type LOOPBACK,
       Cost: 1
       Loopback interface is treated as a stub Host

   Loopback1 is up, line protocol is up
       Internet Address 202.0.0.1/24, Area 1
       Process ID 1, Router ID 194.73.134.24, Network Type LOOPBACK,
       Cost: 1
       Loopback interface is treated as a stub Host

   Serial0 is up, line protocol is up
       Internet Address 172.19.1.2/16, Area 1
       Process ID 1, Router ID 194.73.134.24, Network Type
       POINT_TO_POINT, Cost: 64
       Transmit Delay is 1 sec, State POINT_TO_POINT,
       Timer intervals configured, Hello 10, Dead 40, Wait 40,
       Retransmit 5
         Hello due in 00:00:00
       Index 1/1, flood queue length 0
       Next 0x0(0)/0x0(0)
       Last flood scan length is 1, maximum is 1
       Last flood scan time is 0 msec, maximum is 0 msec
       Neighbor Count is 1, Adjacent neighbor count is 1
         Adjacent with neighbor 194.73.134.23
       Suppress hello for 0 neighbor(s)

   Serial1 is up, line protocol is up
       Internet Address 172.20.1.2/16, Area 1
       Process ID 1, Router ID 194.73.134.24, Network Type
       POINT_TO_POINT, Cost: 64
       Transmit Delay is 1 sec, State POINT_TO_POINT,
       Timer intervals configured, Hello 10, Dead 40, Wait 40,
       Retransmit 5
         Hello due in 00:00:05
       Index 2/2, flood queue length 0
       Next 0x0(0)/0x0(0)
       Last flood scan length is 1, maximum is 1
       Last flood scan time is 0 msec, maximum is 0 msec
       Neighbor Count is 1, Adjacent neighbor count is 1
         Adjacent with neighbor 194.73.134.23
       Suppress hello for 0 neighbor(s)
   Router#
```

This command is used to display explicit routing variables on all interfaces that have IP addresses within the network ranges specified by the OSPF routing protocol. The show ip ospf interface command is important in

OSPF troubleshooting, which is a complex procedure. The identification of the *designated routers* (DR) and *backup designated routers* (BDR) is also important. This command, as you can see, identifies the DR as 194.73.134.24 and shows that no BDR is available on this network. Other useful information, such as the area and neighbor count, is also shown.

Entering the interface name and number after the command, for example, can further restrict this command:

```
Router#sh ip ospf int Ethernet 0
```

and would display the OSPF information only for interface Ethernet 0.

show ip ospf neighbor

The *show ip ospf neighbor* command displays information about the OSPF-adjacent routers. OSPF establishes adjacencies with neighboring routers. This facilitates the sending and receiving of LSPs that make OSPF converge. Here is an example of the command at work:

```
Router#sh ip ospf neigh

Neighbor ID   Pri   State     Dead Time   Address     Interface
10.1.1.1      1     FULL/  -  00:00:34    172.19.1.1  Serial0
10.1.1.1      1     FULL/  -  00:00:34    172.20.1.1  Serial1
```

This command displays the neighbor information on a per-interface basis. We can see from this listing that the only OSPF neighbor has an ID of 10.1.1.1, although it is known about over two interfaces, 172.19.1.1 and 172.20.1.1. This command can also be expanded to show information regarding a specific neighbor by the interface or neighbor ID. The command *show ip ospf neighbor 10.1.1.1* displays the following output:

```
Router#sh ip ospf neigh 10.1.1.1
  Neighbor 10.1.1.1, interface address 172.19.1.1
    In the area 1 via interface Serial0
    Neighbor priority is 1, State is FULL, 6 state changes
    DR is 0.0.0.0 BDR is 0.0.0.0
    Options 2
    Dead timer due in 00:00:30
    Index 1/1, retransmission queue length 0, number of
    retransmission 2
    First 0x0(0)/0x0(0) Next 0x0(0)/0x0(0)
    Last retransmission scan length is 1, maximum is 1
    Last retransmission scan time is 0 msec, maximum is 0 msec
  Neighbor 10.1.1.1, interface address 172.20.1.1
    In the area 1 via interface Serial1
    Neighbor priority is 1, State is FULL, 6 state changes
```

```
DR is 0.0.0.0 BDR is 0.0.0.0
Options 2
Dead timer due in 00:00:30
Index 2/2, retransmission queue length 0, number of
retransmission 1
First 0x0(0)/0x0(0) Next 0x0(0)/0x0(0)
Last retransmission scan length is 1, maximum is 1
Last retransmission scan time is 0 msec, maximum is 0 msec
Router#
```

This command is useful for checking the status of neighboring OSPF routers. By design, OSPF relies upon adjacencies for its correct operation. If a routing update is not propagating from one side of the network to another, it could well be an adjacency problem caused by a media error or something as simple as an access list.

debug ip routing

As discussed earlier, the *debug ip routing* command displays routing information events for the IP routing protocols. To show this in operation, we are going to examine two router listings that show that a new network has been added to OSPF and then removed. This is an OSPF-specific event.

Router A Listing

```
RouterA#debug ip routing
IP routing debugging is on
RouterA#conf t
Enter configuration commands, one per line.  End with CNTL/Z.
RouterA(config)#int lo 2

4w1d: %LINK-3-UPDOWN: Interface Loopback2, changed state to up
4w1d: %LINEPROTO-5-UPDOWN: Line protocol on Interface Loopback2,
                          changed state to up.0.0.1

RouterA(config-if)#ip address 203.0.0.1 255.255.255.0
RouterA(config-if)#

4w1d: is_up: 1 state: 4 sub state: 1 line: 0
4w1d: RT: add 203.0.0.0/24 via 0.0.0.0, connected metric [0/0]
4w1d: RT: interface Loopback2 added to routing table

RouterA(config-if)#exit
RouterA(config)#router ospf 1
RouterA(config-router)#network 203.0.0.0 0.0.0.255 area 1
RouterA(config-router)#exit
RouterA(config)#router ospf 1
RouterA(config-router)#no network 203.0.0.0 0.0.0.255 area 1
RouterA(config-router)#exit
```

```
RouterA(config)#exit
RouterA#no debug all
All possible debugging has been turned off
```

Router B Listing

```
RouterB#debug ip routing
IP routing debugging is on

RouterB#sh ip route
Codes: C - connected, S - static, I - IGRP, R - RIP, M - mobile, B
       - BGP
       D - EIGRP, EX - EIGRP external, O - OSPF, IA - OSPF inter area
       N1 - OSPF NSSA external type 1, N2 - OSPF NSSA external type 2
       E1 - OSPF external type 1, E2 - OSPF external type 2, E - EGP
       i - IS-IS, L1 - IS-IS level-1, L2 - IS-IS level-2, ia - IS-
       IS inter area
       * - candidate default, U - per-user static route, o - ODR
       P - periodic downloaded static route

Gateway of last resort is 172.19.1.2 to network 0.0.0.0

C    194.73.134.0/24 is directly connected, Ethernet0
     201.0.0.0/32 is subnetted, 1 subnets
O       201.0.0.1 [110/65] via 172.20.1.2, 00:00:20, Serial1
                  [110/65] via 172.19.1.2, 00:00:20, Serial0
     202.0.0.0/32 is subnetted, 1 subnets
O       202.0.0.1 [110/65] via 172.20.1.2, 00:00:20, Serial1
                  [110/65] via 172.19.1.2, 00:00:20, Serial0
C    172.19.0.0/16 is directly connected, Serial0
C    172.18.0.0/16 is directly connected, Ethernet0
C    172.20.0.0/16 is directly connected, Serial1
I    172.30.0.0/16 [100/1200] via 194.73.134.24, 00:00:21,
     Ethernet0
C    212.0.0.0/24 is directly connected, Loopback0
R*   0.0.0.0/0 [120/1] via 172.19.1.2, 1d08h, Serial0
               [120/1] via 172.20.1.2, 1d08h, Serial1

RouterB#
RouterB#

4w1d: RT: add 203.0.0.1/32 via 172.20.1.2, ospf metric [110/65]
4w1d: RT: add 203.0.0.1/32 via 172.19.1.2, ospf metric [110/65]

RouterB#sh ip route
Codes: C - connected, S - static, I - IGRP, R - RIP, M - mobile, B
       - BGP
       D - EIGRP, EX - EIGRP external, O - OSPF, IA - OSPF inter area
       N1 - OSPF NSSA external type 1, N2 - OSPF NSSA external type 2
       E1 - OSPF external type 1, E2 - OSPF external type 2, E - EGP
       i - IS-IS, L1 - IS-IS level-1, L2 - IS-IS level-2, ia - IS-
       IS inter area
       * - candidate default, U - per-user static route, o - ODR
       P - periodic downloaded static route

Gateway of last resort is 172.19.1.2 to network 0.0.0.0

C    194.73.134.0/24 is directly connected, Ethernet0
     201.0.0.0/32 is subnetted, 1 subnets
```

```
O        201.0.0.1 [110/65] via 172.20.1.2, 00:00:01, Serial1
                   [110/65] via 172.19.1.2, 00:00:01, Serial0
         202.0.0.0/32 is subnetted, 1 subnets
O        202.0.0.1 [110/65] via 172.20.1.2, 00:00:01, Serial1
                   [110/65] via 172.19.1.2, 00:00:01, Serial0
C     172.19.0.0/16 is directly connected, Serial0
C     172.18.0.0/16 is directly connected, Ethernet0
C     172.20.0.0/16 is directly connected, Serial1
I     172.30.0.0/16 [100/1200] via 194.73.134.24, 00:00:45,
      Ethernet0
         203.0.0.0/32 is subnetted, 1 subnets
O        203.0.0.1 [110/65] via 172.20.1.2, 00:00:01, Serial1
                   [110/65] via 172.19.1.2, 00:00:01, Serial0
C     212.0.0.0/24 is directly connected, Loopback0
R*    0.0.0.0/0 [120/1] via 172.19.1.2, 1d08h, Serial0
                [120/1] via 172.20.1.2, 1d08h, Serial1

RouterB#
RouterB#

4w1d: RT: del 203.0.0.1/32 via 172.20.1.2, ospf metric [110/65]
4w1d: RT: del 203.0.0.1/32 via 172.19.1.2, ospf metric [110/65]
4w1d: RT: delete subnet route to 203.0.0.1/32
4w1d: RT: delete network route to 203.0.0.0

RouterB#sh ip route
Codes: C - connected, S - static, I - IGRP, R - RIP, M - mobile, B
       - BGP
       D - EIGRP, EX - EIGRP external, O - OSPF, IA - OSPF inter area
       N1 - OSPF NSSA external type 1, N2 - OSPF NSSA external type 2
       E1 - OSPF external type 1, E2 - OSPF external type 2, E - EGP
       i - IS-IS, L1 - IS-IS level-1, L2 - IS-IS level-2, ia - IS-
       IS inter area
       * - candidate default, U - per-user static route, o - ODR
       P - periodic downloaded static route

Gateway of last resort is 172.19.1.2 to network 0.0.0.0

C     194.73.134.0/24 is directly connected, Ethernet0
      201.0.0.0/32 is subnetted, 1 subnets
O        201.0.0.1 [110/65] via 172.20.1.2, 00:00:14, Serial1
                   [110/65] via 172.19.1.2, 00:00:14, Serial0
      202.0.0.0/32 is subnetted, 1 subnets
O        202.0.0.1 [110/65] via 172.20.1.2, 00:00:14, Serial1
                   [110/65] via 172.19.1.2, 00:00:14, Serial0
C     172.19.0.0/16 is directly connected, Serial0
C     172.18.0.0/16 is directly connected, Ethernet0
C     172.20.0.0/16 is directly connected, Serial1
I     172.30.0.0/16 [100/1200] via 194.73.134.24, 00:00:15,
      Ethernet0
C     212.0.0.0/24 is directly connected, Loopback0
R*    0.0.0.0/0 [120/1] via 172.19.1.2, 1d08h, Serial0
                [120/1] via 172.20.1.2, 1d08h, Serial1
RouterB#no debug all
All possible debugging has been turned off
```

What we achieve here is the successful entry and removal of an OSPF route into the routing table on Router B. We start by adding a new loopback interface to Router A and giving it the IP address of 203.0.0.1/24. Once the interface is configured, we add this network to the OSPF routing process by entering *network 203.0.0.0 0.0.0.255 area 1* in the OSPF router configuration mode.

We then do a show ip route on Router B and we can see that the network address is available in Router B's routing table as an OSPF route. This confirms that Router B has received the OSPF update. Once the route is established on Router B, we then remove the network from the OSPF process on Router A. As soon as this is done, we can see that Router B receives two RT: del instructions as well as an RT: delete subnet and an RT: delete network. A show ip route after this update shows the immediate release of the 203.0.0.0 network from the internal routing table on Router B. It is interesting to note that this route was immediately removed from Router B's routing table. We covered IGRP and RIP earlier in this chapter and both of these routing protocols place the route into a hold-down.

debug ip ospf events

The *debug ip ospf events* command displays routing information events for the OSPF routing protocol. To show this in operation, we are going to examine two router listings that show a new network was added and removed from OSPF.

Router A Listing

```
RouterA#conf t
Enter configuration commands, one per line.  End with CNTL/Z.
RouterA(config)#int lo 2
RouterA(config-if)#ip address 203.0.0.1 255.255.255.0
RouterA(config-if)#exit
RouterA(config)#exit

RouterA#sh ip route
Codes: C - connected, S - static, I - IGRP, R - RIP, M - mobile, B
       - BGP
       D - EIGRP, EX - EIGRP external, O - OSPF, IA - OSPF inter area
       N1 - OSPF NSSA external type 1, N2 - OSPF NSSA external type 2
       E1 - OSPF external type 1, E2 - OSPF external type 2, E - EGP
       i - IS-IS, L1 - IS-IS level-1, L2 - IS-IS level-2, ia - IS-
       IS inter area
       * - candidate default, U - per-user static route, o - ODR
       P - periodic downloaded static route

Gateway of last resort is 194.73.134.1 to network 0.0.0.0

C    194.73.134.0/24 is directly connected, Ethernet0
C    201.0.0.0/24 is directly connected, Loopback0
C    202.0.0.0/24 is directly connected, Loopback1
C    172.19.0.0/16 is directly connected, Serial0
C    172.18.0.0/16 is directly connected, Ethernet0
C    172.20.0.0/16 is directly connected, Serial1
```

```
C    172.30.0.0/16 is directly connected, Ethernet1
C    203.0.0.0/24 is directly connected, Loopback2
     212.0.0.0/32 is subnetted, 1 subnets
O       212.0.0.1 [110/65] via 172.20.1.1, 00:32:07, Serial1
                   [110/65] via 172.19.1.1, 00:32:07, Serial0
S*   0.0.0.0/0 [1/0] via 194.73.134.1

RouterA#conf t
Enter configuration commands, one per line.  End with CNTL/Z.
RouterA(config)#router ospf 1
RouterA(config-router)#network 203.0.0.0 0.0.0.255 area 1
RouterA(config-router)#exit
RouterA(config)#router ospf 1
RouterA(config-router)#no network 203.0.0.0 0.0.0.255 area 1
RouterA(config-router)#exit
RouterA(config)#exit

RouterA#sh ip route
Codes: C - connected, S - static, I - IGRP, R - RIP, M - mobile, B
       - BGP
       D - EIGRP, EX - EIGRP external, O - OSPF, IA - OSPF inter area
       N1 - OSPF NSSA external type 1, N2 - OSPF NSSA external type 2
       E1 - OSPF external type 1, E2 - OSPF external type 2, E - EGP
       i - IS-IS, L1 - IS-IS level-1, L2 - IS-IS level-2, ia - IS-
       IS inter area
       * - candidate default, U - per-user static route, o - ODR
       P - periodic downloaded static route

Gateway of last resort is 194.73.134.1 to network 0.0.0.0

C    194.73.134.0/24 is directly connected, Ethernet0
C    201.0.0.0/24 is directly connected, Loopback0
C    202.0.0.0/24 is directly connected, Loopback1
C    172.19.0.0/16 is directly connected, Serial0
C    172.18.0.0/16 is directly connected, Ethernet0
C    172.20.0.0/16 is directly connected, Serial1
C    172.30.0.0/16 is directly connected, Ethernet1
C    203.0.0.0/24 is directly connected, Loopback2
     212.0.0.0/32 is subnetted, 1 subnets
O       212.0.0.1 [110/65] via 172.20.1.1, 00:00:00, Serial1
                   [110/65] via 172.19.1.1, 00:00:00, Serial0
S*   0.0.0.0/0 [1/0] via 194.73.134.1
RouterA#
```

Router B Listing

```
RouterB#debug ip ospf event
OSPF events debugging is on
RouterB#
4w1d: OSPF: Rcv hello from 194.73.134.24 area 1 from Serial1
             172.20.1.2
4w1d: OSPF: End of hello processing
4w1d: OSPF: Rcv hello from 194.73.134.24 area 1 from Serial0
             172.19.1.2
4w1d: OSPF: End of hello processing

RouterB#sh ip route
Codes: C - connected, S - static, I - IGRP, R - RIP, M - mobile, B
       - BGP
```

```
         D - EIGRP, EX - EIGRP external, O - OSPF, IA - OSPF inter area
         N1 - OSPF NSSA external type 1, N2 - OSPF NSSA external type 2
         E1 - OSPF external type 1, E2 - OSPF external type 2, E - EGP
         i - IS-IS, L1 - IS-IS level-1, L2 - IS-IS level-2, ia - IS-
         IS inter area
         * - candidate default, U - per-user static route, o - ODR
         P - periodic downloaded static route

Gateway of last resort is 172.19.1.2 to network 0.0.0.0

C    194.73.134.0/24 is directly connected, Ethernet0
     201.0.0.0/32 is subnetted, 1 subnets
O       201.0.0.1 [110/65] via 172.20.1.2, 00:32:22, Serial1
                  [110/65] via 172.19.1.2, 00:32:22, Serial0
     202.0.0.0/32 is subnetted, 1 subnets
O       202.0.0.1 [110/65] via 172.20.1.2, 00:32:22, Serial1
                  [110/65] via 172.19.1.2, 00:32:22, Serial0
C    172.19.0.0/16 is directly connected, Serial0
C    172.18.0.0/16 is directly connected, Ethernet0
C    172.20.0.0/16 is directly connected, Serial1
I    172.30.0.0/16 [100/1200] via 194.73.134.24, 00:00:57,
     Ethernet0
C    212.0.0.0/24 is directly connected, Loopback0
R*   0.0.0.0/0 [120/1] via 172.19.1.2, 1d08h, Serial0
               [120/1] via 172.20.1.2, 1d08h, Serial1
RouterB#

4w1d: OSPF: Rcv hello from 194.73.134.24 area 1 from Serial0
             172.19.1.2
4w1d: OSPF: End of hello processing
4w1d: OSPF: Rcv hello from 194.73.134.24 area 1 from Serial1
             172.20.1.2
4w1d: OSPF: End of hello processing

RouterB#sh ip route
Codes: C - connected, S - static, I - IGRP, R - RIP, M - mobile, B
       - BGP
         D - EIGRP, EX - EIGRP external, O - OSPF, IA - OSPF inter area
         N1 - OSPF NSSA external type 1, N2 - OSPF NSSA external type 2
         E1 - OSPF external type 1, E2 - OSPF external type 2, E - EGP
         i - IS-IS, L1 - IS-IS level-1, L2 - IS-IS level-2, ia - IS-
         IS inter area
         * - candidate default, U - per-user static route, o - ODR
         P - periodic downloaded static route

Gateway of last resort is 172.19.1.2 to network 0.0.0.0

C    194.73.134.0/24 is directly connected, Ethernet0
     201.0.0.0/32 is subnetted, 1 subnets
O       201.0.0.1 [110/65] via 172.20.1.2, 00:00:08, Serial1
                  [110/65] via 172.19.1.2, 00:00:08, Serial0
     202.0.0.0/32 is subnetted, 1 subnets
O       202.0.0.1 [110/65] via 172.20.1.2, 00:00:08, Serial1
                  [110/65] via 172.19.1.2, 00:00:08, Serial0
C    172.19.0.0/16 is directly connected, Serial0
C    172.18.0.0/16 is directly connected, Ethernet0
C    172.20.0.0/16 is directly connected, Serial1
I    172.30.0.0/16 [100/1200] via 194.73.134.24, 00:00:24,
     Ethernet0
     203.0.0.0/32 is subnetted, 1 subnets
```

```
O          203.0.0.1 [110/65] via 172.20.1.2, 00:00:08, Serial1
                     [110/65] via 172.19.1.2, 00:00:08, Serial0
C     212.0.0.0/24 is directly connected, Loopback0
R*    0.0.0.0/0 [120/1] via 172.19.1.2, 1d08h, Serial0
                [120/1] via 172.20.1.2, 1d08h, Serial
1
4w1d: OSPF: Rcv hello from 194.73.134.24 area 1 from Serial1
           172.20.1.2
4w1d: OSPF: End of hello processing
4w1d: OSPF: Rcv hello from 194.73.134.24 area 1 from Serial0
           172.19.1.2
4w1d: OSPF: End of hello processing
4w1d: OSPF: Rcv hello from 194.73.134.24 area 1 from Serial1
           172.20.1.2
4w1d: OSPF: End of hello processing
4w1d: OSPF: Rcv hello from 194.73.134.24 area 1 from Serial0
           172.19.1.2
4w1d: OSPF: End of hello processing

RouterB#sh ip route
Codes: C - connected, S - static, I - IGRP, R - RIP, M - mobile, B
       - BGP
       D - EIGRP, EX - EIGRP external, O - OSPF, IA - OSPF inter area
       N1 - OSPF NSSA external type 1, N2 - OSPF NSSA external type 2
       E1 - OSPF external type 1, E2 - OSPF external type 2, E - EGP
       i - IS-IS, L1 - IS-IS level-1, L2 - IS-IS level-2, ia - IS-
       IS inter area
       * - candidate default, U - per-user static route, o - ODR
       P - periodic downloaded static route

Gateway of last resort is 172.19.1.2 to network 0.0.0.0

C     194.73.134.0/24 is directly connected, Ethernet0
      201.0.0.0/32 is subnetted, 1 subnets
O        201.0.0.1 [110/65] via 172.20.1.2, 00:00:13, Serial1
                   [110/65] via 172.19.1.2, 00:00:13, Serial0
      202.0.0.0/32 is subnetted, 1 subnets
O        202.0.0.1 [110/65] via 172.20.1.2, 00:00:13, Serial1
                   [110/65] via 172.19.1.2, 00:00:13, Serial0
C     172.19.0.0/16 is directly connected, Serial0
C     172.18.0.0/16 is directly connected, Ethernet0
C     172.20.0.0/16 is directly connected, Serial1
I     172.30.0.0/16 [100/1200] via 194.73.134.24, 00:00:10,
      Ethernet0
C     212.0.0.0/24 is directly connected, Loopback0
R*    0.0.0.0/0 [120/1] via 172.19.1.2, 1d08h, Serial0
                [120/1] via 172.20.1.2, 1d08h, Serial1

RouterB#no debug all
All possible debugging has been turned off
```

What we achieve here is the successful entry and removal of an OSPF route into the routing table on Router B. We start by adding a new loopback interface to Router A and giving it the IP address of 203.0.0.1/24. Once the interface is configured, we add this network to the OSPF routing process by entering *network 203.0.0.0 0.0.0.255 area 1* in the OSPF router configuration mode.

We then do a show ip route on Router B and we can see that the network address is available in Router B's routing table as an OSPF route. This is identified as the first and only highlighted section. Our next step is to remove the network from the OSPF process on Router A. We do this with the command, *no network 203.0.0.0 0.0.0.255 area 1.* The next show ip route on Router B confirms that the route has been removed from the routing table.

A point to note is that the output from this debug command does not provide as much information for OSPF as it does for RIP and IGRP. With RIP and IGRP, we can see the route entries occurring, whereas with the *debug ip ospf events*, we only can see frequent hello packet communication. This command does have other extensions, as shown here:

```
Router#debug ip ospf ?
  adj              OSPF adjacency events
  database-timer   OSPF database timer
  events           OSPF events
  flood            OSPF flooding
  lsa-generation   OSPF lsa generation
  packet           OSPF packets
  retransmission   OSPF retransmission events
  spf              OSPF spf
  tree             OSPF database tree
Router#
```

Border Gateway Protocol (BGP)

BGP is a link state dynamic routing protocol designed for interdomain routing. BGP is an *exterior gateway protocol* (EGP) and therefore performs routing between AS. BGP, as defined in RFCs 1163 and 1267, is an EGP. It enables you to set up an interdomain routing system that automatically guarantees the loop-free exchange of routing information between autonomous systems. The latest version of BGP is BGP4 (version 4). This was originally specified in RFC 1654 and updated with RFC 1771.

BGP was created to replace the EGP, which was the standard exterior gateway routing protocol for the Internet, but it had quite a few problems. BGP was designed to address these problems and scale to the Internet's growth more efficiently. BGP performs three main types of routing: inter-autonomous system routing, intra-autonomous system routing, and pass-through autonomous system routing. BGP maintains routing tables, transmits and receives routing updates, and makes routing decisions based on routing metrics in a similar way to other routing protocols. The main difference is that BGP is concerned with network reachability over multiple

AS paths. This is a characteristic of all EGPs. The metric used for BGP routing decisions is based on the degree of preference of a particular link. This metric is usually assigned to each link by the network administrator and is based on the number of autonomous systems that the path crosses through—the stability, the delay, the speed, or the cost of the connection.

Interautonomous system routing occurs between routers running BGP that are located in different AS. This method is used to provide peer routers with a complete view of the network topology. The Internet is an example of interautonomous system routing because it is made up of many autonomous systems. These systems are connected together with routers that are running BGP. Multiple paths can exist and BGP automatically configures the best route and prunes any routing loops.

Intra-autonomous system routing occurs between BGP routers that are located within the same AS. This is used by peer routers within the same AS to maintain a consistent view of the system topology. BGP can provide both inter- and intra- autonomous routing.

Pass-through autonomous system routing occurs between BGP routers that exchange information across non-BGP autonomous systems. This is when BGP uses an AS for packet transportation even when the AS is not running BGP. Therefore, BGP interacts with whatever intra-autonomous routing protocol is being used to transfer traffic through that network. However, the border routers to the AS must be running BGP.

BGP maintains routing tables and transmits routing updates that are based on routing metrics in the same way as any other routing protocol. The main function of BGP is to provide network reachability information over multiple autonomous systems. This produces a graph of the autonomous systems from which routing loops can be pruned and with which autonomous system-level policy levels can be enforced.

Troubleshooting BGP

We are now going to briefly look at troubleshooting BGP and the Cisco IOS commands that are available to assist us in BGP problem resolution. BGP troubleshooting is slightly out of the scope of this chapter and further BGP information can be found in the Webliography at the end of the book.

When starting to troubleshoot a BGP-related problem, you should get a summary snapshot of the BGP routing process. You can ensure that all neighbors are established and that all BGP table versions are synchronized for each neighbor. It is also important to ascertain the length of time each BGP session has been established.

The *show ip bgp summary* command can display the following information:

```
Router#show ip bgp summary
BGT table version is 162305, main routing table version 162305
1028 network entries (2502/3897 paths) using 233200 bytes of memory
204 BGP path attribute entries using 82230 bytes of memory
102 BGP route-map cache entries using 2232 bytes of memory
0 BGP filter-list cache entries using 0 bytes of memory
Neighbor    V  OAS MsgRcvd MsgSent TblVer InQ OutQ Up/Down State/PfxRcd
20.1.1.1    3  1   76783   23422   162305 0   0    2w3d    1059
21.1.1.1    3  2   232332  23344   162305 0   0    2w3d    143
22.1.1.1    3  1   2323    4322    162305 0   0    2w3d    1298
```

From this listing, you should verify that the number of routing entries are what you would expect. This also can prove that routes may have been filtered out. The field headed TblVer is the BGP table version. This value should be the same for each neighbor as seen from the *show ip bgp summary* command. The Up/Down field is the amount of time in weeks (w) and days (d) that the BGP session has been active.

The commands show ip protocols and show ip route are utilized by BGP. The other troubleshooting commands are as follows:

- show ip bgp summary: Displays a summary of all BGP neighbors and their related information.

- show ip bgp x.x.x.x: Displays BGP route information for network x.x.x.x.

- debug ip bgp: Displays real-time debugging information about the BGP routing process.

The full format of the show ip bgp commands is as follows:

```
Router#sh ip bgp ?
  A.B.C.D           IP prefix <network>/<length>, e.g., 35.0.0.0/8
  A.B.C.D           Network in the BGP routing table to display
  cidr-only         Display only routes with non-natural netmasks
  community         Display routes matching the communities
  community-list    Display routes matching the community-list
  dampened-paths    Display paths suppressed due to dampening
  filter-list       Display routes conforming to the filter-list
  flap-statistics   Display flap statistics of routes
  inconsistent-as   Display only routes with inconsistent origin ASs
  neighbors         Detailed information on TCP and BGP neighbor
                    connections
  paths             Path information
  peer-group        Display information on peer-groups
  quote-regexp      Display routes matching the AS path "regular
                    expression"
  regexp            Display routes matching the AS path regular
                    expression
```

```
        summary                 Summary of BGP neighbor status
        vpnv4                   Display VPNv4 NLRI specific information
        |                       Output modifiers
        <cr>
   Router#
```

The full format of the debug ip bgp commands is as follows:

```
Router#debug ip bgp ?
   A.B.C.D                 BGP neighbor address
   dampening               BGP dampening
   events                  BGP events
   in                      BGP Inbound information
   keepalives              BGP keepalives
   out                     BGP Outbound information
   updates                 BGP updates
   vpnv4                   VPNv4 NLRI information
   <cr>
Router#
```

Enhanced Interior Gateway Routing Protocol (EIGRP), the Hybrid Protocol

EIGRP is an evolution of IGRP. EIGRP combines both of the capabilities of distance vector dynamic routing protocols and link state dynamic routing protocols to create a hybrid protocol that meets the demands of diverse large-scale internetworks.

Cisco Systems created EIGRP to improve upon IGRP and to provide an enterprise multi-protocol routing protocol. EIGRP supports AppleTalk, IP, and Novell's IPX/SPX. This integration occurs through the redistribution of routing information between common protocols. AppleTalk support is provided through redistribution with the *routing table maintenance protocol* (RTMP). IP redistributes routes from OSPF, RIP, IS-IS, or BGP. The Novell implementation provides support through redistribution with Novell RIP or the *service advertisement protocol* (SAP).

EIGRP provides seamless compatibility with routers that are currently running IGRP. This occurs via an automatic redistribution mechanism that converts IGRP routes to EIGRP routes and vice versa. This makes the implementation of EIGRP less of an administrative and technical burden because it can coexist with nearly all major routing protocols. EIGRP is a classless routing protocol that supports route summarization and VLSMs.

EIGRP utilizes four key technologies that differentiate it from other routing protocols: Neighbor discovery/recovery, *reliable transport protocol*

(RTP), *diffusing update algorithm* (DUAL) finite state machine, and protocol dependant modules.

Neighbor Discovery/Recovery

Neighbor discovery/recovery is obtained by the sending and receiving of hello packets between directly connected neighbors. This process enables the router to dynamically learn about other routers that are on their directly attached networks. It is used to periodically check the status of these connected routers. If a hello packet is not received from a neighboring router for a pre-determined period of time, it is deemed that this router or link must be down and action is taken.

Reliable Transport Protocol (RTP)

RTP is responsible for the guaranteed delivery of EIGRP packets to the direct neighbors. The RTP has the intelligence to ascertain the type of link and adjust the EIGRP packets accordingly. For example, if you have a multi-access network with multicast capabilities such as Ethernet, it is not necessary to send a hello packet to the direct neighbors individually. Instead, a single multicast packet can be sent to all the required neighbors. RTP can also indicate within the EIGRP packet whether or not it is required that the packet be acknowledged. Hello packets over Ethernet do not need to be acknowledged, whereas other types of packets such as updates always need to be acknowledged.

Diffusing Update Algorithm (DUAL) Finite State Machine

DUAL is the algorithm used by EIGRP to make routing decisions. DUAL uses distance information to select the best loop-free path to the remote network. This information creates a routing table of feasible successors, which are neighboring routers that are used for packet forwarding and are a least-cost path to a destination that is not part of a routing loop.

When a topology change occurs, DUAL tests for feasible successors. If a feasible successor is found for the new network, then DUAL will use this new feasible successor to avoid having to recalculate the route. This conserves CPU time on the router and reduces the new routes that have to be propagated throughout the network. If no feasible successor is found, then DUAL will recalculate the feasible successor.

Protocol Dependant Modules

The protocol dependant modules perform network-layer functions based on the protocol. This takes a data protocol such as IP and ensures that it is dealt with as an IP packet. The IP module would initially receive the EIGRP packet that was encapsulated in IP and inform the DUAL that a new IP packet has been received. DUAL would then make its routing decisions and store the result in the IP routing table. This is the same for the other supported protocols such as AppleTalk and IPX/SPX.

On a Cisco router, simply adding the following command in the global configuration mode enables EIGRP:

```
Router(config)#router eigrp 101
```

This command enables EIGRP for the AS 101. You must specify the AS number when implementing EIGRP.

Networks are advertised and participate in EIGRP routing by entering the following command:

```
Router(config-router)network A.B.C.D E.F.G.H
```

where A.B.C.D is the network address of the network to be advertised via EIGRP. E.F.G.H. is the wildcard mask and this operates as in the access list command.

In addition to the configuration commands listed in the previous sections, EIGRP utilizes the *eigrp* configuration command, which is an EIGRP-specific command. For more information on configuring EIGRP, refer to the ICRC or ACRC course notes.

Troubleshooting EIGRP

If routing inaccuracies occur, it is also advisable to check the router for any misconfigured distribute lists. The wrongful configuration of such a list can render the routing process inoperable.

The EIGRP troubleshooting commands include show ip protocols, show ip route, and debug ip routing. Two other commands are used as well:

- show ip eigrp interface: Displays EIGRP routing protocol information for all EIGRP-configured interfaces.
- debug ip eigrp: Displays debug information about EIGRP updates and routing table entries.

show ip protocols

Here is the show ip protocols command in use:

```
Router#sh ip prot
Routing Protocol is "rip"
  Sending updates every 30 seconds, next due in 19 seconds
  Invalid after 180 seconds, hold down 180, flushed after 240
  Outgoing update filter list for all interfaces is
  Incoming update filter list for all interfaces is
  Redistributing: rip
  Default version control: send version 2, receive version 2
    Interface  Send   Recv   Triggered RIP   Key-chain
    Ethernet0  2      2
    Ethernet1  2      2
    Serial0    2      2
    Serial1    2      2
  Routing for Networks:
    172.18.0.0
    172.19.0.0
    172.20.0.0
    172.30.0.0
    194.73.134.0
  Routing Information Sources:
    Gateway         Distance     Last Update
    194.73.134.26   120          00:00:13
    194.73.134.23   120          00:00:25
    194.73.134.22   120          2d01h
    Gateway         Distance     Last Update
    172.18.0.11     120          00:00:26
    172.20.1.1      120          00:00:26
    172.19.1.1      120          00:00:26
  Distance: (default is 120)

Routing Protocol is "igrp 101"
  Sending updates every 90 seconds, next due in 21 seconds
  Invalid after 270 seconds, hold down 280, flushed after 630
  Outgoing update filter list for all interfaces is
  Incoming update filter list for all interfaces is
  Default networks flagged in outgoing updates
  Default networks accepted from incoming updates
  IGRP metric weight K1=1, K2=0, K3=1, K4=0, K5=0
  IGRP maximum hopcount 100
  IGRP maximum metric variance 1
  Redistributing: igrp 101
  Routing for Networks:
    172.18.0.0
```

```
      172.19.0.0
      172.30.0.0
      194.73.134.0
   Routing Information Sources:
     Gateway         Distance    Last Update
     194.73.134.23   100         1d14h
     172.19.1.1      100         00:00:07
   Distance: (default is 100)

Routing Protocol is "ospf 1"
  Sending updates every 0 seconds
  Invalid after 0 seconds, hold down 0, flushed after 0
  Outgoing update filter list for all interfaces is
  Incoming update filter list for all interfaces is
  Redistributing: ospf 1
  Routing for Networks:
     172.18.0.0
     172.19.0.0
     172.20.0.0
     172.30.0.0
     194.73.134.0
     201.0.0.0
     202.0.0.0
   Routing Information Sources:
     Gateway         Distance    Last Update
     194.73.134.23   110         1d00h
   Distance: (default is 110)

Routing Protocol is "eigrp 20"
  Outgoing update filter list for all interfaces is
  Incoming update filter list for all interfaces is
  Default networks flagged in outgoing updates
  Default networks accepted from incoming updates
  EIGRP metric weight K1=1, K2=0, K3=1, K4=0, K5=0
  EIGRP maximum hopcount 100
  EIGRP maximum metric variance 1
  Redistributing: eigrp 20
  Automatic network summarization is in effect
  Automatic address summarization:
     172.18.0.0/16 for Ethernet1, Loopback0, Loopback1
       Loopback2, Serial0, Serial1
     172.19.0.0/16 for Ethernet0, Ethernet1, Loopback0
       Loopback1, Loopback2, Serial1
     172.20.0.0/16 for Ethernet0, Ethernet1, Loopback0
       Loopback1, Loopback2, Serial0
     172.30.0.0/16 for Ethernet0, Loopback0, Loopback1
       Loopback2, Serial0, Serial1
     201.0.0.0/24 for Ethernet0, Ethernet1, Loopback1
       Loopback2, Serial0, Serial1
     202.0.0.0/24 for Ethernet0, Ethernet1, Loopback0
       Loopback2, Serial0, Serial1
  Routing for Networks:
     172.18.0.0
     172.19.0.0
     172.20.0.0
     172.30.0.0
     201.0.0.0
     202.0.0.0
```

```
Routing Information Sources:
   Gateway          Distance    Last Update
   194.73.134.23    90          06:46:01
   172.20.1.1       90          06:46:01
   172.19.1.1       90          06:46:01
Distance: internal 90 external 170
Router#
```

From this listing, we can see that this router is routing RIP, IGRP, OSPG, and EIGRP. The EIGRP routing process is for AS number 20. We can also see that the EIGRP process on this router is advertising 172.18.0.0, 172.19.0.0, 172.20.0.0, 172.30.0.0, 201.0.0.0, and 202.0.0.0.

show ip route

The following listing displays the usage of the show ip route command in EIGRP:

```
Router#sh ip route
Codes: C - connected, S - static, I - IGRP, R - RIP, M - mobile, B
       - BGP
       D - EIGRP, EX - EIGRP external, O - OSPF, IA - OSPF inter area
       N1 - OSPF NSSA external type 1, N2 - OSPF NSSA external type 2
       E1 - OSPF external type 1, E2 - OSPF external type 2, E - EGP
       i - IS-IS, L1 - IS-IS level-1, L2 - IS-IS level-2, ia - IS-
       IS inter area
       * - candidate default, U - per-user static route, o - ODR
       P - periodic downloaded static route

Gateway of last resort is 172.19.1.2 to network 0.0.0.0

C    194.73.134.0/24 is directly connected, Ethernet0
     201.0.0.0/24 is variably subnetted, 2 subnets, 2 masks
O       201.0.0.1/32 [110/65] via 172.20.1.2, 1d00h, Serial1
                     [110/65] via 172.19.1.2, 1d00h, Serial0
D       201.0.0.0/24 [90/409600] via 194.73.134.24, 06:59:15,
        Ethernet0
     202.0.0.0/24 is variably subnetted, 2 subnets, 2 masks
D       202.0.0.0/24 [90/409600] via 194.73.134.24, 06:59:15,
        Ethernet0
O       202.0.0.1/32 [110/65] via 172.20.1.2, 1d00h, Serial1
                     [110/65] via 172.19.1.2, 1d00h, Serial0
C    172.19.0.0/16 is directly connected, Serial0
C    172.18.0.0/16 is directly connected, Ethernet0
C    172.20.0.0/16 is directly connected, Serial1
D    172.30.0.0/16 [90/307200] via 194.73.134.24, 06:59:15,
     Ethernet0
C    212.0.0.0/24 is directly connected, Loopback0
R*   0.0.0.0/0 [120/1] via 172.19.1.2, 2d09h, Serial0
               [120/1] via 172.20.1.2, 2d09h, Serial1
Router#
```

The first part of this listing indicates all the codes that are used to identify the routing protocols in the actual routing table. This routing table shows three routes that have been received via EIGRP. These are to networks 201.0.0.0, 202.0.0.0, and 172.30.0.0.

This is a small routing table and it is not uncommon for routing tables to be a hundred or more lines long depending on the size of the network. The show ip route command can be further divided by entering the exact route after the command or entering the routing protocol after the command. For example, `Router#show ip route eigrp` would just display routes learned by EIGRP. `Router#show ip route 172.18.10.0` would just display protocol information about network 172.18.10.0

show ip eigrp interface

The *show ip eigrp interface* command displays EIGRP routing protocol information for all EIGRP configured interfaces:

```
Router#sh ip eigrp int
IP-EIGRP interfaces for process 20
                       Xmit Queue   Mean  Pacing Time  Multicast   Pending
Interface   Peers  Un/Reliable  SRTT  Un/Reliable  Flow Timer  Routes
Et0          1      0/0          0     0/10         0           0
Se0          1      0/0          0     0/15         0           0
Se1          1      0/0          1036  0/15         0           0
Et1          0      0/0          0     0/10         0           0
Lo0          0      0/0          0     0/10         0           0
Lo1          0      0/0          0     0/10         0           0
Router#
```

This listing shows the EIGRP interfaces configured on the router. The headings are as follows:

- *Interface* The interface on which EIGRP is enabled

- *Peers* The number of directly connected EIGRP neighbors on this interface.

- *Xmit Queue Un/Reliable* The number of packets in the reliable and unreliable queues.

- *Mean SRTT* SRTT stands for the smooth round trip time. This is the mean time it takes for an EIGRP packet to be sent to a neighbor and an acknowledgement received.

- *Pacing Time Un/Reliable* Determines when EIGRP packets are to be sent out on an interface.

- *Multicast Flow Timer*   The number of seconds before the router will send out EIGRP packets.
- *Pending Routes*   The number of routes in the transmit queue that are waiting to be sent.

This command can be used to determine if misconfigured or failing devices are causing routing problems.

debug ip routing

To show this command in operation, we are going to examine two router listings that show that a new network has been added and removed from EIGRP. The following is an EIGRP-specific event.

Router A Listing

```
RouterA#conf t
Enter configuration commands, one per line.  End with CNTL/Z.
RouterA(config)#int lo3
RouterA(config-if)#ip address 210.0.0.1 255.255.255.0
RouterA(config-if)#exit

4w2d: is_up: 1 state: 4 sub state: 1 line: 0
4w2d: RT: add 210.0.0.0/24 via 0.0.0.0, connected metric [0/0]
4w2d: RT: interface Loopback3 added to routing tablet

RouterA(config)#router eigrp 20
RouterA(config-router)#network 210.0.0.0 0.0.0.255
RouterA(config-router)#
RouterA(config-router)#no network 210.0.0.0 0.0.0.255
RouterA(config-router)#
RouterA(config-router)#exit
RouterA(config)#exit
RouterA#
RouterA#no debug all
All possible debugging has been turned off
RouterA#term no mon
RouterA#
```

Router B Listing

```
RouterB#debug ip routing
IP routing debugging is on
RouterB#
RouterB#sh ip route
Codes: C - connected, S - static, I - IGRP, R - RIP, M - mobile, B
       - BGP
       D - EIGRP, EX - EIGRP external, O - OSPF, IA - OSPF inter area
       N1 - OSPF NSSA external type 1, N2 - OSPF NSSA external type 2
       E1 - OSPF external type 1, E2 - OSPF external type 2, E - EGP
```

```
          i - IS-IS, L1 - IS-IS level-1, L2 - IS-IS level-2, ia - IS-
          IS inter area
          * - candidate default, U - per-user static route, o - ODR
          P - periodic downloaded static route

Gateway of last resort is 172.19.1.2 to network 0.0.0.0

C    194.73.134.0/24 is directly connected, Ethernet0
     201.0.0.0/24 is variably subnetted, 2 subnets, 2 masks
O       201.0.0.1/32 [110/65] via 172.20.1.2, 1d10h, Serial1
                     [110/65] via 172.19.1.2, 1d10h, Serial0
D       201.0.0.0/24 [90/409600] via 194.73.134.24, 00:03:23,
        Ethernet0
     202.0.0.0/24 is variably subnetted, 2 subnets, 2 masks
D       202.0.0.0/24 [90/409600] via 194.73.134.24, 00:03:23,
        Ethernet0
O       202.0.0.1/32 [110/65] via 172.20.1.2, 1d10h, Serial1
                     [110/65] via 172.19.1.2, 1d10h, Serial0
C    172.19.0.0/16 is directly connected, Serial0
C    172.18.0.0/16 is directly connected, Ethernet0
C    172.20.0.0/16 is directly connected, Serial1
I    172.30.0.0/16 [100/1200] via 194.73.134.24, 00:00:14,
     Ethernet0
C    212.0.0.0/24 is directly connected, Loopback0
R*   0.0.0.0/0 [120/1] via 172.19.1.2, 2d19h, Serial0
                 [120/1] via 172.20.1.2, 2d19h, Serial1
RouterB#
RouterB#
4w2d: RT: delete route to 201.0.0.0 via 194.73.134.24, eigrp metric
          [90/409600]
4w2d: RT: no routes to 201.0.0.0
4w2d: RT: add 201.0.0.0/24 via 172.20.1.2, eigrp metric
          [90/2297856]
4w2d: RT: add 201.0.0.0/24 via 172.19.1.2, eigrp metric
          [90/2297856]
4w2d: RT: delete route to 202.0.0.0 via 194.73.134.24, eigrp metric
          [90/409600]
4w2d: RT: no routes to 202.0.0.0
4w2d: RT: add 202.0.0.0/24 via 172.20.1.2, eigrp metric
          [90/2297856]
4w2d: RT: add 202.0.0.0/24 via 172.19.1.2, eigrp metric
          [90/2297856]
4w2d: RT: delete route to 201.0.0.0 via 172.19.1.2, eigrp metric
          [90/2297856]
4w2d: RT: delete route to 202.0.0.0 via 172.19.1.2, eigrp metric
          [90/2297856]
4w2d: RT: add 210.0.0.0/24 via 194.73.134.24, eigrp metric
          [90/409600]
4w2d: RT: delete route to 201.0.0.0 via 172.20.1.2, eigrp metric
          [90/2297856]
4w2d: RT: no routes to 201.0.0.0
4w2d: RT: add 201.0.0.0/24 via 194.73.134.24, eigrp metric
          [90/409600]
4w2d: RT: delete route to 202.0.0.0 via 172.20.1.2, eigrp metric
          [90/2297856]
4w2d: RT: no routes to 202.0.0.0
4w2d: RT: add 202.0.0.0/24 via 194.73.134.24, eigrp metric
          [90/409600]
4w2d: RT: delete route to 210.0.0.0 via 194.73.134.24, eigrp metric
          [90/409600]
```

```
4w2d: RT: no routes to 210.0.0.0
4w2d: RT: add 210.0.0.0/24 via 194.73.134.24, eigrp metric
          [90/409600]
4w2d: RT: delete route to 210.0.0.0 via 194.73.134.24, eigrp metric
          [90/409600]
4w2d: RT: no routes to 210.0.0.0
4w2d: RT: add 210.0.0.0/24 via 194.73.134.24, eigrp metric
          [90/409600]

RouterB#sh ip route
Codes: C - connected, S - static, I - IGRP, R - RIP, M - mobile, B
       - BGP
       D - EIGRP, EX - EIGRP external, O - OSPF, IA - OSPF inter area
       N1 - OSPF NSSA external type 1, N2 - OSPF NSSA external type 2
       E1 - OSPF external type 1, E2 - OSPF external type 2, E - EGP
       i - IS-IS, L1 - IS-IS level-1, L2 - IS-IS level-2, ia - IS-
       IS inter area
       * - candidate default, U - per-user static route, o - ODR
       P - periodic downloaded static route

Gateway of last resort is 172.19.1.2 to network 0.0.0.0

C    194.73.134.0/24 is directly connected, Ethernet0
     201.0.0.0/24 is variably subnetted, 2 subnets, 2 masks
O       201.0.0.1/32 [110/65] via 172.20.1.2, 1d10h, Serial1
                     [110/65] via 172.19.1.2, 1d10h, Serial0
D       201.0.0.0/24 [90/409600] via 194.73.134.24, 00:02:42,
        Ethernet0
     202.0.0.0/24 is variably subnetted, 2 subnets, 2 masks
D       202.0.0.0/24 [90/409600] via 194.73.134.24, 00:02:42,
        Ethernet0
O       202.0.0.1/32 [110/65] via 172.20.1.2, 1d10h, Serial1
                     [110/65] via 172.19.1.2, 1d10h, Serial0
C    172.19.0.0/16 is directly connected, Serial0
C    172.18.0.0/16 is directly connected, Ethernet0
C    172.20.0.0/16 is directly connected, Serial1
I    172.30.0.0/16 [100/1200] via 194.73.134.24, 00:00:45,
     Ethernet0
C    212.0.0.0/24 is directly connected, Loopback0
D    210.0.0.0/24 [90/409600] via 194.73.134.24, 00:02:44,
     Ethernet0
R*   0.0.0.0/0 [120/1] via 172.19.1.2, 2d19h, Serial0
               [120/1] via 172.20.1.2, 2d19h, Serial1
RouterB#

4w2d: RT: delete route to 210.0.0.0 via 194.73.134.24, eigrp metric
          [90/409600]
4w2d: RT: no routes to 210.0.0.0
4w2d: RT: add 210.0.0.0/24 via 172.20.1.2, eigrp metric
          [90/2297856]
4w2d: RT: add 210.0.0.0/24 via 172.19.1.2, eigrp metric
          [90/2297856]
4w2d: RT: delete route to 210.0.0.0 via 172.19.1.2, eigrp metric
          [90/2297856]
4w2d: RT: delete route to 210.0.0.0 via 172.20.1.2, eigrp metric
          [90/2297856]
4w2d: RT: no routes to 210.0.0.0
4w2d: RT: add 210.0.0.0/24 via 172.19.1.2, eigrp metric
          [90/2297856]
```

```
4w2d: RT: delete route to 210.0.0.0 via 172.19.1.2, eigrp metric
        [90/2297856]
4w2d: RT: no routes to 210.0.0.0
4w2d: RT: garbage collecting entry for 210.0.0.0

RouterB#sh ip route
Codes: C - connected, S - static, I - IGRP, R - RIP, M - mobile, B
       - BGP
       D - EIGRP, EX - EIGRP external, O - OSPF, IA - OSPF inter area
       N1 - OSPF NSSA external type 1, N2 - OSPF NSSA external type 2
       E1 - OSPF external type 1, E2 - OSPF external type 2, E - EGP
       i - IS-IS, L1 - IS-IS level-1, L2 - IS-IS level-2, ia - IS-
       IS inter area
       * - candidate default, U - per-user static route, o - ODR
       P - periodic downloaded static route

Gateway of last resort is 172.19.1.2 to network 0.0.0.0

C    194.73.134.0/24 is directly connected, Ethernet0
     201.0.0.0/24 is variably subnetted, 2 subnets, 2 masks
O       201.0.0.1/32 [110/65] via 172.20.1.2, 1d10h, Serial1
                     [110/65] via 172.19.1.2, 1d10h, Serial0
D       201.0.0.0/24 [90/409600] via 194.73.134.24, 00:03:23,
        Ethernet0
     202.0.0.0/24 is variably subnetted, 2 subnets, 2 masks
D       202.0.0.0/24 [90/409600] via 194.73.134.24, 00:03:23,
        Ethernet0
O       202.0.0.1/32 [110/65] via 172.20.1.2, 1d10h, Serial1
                     [110/65] via 172.19.1.2, 1d10h, Serial0
C    172.19.0.0/16 is directly connected, Serial0
C    172.18.0.0/16 is directly connected, Ethernet0
C    172.20.0.0/16 is directly connected, Serial1
I    172.30.0.0/16 [100/1200] via 194.73.134.24, 00:00:14,
     Ethernet0
C    212.0.0.0/24 is directly connected, Loopback0
R*   0.0.0.0/0 [120/1] via 172.19.1.2, 2d19h, Serial0
               [120/1] via 172.20.1.2, 2d19h, Serial1
RouterB#
RouterB#no debug all
All possible debugging has been turned off
RouterB#term no mon
RouterB#
```

What we achieve in this listing is the successful entry and removal of an EIGRP route into the routing table on Router B. We start by adding a new loopback interface to Router A and giving it the IP address of 210.0.0.1/24. As soon as the interface is added, we can see the route getting added to the internal routing table on Router A. Once the interface is configured, we add this network to the EIGRP routing process by entering network 210.0.0.0 0.0.0.255 in the EIGRP router configuration mode for AS number 20.

Router B's listing starts with a show ip route before the new network is added to EIGRP. We can see that there is no advertised route to 210.0.0.0 using any routing protocol. As soon as the route is added to the EIGRP routing process on Router A, Router B receives a RT: addition for the 210.0.0.0 network. A show ip route on Router B clearly indicates the newly received route to the 210.0.0.0 network. This proves that the route has been advertised from Router A and received by Router B. We now remove the network from EIGRP routing on Router B by entering the no network 210.0.0.0 0.0.0.255 command. This immediately removes the route via an RT: deletion and an RT: garbage collection debug message.

debug ip eigrp

The *debug ip eigrp events* command displays routing information events for the EIGRP routing protocol. To show this in operation, we are going to examine two router listings. They show that a new network has been added and then removed from EIGRP.

Router A Listing

```
RouterA#conf t
Enter configuration commands, one per line.  End with CNTL/Z.
RouterA(config)#int lo3
RouterA(config-if)#ip address 210.0.0.1 255.255.255.0
RouterA(config-if)#exit
RouterA(config)#router eigrp 20
RouterA(config-router)#network 210.0.0.0 0.0.0.255
RouterA(config-router)#no network 210.0.0.0 0.0.0.255
RouterA(config-router)#^Z
RouterA#
```

Router B Listing

```
RouterB#debug ip eigrp
IP-EIGRP Route Events debugging is on
RouterB#sh ip route
Codes: C - connected, S - static, I - IGRP, R - RIP, M - mobile, B
       - BGP
       D - EIGRP, EX - EIGRP external, O - OSPF, IA - OSPF inter area
       N1 - OSPF NSSA external type 1, N2 - OSPF NSSA external type 2
       E1 - OSPF external type 1, E2 - OSPF external type 2, E - EGP
       i - IS-IS, L1 - IS-IS level-1, L2 - IS-IS level-2, ia - IS-
       IS inter area
       * - candidate default, U - per-user static route, o - ODR
       P - periodic downloaded static route

Gateway of last resort is 172.19.1.2 to network 0.0.0.0

C    194.73.134.0/24 is directly connected, Ethernet0
     201.0.0.0/24 is variably subnetted, 2 subnets, 2 masks
O       201.0.0.1/32 [110/65] via 172.20.1.2, 1d12h, Serial1
                      [110/65] via 172.19.1.2, 1d12h, Serial0
```

```
D       201.0.0.0/24 [90/409600] via 194.73.134.24, 01:52:32,
        Ethernet0
     202.0.0.0/24 is variably subnetted, 2 subnets, 2 masks
D       202.0.0.0/24 [90/409600] via 194.73.134.24, 01:52:32,
        Ethernet0
O       202.0.0.1/32 [110/65] via 172.20.1.2, 1d12h, Serial1
                     [110/65] via 172.19.1.2, 1d12h, Serial0
C    172.19.0.0/16 is directly connected, Serial0
C    172.18.0.0/16 is directly connected, Ethernet0
C    172.20.0.0/16 is directly connected, Serial1
I    172.30.0.0/16 [100/1200] via 194.73.134.24, 00:00:36,
        Ethernet0
C    212.0.0.0/24 is directly connected, Loopback0
R*   0.0.0.0/0 [120/1] via 172.19.1.2, 2d21h, Serial0
                [120/1] via 172.20.1.2, 2d21h, Serial1

RouterB
#
4w3d: IP-EIGRP: Processing incoming UPDATE packet
4w3d: IP-EIGRP: Int 210.0.0.0/24 M 409600 - 256000 153600 SM 128256
      - 256 128000
4w3d: IP-EIGRP: Processing incoming UPDATE packet
4w3d: IP-EIGRP: Int 210.0.0.0/24 M 2297856 - 1657856 640000 SM
                128256 - 256 128000
4w3d: IP-EIGRP: 210.0.0.0/24 routing table not updated
4w3d: IP-EIGRP: Processing incoming UPDATE packet
4w3d: IP-EIGRP: Int 210.0.0.0/24 M 2297856 - 1657856 640000 SM
                128256 - 256 128000
4w3d: IP-EIGRP: 210.0.0.0/24 routing table not updated
4w3d: IP-EIGRP: 210.0.0.0/24 routing table not updated
4w3d: IP-EIGRP: Int 210.0.0.0/24 metric 409600 - 256000 153600
4w3d: IP-EIGRP: 210.0.0.0/24 - do advertise out Serial0
4w3d: IP-EIGRP: Int 210.0.0.0/24 metric 409600 - 256000 153600
4w3d: IP-EIGRP: 210.0.0.0/24 - do advertise out Serial1
4w3d: IP-EIGRP: Int 210.0.0.0/24 metric 409600 - 256000 153600

RouterB#
RouterB#sh ip route
Codes: C - connected, S - static, I - IGRP, R - RIP, M - mobile, B
       - BGP
       D - EIGRP, EX - EIGRP external, O - OSPF, IA - OSPF inter area
       N1 - OSPF NSSA external type 1, N2 - OSPF NSSA external type 2
       E1 - OSPF external type 1, E2 - OSPF external type 2, E - EGP
       i - IS-IS, L1 - IS-IS level-1, L2 - IS-IS level-2, ia - IS-
       IS inter area
       * - candidate default, U - per-user static route, o - ODR
       P - periodic downloaded static route

Gateway of last resort is 172.19.1.2 to network 0.0.0.0

C    194.73.134.0/24 is directly connected, Ethernet0
     201.0.0.0/24 is variably subnetted, 2 subnets, 2 masks
O       201.0.0.1/32 [110/65] via 172.20.1.2, 1d12h, Serial1
                     [110/65] via 172.19.1.2, 1d12h, Serial0
D       201.0.0.0/24 [90/409600] via 194.73.134.24, 01:53:36,
        Ethernet0
     202.0.0.0/24 is variably subnetted, 2 subnets, 2 masks
D       202.0.0.0/24 [90/409600] via 194.73.134.24, 01:53:36,
        Ethernet0
O       202.0.0.1/32 [110/65] via 172.20.1.2, 1d12h, Serial1
                     [110/65] via 172.19.1.2, 1d12h, Serial0
```

```
C       172.19.0.0/16 is directly connected, Serial0
C       172.18.0.0/16 is directly connected, Ethernet0
C       172.20.0.0/16 is directly connected, Serial1
I       172.30.0.0/16 [100/1200] via 194.73.134.24, 00:00:11,
        Ethernet0
C       212.0.0.0/24 is directly connected, Loopback0
D       210.0.0.0/24 [90/409600] via 194.73.134.24, 00:00:19,
        Ethernet0
R*      0.0.0.0/0 [120/1] via 172.19.1.2, 2d21h, Serial0
                  [120/1] via 172.20.1.2, 2d21h, Serial1
RouterB#

4w3d: IP-EIGRP: Processing incoming QUERY packet
4w3d: IP-EIGRP: Int 210.0.0.0/24 M 4294967295 - 0 4294967295 SM
        4294967295 - 0 4294967295
4w3d: IP-EIGRP: 210.0.0.0/24 routing table not updated
4w3d: IP-EIGRP: Processing incoming QUERY packet
4w3d: IP-EIGRP: Int 210.0.0.0/24 M 4294967295 - 0 4294967295 SM
        4294967295 - 0 4294967295
4w3d: IP-EIGRP: 210.0.0.0/24 routing table not updated
4w3d: IP-EIGRP: 210.0.0.0/24 routing table not updated
4w3d: IP-EIGRP: Processing incoming QUERY packet
4w3d: IP-EIGRP: Int 210.0.0.0/24 M 4294967295 - 0 4294967295 SM
        4294967295 - 0 4294967295
4w3d: IP-EIGRP: 210.0.0.0/24 - do advertise out Ethernet0
4w3d: IP-EIGRP: Int 210.0.0.0/24 metric 4294967295 - 0 4294967295
4w3d: IP-EIGRP: Int 210.0.0.0/24 metric 4294967295 - 0 4294967295
4w3d: IP-EIGRP: 210.0.0.0/24 - do advertise out Serial0
4w3d: IP-EIGRP: Int 210.0.0.0/24 metric 4294967295 - 0 4294967295
4w3d: IP-EIGRP: 210.0.0.0/24 - do advertise out Ethernet0
4w3d: IP-EIGRP: Int 210.0.0.0/24 metric 4294967295 - 0 4294967295
4w3d: IP-EIGRP: 210.0.0.0/24 - do advertise out Serial0
4w3d: IP-EIGRP: Int 210.0.0.0/24 metric 4294967295 - 0 4294967295
4w3d: IP-EIGRP: Processing incoming REPLY packet
4w3d: IP-EIGRP: Int 210.0.0.0/24 M 4294967295 - 0 4294967295 SM
        4294967295 - 0 4294967295
4w3d: IP-EIGRP: Processing incoming REPLY packet
4w3d: IP-EIGRP: Int 210.0.0.0/24 M 4294967295 - 0 4294967295 SM
        4294967295 - 0 4294967295
4w3d: IP-EIGRP: Processing incoming REPLY packet
4w3d: IP-EIGRP: Int 210.0.0.0/24 M 4294967295 - 0 4294967295 SM
        4294967295 - 0 4294967295
4w3d: IP-EIGRP: 210.0.0.0/24 routing table not updated
4w3d: IP-EIGRP: 210.0.0.0/24 - do advertise out Serial1
4w3d: IP-EIGRP: Int 210.0.0.0/24 metric 4294967295 - 0 4294967295

RouterB#sh ip route
Codes: C - connected, S - static, I - IGRP, R - RIP, M - mobile, B
       - BGP
       D - EIGRP, EX - EIGRP external, O - OSPF, IA - OSPF inter area
       N1 - OSPF NSSA external type 1, N2 - OSPF NSSA external type 2
       E1 - OSPF external type 1, E2 - OSPF external type 2, E - EGP
       i - IS-IS, L1 - IS-IS level-1, L2 - IS-IS level-2, ia - IS-
       IS inter area
```

```
          * - candidate default, U - per-user static route, o - ODR
          P - periodic downloaded static route

Gateway of last resort is 172.19.1.2 to network 0.0.0.0

C     194.73.134.0/24 is directly connected, Ethernet0
      201.0.0.0/24 is variably subnetted, 2 subnets, 2 masks
O        201.0.0.1/32 [110/65] via 172.20.1.2, 1d12h, Serial1
                       [110/65] via 172.19.1.2, 1d12h, Serial0
D        201.0.0.0/24 [90/409600] via 194.73.134.24, 01:54:21,
         Ethernet0
      202.0.0.0/24 is variably subnetted, 2 subnets, 2 masks
D        202.0.0.0/24 [90/409600] via 194.73.134.24, 01:54:21,
         Ethernet0
O        202.0.0.1/32 [110/65] via 172.20.1.2, 1d12h, Serial1
                       [110/65] via 172.19.1.2, 1d12h, Serial0
C     172.19.0.0/16 is directly connected, Serial0
C     172.18.0.0/16 is directly connected, Ethernet0
C     172.20.0.0/16 is directly connected, Serial1
I     172.30.0.0/16 [100/1200] via 194.73.134.24, 00:00:57,
      Ethernet0
C     212.0.0.0/24 is directly connected, Loopback0
R*    0.0.0.0/0 [120/1] via 172.19.1.2, 2d21h, Serial0
                 [120/1] via 172.20.1.2, 2d21h, Serial1

RouterB#no debug all
All possible debugging has been turned off
```

What we achieve in this listing is the successful entry and removal of an EIGRP route into the routing table on Router B. We start by adding a new loopback interface to Router A and giving it the IP address of 210.0.0.1/24. Once the interface is configured, we add this network to the EIGRP routing process by entering network 210.0.0.0 0.0.0.255 in the EIGRP router configuration mode.

As soon as this network has been added to the EIGRP routing process on Router A, Router B receives an EIGRP update packet. We can see the result of this after the show ip route command. We can also clearly see the new EIGRP route that has been added to the internal routing table on Router B. This proves that the route to network 210.0.0.0 has been advertised by Router A and is received by Router B.

We then remove network 210.0.0.0 from the EIGRP routing process on Router A with the command no network 210.0.0.0 0.0.0.255. Immediately, we see a EIGRP query message, which tests the validity of the route and eventually removes it from the routing table. This debug command is an excellent tool for diagnosing issues relating to routing updates, metric changes, and advertising requirements.

Chapter Summary

In this chapter, we looked at IP routing protocols and the troubleshooting commands that are available with Cisco IOS. We started by looking at classless and classfull routing protocols and how the differences in operation affect their performance. We provided a technical overview of each routing protocol and moved on to Cisco's show and debug commands, which can be used to interrogate the router to receive real-time reports that will help us in troubleshooting. As in any other troubleshooting situation, always start at the physical layer and work your way up, which can save you a lot of time.

Frequently Asked Questions (FAQ)

Question: What is meant by a classfull routing protocol?

Answer: A classfull routing protocol is a routing protocol that strictly follows the classfull IP addressing scheme.

Question: Can multiple routing protocols be run over the same router at the same time?

Answer: Yes. Multiple routing protocols can coexist, although they, by default, will not transfer or share routing information. You can redistribute routing information by using specific IOS commands.

Case Study

You, as a network engineer, have been given the task of identifying the problem with routing updates on your corporate network.

Scenario

You are the network engineer for a small engineering company with three remote workshops and a central office. You are based at the central office. All remote workshops are connected via leased line services from a local Telco provider. The central site has a Cisco 4500 router and the remote sites have Cisco 2503 routers with ISDN backup.

Until recently, all sites were connected using static routes to the remote networks. Now RIP is implemented to ease the administrative burden that will arise as the company expands and more sites are added to the network. You have just added RIP to the third remote site and now you cannot see the Ethernet network connected to the router at this site.

Approach

You know that communications were working before you removed the static routes and you have successfully re-added them to get the network visible again. You therefore deduce that it must be a RIP configuration error, but you are puzzled because you are sure you set all of these up exactly the same. You look for a way to track exactly what is happening on the router. You decide to run the debug ip rip command on the central router. You considered the debug ip routing command but decided that this wouldn't provide enough RIP specific output. You run the debug ip rip command on the central office 4500 router. Here is the output:

```
07:24:46: RIP: build update entries
07:24:46: 0.0.0.0/0 metric 1, tag 0
07:24:51: RIP: received v2 update from 194.73.134.23 on Ethernet0
07:24:51:        172.19.0.0/16 via 0.0.0.0 in 1 hops
07:24:51:        172.20.0.0/16 via 0.0.0.0 in 1 hops
07:24:51:        172.24.0.0/16 via 0.0.0.0 in 1 hops
07:24:51: RIP: received v2 update from 172.18.0.11 on Ethernet0
07:24:51:        172.19.0.0/16 via 0.0.0.0 in 1 hops
07:24:51:        172.20.0.0/16 via 0.0.0.0 in 1 hops
07:24:51:        172.24.0.0/16 via 0.0.0.0 in 1 hops
07:25:15: RIP: sending v2 update to 224.0.0.9 via Ethernet0
                (194.73.134.22)
07:25:15: RIP: build update entries
07:25:15:        0.0.0.0/0 metric 1, tag 0
```

```
07:25:16: RIP: ignored v1 packet from 192.168.10.1 (illegal
               version)
07:25:16: RIP: ignored v1 packet from 192.168.10.1 (illegal
               version)
07:25:42: RIP: sending v2 update to 224.0.0.9 via Ethernet0
               (194.73.134.22)
07:25:42: RIP: build update entries
07:25:42:      0.0.0.0/0 metric 1, tag 0
07:25:43: RIP: received v2 update from 194.73.134.23 on Ethernet0
07:25:43:      172.19.0.0/16 via 0.0.0.0 in 1 hops
07:25:43:      172.20.0.0/16 via 0.0.0.0 in 1 hops
07:25:43:      172.24.0.0/16 via 0.0.0.0 in 1 hops
07:25:43: RIP: received v2 update from 172.18.0.11 on Ethernet0
07:25:43:      172.19.0.0/16 via 0.0.0.0 in 1 hops
07:25:43:      172.20.0.0/16 via 0.0.0.0 in 1 hops
07:25:43:      172.24.0.0/16 via 0.0.0.0 in 1 hops
07:25:46: RIP: received v2 update from 194.73.134.23 on Ethernet0
07:25:46:      172.24.0.0/16 via 0.0.0.0 in 16 hops  (inaccessible)
07:25:46: RIP: received v2 update from 172.18.0.11 on Ethernet0
07:25:46:      172.24.0.0/16 via 0.0.0.0 in 16 hops  (inaccessible)
07:25:48: RIP: sending v2 flash update to 224.0.0.9 via Ethernet0
               (194.73.134.22)
```

The address of the remote network is 192.168.10.0. The router is 192.168.10.1. After investigating the debug output, you notice that the routing updates received from this router are marked as version 1 and illegal. You have set all RIP processes to use version 2 as you plan to implement VLSMs and route summarization at a later date.

Results

You add the version 2 command to the RIP routing configuration on the remote workshops router. This immediately clears the problem and the dynamic routing activity resumes its normal operation.

Questions

1. Which of the following routing protocols considers the 16th hop unreachable?

   a. RIP

   b. IGRP

   c. EIGRP

   d. IS-IS

2. Which of the following routing protocols is distance vector and the property of Cisco systems?

   a. RIP

   b. OSPF

   c. IGRP

   d. BGP

3. Which command displays the internal IP routing table?

   a. Router#show route

   b. Router(config)#show ip route

   c. Router#show ip route

   d. Router#show all routes ip

4. Which command clears all dynamically learned IP routes from the internal routing table?

   a. Router#clear ip route

   b. Router#clear ip route all

   c. Router(config)#clear ip route

   d. Router#clear ip route *

5. The DUAL algorithm is related to which routing protocol?

   a. OSPF

   b. IGRP

   c. EIGRP

   d. IS-IS

6. Classfull routing protocols enable the subnet mask to be passed with the routing update.

   a. True

   b. False

7. You are using RIP as your routing protocol. You do not follow the class-full IP addressing scheme in your network. To continue using RIP, what should you do?

   a. Set the RIP version to version 2.
   b. Enable RIP VLSM support.
   c. Create a loopback interface.
   d. All of the above.

8. After an IGRP hold-down, which step is performed to remove the route?

   a. Route recover
   b. Garbage collection
   c. Route removal
   d. Route clear

9. Which command displays all the configured routing protocols and their configurations on a router?

   a. Router#show route
   b. Router(config)#show ip protocol
   c. Router#show ip protocol
   d. Router#show all protocols

10. You are running RIP and OSPF on your network. A few networks are not receiving IP packets. Which command would you use to find out which interfaces are running OSPF?

    a. show ip protocols
    b. show ip interface
    c. show ip ospf interface
    d. show ospf all

11. Route redistribution automatically occurs between

    a. OSPF and RIP
    b. EIGRP and IGRP
    c. IS-IS and BGP
    d. EIGRP and OSPF

12. Distribute lists have to relate to an access list number.

    a. True
    b. False

13. The command to enable RIP to utilize VLSMs is

    a. Router(config-router)#vlsm
    b. Router(config-router)#version 2
    c. Router(config-router)#rip vlsm
    d. Router(config-router)#rip vlsm on

14. You have a large interconnected network. The network span from end to end is a possible 23 hops. Which routing protocol wouldn't you use?

    a. IGRP
    b. OSPF
    c. RIP
    d. EIGRP

15. You have a route in the routing table that is shown as 192.168.10.0 [120/1] via Ethernet 0. What does the first value in the brackets identify?

    a. The administrative distance
    b. The cost of the route
    c. The number of hops
    d. The metric

16. The Dijkstra algorithm is related to which routing protocol?

    a. OSPF
    b. EIGRP
    c. RIP
    d. IGRP

17. RIP is an _____ gateway routing protocol.

    a. exterior
    b. anterior
    c. posterior
    d. interior

18. Which command is used to debug all ip routing activity?

    a. debug ip rip
    b. debug routing
    c. debug ip routing
    d. debug ip routing-updates

19. What is a passive interface?

    a. An interface that only accepts outbound routing updates.
    b. An interface that doesn't participate in routing updates.
    c. An interface that only accepts inbound routing updates.
    d. An interface that only accepts routing queries.

20. Which command is used to debug IP RIP routing activity?

    a. debug ip rip
    b. debug routing rip
    c. show rip routing
    d. debug rip all

Answers

1. Answer: a

   RIP considers the 16th hop to be unreachable. This is a major design implication of using RIP in your internetwork.

2. Answer: c

   The *interior gateway routing protocol* (IGRP) is distance vector-based and is also property of Cisco Systems.

3. Answer: c

   The Router#show ip route command displays the internal IP routing table. It is important to get the syntax correct for this command. It can only be entered from the Privileged Exec mode.

4. Answer: d

   The command Router#clear ip route * would clear all dynamically stored routes from the internal routing table. It is important to get the syntax correct for this command. It can only be entered from the Privileged Exec mode.

5. Answer: c

   The DUAL algorithm is related to the EIGRP routing protocol.

6. Answer: b

   Classfull routing protocols do not enable the passing of the subnet mask with the network address within a routing update. Classless routing protocols, however, can perform this function. This is required for route summarization and the implementation of VLSMs.

7. Answer: a

   RIP version 1 is classfull. RIP version 2 is classless and supports route summarization and the implementation of VLSMs.

8. Answer: b

   After a hold-down, garbage collection is performed to remove the route.

9. Answer: c

   The Router#show ip protocol command will display all configured routing protocols on the router along with their specific configuration details.

10. Answer: c

    The show ip ospf interface command will display OSPF information for all configured interfaces on the router.

11. Answer: b

    Route redistribution automatically occurs between EIGRP and IGRP.

12. Answer: a

    Distribute lists have to relate to an access list number.

13. Answer: b

    The command to enable RIP to utilize VLSMs is
    `Router(config-router)#version 2`

14. Answer: c

    You wouldn't use RIP in this network because the maximum hop count of RIP is 15 with the 16th hop considered unreachable. This network spans 23 hops.

15. Answer: a

    The first value identifies the administrative distance.

16. Answer: a

    The Dijkstra algorithm is related to OSFP.

17. Answer: d

    RIP is an *interior gateway routing protocol* (IGRP). The only other valid answer would have been Exterior.

18. Answer: c

    The command debug ip routing will debug all IP routing activity.

19. Answer: b

    A passive interface is an interface that doesn't participate in routing updates.

20. Answer: a

    The command debug ip rip would debug all IP RIP routing activity.

## CHAPTER 13

Troubleshooting ISDN Basic Rate Interface (BRI)

This chapter looks at troubleshooting ISDN *Basic Rate Interface* (BRI) on Cisco router interfaces. We start by looking at the physical layer ISDN troubleshooting techniques and then we progress through the Data-Link layer to finally reach the Network layer. We then look at various IOS commands that help the network troubleshooter identify and rectify common ISDN problems.

Integrated Services Digital Network (ISDN) is becoming very prolific as a wide area network protocol due to its decreasing cost and high availability. It is widely used for Internet access, branch office connection, telecommuting applications, video conferencing, and backup for faster serial WAN interfaces.

ISDN provides a common interface that gives access to digital communications services over the public telephone network. ISDN offers multiple advantages over using traditional analog modems: faster call initiation and authentication, more reliable data transfer, and faster transmission speeds.

ISDN is available as *Basic Rate Interface* (BRI) or *Primary Rate Interface* (PRI).

■ Basic Rate consists of two B-channels and one D-channel. Each B-channel carries data and operates at 64 Kbps. The D-channel is responsible for link management and operates at 16 Kbps. Both of the B-channels can be utilized to offer 128 Kbps of bandwidth. BRI is often referred to as 2B+D.

■ Primary Rate is standard-dependent and thus varies according to country. In North America, PRI has 23 B-channels and one D-channel (23B+D). In Europe, PRI has 30 B-channels and one D-channel (30B+D). The American B- and D-channels operate at an equal rate of 64 Kbps. Consequently, the D-channel is sometimes not activated on certain interfaces, thus allowing the time slot to be used as another B-channel. The 23B+D PRI operates at the CCITT designated rate of 1544 Kbps. The European PRI is comprised of 30 B-channels and one D-channel (30B+D). As in the American PRI, all the channels operate at 64 Kbps. However, the 30B+D PRI operates at the CCITT designated rate of 2048 Kbps.

Local Telco providers provide Basic Rate interface as a service. The first published set of standards was in 1984 by the CCITT. Prior to this document, various geographical areas had already developed ISDN standards, which resulted in a CCITT-defined standard for each country.

This standard has come to be known as the ISDN switch type. Following is a list of Cisco-supported ISDN switch types with their Cisco keyword and geographic location:

■ Basic-1tr6   Germany

■ Basic-5ess   AT&T 5ESS for the US

■ Basic-dms100   Northern DMS-100 switch type

■ Basic-net3   NET3 switch type for U.K. and Europe

■ Basic-nil   National ISDN-1 switch type

■ Basic-nwnet3   NET3 switch type for Norway

■ Basic-nznet3   NET3 switch type for New Zealand

■ Basic-ts013   TS013 switch type for Australia

- Ntt   NTT switch type for Japan
- Vn2   VN2 switch type for France
- Vn3   VN3 and VN4 switch types for France

As in previous chapters, we will cover a methodical approach to troubleshooting BRI that follows the OSI model.

We will start by looking at the Physical layer components and work through Data-Link layer protocols, eventually reaching Network Layer protocols.

ISDN Device and Reference Configuration Devices

ISDN user functions are performed by *Terminal Equipment* (TE). Routers with a BRI interface such as an 801, 802, or 2503 are classed as TE. Terminal Equipment is located at the customer's premises. This equipment is referred to as TE1 and is classed as an ISDN terminal.

Equipment without a built-in BRI interface or equipment that predates ISDN standards can still access ISDN. This equipment is referred to as TE2. In order to communicate with ISDN, TE2 equipment requires a *Terminal Adaptor* (TA). For example, A 2501 router has dual Serial and single Ethernet interfaces. You can connect a Terminal Adapter to one of the Serial interfaces to allow ISDN communications.

Termination

Three termination points exist for ISDN, and they are related to the ISDN reference points:

- A *Network Termination* (NT1) exists between customer TE1/TA and the *Line Termination* (LT).
- Each side of the ISDN network is terminated with an LT.
- The carrier side of the interface is terminated with an *Exchange Termination* (ET).

The following diagram simplifies this process (see Figure 13-1).

Most TE1 equipment has an NT1 built-in. In the U.K., however, the NT1 is provided on the ISDN switch by the Telco. Thus, U.K. TE1 devices do not

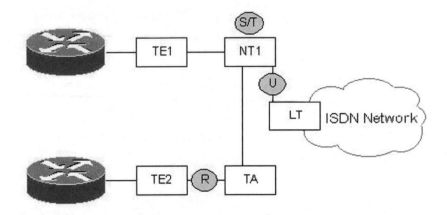

Figure 13-1
ISDN reference points
and termination

have an internal NT1, which makes U.S. and U.K. ISDN equipment incompatible. For example, the 801 ISDN router has an ISDN BRI (S/T) interface and is designed for European markets, and the 802 ISDN router has an ISDN BRI (U) NT1 for North American markets. Although S/T interfaces are still available for use in the U.S., an external NT1 must be used.

ISDN Protocols

The following protocols deal with ISDN issues:

- *E* Specify ISDN on the existing telephone network.
- *I* Specify concepts, terminology, and services.
- *Q* Specify switching and signaling.

Reference Points

ISDN uses five different reference points to define logical interfaces. They are as follows:

- *R* Defines the reference point between non-ISDN equipment and a TA.
- *S* Defines the reference point between user terminals and an NT2.

- ▓ *T*   Defines the reference point between NT1 and NT2 devices.
- ▓ *U*   Defines the reference point between NT1 devices and Line Termination Equipment (North America only).
- ▓ *V*   The termination point within the local loop and switching functions.

Service Profile Identifiers (SPIDs)

Service Profile Identifiers (SPIDs) are used by the carrier to identify what set of services are provided to the customer from the ISDN switch.

SPIDs are mostly used in North America. In other parts of the world, such as Europe, carriers do not assign a specific SPID to the ISDN device. The local Telco provider provides you with the SPID.

SPIDs are usually the 10-digit phone number of the ISDN line, plus a prefix and a suffix that are used to identify services on the line.

On BRI, each B-channel requires a separate SPID.

If the ISDN switch requires a SPID and one is not provided or configured on the ISDN device, Layer 2 initialization will take place, but Layer 3 communication will fail and the device will not connect.

On the Cisco router, the SPID is configured by entering the BRI interface configuration mode and then typing the following commands. For the first B-channel:

```
Router(config-if)#isdn spid1 9999999999999999
```

For the second B-channel:

```
Router(config-if)#isdn spid2 8888888888888888
```

where 8888888888888888 and 9999999999999999 are the Telco provided SPID.

Objectives Covered in This Chapter

This chapter introduces you to troubleshooting Basic Rate Interface.
The following objective is covered:

■ Analyze problem symptoms and resolve resolution strategies in TCP/IP (including the Microsoft 95/NT IP stack), Novell IPX, AppleTalk, Ethernet VLANs, Frame Relay, and ISDN BRI.

■ Use Cisco IOS commands and problem isolation techniques to identify the symptoms of common ISDN BRI problems.

■ Apply diagnostic tools to trouble tickets and solve classroom network ISDN BRI problems that simulate real-life WAN malfunctions.

ISDN in the OSI Model

ISDN maps to the OSI model at the Data-Link and Network layers (see Table 13-1). There are also Physical layer considerations relating to the network termination equipment and the physical links required for call activation and termination.

Physical Layer

Basic Rate Interface is delivered over four twisted pair UTP cabling with an RJ-45 connector. This is specified by the ISO 8877 standard (see Table 13-2).

Table 13-1

ISDN in the OSI model

OSI Layer	ISDN Protocol
Application	
Presentation	
Session	
Transport	
Network	ISDN/Q931
Data Link	LAPD/Q921
Physical	

Table 13-2	Pin	Termination End Point Pin	Network Termination Function
BRI RJ-45 connector— ISO 88//	1	Power Source 3+	Power Sink 3+
	2	Power Source 3-	Power Sink 3-
	3	Transmit +	Receive +
	4	Receive +	Transmit +
	5	Receive -	Transmit -
	6	Transmit -	Receive -
	7	Power Sink 2-	Power Source 2-
	8	Power Sink 2+	Power Source 2+

Data-Link Layer

Layer 2 functions of ISDN define the logical connection between the user terminal equipment and the local network termination. Or, simply the BRI router interface to the ISDN switch.

The ISDN Layer 2 signaling protocol is the Link Access Procedure—Channel D (LAPD). The LAPD protocol is specified in ITU-T Q.920 and ITU-T Q.921.

LAPD

The *Link Access Protocol—Channel D (LAPD)* is a Layer 2 protocol that is defined in ITU-T Q.920/921 (see Figure 13-2). It is primarily responsible for Layer 2 D-channel signaling between two adjacent Layer 2 entities. It provides services to Layer 3 by carrying messages between Layer 3 peers, which it does in conjunction with the Physical layer.

Figure 13-2
LAPD frame structure

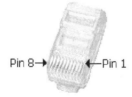

Pin 8→　←Pin 1

Connections between Layer 2 entities occur as either acknowledged or unacknowledged services. These connections are usually acknowledged, but unacknowledged connections are useful when a rapid transfer of information is required.

In acknowledged mode, the Layer 3 information messages are acknowledged by the terminating device. This provides error-free transmission at the protocol level.

In unacknowledged mode, the Layer 3 information messages are transmitted in *Unnumbered Information* (UI) frames. No account is taken of errors, and any error checking must be implemented at the higher layers through software controls.

- *Flag*   The value of the flag is always (0x7E), which ensures that the bit pattern of the frame delimiter flag does not appear in the data field of the frame. The start and end flag are identical.

- *Address Field*   The two bytes after the header flag is the address field. The address field contains several other fields.

  - *SAPI (Service Point Access Identifier)*   The first six bits in the address field. It identifies the point where Layer 2 provides a service to Layer 3.

  - *C/R (Command/Response)*   This next bit identifies whether the frame is a command or response.

  - *EA0 (End Address 0)*   Identifies that it is the end of the first address byte.

  - *TEI*   A 7-bit device identifier.

  - *EA1 (End Address 1)*   Identifies that it is the end of the second address byte.

- *Control Field*   The control field identifies the type of frame as well as including sequence number, control features, and error-tracking according to the frame type.

- *Information*   This is the Layer 3 protocol information and data.

- *FCS*   The Frame Check Sequence (FCS) enables physical error control. The transmitting device calculates the FCS based on the value of the bits in the frame run through an algorithm. The receiving device performs the same calculation to verify the integrity of the frame.

The following command reveals Layer 2 connectivity issues (it is discussed in more depth later in the chapter):

```
Router#debug isdn q921
```

Network Layer

The Layer 3 ISDN signaling protocols are used for call setup, call termination, information, and other messages.

The Layer 3 protocol is specified in ITU-T Q.931. The protocol is known as Q.931.

ISDN Q.931

Q.931 is the Layer 3 ISDN protocol that is responsible for call setup, call termination, information, and other messages.

The messages that are included with this protocol are SETUP, CONNECT, RELEASE, USER INFORMATION, CANCEL, STATUS, and DISCONNECT.

The sequence of Layer 3 messages is as follows:

- SETUP   The caller sends a SETUP to the switch.
- CALL PROC   The switch replies to the caller with a CALL PROC (Call Proceeding).
- SETUP   The switch sends a SETUP to the caller.
- CONNECT   The caller sends a CONNECT to the switch.
- CONNECT   The switch sends a CONNECT to the caller.
- CONNECT ACK   The caller replies with a CONNECT ACK to the switch.
- CONNECT ACK   The switch sends a CONNECT ACK back to the caller.

The following command reveals Layer 3 connectivity issues (we will discuss this in more depth later in the chapter):

```
Router#debug isdn q931
```

Dial-On-Demand Routing

ISDN by its nature is dialup, so it is normally provided where a leased-line or private circuit is cost-prohibitive or unnecessary due to data transfer requirements. Telco's charge connection time for ISDN calls is on a similar scale as standard voice calls. This also applies to long distance or international ISDN calls.

Figure 13-3
DDR Operation

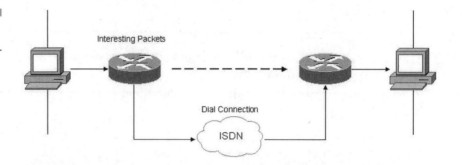

Dial-on-demand Routing (DDR) is when the router only places an ISDN call and brings up the line when it receives what is called interesting traffic (see Figure 13-3).

This connection sequence can be broken down into five distinct phases, as follows:

1. The router receives the packet and looks the destination network up in the routing table. If the outbound interface is a BRI interface, the router checks to see whether the link is already established. If the link is already established, the router sends the packet to the destination network and the process ends.

2. If the link isn't established, the router will check the packet against the access-list that specifies interesting traffic. If the traffic isn't interesting, the packet will be placed in the bit bucket.

3. If the packet is defined by the access-list as interesting traffic, the router will locate the dialing instructions in what is called the dialer map. This will correlate with the destination network.

4. The connection is established using the dialer map information and the router will now transmit both interesting and uninteresting packets.

5. When no interesting traffic is transmitted for the duration specified in the idle-timeout timer, the connection will close.

The command that places the DDR call is the following:

```
Dialer-string 1234567
```

where 1234567 is the destination ISDN number. This is covered in more detail in the ACRC course notes.

If you are faced with a problem where the ISDN router doesn't seem to be initiating a call, it could well be a problem with the specification of interesting traffic.

ISDN is a switched circuit, so the router needs to determine what types of packets should cause the connection to be established and how long the connection should remain established in the absence of these packets. These packets are known as "interesting" packets.

Dialer lists applied to the BRI interface for legacy DDR or the Dialer interface for dialer profiles define interesting packets.

For example, the following would define all IP traffic as interesting where the BRI or Dialer interface is a member of dialer-group 1:

```
Router(config)#dialer-list 1 protocol ip permit
```

There may be instances in which certain traffic is bringing the line up unnecessary such as Windows NT browsing traffic. In this case, it is necessary to create a standard or extended access list and apply this to the dialer-list.

```
Router(config)#access-list 101 deny ip host 172.18.16.20 any
Router(config)#access-list 101 deny ip host 172.18.16.21 any
Router(config)#access-list 101 permit ip any any
Router(config)#dialer-list 1 protocol ip list 101
```

The previous configuration would set IP as interesting traffic, but exclude IP traffic from hosts 172.18.16.20 and 172.18.16.21 as interesting.

Hosts 172.18.16.20 and 172.18.16.21 can still use the BRI connection to communicate; they just cannot bring up the link. This is useful if you have an application running on a host that sends out frequent broadcasts.

Snapshot Routing

If the ISDN router is to take part in routing updates using a routing protocol, care has to be taken.

Static routes are usually recommended for BRI implementations due to the dial-on-demand architecture, although, this may not suit your specific requirements. If you have a large complicated network with frequent topology changes, you probably will want to use a routing protocol such as RIP, IGRP, or OSPF.

Routing protocols that send out frequent hello packets are often inappropriate for ISDN, which include most link state routing protocols such as OSPF. Other routing protocols such as IGRP and RIP allow the connection to be spoofed.

Spoofing is when the local router sends out routing updates to the LAN interfaces as if it were constantly connected to the remote BRI sites. The routing entries remain frozen during periods of inactivity. When interesting traffic brings up the line, routing information is exchanged. This can be forced if the period of activity is over a predetermined limit.

Although this is probably not classed as a problem, incorrectly configured routing protocols on a BRI interface can create a situation in which the link is never closed. At the end of the quarter, this will be reflected by the charge from the Telco for the ISDN use.

PPP

ISDN can use either the *Point to Point Protocol (PPP)* or the *High-Level Data Link Control (HDLC)* as its WAN carrier protocol.

The most common WAN carrier protocol is PPP. PPP operates at Layer 2 of the OSI model and is specified in RFC1548, RFC1661, and RFC1662.

PPP is designed for simple links that transport packets between two peers. These links provide full-duplex, simultaneous, bi-directional operation and are assumed to deliver packets in order.

The PPP connection begins with the *Link Control Protocol (LCP)*, establishing the initial link through configuration and testing. After LCP has connected, one or more *Network Control Protocols (NCPs)* is used to bring up the Layer 3 support for the used protocol suite.

PPP supports TCP/IP, IPX/SPX, and AppleTalk.

PPP is enabled for BRI by entering the following command:

```
Router(config-if)#encapsulation ppp
```

If legacy DDR is used, it only has to be added to the BRI interface. However, if you are using dialer profiles, you also have to add this command to every dialer interface that is created. This is a common configuration fault that is easy to spot and rectify.

PPP Authentication

PPP authentication needs to be established so the router can identify inbound connections and route them to the correct dialer, and also to identify itself on outbound connections.

PPP authentication occurs during session establishment. The two PPP devices communicate and decide on the authentication protocol they will use. Authentication then takes place.

PPP authentication protocols are the *Password Authentication Protocol* (PAP) and the *Challenge Handshake Authentication Protocol* (CHAP). PAP is not recommended because it transmits information in clear text and therefore is considered unsecured. Some older devices will only authenticate using PAP, however.

PAP works by a two-way handshake. After the PPP link establishment phase, the transmitting node repeatedly sends the PAP username and password until authentication is accepted or the receiving node terminates the connection.

CHAP is used at session establishment and also periodically throughout the duration of the session to identify the transmitting node. CHAP follows a three-way handshake that is similar in principle to the TCP/IP three way handshake.

When the PPP nodes establish a session, the receiving node sends a challenge message to the transmitting node. The transmitting node replies with a value that has been calculated using a one-way hash function such as MD5. The receiving node checks this value against its own calculated expected response; if a match occurs, the transmitting node is authenticated. This method is a lot more secure than PAP because it uses a variable challenge value that is unique and unpredictable.

Presenting a username and a password configures authentication.

For example, the following sets the username to be RouterB with a password of qwert321:

```
RouterA(config)#username RouterB password qwert321
```

It is important to note that the passwords must be the same for all authenticating routers.

The username is configured on the router and this is related to the remote node hostname. In the given example, we expect the router called RouterB, which also has a username entry for the router called RouterA. Figure 13-4 explains this configuration.

Then, PPP authentication has to be set. This, like the encapsulation type, must be set for every BRI and every dialer interface that is defined and is to participate in PPP authentication.

```
Router(config-if)#ppp authentication chap
```

The previous command just sets the authentication type to CHAP. You can also configure it for PAP, as follows:

```
Router(config-if)#ppp authentication pap
```

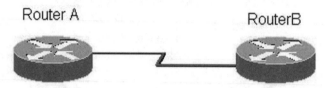

Figure 13-4
RouterA and RouterB
configured for PPP
authentication

```
!
hostname RouterA
!
!
username RouterB password qwert321
!
!
```

```
!
hostname RouterB
!
!
username RouterA password qwert321
!
!
```

The previous command uses PAP only.

```
Router(config-if)#ppp authentication pap chap
```

The previous command uses PAP and then CHAP if PAP authentication fails.

```
Router(config-if)#ppp authentication chap pap
```

The previous command used CHAP and then PAP if CHAP authentication fails. This method is quite frequently used for connecting to Internet service providers where the authentication type can vary depending on the status of the ISP hardware.

If PAP or CHAP PPP authentication is misconfigured, the routers will not be able to establish a connection. Everything else will connect, but the routers will not authenticate. The following command can be used to turn on PPP authentication debugging (this command will be covered later in the chapter):

```
Router#debug ppp authentication
```

Multilink PPP (MPP)

Multilink PPP (MPP) is defined in RFC 1990. It is an industry standard technique that aggregates B-channels at the packet level.

This provides a way to increase bandwidth between two sites by using both channels on a single BRI interface or binding multiple BRI interfaces together.

MPP works by splitting and recombining packets over the channels, thus reducing latency and increasing the effective maximum receive unit (MRU). The receiving end re-creates the data stream in the order it was originally sent by looking at the sequence information sent in each packet.

MPP is established during the PPP LCP negotiation phase. The transmitting device indicates to the receiver that it wants to participate in Multilink PPP by sending the maximum received reconstructed unit (MRRU) as part of the initial LCP negotiation. Before Multilink PPP, there was no standard way to group BRI interfaces and ensure the proper sequencing of packets.

PPP is configured on a Cisco router by enabling MPP on the interface. This has to be done for every BRI interface for legacy DDR or on every Dialer interface when dialer profiles are being used.

```
Router(config-if)#ppp Multilink
```

The previous command enables Multilink PPP on the interface.

```
Router(config-if)#dialer load-threshold 100 outbound
```

The previous command specifies that the interface should reach 39% utilization outbound before bringing up the second line. This figure is worked out on a percentage of 255 (that is, 100/255).

The outbound remark appertains to outbound traffic. This can be set to inbound, outbound, or either.

It is important to ensure both ends of the connection support Multilink PPP before enabling it. If the receiving end doesn't support MPP, you will get spurious packet errors. You may be able to ping the remote hosts but no sustainable traffic will be able to communicate.

ISDN SHOW Commands

Several show commands can be used to view the current BRI configuration of the router. These commands are useful in checking the status of the configuration as well as troubleshooting a range of BRI problems (see Table 13-3).

show interface bri n

The show interface bri n command displays information about the BRI D-channel for BRI interface n:

Table 13-3

Frequently Used
show Commands
for Troubleshooting
BRI Connections

Command	Description
show interface bri n	Displays information about the D-channel on the BRI interface and the relevant counters/statistics.
show interface bri n:x	Displays information about the B-channels on the BRI interface and the relevant counters/statistics.
show controllers bri	Displays the BRI controller information.
show isdn status	Displays the status of the three ISDN layers and the locally configured switch type.
show dialer	Displays information relating to the current dialer state and established connections.
show dialer interface bri n	Displays information relating to the current dialer state and established connections for the given interface.
show dialer interface bri n:x	Displays information relating to the current dialer state and established connections for the given interface and bearer channel.
show ppp multilink	Displays information about the state of ppp Multilink packets.

```
Router#sh interface bri 0/0
BRI0/0 is up, line protocol is up (spoofing)
   Hardware is PQUICC BRI
   Description: connected to Internet
   MTU 1500 bytes, BW 64 Kbit, DLY 20000 usec, rely 255/255, load 1/255
   Encapsulation PPP, loopback not set
   DTR is pulsed for 1 seconds on reset
   Last input 00:00:07, output never, output hang never
   Last clearing of "show interface" counters never
   Input queue: 0/75/0 (size/max/drops); Total output drops: 0
   Queueing strategy: weighted fair
   Output queue: 0/1000/64/0 (size/max total/threshold/drops)
      Conversations  0/1/256 (active/max active/max total)
      Reserved Conversations 0/0 (allocated/max allocated)
   5 minute input rate 0 bits/sec, 0 packets/sec
   5 minute output rate 0 bits/sec, 0 packets/sec
      348 packets input, 2342 bytes, 0 no buffer
      Received 0 broadcasts, 0 runts, 0 giants, 0 throttles
      0 input errors, 0 CRC, 0 frame, 0 overrun, 0 ignored, 0 abort
      504 packets output, 61693 bytes, 0 underruns
      0 output errors, 0 collisions, 7 interface resets
      0 output buffer failures, 0 output buffers swapped out
      5 carrier transitions
Router#
```

The first area indicates that the interface is up and the line protocol is spoofing. This may not mean that the connection is established because spoofing is a way that the D-channel lies to Layer 3 DDR so a routing entry will be maintained in the router.

The second area indicates that we are using PPP as the encapsulation protocol.

The router in the example listing has established a connection and the last input traffic was seven seconds ago.

show interface bri n:x

The `show interface bri n:x` command displays information about the BRI B-channel for BRI interface n and channel x:

```
Router#sh int bri 0/0:1
BRI0/0:1 is up, line protocol is up
  Hardware is PQUICC BRI
  MTU 1500 bytes, BW 64 Kbit, DLY 20000 usec, rely 255/255, load 1/255
  Encapsulation PPP, loopback not set, keepalive set (10 sec)
  DTR is pulsed for 1 seconds on reset
  Time to interface disconnect:  idle 00:59:10
  LCP Open
  Open: IPCP
  Last input 00:00:09, output 00:00:09, output hang never
  Last clearing of "show interface" counters never
  Input queue: 0/75/0 (size/max/drops); Total output drops: 0
  Queueing strategy: weighted fair
  Output queue: 0/1000/64/0 (size/max total/threshold/drops)
     Conversations  0/4/256 (active/max active/max total)
     Reserved Conversations 0/0 (allocated/max allocated)
  5 minute input rate 0 bits/sec, 0 packets/sec
  5 minute output rate 0 bits/sec, 0 packets/sec
     491 packets input, 176884 bytes, 0 no buffer
     Received 0 broadcasts, 0 runts, 0 giants, 0 throttles
     0 input errors, 0 CRC, 0 frame, 0 overrun, 0 ignored, 0 abort
     552 packets output, 67396 bytes, 0 underruns
     0 output errors, 0 collisions, 0 interface resets
     0 output buffer failures, 0 output buffers swapped out
     1 carrier transitions
Router#
```

The first area indicates that the interface is up and the line protocol is up. This indicates that a connection has been established on BRI0/0:1.

The second area indicates the time to disconnect the interface. This is defined as the dialer-idle timeout value less the duration between the last receipt of interesting traffic.

The next example shows BRI0/0:2 on the same router and indicates that this interface is down.

```
Router#sh int bri 0/0:2
BRI0/0:2 is down, line protocol is down
  Hardware is PQUICC BRI
```

```
MTU 1500 bytes, BW 64 Kbit, DLY 20000 usec, rely 255/255, load 1/255
Encapsulation PPP, loopback not set, keepalive set (10 sec)
DTR is pulsed for 1 seconds on reset
LCP Closed
Closed: IPCP
Last input never, output never, output hang never
Last clearing of "show interface" counters never
Input queue: 0/75/0 (size/max/drops); Total output drops: 0
Queueing strategy: weighted fair
Output queue: 0/1000/64/0 (size/max total/threshold/drops)
    Conversations  0/0/256 (active/max active/max total)
    Reserved Conversations 0/0 (allocated/max allocated)
5 minute input rate 0 bits/sec, 0 packets/sec
5 minute output rate 0 bits/sec, 0 packets/sec
    0 packets input, 0 bytes, 0 no buffer
    Received 0 broadcasts, 0 runts, 0 giants, 0 throttles
    0 input errors, 0 CRC, 0 frame, 0 overrun, 0 ignored, 0 abort
    477 packets output, 66183 bytes, 0 underruns
    0 output errors, 0 collisions, 0 interface resets
    0 output buffer failures, 0 output buffers swapped out
    0 carrier transitions
Router#
```

show controllers bri

The show controllers bri command displays the BRI controller information (this includes Physical layer connectivity and several other internal
controller variables):

```
Router#sh controllers bri
BRI unit 0:
Layer 1 is ACTIVATED. (ISDN L1 State F7)
D Channel Information:
idb at 0x8095EF9C, driver data structure at 0x809A43FC
Siemens Chip Version 0x0
SIEMENS Registers:
Status Register [STAR]=0x48, Mode Register [MODE]=0xC9
Serial Port Control Register [SPCR]=0x0
Additional Feature Register [ADF2]=0x80
RX Buffer Descriptor is at 0x809A470C, Buffer size 1524
pak=0x80ADC13C data_ptr=0x158A3F4 partial_size=0x0

TX Buffer Descriptor is at 0x809A4750
pak=0x0 data_ptr=0x0 partial_size=0x0
  0 missed datagrams, 0 overruns
  0 bad datagram encapsulations, 0 memory errors
  0 transmitter underruns  0 d channel collisions


B1 Channel Information:
idb at 0x80964C0C, driver data structure at 0x809A4794
SCC Registers:
General [GSMR]=0x2:0x00000030, Protocol-specific [PSMR]=0x8
Events [SCCE]=0x0000, Mask [SCCM]=0x001F, Status [SCCS]=0x06
Transmit on Demand [TODR]=0x0, Data Sync [DSR]=0x7E7E
[output omitted]
```

```
0 missed datagrams, 0 overruns
  0 bad datagram encapsulations, 0 memory errors
  0 transmitter underruns  0 d channel collisions

B2 Channel Information:
idb at 0x8096A8C0, driver data structure at 0x809A4B78
SCC Registers:
General [GSMR]=0x2:0x00000000, Protocol-specific [PSMR]=0x8
Events [SCCE]=0x0000, Mask [SCCM]=0x0000, Status [SCCS]=0x00
Transmit on Demand [TODR]=0x0, Data Sync [DSR]=0x7E7E
Interrupt Registers:
Config [CICR]=0x00367F80, Pending [CIPR]=0x00000002
Mask   [CIMR]=0x40200000, In-srv  [CISR]=0x00000000
Command register [CR]=0x600
Port A [PADIR]=0x04C0, [PAPAR]=0xFFFF
       [PAODR]=0x0040, [PADAT]=0xFBFD
Port B [PBDIR]=0x0220F, [PBPAR]=0x0D00E
       [PBODR]=0x0000E, [PBDAT]=0x32FFD
Port C [PCDIR]=0x00C, [PCPAR]=0x800
       [PCSO]=0x080,   [PCDAT]=0x7F0, [PCINT]=0x00F
[output omitted]
0 missed datagrams, 0 overruns
  0 bad datagram encapsulations, 0 memory errors
  0 transmitter underruns  0 d channel collisions
```

The first area indicates that Layer 1 is activated. The second area then provides you with the D-channel information. This is then followed by the B1- and B2-channel information.

You are also provided with information relating to datagram errors: missed datagrams, overruns, bad datagram encapsulations, memory errors, transmitter underruns, and channel collisions.

show isdn status

The show isdn status command displays the status of the three ISDN layers and the locally configured switch type:

```
Router# sh isdn stat
Global ISDN Switchtype = basic-net3
ISDN BRI0/0 interface
      dsl 0, interface ISDN Switchtype = basic-net3
   Layer 1 Status:
      ACTIVE
   Layer 2 Status:
      TEI = 114, Ces = 1, SAPI = 0, State =
      MULTIPLE_FRAME_ESTABLISHED
   Layer 3 Status:
      1 Active Layer 3 Call(s)
   Activated dsl 0 CCBs = 1
      CCB:callid=0x8001, sapi=0x0, ces=0x1, B-chan=1
   The Free Channel Mask:  0x80000002
   Total Allocated ISDN CCBs = 1
Router#
```

The first and second areas indicate which ISDN switch type is used both globally and at the BRI0/0 interface level.

The next areas indicate the status of Layer 1, Layer 2, and Layer 3. As seen in this example, Layers 1, 2, and 3 are all active with one Layer 3 call placed. This output is very important in BRI troubleshooting as a quick way of determining whether the BRI interface is communicating with the Telco's ISDN equipment.

show dialer

The show dialer command displays information relating to the current dialer state and established connections.

```
Router#sh dialer
BRI0/0 - dialer type = ISDN
Rotary group 1, priority = 0
0 incoming call(s) have been screened.
0 incoming call(s) rejected for callback.
BRI0/0:1 - dialer type = ISDN
Idle timer (3600 secs), Fast idle timer (20 secs)
Wait for carrier (30 secs), Re-enable (15 secs)
Dialer state is data link layer up
Dial reason: ip (s=192.168.10.26, d=216.156.2.60)
Time until disconnect 3559 secs
Current call connected 00:14:50
Connected to 08456621349
BRI0/0:2 - dialer type = ISDN
Idle timer (3600 secs), Fast idle timer (20 secs)
Wait for carrier (30 secs), Re-enable (15 secs)
Dialer state is idle
Dialer1 - dialer type = IN-BAND SYNC NO-PARITY
Load threshold for dialing additional calls is 255
Idle timer (3600 secs), Fast idle timer (20 secs)
Wait for carrier (30 secs), Re-enable (15 secs)
Dial String    Successes  Failures  Last called  Last status
08456621349           1         0  00:14:52     successful Default
Router#
```

The first area indicates that no incoming calls have been received by the BRI interface. This is normal if the router is only used for outbound connections such as an Internet connection.

The next area indicates the start of information relating to the BRI interface 0/0 and channel 1. We can see that the idle timer is 3600 seconds and it will disconnect in 3559 seconds. This indicates that interesting traffic was received just one second ago. The dial reason indicates the source IP address of the host that sent the first interesting packet that brought up the link. The destination address is also included.

You can see that this call has been active for 14 minutes and 50 seconds, and the current call is connected to the number 08456621349.

Interface BRI0/0 channel 2 is displayed next. From the output, we can see that this channel is currently down and in the idle state waiting for a connection. We can also see that the dialer load-threshold for the dialer interface is set at 255. This tells us that the second channel will never be brought up as part of this dialer interface.

The last highlighted area indicates the dial string, along with historical information appertaining to the successes and failures on this connection.

The following example shows you the output from

```
Router#sh dialer int bri 0/0
BRI0/0 - dialer type = ISDN
Rotary group 1, priority = 0
0 incoming call(s) have been screened.
0 incoming call(s) rejected for callback.
BRI0/0:1 - dialer type = ISDN
Idle timer (3600 secs), Fast idle timer (20 secs)
Wait for carrier (30 secs), Re-enable (15 secs)
Dialer state is data link layer up
Dial reason: ip (s=192.168.10.26, d=216.156.2.60)
Time until disconnect 3530 secs
Current call connected 00:15:19
Connected to 08456621349
BRI0/0:2 - dialer type = ISDN
Idle timer (3600 secs), Fast idle timer (20 secs)
Wait for carrier (30 secs), Re-enable (15 secs)
Dialer state is idle
Router#
```

The following example shows you the output from

```
Router#sh dialer int bri 0/0:1
BRI0/0:1 - dialer type = ISDN
Idle timer (3600 secs), Fast idle timer (20 secs)
Wait for carrier (30 secs), Re-enable (15 secs)
Dialer state is data link layer up
Dial reason: ip (s=192.168.10.26, d=216.156.2.60)
Time until disconnect 3503 secs
Current call connected 00:15:46
Connected to 08456621349
Router#
```

The following example shows you the output from

```
Router#sh dialer int bri 0/0:2
BRI0/0:2 - dialer type = ISDN
Idle timer (3600 secs), Fast idle timer (20 secs)
Wait for carrier (30 secs), Re-enable (15 secs)
Dialer state is idle
Router#
```

This shows you that the interfaces can be displayed all together or individually.

As you can see, you can extract a lot of information from the `show dialer` command. This is a very important command to master and is useful for troubleshooting BRI connections because it displays a lot of information about the dialer connection.

show ppp multilink

The `show ppp multilink` command displays information about the state of ppp multilink packets:

```
Router#sh ppp multilink

Bundle 0010.bc01.7f40, 1 member, Master link is Virtual-Access1
Dialer Interface is Dialer1
  1 lost fragments, 1 reordered, 0 unassigned, sequence 0xA/0x0
    rcvd/sent
  0 discarded, 0 lost received, 1/255 load

Member Link: 1 (max not set, min not set)
BRI0/0:1
Router#
```

This command is used to verify that multilink bundles have been activated correctly. From the output, you can see that one lost fragment has occurred and one bundle has been reordered.

ISDN DEBUG Commands

The `debug` commands are an excellent way to interrogate the router and receive real-time information regarding the state of ISDN connections at various OSI layers (see Table 13-4).

As always, only use `debug` commands when it is necessary to do so and be careful when using them on busy core production routers. Debugging puts a load on the router CPU and can have a detrimental effect on the network.

After every debugging session, always use the `Router#no debug all` command to turn off all debug events.

	Command	Description
Table 13-4		
Frequently Used debug Commands for Troubleshooting BRI Connections	`debug bri`	Displays debug information about the physical layer activation of the B-channels.
	`debug isdn q921`	Displays debug information about the Q.921 Data-Link layer access procedures.
	`debug isdn q931`	Displays debug information about the Q.931 Network layer call setup and teardown.
	`debug ppp negotiation`	Displays debug information on LCP and PPP packets.
	`debug ppp authentication`	Displays debug information on the PPP authentication phase.
	`debug dialer`	Displays debug information about dial-on-demand routing.
	`debug isdn`	Displays debug information on Q.931 call establishment.
	`debug ppp packet`	Displays debug information on PPP packets.

debug bri

The `debug bri` command displays debug information about the Physical layer activation of the B-channels:

```
Router#debug bri
BRI: write_sid: wrote 1B for subunit 0, slot 1.
BRI: write_sid: wrote 15 for subunit 0, slot 1.
BRI: write_sid: wrote 17 for subunit 0, slot 1.
BRI: write_sid: wrote 6 for subunit 0, slot 1.
BRI: write_sid: wrote 8 for subunit 0, slot 1.
BRI: write_sid: wrote 11 for subunit 0, slot 1.
BRI: write_sid: wrote 13 for subunit 0, slot 1.
BRI: write_sid: wrote 29 for subunit 0, slot 1.
BRI: write_sid: wrote 1B for subunit 0, slot 1.
BRI: write_sid: wrote 15 for subunit 0, slot 1.
BRI: write_sid: wrote 17 for subunit 0, slot 1.
BRI: write_sid: wrote 20 for subunit 0, slot 1.
BRI: Starting Power Up timer for unit = 0.
BRI: write_sid: wrote 3 for subunit 0, slot 1.
BRI: Starting T3 timer after expiry of PUP timeout for unit = 0,
    current state is F4.
BRI: write_sid: wrote FF for subunit 0, slot 1.
BRI: Activation for unit = 0, current state is F7.
BRI: enable channel B1
BRI: write_sid: wrote 14 for subunit 0, slot 1.
%LINK-3-UPDOWN: Interface BRI0: B-Channel 1, changed state to up
%LINK-5-CHANGED: Interface BRI0: B-Channel 1, changed state to up.!!!
BRI: disable channel B1
```

```
BRI: write_sid: wrote 15 for subunit 0, slot 1.
%LINK-3-UPDOWN: Interface BRI0: B-Channel 1, changed state to down
%LINK-5-CHANGED: Interface BRI0: B-Channel 1, changed state to down
%LINEPROTO-5-UPDOWN: Line protocol on Interface BRI0: B-Channel 1,
                changed state to down
```

This command displays the internal Physical layer code used to initialize outgoing calls. This debug command produces a significant amount of
output and is usually performed under instruction from a TAC engineer.

The following line indicates that an internal command was written to the
interface controller (the subunit identifies the first interface in the slot):

```
BRI: write_sid: wrote 1B for subunit 0, slot 1.
```

The following line indicates that the power up timer was started for the
named unit:

```
BRI: Starting Power Up timer for unit = 0.
```

The following lines indicate that the channel or the protocol on the interface changed state:

```
%LINK-3-UPDOWN: Interface BRI0: B-Channel 1, changed state to up
%LINK-5-CHANGED: Interface BRI0: B-Channel 1, changed state to up.!!!
%LINEPROTO-5-UPDOWN: Line protocol on Interface BRI0: B-Channel 1,
                changed state to down
```

The following line indicates that the channel was disabled:

```
BRI: disable channel B1
```

debug isdn q921

The debug isdn q921 command displays debug information about the
Q.921 Data-Link layer access procedures:

```
Router#debug isdn q921
ISDN Q921 packets debugging is on
Router#
00:36:15: ISDN BR0/0: TX ->  RRp sapi = 0  tei = 114 nr = 5
00:36:64424509440: ISDN BR0/0: RX <-  RRp sapi = 0  tei = 114  nr = 3
00:36:15:          ISDN BR0/0: TX -> RRf sapi = 0  tei = 114  nr = 5
00:36:64424550400: ISDN BR0/0: RX <-  RRf sapi = 0  tei = 114  nr = 3
00:36:77309452288: ISDN BR0/0: RX <-  RRp sapi = 0  tei = 116  nr = 1
00:36:77309452288: ISDN BR0/0: RX <-  RRf sapi = 0  tei = 116  nr = 1
00:36:98806703255: %ISDN-6-DISCONNECT: Interface BRI0/0:1
                disconnected from 08456621349 , call lasted 108
                seconds
00:36:100940167231: %LINK-3-UPDOWN: Interface BRI0/0:1, changed
                state to down
```

```
00:36:24: %LINEPROTO-5-UPDOWN: Line protocol on Interface BRI0/0:1,
           changed state to down
00:36:24: ISDN BR0/0: TX ->  SABMEp sapi = 0  tei = 114
00:36:105237151076: ISDN BR0/0: RX <-  UAf sapi = 0  tei = 114
00:36:24: %ISDN-6-LAYER2UP: Layer 2 for Interface BR0/0, TEI 114
           changed to up
00:36:103079256064: ISDN BR0/0: RX <-  SABMEp sapi = 0  tei = 114
00:36:24: ISDN BR0/0: TX ->  UAf sapi = 0  tei = 114
00:36:105235134204: ISDN BR0/0: RX <-  INFOc sapi = 0  tei = 114
                    ns = 0  nr = 0  i = 0x08018875
00:36:24: ISDN BR0/0: TX ->  RRr sapi = 0  tei = 114  nr = 1
00:36:24: ISDN BR0/0: TX ->  INFOc sapi = 0  tei = 114  ns = 0  nr
           = 1  i = 0x0801084D080280D1
00:36:107374182400: ISDN BR0/0: RX <-  RRr sapi = 0  tei = 114  nr = 1
00:36:109530101500: ISDN BR0/0: RX <-  INFOc sapi = 0  tei = 114
                    ns = 1  nr = 1  i = 0x0801885A
00:36:25: ISDN BR0/0: TX ->  RRr sapi = 0  tei = 114  nr = 2
00:36:120259084288: ISDN BR0/0: RX <-  RRp sapi = 0  tei = 116 nr = 1
00:36:120259125248: ISDN BR0/0: RX <-  RRf sapi = 0  tei = 116  nr = 1
00:36:35: ISDN BR0/0: TX ->  RRp sapi = 0  tei = 114 nr = 2
00:36:150323896320: ISDN BR0/0: RX <-  RRf sapi = 0  tei = 114  nr = 1
00:36:36: ISDN BR0/0: TX ->  INFOc sapi = 0  tei = 114  ns = 1  nr
           = 2  i = 0x08010905040288901801837000
                  C80303834353636323133439
00:36:154618863616: ISDN BR0/0: RX <-  RRr sapi = 0  tei = 114  nr = 2
00:36:156774741756: ISDN BR0/0: RX <-  INFOc sapi = 0  tei = 114
                    ns = 2  nr = 2  i = 0x08018902180189
00:36:36: ISDN BR0/0: TX ->  RRr sapi = 0  tei = 114  nr = 3
00:36:158913830912: ISDN BR0/0: RX <-  INFOc sapi = 0  tei = 114
                    ns = 3  nr = 2  i = 0x08018901
00:36:37: ISDN BR0/0: TX ->  RRr sapi = 0  tei = 114  nr = 4
00:36:158913830912: ISDN BR0/0: RX <-  INFOc sapi = 0  tei = 114
                    ns = 4  nr = 2  i = 0x08018907
00:36:37: ISDN BR0/0: TX ->  RRr sapi = 0  tei = 114  nr = 5
00:36:37: %LINK-3-UPDOWN: Interface BRI0/0:1, changed state to up
00:36:37: %ISDN-6-CONNECT: Interface BRI0/0:1 is now connected to
           08456621349
00:36:37: ISDN BR0/0: TX ->  INFOc sapi = 0  tei = 114  ns = 2  nr
           = 5  i = 0x0801090F
00:36:158913789952: ISDN BR0/0: RX <-  RRr sapi = 0  tei = 114  nr = 3
00:36:38: %LINEPROTO-5-UPDOWN: Line protocol on Interface BRI0/0:1,
           changed state to up
00:36:163208798208: ISDN BR0/0: RX <-  RRp sapi = 0  tei = 116 nr = 1
00:36:163208798208: ISDN BR0/0: RX <-  RRf sapi = 0  tei = 116  nr = 1
00:36:43: %ISDN-6-CONNECT: Interface BRI0/0:1 is now connected to
           08456621349
Router#
00:36:47: ISDN BR0/0: TX ->  RRp sapi = 0  tei = 114 nr = 5
00:36:201863503872: ISDN BR0/0: RX <-  RRp sapi = 0  tei = 114  nr = 3
00:36:47: ISDN BR0/0: TX ->  RRf sapi = 0  tei = 114  nr = 5
00:36:201863503872: ISDN BR0/0: RX <-  RRf sapi = 0  tei = 114  nr = 3
00:36:206158471168: ISDN BR0/0: RX <-  RRp sapi = 0  tei = 116 nr = 1
00:36:206158471168: ISDN BR0/0: RX <-  RRf sapi = 0  tei = 116  nr = 1
Router#no debug all
All possible debugging has been turned off
```

This command displays the communication process for the ISDN Link Access Protocol—D Channel (LAPD) signaling protocol on the D-channel. The output will vary, depending on the role of the router. If the router is making a connection, you will see information appertaining to the outbound connection. If the router is receiving a connection, you will see information appertaining to the inbound connection.

The previous example output is taken during outbound call connection to 08456621349.

This `debug` command produces a lot of output and it is difficult to use for troubleshooting purposes.

Two of the common reasons why errors occur at Layer 2 for ISDN are poor D-channel line quality and mismatched switch type.

The Layer 2 connection establishment procedure consists of six steps outlined as follows:

1. *Receive Ready* (RR) frames are exchanged between the *Terminal Endpoint* (TE) and the network. These frames are listening for a connection.

2. An *Unnumbered Information* (UI) frame is sent by the TE. This UI frame includes a *Service Access Point Identifier* (SAPI) of 63 and a *Terminal Endpoint Identifier* (TEI) of 127. A TEI of 127 is a broadcast.

3. An available TEI is assigned between 64 and 126.

4. The TE sends a *Set Asynchronous Balanced Mode* (SABME) frame with a SAPI of 0 and a TEI that has been assigned by the network. The SAPI of 0 indicates the initiation of a call setup.

5. An *Unnumbered Acknowledgment* (UA) is sent to the TE from the network.

6. Layer 2 connection is now completed and we are ready for Layer 3 setup.

debug isdn q931

The `debug isdn q931` command displays debug information about the Q.931 network layer call setup and teardown:

```
Router#debug isdn q931

ISDN Q931 packets debugging is on
00:34:55834574850: ISDN BR0/0: RX <-   STATUS_ENQ pd = 8   callref =
                    0x87
00:34:13: ISDN BR0/0: TX ->   RELEASE pd = 8   callref = 0x07
00:34:13:          Cause i = 0x80D1 - Invalid call reference value
00:34:55834615808: ISDN BR0/0: RX <-   RELEASE_COMP pd = 8   callref
                    = 0x87
00:34:33: ISDN BR0/0: TX ->   SETUP pd = 8   callref = 0x08
00:34:33:          Bearer Capability i = 0x8890
00:34:33:          Channel ID i = 0x83
00:34:33:          Called Party Number i = 0x80, '08456621349'
```

```
00:34:141733961728: ISDN BR0/0: RX <-  CALL_PROC pd = 8  callref =
                      0x88
00:34:141733920768:          Channel ID i = 0x89
00:34:146028929024: ISDN BR0/0: RX <-  ALERTING pd = 8  callref = 0x88
00:34:150323896320: ISDN BR0/0: RX <-  CONNECT pd = 8  callref = 0x88
00:34:35: %LINK-3-UPDOWN: Interface BRI0/0:1, changed state to up
00:34:35: %ISDN-6-CONNECT: Interface BRI0/0:1 is now connected to
                      08456621349
00:34:35: ISDN BR0/0: TX ->  CONNECT_ACK pd = 8  callref = 0x08
00:34:37: %LINEPROTO-5-UPDOWN: Line protocol on Interface BRI0/0:1,
          changed state to up
00:34:41: %ISDN-6-CONNECT: Interface BRI0/0:1 is now connected to
          08456621349
Router#
```

The Q.931 standard defines the Network layer protocols for user-to-user circuit-switched connections for D-channel communications.

This includes the setup, connection, release, and disconnection of calls between the terminal equipment (TE) and the Telco's ISDN switch.

This debug command displays the call establishment information transmitted between these two devices.

Q931 debugging is useful for tracking any configuration problems such as ISDN switch types or SPID configurations.

Every ISDN call should go through the following Layer 3 stages:

- SETUP   The caller sends a SETUP to the switch.

- CALL PROC   The switch replies to the caller with a CALL PROC (Call Proceeding).

- SETUP   The switch sends a SETUP to the caller.

- CONNECT   The caller sends a CONNECT to the switch.

- CONNECT   The switch sends a CONNECT to the caller.

- CONNECT ACK   The caller replies with a CONNECT ACK to the switch.

- CONNECT ACK   The switch sends a CONNECT ACK back to the caller.

These stages are all available via the debug isdn q931 command.

debug ppp negotiation

The debug ppp negotiation command displays debug information on LCP and PPP packets:

```
Router#debug ppp negot
PPP protocol negotiation debugging is on
00:23:42: BR0/0:1 PPP: Treating connection as a callout
```

```
00:23:42: BR0/0:1 PPP: Phase is ESTABLISHING, Active Open
00:23:42: BR0/0:1 PPP: No remote authentication for call-out
00:23:42: BR0/0:1 LCP: O CONFREQ [Closed] id 9 len 10
00:23:42: BR0/0:1 LCP:    MagicNumber 0xD0D00BDE (0x0506D0D00BDE)
00:23:42: BR0/0:1 LCP: I CONFREQ [REQsent] id 1 len 35
00:23:42: BR0/0:1 LCP:    MRU 1500 (0x010405DC)
00:23:42: BR0/0:1 LCP:    AuthProto PAP (0x0304C023)
00:23:42: BR0/0:1 LCP:    MagicNumber 0xA924130B (0x0506A924130B)
00:23:42: BR0/0:1 LCP:    PFC (0x0702)
00:23:42: BR0/0:1 LCP:    ACFC (0x0802)
00:23:42: BR0/0:1 LCP:    MRRU 1506 (0x110405E2)
00:23:42: BR0/0:1 LCP:    EndpointDisc 3 0010.bc01.7f40
                            (0x1309030010BC017F40)
00:23:42: BR0/0:1 LCP: O CONFREJ [REQsent] id 1 len 17
00:23:42: BR0/0:1 LCP:    MRRU 1506 (0x110405E2)
00:23:42: BR0/0:1 LCP:    EndpointDisc 3 0010.bc01.7f40
                            (0x1309030010BC017F40)
00:23:42: BR0/0:1 LCP: I CONFACK [REQsent] id 9 len 10
00:23:42: BR0/0:1 LCP:    MagicNumber 0xD0D00BDE (0x0506D0D00BDE)
00:23:42: BR0/0:1 LCP: I CONFREQ [ACKrcvd] id 2 len 22
00:23:42: BR0/0:1 LCP:    MRU 1500 (0x010405DC)
00:23:42: BR0/0:1 LCP:    AuthProto PAP (0x0304C023)
00:23:42: BR0/0:1 LCP:    MagicNumber 0xA924130B (0x0506A924130B)
00:23:42: BR0/0:1 LCP:    PFC (0x0702)
00:23:42: BR0/0:1 LCP:    ACFC (0x0802)
00:23:42: BR0/0:1 LCP: O CONFACK [ACKrcvd] id 2 len 22
00:23:42: BR0/0:1 LCP:    MRU 1500 (0x010405DC)
00:23:42: BR0/0:1 LCP:    AuthProto PAP (0x0304C023)
00:23:42: BR0/0:1 LCP:    MagicNumber 0xA924130B (0x0506A924130B)
00:23:42: BR0/0:1 LCP:    PFC (0x0702)
00:23:42: BR0/0:1 LCP:    ACFC (0x0802)
00:23:42: BR0/0:1 LCP: State is Open
00:23:42: BR0/0:1 PPP: Phase is AUTHENTICATING, by the peer
00:23:42: BR0/0:1 PAP: O AUTH-REQ id 5 len 20 from "agmason"
00:23:42: BR0/0:1 PAP: I AUTH-ACK id 5 len 5
00:23:42: BR0/0:1 PPP: Phase is UP
00:23:42: BR0/0:1 IPCP: O CONFREQ [Closed] id 9 len 10
00:23:42: BR0/0:1 IPCP:    Address 0.0.0.0 (0x030600000000)
00:23:42: BR0/0:1 IPCP: I CONFREQ [REQsent] id 1 len 4
00:23:42: BR0/0:1 IPCP: O CONFACK [REQsent] id 1 len 4
00:23:42: BR0/0:1 IPCP: I CONFNAK [ACKsent] id 9 len 10
00:23:42: BR0/0:1 IPCP:    Address 212.1.159.45 (0x0306D4019F2D)
00:23:42: BR0/0:1 IPCP: O CONFREQ [ACKsent] id 10 len 10
00:23:42: BR0/0:1 IPCP:    Address 212.1.159.45 (0x0306D4019F2D)
00:23:42: BR0/0:1 IPCP: I CONFACK [ACKsent] id 10 len 10
00:23:42: BR0/0:1 IPCP:    Address 212.1.159.45 (0x0306D4019F2D)
00:23:42: BR0/0:1 IPCP: State is Open
00:23:42: Di1 IPCP: Install negotiated IP interface address
                        212.1.159.45
00:23:42: BR0/0:1 CCP: I CONFREQ [Not negotiated] id 1 len 10
00:23:42: BR0/0:1 CCP:    MS-PPC supported bits 0x00000001
                            (0x120600000001)
00:23:42: BR0/0:1 LCP: O PROTREJ [Open] id 10 len 16 protocol CCP
                            (0x80FD0101000A120600000001)
00:23:43: %LINEPROTO-5-UPDOWN: Line protocol on Interface BRI0/0:1,
                            changed state to up
00:23:48: %ISDN-6-CONNECT: Interface BRI0/0:1 is now connected to
                            08456621349
```

When PPP establishes a connection, both communication partners agree on the Link Control Protocol (LCP) variables. The `debug ppp negotiation` command outputs these initial packets.

The router sends a CONFREQ message, which is a configuration request. This gets a response of either a CONFACK or CONFNAK. A CONFACK message is a configuration acknowledgment; a CONFNAK message is a configuration not acknowledged and is an indication of a mismatched configuration.

It is interesting to see from this example output that this router is authenticating against PPP PAP. The router is set up for CHAP and then PAP authentication; this can indicate a problem with the CHAP configuration at the receiving end.

debug ppp authentication

The `debug ppp authentication` command displays debug information on the PPP authentication phase of session establishment:

```
Router#debug ppp auth
PPP authentication debugging is on
Router#
00:20:23: %ISDN-6-LAYER2UP: Layer 2 for Interface BR0/0, TEI 114
          changed to up
00:20:37: %LINK-3-UPDOWN: Interface BRI0/0:1, changed state to up
00:20:37: %ISDN-6-CONNECT: Interface BRI0/0:1 is now connected to
          08456621349
00:20:37: BR0/0:1 PPP: Treating connection as a callout
00:20:37: BR0/0:1 PPP: Phase is AUTHENTICATING, by the peer
00:20:37: BR0/0:1 PAP: O AUTH-REQ id 3 len 20 from "agmason"
00:20:37: BR0/0:1 PAP: I AUTH-ACK id 3 len 5
00:20:38: %LINEPROTO-5-UPDOWN: Line protocol on Interface BRI0/0:1,
          changed state to up
00:20:43: %ISDN-6-CONNECT: Interface BRI0/0:1 is now connected to
          08456621349
Router#
```

This command provides information about the PPP authentication phase. Authentication occurs after the initial LCP connection has been established.

You can see from the previous example output that the router is authenticating against PPP PAP and the username is "agmason."

The AUTH-ACK acknowledged positive authentication. An AUTH-NCK would indicate a failure of authentication.

This command is very useful to trace any PPP authentication problems with the router. You can see the authentication protocol, as well as the sent username and dialer string.

A visual acknowledgment is sent, indicating that the user has been authenticated.

As previously stated, this router is set up to use CHAP first and then PAP as the PPP authentication protocols. You may be wondering why CHAP isn't selected here and shown to be failing before PAP is initiated.

As shown in the output from the `debug ppp negotiation` command, PAP is agreed-upon during the LCP negotiation phase. This indicates a problem with the CHAP configuration at one end of the link.

debug ppp packet

The `debug ppp packet` command displays debug information for ppp packets:

```
Router#debug ppp packet
PPP packet display debugging is on
00:26:20: BR0/0:1 PPP: I pkt type 0x0021, datagramsize 580
00:26:20: BR0/0:1 PPP: O pkt type 0x0021, datagramsize 44
00:26:22: BR0/0:1 PPP: I pkt type 0x0021, datagramsize 580
00:26:22: BR0/0:1 PPP: O pkt type 0x0021, datagramsize 44
00:26:23: BR0/0:1 LCP: O ECHOREQ [Open] id 5 len 12 magic
         0xD0D1CFF8
00:26:23: BR0/0:1 PPP: I pkt type 0xC021, datagramsize 16
00:26:23: BR0/0:1 LCP: I ECHOREP [Open] id 5 len 12 magic
         0xB4CFC3A0
00:26:23: BR0/0:1 LCP: Received id 5, sent id 5, line up
00:26:33: BR0/0:1 LCP: O ECHOREQ [Open] id 6 len 12 magic
         0xD0D1CFF8
00:26:33: BR0/0:1 PPP: I pkt type 0xC021, datagramsize 16
00:26:33: BR0/0:1 LCP: I ECHOREP [Open] id 6 len 12 magic
         0xB4CFC3A0
00:26:33: BR0/0:1 LCP: Received id 6, sent id 6, line up
00:26:36: BR0/0:1 PPP: O pkt type 0x0021, datagramsize 100
00:26:37: BR0/0:1 PPP: O pkt type 0x0021, datagramsize 100
00:26:39: BR0/0:1 PPP: O pkt type 0x0021, datagramsize 100
00:26:41: BR0/0:1 PPP: O pkt type 0x0021, datagramsize 66
00:26:41: BR0/0:1 PPP: O pkt type 0x0021, datagramsize 66
00:26:41: BR0/0:1 PPP: I pkt type 0x0021, datagramsize 177
00:26:41: BR0/0:1 PPP: O pkt type 0x0021, datagramsize 64
00:26:41: BR0/0:1 PPP: I pkt type 0x0021, datagramsize 177
00:26:43: BR0/0:1 LCP: O ECHOREQ [Open] id 7 len 12 magic
         0xD0D1CFF8
00:26:43: BR0/0:1 PPP: I pkt type 0xC021, datagramsize 16
00:26:43: BR0/0:1 LCP: I ECHOREP [Open] id 7 len 12 magic
         0xB4CFC3A0
00:26:43: BR0/0:1 LCP: Received id 7, sent id 7, line up
Router#no debug all
All possible debugging has been turned off
Router#
```

This command displays all PPP packets that are sent and received. This is very low-level information and is not as useful as other debug commands for troubleshooting BRI. It can be used when a link is already established to look at the bi-directional flow of packets. debug ppp negotiation and debug ppp authentication can be used only during the initial phase of link establishment.

debug dialer

The debug dialer command displays debug information about dial-on-demand routing (DDR):

```
Router#debug dialer events
Dial on demand events debugging is on
Router#
00:25:81604378623: %ISDN-6-DISCONNECT: Interface BRI0/0:1
                    disconnected from 08456621349 , call lasted 96
                    seconds
00:25:79465330751: %LINK-3-UPDOWN: Interface BRI0/0:1, changed
                    state to down
00:25:78165049344: BRI0/0:1 DDR: disconnecting call
00:25:77309452288: BRI0/0:2 DDR: disconnecting call
00:25:19: %LINEPROTO-5-UPDOWN: Line protocol on Interface BRI0/0:1,
                    changed state to down
00:25:20: %ISDN-6-LAYER2UP: Layer 2 for Interface BR0/0, TEI 114
                    changed to up
Router#
00:25:36: BRI0/0 DDR: rotor dialout [priority]
00:25:36: BRI0/0 DDR: Dialing cause ip (s=192.168.10.26,
                    d=195.8.69.77)
00:25:36: BRI0/0 DDR: Attempting to dial 08456621349
00:25:37: %LINK-3-UPDOWN: Interface BRI0/0:1, changed state to up
00:25:37: %ISDN-6-CONNECT: Interface BRI0/0:1 is now connected to
                    08456621349
00:25:39: BRI0/0:1 DDR: dialer protocol up
00:25:40: %LINEPROTO-5-UPDOWN: Line protocol on Interface BRI0/0:1,
                    changed state to up
00:25:43: %ISDN-6-CONNECT: Interface BRI0/0:1 is now connected to
                    08456621349
Router#
```

You can clearly see from this debug output that the dialer interface has called 08456621349 due to the interesting traffic from IP=192.168.10.26 to IP=105.8.69.77 and the call is connected successfully.

The output from this command is very similar to the show dialer command and this is very useful for troubleshooting dialer problems when the router just doesn't dial.

This debug command is very similar to the show dialer command. However, with the debug command, you see the dialer status in real time.

debug isdn

The debug isdn command displays debug information on Q931 call establishment:

```
Router#debug isdn
ISDN events debugging is on
Router#
00:32:210453397522: ISDN BR0/0: Recvd MPH_EI1_IND from L1
00:32:214748364799: %ISDN-6-DISCONNECT: Interface BRI0/0:1
                    disconnected from 08456621349 , call lasted 432
                    seconds
00:32:212609316927: %LINK-3-UPDOWN: Interface BRI0/0:1, changed
                    state to down
00:32:210453397522: ISDN BR0/0: Physical layer is IF_DOWN
00:32:49: ISDN BR0/0: Shutting down ME
00:32:49: ISDN BR0/0: Shutting down ISDN Layer 3
00:32:214748405760: ISDN BR0/0: L1 is IF_ACTIVE
00:32:50: %ISDN-6-LAYER2UP: Layer 2 for Interface BR0/0, TEI 114
          changed to up
00:32:50: L3: L3_GetUser_NLCB failed, message ignored cid 0x0 cr
          0x6 ev 0x75 ces 1 dsl 0
00:32:50: L3: L3_GetUser_NLCB failed, message ignored cid 0x0 cr
          0x6 ev 0x5A ces 1 dsl 0
00:32:50: %LINEPROTO-5-UPDOWN: Line protocol on Interface BRI0/0:1,
          changed state to down
00:33:07: ISDN BR0/0: Outgoing call id = 0x8007
00:33:30064771072: ISDN BR0/0: Event: Call to 08456621349 at 64 Kb/s
00:33:07: ISDN BR0/0: received HOST_PROCEEDING call_id 0x8007
00:33:08: ISDN BR0/0: received HOST_ALERTING call_id 0x8007
00:33:08: ISDN BR0/0: received HOST_CONNECT call_id 0x8007
00:33:08: %LINK-3-UPDOWN: Interface BRI0/0:1, changed state to up
00:33:08: %ISDN-6-CONNECT: Interface BRI0/0:1 is now connected to
          08456621349
00:33:08: ISDN BR0/0: Event: Connected to 08456621349 on B1 at 64 Kb/s
00:33:10: %LINEPROTO-5-UPDOWN: Line protocol on Interface BRI0/0:1,
          changed state to up
Router#
00:33:14: %ISDN-6-CONNECT: Interface BRI0/0:1 is now connected to
          08456621349
Router#
```

This command is used to troubleshoot Layer 3 connection problems. The highlighted areas show that the router has connected successfully to 08456621349. This is very useful to check for incorrectly configured SPIDs.

This debug command is best used in conjunction with the debug isdn q931 command.

Other ISDN Troubleshooting Commands

We have now covered the show and debug commands that are associated with debugging BRI. There are a few other commands that can be used to help troubleshoot the problem.

The first commands that can be used are the ping and trace commands. These can be used to check the connectivity and also to provide debug information against the events you have selected to debug.

Another useful command is the clear interface bri command, which sets all the BRI interface counters to zero. This command is useful for keeping track of the counters against a timed period for performance and error identification.

Here is the output of the show interface bri command:

```
Router#sh int bri 0/0
BRI0/0 is up, line protocol is up (spoofing)
  Hardware is PQUICC BRI
  Description: connected to Internet
  MTU 1500 bytes, BW 64 Kbit, DLY 20000 usec, rely 255/255, load 1/255
  Encapsulation PPP, loopback not set
  DTR is pulsed for 1 seconds on reset
  Last input 00:00:08, output never, output hang never
  Last clearing of "show interface" counters never
  Input queue: 0/75/0 (size/max/drops); Total output drops: 0
  Queueing strategy: weighted fair
  Output queue: 0/1000/64/0 (size/max total/threshold/drops)
     Conversations  0/1/256 (active/max active/max total)
     Reserved Conversations 0/0 (allocated/max allocated)
  5 minute input rate 0 bits/sec, 0 packets/sec
  5 minute output rate 0 bits/sec, 0 packets/sec
     419 packets input, 2626 bytes, 0 no buffer
     Received 0 broadcasts, 0 runts, 0 giants, 0 throttles
     0 input errors, 0 CRC, 0 frame, 0 overrun, 0 ignored, 0 abort
     664 packets output, 66967 bytes, 0 underruns
     0 output errors, 0 collisions, 7 interface resets
     0 output buffer failures, 0 output buffers swapped out
     5 carrier transitions
Router#
```

We will now clear the counters on interface bri:

```
Router#clear counters bri 0/0
Clear "show interface" counters on this interface [confirm]
Router#
```

Here is the new show interface bri command output:

```
Router#sh int bri 0/0
BRI0/0 is up, line protocol is up (spoofing)
  Hardware is PQUICC BRI
  Description: connected to Internet
  MTU 1500 bytes, BW 64 Kbit, DLY 20000 usec, rely 255/255, load 1/255
  Encapsulation PPP, loopback not set
  DTR is pulsed for 1 seconds on reset
  Last input 00:00:03, output never, output hang never
  Last clearing of "show interface" counters 00:00:13
  Input queue: 0/75/0 (size/max/drops); Total output drops: 0
  Queueing strategy: weighted fair
  Output queue: 0/1000/64/0 (size/max total/threshold/drops)
     Conversations  0/1/256 (active/max active/max total)
     Reserved Conversations 0/0 (allocated/max allocated)
  5 minute input rate 0 bits/sec, 0 packets/sec
  5 minute output rate 0 bits/sec, 0 packets/sec
     2 packets input, 8 bytes, 0 no buffer
     Received 0 broadcasts, 0 runts, 0 giants, 0 throttles
     0 input errors, 0 CRC, 0 frame, 0 overrun, 0 ignored, 0 abort
     2 packets output, 8 bytes, 0 underruns
     0 output errors, 0 collisions, 0 interface resets
     0 output buffer failures, 0 output buffers swapped out
     0 carrier transitions
Router#
```

As you can see, all of the counters have been reset to zero.

Chapter Summary

In this chapter, we looked at Basic Rate Interface and the troubleshooting commands that are available at the three layers of the OSI model that ISDN correlates to.

We started with a technical overview of ISDN and moved on to the Cisco show and debug commands that can be used to interrogate the router to receive real-time reports to help in the troubleshooting process.

As in any other troubleshooting situation, always start at the Physical layer and work your way up. This method of troubleshooting is logical and can save you a lot of time.

Common BRI Problems

Some common BRI problems are shown in Table 13-5.

Table 13-5	**Symptom**	**Action**
Common BRI Problems	Remote router does not answer call	Verify the telephone number and SPIDs.
	Dialing cannot occur	Check configuration, including dialer-list, dialer-group, dialer map, dialer string, etc.
	CHAP authentication failed	Check username and passwords for correct spelling and case. Check the `dialer map` command for name keyword and correct hostname.
	PAP authentication failed	Check username and passwords for correct spelling and case. Check the `dialer map` command for name keyword and correct hostname.
	Call connects but then disconnects	Turn on `debug ppp negotiation` and `debug ppp authentication` to check the PPP initial session establishment phase.
	Router is sending IDREQ requests to the switch but does not get a response from the switch. Shown under `debug isdn q921`.	Check and verify the SPID configuration with the Telco.
	The remote device does not authenticate itself. Can be a problem with non-Cisco devices.	Use the `ppp authentication chap callin` or `ppp authentication pap callin` commands.
	Router connects but users cannot connect	Check the router LAN interface and the user's Network layer protocol settings.
	Second ISDN B-channel will not come up	Check the dialer load-threshold command.

Frequently Asked Questions (FAQ)

Question: With BRI. What is the fastest connection I can establish?

Answer: You can aggregate both of the B-channels to attain 128 Kbps.

Question: Why do differing switch types exist per geographical region?

Answer: Most local Telcos established their own standards before the 1984 standards were introduced.

Question: What is the speed of the B-channel?

Answer: The B-channel transmits at 64 Kbps.

Question: Can the D-channel be utilized for data transfer?

Answer: Under normal circumstances, the D-channel cannot be used for data transfer or aggregation with the B-channels. However, in special circumstances, protocols allow this to happen.

Question: What are the advantages of CHAP over PAP for PPP authentication?

Answer: CHAP is more secure than PAP for password authentication. CHAP uses a three-way handshake to authenticate that includes a one-way hash function.

Case Study

You, as network engineer, have been tasked to identify a problem with connectivity to one of your remote retail stores.

Scenario   You are the network engineer for a small retail company with seven remote retail outlets and a central office. You are based at the central office. All remote retail outlets are running PC Till-based EPOS and they connect to the head office every hour to upload sales figures. The outlets are using Cisco 801 ISDN routers. The central office is running a Cisco 2621 with an eight-port BRI network module installed.

Recently, you have lost communication with one of the outlets, which is based in Tucson, AZ. This has led to sales data being sent daily through the postal service on floppy disks. All of the other stores are still communicating with the central office on an hourly basis.

Approach   You deduce that because communication is still occurring with the other six retail outlets, it is most probably a problem with the configuration of the 801 router at Tucson.

You decide to examine the running configurations on both the central office and Tucson routers.

The following config is from the central office router:

```
version 12.0
service udp-small-servers
service tcp-small-servers
!
hostname Central
!
enable secret cisco
!
username Tucson password shoedepot
isdn switch-type basic-5ess
!
interface Ethernet0
 ip address 20.1.1.1 255.0.0.0
!
interface BRI0
 no ip address
 encapsulation ppp
 dialer rotary-group 0
 isdn spid1 0155533330 5553333
 isdn spid2 0155533330 5554444
!
interface Dialer0
 ip unnumbered Ethernet0
 encapsulation ppp
 dialer in-band
 dialer idle-timeout 300
 dialer map ip 10.1.1.1 name Tucson speed 56 14045551111
```

```
       dialer map ip 10.1.1.1 name Tucson speed 56 14045552222
       dialer hold-queue 10
       dialer load-threshold 200 either
       dialer-group 1
       no fair-queue
       no cdp enable
       ppp authentication chap
       ppp multilink
      !
      ip classless
      ip route 10.0.0.0 255.0.0.0 Dialer0
      ip http server
      !
      dialer-list 1 protocol ip permit
      !
      line con 0
       password console
       login
      line aux 0
      line vty 0 4
       password telnet
       login
      !
      end
```

The config below is from the Tucson router:

```
      version 12.0
      service udp-small-servers
      service tcp-small-servers
      !
      hostname Tucson
      !
      enable secret cisco
      !
      username Central password shoedepo
      ip subnet-zero
      isdn switch-type basic-ni1
      !
      interface Ethernet0
       ip address 10.1.1.1 255.0.0.0
      !
      interface BRI0
       no ip address
       encapsulation ppp
       dialer rotary-group 0
       isdn spid1 014045551111000 5551111
       isdn spid2 014045552222000 5552222
      !
      interface Dialer0
       ip unnumbered Ethernet0
       encapsulation ppp
       dialer in-band
       dialer idle-timeout 300
       dialer map ip 20.1.1.1 name Central speed 56 16175553333
       dialer map ip 20.1.1.1 name Central speed 56 16175554444
       dialer hold-queue 10
```

```
dialer load-threshold 200 either
dialer-group 1
no fair-queue
no cdp enable
ppp authentication chap
ppp multilink
!
ip classless
ip route 20.0.0.0 255.0.0.0 Dialer0
ip http server
!
dialer-list 1 protocol ip permit
!
line con 0
 password console
 login
line aux 0
line vty 0 4
 password telnet
 login
!
end
```

Upon inspecting both of these configuration files, it is evident that the password has a character truncated off the end. The password should be set to shoedepot. The password on the Tucson router was set to shoedepo.

Results   After you make the password change on the router, the connection is established once again. Passwords have to be set the same on both ends of the connection for PAP or CHAP PPP authentication to take place.

Questions

1. What is BRI also referred to as?

   a. B+D
   b. 2B+2D
   c. 2B+D
   d. 2D+B

2. Which `debug` command displays information about Layer 3 call establishments? (Choose two)

   a. `debug isdn q921`
   b. `debug isdn`
   c. `debug isdn calls`
   d. `debug isdn q931`

3. What does the ISDN reference model require non-ISDN devices to connect to?

   a. NT1
   b. TEI
   c. TE1
   d. TA

4. How do you reset the counters on the BRI interface?

   a. `clear counters interface bri`
   b. `clear bri`
   c. `clear bri counters`
   d. `clear all counters`

5. What configuration mode should you be in to set ppp mulitlink?

   a. Global
   b. Interface
   c. Line
   d. Router

6. Which authentication protocol operates a three way handshake?

   a. PAP
   b. CHAP
   c. DES
   d. PPP-SEC

7. Which show command displays information on the B-channels, the dialer string, and idle timeout values?

   a. show inter bri
   b. sh isdn
   c. sh dialer
   d. sho all bri info

8. What is the standard that defines LAPD?

   a. Q.931
   b. Q.921
   c. RS-232
   d. CCITTQ1

9. At what speed does the data channel operate?

   a. 24 Kbps
   b. 64 Kbps
   c. 16 Kbps
   d. 1024 Kbps

10. What IOS command would stop the second B-channel from ever aggregating with the first?

   a. Router(config)#dialer load-thre 255
   b. Router#dialer load-thresh 255
   c. Router(config-if)#dial load-thres 1
   d. Router(config-if)#dial load-thres 255

11. What IOS command displays information as to the status of all three OSI layers in relation to BRI?

   a. sh isdn
   b. sh dialer
   c. sh int bri
   d. show interface bri all

12. OSPF is an ideal routing protocol for BRI DDR networks. True or false?

   a. True
   b. False

13. Which debug command displays information about PAP and CHAP authentication?

   a. debug ppp auth
   b. debug ppp negot
   c. debug ppp pack
   d. debug ppp event

14. What is the default encapsulation protocol for a BRI interface?

    a. PPP
    b. HDLC
    c. SDLC
    d. Frame Relay

15. What `debug` command displays information about the Data-Link layer access procedures?

    a. `debug isdn events`
    b. `debug isdn q931`
    c. `debug isdn q921`
    d. `debug ppp nego`

16. What is the first Layer 3 message sent via Q.931 for session establishment?

    a. CALL PROC
    b. SETUP
    c. CONNECT
    d. CONNECT ACK

17. After you have finished a debug session, what command should you always enter ?

    a. `terminal no monitor`
    b. `debug off`
    c. `no debug all`
    d. `no debug`

18. What channel is spoofing used on?

    a. B
    b. D

19. What is spoofing used for?

    a. To prevent routing loops
    b. To permit BRI traffic
    c. To fool Layer 3 into thinking a connection exists
    d. To create a virtual interface between Layer 2 LAPD and Layer 3

20. You notice that your BRI connection never drops. You are sure that no traffic is going across the link. What command should you check on the router?

    a. `dialer timeout`
    b. `dialer fast-timeout`
    c. `dialer idle-timeout`
    d. `dialer drop`

Answers

1. Answer: c

   BRI is also referred to as 2B+D. This is because BRI has two Bearer channels and one Data channel.

2. Answer: b and c

   The correct `debug` commands to display Layer 3 call establishment information are `debug isdn` and `debug isdn q931`.

3. Answer: d

   The ISDN reference model requires non-ISDN devices to connect to a Terminal Adapter.

4. Answer: a

   The correct command is `clear counters interface bri`. This must be done from the exec mode. This will reset all statistical counters on the interface to zero. You will be prompted to confirm your actions.

5. Answer: b

   Multilink PPP has to be enabled at the interface configuration mode. You enable Multilink PPP with the following command:

   ```
   Router(config-if)#ppp multilink
   ```

6. Answer: b

   CHAP provides a three-way challenge handshake. The other option was PAP. PAP is just a two-way authentication procedure.

7. Answer: c

   The `show dialer` command displays B channel information as well as the dialer string and idle timeout values.

8. Answer: b

   Q.921 defines LAPD.

9. Answer: c

   The Data channel operates at 16 Kbps. The Bearer channels operate at 64 Kbps.

10. Answer: d

    The following command would stop the second B channel from ever aggregating with the first:

    ```
    Router(config-if)#dialer load-threshold 255
    ```

    The key was that you have to be in interface configuration mode.

11. Answer: a

   The `sh isdn` command displays active information about all three of the OSI layers appertaining to ISDN.

12. Answer: b

   OSPF is link state and so not ideal for DDR. This is due to the frequency of the "hello" packets that OSPF requires to operate.

13. Answer: a

   The command `debug ppp auth` enables PPP authentication debugging. This displays information for PAP and CHAP authentication over PPP.

14. Answer: b

   The default encapsulation for all serial interfaces on Cisco equipment is HDLC. You are advised to use PPP due to its authentication.

15. Answer: c

   The command `debug isdn q921` would display information about the Data-Link layer access procedures.

16. Answer: b

   The first Q931 Layer 3 message to be sent for call establishment is SETUP.

17. Answer: c

   ALWAYS enter the command `no debug all` after every debugging session. Debugging is very CPU-intensive and can have a detrimental effect on the performance of a core router.

18. Answer: b

   Spoofing is on the D channel.

19. Answer: c

   Spoofing fools Layer 3 into thinking that the link is active, even when it isn't. This is to ensure that routing updates are propagated out on the other active interfaces. See Snapshot Routing.

20. Answer: c

   The `dialer idle-timeout` command specifies an idle duration, after which the router drops the connection.

PART

5

Advanced
Troubleshooting

14

Cisco Support

This chapter provides information about the support options that are provided by Cisco Systems, Inc. for troubleshooting internetworking problems relating to Cisco devices. We will look at the online tools and resources that are available via the *Cisco Connection Online* (CCO) web site, as well as the services that complement this resource.

Every new Cisco product comes with a copy of the Cisco Documentation CD. This includes a wealth of product- and technology-related documents that can be used when troubleshooting specific problems in your internetwork. We will give an overview of what the CD has to offer as well as an explanation of how to fully utilize the search capabilities. We will then look at the *Technical Assistance Center* (TAC), which is the central repository for support offered by Cisco on its internetworking devices. TAC includes an online web site and a worldwide call center/helpdesk for dealing with support issues on Cisco equipment.

Rather than focusing on the technical aspects of troubleshooting, this chapter will approach the support offerings that are available from Cisco. These resources should be used (in conjunction with troubleshooting techniques learned in this book relating to the specific technology) to attempt a successful fault resolve. If all else fails, a call to the *Technical Assistance Center* (TAC) should provide a timely resolution.

Objectives Covered in This Chapter

This chapter introduces you to the support options that are provided by Cisco Systems, Inc.

The following objectives will be covered:

- Describe information-gathering and communications to get the best use of Cisco's service and support services.

- Describe and use the Cisco information resources (especially those in the CCO CD or World Wide Web site) that can assist with troubleshooting processes.

- List the preferred methods for escalation of troubleshooting issues to Cisco's service and support programs.

- Describe the necessary steps to execute a (manual) core dump.

On Line Support—Cisco Connection Online (CCO)

Cisco offers an award-winning web site with a very comprehensive range of support options. The Cisco web site is called Cisco Connection Online and can be found at http://www.cisco.com. (See Figure 14-1.)

This is a global site for Cisco Systems, Inc., and there are various branches for different geographical regions such as http://www.cisco.com/uk/ for the U.K. and Ireland (as shown in Figure 14-2).

CCO is also available in multiple languages. The link to http://www.cisco.com/public/countries_languages.shtml is the site where you can choose your geographical region and language for CCO. Figure 14-3 shows the Spanish language version.

Figure 14-1
Cisco Connection
Online (CCO)

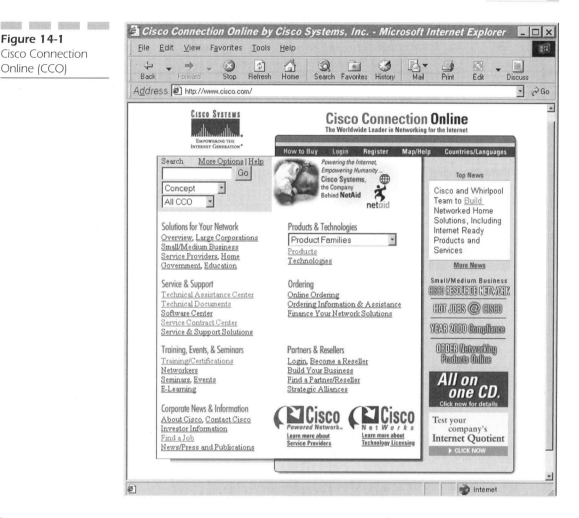

The home page of CCO is a portal to a whole range of information relating to Cisco products, technologies, and the market they operate in. There are two levels of general access to CCO: guest users and registered users. There are also many more specific levels available for software downloads. Guest users of CCO have the ability to access general areas on CCO, including basic information about Cisco and its networking solutions, services, and programs. Selected areas of the software center can be browsed, and selected trial software can be downloaded for trial and evaluation purposes.

Most resources that require registered CCO access will either indicate this as (CCO Access Required) or the link will display a padlock next to it.

Figure 14-2
Cisco Connection
Online (CCO—U.K.
and Ireland site

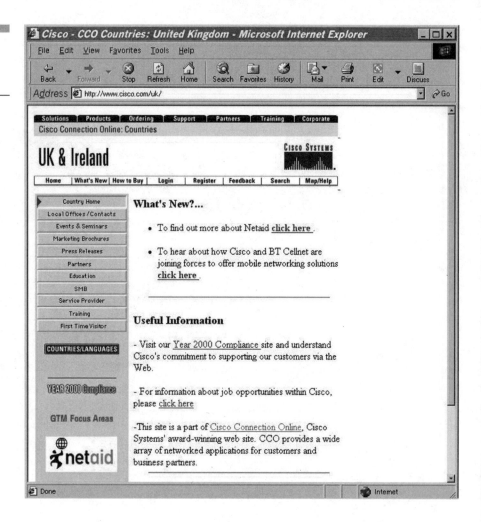

If you try to access a registered user only page you will see the screen shown in Figure 14-4.

As you can see from this screen, access has been denied to this resource because you have not logged on to CCO as a registered user. At this point, you are offered the opportunity to register (as long as you meet the requirements) and you can see the advantages of registering.

To become a registered user of CCO, you have to meet one of the following criteria:

■ Hold the Cisco Certified Internetworking Expert (CCIE) qualification.

■ Hold a Cisco service contract.

Figure 14-3
Cisco Connection
Online (CCO)—
Spanish version

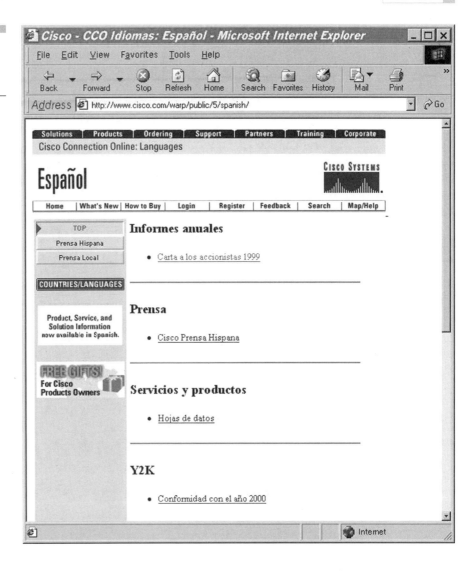

- Be a Cisco reseller.
- Be a Cisco Partner: Premier, Silver, or Gold.
- Be an employee of Cisco Systems, Inc.
- Hold a direct purchasing agreement with Cisco.

If you meet one of these criteria, you can use your previously provided information to create an account on CCO. Upon visiting the CCO site, you have the option to "log in" to the site on the home page via the green text

Figure 14-4
Failed CCO
authentication

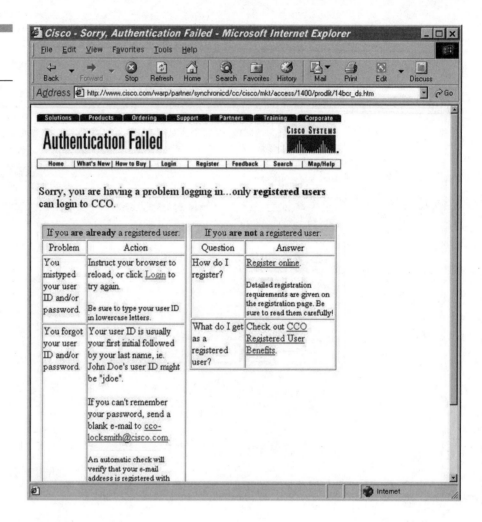

link on the menu bar at the top. After you are logged in, your user information appears in the top-left corner and the CCO home page is customized
with more options available that reflect your level of CCO access.

Over and above the guest user, you now have access to the full range of
tools and services available on the CCO web site, complete product details
and support documentation, and various benefits specific to your registered
relationship with Cisco.

The main areas on CCO that we are concerned about with relation to
support are the following:

- Cisco Marketplace
- Online Technical Documents

■ Software Center

■ Technical Assistance Center

We are going to look at each of these offerings in detail.

Cisco Marketplace

The Cisco Marketplace can be reached by accessing the web site `http://www.cisco.com/marketplace` (see Figure 14-5). You can also click on the **Online Ordering** link under the **Ordering** header at the main CCO home page.

Figure 14-5
The Cisco
marketplace

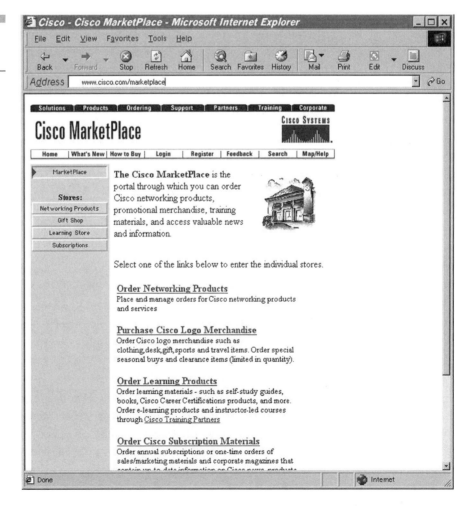

The Cisco Marketplace is the part of CCO that offers 24-hours a day, 7-days-a-week online ordering of Cisco products and related materials. This is done over a secure Internet connection straight from the customer's Internet browser. The purchasing process uses Cisco Commerce Agents, which were designed with the Cisco customer in mind. The Commerce agents include the following:

- *Status Agent*   The Status Agent provides information about any current orders that you have with Cisco. This information is available 24×7 and includes detailed tracking information applicable to your orders.

- *Pricing Agent*   The Pricing Agent provides access to the current Cisco online price list. A full search facility is provided with a range of options. You can also download the full price list to your personal computer.

- *Configuration Agent*   The Configuration Agent is a tool that allows you to create configurations online for the Cisco equipment you are purchasing.

- *Service Order Agent*   The Service Order Agent provides detailed information and tracking relating to your service orders and TAC cases.

These facilities are available only after you have signed up to the Marketplace service. This is available online at `http://www.cisco.com/public/npm/direct_advantage.html`. To register, you need to complete the *Internet Commerce Agreement* (ICA).

Besides Cisco networking products, you can also order promotional merchandise, order training materials, and access valuable news and information.

Technical Documents

Access to the Cisco technical documents online can be from two main sources. You can either browse through the CCO home page to the required document or you can perform a search using the search facility provided on the main CCO home page.

To browse the online documents, click on the `Technical Documents` link under the `Service & Support` section on the home page of CCO. This takes you to the main Technical Documents index. (See Figure 14-6.)

From this page, you have access to the following sub-sections of documentation:

Figure 14-6
The Technical
Documents home
page

- Documentation Home Page
- Security Advisories
- Field Notices
- Product Bulletins
- New Product Releases
- Cisco Product Documentation
- Cisco Product Catalog
- Hardware Technical Tips

- Software Technical Tips
- Data Sheets
- Product Categories
- Internetworking Technologies Overview
- Sample Configurations
- Internetworking Design Guide
- Internetworking Terms and Acronyms
- Internetworking Technical Tips
- Cisco Press Publications
- References and RFC's
- Packet Magazine
- Internetworking Case Studies
- Cisco Site Preparation Guide
- Cisco IOS Configuration
- Dial Solutions Configuration Guide
- Cisco Access Dial Cookbook
- Router Configuration Tools
- Hot Tips
- Frequently Asked Questions (FAQ)
- Internetworking Troubleshooting Guide
- Troubleshooting Internetworking Systems

As you can see from this list of subjects, CCO has a lot of resources available online. You can access complete product catalogs and configuration manuals for all current and many obsolete Cisco networking devices and technologies. From a troubleshooting point of view, the last two documents are excellent troubleshooting references; they are large volumes that address a range of networking technologies and common faults that occur with possible solutions.

As well as browsing for subject matter, you can also perform a search of the CCO web site to find documents and information that you require. You can search from the home page of CCO or from any other main index page contained within the CCO web site. The search facility contains three fields: the search string, the search type, and the search location.

The search string is the actual text that you are searching for on CCO. This follows the advanced entry features common in most Internet Search

Figure 14-7
Boolean Search
Syntax

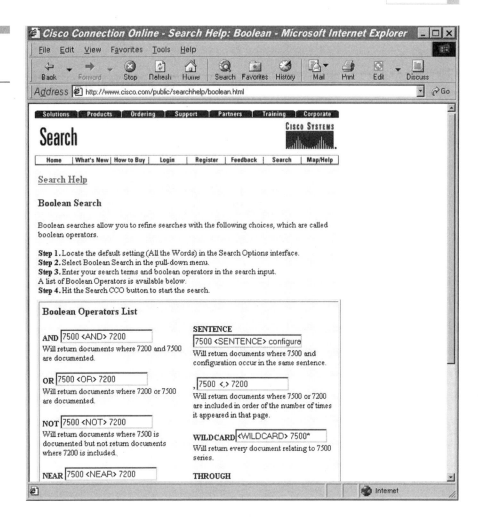

Engines such as AltaVista and Yahoo. You can also use Boolean searches to further restrict the search results (see Figure 14-7).

You can specify that you wish to find the Concept, All Words, Any Phrase, Exact Phrase, or Boolean with respect to the search string. This also affects the way the search is returned. The last option is the choice to search the Whole of CCO, Solutions, Products, Ordering, Support, Partners, Training, Corporate, or Tech Docs. This further limits the results by restricting the search to a specific section on CCO.

Full help for the search facilities on CCO can be found at the URL http://www.cisco.com/public/search_help.html.

After you have entered your search, you will be presented with a screen of the results against the search criteria that you entered. Entering a new search string can further narrow these results down. This new search is made from the content that the previous search returned. This is an excellent way of picking out a particular topic from the online documentation. Figure 14-8 shows the results returned when searching the whole of CCO for "Reverse Telnet."

You can see from this screen shot that 12489 results were returned against this search. Obviously, this search needs refining in order to get a smaller, more related section of articles.

The online documents and the tools for interrogating them really make CCO an excellent ally to have in your troubleshooting tool cupboard. You can find out whether the problem you are experiencing is caused by a known bug in the IOS version, as well as finding out configuration and technological information to support you in the troubleshooting process.

Figure 14-8

Results of a search on CCO

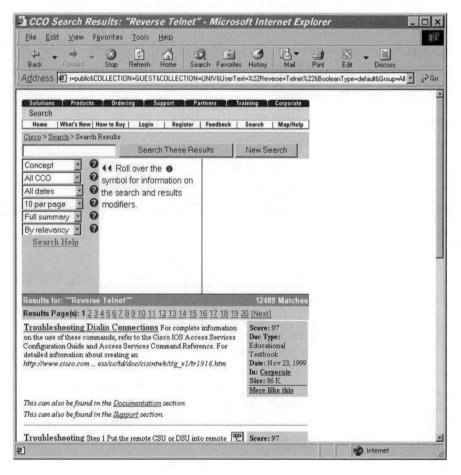

Software Center

The Software Center on CCO can be accessed by clicking on the Software Center link under the Service & Support section of the CCO home page. Figure 14-9 shows the home page of the Software Center.

The Software Center contains the latest releases of Cisco IOS software along with other technical and support-related software. For Cisco IOS software, you have access to upgrade planners that take you step-by-step through the upgrade process to ensure you have opted for the right IOS version. The latest releases of Cisco IOS are available, as well as old versions back to IOS 10.3. The IOS software can be grouped and viewed by Main IOS Version (10, 11, etc.), IOS Release (12.01, 12.02, etc.), Product (2500, 2600, etc.), and IOS Feature Set (IP, IP Plus, etc.). There is also software for the

Figure 14-9
Cisco Software center

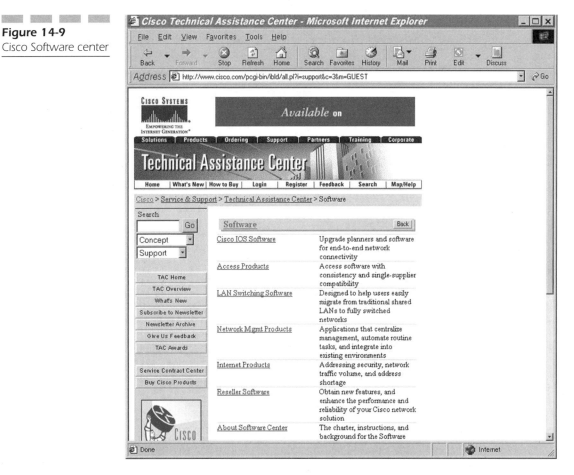

Catalyst range of switches and other systems such as the 700 series routers that don't use standard IOS.

Other software, such as trial versions of the Cisco Works network management suite, can be downloaded from the software center. This software is located under the Network Management Products link from the Software Center home page.

Technical Assistance Center (TAC)

The Technical Assistance Center is the support arm of Cisco Systems, Inc. Cisco offers packaged services to its customers that include support options at various levels for all of the Cisco product range. One example of this is Cisco SMARTnet. With SMARTnet, you get access to a pre-paid level of support. You can opt for an onsite 24x7x4 that guarantees an engineer on-site within 4 hours, 24 hours a day, 7 days a week. Incidents covered under these agreements are raised with the TAC. To raise a fault with the TAC, you can send an email to tac@cisco.com (or euro-tac@cisco.com if you are based in Europe). Alternatively, you can call TAC: 1-800-553-2447 (or 32-2-778-4242 if you are based in Europe). The first time you contact TAC, you are sent a welcoming email. Following is a copy of the welcome email.

```
Date

Dear Name,

You recently contacted Cisco Systems Technical Assistance Center
(TAC). Since this is your first contact with the TAC, we want to
ensure you can use our services to your best advantage. The
following resources, suggestions, and information sources will help
streamline the case resolution process. First, it may help to
clarify the service resources available to Cisco's customers:
Technical Assistance Center (TAC)
A worldwide network of 600 support specialists providing around-
the-clock support in over 144 languages. Here are your local phone
numbers and email addresses for reaching the TAC 24 hours a day 7
days a week:
North America     1-800-553-2447/ tac@cisco.com
Europe            32-2-778-4242/ euro-tac@cisco.com
Asia Pacific      61-2-9935-4107/ asiapac-tac@cisco.com
USA Non-Domestic  1-408-526-7209
Australia         1 800-805-227
China             10800 3578    Beijing & Shanghai only or 10810,
                  then 800 501 2306 Mandarin or 10811, then
                  800 501 2306 English
Hong Kong         800 96 5910
India             000 117, then 888 861 6453
Indonesia         001 800 61 838
```

```
Japan              0066 33 800 926
Korea              00798 611 0712 or 00911, then 888 861 5146
Malaysia           1800 805 880
New Zealand        0800 44 6237
Philippines        1 800 611 0056
Singapore          800 6161 356
Taiwan             0080 61 1206
Thailand           001 800 61 0754
South America      408 526 7209
Mexico/
Caribbean
```

Cisco Connection Online (CCO) www.cisco.com

CCO's industry-leading interactive web site providing technical information and Technical Assistance Tools that help save customers time by solving common technical problems online. CCO is available to all Cisco customers. Special features such as Technical Assistance Tools and the Software Library are available only to registered service customers. Check with your network operations center for valid CCO registered user information or refer to http://www.cisco.com/public/registration.shtml

For assistance using CCO: cco-team@cisco.com

On-Site Services (OSS)

Depending on the type and level of contract, a Cisco-supported field engineer can be available for 4-hour to next-day response if you have purchased an enhanced SMARTnet contract. The TAC will dispatch OSS personnel if your service contract covers that service. If not, Time and Materials service can be purchased where available.

Before You Call

You may wish to check with your network operations center to determine which services (for example; SMARTnet, SMARTnet Onsite or NSA) you are entitled to and record any contract numbers here for future reference:

Contract type: _____
Contract number: _____
Contract expiration date: _____
Product Serial Number(s):_____

TAC Terminology:

Case: This is how we track issues related to individual issues that you may have.

Case Number: This is the unique tracking number we assign to your issue (e.g. K01234).

Case Priority: P1, P2, P3, P4
Priority 1
Production network is down, causing critical impact to business operations if service is not restored quickly. No workaround is available. Cisco and the Customer are willing to commit substantial resources around the clock to resolve the situation.

Priority 2
Production network is severely degraded, impacting significant
aspects of your business operations. No workaround is available.
Cisco and Customer are willing to commit full-time resources during
business hours to resolve the situation.

Priority 3
Network performance is degraded. Network functionality is
noticeably impaired, but most business operations continue.

Priority 4
Customer requires information or assistance on Cisco product
capabilities, installation or configuration."

Contract Number: This is the number that we use to track your level
of services.

Bug ID: This is a tracking number that our development engineering
organization uses to track errors (e.g. CSCdi15001).

Duty Manager: Your escalation resource in the TAC. The duty manager
ensures that the right resources are available to solve the
problem.

Making the Call

When calling for technical support please have the following
information available: Service Entitlement, Contract Number, and
Serial Number of the Device.

Please be aware, either access to the product experiencing the
problem or additional information may be required, including:

History of the problem
Network topology and explanation
Problem and symptoms description
Software version and types of hardware
Physical router configuration
Error or debugging messages logged by or on the product's console
display.

In the course of resolving a problem, an Engineer may access your
site via the Internet or dial up. All Engineers have fax, email,
modem and Internet access. Please inform the Engineer of your
preferred method for exchanging product information.

Other Important Phone Numbers

For order inquiry, shipping information, technical documentation,
product literature, express orders, web (CCO) registration and
questions, technical training/CCIE, and general company
information call:

Customer Service   800 553 NETS (6387)
International   408 526 7208
Email   cs-rep@cisco.com

For information on service plans and for service contracts
questions call:

```
Service Contracts  800 553 NETS (6387)
International       408 526 7208

Additional Information and Tools
All of this information is available to you on the web via the
Cisco Support Solutions Quick Reference Card at:

http://www.cisco.com/warp/customer/437/supps_sm.htm

To be able to access "customer" data on our web site you will need
to register on line. You can use your contract number to start this
process (http://www.cisco.com/public/registration.shtml).

We have also provided you with many tools and technical tips via
the web (registered users only):

            our service & support home page
                    http://www.cisco.com/kobayashi/Support_root.shtml

            technical tips
                    http://www.cisco.com/kobayashi/serv_tips.shtml

            a troubleshooting engine for help with common technical
            problems
                    http://www.cisco.com/diag/te_start.shtml

            our forum for you to discuss problems with Cisco Certified
            Internetworking Experts (CCIEs) worldwide
                    http://www.cisco.com/openf/openproj.shtml

            a brief overview of the TAC and our role at Cisco
                    http://www.cisco.com/kobayashi/support/help.shtml

We hope your initial experience was positive and that this
information will ensure that all future contact with Cisco will be
timely, straight-forward, and successful.

Thank you,

Cisco Systems
```

This email provides a lot of information and is the best way to understand what Cisco requires before you raise an incident with the TAC.

When you raise a call with the TAC, you are assigned a unique case number and a *Cisco Support Engineer* (CSE) takes ownership of the call. The CSE is guaranteed to have a Bachelors Degree in electrical engineering or equivalent, and one out of every three CSEs have attained the prestigious Cisco CCIE qualification. Your call will be assigned a priority level. (These levels are explained in detail in the welcome email). Depending upon the priority level, you are notified of the status of your incident at frequent intervals.

You will then receive an email with the status indicated as Cust-Pend. Following is an example:

```
Error! No table of contents entries found. CASE: XXXXXXX
TITLE: C2610: Keeps Rebooting
PRIORITY: 2
STATUS: Cust-Pend
Name.
```

This is a Customer Case Update Notification from Cisco Systems regarding Case Number XXXXXXX, which you opened with the Cisco Technical Assistance Center.

Case XXXXXXX has been changed to a status of Cust-Pend. This status indicates the Cisco Customer Support Engineer assigned to your case has requested information from you and is awaiting your response. No Work Around has been determined at this time.

Since this is a Priority 2 case, you will receive ongoing email notification until it is closed. Priority 1 and 2 case notifications occur every 24 hours, Priority 3 every 72 hours (3 days), Priority 4 every 120 hours (5 days).

CSE Name is the Customer Support Engineer at Cisco who owns your case XXXXXXX. If you need to discuss this case further, CSE Name can be reached by email at CSE@cisco.com or by phone at 99 9999 99999.

You can also reach CSE Name or the Cisco Technical Assistance Center through the following methods:

```
North America:      1-800-553-2447
Europe:             32-2-704-5555
Asia Pacific:       61-2-9935-4107
Australia:          1-800-805-227
USA Non-Domestic:   1-408-526-7209
```

To disable these email notifications or to update or check the status of your case over the Internet using Cisco Connection Online (CCO), registered CCO users may point their web browser to:

    http://www.cisco.com/kobayashi/Tech_support.shtml

                            ****
For information on Year 2000 issues concerning Cisco products, please visit our Year 2000 Web Site located at http://www.cisco.com/warp/public/752/2000/. Our Product Compliance Matrix, Frequently Asked Questions, and contact information for our Year 2000 Support Team is located on this web site. Year 2000 questions and inquiries may be sent to year2000@cisco.com. This information is provided as a part of Cisco's Year 2000 Readiness Disclosure Statement.

Sincerely,

Technical Assistance Center
Cisco Systems, Inc.

This email explains that the case has been received and allocated to a CSE. You would be given the CSE's name, email, and direct line in a real case. The Cust-Pend state refers to the fact that no solution has been provided.

After a solution has been provided, your case turns into the Close-Pend state. You will receive the following email:

```
Error! No table of contents entries found. CASE: XXXXXXX
TITLE: C2610 keeps on rebooting
PRIORITY: 2
STATUS: Close-Pend

Name,

This is a Customer Case Update Notification from Cisco Systems
regarding Case Number XXXXXXX, which you opened with the Cisco
Technical Assistance Center.

Case XXXXXXX has been changed to a status of Close-Pend. This
status indicates the Cisco Customer Support Engineer has provided
you with an answer/solution with which they feel confident will
answer your question or solve your problem. Contact the assigned
engineer if you feel your problem has not been solved.

Since this is a Priority 2 case, you will receive ongoing email
notification until it is closed.  Priority 1 and 2 case
notifications occur every 24 hours, Priority 3 every 72 hours (3
days), Priority 4 every 120 hours (5 days).

CSE Name is the Customer Support Engineer at Cisco who owns your
case XXXXXXX. If you need to discuss this case further, CSE Name
can be reached by email at CSE@cisco.com or by phone at 99 9999
999999.

You can also reach CSE Name or the Cisco Technical Assistance
Center through the following methods:

North America:      1-800-553-2447
Europe:             32-2-704-5555
Asia Pacific:       61-2-9935-4107
Australia:          1-800-805-227
USA Non-Domestic:   1-408-526-7209

To disable these email notifications or to update or check the
status of your case over the Internet using Cisco Connection Online
(CCO), registered CCO users may point their web browser to:

    http://www.cisco.com/kobayashi/Tech_support.shtml

                        *********
For information on Year 2000 issues concerning Cisco products,
please visit our Year 2000 Web Site located at http://
www.cisco.com/warp/public/752/2000/. Our Product Compliance Matrix,
Frequently Asked Questions, and contact information for our Year
2000 Support Team is located on this web site. Year 2000 questions
and inquiries may be sent to year2000@cisco.com. This information
is provided as a part of Cisco's Year 2000 Readiness Disclosure
Statement.

Sincerely,

Technical Assistance Center
Cisco Systems, Inc.
```

Your case will then stay in the Close-Pend state until you contact TAC to inform them that the solution they provided has worked. The case is then closed.

Table 14-1 displays the automatic escalation path for priority 1 and 2 cases, based on how long a case is unresolved. Priority 3 and priority 4 cases do not have an automatic escalation path.

Besides the TAC Global Call Center there is also a TAC web site. This web site can be found by clicking on the `Technical Assistance Center` link under the `Service & Support` section of the CCO home page. Figure 14-10 shows you the main TAC home page.

The TAC web site is split into four main sections:

- *Products* Here, you find information relating to the hardware and software configuration of all Cisco equipment. The web pages are all sorted by product technology and then down to product and the specific product features. This organization makes it very easy to find out technical information about the product you are looking for.

- *Tools* Here, you will find the TAC newsletter, information on the Cisco Interactive Mentor, and the worldwide TAC support contacts.

- *Documents* The Documents section contains the same information already covered in the Technical Documents section.

- *Software* The Software section provides IOS image upgrades as well as performance monitoring and optimization tools to help you perform troubleshooting tasks on the network and its attached devices.

- *Escalate* The Escalate section gives an overview of the process you should take to escalate a problem with the TAC.

Table 14-1

TAC Escalation Process for Priority 1 and 2 Cases

Elapsed Time	Priority 1	Priority 2
1 Hour	CSE Team	
2 Hours	CSE Manager	
4 Hours	Tech Support Director	CSE Team
5 Hours		CSE Manager
12 Hours	Tech Support Director	
24 Hours	Vice President of TAC	Tech Support Director
48 Hours	President (CEO)	Vice President of TAC
96 Hours		President (CEO)

Figure 14-10
Cisco TAC Home
page

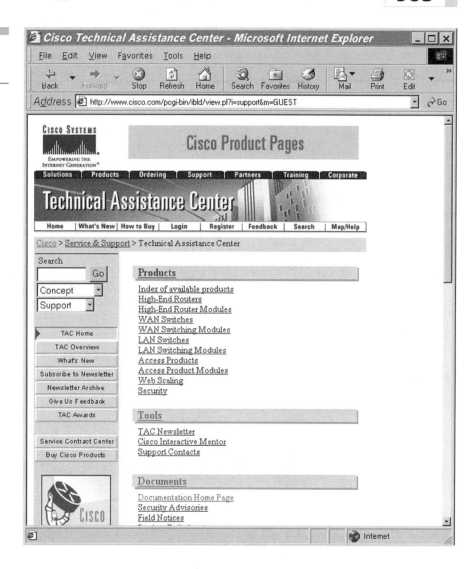

Documentation CD

Cisco provides a documentation CD with every piece of hardware that you purchase. This CD is updated frequently and the version can be told by looking at the date sticker on the back of the CD case. The CD contains numerous documents and tools, split into the following categories:

- Cisco Product Documentation
- Router Configuration Tools

- Technology Information
- Cisco Product Catalog
- Cisco Product Quick Reference Guide
- Packet Magazine (Online)
- Cisco Connection Online (Online)

The items marked (Online) require Internet access to fully function. The pack contains two CDs; the first CD has the software installer.

Running this CD installs Netscape Communicator v4.05, Adobe Acrobat Reader v3.0, Apple QuickTime v2.12 and Plug-In v1.1, and the Verity CD Web Publisher v3.0. Your current system is scanned and if you already have the same or later version of any of the software, you are given the choice to not install that piece of the software.

Once installed, you can launch the documentation CD-ROM from the second CD.

A current version of the contents of the CD is always available over the Internet at `http://www.cisco.com/univercd/home/home.htm`.

Searching the CD

The documentation CD has a built-in search facility that is similar to the facility offered on CCO. The CD search is not as powerful as the CCO

Figure 14-11
Master Setup

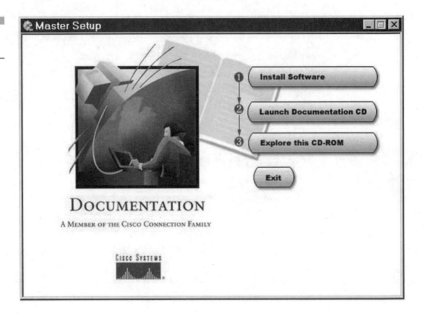

Figure 14-12

Cisco connection
documentation

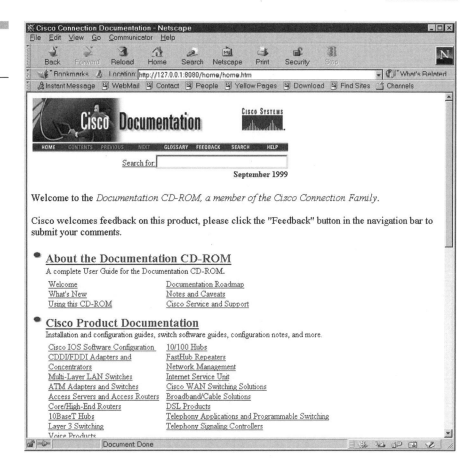

search, but it is still an excellent tool for interrogating the contents of the CD. You can see the search text box at the top of Figure 14-11. We have typed "Reverse Telnet" into this search box and here are the results.

You can see in the figure that (as with the CCO search) you have the ability to narrow your search by searching within the original returned results.

The documentation CD is a very handy tool to become familiar with. There may be occasions when Internet access is not available for some reason. In this case, you will have to turn to the books or the Documentation CD for reference. The power of the in-built search on the documentation CD makes it the best offline option for your troubleshooting questions.

Figure 14-13

Cisco Connection
Documentation—
Search

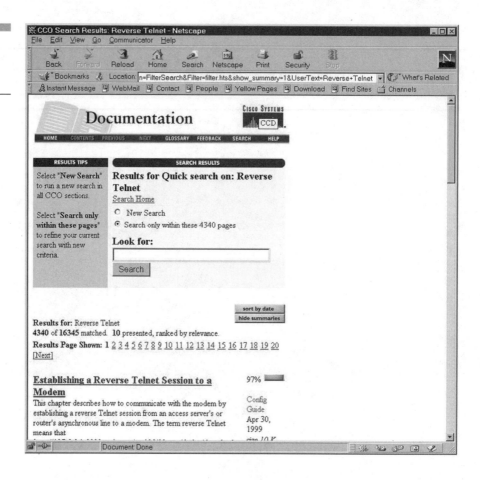

Support Commands

When reporting an error to the Technical Assistance Center, you will probably be asked to provide two sources of information for the Cisco Systems Engineers to look at in order to deduce what the problem is. These sources are the results of a show tech-support and also the core dump file.

Show Tech-Support

The show tech-support command is a Cisco IOS command that is available in privileged EXEC mode. The command syntax is as follows:

```
Router#sh tech-support ?
  page          Page through output
  password      Include passwords
```

The output below is the result of a show tech-support command run on a Cisco 2505 router.

```
Router#sh tech-support

------------------ show version ------------------

Cisco Internetwork Operating System Software
IOS (tm) 2500 Software (C2500-I-L), Version 11.2(2), RELEASE
SOFTWARE (fc1)
Copyright (c) 1986-1996 by cisco Systems, Inc.
Compiled Wed 13-Nov-96 07:37 by ajchopra
Image text-base: 0x030217A4, data-base: 0x00001000

ROM: System Bootstrap, Version 5.2(8a), RELEASE SOFTWARE
ROM: 3000 Bootstrap Software (IGS-RXBOOT), Version 10.2(8a),
RELEASE SOFTWARE (f
c1)

Router uptime is 9 minutes
System restarted by power-on
System image file is "flash:ie11220n", booted via flash

cisco 2505 (68030) processor (revision C) with 4096K/2048K bytes of
memory.
Processor board ID 02386215, with hardware revision 00000000
Bridging software.
X.25 software, Version 2.0, NET2, BFE and GOSIP compliant.
1 Ethernet/IEEE 802.3 interface(s)
8 Ethernet/IEEE 802.3 repeater port(s)
2 Serial network interface(s)
32K bytes of non-volatile configuration memory.
8192K bytes of processor board System flash (Read ONLY)

Configuration register is 0x2102

------------------ show running-config ------------------

Building configuration...

Current configuration:
!
version 11.2
!
hostname Router
!
enable secret 5 <removed>
enable password <removed>
!
!
hub ether 0 1
 link-test
 auto-polarity
 shutdown
!
```

```
hub ether 0 2
 link-test
 auto-polarity
 shutdown
!
hub ether 0 3
 link-test
 auto-polarity
 shutdown
!
hub ether 0 4
 link-test
 auto-polarity
 shutdown
!
hub ether 0 5
 link-test
 auto-polarity
 shutdown
!
hub ether 0 6
 link-test
 auto-polarity
 shutdown
!
hub ether 0 7
 link-test
 auto-polarity
 shutdown
!
hub ether 0 8
 link-test
 auto-polarity
 shutdown
!
interface Ethernet0
 ip address 10.0.0.1 255.0.0.0
 no ip mroute-cache
!
interface Serial0
 ip address 192.168.10.1 255.255.255.0
 no ip mroute-cache
 encapsulation ppp
!
interface Serial1
 description Intenet Link
 ip address 192.168.20.2 255.255.255.0
 no ip mroute-cache
 encapsulation ppp
 ppp authentication chap
!
router rip
 version 2
 network 192.168.10.0
 network 192.168.20.0
 network 10.0.0.0
!
no ip classless
ip route 0.0.0.0 0.0.0.0 192.168.20.1
!
```

```
line con 0
line aux 0
line vty 0 4
 password <removed>
 login
!
end

----------------- show controllers -----------------

LANCE unit 0, idb 0x88D4C, ds 0x8A770, regaddr = 0x2130000,
reset_mask 0x2
IB at 0x406DAC: mode=0x0000, mcfilter 0000/0000/0100/0020
station address 0060.3e69.da1e  default station address
0060.3e69.da1e
buffer size 1524
RX ring with 16 entries at 0x406DF0
Rxhead = 0x406DF0 (0), Rxp = 0x8A78C (0)
00 pak=0x08D390 ds=0x410A2E status=0x80 max_size=1524 pak_size=0
01 pak=0x08D1C4 ds=0x410376 status=0x80 max_size=1524 pak_size=0
02 pak=0x08CFF8 ds=0x40FCBE status=0x80 max_size=1524 pak_size=0
03 pak=0x08CE2C ds=0x40F606 status=0x80 max_size=1524 pak_size=0
04 pak=0x08CC60 ds=0x40EF4E status=0x80 max_size=1524 pak_size=0
05 pak=0x08CA94 ds=0x40E896 status=0x80 max_size=1524 pak_size=0
06 pak=0x08C8C8 ds=0x40E1DE status=0x80 max_size=1524 pak_size=0
07 pak=0x08C6FC ds=0x40DB26 status=0x80 max_size=1524 pak_size=0
08 pak=0x08C530 ds=0x40D46E status=0x80 max_size=1524 pak_size=0
09 pak=0x08C364 ds=0x40CDB6 status=0x80 max_size=1524 pak_size=0
10 pak=0x08C198 ds=0x40C6FE status=0x80 max_size=1524 pak_size=0
11 pak=0x08BFCC ds=0x40C046 status=0x80 max_size=1524 pak_size=0
12 pak=0x08BE00 ds=0x40B98E status=0x80 max_size=1524 pak_size=0
13 pak=0x08BC34 ds=0x40B2D6 status=0x80 max_size=1524 pak_size=0
14 pak=0x08BA68 ds=0x40AC1E status=0x80 max_size=1524 pak_size=0
15 pak=0x08B89C ds=0x40A566 status=0x80 max_size=1524 pak_size=0
TX ring with 4 entries at 0x406EA8, tx_count = 0
tx_head = 0x406EC0 (3), head_txp = 0x8A7EC (3)
tx_tail = 0x406EC0 (3), tail_txp = 0x8A7EC (3)
00 pak=0x000000 ds=0x43195A status=0x03 status2=0x0000 pak_size=60
01 pak=0x000000 ds=0x43195A status=0x03 status2=0x0000 pak_size=60
02 pak=0x000000 ds=0x43195A status=0x03 status2=0x0000 pak_size=60
03 pak=0x000000 ds=0x000000 status=0x03 status2=0x0000 pak_size=0
0 missed datagrams, 0 overruns
0 transmitter underruns, 0 excessive collisions
0 single collisions, 0 multiple collisions
0 dma memory errors, 0 CRC errors

0 alignment errors, 0 runts, 0 giants
0 tdr, 0 spurious initialization done interrupts
0 no enp status, 0 buffer errors, 0 overflow errors
0 tx_buff, 0 throttled, 0 enabled
Lance csr0 = 0x73
HD unit 0, idb = 0x8F3B4, driver structure at 0x92FE0
buffer size 1524  HD unit 0, No cable
cpb = 0x41, eda = 0x4940, cda = 0x4800
RX ring with 16 entries at 0x414800
00 bd_ptr=0x4800 pak=0x095B58 ds=0x41EC68 status=80 pak_size=0
01 bd_ptr=0x4814 pak=0x09598C ds=0x41E5B0 status=80 pak_size=0
02 bd_ptr=0x4828 pak=0x0957C0 ds=0x41DEF8 status=80 pak_size=0
03 bd_ptr=0x483C pak=0x0955F4 ds=0x41D840 status=80 pak_size=0
04 bd_ptr=0x4850 pak=0x095428 ds=0x41D188 status=80 pak_size=0
```

```
05 bd_ptr=0x4864 pak=0x09525C ds=0x41CAD0 status=80 pak_size=0
06 bd_ptr=0x4878 pak=0x095090 ds=0x41C418 status=80 pak_size=0
07 bd_ptr=0x488C pak=0x094EC4 ds=0x41BD60 status=80 pak_size=0
08 bd_ptr=0x48A0 pak=0x094CF8 ds=0x41B6A8 status=80 pak_size=0
09 bd_ptr=0x48B4 pak=0x094B2C ds=0x41AFF0 status=80 pak_size=0
10 bd_ptr=0x48C8 pak=0x094960 ds=0x41A938 status=80 pak_size=0
11 bd_ptr=0x48DC pak=0x094794 ds=0x41A280 status=80 pak_size=0
12 bd_ptr=0x48F0 pak=0x0945C8 ds=0x419BC8 status=80 pak_size=0
13 bd_ptr=0x4904 pak=0x0943FC ds=0x419510 status=80 pak_size=0
14 bd_ptr=0x4918 pak=0x094230 ds=0x418E58 status=80 pak_size=0
15 bd_ptr=0x492C pak=0x094064 ds=0x4187A0 status=80 pak_size=0
16 bd_ptr=0x4940 pak=0x093E98 ds=0x4180E8 status=80 pak_size=0
cpb = 0x41, eda = 0x5000, cda = 0x5000
TX ring with 2 entries at 0x415000
00 bd_ptr=0x5000 pak=0x000000 ds=0x000000 status=80 pak_size=0
01 bd_ptr=0x5014 pak=0x000000 ds=0x000000 status=80 pak_size=0
02 bd_ptr=0x5028 pak=0x000000 ds=0x000000 status=80 pak_size=0
0 missed datagrams, 0 overruns
0 bad datagram encapsulations, 0 memory errors
0 transmitter underruns
0 residual bit errors
HD unit 1, idb = 0x96BCC, driver structure at 0x9A7F8
buffer size 1524   HD unit 1, No cable
cpb = 0x42, eda = 0x3140, cda = 0x3000
RX ring with 16 entries at 0x423000
00 bd_ptr=0x3000 pak=0x09D370 ds=0x42CDB0 status=80 pak_size=0
01 bd_ptr=0x3014 pak=0x09D1A4 ds=0x42C6F8 status=80 pak_size=0
02 bd_ptr=0x3028 pak=0x09CFD8 ds=0x42C040 status=80 pak_size=0
03 bd_ptr=0x303C pak=0x09CE0C ds=0x42B988 status=80 pak_size=0
04 bd_ptr=0x3050 pak=0x09CC40 ds=0x42B2D0 status=80 pak_size=0
05 bd_ptr=0x3064 pak=0x09CA74 ds=0x42AC18 status=80 pak_size=0
06 bd_ptr=0x3078 pak=0x09C8A8 ds=0x42A560 status=80 pak_size=0
07 bd_ptr=0x308C pak=0x09C6DC ds=0x429EA8 status=80 pak_size=0
08 bd_ptr=0x30A0 pak=0x09C510 ds=0x4297F0 status=80 pak_size=0
09 bd_ptr=0x30B4 pak=0x09C344 ds=0x429138 status=80 pak_size=0
10 bd_ptr=0x30C8 pak=0x09C178 ds=0x428A80 status=80 pak_size=0
11 bd_ptr=0x30DC pak=0x09BFAC ds=0x4283C8 status=80 pak_size=0
12 bd_ptr=0x30F0 pak=0x09BDE0 ds=0x427D10 status=80 pak_size=0
13 bd_ptr=0x3104 pak=0x09BC14 ds=0x427658 status=80 pak_size=0
14 bd_ptr=0x3118 pak=0x09BA48 ds=0x426FA0 status=80 pak_size=0
15 bd_ptr=0x312C pak=0x09B87C ds=0x4268E8 status=80 pak_size=0
16 bd_ptr=0x3140 pak=0x09B6B0 ds=0x426230 status=80 pak_size=0
cpb = 0x42, eda = 0x3800, cda = 0x3800
TX ring with 2 entries at 0x423800
00 bd_ptr=0x3800 pak=0x000000 ds=0x000000 status=80 pak_size=0
01 bd_ptr=0x3814 pak=0x000000 ds=0x000000 status=80 pak_size=0
02 bd_ptr=0x3828 pak=0x000000 ds=0x000000 status=80 pak_size=0
0 missed datagrams, 0 overruns
0 bad datagram encapsulations, 0 memory errors
0 transmitter underruns
0 residual bit errors


----------------- show stacks ------------------

Minimum process stacks:
  Free/Size      Name
  2764/3000      IP Background
  2768/4000      Init
  1420/2000      Router Init
```

```
Interrupt level stacks:
Level   Called  Unused/Size     Name
  2      0      2000/2000       HUB interrupt
  3      0      2000/2000       Serial interface state change
interrupt
  4      21     1780/2000       Network interfaces
  5      23699  1872/2000       Console Uart


----------------- show interfaces ------------------


Ethernet0 is up, line protocol is up , using hub 0
  Hardware is Lance, address is 0060.3e69.da1e (bia 0060.3e69.da1e)
  Internet address is 10.0.0.1/8
  MTU 1500 bytes, BW 10000 Kbit, DLY 1000 usec, rely 255/255, load
  1/255
  Encapsulation ARPA, loopback not set, keepalive set (10 sec)
  ARP type: ARPA, ARP Timeout 04:00:00
  Last input never, output 00:00:02, output hang never
  Last clearing of "show interface" counters never
  Queueing strategy: fifo
  Output queue 0/40, 0 drops; input queue 0/75, 0 drops
  5 minute input rate 0 bits/sec, 0 packets/sec
  5 minute output rate 0 bits/seec
     0 packets input, 0 bytes, 0 no buffer
     Received 0 broadcasts, 0 runts, 0 giants
     0 input errors, 0 CRC, 0 frame, 0 overrun, 0 ignored, 0 abort
     0 input packets with dribble condition detected
     21 packets output, 2456 bytes, 0 underruns
     0 output errors, 0 collisions, 4 interface resets
     0 babbles, 0 late collision, 0 deferred
     0 lost carrier, 0 no carrier
     0 output buffer failures, 0 output buffers swapped out
Serial0 is down, line protocol is down
  Hardware is HD64570
  Internet address is 192.168.10.1/24
  MTU 1500 bytes, BW 1544 Kbit, DLY 20000 usec, rely 255/255, load
  1/255
  Encapsulation PPP, loopback not set, keepalive set (10 sec)
  LCP Closed
  Closed: IPCP, CDP
  Last input never, output never, output hang never
  Last clearing of "show interface" counters never
  Input queue: 0/75/0 (size/max/drops); Total output drops: 0
  Queueing strategy: weighted fair
  Output queue: 0/64/0 (size/threshold/drops)
     Conversations  0/0 (active/max active)
     Reserved Conversations 0/0 (allocated/max allocated)
  5 minute input rate 0 bits/sec, 0 packets/sec
  5 minute output rate 0 bits/sec, 0 packets/sec
     0 packets input, 0 bytes, 0 no buffer
     Received 0 broadcasts, 0 runts, 0 giants
     0 input errors, 0 CRC, 0 frame, 0 overrun, 0 ignored, 0 abort
     0 packets output, 0 bytes, 0 underruns
     0 output errors, 0 collisions, 8 interface resets
     0 output buffer failures, 0 output buffers swapped out
     0 carrier transitions
     DCD=down  DSR=down  DTR=down  RTS=down  CTS=down
Serial1 is down, line protocol is down
  Hardware is HD64570
```

```
Description: Intenet Link
Internet address is 192.168.20.2/24
MTU 1500 bytes, BW 1544 Kbit, DLY 20000 usec, rely 255/255, load
1/255
Encapsulation PPP, loopback not set, keepalive set (10 sec)
LCP Closed
Closed: IPCP, CDP
Last input never, output never, output hang never
Last clearing of "show interface" counters never
Input queue: 0/75/0 (size/max/drops); Total output drops: 0
Queueing strategy: weighted fair
Output queue: 0/64/0 (size/threshold/drops)
   Conversations  0/0 (active/max active)
   Reserved Conversations 0/0 (allocated/max allocated)
5 minute input rate 0 bits/sec, 0 packets/sec
5 minute output rate 0 bits/sec, 0 packets/sec
   0 packets input, 0 bytes, 0 no buffer
   Received 0 broadcasts, 0 runts, 0 giants
   0 input errors, 0 CRC, 0 frame, 0 overrun, 0 ignored, 0 abort
   0 packets output, 0 bytes, 0 underruns
   0 output errors, 0 collisions, 8 interface resets
   0 output buffer failures, 0 output buffers swapped out
   0 carrier transitions
   DCD=down  DSR=down  DTR=down  RTS=down  CTS=down


----------------- show process memory -----------------
Total: 6005032, Used: 1011336, Free: 4993696
```

PID	TTY	Allocated	Freed	Holding	Getbufs	Retbufs	Process
0	0	155988	1236	889832	0	0	*Init*
0	0	252	16580	252	0	0	*Sched*
0	0	936212	139136	300	323940	0	*Dead*
1	0	252	252	1716	0	0	Load Meter
2	0	303740	248300	24308	0	0	Exec
3	0	0	0	2716	0	0	Check heaps
4	0	92	0	2808	0	0	Pool Manager
5	0	252	252	2716	0	0	Timers
6	0	92	0	2808	0	0	ARP Input
7	0	92	0	2808	0	0	SERIAL A'detect
8	0	128	0	4844	0	0	IP Input
9	0	520	260	2976	0	0	CDP Protocol
10	0	0	0	2716	0	0	TCP Timer
11	0	748	0	3464	0	0	TCP Protocols
12	0	232	0	2948	0	0	Probe Input
13	0	92	0	2808	0	0	RARP Input
14	0	744	0	3460	0	0	BOOTP Server
15	0	232	0	2948	0	0	CCP manager
16	0	0	0	2716	0	0	IP Cache Ager
17	0	128	0	2844	0	0	Critical Bkgnd
18	0	7492	0	3060	0	0	Net Background
19	0	344	252	2808	0	0	Logger
20	0	6548	1748	2800	0	0	TTY Background
21	0	184	0	2900	0	0	Net Input
22	0	252	52	1716	0	0	Compute load avgs

```
 23  0      0        0      2716     0       0      Per-minute
                                                    Jobs
 24  0      232      0      2948     0       0      PPP manager
 25  0      232      0      2948     0       0      Multilink
                                                    PPP
 26  0      232      0      2948     0       0      Multilink
                                                    PPP out
 27  0      248      0      3972     0       0      IP
                                                    Background
 28  0      184      0      2900     0       0      IP-RT
                                                    Background
 29  0      92       0      2852     0       0      RIP Send
 30  0      3480     0      14492    0       0      RIP Router
                                   1011048 Total
```

```
----------------- show process cpu ------------------

CPU utilization for five seconds: 23%/17%; one minute: 21%; five
minutes: 14%
 PID  Runtime(ms) Invoked  uSecs  5Sec   1Min   5Min  TTY  Process
   1  4           111      36     0.00%  0.00%  0.00%  0   Load Meter
   2  15980       776      20592  6.85%  7.11%  3.52%  0   Exec
   3  708         19       37263  0.00%  0.10%  0.08%  0   Check
                                                          heaps
   4  0           1        0      0.00%  0.00%  0.00%  0   Pool
                                                          Manager
   5  4           2        2000   0.00%  0.00%  0.00%  0   Timers
   6  0           10       0      0.00%  0.00%  0.00%  0   ARP Input
   7  0           1        0      0.00%  0.00%  0.00%  0   SERIAL
                                                          A'detect
   8  0           10       0      0.00%  0.00%  0.00%  0   IP Input
   9  8           57       140    0.00%  0.00%  0.00%  0   CDP
                                                          Protocol
  10  4           112      35     0.00%  0.00%  0.00%  0   TCP Timer
  11  0           2        0      0.00%  0.00%  0.00%  0   TCP
                                                          Protocols
  12  0           1        0      0.00%  0.00%  0.00%  0   Probe
                                                          Input
  13  0           1        0      0.00%  0.00%  0.00%  0   RARP Input
  14  4           1        4000   0.00%  0.00%  0.00%  0   BOOTP
                                                          Server
  15  0           1        0      0.00%  0.00%  0.00%  0   CCP
                                                          manager
  16  0           10       0      0.00%  0.00%  0.00%  0   IP Cache
                                                          Ager
  17  0           1        0      0.00%  0.00%  0.00%  0   Critical
                                                          Bkgnd
  18  56          18       3111   0.00%  0.00%  0.00%  0   Net
                                                          Background
  19  20          20       1000   0.00%  0.00%  0.00%  0   Logger
  20  276         553      499    0.00%  0.00%  0.00%  0   TTY
                                                          Background
  21  0           1        0      0.00%  0.00%  0.00%  0   Net Input
  22  12          112      107    0.00%  0.00%  0.00%  0   Compute
                                                          load avgs
  23  268         10       26800  0.00%  0.06%  0.01%  0   Per-minute
                                                          Jobs
  24  0           1        0      0.00%  0.00%  0.00%  0   PPP
                                                          manager
```

25	16	172	93	0.00%	0.00%	0.00%	0	Multilink PPP
26	0	1	0	0.00%	0.00%	0.00%	0	Multilink PPP out
27	92	69	1333	0.00%	0.00%	0.00%	0	IP Background
28	4	4	1000	0.00%	0.00%	0.00%	0	IP-RT Background
29	0	1	0	0.00%	0.00%	0.00%	0	RIP Send
30	28	4	7000	0.00%	0.02%	0.00%	0	RIP Router

```
----------------- show buffers ------------------

Buffer elements:
     500 in free list (500 max allowed)
     66 hits, 0 misses, 0 created

Public buffer pools:
Small buffers, 104 bytes (total 50, permanent 50):
     50 in free list (20 min, 150 max allowed)
     17 hits, 0 misses, 0 trims, 0 created
     0 failures (0 no memory)
Middle buffers, 600 bytes (total 25, permanent 25):
     25 in free list (10 min, 150 max allowed)
     22 hits, 0 misses, 0 trims, 0 created
     0 failures (0 no memory)
Big buffers, 1524 bytes (total 50, permanent 50):
     50 in free list (5 min, 150 max allowed)
     11 hits, 0 misses, 0 trims, 0 created
     0 failures (0 no memory)
VeryBig buffers, 4520 bytes (total 10, permanent 10):
     10 in free list (0 min, 100 max allowed)
     0 hits, 0 misses, 0 trims, 0 created
     0 failures (0 no memory)
Large buffers, 5024 bytes (total 0, permanent 0):
     0 in free list (0 min, 10 max allowed)
     0 hits, 0 misses, 0 trims, 0 created
     0 failures (0 no memory)
Huge buffers, 18024 bytes (total 0, permanent 0):
     0 in free list (0 min, 4 max allowed)
     0 hits, 0 misses, 0 trims, 0 created
     0 failures (0 no memory)

Interface buffer pools:
Ethernet0 buffers, 1524 bytes (total 32, permanent 32):
     8 in free list (0 min, 32 max allowed)
     24 hits, 0 fallbacks
     8 max cache size, 8 in cache
Serial0 buffers, 1524 bytes (total 32, permanent 32):
     7 in free list (0 min, 32 max allowed)
     25 hits, 0 fallbacks
     8 max cache size, 8 in cache
Serial1 buffers, 1524 bytes (total 32, permanent 32):
     7 in free list (0 min, 32 max allowed)
     25 hits, 0 fallbacks
     8 max cache size, 8 in cache

Router#
```

As you can see, this command produces a lot of output. It is important to familiarize yourself with this command because this command can produce almost everything you need to check a configuration out on a router. If you are asking someone to send you a router configuration, you are much better asking them for a `show tech-support` because this includes a lot more information than just a `show running-config`.

This command provides you with the equivalent output of the following IOS commands:

- `show version`
- `show running-config`
- `show controllers`
- `show stacks`
- `show interface`
- `show process`
- `show process cpu`
- `show buffers`

For TAC purposes, it is recommended that you log this output to a file and then either email the log file to your TAC Systems Engineer or copy and paste the output into an email message addressed to the TAC Systems Engineer.

Core Dumps

Core dumps are full dumps of the routers memory image. This image file is not much use to the untrained eye, but the TAC Systems Engineers are trained to analyze them to ascertain the cause of a router crash. You may be asked to provide a core dump file if you have reported a router crash problem to the TAC.

The command to produce a core dump is **write core**. One interesting point is that this command cannot be viewed by using the online help.

```
Router#wr ?
  erase      Erase NV memory
  memory     Write to NV memory
  network    Write to network TFTP server
  terminal   Write to terminal
  <cr>

Router#
```

As you can see from the output, there is no mention of the command **write core**. This is a command that can be run only in privileged EXEC mode and it copies the router memory dump to a TFTP server. The correct commands to produce a core dump are as follows:

```
Router#wr core
Remote host? 192.168.10.1
Name of core file to write [Router-core]?
Write file Router-core on host 1.1.1.1? [confirm]
Writing Router-core
!!!!!!!!!!!!!!!!!!!!!!!!!!!!!!!!!!!!!!!!!!!!!!!!!!!!!!!!!!!!!!!!!!!!!!!
!!!!!!!!!!!
!!!!!!!!!!!!!!!!!!!!!!!!!!!!!!!!!!!!!!!!!!!!!!!!!!!!!!!!!!!!!!!!!!!!!!!
!!!!!!!!!!!!!!!!!!!!!!!!!!!!!!!!!!!!!!!!!!!!!!!!!!!!!!!!!!!!!!!!!!!!!!!
!!!!!!!!!!!!!!!!!!!!!!!!!!!!!!!!!!!!!!!!!!!!!!!!!!!!!!!!!!!!!!!!!!!!!!!
!!!!!!!!!!!!!!!!!!!!!!!!!!!!!!!!!!!!!!!!!!!!!!!!!!!!!!!!! [OK]
Router#
```

The output shows the core dump being written to the TFTP server 192.168.10.1 and the file will be named Router-core.

Chapter Summary

In this chapter, we have looked at the support offerings that Cisco offers to aid the troubleshooting process. We have looked at the Cisco Connection Online web site and the major parts that make up the site. We then looked at the Technical Assistance Center and the procedures for getting support issues resolved.

The documentation CD, which is provided with every Cisco product and also available on CCO, was explained along with the best ways to utilize the CD for troubleshooting. We then finished off the chapter with a look at two commands that are useful in troubleshooting and the output that is required for the TAC Systems Engineer to progress a reported TAC incident.

Besides these mentioned resources, there are other web sites that are dedicated to building online communities. They can be used as a source of information as well as a way of getting questions answered by technical peers. Such sites include www.brainbuzz.com and www.netcerts.com. Numerous news servers exist that provide excellent feeds for the Cisco community. The most frequented of these are the news servers run by www.groupstudy.com.

Frequently Asked Questions (FAQ)

Question: What is the difference between a `show tech-support` and a core dump?

Answer: A `show tech-support` is a collection of the output from various `show` commands, in which the core dump is a file that represents a dump of the router's memory at the time of application of the command.

Question: Does the CCNA or CCNP provide a CCO account?

Answer: No, the only qualification that provides full CCO access is CCIE.

Question: Can anybody download Cisco IOS images from the Software Center section on CCO?

Answer: No, each registered CCO account has specific privileges appertaining to that user. If you hold a TAC agreement, you may be able to download specific software but not others. If you hold a Cisco Employee CCO login, you may have full download capabilities to all areas on CCO.

Questions

1. Which command performs a core dump ?

    a. write dump

    b. run dump

    c. run core

    d. write core

2. What mode must you be in to perform a core dump?

    a. User

    b. Privileged

    c. Global Configuration

    d. Interface Configuration

3. An incident where the production network is severely degraded and impacts significant aspects of your business operations would be classed as which TAC case priority?

    a. 1

    b. 3

    c. 2

    d. 4

4. With a TAC priority of 1, you are notified of the status of the problem every ... ?

    a. 36 hours

    b. 24 hours

    c. 12 hours

    d. 36 hours

5. What is the last state a TAC case enters before being closed?

    a. Resolution

    b. Cust-Pend

    c. Close-Pend

    d. Close

6. The Cisco Connection Online is available in other languages than English. True or false?

    a. True

    b. False

7. What mode must you be in to perform a `show tech-support`?

    a. User

    b. Global Configuration

    c. Interface Configuration

    d. Privileged

8. If you wanted to download the latest IOS version, as outlined in your SMARTnet agreement, which part of CCO would you go to?

    a. Software Center

    b. Technical Documents

    c. Marketplace

    d. Locate a reseller

9. What is the URL of the Cisco Connection Online?

    a. `www.cisco.com`

    b. `www.cco.com`

    c. `www.ciscocco.com`

    d. `www.ciscotac.com`

10. When you perform a write core, what must you specify? (Choose two.)

    a. IP address of a TFTP server

    b. IP address of the FTP server

    c. Name of the core file

    d. Memory buffers required

11. Which of the following outputs are not included in a `show tech-support`?

    a. `show version`

    b. `show ip route`

    c. `show interface`

    d. `show process`

12. How many CDs are in the Documentation CD pack?

    a. 1

    b. 2

    c. 3

    d. 4

13. Which part of CCO provides 24x7 access to online ordering of Cisco equipment?

    a. Cisco TAC

    b. Cisco Software Center

    c. Documents Online

    d. Cisco Marketplace

14. If you raise a call with TAC for advice on a product, what priority is assigned to it?

    a. 2
    b. 1
    c. 4
    d. 3

15. With a TAC priority of 3, how often are you notified of the status of the problem?

    a. Every 24 hours
    b. Every 12 hours
    c. Every 48 hours
    d. Every 72 hours

16. What does CCO stand for?

    a. Cisco Center Online
    b. Cisco Correction Online
    c. Cisco Career Offers
    d. Cisco Connection Online

17. With a TAC priority of 4, how often are you notified of the status of the problem?

    a. Every 60 hours
    b. Every 48 hours
    c. Every 72 hours
    d. Every 120 hours

18. Which of the following Cisco Career Certifications gets you a CCO login?

    a. CCIE
    b. CCNA
    c. CCNP
    d. CCDP

19. Which Cisco TAC priority is classed as the most important?

    a. 1
    b. A
    c. D
    d. 2

20. What are you assigned when you raise a TAC case? (Choose two.)

    a. CSE
    b. Case number
    c. TAC code
    d. TAC number

Answers

1. Answer: d

   The command **write core** performs a core dump.

2. Answer: b

   This must be run from the Privileged EXEC mode.

3. Answer: c

   An incident where the production network is severely degraded and impacts significant aspects of your business operations would be classed as a priority 2 case.

4. Answer: b

   With a TAC priority of 1, you are notified of the status of the problem every 24 hours.

5. Answer: c

   The last state a TAC case enters before being closed is Close-Pend.

6. Answer: a

   This is True. CCO is available in many foreign languages as well as English.

7. Answer: d

   To run a `show tech-support`, you must be in privileged EXEC mode.

8. Answer: a

   If you want to download the latest IOS version as outlined in your SMARTnet agreement, you would go to the Software Center.

9. Answer: a

   The correct URL for CCO is www.cisco.com.

10. Answers: a and c

    When you perform a write core. You must specify the IP address of the TFTP server and the name of the core file.

11. Answer: b

    The results from a `show ip route` command are not included in the output of a `show tech-support`.

12. Answer: b

    There are two CDs in the Documentation CD pack: the Installer CD and the Documentation CD.

13. Answer: d

The Cisco Marketplace provides 24×7 access to online ordering of Cisco equipment.

14. Answer: c

If you raise a call with TAC for advice on a product, it is assigned a priority of 4.

15. Answer: d

With a TAC priority of 3, you are notified of the status of the problem every 72 hours.

16. Answer: d

CCO stands for Cisco Connection Online.

17. Answer: d

With a TAC priority of 4, you are notified of the status of the problem every 120 hours.

18. Answer: a

You get a CCO login only after passing the CCIE qualification.

19. Answer: aq

The most important priority of a TAC case is priority 1.

20. Answers: a and b

When you raise a TAC case, you are assigned a unique case number and also a Cisco Support Engineer (CSE).

15

Advanced Troubleshooting Techniques

This chapter will present you with tricks, tips, and techniques that are grounded on the information presented in previous chapters. A single test objective is covered in this chapter. The focus of this chapter is to help the administrator in their daily efforts at maintaining the network.

It is important that the information presented in this chapter is not taken without regard to what was previously presented. For instance, looking at the section in this chapter regarding ping will not give you the information necessary to really understand it unless you have read the previous chapters. The Traceroute examples also presuppose knowledge of both routing protocols and the routing process. If you have not grasped the concepts and methodologies previously presented, this chapter will not help you in your troubleshooting efforts.

However, if you have read the previous chapters and understand the basic concepts and methodologies, this chapter will give you additional material designed to make your everyday troubleshooting easier. It will also explore some of the underutilized commands and show some ways to avoid making the same mistakes that many others have made in the past.

Objectives Covered in the Chapter

This chapter's objective is to obtain protocol troubleshooting information by capturing and interpreting data with a third-party protocol analyzer.

Reading Protocol Analyzer Outputs

There is no real secret to reading output received from protocol analyzers. As long as we know what the fields are supposed to be, we can easily adapt to seeing the output in whatever form the source code is shown to us by our analyzer. Now would be a good time to go back over the previous chapters if you are not totally sure of how each protocol should look. Protocol analyzers can give us misleading information if we are not positive about what we are seeing.

Most analyzers produced these days will automatically decipher the packets received and tell you exactly what we are seeing. Let's take a look at the following output in Figure 15-1 and decipher exactly what the analyzer has shown us.

In the output, our analyzer shows that this is a broadcast packet. We can verify this by looking at the *media access control* (MAC) destination address. If all bits are set to 1, this is a broadcast address. This will show in hex as a MAC destination address consisting of FF-FF-FF-FF-FF-FF-FF-FF, as is shown in the output. The source address is the MAC address of 00-C0-02-A3-14-10.

Now, let's examine a few other items that are shown. The first question we raise is, "Are we using a *Subnetwork Access Protocol* (SNAP) header in this output?" The answer is no because our *Destination Service Access Point* (DSAP) is set to EO and our SSAP is set to EO. In order to use a SNAP header, we need to have both the DSAP and SSAP set to AA. If you do not already know this, you need to review Chapter 4, "Basic Diagnostic Commands," which discusses Ethernet protocols.

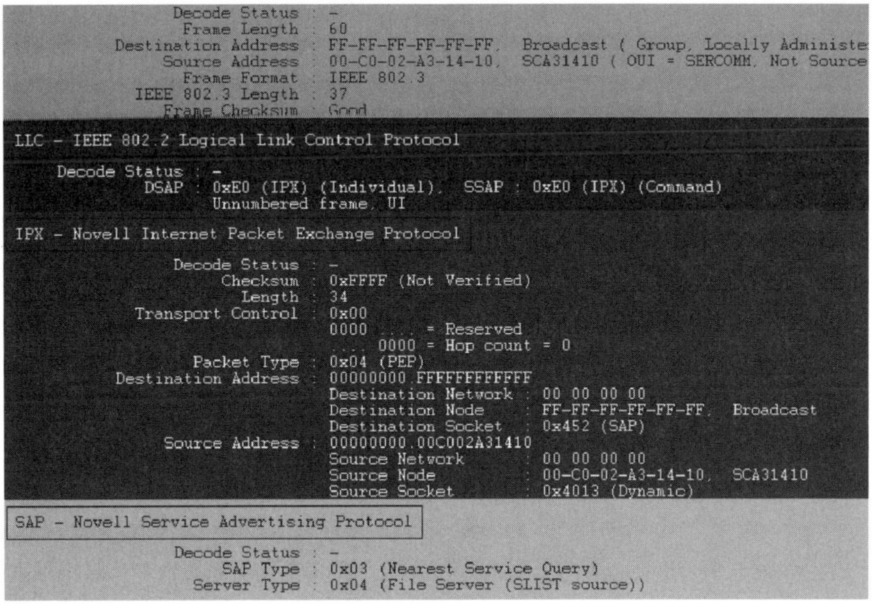

Figure 15-1
An apple broadcast

```
              Decode Status : -
               Frame Length : 60
         Destination Address : FF-FF-FF-FF-FF-FF, Broadcast ( Group, Locally Administe
              Source Address : 00-C0-02-A3-14-10, SCA31410 ( OUI = SERCOMM, Not Source
                Frame Format : IEEE 802.3
            IEEE 802.3 Length : 37
              Frame Checksum : Good

LLC - IEEE 802.2 Logical Link Control Protocol

       Decode Status : -
                DSAP : 0xE0 (IPX) (Individual), SSAP : 0xE0 (IPX) (Command)
                       Unnumbered frame, UI

IPX - Novell Internet Packet Exchange Protocol

            Decode Status : -
                Checksum : 0xFFFF (Not Verified)
                  Length : 34
       Transport Control : 0x00
                           0000     = Reserved
                               0000 = Hop count = 0
             Packet Type : 0x04 (PEP)
       Destination Address : 00000000.FFFFFFFFFFFF
                           Destination Network : 00-00-00-00
                           Destination Node    : FF-FF-FF-FF-FF-FF, Broadcast
                           Destination Socket  : 0x452 (SAP)
            Source Address : 00000000.00C002A31410
                           Source Network : 00-00-00-00
                           Source Node    : 00-C0-02-A3-14-10, SCA31410
                           Source Socket  : 0x4013 (Dynamic)

SAP - Novell Service Advertising Protocol

            Decode Status : -
                SAP Type : 0x03 (Nearest Service Query)
             Server Type : 0x04 (File Server (SLIST source))
```

Notice that the full destination network address, which is a combination of the network number and the MAC address is 00000000.FFFFFFFF. In other words, we know that this packet is destined for Novell network number 00000000, which is also the default network number. The source address is on the same Novell network. Therefore, this packet has not crossed a router.

Let's examine another Apple example. In this example, shown in Figure 15-2, one of the first things we should notice is that a SNAP header is being run. Besides the analyzer telling us this, we can verify it by looking at the SSAP and DSAP fields. Since both are set to AA, this must be a SNAP header.

However, the analyzer from the output tells us that this is a broadcast packet, but the destination MAC address is not FF-FF-FF-FF-FF-FF. How can this be? It is actually a limitation of the analyzer, which does not distinguish between a multicast and broadcast address. Part of the reason the analyzer does not make a distinction is because a multicast is generally considered a form of broadcast. This is an example of why it is important that we understand what we should be seeing so that we can compare it to what we actually see.

The next example in Figure 15-3 shows us a packet sent to a Web site. This is known because our destination port is 80 (HTTP). If our source port were 80, we would know that the source of the packet was from a Web site. When analyzing protocols, it is critical to remember that we attach to

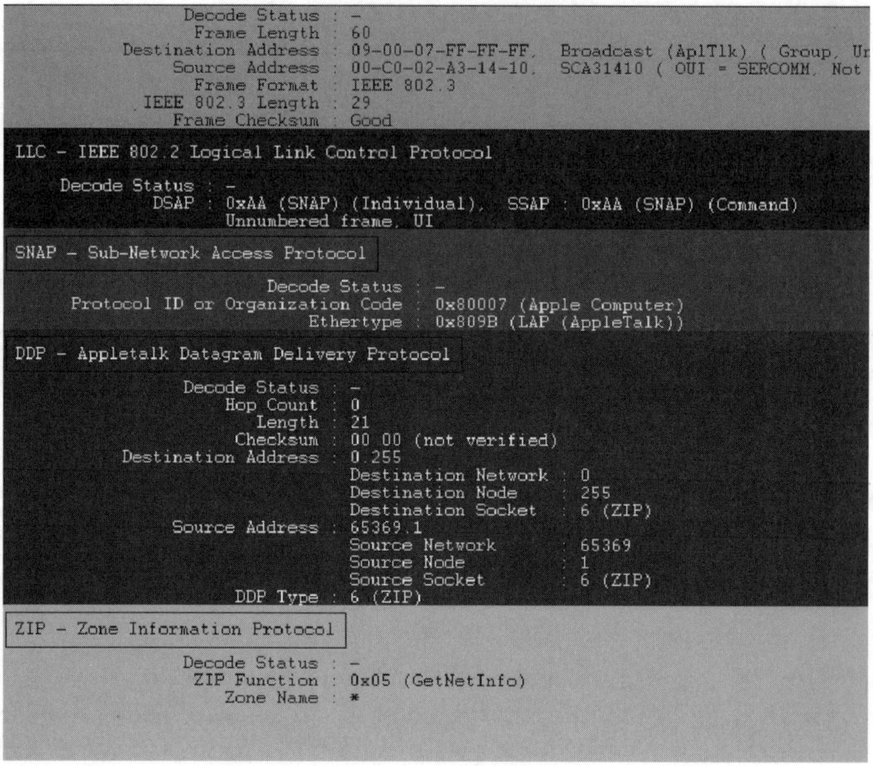

Figure 15-2
AppleTalk SAP

```
                  Decode Status : -
                   Frame Length : 60
              Destination Address : 09-00-07-FF-FF-FF.  Broadcast (AplTlk) ( Group, Ur
                    Source Address : 00-C0-02-A3-14-10.  SCA31410 ( OUI = SERCOMM, Not
                      Frame Format : IEEE 802.3
               IEEE 802.3 Length : 29
                  Frame Checksum : Good

 LLC - IEEE 802.2 Logical Link Control Protocol

      Decode Status : -
                DSAP : 0xAA (SNAP) (Individual),  SSAP : 0xAA (SNAP) (Command)
                        Unnumbered frame, UI

 SNAP - Sub-Network Access Protocol

                      Decode Status : -
        Protocol ID or Organization Code : 0x80007 (Apple Computer)
                        Ethertype : 0x809B (LAP (AppleTalk))

 DDP - Appletalk Datagram Delivery Protocol

                  Decode Status : -
                       Hop Count : 0
                          Length : 21
                        Checksum : 00 00 (not verified)
              Destination Address : 0.255
                                     Destination Network : 0
                                     Destination Node    : 255
                                     Destination Socket  : 6 (ZIP)
                  Source Address : 65369.1
                                     Source Network : 65369
                                     Source Node    : 1
                                     Source Socket  : 6 (ZIP)
                        DDP Type : 6 (ZIP)

 ZIP - Zone Information Protocol

                  Decode Status : -
                    ZIP Function : 0x05 (GetNetInfo)
                       Zone Name : *
```

known ports. We are sent back information from the known port to a different port number, which may not be known.

It is important in real life as well as on a test to make sure that you really study the data presented. Take a look at Figure 15-4, a BPDU packet. One question that is likely to come up is whether this packet has traversed over a bridge or if it was generated locally. An easy way to tell is to compare the root MAC address with the bridge MAC address. Also, the root ID and the bridge ID are identical. In either case, if both are the same, then this could not have traversed over a bridge.

One final example of what to expect from a protocol analyzer and the test is shown in Figure 15-5. Study this carefully and then we'll ask a few questions after we have studied it.

Now, cover up the figure and see how many of these questions you can answer:

1. Was this a broadcast packet, a multicast packet, or was it sent to an individual workstation?

2. Was this packet part of a larger packet that was fragmented?

Figure 15-3

HTTP

```
             Decode Status : -
              Frame Length : 60
        Destination Address : 00-00-C5-73-1F-0C,  Farallon 73-1F-0C ( OUI = FARALL
             Source Address : 00-E0-29-35-4F-F0,  EUROPA          ( OUI = Unknown
               Frame Format : Ethernet DIX V2
                  Ethertype : 0x800 (IP)
             Frame Checksum : Good

IP - Internet Protocol

              Decode Status : -
                    Version : 4,  Header length : 20
            Type of Service : 0x00
                              000. .... = Routine Precedence
                              ...0 .... = Normal Delay
                              .... 0... = Normal Throughput
                              .... .0.. = Normal Reliability
                              .... ..00 = Reserved
               Total length : 40 bytes
             Identification : 28316
           Fragment Control : 0x4000
                              0... .... .... .... = Reserved
                              .1.. .... .... .... = Don't Fragment
                              ..0. .... .... .... = Last Fragment
                              ...0 0000 0000 0000 = Fragment Offset = 0 bytes
               Time to Live : 128 seconds/hops
                   Protocol : 6 (TCP)
                   Checksum : 0x201E (Checksum Good)
             Source Address : 10.1.1.19
        Destination Address : 192.215.160.42
No IP options

TCP - Transmission Control Protocol

              Decode Status : -
                Source Port : 4171 (Unknown)
           Destination Port : 80 (HTTP)
            Sequence Number : 1212000296
      Acknowledgement Number : 1034244
                Data Offset : 0x50
                              0101 .... = Header length = 20
                      Flags : 0x10
                              ..0. .... = No Urgent pointer
                              ...1 .... = Acknowledgement
                              .... 0... = No Push
```

Figure 15-4

A BPDU packet

```
IEEE 802.3/Ethernet DIX V2 Header

              Decode Status : -
              Frame Length : 60
        Destination Address : 01-80-C2-00-00-00,  IEEE 802.1D Bridge Group Addr ( Group.
             Source Address : 00-E0-1E-6A-67-98,  Cisco     6A-67-98 ( OUI = Unknown OUI.
               Frame Format : IEEE 802.3
           IEEE 802.3 Length : 38
             Frame Checksum : Good

LLC - IEEE 802.2 Logical Link Control Protocol

Decode Status : -
         DSAP : 0x42 (BPDU) (Individual),  SSAP : 0x42 (BPDU) (Command)
                Unnumbered frame, UI

BPDU - Bridge Spanning Tree Protocol

              Decode Status : -
        Protocol Identifier : 0x00
          Protocol Version : 0x00
                  BPDU Type : 0x00 (Configuration)
                      Flags : 0x00
                              0... .... = Not Topology Change Acknowledgment
                              .... ...0 = Not Topology Change
            Root Identifier : 0x80000010F6C6D100
                   Priority : 0x8000
            Root MAC Address : 00-10-F6-C6-D1-00
             Root Path Cost : 0
                  Bridge ID : 0x80000010F6C6D100
                   Priority : 0x8000
          Bridge MAC Address : 00-10-F6-C6-D1-00
                       Port : 0x80E9
                Message Age : 0x00  (0.00 Seconds)
        Information Lifetime : 0x1400  (20.00 Seconds)
            Root Hello Time : 0x200  (2.00 Seconds)
              Forward Delay : 0xF00  (15.00 Seconds)
```

Figure 15-5
TCP/IP

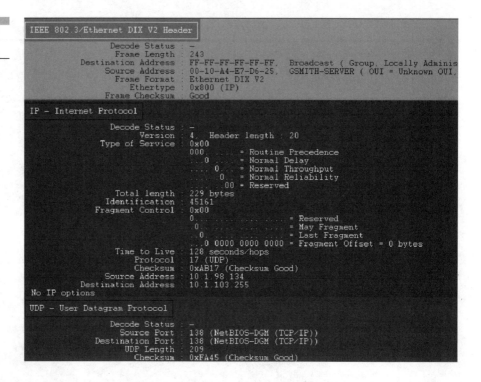

```
IEEE 802.3/Ethernet DIX V2 Header
                Decode Status : -
                 Frame Length : 243
           Destination Address : FF-FF-FF-FF-FF-FF,  Broadcast ( Group, Locally Adminis
                Source Address : 00-10-A4-E7-D6-25,  GSMITH-SERVER ( OUI = Unknown OUI,
                  Frame Format : Ethernet DIX V2
                     Ethertype : 0x800 (IP)
                Frame Checksum : Good

IP - Internet Protocol
                Decode Status : -
                      Version : 4,  Header length : 20
              Type of Service : 0x00
                                000. .... = Routine Precedence
                                ...0 .... = Normal Delay
                                .... 0... = Normal Throughput
                                .... .0.. = Normal Reliability
                                .... ..00 = Reserved
                 Total length : 229 bytes
               Identification : 45161
             Fragment Control : 0x00
                                0... .... .... .... = Reserved
                                .0.. .... .... .... = May Fragment
                                ..0. .... .... .... = Last Fragment
                                ...0 0000 0000 0000 = Fragment Offset = 0 bytes
                 Time to Live : 128 seconds/hops
                     Protocol : 17 (UDP)
                     Checksum : 0xAB17 (Checksum Good)
               Source Address : 10.1.98.134
          Destination Address : 10.1.103.255
No IP options

UDP - User Datagram Protocol
                Decode Status : -
                  Source Port : 138 (NetBIOS-DGM (TCP/IP))
             Destination Port : 138 (NetBIOS-DGM (TCP/IP))
                   UDP Length : 209
                     Checksum : 0xFA45 (Checksum Good)
```

3. How long was the Ethernet frame?

4. How could you tell if this includes the pre-amble?

5. What protocol number is associated with UDP?

6. What is the port associated with NetBIOS?

7. What is the largest number of bits allowable on the subnet mask for this network?

8. How long is the UDP packet?

All of the information required to answer the questions is included within the example above assuming that you know what to look for. Actually, five or six more questions could be asked based on this one example. Study the previous chapters regarding protocols, frames, and packet definitions if you are still unsure of the correct answers to these questions. Practice looking at the examples above, restudying the previous chapters, and become prepared to learn the meaning of every line of an analyzer's output.

On the test you may see a question regarding the type of frame being shown (AppleTalk, Ethernet, SNAP, and so on). The trick to answering such a question correctly is not in knowing how to read the output, but that knowing if the frame is considered to be a SNAP frame when both the DSAP and SSAP fields are set to AA.

The answers are as follows:

1. This was a broadcast packet because the destination MAC address was FF-FF-FF-FF-FF-FF.

2. No, we know this because the fragment offset was set to all zeroes. If this was a fragmented packet, the offset could not be zero.

3. 243 bytes. See the second line in the output.

4. Check the shortest packets you get with the analyzer. Go back to Chapter 5, "Troubleshooting Local Area Networks (LANs)," if you do not remember the specifics of how the pre-amble works.

5. Inside the IP section, find the line that says "Protocol". Notice that the analyzer shows that this is type 17 (UDP).

6. 138. See the UDP section on the line labeled "Source Port."

7. This one takes a little more intuition than the others. Remember that this was a broadcast with a destination MAC address of FF-FF-FF-FF-FF-FF. This means that the Ethernet protocols treat it as a broadcast. Notice how the IP destination address is set. This UDP packet is also an IP broadcast as well as an Ethernet broadcast. The destination IP address is 10.1.103.255. We know that the next network will start at the address one higher than the broadcast address of 10.1.103.255 (one above this is 10.1.104.0). Therefore, our question becomes, what is the largest number of bits in a subnet mask that will include at least 10.1.98.134 (the source address) and still stop at 10.1.103.255 (the destination address)? The answer is 255.255.248.0 or 21 bits. Review Chapters 5 and 9, "Transmission Control Protocol/Internet Protocol (TCP/IP)," if you are unsure of how we arrived at this answer.

8. 209 bytes.

Using a protocol analyzer is no different than using almost any other program. Without the background necessary to interpret the data presented, the program is of little use. If you are unsure of what your protocol analyzer is showing, go back over the previous chapters and research the protocol structures.

Common Symptoms and Causes

Table 15-1 provides a quick way to associate issues with the most common solutions. Although this chart is by no means comprehensive, it will give you a few quick things to check for while troubleshooting. We encourage you to make your own list and add to it as you learn more techniques and develop new ones.

The table is not meant to show what may not be an issue, but rather its purpose is to show the most commonly related issues to particular symptoms. For example, an improperly configured access list may produce almost any of the symptoms listed below, but there may be other causes that are more likely.

Table 15-1

Common symptoms and causes

Symptom	Likely Causes
A single host cannot see the LAN.	Check physical cabling, the hub or switch connection, the host for configuration, or the *virtual local area network* (VLAN) configuration.
An associated group of hosts cannot see the LAN.	Check the hubs or switches for that group. Use Traceroute to isolate the failure point.
An associated group of hosts can see each other but not any other part of a LAN or *wide area network* (WAN).	Check the uplinks between workgroup hub/switch and the main switch or the VLAN.
DHCP does not work.	Check the DHCP server configuration and reachability, the VLAN, or the IP helper address. Ensure that portfast is enabled.
A single host cannot see the WAN.	Check the default gateway.
An associated group of hosts cannot see parts of the WAN.	Check the access lists and use Traceroute to isolate the failure point.
An associated group of hosts cannot see the WAN.	Check the connection from group to router or check the router.
All hosts cannot see parts of the WAN.	Check the router, the remote site, or the routing protocols.
All hosts cannot see a specific part of the WAN.	Check the core router or the serial connections, or check for routing loops.
Slow WAN response.	Check the router configuration and make sure that debugging is off. Also check the CDP neighbors and the serial connections.

Common False Assumptions

False assumptions only slow the troubleshooting process. A good troubleshooter will assume nothing because he knows that most assumptions are not necessarily true. Let's look at a few false assumptions, how they can hurt our troubleshooting efforts, and discuss how to avoid making false assumptions.

We have all seen administrators who are called upon to diagnose a problem and appear to instantly solve that problem by either magic or intuition. The truth is that they are not using either magic or intuition; they are relying on the same basic troubleshooting principles shown throughout this book. They know where the protocols reside in relation to each other, they work with a problem-solving method similar to the one promoted by Cisco, and, most importantly, do not make false assumptions.

The secret to avoiding assumptions is to slow down, be thorough, and ask yourself why you believe that something is true. If you are unsure of how something works, take the time and research the topic before continuing. The time spent researching will be made up by the time saved because you know how the system is working.

The "I can see you, therefore, you can see me" Assumption

While trying to diagnose a problem, the administrators issue a *show cdp neighbors* command. They see that all of the neighbors are reporting in as expected. The administrators even go so far as to debug the CDP neighbor packets that are being received. The administrators then falsely assume that the issue is not related to either a physical connection or access list issue between the routers because they are receiving updates in the proper manner at the proper times.

Two scenarios come to mind immediately that could cause the assumptions to be proven false. The first scenario in which this could happen is that the remote router could have an access list filter applied to an inbound interface. This access list could be preventing this router from receiving CDP neighbor packets. This would not prevent the router from sending out CDP packets, only from receiving them.

The second scenario where this could happen would be if the physical cabling on the remote router is not working correctly. If the two routers were connected through Ethernet ports, it is possible that the remote router's Ethernet cable had the receive wires broken. In this case, the remote router would still send CDP updates but never receive them.

The best way to avoid falling into this false assumption is to telnet to the remote router and do the same show cdp neighbors command. Pinging the remote router will not necessarily work because a ping will not directly tell you over which route the connection is made. A Traceroute would tell you which routes were taken and therefore may be useful unless you are limiting responses through access lists.

It is almost always worth the time and effort taken to open up a telnet session to the remote router so that you can see what is happening on both routers simultaneously if possible. Do not assume that just because router A can see router B that the reverse is true. While this telnet session is open, take a moment to look at the distance and route taken to a remote network. The distance should be shorter from an intermediate router than from an end router. If it is not, then you may have run telnet to the wrong router.

The "I know how this is configured" Assumption

This assumption occurs most often when one person routinely maintains the network and others do occasionally. Failure to either accurately document changes or to look at the network configuration documents and running configuration before starting work on the issue will increase the possibility of wasting time making changes that should not be made.

When an administrator believes that they know how a piece of equipment is configured without verifying that belief, they are merely assuming that they know how the equipment is configured. Unless you have actually checked the running configuration of the router, there is no way to know for a fact how the router is configured. The way to combat this false assumption is to always thoroughly document any changes as they are made and always look at both the documentation and the running configuration before starting on complex problems.

The "I can ping, so there are no TCP/IP issues" Assumption

This assumption is built on a lack of knowledge regarding TCP/IP. Although IP and the ping utility both work at layer 3 of the OSI model, TCP, UDP, and many other protocols and utilities commonly associated with TCP/IP work at layer 4 of the OSI model. Just because a layer of the OSI model is working properly, it has no relationship to any other higher level of the OSI model. In other words, if layer 3 is working, there is no guarantee that layer 4 will work. The only valid relationship works in the opposite manner. A properly working layer of the OSI model will guarantee that all of the lower layers are working.

If you do not instinctively know where each protocol sits in relationship to others, make a chart consisting of all the protocols you commonly use and the relationship between these protocols.

The "I have a link light, therefore, there is a good physical connection" Assumption

This assumption does not allow for the fact that the link light merely shows a physical connection, not a fully functional and properly configured physical connection. The cable may only be good enough to provide the voltage necessary to enable the light but not reliably transfer data.

When there is any doubt as to the physical connection, it should be tested. Replacing an Ethernet cable suspected of being poor quality may cost only a few dollars and save many man-hours in the debugging process.

The "I took a quick look and that is not the issue" Assumption

This assumption is made when taking a quick and non-thorough look at a possible cause. For example, it is easy to think that showing the configuration and then pinging the destination checked a route. The reality is that unless enough time and concentration is devoted to looking at the configuration and route, you can assume that what you saw was what was really being presented. In other words, if you are looking for an IP address of 172.31.1.1 and you see the IP address of 172.81.1.1, you could inadvertently see what was expected instead of what was actually there. Slowing down and concentrating on the immediate task will help overcome any problems.

Debug

As previously discussed, debugging may have a negative impact on your router and connections. Running debug on a busy router may cause more problems than are solved in terms of lost routing update packets, lost routes, and extremely poor performance. Since virtually every router is critical to the daily operations of a company, it is not usually the case that routers may go offline at will. The question becomes how does someone use debug on a production router that is already under a heavy load? Three basic techniques can enable an administrator to debug a production router while minimizing the impact on the network as a whole.

First, make sure that logging is set in such a way that it minimizes impact. Review the section in Chapter 4 labeled "Debug and Performance." This section provides the key performance tips that need to be remembered while debugging. The most important of these tips is that a syslog server minimizes the amount of processing required by the router. Enabling logging buffering with the *logging buffered* command and assigning a syslog server will greatly reduce the chances of disrupting your network during the debugging process.

A second technique is to only enable debugging for a short amount of time, such as less than five seconds. By keeping the amount of time short enough, the administrator eliminates the possibility of routes disappearing due to an inability to process the keep-alive and routing update packets. This may require that several debugging sessions be run, but you will eventually receive the data that you seek. The problem with this technique is that the processor may be so overloaded processing debugging information that you may not be able to turn off the debugging. The third technique overcomes this problem.

This third technique is to log on to the router with two different connections. On the first terminal (telnet into the router), the command *no debug all* is entered, but the Return key is not pressed. Immediately after starting the debug session on the second terminal (attached to the console port), the Return key is pressed on the first terminal. This enables a small amount of debugging data to be gathered while minimizing the possibility that debugging will not be able to be turned off.

Even when using these tips, it is still possible to overload a router to the point where the only choice left is to reboot it. The best policy for debugging is to implement only as much debugging as necessary, limit the time debugging is enabled, and use the least intrusive method of recording debugging information that is available.

However, even with the possibility of causing problems, debugging is the most useful tool available to the network administrator. Instead of thinking if one should debug to solve a problem, a more proactive approach would be to ask how running debug will provide the information needed. If there is not a likelihood of crashing the system due to debugging, the administrator should not hesitate to use debugging to find the root causes of the issue.

Debugging Access Lists

Incorrectly configured access lists may cause more problems than any other configuration option available through the Cisco IOS. Whenever there is doubt that an access list may be adversely affecting the network, the administrator should either temporarily remove the access list or debug the access list. This is especially true of complex extended access lists because of the options available for filtering using an extended access list.

One of the most widely underused debug commands is related to access lists. Most administrators would not even think of debugging an access list if an active one was not on the interface. However, adding and then debugging an access list may prove invaluable, especially if you are trying to debug a problem while using the *Network Address Translations* (NAT) functions. A simple three-step process can enable you to see exactly which addresses are passing through an interface. The following is a quick means of determining the traffic that is traveling through the interface without causing a large amount of CPU cycles to be used in the debugging process:

1. Add an access list to the interface that will enable all traffic to traverse the interface:

   ```
   Router(config)#Access-list 1 permit any any
   ```

2. Assign the access list to an (sub)interface:

   ```
   Router(config)#int s1.1
   Router(config-if)#ip access-group 1 in
   Router(config-if)#^Z
   ```

3. Turn debugging on for that access list:

   ```
   Router#Debug access-group 1
   ```

This will show every time an inbound packet crosses the interface and the source address of the packet. The best features of this process are that it is quick to implement and uses few CPU cycles because the access list is short and we are only debugging exactly what we need. Depending upon the traffic flowing through this interface, simply debugging the whole interface may overload the router. Debugging both incoming and outgoing packets is a waste of effort if we are only interested in the incoming packets.

Routing Issues

While working on dynamic routing protocols, it is important to keep in mind the default timings for the protocol on which you are working. This is especially true if you are redistributing between differing protocols. For example, if you are debugging an RIP issue and see updates every 60 seconds, you should become alerted because the default update period for RIP is 30 seconds. Although it is possible to change these default values, any change from the default should raise questions such as whether all participating routers have been changed and why the change was originally made.

Another problem commonly experienced is routing loops due to running multiple protocols. Some administrators mistakenly believe that running more than one protocol simultaneously will enable the second protocol to take over if the primary protocol fails. This will regularly cause more problems than solve them. It is not uncommon for routing loops to develop in this situation when a new router is added to the system. This is usually a result of the differing update periods between the routing protocols. Instead, the administrator should be redistributing the routes between the protocols.

The redistribution of routes also has its own pitfalls. Redistributing without paying attention to the default costs of redistribution can cause undesired behavior such as an alternate route being chosen. Knowing the default administrative distances based upon the routing protocol used can help solve many questions regarding why a particular route is chosen by a dynamic protocol. As a reminder, default administrative distances are shown in Table 15-2.

Static Routes

Many books and documents you read will gloss over static routes because we have all been taught to avoid them. The reason for this is because if they are implemented incorrectly they can cause nightmares for the administrator. However, static routes are a valuable and sometimes necessary part of router configuration. Before giving a few pointers on working with static routes, we will review when static routes are desirable and when they are not desirable.

Static routes should be used in the following situations:

Table 15-2	Routing Information Source	Default Administrative Distance
Default administrative distances	Directly connected interface	0
	Static route	1
	EIGRP summary route	5
	External BGP	20
	Internal enhanced IGRP	90
	IGRP	100
	OSPF	110
	IS-IS	115
	RIP	120
	EGP	140
	Internal BGP	200
	Untrusted or unknown route	255

- To reduce dynamic protocol traffic over connections that service large areas of the network with the desire to relieve routing update traffic over this link.
- When there is only a single pathway that data should travel if that data is destined for any place other than the local network.
- To assign a backup route in case the main route fails.

Static routes should never be used in attempt to correct problems with dynamic routing protocols. Using a static route in this fashion will merely cover up the symptom instead of curing the underlying problem.

It is important to know the administrative distance for a static route. The administrative distance for a static route changes depending upon how the route is configured. This is true even when no administrative distance is specified in the configuration. The determining factor is a combination of whether the static route is configured as a "floating" static route or merely a static route and if an administrative distance is specified. Look at the three entries below:

```
Router(config)#ip route 172.30.1.0 255.255.255.0 172.28.234.7
Router(config)#ip route 172.30.1.0 255.255.255.0 172.28.211.30 201
Router(config)#ip route 172.30.1.0 255.255.255.0 int s1.1
```

Given the above, the third entry will be used unless interface s1.1 is down. The reason for this is that the administrative distance is set to zero if you specify the interface as opposed to the next hop router. In this case, the attached network has an administrative distance set as if the network were directly connected (zero). If an IP address of the next hop router is specified instead, the administrative distance is one.

If both interface s1.1 and the path to 172.28.234.7 are unusable, data destined for 172.30.1.0 will go out the interface associated with 172.28.211.30.

If you are configuring static routes to be used in case a primary route is lost, it is strongly advised to set the administrative distance to at least 201. Internal BGP, which has the highest administrative distance of all dynamic routing protocols, uses an administrative distance of 200. By setting static routes designed for backup purposes to a higher number than all dynamic protocols, you will ensure that the static routes do not interfere with dynamic protocols, even if these routing protocols used are changed.

Ping and Traceroute

Ping and Traceroute remain powerful tools for testing connectivity. Know how and when to use each of them. Experiment with each of these in both the default and extended modes until you are thoroughly familiar with both the expected output and what they mean.

Let's look for differences between pinging using the default size and pinging using the maximum size. For example, compare the following two outputs:

```
Router#ping
Protocol [ip]:
Target IP address: 172.31.1.1
Repeat count [5]: 50
Datagram size [100]:
Timeout in seconds [2]:
Extended commands [n]: y
Source address or interface: 172.30.1.3
Type of service [0]:
Set DF bit in IP header? [no]:
Validate reply data? [no]:
Data pattern [0xABCD]:
Loose, Strict, Record, Timestamp, Verbose[none]:
Sweep range of sizes [n]:
Type escape sequence to abort.
Sending 50, 100-byte ICMP Echos to 172.30.1.1, timeout is 2
seconds:
!!!!!!!!!!!!!!!!!!!!!!!!!!!!!!!!!!!!!!!!!!!!!!!!!!!!!!
```

```
Success rate is 100 percent (50/50), round-trip min/avg/max =
10/20/40 ms

Router#ping
Protocol [ip]:
Target IP address: 172.31.1.1
Repeat count [5]: 50
Datagram size [100]: 18024
Timeout in seconds [2]:
Extended commands [n]: y
Source address or interface: 172.30.1.3
Type of service [0]:
Set DF bit in IP header? [no]:
Validate reply data? [no]:
Data pattern [0xABCD]:
Loose, Strict, Record, Timestamp, Verbose[none]:
Sweep range of sizes [n]:
Type escape sequence to abort.
Sending 50, 18024-byte ICMP Echos to 172.30.1.1, timeout is 2
seconds:
!!!!!!!!!!!!!!!!!!!!!!........!!!!!!!!!!!!!!!!!!!!!!
Success rate is 80 percent (40/50), round-trip min/avg/max =
60/80/100 ms
```

What could cause 10 pings in the middle of a number of pings to fail? One likely answer is that this is a congested line. During the period where the pings were not successful, other traffic took precedence. What traffic was it? In this case, a routing update was received from the remote routing running RIP as the routing protocol, but the only way we know this is because a protocol analyzer was watching the connection during this example.

Here is another example:

```
Router#ping
Protocol [ip]:
Target IP address: 172.31.1.1
Repeat count [5]: 5000
Datagram size [100]: 18024
Timeout in seconds [2]: 20
Extended commands [n]: y
Source address or interface: 172.30.1.3
Type of service [0]:
Set DF bit in IP header? [no]:
Validate reply data? [no]:
Data pattern [0xABCD]:
Loose, Strict, Record, Timestamp, Verbose[none]:
Sweep range of sizes [n]:
Type escape sequence to abort.
Sending 5000, 18024-byte ICMP Echos to 172.30.1.1, timeout is 20
seconds:
!!!!!!!!!!!!!!!!!!!!!................. (output truncated)
....U.U.U.UUUUUUUUUUUU (output truncated)UU!!!!!!!!!!!!!!!!!!!!!
```

This example shows what happens when a route is lost and then recovered. For purposes of clarity, the output was greatly abbreviated. We were running a protocol analyzer at the same time as this ping, so we know more than is shown in just the ping output. Notice that a few packets were lost before we received a "Destination network unknown" response. The route went down and the pings timed out. When RIP updates were not received, the router marked the destination network as unknown. When the router connection was reestablished and RIP updates were received, the network was once again marked as reachable and ping packets were successfully transmitted.

Traceroute may also sometimes give unexpected results. For instance, in the following Traceroute example, three routers are all directly connected through FastEthernet ports via cross-over cables. No equipment exists between the three routers. These are Cisco 3640 routers that are not under any appreciable load.

```
Router#traceroute
Protocol [ip]:
Target IP address: 172.28.237.1
Source address: 172.30.100.1
Numeric display [n]: y
Timeout in seconds [3]: 3
Probe count [3]: 5
Minimum Time to Live [1]:
Maximum Time to Live [30]: 60
Port Number [33434]:
Loose, Strict, Record, Timestamp, Verbose[none]:
Type escape sequence to abort.
Tracing the route to 172.28.237.1

  1 172.30.101.1 4 msec * * * *
  2 172.31.252.13 5 msec 8 msec 6 msec 4 msec 5 msec
```

Why, if the routers are large and powerful, are not under any load, and are directly connected, should there be timed-out messages (*) received? The answer lies in a built-in feature of Cisco routers designed to combat denial of service attacks. The router at address 172.30.101.1 did not reply to three of the ICMP messages because the time between the requests was too small. In other words, a Traceroute may show that the packet has timed-out if the packet was processed either too slowly or too fast.

Another anomaly you may see while using Traceroute is that the route seems to change whenever you are testing it. Look at the following two outputs that were run directly after the other and try to figure out why the paths chosen are different:

```
Router#traceroute 172.31.238.1

Type escape sequence to abort.
Tracing the route to 172.28.238.1
```

```
1 172.30.100.2 0 msec 0 msec 4 msec
2 172.31.252.13 92 msec 92 msec 92 msec
3 172.31.252.6 100 msec 100 msec 100 msec

Router#traceroute 172.28.238.1
Type escape sequence to abort.
Tracing the route to 172.28.238.1

1 172.30.100.2 0 msec 0 msec 4 msec
2 172.31.248.3 17 msec 38 msec 42 msec
3 172.31.142.9 38 msec 45 msec 45 msec
4 172.28.233.53 100 msec 100 msec 110 msec
```

Why does the first Traceroute travel through 172.31.252.13, while the second Traceroute travels through 172.31.248.13? Have we misconfigured one of the routers? Are our routing tables messed up? Do we have routing issues? The answer is that there are likely not any routing issues, but there is probably a configuration issue. This is almost certainly caused by a combination of two configuration choices. The first choice made was to balance loads between the sites over two different lines. As long as the costs are equal between the two routes, the router will balance the load between the routes.

The configuration issue we should be aware of is indicated by the fact that immediately subsequent Traceroutes travel over different paths. If we look back at Chapter 4 in the "Fast Switching" section, we will see that the default fast switching method uses the cache for all packets after the first one. A *no ip route-cache* has been entered on the router with the IP address of 172.30.100.2. This forces the router to determine the path for each packet, slows down the switching process, and puts a large load on the CPU for the router. Since the no ip route-cache command is generally associated with the debugging process, it appears that the router was not returned to its original state after some issue was resolved.

Working with Your Service Provider

Working with your service provider can be a rewarding or frustrating experience depending on your attitude, your service-level agreement, and the initiative of the technicians working for your service provider. The administrator must find a balance between calling the provider every time a problem they should be able to solve arises and not calling the provider soon enough when issues caused by the provider are involved. Our suggestion is that the service provider be called either when you have stopped making progress or when you have proven that the issue lies within the service provider's network.

Point out to the provider all the issues you have looked at, including the debugging information you have gathered, and ask for their advice. Enlist their support for your own network and use them as you would any consultant. If you have properly documented and are able to list all of your debugging attempts, the service provider should be impressed with your thoroughness. This will also help them to resolve the problem. Do not hesitate to bring Cisco *type approval code* (TAC) into your phone conversations if you stop making progress with your service provider.

Line Monitoring

One of the benefits of using a service provider for troubleshooting problems is that it can provide all the equipment that you have only dreamed of owning. If a *bit error rate test* (BERT), a *Time Domain Reflectometer* (TDR), or an *Optical Time Domain Reflectometer* (OTDR) are needed, they will almost certainly have one available. The service provider will also be able to monitor all the conditions on your line and provide you with an analysis that includes all of the parts of the *wide area network* (WAN) that you are unable to see.

Escalation

Eventually, the level of service you are receiving on an issue will seem inadequate. This is the time to review your *Service-Level Agreement* (SLA). This document, usually signed when services are first contracted, should show the specific terms of how the escalation of issues will occur and exactly what services will be provided to the end user. Your company is paying for a certain level of service and it is your job to make sure that your company gets what it is paying for.

Do not hesitate to ask management on either side to become involved if the expertise expected is not apparent or the issues do not seem to be moving towards resolution. Even if the SLA does not require the provider to perform certain functions or work after hours, it is still possible to get the service provider to provide you with the help that is needed. This can be accomplished through either asking the provider to "go the extra mile" or by agreeing to pay for the additional services received. In addition, using Cisco TAC personnel to emphasize that the problem does not lie in your equipment can go a long way towards convincing the service provider that they need to push harder towards problem resolution.

Additionally, if you are a large buyer of Cisco equipment, your local Cisco sales representative should be able to provide the assistance of a Cisco engineer (usually a *Cisco Certified Internetwork Expert* [CCIE]) free of charge to help resolve the really tough problems that all administrators experience. The primary responsibility of your local Cisco sales office is to sell products. Convincing them that this will help them make sales will ensure that they do everything possible to ensure your satisfaction.

Chapter Summary

This chapter started by looking at protocol analyzer output before exploring a few of the common network symptoms and causes associated with these symptoms. The chart presented should be expanded and refined as experience is gained on your own network.

Next, some common false assumptions were explored in order to teach the reader to not jump to conclusions when troubleshooting. Remaining methodical, thorough, and patient during the troubleshooting process is critical, especially as the seriousness of the situation increases. Remember that the professional is the one who keeps calm while others panic.

Debugging was reexamined with a special focus on the dangers of overloading equipment through the use of debugging utilities. We also looked at the usefulness of access lists in the debugging process. We have reemphasized that the debugging utilities are the most powerful tools available to the network administrator.

We looked at issues common to all routing and have given a few hints on how to think about routing issues. We have also shown a few common mistakes and demonstrated that truly knowing how a routing protocol works is invaluable to troubleshooting.

We explored how Ping and Traceroute can sometimes show us more than merely if and how remote sites are connected. These commands can also show us how a link is congested and the configuration of intermediate equipment.

Finally, we provided some guidelines on how to work with your service provider and gave given some advice on how to resolve the tough issues that all administrators eventually face.

Now, in the final chapter of the book, we are ready to reveal the "secrets" that separate great troubleshooters from the mere mediocre. The secrets do not really have anything to do with vastly superior knowledge or experience and can be boiled down to just seven rules:

1. Always approach the problem in a predefined, methodical manner.
2. Know the basics.
3. If you are unsure how it should work, look it up.
4. Never assume that anything works.
5. Always ask, "What else could be causing this?"
6. Bring in additional help as needed.
7. Never panic.

Good luck in your troubleshooting endeavors.

APPENDIX A

Glossary

2B+D The *Basic Rate Interface* (BRI) in ISDN. A single ISDN circuit is divided into two 64Kbps digital channels for voice or data and one 16Kbps channel for low-speed data and signaling. In ISDN, 2B+D is carried on one or two pairs of wires (depending on the interface), the same wire pairs that today bring a single voice circuit into your home or office.

802.2 An IEEE standard used in Ethernet networks.

802.3 An *Institute of Electrical and Electronics Engineers* (IEEE) standard used in Ethernet networks. This is distinguished from 802.2 by the use of the Logical Link Control (LLC) layer.

802.5 An IEEE standard commonly called Token Ring.

AARP AppleTalk Address Resolution Protocol. A connectionless layer 2 protocol that maps a known layer 2 address to a layer 3 address.

Access list A filtering mechanism used on routers to disable some traffic through an interface while enabling other types of traffic. Access lists can filter based upon host or source addresses, the type of service, or other criteria.

ADSP AppleTalk Data Stream Protocol. A layer 5 protocol that controls full-duplex sessions.

AFP AppleTalk File Protocol. A layer 6 and 7 protocol that enables the sharing of files.

AppleTalk This is a set of communication protocols developed by Apple Computer. Two versions of AppleTalk exist: Phase I and Phase II.

Application layer Layer 7 of the *Open Standards Interface* (OSI) model. The application layer is also responsible for determining the availability of local resources and combining the functionality of different programs.

ARP Address Resolution Protocol. The protocol used at the data-link layer of the *Open Standards Interface* (OSI) model to resolve IP addresses to MAC addresses.

ASP AppleTalk Session Protocol. A connectionless layer 5 (session) protocol that establishes and maintains sessions between AppleTalk clients and servers.

Asynchronous Transfer Mode (ATM)   A standard for transporting data that relies upon 53-byte cells where the first five bytes contain the header information and the following 48 bytes contain data. This standard was designed to transport all forms of data including voice, video, and data. The delays present in the system are reduced by the use of fixed-length cells that enable processing to occur at the chip level.

AURP   Apple Update-Based Routing Protocol. A routing protocol used in conjunction with the *Route Table Maintenance Protocol* (RTMP) and TCP/IP that utilizes tunneling technologies.

Autonomous switching   A feature that provides faster packet processing by enabling the bus to switch packets independently without interrupting the system processor.

Backoff algorithm   The method used to enforce retransmission delay enforced by contentious *media access control* (MAC) protocols after a collision.

Backplane   The physical connection between an interface processor or card and the data buses inside a router.

B channel   An ISDN communication channel that bears or carries voice, circuit, or packet conversations. The B channel is the fundamental component of ISDN interfaces. It carries 64,000 bits per seconds in either direction.

BECN   Backward Explicit Congestion Notification. A one-bit field found in the Frame Relay header that is concerned with congestion management.

BERT   Bit/Block Error Rate Tester. A device for testing serial and parallel cables and pinouts.

BRI   Basic Rate Interface. Two 64-Kbps bearer channels and one 16Kbps data channel. An international standard for communicating digitally over the *Public Switched Telephone Network* (PSTN).

Bridge Protocol Data Units (BPDU)   A type of packet used with the Spanning Tree protocol. Also called Spanning Tree Frames.

Broadcast   A packet that is sent to all hosts on a network.

Broadcast   Data packet that will be sent to all nodes on a network. Broadcasts are identified by a broadcast address of FF-FF-FF-FF-FF-FF.

Broadcast domain   A set of all the devices that will receive broadcast frames originating from any device within the set.

Cable range   In an AppleTalk network, this is the range of numbers allocated for use by the hosts within the network. The value of the network set by the cable range can be anywhere from zero to 65,279. The cable range can consist of a single or multiple network numbers.

CDDI   Copper Distributed Data Interface. This is an implementation of *Fiber Distributed Data Interface* (FDDI) protocols over *Signal Transfer Point* (STP) and *Unshielded Twisted Pair* (UTP) cabling.

Cisco Discovery Protocol (CDP)   Cisco's proprietary protocol that is used to transfer information between adjacent Cisco devices.

CCO   Cisco Connection Online located at www.cisco.com.

Cisco Express Forwarding   A switching method that relies upon two tables instead of a cache.

Collision   In Ethernet, the result of two nodes transmitting simultaneously. The frames from each device are damaged when they meet on the physical media.

Collision domain   In Ethernet, the network area where frames that have collided are seen. Repeaters and hubs pass along collisions.

CSMA/CD   Carrier Sense Multiple Access/Collision Detect. A media access mechanism where devices ready to transmit data first check the channel for a carrier. If no carrier is sensed for a specific period of time, a device can transmit. If two devices transmit at once, a collision occurs and is detected by all colliding devices.

Data-link layer (DLL)   Layer 2 of the *Open Standards Interface* (OSI) model. The DLL transfers messages between the network and physical layers.

DCE   Data Circuit-Terminating Equipment. The equipment that provides the carrier for the network. Usually property of the Telco.

D channel   An ISDN communication channel used for sending information between the ISDN equipment and the ISDN central office switch. The D channel can also carry "user" packet data at rates up to 9.6 Kbps.

DDP   Datagram Delivery Protocol. An unreliable layer 3 protocol responsible for selecting a unique node ID.

DDR   Dial-on-demand routing. The way that ISDN connects only when it is required to do so.

DE   Discard Eligibility. A one-bit field found in the Frame Relay header that is concerned with congestion management.

DHCP   Dynamic Host Configuration Protocol. This is used to assign an IP address, subnet mask, default gateway, and optionally *Windows Internet Naming Service* (WINS) and *Domain Name System* (DNS) servers to a host computer. It is an automated way of "leasing" an IP address to a host.

Distribute switching Switching that occurs on the *Versatile Interface Processor* (VIP) card installed in the router.

DLCI Data Link Connection Identifier. The value of this identifies the Frame Relay *permanent virtual circuit* (PVC) or *switched virtual circuit* (SVC).

DNS Domain Name Server.

DTE Data Terminal Equipment. The devices that connect to other DTE devices through *Data Circuit-Terminating Equipment* (DCE) devices to provide an endpoint for the network carrier.

EARL Encoded Address Recognition Logic. This is responsible for giving permission for a frame to leave a port. The EARL builds a table containing the *media access control* (MAC) address, the port the MAC address sits on, and the *virtual local area network* (VLAN) ID associated with the MAC address.

EIGRP Enhanced Interior Gateway Routing Protocol. A hybrid routing protocol that supports multiprotocols.

Emulated LAN (ELAN) An *Asynchronous Transfer Mode* (ATM) network that is configured to emulate either a Token Ring or an Ethernet *local area network* (LAN).

Enhanced Switched Port Analyzer (ESPAN) An enhancement of the Switched Port Analyzer (SPAN). ESPAN enables the same functionality as SPAN with the added benefit of working across virtual local area networks (VLANs).

Ethernet A baseband *local area network* (LAN) specification invented by Xerox Corporation and developed jointly by Xerox, Intel, and Digital Equipment Corporation. Ethernet networks use *Carrier Sense Multiple Access / Collision Detect* (CSMA/CD) and run over a variety of cable types.

Ethernet_II An Ethernet protocol distinguished by the fact that it uses a type field instead of a length field.

FastEtherChannel A Cisco proprietary means of link aggregation. Members of a FastEtherChannel group act as if they were a single port.

Fast Switching A Cisco feature whereby a route cache is used to expedite packet switching through a router.

FDDI Fiber Distributed Data Interface. A *local area network* (LAN) standard using a 100-Mbps token-passing network using fiber-optic cable over two physical and logical rings.

FECN Forward Explicit Congestion Notification. A one-bit field found in the Frame Relay header that is concerned with congestion management.

File Transfer Protocol (FTP) A layer 4 protocol used to transfer files from remote hosts.

GNS Get Nearest Server. Packets sent by Netware clients upon boot-up to locate local servers and resources.

HDLC High-Level Data Link Control. The default encapsulation on Cisco interfaces. A bit-orientated synchronous data link control protocol developed from the *Synchronous Data Link Control* (SDLC).

IGRP Interior Gateway Routing Protocol. A Cisco propriety distance vector-based routing protocol that uses a combination of values such as bandwidth, hops, delay, and the *maximum transmission unit* (MTU) as its metric.

IPX Internet Packet Exchange. A network layer delivery protocol. Similar in operation to IP.

ISDN Integrated Services Digital Network.

Jabber An error condition in which a network device continually transmits continuous, meaningless data onto the network.

LAPB Link Access Procedure Balanced. The X.25 bit-orientated data-link layer protocol that was developed from the *High-Level Data Link Control* (HDLC).

LAPD Link Access Procedure D Channel. The ISDN bit-orientated data link layer protocol that was developed from the *Link Access Procedure Balanced* (LAPB) protocol. Used for signaling over the D channel for ISDN. Referred to as Q.921.

Latency The amount of time that a packet is delayed before being sent to the destination. Latency is usually caused by equipment that must store the data in order to check the validity or to determine where to send the data before transferring it to the destination.

LMI Local Management Interface. A set of Frame Relay extensions that include global addressing, virtual circuit status messages, and multicasting.

LT Line Termination. A physical connection to the ISDN switch.

MAC   Media access control. A 48 bit-addressing scheme used to uniquely identify every host on the network.

Maximum Transmission Unit (MTU)   The maximum size that a data unit can achieve. This is usually limited by the specifications of the media in use.

Microsegmentation   The division of a network into smaller segments, usually with the intention of increasing aggregate bandwidth to network devices.

MPP   Multilink Point-to-Point Protocol. An international standard for aggregating the ISDN B Channels.

Multicast   Single packets copied by the network and sent to a specific subset of network addresses.

NBP   Name Binding Protocol. A layer 4 connectionless protocol used to build a list of hosts by mapping the hostnames to the network.

NCP   Netware Core Protocol. A collection of file server functions for remote file access and printing on Netware servers. Very similar to the Microsoft SMB protocol.

NetFlow Switching   Network flow is defined as a unidirectional sequence of packets between given source and destination endpoints.

Network Layer   Layer 3 of the *Open Standards Interface* (OSI) model. Responsible for determining the best path through a network. Routing protocols use this layer.

NIC   Network Interface Card. The PC card that connects the PC to the network at the physical layer of the *Open Standards Interface* (OSI) model.

NLSP   Netware Link Services Protocol. A link state protocol designed by Novell Inc., based upon the *Open Standards Interface* (OSI) *Intermediate System-to-Intermediate System* (IS-IS) routing protocol.

NT1   Network Termination 1. A device that is required to connect ISDN terminal equipment to an ISDN line. The NT-1 connects to the two-wire line (twisted pair copper wiring) that your telephone company has assigned for your ISDN service. Your ISDN service will not work if the NT-1's plug is not connected to a working electrical outlet.

Optimum switching   Switching where all processing is carried out on the interface processor, including the *cyclic redundancy check* (CRC).

OSPF   Open Shortest Path First. A link state routing protocol that exists in the public domain.

OTDR Optical Time Domain Reflectometer. A device that is used to check fiber-optic cables for inconsistencies and faults such as breaks, crimps, and opens. It can also be used for checking cable length.

OSI Model *Open Standards Interface* (OSI) model. A method of breaking the functions of a computer system into reliable and easily usable parts.

PAP Printer Access Protocol. A connection-oriented layer five protocol to establish and maintain printing sessions.

Phase I In an AppleTalk network, this is the older protocol that supports only a single logical network within a single physical network. Therefore, a network may reside on only one zone.

Phase II In an AppleTalk network, this is the newer protocol that supports multiple logical networks within a single physical network, thereby allowing a network to reside on more than one zone.

Phoenix The *Application-Specific Integrated Circuit* (ASIC) responsible for connecting the three backplanes within the Catalyst 5500 chassis. This connection is known as the "crossbar fabric" of the switch and transfers data between the three backplanes.

Physical layer The lowest layer of the *Open Standards Interface* (OSI) model, layer 1. The physical layer has three responsibilities: to send and receive bits of data and provide proper physical connections.

PING Packet Internet Groper. A tool that is used to check the remote status of a host running the TCP/IP protocol stack.

PPP Point-to-Point Protocol. An ISDN carrier protocol at layer 2 of the OSI model. PPP is designed for simple links that transport packets between two peers. These links provide full-duplex simultaneous bidirectional operations and are assumed to deliver packets in order.

Presentation layer Layer 6 of the OSI model. The presentation layer is used as a translator service.

Process switching An operation that provides full route evaluation and per-packet load balancing across parallel *wide area network* (WAN) links.

PSTN Public Switched Telephone Network. The public telephone infrastructure that BRI uses as its medium.

PVC Permanent Virtual Circuit. A permanent circuit that is constantly active and takes the same route through the carrier's network every time.

Q921 The specification for LAPD. Responsible for layer 2, D-channel signaling between two adjacent layer 2 entities.

Q931 The ISDN protocol responsible for call setup, call termination, and call teardown. Operates over the D channel.

RARP Reverse Address Resolution Protocol. The protocol used at the data-link layer of the *Open Standards Interface* (OSI) model to resolve *media access control* (MAC) addresses to IP addresses.

RIP Routing Information Protocol. A distance vector-based routing protocol that uses hop counts as its metric.

RTMP Route Table Maintenance Protocol. Used in an AppleTalk network, this is a distance-vector algorithm routing protocol.

Runt A packet shorter than the minimum specified by a protocol.

SAGE The Synergy Advanced Gate-Array Engine handles switching for *Fiber Distributed Data Interface* (FDDI), *Asynchronous Transfer Mode* (ATM) Lane, and Token Ring, as well as ISL encapsulation.

SAINT The Synergy Advanced Interface and Network Termination works similarly to the *Synergy Advanced Gate-Array Engine* (SAGE) except only dealing with Ethernet.

SAMBA The Synergy Advanced Multipurpose Bus Arbiter is an *Application-Specific Integrated Circuit* (ASIC) working in either master or slave mode. The purpose of the SAMBA is to suppress broadcasts above the thresholds set by the administrator.

SAP Service Advertisement Protocol.

Session layer Layer 5 of the *Open Standards Interface* (OSI) model. The session layer is concerned with the coordination of dialog between hosts.

Silicon switching Switching based on the silicon switching engine, enabling the processing of packets independent of the *Silicon Switch Processor* (SSP) system processor. Silicon switching provides high-speed, dedicated packet switching.

SMDS Switched Multimegabit Data Service. A high-speed, packet-switched datagram service offered by telephone companies.

Spanning Tree Protocol A protocol that uses the Spanning Tree Algorithm and enables a single connection between two devices to be active, although more than one physical connection exists. When the active connection is severed, a new connection is made, utilizing a redundant physical connection.

SPID   Service Profile Identifier. A tool that provides the ISDN switch with a unique identification number for each ISDN set to which it sends calls and signals.

SPX   Sequenced Packet Exchange. A transport layer connection-orientated protocol. Similar in operation to TCP.

S/T interface   A four-wire ISDN circuit. The S/T interface is the part of a ISDN line that connects to the terminal equipment.

Subnetwork Access Protocol (SNAP)   SNAP is an *Institute of Electrical and Electronics Engineers* (IEEE) standard that resembles 802.3.

SVC   Switched Virtual Circuit. A circuit that is switched so changes are routed upon every connection. An SVC requires call setup and termination.

Switched Port Analyzer (SPAN)   A tool that enables frames to be additionally forwarded to another port for analysis purposes. By default, a switch will only forward frames to the destination port.

TCP/IP   Transmission Control Protocol/Internet Protocol. A multi-layer protocol.

TDR   Time Domain Reflectometer. A device that is used to check copper cables for inconsistencies and faults such as breaks, crimps, and opens. It can also be used for checking cable length.

TE1   Terminal Equipment 1. A device that is classified as an ISDN terminal in that it can directly connect to the ISDN network.

TE2   Terminal Equipment 2. A device that is not classified as an ISDN terminal and has to connect using a *terminal adapter* (TA).

Technical Assistance Center (TAC)   The TAC is a Cisco service that enables end users to gain official Cisco assistance with issues they are experiencing related to configuration and hardware.

Token Ring   Token-passing *local area network* (LAN) developed and supported by IBM running at four or 16 Mbps over a ring topology.

Topology   An arrangement of network nodes and media within an enterprise networking structure.

Transport layer   Layer 4 of the Open Standards Interface (OSI) model. The transport layer is the first layer where a connection-oriented session can be established.

TTL   Time to Live. A field in the IP header that prevents routing loops. TTL is also used to report router names for the Trace command.

U-interface A two-wire ISDN circuit. Essentially, today's standard one-pair telephone company local loop made of twisted wire. The U interface is the most common ISDN interface and extends from the central office.

Unicast A packet that is intended for à specific host on the network.

Virtual LANs (VLANs) A group of devices that comprise a single broadcast domain despite the fact that the physical network is larger than the VLAN (a virtual LAN as opposed to a physical LAN). A VLAN is configured arbitrarily and is not related to the physical structure of the network.

VLSM Variable Length Subnet Mask. When you implement multiple subnet masks within a single network, VLSMs can conserve IP addresses on *wide area network* (WAN) links.

ZIP Zone Information Protocol. In an AppleTalk network, this is used to map network numbers to zone names. This is a session-layer protocol.

ZIP Storm In an AppleTalk network, this is a broadcast storm caused by the improper configuration of a router. The storm is an excess amount of broadcasts using the *Zone Information Protocol* (ZIP).

ZIT Zone Information Table. In an AppleTalk network, the ZIT is where a map of the zones is held.

Zone In an AppleTalk network, the zone is a logical grouping of network devices.

APPENDIX B

Bibliography

Casad, Joe. *MCSE Study Guide Windows 95 & Networking Essentials*. Indianapolis, IN: New Riders, 1996.

Caslow, Bruce. *Cisco Certification—Bridges, Routers, and Switches for CCIE*. Upper Saddle River, NJ: Prentice Hall, 1999.

Chappell, Laura. *Advanced Cisco Router Configuration*. Indianapolis, IN: Cisco Press, 1999.

Cisco Internetwork Troubleshooting. Indianapolis, IN: Cisco Press, 1999.

Giles, Roosevelt. *Cisco CCIE Study Guide*. New York, NY: McGraw-Hill, 1998.

Cisco IOS Software Command Summary. Cisco Systems, Inc., 1997.

Comer, Douglas E. *Internetworking with TCP/IP, Volume I, Third Edition*. Englewood Cliffs, NJ: Prentice Hall, 1995.

Hein, Mathias and David Griffiths. *Switching Technology in the Local Network*, Boston, MA: International Thompson Publishing, 1997.

McDysan, David and Darren Spohn. *ATM Theory and Application*. New York, NY: McGraw-Hill, 1998.

Nemzow, Martin. *Fast Ethernet Implementation and Migration Solutions*. New York, NY: McGraw-Hill 1997.

Oppenheimer, Pricilla. *Top-Down Network Design*. Indianapolis, IN: Cisco Press 1999.

Russell, Ryan. *CCNP Cisco Internetwork Troubleshooting Handbook*. Berkeley, CA: Osborne/McGraw-Hill, 1999.

Siyan, Karanjit. *Windows NT TCP/IP*. Indianapolis, IN: New Riders, 1998.

Smith, Marina. *Virtual LANs*. New York, NY: McGraw-Hill, 1998.

Stewart III, John W. *BGP4 Inter-Domain Routing in the Internet*. New York, NY: Addison Wesley Longman, 1999.

Tripod, Mark. *Cisco Router Configuration & Troubleshooting*. Indianapolis, IN: New Riders, 1999.

APPENDIX C

Webliography

http://www.cisco.com/univercd/cc/td/doc/cisintwk/itg_v1/
index.htm, October 1999

http://www.cisco.com/univercd/cc/td/doc/cisintwk/itg_v1/
itg_hard.htm, October 1999

http://www.cisco.com/public/sw-center/sw-netmgmt.shtml,
Cisco Network Management Home Page

http://www.cisco.com/warp/public/701/index.shtml,
September 1999

http://www.host.ots.utexas.edu/ethernet/ethernet-home.
html, September 1999

http://www.clark.net/pub/rbenn/cisco.html, September 1999

http://www.alliancedatacom.com/frame-relay-tutorials.htm,
September 1999

http://www.cisco.com/univercd/cc/td/doc/cisintwk/ito_doc/
index.htm, September 1999

http://www.protocols.com, September 1999

http://www.itprc.com, September 1999

http://www.cisco.com/univercd/cc/td/doc/product/
software/ios112/dbook, September 1999

http://www.cisco.com/warp/public/701/index.shtml,
September 1999

http://wwwhost.ots.utexas.edu/ethernet/ethernet-home.html,
September 1999

http://www.alliancedatacom.com/frame-relay-tutorials.htm,
September 1999

http://www.itprc.com, September 1999

http://www.cisco.com/univercd/cc/td/doc/product/software/
ios112/dbook, September 1999

http://wwwhost.ots.utexas.edu/ethernet/ethernet-home.html,
September 1999

`http://www.cisco.com/univercd/cc/td/doc/pcat`, December, 1999

`http://www.cisco.com/univercd/cc/td/doc/pcat/159.htm`,
December, 1999

`http://www.cisco.com/univercd/cc/td/doc/pcat/164.htm`,
December, 1999

`http://www.cisco.com/univercd/cc/td/doc/pcat/177.htm`,
December, 1999

`http://www.cisco.com/univercd/cc/td/doc/pcat/179.htm`,
December, 1999

`http://www.cisco.com/univercd/cc/td/doc/pcat/157.htm`,
December, 1999

`http://www.cisco.com/warp/public/701/index.shtml`,
December, 1999

`http://wwwhost.ots.utexas.edu/ethernet/ethernet-home.html`,
December, 1999

`http://www.clark.net/pub/rbenn/cisco.html`, December, 1999

`http://www.cisco.com/univercd/cc/td/doc/cisintwk/ito_doc/
index.htm`, December, 1999

`http://www.protocols.com`, December, 1999

`http://www.itprc.com`, December, 1999

`http://www.protocols.com/pbook/tcpip.htm`, TCP/IP information
from Protocols.com

`http://www.cisco.com/univercd/cc/td/doc/cisintwk/itg_v1/
itg_ip.htm`, Troubleshooting TCP/IP from Cisco Systems, Inc.

`http://www.cisco.com/univercd/cc/td/doc/product/iaabu/
centri4/user/scf4ap1.htm`, Understanding TCP/IP from Cisco
Systems Inc.

`http://www.protocols.com/pbook/appletalk.htm`, September 1999

`http://www.cisco.com/univercd/cc/td/doc/cisintwk/ito_doc/
applet.htm`, September 1999

`http://www.cisco.com/univercd/cc/td/doc/product/access/
acs_fix/cis2500/2509/acsvrug/techovr.htm#xtocid2006745`,
September 1999

`http://www.cisco.com/univercd/cc/td/doc/product/iaabu/
centri4/user/scf4ap1.htm`, Understanding TCP/IP from Cisco
Systems, Inc.

http://www.cisco.com/univercd/cc/td/doc/product/software/ios113ed/113ed_cr/np1_c/1cbgp.htm, Configuring BGP from Cisco Systems

http://www.academ.com/nanog/feb1997/BGPTutorial/index.htm, An introduction to BGP

http://www.protocols.com/pbook/novel.htm, Novell information from Protocols.com

http://www.cisco.com/univercd/cc/td/doc/product/software/ios100/rpcg/41225.htm, Configuring Novell IPX/SPX from Cisco.com

http://www.protocols.com/pbook/isdn.htm, ISDN information from Protocols.com

http://www.cisco.com/warp/public/2/ISDN.html, Cisco ISDN Solutions Homepage

http://www.protocols.com/pbook/frame.htm, Frame Relay overview from Protocols.com

http://www.protocols.com/pbook/x25.htm, X.25 overview from Protocols.com

http://www.cisco.com, Various documents on Frame Relay and X.25

http://www.cisco.com, The main CCO homepage

http://www.brainbuzz.com, The Brainbuzz Network Engineers online community

http://www.netcerts.com, The NetCerts Network Engineers online community

http://www.cpaw.org, The Cisco Professionals Association Worldwide

http://www.groupstudy.com, The home of the Groupstudy news servers

APPENDIX D

OSI Model

The OSI Model is used to describe how information from one application on one computer can move to an application on another computer. Developed by the *International Organization for Standardization* (ISO) in 1984, it is the primary architectural model for internetworking communications. The OSI Model has seven layers:

- Physical layer
- Data link layer
- Network layer
- Transport layer
- Session layer
- Presentation layer
- Application layer

We will now take a look at their purposes within the OSI Model and give an example of a technology that correlates to that particular layer.

Layer 1: The Physical Layer

The definition of the physical layer is that it is Layer 1 of the OSI Reference Model. The physical layer defines the electrical, mechanical, procedural, and functional specifications for activating, maintaining, and deactivating the physical link between end systems. It is comprised of three components. These components, in some instances, are the same in *Local Area Network* (LAN) and *Wide Area Network* (WAN) environments. They are cables or wires, connectors, and encoding.

Cables and Wires

The majority of the cable in place today falls into three types: *Unshielded Twisted Pair* (UTP), coaxial, and fiber optic. The majority of modern internal cable plant wiring is UTP. However, coaxial cable is still used today for specific LAN applications as well as for some high-speed WAN applications. Finally, the high-speed cable of choice is fiber. Fiber is used as the backbone for all high-speed LAN and WAN connections today.

Unshielded Twisted Pair (UTP) UTP has many uses. It is used for voice communication, key card readers, alarm systems, and data communications. The first distinction in the type of UTP that can be used is the rating of the cable. UTP cable is rated for *either* or *plenum* use. If an area is a plenum or air return space, plenum rated cable must be used. Otherwise, standard cable is acceptable for use.

NOTE: *Plenum-rated cable is approximately twice the cost of standard UTP cable.*

The next distinction, and probably most important, is the category designator. The category, often abbreviated as CAT, levels officially run from Category 1 to Category 5:

- *CAT 1* Here cable performance is intended for basic communications and power-limited circuit cable. No performance criteria exist for cable at this level.

- *CAT 2* Low performance UTP. Typical applications are voice and low-speed data. This is not specified in the *Electronic Industries Association / Telecommunications Industry Association* (EIA/TIA) 568A for data use.

- *CAT 3* This is data cable that complies with the transmission requirements in the EIA/TIA 568A. It has a maximum transmission speed of 16Mbps. In current installations, this is the grade most often used for voice cabling.

- *CAT 4* An infrequently used category. It has a maximum transmission speed of 20Mbps.

- *CAT 5* The most commonly used UTP category. Its maximum transmission speed is 100Mbps.

Coaxial cable The coaxial cable used in networks is a relative of the coax cable used in many households for cable TV reception. Just like UTP, there can be both PVC and plenum-rated varieties for each variation. Many variations of this cable exist, but only three are used for data communications. The impedance or resistance of the cable is the item that differentiates the specific cables. RG58, RG59, and RG62 have approximately the same diameter, but each cable has a different amount of impedance. Table D-1 summarizes the coax categories, as follows:

- *RG58*   Also called ThinNet. Rated for 10MHz transmissions over a distance of 185 meters.
- *RG8*   Also called ThickNet. Rated for 10MHz transmissions over a distance of 500 meters.
- *RG62*   Used for IBM controller cabling.
- *RG59*   Not used for data transmissions. Used primarily for video transmissions and household cable TV.

Fiber optic cable   Fiber optic cable is the cable of choice for high-speed, long-distance communications. Simply put, a light source such as a low-powered laser is used to generate the optical or light signals down this type of cable. These cables are constructed out of small, thin strands of glass that look like fibers. The distance limitation of fiber is often measured in kilometers. Fiber optic cable, like UTP and coax, is rated either for PVC or plenum use. Two different types of fiber optic cable exist:

- *Multimode Fiber (MMF)*   Multimode fiber enables light to travel over one of many possible paths. Light, for example, could bounce under various angles in the core of the multimode cable. Because of the larger diameter of the core, it is much easier to get the light within it, allowing for less expensive electronics and connectors. The maximum distance for MMF is two km.

Table D-1

Coaxial Cable
Variations

Type of Coaxial Cable	Impedance	Cable Diameter	Usage
RG8	50 Ohm	10mm	10Base5, Thick Ethernet
RG58	50 Ohm	5mm	10 Base2, Thin Ethernet
RG59	75 Ohm	6mm	Video
RG62	93 Ohm	6mm	IBM 3270, Arcnet

■ *Single Mode Fiber (SMF)*   This offers the light only one route to travel through. SMF has a much smaller core than MMF (eight micron for SMF versus 50 or 62.5 micron for MMF). The smaller core enables much longer distances than MMF. Telephone companies interconnect their network equipment with SMF. The typical distance is between five and 1,000 miles. Simply put, if you want more distance, use a stronger laser.

NOTE: *SMF equipment is much more expensive than the equipment for MMF.*

Physical Terminations and Connectors

Without connectors and terminations, cables would have to be "hard-wired" to the end device. This would make quick disconnects and reconnects impossible. Connectors usually vary depending on the media type.

UTP   Four basic modular jack styles are used in UTP. Figure D-1 shows the eight-position and eight-position keyed modular jacks. These jacks are commonly and incorrectly referred to as RJ45 and keyed RJ45 respectively.

The six-position modular jack is commonly referred to as RJ11. Using these terms can sometimes lead to confusion since the RJ designations actually refer to specific wiring configurations called *Universal Service Ordering Codes* (USOC).

Figure D-1
UTP jacks

8-position   8-position keyed

6-position   6-position modified

The designation RJ means "registered jack." Each of these three basic jack styles can be wired for different RJ configurations. For example, the six-position jack can be wired as an RJ11C (one-pair), RJ14C (two-pair), or RJ25C (three-pair) configuration. An eight-position jack can be wired for configurations such as RJ61C (four-pair) and RJ48C. The keyed eight-position jack can be wired for RJ45S, RJ46S, and RJ47S.

The fourth modular jack style is a modified version of the six-position jack (modified modular jack or MMJ). It was designed by *Digital Equipment Corporation*® (DEC) along with the *modified modular plug* (MMP) to eliminate the possibility of connecting DEC data equipment to voice lines and vice versa.

Cable Termination Practices for UTP Two primary wiring standards exist. One set of standards is set by the EIA/TIA; the other is set by the USOC. The various pinouts are detailed in Figure D-2.

Two wiring schemes have been adopted by the EIA/TIA 568-A standard. They are nearly identical, except that pairs two and three are reversed. T568A is the preferred scheme because it is compatible with one or two-pair USOC systems. Either configuration can be used for *Integrated Services Digital Network* (ISDN) and high-speed data applications.

USOC wiring is available for one-, two-, three-, or four-pair systems. Pair 1 occupies the center conductors; pair 2 occupies the next two contacts out, and so on. One advantage to this scheme is that a six-position plug configured with one or two pairs can be inserted into an eight-position jack and maintain pair continuity.

Ethernet uses either of the EIA/TIA standards in an eight-position jack. However, only two pairs are used. On the other hand, Token Ring wiring uses

Figure D-2
EIA/TIA and USOC
jack pinouts

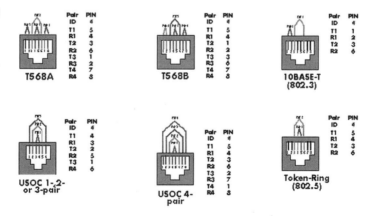

either an eight-position or six-position jack. The eight-position format is compatible with T568A, T568B, and USOC wiring schemes. The six-position format is compatible with one- or two-pair USOC wiring.

Coaxial connectors   Coaxial cables use two different connectors. One type is used specifically for ThickNet. All other types of coax use the same type of connector.

All ThinNet and other coax cables, except RG8 (ThickNet), use the *Bayonet Neil-Concelman* (BNC) connector, shown in Figure D-3. The acronym BNC has also been purported to mean British Naval Connector and Bayonet Nut Connector, but those references are incorrect.

NOTE: *If the connector is not firmly connected to the cable, the connection will have intermittent connection issues. This is not acceptable for DS3 WAN circuits.*

ThickNet (RG8) uses an *Attachment Unit Interface* (AUI) connector to connect devices to the cable. The AUI connector itself is a standard male DB-15M with studs instead of mounting screws; the female is a DB-15F with a slide-clip that attempts to lock onto the studs. Table D-2 lists the pinouts for an AUI connector as well as an RJ45-pinned connector.

Fiber optic connectors   Five popular types of fiber connectors exist. They can be used for both MMF and SMF. The most common types of connectors, ST, SC, and MIC, are pictured in Figure D-4. The less common connector types are ESCON and MT-RJ. The following is a brief description of each of the connectors:

Figure D-3
BNC connector for
coaxial cable

	AUI Pin No.	Ethernet V2.0	IEEE 802.3	RJ45 (EIA/TIA568A) Pin #
Table D-2	1	Shield	Control in Shield	
AUI and RJ45 Pinouts	2	Collision Presence +	Control in A	
	3	Transmit +	Data out A	1
	4	Reserved	Data in Shield	
	5	Receive +	Data in A	3
	6	Power Return	Voltage Common	
	7	Reserved	Control out A	
	8	Reserved	Control out Shield	
	9	Collision Presence −	Control in B	
	10	Transmit −	Data out B	2
	11	Reserved	Data out Shield	
	12	Receive −	Data in B	6
	13	Power	Voltage	
	14	Reserved	Voltage Shield	
	15	Reserved	Control out B	
	Connector Shield ———————————————— Protective Ground			

Figure D-4
Common types of
fiber connectors

A) ST Connector   B) SC Connector

C) MIC Connector

■ *ST*   A commonly used connector in the earlier days of fiber installations.

■ *SC*   The most commonly used connector type today. Almost every connector on Cisco equipment uses an SC connector.

■ *MIC/FSD*   The *Medium Interface Connector/Fiber Shroud Duplex* (MIC/FSD) connector is used for fiber-based Fiber Distributed Data

Interfaces (FDDI) connections. It is polarized so that TX/RX are always correct.

- *ESCON*   This is used to connect to IBM equipment as well as channel interface processors.
- *MT-RJ*   A new fiber connector that is able to fit into a standard 110 patch panel. It almost doubles the port capacity of an SC module.

Physical Encoding Methods

An encoding method is the method that a device uses to put data on the media. Although the media and connectors for LANs and WANs are similar, the encoding variations for LANs and WANs are different.

LAN encoding   Four basic LAN encoding schemes exist. The first encoding scheme is the foundation for all the other encoding schemes. Thus, it is important that you understand the basic encoding scheme that everything is based on, the *Non-Return To Zero-Level* (NRZ-L). Figure D-5 shows how the various encoding methods reduce the binary numbers to electrical or optical signals.

The common encoding methods are as follows:

- *Non-Return to Zero-Level (NRZ-L)*   This is the basic type of encoding upon which all others are based. A *one* is positive voltage; a *zero* is no voltage. The problem with this is that timing information cannot be retrieved from a string of zeros. Thus, other encoding methods have been developed to overcome this problem.
- *Non-Return to Zero Inverted (NRZI)*   Used in 100Base-Fx fiber networks, NRZI uses a change in signal to represent a one.

Figure D-5
Common encoding methods

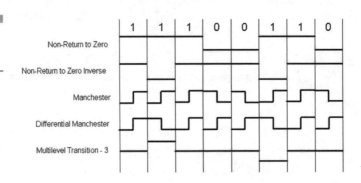

- *Manchester*   Used in Ethernet, this encoding is based on the signal transition in the middle of the bit. An upward transition is a one. A downward transition represents a zero.

- *Differential Manchester*   Used in Token Ring networks, this always has a transition in the middle. However, the encoding is based on the transition at the bit boundaries. A transition indicates a zero. No transition indicates a one.

- *MLT-3*   Used in Fast Ethernet Networks. Instead of two voltage levels (voltage and no voltage), MLT-3 uses three layers: positive voltage, no voltage, and negative voltage. Changing the voltage represents a one. For instance, a series of ones would be represented as $0,1,0,-1,0,1,0.-1$.

WAN connectors   Remember that the same types of media are used in WANs as LANs. However, the connectors used in WANs differ depending upon their use. Too many WAN connectors exist for us to cover every type, but the most common WAN connectors terminate T1 and E1 lines. Table D-3 displays the pinouts of T1 and E1 Lines.

NOTE: *The use of the terms tip and ring are typically not used today. Their usage is historical in perspective when testing was done with a tone tester. This test would allow a different tone to be present depending on which tip or ring was tested.*

Table D-3

The Pinouts of T1 and E1 Lines

Eight Position Jack Pinouts	T1/EI
1	Receive (tip)
2	Receive (ring)
3	Not used
4	Transmit (tip)
5	Transmit (ring)
6	Not used
7	Not used
8	Not used

WAN encoding   Before the topic of WAN encoding can be addressed, the concept of the digital hierarchy must be familiar to the reader. The digital hierarchy is a classification of circuit speeds. In North America, it is called the North American Digital Hierarchy. In Europe and the majority of the world, it is called the CCITT Digital Hierarchy. Both begin at the DS0 level with a single 64Kbps circuit. Then differences appear in the two systems.

In the North American Digital Hierarchy, this DS0 circuit is multiplied 24 times into a DS1 circuit with a speed of 1.544Mbps. This DS1 is then multiplied 28 times into a DS3 circuit with a speed of over 44Mbps.

The CCITT Digital Hierarchy combines 30 DS0s into an E1 circuit with a speed of 2.048Mbps. Next, 16 E1 circuits are combined to form an E3 circuit with a speed of over 34Mbps.

The WAN media type used depends on the circuit speed. T1 and E1 circuits generally use UTP. DS3 and E3 circuits use coax. However, all speeds above DS3/E3 require the use of fiber optic cables. The terms *North American Synchronous Optical Network* (SONET) and *International Synchronous Digital Network* (SDH) identify the circuits in this range. Table D-4 denotes the various circuit names and speeds.

The variations in WAN encoding first occur at the DS1 level. When a DS1 line is ordered, it is necessary to specify the framing and line coding. These settings must match the Channel Service Unit/Data Service Unit (CSU/DSU) and the other end of the circuit.

NOTE: *One of the most difficult issues to troubleshoot is the incorrect encoding of a circuit. More that once, I have seen a service provider finally determine that the cause of a line fault is improper encoding at one end of the circuit.*

Table D-4

Various Circuit
Names and Speeds

Optical Circuit	Speed
OC-1	51.8Mbps
OC-3	155.5Mbps
OC-12	622.1Mbps
OC-48	2488.3Mbps

The two frame types available for DS1s are *D4/Super Frame* (SF) and *Extended Super Frame* (ESF). The two frame types for E1s are CRC4 and no CRC4.

The available line codings for DS1s are *Alternate Mark Inversion* (AMI) and *Bipolar Eight-Zero Substitution* (B8ZS). The only available line codings for E1s are AMI and *High-Density Bipolar 3* (HDB3).

Conclusion

The physical layer may be seen as the most trivial or least important of the seven layers. After all, no fancy things like routing or switching happen at this layer. No addresses are used at the physical layer. However, many of the issues faced in the networking world are solved at the physical layer. A UTP cable might run too close to a fluorescent light or an OC-3 fiber patch cord might get accidentally crushed. When troubleshooting network problems, one of the most effective methods is to follow the OSI Model and troubleshoot by layers. Thus, you would start at the physical layer and move up once you have determined each layer is operating correctly.

Layer 2: The Data Link Layer

Layer 2 of the OSI Reference Model is the data link layer. Figure D-6 shows the placement of the network layer in the OSI Reference Model.

The data link layer is responsible for describing the specifications for topology and communication between local systems. Many examples of data link layer technology exist:

- Ethernet
- Fast Ethernet
- Token Ring
- Frame Relay
- HDLC
- Point-to-Point Protocol (PPP)
- Serial Line Interface Protocol (SLIP)

Figure D-6
The data link layer in
the OSI Reference
Model

7	Application Layer
6	Presentation Layer
5	Session Layer
4	Transport Layer
3	Network Layer
2	**Data Link Layer**
1	Physical Layer

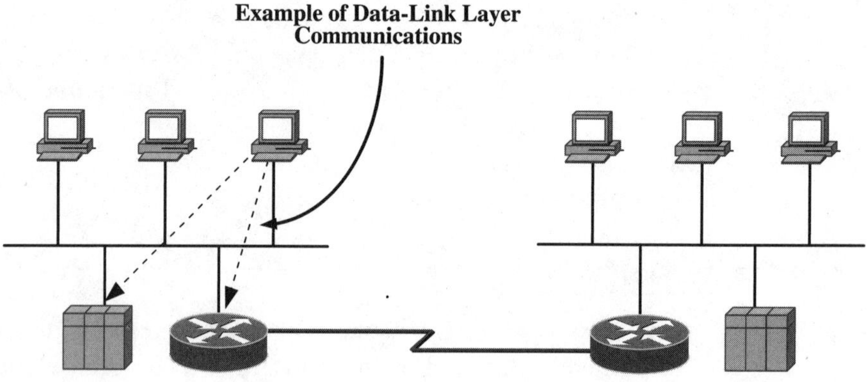

Figure D-7
An example of data
link layer
conversations

Example of Data-Link Layer Communications

All of these services describe how conversations take place between two devices on the same media. Remember that the data link layer implementation used is independent of the physical layer. For example, Ethernet can use UTP or coaxial cable. It does not matter which physical layer media it uses; the rules that govern the technology are the same. This is the beauty of the OSI Model: any layer can be replaced without concerns about the lower or upper layers.

Communication at the data link layer is between two hosts on the same network. Those two hosts can be a desktop computer communicating with a local file server or a local host sending data to a router that is destined for a remote host (see Figure D-7).

Data Link Layer Example

The following section focuses on Ethernet, one of the most commonly used data link layer standards. If we look at the frame format of an Ethernet frame, we can get a better understanding of each component's purpose. In Figure D-8, we see a standard IEEE 802.3 Ethernet frame format. If we look at each component, we can easily see its purpose.

Preamble The preamble is an alternating pattern of ones and zeros. It tells the other stations on the media that a frame is coming. The IEEE 802.3 preamble ends with two consecutive ones, which serves to synchronize the frame reception of all stations on the LAN.

Data link layer addressing (Destination and source address) The capability to distinguish one host from another is critical when multiple hosts have access to the same media. Compare that to point-to-point connections in which the capability to distinguish the end point is irrelevant because there is only one other node on the network that can hear the data.

The address used by end hosts to identify each other is called the *Media Access Control* (MAC) address. It is often referred to as the physical address, burned-in address, or hardware address. The MAC address of each Ethernet *Network Interface Card* (NIC) is by definition unique. It is a 48-bit address built into the NIC that uniquely identifies the station. It is generally represented in one of three formats:

- 00-60-94-EB-41-9F

- 00:60:94:EB:41:9F

- 0060.94EB.419F

If we look closely at the MAC address, we will see that it can be broken down into two distinct components: the vendor's address and a unique host

Figure D-8
Ethernet frame
format

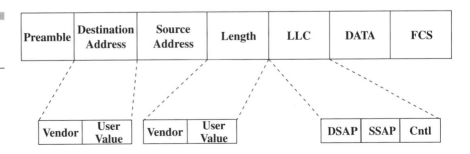

identifier. The first three octets (24 bits) identify the vendor. Using the example listed above, we can look up 00-60-94 at `http://standards.ieee.org/regauth/oui/oui.txt`.

We can see that this NIC was manufactured by IBM. This can be useful when attempting to locate a device on the network that is malfunctioning.

Length   The Length field indicates the number of bytes contained in the Data field. Although all of the other fields are of a predetermined length (the Destination and Source addresses are six bytes) the Data field can be up to 1,500 bytes. If the data in the frame is insufficient to fill the frame to a minimum 64-byte size, the frame is padded to ensure at least a 64-byte frame.

Logical Link Control (LLC)   The IEEE 802.2 *Logical Link Control* (LLC) header is used to specify which upper layer protocol is contained in the data. Without the capability to distinguish which upper layer protocol a packet belongs to, it is impossible to carry multiple network layer protocols over a data link layer implementation. For example, because Novell's 802.3 RAW frame format does not have a method to distinguish between network layer protocols, it could only carry a single network layer protocol. This is one of the reasons why Novell's 802.3 frame format is generally not employed.

Another example of a data link layer technology not using a type field is SLIP. Even though it enjoyed some success in the late '80s and early '90s as a dialup protocol, its incapability to distinguish between different network layer protocols has allowed PPP to become the standard dialup protocol.

The following fields all play a part in LLC identification:

- *DSAP*   The *Destination Service Access Point* (DSAP) is a one-byte field that acts like a pointer in the receiving station. It tells the receiving NIC which buffer to put this information in. This function is critical when users are running multiple network layer protocols.

- *SSAP*   The *Source Service Access Point* (SSAP) is identical to the DSAP, except that it indicates the source of the sending application.

- *Control*   This one-byte field is used to indicate the type of LLC frame of this data frame. Three different types of LLC frames exist:

  - *LLC1*   An unacknowledged connectionless service. It uses unsequenced information to set up communication between two network stations. This type of LLC is generally used with Novell's *Internetwork Packet Exchange* (IPX), TCP/IP, and Vines IP.

- *LLC2*   A connection-oriented service between two network stations. This type of service is generally used in SNA and NetBIOS sessions.

- *LLC3*   A connectionless but acknowledged-oriented service between two different stations. This type of service can be used by SDLC.

Data   The Data field in an IEEE 802.3 frame can be between 43 and 1,497 bytes. However, depending upon the type of frame being used, this size can vary. For example, an Ethernet II frame can hold between 46 and 1,497 bytes of data, while a frame using Novell's RAW 802.3 frame format can hold between 46 and 1,500 bytes of data.

Frame Check Sequence (FCS)   The last four bytes of a IEEE 802.3 frame are used to verify that the frame is not corrupt. By using a complex polynomial, the NIC can detect errors in the frame. If errors are detected, then the frame is discarded and it never reaches the memory buffers.

Now that we understand the frame format of an IEEE 802.3 frame, we need to discuss how those frames get on the wire.

Carrier Sense Media Access with Collision Detection (CSMA/CD)
Ethernet is one of the most common network topologies. The basic rule behind Ethernet communication is called *Carrier Sense Multiple Access with Collision Detection* (CSMA/CD). If we break down each phrase, we can interpret its meaning:

- *Carrier Sense*   All Ethernet stations are required to listen to the network to see if any other devices are sending data. This serves two purposes: one, it keeps the station from sending data when someone else is sending data and, two, it enables the station to be ready when another station wants to send it data.

- *Multiple Access*   This means more than two stations can be connected to the same network at the same time and that all stations can transmit data whenever the network is free. In order for data to be transmitted, the station must wait until the Ethernet channel is idle. Once the channel is idle, the station can transmit a frame, but it must listen to see if there is a collision.

- *Collision Detection*   If there is a collision, then both stations must immediately back off and use a backoff algorithm to randomly determine how long they should wait before trying to transmit again. It is important that a random number be generated for this timer, because if some standard number were used, then both stations would wait the same length of time and then attempt to transmit again, thus causing another collision.

NOTE: *A collision is the simultaneous transmitting of a frame by two different stations. A station can detect a collision within the first 64 bytes of the transmission.*

Conclusion

Many different types of data link layer technologies exist, and Ethernet is one of those technologies. Although a data link layer technology can theoretically use any physical layer implementation, generally the actual implementation of a data link layer technology goes hand in hand with the physical layer implementation. For example, PPP is generally used over dialup networks or WAN networks, while Ethernet and Token Ring are used in LAN environments. This means that you probably won't see very many implementations of PPP using CAT 5 cable for its wiring infrastructure. Likewise, you probably won't see Token Ring being deployed from a corporate office to a telecommuter's home using the Telco's wiring infrastructure.

Layer 3: Network Layer

Layer 3 of the OSI Reference Model is the network layer. Figure D-9 shows the placement of the network layer in the OSI Reference Model.

This layer is responsible for providing routing for the network. Routing, in a generic sense, is simply finding a path to a destination. In the context of the network layer, routing means finding a path to a destination that is a member of a different Layer 2 network than the source. Physical networks can be connected together with bridges to form larger Layer 2 networks. Unfortunately, Layer 2 networks cannot scale to an infinite size. As these networks grow, more bandwidth is used to transmit broadcast packets that flood the entire Layer 2 network. These broadcast packets are used to find the destination host.

Figure D-9
The network layer
and the OSI
Reference Model

7	Application Layer
6	Presentation Layer
5	Session Layer
4	Transport Layer
3	**Network Layer**
2	Data Link Layer
1	Physical Layer

Routing enables Layer 2 networks to be broken into smaller segments, enabling the network to grow to support more hosts. Figure D-10 shows the concept of routing.

The data link control layer passes packets up to the network layer. These packets have headers to define the source and destination addresses and other network layer parameters of the data in the packet. The network layer only uses the data in the network layer packet header for information to perform its functions. This maintains the modularity of the network layer. Therefore, there is no dependency on the information from the data link control layer headers and the transport layer headers.

Network layer communication is not guaranteed. This means that there is no mechanism to determine if the destination node received the network layer packets. Guaranteed delivery is maintained at other layers in the OSI Reference Model. The most obvious reason for not implementing guaranteed delivery at the network layer is because this layer has no concept of end-to-end delivery. It would be more appropriate for upper layer protocols that implement more connection-oriented services to make sure that the data reaches its destination. The network layer routes data on a packet-by-packet basis.

Only one network layer process exists for each network node. Several data link control layer processes may be found below the network layer, depending on the number of physical interfaces in the node, and several transport layer processes may be found above the network layer, depending

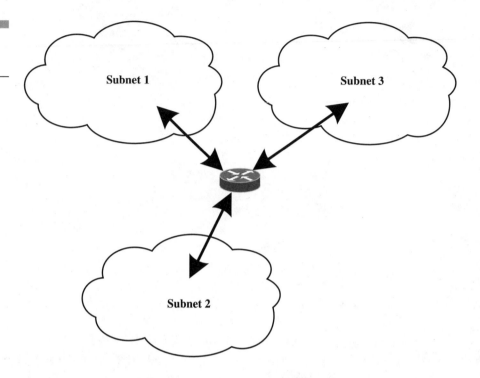

on the number of connection-oriented streams terminating at the node. Several network layer protocols may be running on a node, but each of these protocols corresponds to a separate logical internetwork and they do not intercommunicate.

A special node called a *gateway* connects logical networks formed by network layer addressing schemes. Gateways have a special sublayer in the upper portion of the network layer called the *Internet sublayer*. This sublayer handles the intercommunication between subnets. When a packet arrives from one subnet that is destined for another, the packet will be passed from the network layer to the Internet sublayer. The Internet sublayer in turn determines the destination subnet and forwards the packet back down to the lower portion of the network layer to the destination subnet. This is the basic idea behind routing. Figure D-11 illustrates the concept of a network node.

Each network layer process at each node is a peer process. These peer processes work together to implement distributed algorithms. These distributed algorithms are the routing algorithms corresponding to various routing protocols. These protocols provide a means to automatically discover and transmit routing information between gateways.

Figure D-11
Network node model

	Internet Sublayer
3	-------------------------------------
	Network Layer
2	Data Link Layer
1	Physical Layer

The Internet Protocol (IP)

The most familiar protocol that operates at the network layer is the *Internet Protocol* (IP). IP is by far the most widely deployed network layer protocol due to the success of the Internet. This protocol is the foundation of the Internet in terms of addressing and packet routing. The Internet employs multiple protocols in the other OSI Reference Model layers, but it only uses IP in the network layer.

Another example of a network protocol is Novell's *Internet Packet Exchange* (IPX). Novell has since refined NetWare to use IP as the native network layer protocol instead of IPX.

IP Node Operation

If an IP host wants to communicate with another IP host, the transmitting IP source must determine if the destination IP address is in the same subnet or not. If the destination is in the same subnet, the host must send an *Address Resolution Protocol* (ARP) request packet to obtain the MAC address of the destination, assuming the destination MAC address isn't already in its ARP table. If the destination is not in the same subnet as the source, the source must send the packet to the MAC address of the gateway for that subnet. Most IP hosts have one IP address to send their packets to if they are destined for any subnet other than their own. This is called the *default gateway* or *default router address*. The user configures the default gateway address.

Once the default gateway (router) gets the packet and sees that the packet is destined for its own MAC address and at the same time destined for another IP host, the router knows that it must forward the packet to another interface to move the packet closer to its destination.

The mechanism for determining if the destination IP host is in the same subnet is as follows. The subnet mask is bitwise ANDed with both the source IP address and the destination IP address. The logic table for the AND operation is shown in Table D-5.

The result of these two functions is exclusively ORed (XORed). If this final result is not zero, then the destination IP address is in another subnet. The logic table for the XOR operation is shown in Table D-6.

Here is an example of determining if the destination address is in the same subnet as the host:

Source IP address:

$(100.1.43.1)_{\text{dotted-decimal}}$ $(01100100.00000001.00101011.00000001)_{\text{binary}}$

Subnet mask:

$(255.255.255.0)_{\text{dotted-decimal}}$ $(11111111.11111111.11111111.00000000)_{\text{binary}}$

Destination IP address:

$(100.1.44.2)_{\text{dotted-decimal}}$ $(01100100.00000001.00101100.00000010)_{\text{binary}}$

Table D-5

Logic table for AND operations

	1	0
1	1	0
0	0	0

Table D-6

Logic table for OR operations

	1	0
1	0	1
0	1	0

Source IP address ANDed with subnet mask:

01100100.00000001.00101011.00000001

<u>11111111.11111111.11111111.00000000</u>

01100100.00000001.00101011.00000000

Destination IP address ANDed with subnet mask:

01100100.00000001.00101100.00000010

<u>11111111.11111111.11111111.00000000</u>

01100100.00000001.00101100.00000000

The two results XORed:

01100100.00000001.00101011.00000000

<u>01100100.00000001.00101100.00000000</u>

00000000.00000000.00000111.00000000

The result of the XOR function is not zero. Therefore, the destination IP address is in another subnet than the source and the packet must be sent to the default gateway to be routed to the destination subnet.

When the router gets a packet to be forwarded to another subnet, the router must manipulate the MAC and IP header fields to ensure that the packet is forwarded toward its destination.

Three things must happen when the router forwards the packet at the network layer:

- The interface to forward the packet to must be determined.
- The destination MAC address must be updated with the MAC address of the next-hop router or destination host.
- The *Time to Live* (TTL) field must be decremented in the IP header.

The interface that the packet is forwarded out of is determined by looking through the route table that the router maintains. This route table associates a route to a destination with a physical interface.

The destination MAC address must be updated with the MAC address of the destination IP host if the host is directly connected to the router. If the destination host is not directly connected to one of the ports of the router, the router must forward the packet to the next router to move the packet toward the destination IP host. In either case, if the router doesn't know the

MAC address of the next hop toward the destination, it must ARP for the MAC address.

The TTL field is then decremented. This field provides a mechanism for the packet to be removed from the network if it gets caught in a loop. Without such a mechanism, the packet may be forwarded for as long as the routing loop is active. The packet is removed by a router if its TTL field is zero.

Internetwork Packet Exchange (IPX) Operation

Another example of a Layer 3 protocol is the IPX protocol. The IPX protocol was developed by Novell NetWare. Novell NetWare is a *Network Operating System* (NOS) that provides network file and print services. IPX is quickly being replaced by IP since NetWare now provides native IP support, but there remains a large installed base of IPX networks in campus networks.

Unlike IP, IPX has no concept of multiple subnets per the Layer 2 network. Instead, IPX has only one address per physical network called a *network number*. The full network layer address for a network device is made of two parts: the 32-bit network number and the node's 48-bit MAC address.

Some argue that the combination of Layer 2 and Layer 3 addresses to form a Layer 3 address undermines the modularity of the OSI Reference Model. This is due to the fact that IPX (Layer 3) network numbers depend on the Layer 2 addressing scheme. This argument is purely academic since the MAC address scheme is so prevalent. The real limitation to IPX is its inability to logically subnet hosts on the same physical network.

Layer 4: Transport Layer

Layer 4 of the OSI Reference Model is the transport layer. Figure D-12 shows the placement of the network layer in the OSI Reference Model.

The transport layer is responsible for data transfer issues such as reliability of the connection, establishing error detections, recovery, and flow control. In addition, this layer is responsible for delivering packets from the network layer to the upper layers of the OSI Model.

If we think of the network layer as responsible for delivering packets from one host to another, the transport layer is responsible for identifying the conversations between two hosts. For example, Figure D-13 shows an

Figure D-12
The transport layer
and the OSI
Reference Model

7	Application Layer
6	Presentation Layer
5	Session Layer
4	**Transport Layer**
3	Network Layer
2	Data Link Layer
1	Physical Layer

Figure D-13
The transport layer
differentiating
between
conversations

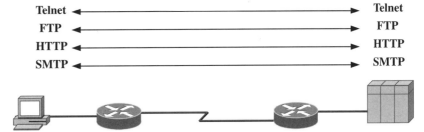

SERVICES REQUESTED   SERVICES ON HOST

Telnet ←————————————————————→ Telnet
FTP   ←————————————————————→ FTP
HTTP   ←————————————————————→ HTTP
SMTP   ←————————————————————→ SMTP

example of how the transport layer keeps the conversations between the different applications separate.

Two different variants of transport layer protocols are used. The first provides a reliable, connection-oriented service, while the second method is a best-effort delivery. The difference between these two protocols dictates the paradigm in which they operate. When using TCP/IP, the two different protocols are TCP and UDP. Inside an IP packet is a protocol number that enables the host to identify whether the packet contains a TCP message or a UDP message. The TCP protocol value is 6 and for UDP it is 17. Many other (~130) protocols types exist, but these two are commonly used to transport user messages from one host to another.

Transport Layer Protocol Examples

In this section, we'll examine some examples of transport layer protocols.

Transmission Control Protocol (TCP)   The TCP described in RFC 793 provides applications with a reliable connection-oriented service. Three basic instruments are used to make TCP a connection-oriented service:

- Sequence numbers
- Acknowledgments
- Windowing

In order for data to be handed down to the network layer, the data must be broken down into messages. These messages are then given a sequence number by TCP before being handed off to the network layer. The purpose of the sequence number is so that in case the packets arrive out of order the remote host can reassemble the data using the sequence numbers. This only guarantees that the data is reassembled correctly.

In addition to sequence numbers, acknowledgements are used by the remote host to tell the local host that the data was received, guaranteeing the delivery of data. If, for whatever reason, a packet gets dropped along the way, the remote host can see that it is missing a message and request it again, as shown in Figure D-14.

Although windowing enables TCP to regulate the flow of packets between two hosts, this minimizes the chances of packets being dropped because the buffers are full in the remote host.

Figure D-14
Using
acknowledgements
for guaranteed
delivery

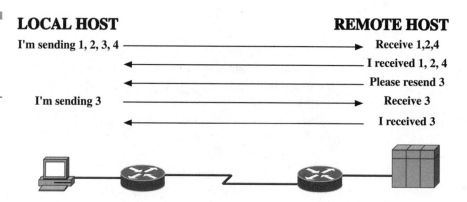

LOCAL HOST

I'm sending 1, 2, 3, 4 ⟶ Receive 1,2,4

⟵ I received 1, 2, 4

⟵ Please resend 3

I'm sending 3 ⟶ Receive 3

⟵ I received 3

REMOTE HOST

In order for a TCP connection to be established, a three-step handshake is exchanged between the local host and the remote host. This three-way handshake starts with the local host initiating a conversation by sending a *Synchronize Sequence Numbers* (SYN) packet to the remote host, as shown in Figure D-15.

The remote host acknowledges the SYN and sends an SYN acknowledgement back to the local host. The local host responds by sending an acknowledgement and then starts sending data. The purpose of this handshake is to synchronize the sequence numbers that identify the proper order used to reconstruct the messages throughout the conversation.

User Datagram Protocol (UDP)   The UDP, as described in RFC 768, provides applications with a connectionless best-effort delivery service. Because there is no time wasted setting up a connection, applications that utilize UDP are very fast. Applications that send short bursts of data can take advantage of UDP's speed, but if the messages get delivered out of order or a message gets dropped, then the entire message fails.

Well-Known Ports   We've seen how we can guarantee the delivery of a packet through the use of TCP and how we can improve throughput by using a connectionless delivery service, but how are discrete conversations between two hosts handled? Both TCP and UDP utilize a mechanism called a port (also known as a socket). By utilizing a source port and a destination port, two hosts can distinguish between multiple conversations.

In order to provide services to unknown callers, a host will use a well-known port number. Well-known port numbers are assigned by the *Internet Assigned Numbers Authority* (IANA). By adhering to the well-known port numbers published by the IANA, we can make sure that various services do not utilize the same port. Both TCP and UDP use port numbers and when

Figure D-15
Three-way
handshake to initiate
a connection

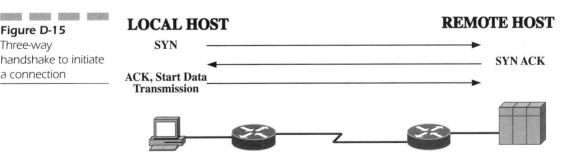

Table D-7

Well-Known Port
Numbers

Port Number	Service
20	FTP (Data)
21	FTP (Control)
23	Telnet
25	SMTP
42	Host Name Server
53	Domain Name Service
80	HTTP

a service can utilize both TCP and UDP, the port number is identical. Table D-7 shows us a sampling of the well-known port numbers.

Until recently, the assigned port range was from 0 to 255. However, the range has been expanded from 0 to 1,023.

Conclusion

The transport layer protocol helps end devices distinguish between simultaneous conversations between the same two hosts. The protocol that is used, connection-oriented or connectionless, is dependent upon the needs of the upper layer application. Some applications want the speed of UDP and will implement their own form of reliability-checking in an effort to speed up the transmission of the data. Although this obviously adds a lot of overhead to the programmer's job, it can be worth it, depending upon the applications requirements.

Layer 5: Session Layer

Layer 5 of the OSI Reference Model is the session layer. Figure D-16 shows the placement of the session layer in the OSI Reference Model.

The session layer is responsible for providing such functions as directory service and access rights. The session layer has a defined role in the OSI Reference Model, but its functions are not as critical as the lower layers to all networks. For example, a network without the physical layer, the data

Figure D-16
The session layer and
the OSI Reference
Model

7	Application Layer
6	Presentation Layer
5	**Session Layer**
4	Transport Layer
3	Network Layer
2	Data Link Layer
1	Physical Layer

link layer, network layer, or the transport layer would be lacking basic functionality that would make the network useful. Until recently, the session layer has been ignored or at least not seen as absolutely necessary in data networks. Session layer functionality has been seen as a host responsibility, not a network function. As networks become larger and more secure, functions such as directory services and access rights become more necessary.

Access rights functionality deals with a user's access to various network resources such as computer access and authentication, file access, and printer access. Devices providing the service such as file and print servers have typically implemented access rights. There has been a shift in responsibility for these functions in recent years. Authentication can now be distributed using authentication services such as Kerberos. File and print service access control is moving to network directory services such as Novell's *Network Directory Service* (NDS) or Microsoft's *Active Directory Services* (ADS). These services control what resources a host may access.

Directory services are services that find resources on the network. Typically, a user would have to have prior knowledge of a service to gain access to the service. Some services have the capability of broadcasting their presence, but that methodology does not scale well in a large network with many hosts and many services. True directory services act as a redirection point for hosts to be given addressing information to find a particular resource. Novell's NDS or Microsoft's ADS can act as directory services as well as define a user's access rights, as mentioned above.

The session layer has no hard and fast rules for interfacing with the presentation layer since the presentation layer is optional in many cases. The session layer services are typically accessed via TCP or UDP port numbers, therefore defining the interface to the transport layer.

Layer 6: Presentation Layer

Layer 6 of the OSI Reference Model is the presentation layer. Figure D-17 shows the placement of the network layer in the OSI Reference Model.

The presentation layer is responsible for providing data encryption, data compression, and code conversion. The functions in this layer have not been considered a function of the network and have been handled by various applications. In recent years, data encryption, compression, and code conversion have moved into the mainstream of the network protocol functionality.

Data encryption is moving to the forefront of networking since networks are carrying more sensitive data. Encryption can be handled in a number of ways. The easiest and most secure method for encrypting data is to encrypt all the data on a particular link. This requires a device on both ends of a path to encrypt and decrypt the payload of each packet that passes over the link. This requires that sensitive data always pass over a path installed with an encryption device. This does not scale well for a large network. The more scalable method for encryption is for the applications at both ends of

Figure D-17
The presentation
layer and the OSI
Reference Model

7	Application Layer
6	**Presentation Layer**
5	Session Layer
4	Transport Layer
3	Network Layer
2	Data Link Layer
1	Physical Layer

a session to set up a means for encrypting the data. This method of encryption requires that a device have more processing power to handle the application and the data encryption in real time.

Data compression conserves bandwidth over a link. Like data encryption, data compression can be done on both ends of a path through a network. This requires an external device to compress the network data. This method does not scale well in large networks where there can be many paths through a network. A more scalable method for data compression is to allow the application at both ends of a session to compress the data. The tradeoff in this method is more processing power is required on the host to support the application and real-time compression/decompression.

Code conversion involves converting a set of data or a data stream from one format to another. Data formats can be for character sets, video formats, graphics formats, and presentation formats. Examples of character set formats are ASCII and EBCDIC, video formats are MPEG and MJPEG, graphics formats are GIF, TIFF, JPEG, and bitmap, and presentation formats are HTML, XML, and SHTML.

No hard and fast rules define the interface between the presentation layer and the session layer since the session layer may be optional for a particular network. The presentation layer communicates to the application layer by addressing the application with an appropriate transport layer (session) address such as a TCP port number.

Layer 7: Application Layer

The final layer, Layer 7, of the OSI Model is the application layer. This section will define the application layer and examine in moderate detail what takes place at Layer 7.

The application layer consists of an application that requires the use of a network to perform its task. Communication between applications takes place at Layer 7. As with the previous layers, Layer 7 exchanges messages with Layer 7 only. Restated, an application communicates with only a peer application. Figure D-18 depicts this layer-to-layer communication.

An example application could be something as simple as a *chat* program. The application connects to its peer application and sends characters that are entered on the keyboard. It also displays characters received from the peer application. The applications communicating at Layer 7 use the lower layers and the services they provide to send and receive application-specific information.

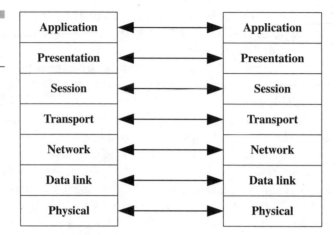

Figure D-18
Layer 7 application
communication

Furthermore, it is common for applications to further define the contents of the data that is being exchanged. Even with the simple chat program, a protocol is defined: "Each message received from a peer application contains a single character." This creates a challenge for troubleshooting network-related problems.

Although only a handful of protocols are used at the lower layers, the protocols are usually well specified. As you can see, anyone can define a new protocol for his or her specific application. This makes it difficult for vendors that develop network analyzers to provide the capability of troubleshooting application, or Layer 7, problems.

As you can see, this layer can be any application that requires network communication. The application communicates with its peer application at Layer 7, and an application may arbitrarily define a protocol that specifies application-to-application communication.

Conclusion

It is important to remember that the OSI Model is only for reference. Not all protocols and technologies have a direct correlation to one of the seven layers. Frequently, a protocol may straddle different layers, such as ARP, which is used when a computer knows the IP address it needs to communicate with (network layer) but it doesn't know its MAC address (data link layer). ARP enables a computer to map an IP address to a MAC address. So is ARP a data link layer-protocol or a network-layer protocol? Technically, it straddles both layers, so it doesn't really fit the OSI Model, but without it IP communication on a LAN couldn't happen.

INDEX

Symbols

80/20 rule, 155
802.1q frames, 192

A

AAL (ATM Adaptation Layer), 175
AARP (AppleTalk Address Resolution
        Protocol), 357
access lists
    AppleTalk commands, 372
    debugging, 595
    IP
        clearing counters, 329
        viewing, 319-320
    IPX, 404
    ISDN BRI, 507
    SAP filtering, 389
access-list command, 389
Acknowledged mode, LAPD, 504
ACL Manager, 67
action plans, Cisco problem-solving method, 29
active monitors, Token Ring, 157
adapters, promiscuous mode, 154
Address field
    LAPB frames, 267
    LAPD frames, 504
addresses, AppleTalk
    assigning, 355-356
    gleaning, 364
    IP, *see* IP addresses.
    IPX, 384
adjacency tables, CEF, 84
ADSP (AppleTalk data stream protocol), 358
advanced troubleshooting, 584
    Apple protocol analysis, 585
    CCO Web site, 544
    common symptoms and causes, 590
    debugging
        access lists, 595
        techniques, 594

false assumptions, 591-593
line monitoring, 602
NetWare protocol analysis, 585
ping, 598
routing issues, 596
service providers, 601-602
static routes, 596
Traceroute, 600
advertisements, SAP, 387
AFP (AppleTalk file protocol), 362
agents, RMON, 223
AIX NetSys SLM suite, 70
algorithms
    Backoff, Etherent, 152
    Bellman-Ford, 430
    Dijkstra, 456
    DUAL, 474
    SPF, 455
AMT (address maintenance table), 357
analyzing problems, Cisco problem-solving
        method, 29
AppleTalk
    access list commands, 372
    addresses
        assigning, 355-356
        gleaning, 364
        maintenance table, 357
    ARP cache
        timeouts, 357
        viewing contents, 357
    ARP table, 357
    ARP-TIMEOUT command, 358
    Arp interval command, 358
    Arp retransmit command, 358
    cable-range command, 352
    cable ranges, 352, 355
    configuring, 352
    event dumps, 369
    hosts
        extended ping, 125
        ping, 122
    interfaces, 364
    names, 360
    nodes, 355

protocols, 354
  analyzer output, 585
  routing, 353
routing AURP command, 362
routing RTMP command, 361
Split Horizon, 361
troubleshooting, 350
viewing
  all traffic, 369-370
  neighbors, 366
  traffic data, 365-366
ZIP updates, 371
zone name command, 353
zones, 350-351
Application layer, OSI model, 288
ARP (Address Resolution Protocol), 296
  broadcast storms, 298
  converting IP addresses to MAC addresses, 296
  directed broadcasts, 298
  flooding, 298
  transaction debug data, 323-324
ARP cache
  AppleTalk, 357
  clearing, 328
  hosts, 297
  routers, 297
  viewing address resolutions, 318
  Windows NT, 306
arp command, syntax, 307
ASICs (Application Specific Integrated Circuits),
    Catalyst switches, 225
ASP (AppleTalk session protocol), 362
assigning AppleTalk addresses, 355-356
asymmetrical routing, 118
ATM networks (Asynchronous Transfer Mode), 175
  cells, 175–177
  ELANs, 178
  OSI model, 177
attenuation, 61
audience of book, 4
AURP (Apple Update-based Routing
    Protocol), 361
authentication, PPP, ISDN BRI, 508-509
autonomous switching, 82

B

B channel, ISDN BRI, 513, 519-520
backoff algorithms, Etherent, 152
baselines of performance, 21-22
BDRs (backup designated routers), OSPF, 462
beacons, Token Ring, 158
BECN field, Frame Relay, 255
Bellman-Ford algorithm, 430
BERTs (Bit/Block Error Rate Testers), 63
BGP (Border Gateway Protocol), 470–471
BPDUs (Bridge Protocol Data Units), 188, 586
bridges, Ethernet, 180
broadcast domains, 154–155
Broadcast keyword, debug frame-relay packet
    command, 263
broadcast storms, ARP, 298
broadcasts
  ARP, 298
  Ethernet, 154
  SAP, 389
buffer pool statistics, routers, 247
buffers, message logging parameters, 88
bus system, 144

C

cable ranges, AppleTalk, 352, 355
cable testers, checking cabling continuity, 60
cabling, 147
  checking, TDRs, 61
  continuity, 60
  cross-over cables, 150
  electrical interference, 149
  length limits, 147
  near-end cross talk, 148
  patch cables, 147
cache, AR. *See* ARP cache.
captures, network analyzers, 66
carrier transitions, 109
Catalyst switches, 206–207
  ASICs, 225
  EARL chip, 226
  internal components, 225
  Phoenix ASIC, 227

SAGE chip, 226
SAINT chip, 226
SAMBA chips, 227
CCNP requirements, 8-9
CCO Web site (Cisco Connection Online), 543
  advanced troubleshooting options, 544
  Cisco Marketplace, 549
  Commerce Agents, 550
  overview, 545
  registered users, 546-547
  searches, 552-553
  Software Center, 555
  technical documents, 550–552
CD. *See* Cisco, Documentation CD.
CDP packets (Cisco Discovery Protocol), 188, 591
CEF (Cisco Express forwarding), 83
cells, ATM
  fields, 175
  processing, 177
CHAP (Challenge Handshake Authentication
    Protocol), 509
Checksum field, ICMP messages, 294
circular routes, 129
Cisco
  CCNP requirements, 8-9
  Cisco Management Connection, 68
  Cisco Marketplace, 549
  Cisco NetSys Network Management Suites, 69
  Cisco View, 67
  Cisco Works Blue Maps, 69
  Cisco Works, network management tools, 66–69
  Documentation CD, 543, 563-564
    searches, 565
  problem-solving method, 22
    action plans, 29
    defining problem, 22–26
    documenting solution, 31
    evaluating causes, 28
    evaluating results, 30
    gathering facts, 27
    repeating until problem is solved, 30-31
CIT exam (Cisco Internetwork Troubleshooting)
  retaking test, 15
  taking test, 12-14
  test objectives, 10–12
classful routing protocols, 428
classless routing protocols, 429

clear arp-cache command, 328
clear counters bri command, 529
clear counters command, 110
clear ip access-list counters command, 329
clear ip route command, 331
clearing
  ARP cache, 328
  fast-switching cache, 328
  IP routing table entries, 331
CLI (Command-Line Interface), switches, 209
climbing the ladder problem-solving method, 41
Code field, ICMP messages, 294
collision detection, Ethernet, 152
collision domains
  Ethernet, 181
  networks, 153
commands
  access-list, 389
  apple arp-timeout, 358
  appletalk arp interval, 358
  appletalk Arp retransmit, 358
  appletalk cable-range, 352
  appletalk routing AURP, 362
  appletalk routing RTMP, 361
  appletalk zone name, 353
  arp, 297
  clear arp-cache, 328
  clear counters, 110
  clear counters bri, 529
  clear ip access-list counters, 329
  clear ip route, 331
  core dumps, 110
  debug, 85
  debug all, 91
  debug apple events, 369
  debug apple nbp, 360
  debug apple packet, 369-370
  debug apple zip, 363, 371
  debug arp, 323-324
  debug bri, 519-520
  debug dialer, 527
  debug frame-relay events, 261
  debug frame-relay lmi, 262
  debug frame-relay packet, 263
  debug ip bgp, 473
  debug ip eigrp events, 484
  debug ip icmp, 296, 324

debug ip igrp events, 448–453
debug ip ospf events, 466–470
debug ip packet, 325
debug ip rip, 440–442
debug ip routing, 326-327, 438-439, 446,
    463-464, 480–483
debug ipx packet, 407
debug ipx routing events, 408–411
debug ipx sap events, 407
debug isdn, 528
debug isdn q921, 520–522
debug isdn q931, 522
debug ppp authentication, 525
debug ppp negotiation, 523–525
debug ppp packet, 526
debug serial interface, 92, 248-249, 263-264
debug serial packet, 94
debug service-module, 94
debug x25 all, 273
debug x25 events, 272
diagnostic, 79-80
dialer load-threshold, 511
dialer-list, 507
duplex full, 218
eigrp configuration, 475
encapsulation, 241
encapsulation ppp, 508
exception core-file, 111
exception dump, 111
exception memory, 112
exception protocol, 111
extended ping, 122-125, 330
extended traceroute, 128
global, 103
IGRP configuration, 443
interface, 106
ip domain-lookup, 300
ip forward-protocol, 303
ip helper-address, 301
ip name-server, 300
ipconfig, 303-304
ipconfig/all, 303
ipx encapsulation, 396
ipx input-sap-filter, 389
ipx network, 385
ipx output-sap-filter, 389
ipx rip, 392

ipx router eigrp, 394
ipx router nlsp, 393
ipx router rip, 392
ipx sap-incremental eigrp, 390
logging, 86
logging buffered, 88
logging console, 87
logging ip-address, 88
logging monitor, 88
logging trap, 88
no appletalk zone, 353
no appletalk zone name, 353
no logging buffered, 88
no network, 447
no shut, 110
OSPF configuration, 457
ping, 112, 296, 304
    IPX, 412
    time-out process, 116
    user form, 120-122
    Windows systems, 125-126
port group, 218
port monitor, 217
ppp authentication, 509
ppp multilink, 511
router eigrp, 475
router igrp, 443
router network, 394
router ospf, 457
router rip, 433
show, 94, 96
show apple arp, 357
show appletalk, 368
show appletalk globals, 364
show appletalk interface, 364
show appletalk neighbors, 366
show appletalk traffic, 365
show ARP, 103
show async, 96
show buffers, 98, 247
show cdp, 211
show cdp neighbors detail, 211–213
show config, 214–218
show controllers, 106, 245–247
show controllers bri, 514
show debugging, 104
show dialer, 516-517

show flash, 102
show frame-relay lmi, 104, 256
show frame-relay map, 105, 257
show frame-relay pvc, 105, 258
show int ser 0, 244
show interface, 242–244, 250, 259-260,
    269, 312
  IPX/SPX settings, 397
show interface ?, 221
show interface bri, 511–513, 529
show interface serial, 109
show interfaces, 107-108, 221-222
show ip access-lists, 319
show ip arp, 318
show ip bgp, 472
show ip bgp summary, 472
show ip eigrp interface, 479
show ip interface, 314
show ip interface brief, 316
show ip ospf interface, 460
show ip ospf neighbor, 462-463
show ip protocols, 317, 435, 444-445, 458, 476
show ip rip database, 438
show ip route, 318, 437, 445, 459-460, 478-479
show IP traffic, 102-103, 321
show ipx access-lists, 404
show ipx eigrp interface, 405
show ipx eigrp neighbors, 405
show ipx int, 385
show ipx interface, 398
show ipx interface brief, 400
show ipx route, 403-404
show ipx servers, 401
show ipx traffic, 402
show isdn status, 515
show logging, 88
show MAC, 213
show port group, 218
show port monitor, 219
show ppp multilink, 518
show process CPU, 101
show process memory, 100
show running-config, 98
show spantree, 220
show stacks, 98
show tech, 96, 223
show tech-support, 566–568, 570–572, 575

show version, 97, 222
show x25 route, 270
show x25 vc, 270-271
speed 100, 218
trace, 333
    ping, 413
traceroute, 127
tracert, 130, 305
undebug, 85
username, 509
write core, 112, 575
Commerce Agents, CCO Web site, 550
common false assumptions, 591-593
common symptoms and causes, 590
computer names, Windows NT. *See* NetBIOS
    name resolution.
Configuration Agent, 550
configuration commands
    EIGRP, 395
    IGRP, 443
    NLSP, 393
    OSPF, 457
    RIP, 434
configuring
    routers, AppleTalk, 352
    TCP/IP, viewing settings, 312
congestion management, Frame Relay, 255
connectionless protocols, 290
connections
    checking physical, 59
    Ethernet, 193–194
    networks, 331–333
contention modes, Token Ring, 157
continuity of cabling, 60
Control field
    LAPB frames, 267
    LAPD frames, 504
controllers
    ISDN BRI, viewing data, 514
    serial interfaces, viewing status, 245–247
convergence, static routes, 424
converting IP addresses to MAC addresses, 296
core dumps, 110-111, 575
counters, IP access lists, clearing, 329
CPU halt light, RSM module, 225
CRCs (Cyclic Redundancy Checks)
    fast switching, 82

Frame Relay, 251
viewing errors, 109
cross-over cables, 150
crosstalk, 61
CSEs (Cisco Support Engineers), 559
CSMA/CD (Carrier Sense Multiple Access/Collision Detect), 152
CSU/DSUs (channel service unit /data service units), 94
CWSI Campus (Cisco Works For Switched Internetworks), 67

D

D channel, ISDN BRI, viewing, 511
DASs (dual attached stations), FDDI, 159
Data field, LAPB frames, 267
Data Link layer
  ISDN BRI, 503
  OSI model, troubleshooting, 34-36
  switched LANs, 173
datagram sizes, extended ping, 123
DCE (Data Circuit Terminating Equipment), 251
  Frame Relay, 253
  X.25, 267
DDP (datagram delivery protocol), 359
DDR (Dial-on-Demand Routing), ISDN BRI, 506, 527
DE field, Frame Relay, 255
debug all command, 91
debug apple events command, 369
debug apple nbp command, 360
debug apple packet command, 369-370
debug apple zip command, 363, 370
debug arp command, 323-324
debug bri command, 519-520
debug commands, 85, 89, 248
  differences from show commands, 84, 96
debug dialer command, 527
debug frame-relay events command, 261
debug frame-relay lmi command, 262
debug frame-relay packet command, 263
debug ip bgp commands, 473
debug ip eigrp events command, 484
debug ip icmp command, 296, 324
debug ip igrp events command, 448-453
debug ip ospf events command, 466-470

debug ip packet command, 325
debug ip rip command, 440-442
debug ip routing command, 326-327, 438-439, 446, 463-464, 480-483
debug ipx packet command, 407
debug ipx routing events command, 408-411
debug ipx sap events command, 407
debug isdn command, 528
debug isdn q921 command, 520-522
debug isdn q931 command, 522
debug ppp authentication command, 525
debug ppp negotiation command, 523-525
debug ppp packet command, 526
debug serial interface command, 92, 248-249, 263-264
debug serial packet command, 94
debug service-module command, 94
debug x25 all command, 273
debug x25 events command, 272
debugging
  access lists, 595
  available debug areas, 89-90
  CSU/DSUs, 94
  Ethernet interfaces, 107-108
  IPX
    packets, 405
    routing, 406-409
  message logging parameters, 87
  overruns, 106-107
  performance impact, 85-86
  ping, 598
  routing issues, 596
  serial interfaces, 91-92
  static routes, 596
  Traceroute, 600
  underruns, 106
  useful techniques, 594
defining problem, Cisco problem-solving method, 22-26
designing action plans, Cisco problem-solving method, 29
Destination Address, IP packets, 292
destination hosts, traceroute, 127
diagnostic commands, 79-80
diagrams of network layout, 20
dialer interface, ISDN BRI, 507, 516-517
dialer load-threshold command, 511
dialer-list command, 507

dialer lists, ISDN BRI, 507
Dijkstra algorithm, 456
discovering neighbors, distance vector
    protocols, 431
distance vector protocols, 427, 430
  hold-down timers, 432
  hop counts, 431
  maximum hop count, 432
  neighbor discovery, 431
  routing loops, 432
  Split Horizon, 432
  triggered updates, 432
distributed switching, 83
distribution lists
  IGRP, 444-445
  RIP, 435
divide and conquer problem-solving method, 42
DLCI (Data Link Connection Identifier), Frame
    Relay, 252
DNS (Domain Name Servers), 299-300
documentation, network layout, 20
documentation CD, 563-564
  searches, 565
documenting solution, Cisco problem-solving
    method, 31
domains, collision, 153
DRs (designated routers), OSPF, 462
DSAPs (Destination Service Access Points), 584
DTE (Data Terminating Equipment), 251
  Frame Relay, 253
  X.25, 267
DUAL (Diffusing Update Algorithm), 474
dumping router core, 110-111
duplex full command, 218
dynamic routes, 426

E

EARL chip (Encoded Address Recognition
    Logic), 226
echo replies, ICMP, 114, 331
echo requests, ICMP, 114, 331
EIGRP (Enhanced IGRP), 394, 473
  configuration commands, 395, 474
  DUAL, 474
  incremental SAP updates, 390

interfaces, viewing, 405, 479
neighbors
  discovery/recovery, 474
  viewing, 405
protocol dependent modules, 475
routing events, 484-486
routing tables, 479
  adding entries, 480-483
Eigrp configuration command, 475
ELANs (Emulated LANs), 178
electrical interference, cabling, 149
encapsulation
  Ethernet, 395
  HDLC, troubleshooting, 242
  IPX, 383, 395
encapsulation command, WAN interface
    protocols, 241
encapsulation ppp command, 508
enhanced mode, debug commands, 89
error correction
  Frame Relay, 2451
  Token Ring, 158
error messages, debug serial interface
    command, 93
error reporting protocols, ICMP, 113-114
ESPAN (Enhanced Switched Port Analyzer), 193
ET (Exchange Termination), ISDN, 499
EtherChannel, 190
Ethernet, 145
  backoff algorithms, 152
  broadcast packets, comparing to baseline
    analysis, 155
  collision detection, 152
  frames, IPX encapsulation, 395
  hosts, pinging, 122
  hubs, 145
  interfaces, debugging, 107-108
  interframe gap, 152
  jabbering, 156
  late collisions, 147
  multicast packets, 154
  networks
    bridges, 180
    collision domains, 181
    hubs, 179
    switch fabric, 183
    switches, 183
    switching methods, 184-185

topologies, 151-153
troubleshooting, 192
connection speeds, 193-194
full duplex, 194
EtherTalk, 357
evaluating causes, Cisco problem-solving method, 28
evaluating results, Cisco problem-solving method, 30
events
AppleTalk, viewing, 369
RMON, 225
exception core-file command, 111
exception dump command, 111
exception memory command, 112
exception protocol command, 111
extended DDP packets, 359
extended ping command, 122, 332
datagram sizes, 123
repeat counts, 123
source address variable, 125
timeouts, 124
extended traceroute, 128

F

failing test, 15
false assumptions, 591-593
FAQs
AppleTalk, 373
Cisco support options, 577
diagnostic commands, 131
Frame Relay, 275
IPX/SPX, 415
ISDN BRI, 532
LAN troubleshooting, 164
routing protocosl, 489
serial interfaces, 275
switched LANs, 197
switches, 229
TCP/IP, 337
troubleshooting, 48, 71
fast switching, 82
fast-switching cache, clearing, 328
FastEtherChannel, 190
faults in cabling, 61

FCS field
LAPB frames, 267
LAPD frames, 504
FDDI networks (Fiber Distributed Data Interface), 145, 158
DASs (dual attached stations), 159
OSI specifications, 160
port states, 160
SASs (single attached stations), 159
FDDITalk, 357
FECN field, Frame Relay, 255
FIB (forwarding information base), CEF, 84
fields
ATM cells, 175
DDP packets, 359
files
core dumps, 575
HOSTS, Windows NT, 311
LMHOSTS, Windows NT, 310-311
filtering access lists, SAP, 388-389
Flag field
IP packets, 291
LAPB frames, 267
LAPD frames, 504
flash updates, IGRP, 443
flooding, ARP, 298
flow control
Frame Relay, 251
TCP, 293
Fragment Offset field, IP packets, 292
Fragment-Free Cut-Through switching, 185
Frame Relay, 251
BECN field, 255
congestion management, 255
CRC, 251
DCE devices, 253
DE field, 255
DLCI, 252
DLCI to protocol mapping, 258
DTE devices, 253
error correction, 251
FECN field, 255
flow control, 251
headers, 252-253
LMI, 252, 255
configuration data, 256
packet debug data, 262
packet debug data, 263

PVCs, 254
  viewing status data, 259
serial interfaces
  debug data, 263-264
  viewing data, 259-260
SVCs, 254
viewing transmission/reception events, 261
virtual circuits, 253
frames
  802.1q, 192
  Ethernet, IPX encapsulation, 395
  ISL, 192
  protocol analyzers, 589
full-duplex Ethernet, 194

G

gathering facts, Cisco problem-solving method, 27
GFI (General Format Identifier), PLP
  packets, 266
global commands, 103
GNS requests (Get Nearest Server), 388
green indicator lights on switches, 225

H

hard errors, Token Ring, 158
HDLC (High-Level Data Link Control), 240
  encapsulation, troubleshooting, 242
  fields, debug serial interface command, 93
Header Checksum field, IP packets, 292
headers, Frame Relay, 252-253
helper addresses, IP, 300
History RMON, 224
hold-down timers, distance vector protocols, 432
hop counts
  distance vector protocols, 431
  RIP, 433
hosts
  ARP cache, 297
  extended ping, 123
  name resolution, 299-300
    Windows NT, 309
  pinging, 120-122
HOSTS files, Windows NT, 311

HP-UX, NetSys SLM suite, 70
hubs, 145, 179

I

I frames, LAPB, 267
ICMP (Internet Control Messzage Protocol),
  113, 294
  echo replies, 114, 331
  echo requests, 114, 331
  error reporting protocol, 113-114
  messages, 115, 294-295
  transaction debug data, 324
Identification field, IP packets, 291
IGP (Interior Gateway Protocol), 391
IGRP (Interior Gateway Routing Protocol),
  394, 442-443
  adding networks, 446
  configuration commands, 443
  distribution lists, viewing, 444-445
  flash updates, 443
  IP routing tables, viewing, 445
  routing events, viewing, 448-453
  troubleshooting, 443
IHL field, IP packets, 291
ILAPD, acknowledged mode, 504
implementing action plans, Cisco problem-solving
  method, 29
incremental updates, SAP, 390
indicator lights on devices, 225
Information field, LAPD frames, 504
input statistics, serial interfaces, 245
interautonomous system routing, BGP, 471
interesting packets, ISDN BRI, 506-507
interfaces
  AppleTalk, 364
  carrier transitions, 109
  commands, 106
  EIGRP, 479
  IPX/SPX, 397-400
  jabbering, 156
  LANs, 240
  OSPF, routing data, 460
  serial
    controller status, 245-247
    debugging, 91-92

input/output statistics, 245
viewing configuration, 242
TCP/IP, viewing settings, 314-316
viewing status, 108
WANs, 240-241
interframe gap, Ethernet, 152
internal components, Catalyst 5000 switches, 225
Internet layer, OSImodel, 288
Internetwork Status Monitor, 68
intra-autonomous system routing, BGP, 471
IP (Internet Protocol), 287-288
access lists
clearing counters, 329
viewing, 319-320
addresses
converting to MAC addresses, 296
helper addresses, 300
hosts
extended ping, 123
pinging, 120-121
packets
debug data, 325
ICMP messages, 114
multicasts, 299
routing, 289-290
unicasts, 299
RIP
database, viewing, 438
routing events, 440-442
routing events, 438-439
routing tables
clearing, 331
debug data, 326-327
viewing, 437
viewing
routing table, 318
settings, 317
traffic data, 321
ip forward-protocol command, 301
ip helper-address command, 301
ip name-server command, 300
ipconfig command, 303-304
ipconfig/all command, 303
IPM (Internetwork Performance Monitor), 68-69
IPX (Internet Packet Exchange), 383
access lists, 404
EIGRP interfaces and neighbors, 405

encapsulation, 383, 395
Ethernet frames, 395
extended ping, 412
packets, debug data, 407
routers, traffic data, 402
routing, debug data, 408-411
routing tables, 403-404
SAP
advertisements, 387
updates, 407
servers, viewing, 401
trace command, 413
ipx encapsulation command, 396
ipx input-sap-filter command, 389
ipx network command, 385
ipx output-sap-filter command, 389
IPX RIP (Internet Packet Exchange/Routing
Information Protocol)
configuration commands, 392
enabling, 392
routing updates, 391
VLSMs, 391
ipx router nlsp command, 393
ipx router rip command, 392
ipx routers eigrp command, 394
ipx sap-incremental eigrp command, 390
IPX/SPX (Internet Packet Exchange/Sequenced
Packet Exchange), 382
addresses, 384
interfaces, viewing data, 397-400
IS-IS protocol (intermediate system-to-
intermediate system), 454
ISDN (Integrated Services Digital Network), 497
connections, pinging, 121
ET (Exchange Termination), 499
LT (Line Termination), 499
NT1 (Network Termination), 499
protocols, 500
reference points, 500
switch types, 498
TAs (Terminal Adaptors), 499
TE1 (Terminal Equipment), 499
TE2 (Terminal Equipment), 499
ISDN BRI (Integrated Services Digital Network
Basic Rate Interface), 497-498
access lists, 507
B channel, 513

common problems, 531
controllers, viewing data, 514
D channel, viewing, 511
data link layer, 503
DDR (Dial-on-Demand Routing), 506, 527
Dialer interface, 507
dialer lists, 507
dialer status, 516-517
interesting packets, 506-507
Layer 2 connection establishment, 522
layer status, 515
LCP/PPP packet debug data, 523-525
MPP, 510-511
network layer, 505
    call data, 522
physical layer, 502
    B channel debug data, 519-520
PPP, 508
    authentication, 508-509
    debug data, 525
    multilink packet status, 518
    packets, debug data, 526
Q.931 protocol, 509
    debug data, 520-522, 528
    message sequence, 505
sessions, establishment, 508
SPIDs (Service Profile Identifiers), 501
spoofing, 507
static routing, 507
switch types, 515
troubleshooting, 499-501
ISDN PRI (Primary Rate Interface), 498
ISL (InterSwitch Link), 192

J–L

jabbers, 156
LANE (LAN Emulation), 178
language options for troubleshooting, 544
LANs (Local Area Networks)
ATM
    cell fields, 175
    cell processing, 177
    ELANs, 178
    OSI model, 177

cabling
    electrical interference, 149
    length limits, 147
collision domains, 153
cross-over cables, 150
Ethernet
    bridges, 180
    collision domains, 181
    connection speeds, 193-194
    full duplex, 194
    hubs, 179
    switch fabric, 183
    switches, 183
    switching methods, 184-185
    troubleshooting, 192
FDDI, 145, 158
    DASs (dual attached stations, 159
    OSI specifications, 160
    port states, 160
    SASs (single attached stations, 159
hubs, 145
interfaces, 240
jabbering, 156
microsegmentation, 153
NEXT (near-end cross talk), 148
patch panels, 147
ring, 145
star, 145
switched. *See* switched LANs.
Token Ring, 156
    active monitors, 157
    beacons, 158
    contention repeat mode, 157
    contention transmit mode, 157
    error correction, 158
    monitor contention process, 157
    tokens, 158
topologies, 151-153
troubleshooting, 144
VLANs, 186-188
LAPB (Link-Access Procedure Balanced), 265-267
LAPD (Link Access Procedure-D Channel), 252,
        503-504
late collisions, 147
layers, ISDN BRI
    connections, 522
    status, 515

LCI (Logical Channel Identifier), PLP
packets, 266
LCP (Link Control Protocol), 508, 523-525
length limits, cabling, 147
lights on equipment, 225
line monitoring, 602
link lights
checking cable connectivity, 150
false assumptions, 593
link state flooding, 455
link state routing protocols, 427, 454-455
LMHOSTS files, Windows NT, 310-311
LMI (Local Management Interface), Frame
Relay, 252-255
configuration data, 256
packets, debug data, 262
LocalTalk, 354
locating resources, CCO Web site, 552
logging, enabling, 86
logging buffered command, 88
logging command, 86
logging console command, message logging
parameters, 87
logging ip-address command, 88
logging monitor commands, 88
logging trap command, 88
logical bus systems, 144
loops, routing, 130
LSAs (link state advertisements), 456
LSPs (link state packets), 454-455
LT (Line Termination), ISDN, 499

M

MAC addresses (media access control), 154, 296
converting IP addresses, 296
Macintosh. *See* Apple.
management tools, 66-69
MAUs (media access units), 146
maximum hop count, distance vector
protocols, 432
memory, core dumps, 110-111
messages, ICMP, 294-295
MIB (Management Information Base), 223
microsegmentation, 153

Microsoft
Network Monitor, 66
SMS (Systems Management Server), 66
Windows, TCP/IP, 301
monitor contention process, Token Ring, 157
MPP (Multilink PPP), 510-511
multi meters, checking cable continuity, 59-60
multi-point AURP tunnels, 361
multicasts, 299
Ethernet packets, 154

N

name resolution
host to IP address, 299-300
Windows NT, 309
names, AppleTalk, 360
NBP (name binding protocol), 360
NCP (NetWare Core Protocol), 388
neighbor discovery
distance vector protocols, 431
EIGRP, 474
neighbors
AppleTalk, viewing, 366
OSPF, 462-463
NetBIOS name resolution, Windows NT, 309
Netflow switching, 82
NetSys Baseliner, 69
NetSys SLM suite, 70
NetWare
encapsulation, 383
GNS requests, 388
IPX/SPX, 382
protocol analyzer output, 585
SAP
advertisements, 387
broadcasts, 389
network analyzers, 65-66
Network Associates Sniffer Pro, 66
network layer
ISDN BRI, 505
call setup data, 522
OSI model, 288
troubleshooting, 37
switched LANs, 175

network maps, documenting network layout/configuration, 20-21
Network Monitor (Microsoft), 66
network monitors, 64
networks
  80/20 rule, 155
  adding to IGRP, 446
  AppleTalk. *See* AppleTalk.
  ATM
    cell fields, 175
    cell processing, 177
    ELANs, 178
    OSI model, 177
  cabling
    electrical interference, 149
    length limits, 147
  collision domains, 153
  connections, testing, 59, 331-333
  cross-over cables, 150
  Ethernet
    bridges, 180
    collision domains, 181
    connection speeds, 193-194
    full duplex, 194
    hubs, 179
    switch fabric, 183
    switches, 183
    switching methods, 184-185
    topologies, 151-153
    troubleshooting, 192
  FDDI, 145, 158
    DASs (dual attached stations), 159
    OSI specifications, 160
    port states, 160
    SASs (single attached stations), 159
  Frame Relay, 251
  hubs, 145
  jabbering, 156
  management tools, 66-69
  microsegmentation, 153
  NEXT (near-end cross talk), 148
  patch panels, 147
  performance baselines, 21-22
  ring, 145
  star, 145
  Token Ring, 146, 156–158
    active monitors, 157

    beacons, 158
    contention repeat mode, 157
    contention transmit mode, 157
    error correction, 158
    monitor contention process, 157
    tokens, 158
  VLANs, 186-188
  Windows NT, troubleshooting, 304
  X.25, 265
NEXT (near-end cross talk), 148
NLSP (NetWare Link Services Protocol)
  configuration commands, 393
  routing process, 392
no appletalk zone command, 353
no appletalk zone name command, 353
no logging buffered command, 88
no network command, 447
no shut command, 110
nodes, AppleTalk, 355
noise on cables, 61, 149
Novell
  IPX/SPX. *See* IPX/SPX.
  protocol analyzer output, 585
  See also NetWare.
NT1 (Network Termination), ISDN, 499

O

optimum switching, 83
Options field, IP packets, 292
OSI model
  application layer, 41
  ATM networks, 177
  data link layer, 34-36
  FDDI specifications, 160
  ISDN BRI, 504
  network layer, 37
  physical layer, 32-34
  presentation layer, 40
  routing protocols, 427
  session layer, 40
  switched LANs, 174
  TCP/IP, 287-288
  transport layer, 38
OSPF (open shortest path first), 307, 456
  BDRs (backup designated routers), 462

configuration commands, 457
DRs (designated routers), 462
interfaces, routing data, 460
IP routing events, 463-464
link state advertisements, 456
neighbors, viewing, 462-463
routing events, 466
routing tables, viewing, 460
troubleshooting, 457
OTDRs (Optical Time Domain
    Reflectometers), 61
output statistics, serial interfaces, 245
overruns, debugging, 106-107
overview of CCO Web site, 545

P

packets
    broadcast
        comparing to baseline analysis, 155
        Ethernet, 154
    DDP, 359
    Frame Relay, debug data, 263
    IP, 290
        debug data, 325
        ICMP messages, 114
    IPX, debug data, 407
    multicast, Ethernet, 154
    NBP, 360
    PLP, 266
    ppp multilink, 518
    routing, IP, 289-290
    runts, 156
    tracing routes, Windows NT systems, 305
    ZIP, 362
Padding field, IP packets, 292
PADs (Packet Assembler/Disassembler), X.25, 267
PAP
    Password Authentication Protocol, 509
    Printer Access Protocol, 362
pass-through autonomous system routing,
    BGP, 471
Passive mode, Token Ring, 157
patch cables, 147
patch panels, 147
path determination, routing processes, 80

performance
    baselines, 21-22
    debug command impact, 85-86
Phoenix ASIC, 227
physical cabling system. *See* bus system.
physical connections, testing, 59
physical layer
    ISDN BRI, 502
    OSI model, 32-34
physical troubleshooting tools, 58-59
PIDs (process identifiers), traceroute, 129
ping, 112
    debugging, 598
    echo replies, 331-332
    echo requests, 331-332
    false assumptions, 592
    IPX, 412
    syntax, 305
    testing
        remote nodes, 296
        Windows NT remote hosts, 304
    time-out process, 116
    user form, 120-122
    Windows systems, 125-126
PLP (Packet-Layer Protocol), 265-266
point-to-point AURP tunnels, 361
port group command, 218
port monitor command, 219
ports
    SPAN, 195
    states, FDDI networks, 160
    TCP, 301
    UDP, 301
PPP (Point to Point Protocol), 508
    ISDN BRI
        authentication, 508-509, 525
        debug data, 525
        multilink packets, 518
        packet debug data, 523-526
ppp authentication command, 509
ppp multilink command, 511
Presentation layer, OSI model,
    troubleshooting, 40
Pricing Agent, 550
Privileged mode, show commands, 94
problem solving. *See* Cisco problem-solving
    method.
processes, viewing utilization, 101

promiscuous mode, adapters, 154
protocol analyzers, 65-66, 588
  Apple output, 585
  BPDU packets, 586
  frame analysis, 589
  NetWare output, 585
  UDP packets, 589
  Web site packets, 585
protocol dependent modules, EIGRP, 475
Protocol field, IP packets, 292
protocols
  AARP, 357
  ADSP, 358
  AFP, 362
  AppleTalk, 356
  ARP, 296
  ASP, 362
  AURP, 361
  BGP, 470
  CDP, 188
  CHAP, 509
  DDP, 359
  distance vector, 430-431
  EIGRP, 473
  Frame Relay, 251
  ICMP, 113, 294
  IGP, 391
  IGRP, 394, 442-443
  IP, 287-288
  IPX, 383
  IPX RIP, 391
  IPX/SPX, 382
  IS-IS, 454
  ISDN, 500
  ISL, 192
  LAPB, 265
  LAPD, 252, 503
  LCP, 508
  link state, 454
  MPP, 510
  NBP, 360
  NCP, 388
  NLSP, 392
  OSPF, 307, 456
  PAP, 362, 515
  PLP, 265
  PPP, 514
  Q.931, 505
  RIP, 307, 433-437
  routing, 425
  RTMP, 361, 394
  RTP, 474
  SAP, 387
  SNAP, 384
  Spanning Tree, 188
  SPX, 386
  TCP, 293
  TCP/IP, 285
  X.25, 265
  ZIP, 352
PSE devices (Packet Switching Equipment),
      X.25, 267
PTI (Packet Type Identifier), PLP packets, 266
PVCs (Permanent Virtual Circuits), Frame
      Relay, 254, 259

Q

Q.921 debug data, ISDN BRI, 520-522
Q.931 protocol, message sequence, 505

R

reception events, Frame Relay, 261
red indicator lights, 225
reference points, ISDN, 500
registered users, CCO Web site, 546-547
remote hosts, pinging, 120
repeat counts, extended ping, 123
repeat until problem is solved, Cisco
      problem-solving method, 30-31
requests, GNS, 388
resets, serial interfaces, 250
resolving host names to IP addresses, 299-300
Resource Manager Essentials, 67
ring networks, 145
RIP (routing information protocol), 307, 433
  configuration commands, 434
  distribution lists, 435
  hop counts, 433
  routing
    IP events, 440-442

protocols, 435-437
  routing updates, 433
troubleshooting, 434-435
viewing IP database, 438
VLSMs, 433
RMON (Remote Monitoring), 222
  Alarms service, 224
  Events service, 225
  History service, 224
  Statistics service, 224
  Route command, 308
router eigrp command, 475
router igrp command, 443
router network command, 394
router ospf command, 457
router rip command, 433
router switching, 81
routers
  ARP cache, 297
  buffer pool statistics, 247
  configuring, AppleTalk, 352
  core dumps, 110-111
  differences from switches, 209
  interfaces, 240
  IPX, traffic data, 402
  RMON (Remote Monitoring), 223
routing
  asymmetrical, 120
  debugging, 596
  events
    EIGRP, 484-486
    IGRP, 448-453
    OSPF, 463-470
  IP
    packets, 289-290
    viewing events, 438-439
  IPX, debug data, 408-411
  ISDN BRI, static routes, 513
  loops, 130, 432
  NLSP, 392
  processes
    path determination, 80
    switching process, 81
routing protocols, 425-426
  AppleTalk, 353
  classful, 428
  classless, 429

OSI model, 427
RIP, 435-437
See also protocols.
routing tables
  EIGRP, 479
    adding entries, 480-483
  IGRP, viewing, 445
  IP
    clearing, 331
    debug data, 326-327
    viewing, 318, 437
  IPX, viewing, 403-404
  OSPF, 460
  RTMP, 361
  Windows NT, 307
  X.25, viewing, 270
routing updates
  IPX RIP, 391
  RIP, 432
RSMs (Router Switching Modules)
  CPU halt light, 225
  VLANs, 186
RTMP (Routing Table Maintenance Protocol),
    361, 394
RTP (Reliable Transport Protocol), EIGRP packet
    delivery, 474
runts, 156

S

S frames, LAPB, 267
SAGE chips (Synergy Advanced Gate-Array
    Engine), 226
SAINT chips (Synergy Advanced Interface and
    Network Termination), 226
SAMBA chips (Synergy Advanced Multipurpose
    Bus Arbiter), 227
SAP (Service Advertisement Protocol), 387
  advertisements, 387
  broadcasts, 389
  filtering access lists, 388-389
  incremental updates, 390
  updates, viewing, 407
SASs (single attached stations), FDDI, 159
scenarios, troubleshooting, 49, 72

searches
  CCO Web site, 552-553
  Cisco documentation CD, 565
serial interfaces, 240
  controller status, 245-247
  debug event data, 248
  debugging, 91-92
  Frame Relay
    debug data, 263-264
    viewing data, 259-260
  input/output statistics, 245
  interface resets, 250
  timing problems, 249
  viewing configuration, 242
serial lines, checking via BERTs, 63
servers
  IPX, viewing, 401
  NetWare, SAP broadcasts, 387-389
Service Order Agent, 550
service providers
  line monitoring, 602
  troubleshooting, 601-602
Session layer, OSI model, troubleshooting, 40
sessions, ISDN BRI, 508
short DDP packets, 359
show apple arp command, 357
show appletalk globals command, 364
show appletalk interface command, 364
show appletalk neighbors command, 366
show appletalk traffic command, 365
show arp command, 103, 297
show async command, 96
show buffers command, 98, 247
show cdp command, 211
show cdp neighbors detail command, 211-213
show commands, 94
  AppleTalk, 364
  available debug areas, 94-96
  differences from debug commands, 84, 96
  sample output, 210
show config command, 214-218
show controllers bri command, 514
show controllers command, 106, 245-247
show debugging command, 104
show dialer command, 516-517
show flash command, 102
show frame-relay lmi command, 104, 256

show frame-relay map command, 105, 257
show frame-relay pvc command, 105, 258
show int ser command, 244
show interface ? command, 221
show interface bri command, 511-513, 529
show interface command, 107-108, 221-222,
    241-244, 250, 259-260, 269, 312, 397
show interface serial command, 109
show ip access-lists command, 319
show ip arp command, 318
show ip bgp commands, 472
show ip bgp summary command, 472
show ip eigrp interface command, 479
show ip interface brief command, 316
show ip interface command, 314
show ip ospf interface command, 460
show ip ospf neighbor command, 462-463
show ip protocols command, 317, 435, 444-445,
    458, 476
show ip rip database command, 438
show ip route command, 318, 437, 445, 459-460,
    478-479
show ip traffic command, 102-103, 321
show ipx access-lists command, 404
show ipx eigrp interface command, 405
show ipx eigrp neighbors command, 405
show ipx int command, 385
show ipx interface brief command, 400
show ipx interface command, 398
show ipx route command, 403-404
show ipx servers command, 401
show ipx traffic command, 402
show isdn status command, 515
show logging command, 88
show MAC command, 213
show port group command, 218
show port monitor command, 219
show ppp multilink command, 518
show process CPU command, 101
show process memory command, 100
show running-config command, 98
show spantree command, 220
show stacks command, 98
show tech command, 96, 223
show tech-support command, 566-572, 575
show version command, 97, 222
show x25 route command, 267

show x25 vc command, 270-271
silicon switching, 83
site areas, TAC, 556
SLAs (Service-Level Agreements), 602
SMDS (Switched Multimegabit Data Service), 240
SNA View, 69
SNAP (Subnetwork Access Protocol), 384, 584
Sniffer Pro (Network Associates), 66
SNMP (simple network monitoring protocol), 64
soft errors, Token Ring, 157
software, troubleshooting tools, 64
Software Center, CCO Web site, 555
Solaris NetSys SLM suite, 70
source addresses, IP packets, 292
source address variable, extended ping, 125
source quench messages, ICMP, 115
SPAN (Switched Port Analyzer), 191
Spanning Tree protocol, 188
speed 100 command, 218
SPF algorithm, 455
SPIDs (Service Profile Identifiers), ISDN, 501
Split Horizon
   AppleTalk RTMP/AURP, 361
   distance vector protocols, 432
spoofing, ISDN BRI, 507
SPX (Sequenced Packet Exchange), 386
SSE (silicon switching engine), 83
SSP (silicon switch processor), 83
Standard Ethernet, 144
star networks, 145
starting logging, 86
static routes
   convergence, 426
   debugging, 596
   ISDN BRI, 511
Statistics RMON, 224
Status Agent, 550
Store-and-Forward switching, 185
storms, ZIP, 364
SunOS, NetSys SLM suite, 70
SVCs (Switched Virtual Circuits), Frame Relay, 254
switch fabric, Ethernet, 183
switch types
   ISDN, 498
   ISDN BRI, 515

switched LANs, 174-175
switches
   Catalyst series, 206-208
      internal components, 225
   CLI (Command-Line Interface), 209
   connection speeds, 194
   differences from routers, 209
   EARL chip, 226
   Ethernet, 181
   Phoenix ASIC, 227
   SAGE chip, 226
   SAINT chip, 226
   SAMBA chips, 227
switching
   autonomous, 82
   distributed, 83
   Ethernet, 184-185
   fast, 82
   Fragment-Free Cut-Through, 185
   netflow, 82
   optimum, 83
   router, 81
   silicon, 83
   Store-and-Forward, 185
symptoms and causes, 590
syntax
   arp command, 307
   ipconfig command, 304
   ping command, 305
   route command, 308
   tracert command, 306
syslog servers, message logging parameters, 88
Systems Management Server (Microsoft), 66

T

TAC (Technical Assistance Center), 549, 562-568
TAs (Terminal Adaptors), ISDN, 505
TCP (Transmission Control Protocol)
   flow control, 293
   ports, 301
TCP/IP (Transmission Control Protocol/Internet Protocol), 285-287
   configuration settings, 312

interfaces, viewing settings, 314-316
    OSI model, 287-288
TDRs (Time Domain Reflectometers), 61
TE1 (Terminal Equipment), ISDN, 499
TE2 (Terminal Equipment), ISDN, 499
technical documents, CCO Web site, 550-552
termination, ISDN, 499
test objectives, 10-12
testing tools, physical layer, 58-59
Thicknet, 144
Thinnet, 144
time-exceeded messages, ICMP, 115
time-out process, ping command, 116
timeouts
    ARP cache, AppleTalk, 357
    extended ping, 124
Token Ring networks, 156
    active monitors, 157
    beacons, 158
    cabling, length limits, 147
    contention repeat mode, 157
    contention transmit mode, 157
    error correction, 158
    MAUs, 146
    monitor contention process, 157
    tokens, 158
TokenTalk, 357
tools, troubleshooting, 58
topologies
    Ethernet, 151-153
    Token Ring, 156
TOS field, IP packets, 291
Total Length field, IP packets, 291
trace command, 333, 413
traceroute, 127
    circular routes, 129
    debugging, 600
    extended, 128
tracert command, 130, 305-306
tracing packet routes, Windows NT, 305
traffic data
    AppleTalk, viewing, 365-366, 369-370
    IPX servers, 402
    X.25, 273
transactions, debug data
    ARP, 323-324
    ICMP, 324

transmission events, Frame Relay, 261
Transport layer, OSI model, 38, 288
triggered updates, distance vector protocols, 432
troubleshooting, 19
    advanced options. See advanced troubleshooting.
    AppleTalk, 350
    avoiding panic, 45
    BERTs (Bit/Block Error Rate Testers), 63
    BGP, 471
    Cisco problem-solving method, 22
    climbing the ladder problem-solving method, 41
    core dumps, 575
    debug techniques, 594
    divide and conquer problem-solving method, 42
    Ethernet, 192
        connection speeds, 193-194
        full duplex, 194
    HDLC encapsulation, 242
    IGRP, 443
    ISDN BRI, 499-501
    LANs, 144
    line monitoring, 602
    network analyzers, 65-66
    network connections
        ping, 331-332
        trace command, 333
    network monitors, 64
    OSI model
        application layer, 41
        data link layer, 34-36
        network layer, 37
        physical layer, 32-34
        presentation layer, 40
        session layer, 40
        transport layer, 38
    OSPF, 457
    OTDRs (Optical Time Domain
        Reflectometers), 61
    physical tools, 58-59
    protocol analyzers, 65-66
    raising calls to Technical Assistance Center,
        556-562
    RIP, 434-435
    scenarios, 49
    service providers, 601-602
    show tech-support output, 566-568, 575
    software options, 64

TDRs (Time Domain Reflectometers), 61
tools, 58
Windows NT, host-to-host communication, 303
TTL field, IP packets, 292
tunneling, AURP, 361
Type field, ICMP messages, 294

U

U frames, LAPB, 267
UDP (User Datagram Protocol)
packets, protocol analysis, 589
ports, 301
UI frames (Unnumbered Information), LAPD, 504
Unacknowledged mode, LAPD BRI, 504
undebug command, 85
underruns, debugging, 106
unicasts, 299
unreliability, IP, 290
updates
routing, IPX RIP, 391
SAP, incremental, 390
ZIP, AppleTalk, 371
URT (User Registration Tool), 68
User Data field, PLP packets, 266
user form, ping command, 120-122
username command, 509
utilities, troubleshooting, 58

V

VCs (Virtual Circuits), X.25, viewing data,
270-271
Version field, IP packets, 291
viewing
AppleTalk
all traffic, 369-370
events, 369
interface configuration, 364
interfaces, 364
neighbors, 366
traffic data, 365-366
ARP cache
address resolutions, 318
AppleTalk, 357

ARP transactions, debug data, 323
CRC errors, 109
EIGRP
interfaces, 405, 479
neighbors, 405
routing events, 484-486
routing tables, 479
ICMP transactions, debug data, 324
IGRP
distribution lists, 444-445
routing events, 448-453
routing tables, 445
interfaces, status, 108
IP
access lists, 319-320
RIP database, 438
routing events, 438-439
routing tables, 318, 326-327, 437
settings, 317
traffic data, 321
IP packets, debug data, 325
IPX
access lists, 404
routing tables, 403-404
servers, 401
IPX/SPX interface data, 397-400
ISDN BRI
B channel, 513
controller data, 514
D channel, 511
Dialer interface, 516-517
OSPF
neighbors, 462-463
routing events, 462-464
routing events, 466-470
routing tables, 460
processor utilization, 101
RIP
IP routing events, 440-442
routing protocols, 435-437
SAP updates, 407
serial interface configuration, 242
TCP/IP configuration settings, 312
TCP/IP interface settings, 314, 316
VIP cards (versatile interface processor), 83
virtual circuts, Frame Relay, 252
virtual terminals, message logging
parameters, 88

VlanDirector, 186
VLANs (Virtual LANs), 155, 180, 186
    MTUs (Maximum Transmission Units), 188
    RSMs (Router Switching Modules), 186
VLSMs (Variable Length Subnet Masks)
    IPX RIP, 391
    RIP support, 433
volt ohm meters, 59

W

WANs (Wide Area Networks), 239
    Frame Relay, 251
    interfaces, 240-241
    X.25, 265
web sites
    CCO
        Cisco Marketplace, 549
        overview, 545
        searches, 552-553
        Software Center, 555
        technical documents, 550-552
    TAC, 556-562
Windows NT
    ARP cache, 306
    HOSTS files, 311
    LMHOSTS files, 310-311
    name resolution, 309
    NetSys Baseliner, 69
    pining remote hosts, 304
    routing tables, 307

tracking packet routes, 305
troubleshooting host-to-host communication, 303
Windows systems
    ping command, 125-126
    TCP/IP, 301
write core command, 112, 575

X–Y

X.25, 265
    DCE devices, 267
    DTE devices, 267
    PADs, 267
    PSE devices, 267
    routing tables, viewing, 270
    traffic data, 273
    VCs, viewing data, 270-271
    viewing traffic data, 272
yellow indicator lights, 225

Z

ZIP (zone information protocol), AppleTalk,
    352, 371
    packets, 362
    storms, 364
    updates, 371
ZITs (zone information tables), 352
Zones, AppleTalk, 350-351

ABOUT THE CD-ROM

FastTrakExpress™

FastTrak Express provides interactive certification exams to help you prepare for certification. With the enclosed CD, you can test your knowledge of the topics covered in this book with over 200 multiple choice questions.

To Install FastTrak Express:

1. Insert the CD-ROM in your CD-ROM drive.
2. FastTrak Express Setup will launch automatically. Follow the instructions to complete the Setup.
3. When the Setup is finished, you may immediately begin using FastTrak Express.

FastTrak Express offers two testing options: the Adaptive exam and the Standard exam.

The Adaptive Exam

The Adaptive exam style does not simulate all of the exam environments that are found on certification exams. You cannot choose specific subcategories for the adaptive exam and once a question has been answered you cannot go back to a previous question.

You have a time limit in which to complete the adaptive exam. This time varies from subject to subject, although it is usually 15 to 25 questions in 30 minutes. When the time limit has been reached, your exam automatically ends.

To take the Adaptive Exam:

1. Click the Adaptive Exam button from the Main window. The Adaptive Exam window will appear.
2. Click the circle or square to the left of the correct answer.

NOTE: *There may be more than one correct answer. The text in the bottom left corner of the window instructs you to Choose the Best Answer (if there is only one answer) or Mark All Correct Answers (if there is more than one correct answer.*

3. Click the Next button to continue.
4. To quit the test at any time, click the Finish button. After about 30 minutes, the exam exits to review mode.

After you have completed the Adaptive exam, FastTrak Express displays your score and the passing score required for the test.

■ Click Details to display a chapter-by-chapter review of your exam results.
■ Click on Report to get a full analysis of your score.

To review the Adaptive exam After you have taken an Adaptive exam, you can review the questions, your answers, and the correct answers. You may only review your questions immediately after an Adaptive exam. To review your questions:

1. Click the Correct Answer button.
2. To see your answer, click the Your Answer button.

The Standard Exam

After you have learned about your subject using the Adaptive sessions, you can take a Standard exam. This mode simulates the environment that might be found on an actual certification exam.

You cannot choose subcategories for a Standard exam. You have a time limit (this time varies from subject to subject, although it is usually 75 minutes) to complete the Standard exam. When this time limit has been reached, your exam automatically ends.

To take the Standard exam:

1. Click the Standard Exam button from the Main window. The Standard Exam window will appear.
2. Click the circle or square to the left of the correct answer.

NOTE: *There may be more than one correct answer. The text in the bottom left corner of the window instructs you to Choose the Best Answer (if there is only one answer) or Mark All Correct Answers (if there is more than one correct answer).*

3. If you are unsure of the answer and wish to mark the question so you can return to it later, check the Mark box in the upper left hand corner.
4. To review which questions you have marked, which you have answered, and which you have not answered, click the Review button.
5. Click the Next button to continue.
6. To quit the test at any time, click the Finish button. After about 75 minutes, the exam exits to review mode.

After you have completed the Standard exam, FastTrak Express displays your score and the passing score required for the test.

▓ Click Details to display a chapter-by-chapter review of your exam results.
▓ Click on Report to get a full analysis of your score.

To review a Standard Exam After you have taken a Standard exam, you can review the questions, your answers, and the correct answers.

You may only review your questions immediately after a Standard exam.

To review your questions:

1. Click the Correct Answer button.
2. To see your answer, click the Your Answer button.

Changing Exams FastTrakExpress provides several practice exams to test your knowledge. To change exams:

1. Select the exam for the test you want to run from the Select Exam window.

If you experience technical difficulties please call (888) 992-3131. Outside the U.S. call (281) 992-3131. Or, you may e-mail brucem@bfq.com. For more information, visit the BeachFrontQuizzer site at www.bfq.com.